Directory of European Porcelain

Marks, Makers and Factories

(Fourth Edition)

The *Directory of European Porcelain* is one of the most comprehensive reference books on European porcelain marks, makers and factories. In this, the new English translation of the fourth edition, Ludwig Danckert's book contains the most up-to-date information available. There are now 4,765 marks, some of them published for the first time, and it has a special section on dolls and dolls' heads which are becoming an increasingly important study area.

The Directory will appeal to collectors for its detailed coverage of European marks, including those from the late 19th and early 20th century, the inclusion of records and marks of porcelain decorating studios, for details on the Imperial Monarchy of Bohemia before 1918 and for previously restricted information from the DDR on Meissen designs.

The Directory will also appeal to social and art historians since it provides a vast amount of background information not usually found in such works. Its terms of reference cover the history of art, manners, industry and fashion. Not only does the Directory go further than any other book on the subject but, most importantly, it has a 'feel' for porcelain that never allows design to be considered separately from artistic achievement.

DIRECTORY OF EUROPEAN PORCELAIN

Marks, Makers and Factories

Ludwig Danckert

Translated by Rita Kipling
Consultant editor: Pietro Raffo
(Christies Fine Arts Course)

N.A.G. Press Ltd
Colchester, Essex

Published (in English) 1981
Reprinted 1990
Reprinted 1992
Reprinted 1993

Translated from the Fourth Edition of 'Handbuch des
Europäischen Porzellans' (published by Prestel-Verlag,
Munich) with additional material.

ISBN 7198 0003 X

Printed and bound in Great Britain by
J.B. Offset Printers (Marks Tey) Ltd, Colchester.

Contents

Preface to the Fourth Edition

Since its publication in 1954, this book has gained many devoted readers. The First Edition departed from the style and content of the porcelain literature of the time by including manufacturers and production of the 19th and 20th centuries. The Second and Third Editions subsequently gave further emphasis to these areas, which are of prime interest to scientists and collectors.

Meanwhile research has continued and the sheer weight of new information has demanded that this work be revised completely. This has given the author the opportunity to include important improvements and additions to the text which have come to light, both as a result of 25 years' continuous contact with collectors, and his long and fruitful exchange of correspondence with various factories and specialists. Of particular interest are the new details concerning the Imperial Monarchy of Bohemia before 1918, which have been gleaned from the former managers of the Bohemian factories which clustered around Carlsbad. Through official channels the porcelain industry of East Germany has supplied the author with extensive documentation up until 1977. The VEB Porzellanmanufaktur Meissen have clarified long-accepted facts with archival evidence in their Publication, *Meissen 75,* by J. Schärer.

The inclusion of records and marks of porcelain decorating studios (for Dresden alone there are about 30) is an innovation which will be of great interest to many collectors. Lastly, account has been taken of a whole new collector's field which has received international recognition over the past few years, that of dolls with heads of porcelain. The factories and so-called neck marks of these heads (which are mainly produced in biscuit porcelain by Thüringian factories) have been traced and their histories are given in as much detail as possible.

The number of marks recorded has therefore risen from the original 3,500 to 4,765, among which there are several which have never appeared in porcelain literature before. This is due partly to the increased access to the sources mentioned above, and partly to an intensive search by the author through European trademark registers.

I should like to dedicate this new edition to my friends, fellow workers and colleagues.

Dr. Alois Bergmann, Nittenau; Marcel de Chavonne, Limoges; Jens A. Cuyper, Copenhagen; Ursel Danckert, Ravenstein; Heinrich Dechamps, Munich; Professor Dr. Erich Köllmann, Cologne; Ekkehard Kraemer, Berlin, East Germany; Helmut Kunz, Leipzig; Dr. Hans Leichter, West Berlin; Dr. Fritz and Frau Johanna Müller, Coburg; Dr. Waltraud Neuwirth, Vienna; Leslie Parr-Armstrong,

London; Dir. Paul Pöttig, Töging; Tamara Preaut, Paris; Dr. Gunter Reinheckel, Dresden; Dr. Wolfgang Scheffler, West Berlin; Clifford Schlegelmilch, Flinn, USA; Professor Dr. Arno Schönberger, Nürnberg; Dr. Marian Swinarski, Posen; Professor Heinrich Zimmermann, Elbogen.

Ravenstein 1978
L.D.

From the Preface to the First Edition

Literature pertaining to European porcelain is almost as old as the porcelain itself. Early arcanists and colour technicians rapidly published their experiences and recipes, though these writings can rarely be regarded as reliable sources. Business records and catalogues of early factories, which contain details of the volume of production, techniques, artists and specialities, are far more enlightening and interesting. Instruction manuals and detailed publications regarding individual factories only appeared as late as the 19th century. Their value to the ever-expanding field of research is proven by the many editions of such works as W. Chaffer's, *Marks and Monograms on European and Oriental Pottery and Porcelain,* and Grasse's, *Guide de l'Amateur de Porcelaines et de Faiences.*

Collectors soon became aware that the practical difficulties involved in keeping abreast with the expanding production of most factories of the 19th and 20th centuries, together with the increasing amount of information available, could not be met by any of the many existing monographs and handbooks. Thus the need arose for a condensed reference book containing all the most up-to-date information. In setting out to provide such a book the author had to keep two essential requirements constantly in mind: the need to be able to identify an object as quickly as possible, and the need for short pieces of text summarising the individual characteristics of each mark. Such needs were best met by the simplest and most logical form of publication, a dictionary. The sections containing reproductions of the marks had to be as informative as possible at the expense of unnecessary detail, while the paragraphs of text had to satisfy a readership which had grown accustomed to accuracy. Bearing all these factors in mind the author also endeavoured to include all the recent developments which had been previously neglected.

Since the intrinsic worth of a porcelain object, as appreciated by sight and touch, cannot be conveyed in words, this book only becomes truly valuable when its contents have been illuminated by contact with the actual objects.

Cologne 1954
L.D.

Directory of Keywords

Abbreviations used in the Directory

b.	born
bros.	brothers
c.	century
c.	circa
d.	Derby
d.	died
f.	founded
fg.	figure
Jos.	Joseph
Jr.	junior
no.	number
nr.	near
p.	page
q.v.	which see
reg.	registered
Sr.	senior

Aachen (1) (Germany). E. Haselhuhn, porcelain decorator from 1921. Still in existence 1930. The following mark, under the number 292212, was entered in the Register of Trademarks of the German Reich on 22 February 1922.

Aachen (2) (Germany). Ferdinand Schmetz, porcelain decorator, 1930–4.

Aaron, Michel Isaac, père, see Chantilly (2) and Paris (32).
Absolon, English decorator of the early 19th c.
Achard, see 'Bleu mourant'.
Acier, Michel-Victor (20 January 1736, Versailles–16 February 1795, Dresden). Sculptor and porcelain modeller. Appointed as modelling master to the Meissen Porcelain works in 1764, and employed there until he received a pension in 1781. He created many groups and figures, particularly allegorical-mythological scenes and scenes of children. His work set the style of production which came between rococo and classicism.

Äcker, founder of Arzberg, see Arzberg (3) and Hohenberg.
Ackermann & Fritze, see Rudolstadt Volkstedt (9).
Adam, Charles, see Sèvres (1) and Vincennes (1).
Adam, Elias (1669 or 70–1745). Goldsmith from Augsburg, his master-stamp 'EA' is frequently found on the precious metalmounts adorning Meissen porcelain.
Adam, Heinrich-Albert. Painter in St. Petersburg in the early 19th c. He copied oil paintings on to porcelain vases.
Adams, E., see Lustre Glaze.
Adams & Cooper, see Longton (1).
Adderley Floral & Figurine China Co. Ltd., see Longton (2).

Adderleys Ltd., G. E. Wotherspoon, see Longton (3).

Adelmann, Christian, mentioned in the *Meissener Chronicles* in 1760 as a modeller.

Adler, Christian (1787–1850). Porcelain decorator. In 1811 he was recruited by the Nymphenburg factory; in 1815 promoted to painter overseer; in 1827 commissioned by Ludwig I to copy the paintings of the Royal Gallery on to porcelain. He received his pension as painter overseer in 1838, but remained active in the factory as a decorator until his death.

Adler, Woldemar, see Berchtesgaden.

Advenier, see Paris (3).

Agate Wares. Ceramic imitation of marble and agate made by kneading together variously coloured clays or by appropriate painting. This technique is also used in the art of glassmaking and has been known since antiquity. In the 18th and early 19th c. it was employed particularly in Staffordshire and by Wedgwood, but was also used by continental factories.

Aich nr. Karlsbad (Bohemia, now Doubi). Johan Möhling (from Schlagenwald) founded a porcelain factory here which produced mainly figures. He was also the first to produce porcelain coins (surrogate money in circulation during economic crises); later produced utility and luxury porcelain. Sold to A. C. Anger c. 1862. Before this a Baron von Ziegler was the owner for a short time. From 1918–23 Menzel & Co. owned the factory, the partners being Leo Hähnl and Eduard Wolf. It was incorporated into the Verband der EPIAG in 1923. Closed in 1933.

1 incised stamp – 2 incised stamp on figures (Moehling) – 3 incised stamp, A. C. Anger until 1901 – 4 modern mark

d'Aigmont-Desmares, see Caen.

Aigner, Ph., see Vienna (2).

Aktiengesellschaft Porzellanfabrik Rudolstadt, see Rudolstadt Volkstedt (10).

Alant pitchers. Pitcher-like vessels to hold Alant wine (spiced wine), which, like the present-day aperitif, was said to stimulate appetite.

A la Pologne, see Paris (111).

Albarello. Cylindrical pharmaceutical jars, originally in tin-glazed earthenware, probably introduced from the Orient. In use in Spain and Italy since the 16th c. Prototype for the cylindrical porcelain jars used in European pharmacies since about 1827 and still found today, serving as ornaments and sought-after antiques.

Albersweiler (Germany, Bavaria). Robert Lutz porcelain factory operating about 1894. Utility pottery, international representatives.

Albert, C. G. Painter *par excellence* of birds. Recorded in Fuerstenberg from 1768–72, probably later in Copenhagen with the Luplau brothers.
Alberti, Carl, see Uhlstädt.
Alcock, S. & Co., see Burslem (1).
Alcock & Diggory (earlier Hill), see Burslem (1).
Alcora (Spain). In the Spanish faience factory experiments in search of frit porcelain began in 1751, conducted by two Frenchmen, François Haly and François Martin and the Meissen arcanist Knipffer. This was however, not discovered until 1764 under Count Aranda. In 1784 two potters, Christobal Pastor and Vincente Alvaro, were sent to study the porcelain factories in Paris. But it was probably only after the appointment of Pierre Closterman, also from Paris, that the enterprise became successful. See also Bachero, V. amd Soliva, M.

1 brown or black – 2 incised – 3 gold – 4 red, A stamped into the unfired paste – 5 first A in gold, second A stamped – 6 printed in various colours

Aldred, see Lowestoft.
Alexandra. Name of pattern, registered as 259362, 26 January 1921, by P. F. Thomas' factory at Marktredwitz.
Alexandra Porcelain Works, Ernst Wahliss, see Turn 10.
Alexandrinenthal (1) near Oeslau (Germany, Upper Frankonia). Th. Recknagel, porcelain factory Alexandrinenthal, f. 1886. Vases, bowls etc., dolls and dolls' heads.

Halsmarke

Alexandrinenthal (2) near Oeslau (Germany, Upper Frankonia). Th. Recknagel, porcelain painter.

Aliver & Brouhaut, see Saou (1).
Alka porcelain factories, Alboth & Kaiser KG, see Staffelstein.
Allach nr. Munich (Germany, Bavaria). Porcelain works Allach-Munich GmbH, founded 1935. Figurative porcelain.

Allard, see Paris (2).

Allen, Robert (1744–1835). At Lowestoft from 1757 as a painter and from 1780–1802 as Director. Later he worked as an independent painter of porcelain.

Allerlei, see Quodlibet.

Allerton, Charles & Sons, see Longton (4).

Allgäuer porcelain painters, see Sonthofen.

Alluaud, François, Director at Limoges, partner in the Bordeaux works, see Bordeaux and Limoges (2) and (3).

'Alp' GmbH, see Lubau.

Alt, Beck & Goldschalck GmbH, see Nauendorf.

Altar-Garnitur, see Meissen (1) and Kändler, J. J.

Altbrandensteinmuster. A Meissen porcelain pattern, introduced in 1741. The curved rim, finished with a ridged edge, is divided into eight sections. Four of these are filled with a wide-meshed grid pattern, alternating with four segments which are each divided into three. Each of the twelve squares is ornamented with a single rosette, all arranged around to frame an equally broad, undecorated section.

Altenkunstadt (1) (Germany, Oberfranken). Karl Nehmzow GmbH, porcelain factory, f. 1933. Taken over by the Altenkunstadt Rothemund & Co. porcelain factory. Artistic porcelain.

     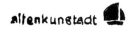

Altenkunstadt (2) (Germany, Oberfranken). Rothemund, Hager & Co., porcelain factory.

ÄLTESTE VOLKSTEDTER PORZELLAN FABRIK. Since a number of porcelain factories trade under this name, they are here dealt with together and ordered according to their geographical positions.

Älteste Volkstedter (1) porcelain factory AG, f. 1762. In operation as Staatlich Thüringsche Porcelain Works from 1945; formerly Älteste Volkstedter GmbH, Volkstedt Rudolstadt.

Älteste Volkstedter (2) porcelain factory AG Abtlg. Eckert, formerly Richard Eckert & Co., Volkstedt Rudolstadt AG, f. 1895. Closed in 1949.

Älteste Volkstedter (3) porcelain factory AG branch Neuhaus a. Rennweg (Germany, Thuringia), formerly Rudolf Heinz & Co. F. as a decorating shop in 1859, it became a porcelain factory in 1885; still extant in 1949.

Älteste Volkstedter (4) porcelain factory, formerly Dressel, Kister & Co., AG Passau. It is not known when the 'Älteste' (prefix) became part of the name. F. 1840. From 1937–42 in operation as the Passau Philipp Dietrich porcelain factory and still called 'Porzellan-Fabrik Passau – Innstadt' in the 'Keramadressbuch' in 1949. Factory for luxury porcelain. It is no longer listed in the 'Keramadressbuch' of 1954/5.

Älteste Volkstedter (5) porcelain factory, formerly Triebner. See Unterweissbach porcelain factory, formerly Mann & Porzelius AG.

Alt-Haldensleben (Prussia, Prov. Sachsen). Porcelain factory f. 1826 by Nathusius.

Althaldensleben (Prussia, Prov. Saxony). Schmelzer & Gericke, porcelain decorators studio, f. 1885.

Alton China Co. Ltd., see Longton (5).

Altrohlau (1) (Bohemia, now Stará Role). F. 1814 by Benedikt Hasslacher, former director of Dallwitz, a stoneware factory, which he leased in 1820 to Schwengsbier and sold three years later to August Novotny. The latter introduced transfer printing, but did not begin the manufacture of porcelain until 1838. Main markets in Vienna and Hungary. The 'little flower' decoration was mostly used on their ordinary ware but also sometimes on earthenware, the outlines of the pattern being transferred and the colours hand painted. Views were also used. In 1884 the banker Moritz Zdekauer took the business over. Later, after it was acquired in 1909 by C. M. Hutschenreuther from Hohenberg, the enterprise was called 'Altrohlauer Porcelain Factory AG', and from 1945 it was known as 'Starolský porcelán národni podnik Stará Role'. Utility porcelain.

1   2   3   4

1–5 blind embossed, mark of the Benedict Hasslacher 1813–23 – 6 blind embossed after 1823 – 7–8 blue underglaze – 9–14 blind-mark of August Nowotny 1823–84 – 15–18 Moritz Zdekauer – 19–21 1920–38 (Hutschenreuther marks) – 22 1938–45 – 23 since 1945

Altrohlau (2) (Bohemia, now Stará Role). The Ing. Fritsch & Weidermann porcelain factory had its origin in a porcelain painters workshop founded in 1876. It is not known when the Fritsch and Weidermann factory, first mentioned in 1921, began to produce porcelain. Utility ware.

Altrohlau (3) (Bohemia, now Stará Role). Viktoria AG porcelain factory, formerly Schmidt & Co., f. 1883. Keepsakes and utility ware. The last mark for porcelain wares (oval mark with angel) was registered as No. 164 on 20 August 1891 with the Chamber of Trade and Commerce in Eger by Schmidt & Co. Quite possibly this may be the oldest mark used.

Altrohlau (4) (Bohemia, now Stará Role). Oskar and Edgar Gutherz f. a porcelain factory here in 1887. Production consisted of coffee, tea and dinner services, also utility articles. From 1918 the factory was incorporated into the EPIAG; see Carlsbad (2).

Altrohlau (5) (Bohemia, now Stará Role). Josef Plass, who had a porcelain painting shop, registered the following marks with the Chamber of Trade in Eger on 13 August 1897. He received the Reg. No. 562 for porcelain wares of all kinds. This mark appears on the reverse of the ware in red and black.

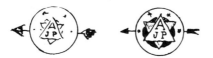

Altrohlau (6) (Bohemia, now Stará Role). Schneider & Co. porcelain factory, f. 1904; successor: Josef Lenharts Erben. Utility ware.

Altrohlau (7) (Bohemia, now Stará Role). Holdschick, formerly Dutz & Co., f. a porcelain factory here in 1926. In 1936 it was taken over by Franz Manka and expanded into a master workshop. Utility ware.

Altwasser (1) (Germany, Silesia). The Heubach, Kampa and Sonntag-factory produced porcelain here from about 1870.
Altwasser (2) (Germany, Silesia). With the help of a sleeping partner, C. Thielsch f. a porcelain factory in 1845, in Altwasser nr. Waldenburg, the second porcelain factory of Silesia. As an addition to his factory Thielsch later bought the porcelain factory of the merchant and builder Silber. After the death of the Councillor of Commerce Thielsch the works were transferred to his son Egmont von Thielsch in 1882. Under his direction another factory was built in Altwasser, which began to operate 1 January 1906. In 1918 it was taken over by C. M. Hutschenreuther from Hohenberg. In 1906 the director G. Feist developed the earliest tunnel oven for porcelain, together with Fougeron from Montereau (France) and the Vereinigten Chamotte factories, formerly Kulmiz GmbH Saarau. Its length was 64 m and it was heated by direct coal-firing.
See also: Walbryzych.

Alt-Wien-Vergoldung (old Viennese gilding). A method of decoration used mostly for luxury items, where several layers of gold were applied one on top of the other, creating a gold relief.
Alvaro. Family of painters in Alcora. Signed pieces by 'Vicente Alvaro Ferrando' are from the late 18th c.
Alvaro, Vicente, painter, see Alcora.
Alvier, see Saou.
Amberg (Germany, Bavaria). A faience factory was f. here in 1759 and first produced stoneware in about 1790. Ownership changed frequently as follows: from 1836 the factory was owned by Stephan Mayer and Son until 1850 when it was bought by Eduard Kick who passed it to his brother in law, W. Kasel, in 1880. The factory was active until 1910. In the 19th c. there was a large

production of utility stoneware and porcelain. Black or blue overprint decoration, in the 1880s presentation vases in renaissance style. C. 1850 acquisition of 97 moulds from the Ludwigsburger porcelain works, which after its closure (1824) had been sold to the Schwerdtner porcelain factory in Regensburg. Mostly with double numbering, rarely with stamp 'Amberg'.

Amberg $Amberg\atop 4$

Blindstamping

Amberg, Adolf (1874–1913). Sculptor and modeller. Submitted the designs for the Hochzeitszug (wedding procession) *q.v.* of the KPM Berlin, c. 20 figure-groups.
Amison, C. & Co. Ltd. China manufacturers, Stanley China Works, see Longton (6).
Amphora, see Oegstgeest.
Amphorawerke Riessner, see Turn (5).
Amsterdam (Holland). Porcelain factory reputed to have been in existence in about 1810, using the mark 'A. Lafond & Comp. à Amsterdam'.

A Lafond & Comp
à Amsterdam

Anchor Porcelain Co. Ltd., see Longton (7).
Ancienne Maison Demay, Avignon, see Bruère-Allichamps.
Anciennes Maisons Chauffriasse, see Limoges (26).
Anciennes Maisons Pillivuyt & Fils, see Limoges (26).
'Anciennes Usines de Fuisseaux' SA, see Baudour (1).
Anciens Etablissements Noublanche, see Paris (3).
Andenne (Belgium). In the mid 19th c. Winand and Camille Renard ran a porcelain factory here.
André, see Paris (4).
André & Cottier, see Paris (5).
Anger, A. C., see Aich.
Angoulême (France). Mouchard had a studio here around 1819, in which porcelain was decorated.

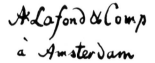

Angoulême-pattern (cornflower-design), see Paris (41).
Anhäuser, Karl, see Dresden (1).
Anliczek, Dominicus, see Pearl Service.
Anochin, see Moscow.
Anreiter, Anton, son of Johann-Karl W., painter and independent decorator in
Florence and Vienna. From c. 1754 he was cheif decorator at the Vienna works.

$$Anl^{us}Anreiter$$
$$VZ:1755$$

Anreiter von Zirnfeld, Johann Karl Wendelin (1702 to 4 October 1747).
Viennese arcanist and painter in the porcelain factory of the Marquess Carlo
Ginori in Doccia. It is said of him that 'few such workers can be found in Europe
whose skill equals his in form, artistry and beauty'. He died in Vienna prior to a
proposed transfer to Munich, where he was expected to facilitate the production
of porcelain.

$$J:Carl Wendelin Anreiter vz$$

Ansbach (Germany). On Markgrave Karl Alexander's initiative, the Ansbacher
faience factory which had existed since 1710, produced porcelain for the first
time in 1758–9 with the help of Meissen workers. By 1762 the rapidly expanding
concern had already moved into the princely hunting-lodge, Bruckberg. The
artistic direction was in the hands of Johann Friedrich Kändler, a cousin of the
then famous Meissen master modeller, and was flourishing particularly well at
the beginning of the Rococo period, from c. 1758–77. The plastic modelling
shows strong affinity with contemporary leading factories. Of particular interest
is the decorating of porcelain by the painter Schöllhammer and the landscape
artist Stenglein, with the use of a superb purple and soft blue. Kahl and
Schreimüller are named as flower painters. A great amount of Ansbach white
porcelain was delivered to Leichner (also Lynker), at the Haag, who had it
painted in his factory and marked with the sign of the stork. With few
exceptions, this porcelain stands out through its brilliant whiteness. The
business closed down as late as 1860, after having been in private ownership
since before 1807.
See also Gerlach, K., Löwenfinck, A., Taglieb, G.

1   2   3   4   5   6   7   8

A = Alexander – 1 impressed mark, cartouche of Ansbach on figures – 2–8 all blue
underglaze – 4 c. 1765 – 8 palace mark

Ansbach, Karl Alexander, Markgraf von (1736–1806), see Ansbach.
'Ansbacher Muster'. Name of the pattern for a service of the porcelain ware of Ansbach in which the faces of the plates were left completely plain, but on the rims fields of plaiting were arranged between four cartouches. This is one of the most refined German porcelain patterns. It was produced for many decades and occurs in many variations.
Anspach (Germany, Thuringia). Porcelain was produced here c. 1870.

Anstett, Charles-Armand (b. 1771), see Colmar.
Anstett, François-Antoine I. Painter and ceramicist, pupil of Paul Hannong, director in Niderviller 1754–79.
Anstett, François-Michel. Brother of François-Antoine I, painter in Niderviller 1759–71.
Antikzierat. Famous relief pattern on Berlin services from 1767–1798. The borders are decorated with bundled reeds in relief work.
Antonibona, Pasquale. Proprietor of the Nove faience factory, which began to produce porcelain in 1752. See Nove.
Antonio, Maestro di San Simone. From Venice. He is reputed to have succeeded in producing porcelain in Venice in 1470, using clays from Bologna. See Venice (1).
Antwerp. By 1560, Italian potters were producing Italian style majolica here.
Apollo candlestick, see Ludwigsburg and Göz, J.
Aponte, Francisco de, see Seville.
Aprey (France, Haute Marne). Joseph Lallemant de Villehaut produced life sized figures in biscuit porcelain here (c. 1772 and later). To this day important examples of his work have not been authenticated, so it is assumed that the production was only small.
Aqua Regia. Mixture of three parts concentrated hydrochloride with one part concentrated nitro-hydrochloride, which, because of its contents of free chloride and nitrosylchloride, (NOCl), can dissolve gold and platinum.
Arabesque Service, St. Petersburg, 1784. The famous Katharina II Service of Sèvres porcelain, made in 1778, inspired the master modeller Rachette's service. It included an extensive table centre piece in the antique taste, with frescoes and comprising 937 pieces for 60 table settings. Similar in form were the Cabinet Service, decorated with wild flowers and Italian verdute and the Yacht Service commemorating the sea victories of the Empress (Köllmann).
Arabia Porcelain factory, see Helsinki.
Aranda, Count of, Don Pedro Pablo (1798). Owner of the Spanish faience factory of Alcora, which, in the mid 18th c. also produced porcelain. See Alcora.
Arboras (France, Rhone). The Decaen brothers managed a porcelain factory here about 1839.

Arcadian Service, produced by Staatliche porcelain works, Berlin (originally only tea-services were made). In 1938, form by Trude Petri and reliefs by Siegmund Schütz. Biscuit medallions on smooth glazed ground, unpainted. In the classical idiom, a timeless, beautiful service (Köllman).

Arcanum. In alchemy this was a general term meaning 'our own' or 'secret remedy'. In the 18th c., after the discovery of porcelain, the word Arcanum was applied in particular to the formula for porcelain making. Up to the late 19th c. those who professed knowledge of this secret, called themselves 'Arcanists'.

Archangelskoje (Russia). The porcelain factory of Prince Nicolas Yussupoff existed here from 1814 until 1831.

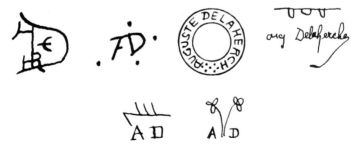

Ardouin, see Grigny.
'Argenta' (silver-decoration), see Gustavsberg (1).
Aristocrat Florals & Fancies, see Longton (8).
Arita. Village in Japan, trading post of the Japanese porcelain industry.
Arita porcelain, see Imari porcelain.
Arkanist, see Arcanum.
Armentières (France). La Chapelle-aux-Pots. Auguste Delaherche produced faience, stoneware and enamelled porcelain here from about 1896.

Armstrong, R. W., see Beleek.
Arnold, Samuel, see Vine wreath.
Arnoldi, C. E. and F., see Henneberg.
Arnoldi, E. and F. C., see Elgersburg (1).

Arnstadt (1) (Germany, Thuringia). It is suggested that a small porcelain factory was founded here in 1790.

Arnstadt (2) (Germany, Thuringia). Arnstadt, Marsdorf & Bandorf KG porcelain factory f. 1905; ointment jars, vases, bonbonnières (no tableware).

Arras. Joseph François Boussomaert f. a porcelain factory here in 1770 under the protection of 'Intendant de Flandre et d'Artois', M. de Calonne. Intended to compete with Tournai. Soft paste porcelain (only general ware) of medium quality was produced. The pieces are related to Chantilly, Tournai and Sèvres. Some time after it had been passed to the brother and sister Delemer (who were engaged in trading with ceramic products), the concern was closed in 1790.

$$AR \quad \overset{AR}{\underset{\textbf{I}}{}} \quad AA \quad \overset{A \cdot R}{\underset{P}{}} \quad AR \quad 2O$$

Arzberg (1) (Germany, Bavaria). Äcker's porcelain factory, f. 1839, was incorporated into the C. M. (Carl Magnus) Hutschenreuther AG Arzberg in 1918. After the amalgamation of Lorenz Hutschenreuther Selb and C. M. Hutschenreuther Hohenberg the Arzberg porcelain factory used the last of the marks, as shown.

Arzberg (2) (Germany, Bavaria). Carl Auvera f. a porcelain factory here in 1884. Pipe bowls. This concern no longer exists.

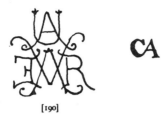

[190]

Arzberg (3) (Germany, Bavaria). In 1886 Theodor Lehmann f. the Arzberg porcelain factory which was taken over on 22 July 1927 by the Kahla porcelain factory. On 22 December 1928 it assumed its present title: the Arzberg AG porcelain factory. Coffee, tea and table ware; also vases.

Arzberg (4) (Germany, Bavaria). Carl Schumann AG porcelain factory, f. 1881. Table and coffee ware, vases, shallow bowls and gift articles, perforated porcelain. Strawflower pattern. Since 1926 this firm has been a joint-stock company.

Arzberg (5) (Germany, Bavaria). Strebel produced porcelain here in 1867.
Asch (Bohemia). Rudolf Hoffmann f. a porcelain factory here in 1920.
Aschaffenburg, see Damm.
Aschuat (Russia). Polivanoff f. a porcelain factory here about 1820 (after he had severed his connections with the Moscow-based factory Vsevolojsky & Polivanoff). Nothing is known of the produce.
Askew, Richard. A painter in Chelsea in 1772, later in Derby and Birmingham. No signed piece of his extant.
Asnières (France). Marcel Guillard porcelain works; artistic and luxury porcelain. This factory no longer exists.
Assay-le-Chateau (France, Allier). Seigle and Chaviot produced porcelain here in about 1870. The products bore no factory marks.
Association of German porcelain factory owners, see Berlin (6).
Asturiana, La, see Gijon.
Atlas China Co., see Fenton (1).
Atmography, see Enamel printing and Transfer printing.
'Aubergine-Glaze'. The dark violet coloured glaze on Chinese porcelain,

named after the colour of the egg-plant. The glaze was known to the Kunyao since the time of the Sung and was especially popular in the 18th c.

Aubiez, Maurice, see Vincennes (2).

Auer, Anton (1778–1814). Engaged as painter in Nymphenburg in 1795 and in 1809 became chief painter. From 1823 his son, Max Joseph Auer, also worked in the Nymphenburg factory.

Aufenwerth (also Auffem Werth), Johann (d. 1728). Decorator with the Augsburg firm, who painted in his own workshop, decorating Meissen porcelain with chinoiseries. He also worked with oriental porcelain and faience with gold and silver, with landscapes and repoussoir figures. Etchings in gold were also made. His daughter Sabina and one Anna Elisabeth Aufenwerth, later married to Wald, were also active as porcelain painters. See Gold chinoiseries.

Augarten, see Vienna (3).

Augsburger gold-chinese, see Gold-chinoiseries. Aufenwerth and Seuter.

Auguste Victoria. Name of pattern number 265978 registered on 26 May 1921 by P. F. Rosenthal, Selb.

Auliczek, Dominikus. (1 August 1734, Policzka in Bohemia to 15 April 1804, Munich). Sculptor and porcelain modeller. After visits to the Academies of Vienna, Paris, London and Rome, he succeeded Bustelli as master modeller at the Nymphenburg factory in 1763. In 1774 he became factory inspector. Up to the time of receiving his pension in 1797, he modelled many animal groups and a series of larger figures of mythological gods. As a court sculptor, he created several statues for the park at Nymphenburg Castle.

Auliczek, Dominikus the Younger (b. 17 November 1775, Nymphenburg). Son of Dominikus Auliczek the Elder, porcelain painter and modeller. In 1797 rose to the rank of factory inspector in Nymphenburg but was dismissed in the same year. After his reinstating as a provisional inspector, in 1808, he was again dismissed in 1809. In 1829, he was the owner of the porcelain and stoneware factory in Regensburg which in 1835 was absorbed by the firm Schwerdtner.

Aurnhammer, Alfred, see Brambach.

Aussig a. d. Elbe (Bohemia). Rudolf Kindler, porcelain, stoneware and earthenware factory, f. 1881. Domestic ware.

R K
A

Austrian porcelain factories at Mildeneichen and Raspenan, G. Robreicht, see Mildeneichen.

Austrian Service. A table service from the KPM Vienna factory in the Louis XVI style, decorated with portraits in imitation of onyx cameos. The paintings by Claudius and Lorenz Herr are after paintings by Peter Krafft. It was presented on behalf of the Austrian Emperor Franz I to the Duke of Wellington in the autumn of 1820. The service is made up of 195 pieces and the cost was 40,000 Fl.
See Wellington Service.

Autriau, Gérard, see Villenauxe (1).

Auvera, Carl, see Arzberg (2).

Avignon, see La Celle-Bruère and Bruère-Allichamps.

Aynsley China, John Aynsley & Sons Ltd., see Longton (9).

Azier, see Acier.

Bachelier, Jean Jacques (1724–1805). Directed the painter's studios of Sèvres from 1751–93 and was the successor of Falconet after the latter went to Russia. Master modeller from 1766–73. It is uncertain whether he himself painted on porcelain; most likely he was primarily a teacher supplying drawings for porcelain vases and sculptured figures.

Bachero, Vicente. He was regarded as the most important painter of the Alcora factory in the 18th c.

Bacon the Elder, John. English sculptor, who from 1755–62 worked at Bow, 1769 at Derby and 1777 at Wedgwood.

Baden-Baden (Germany). Contrary to previous opinion that a factory had been f. in 1750 or 1753, the current view is that during that time only abortive trials were conducted by Jeremias Bitsch and Susanna Sperl. Apparently the works were not f. until 1770 by Zacharias Pfalzer, who had worked in Strassburg.

1–2 blue underglaze 1770–8 – 3–4 in gold, later 18th c.

Bader, porcelain painter, see Schäffler, J. C.

Baeck, Elias (b. 1679), engraver, see also Callot, J.

Baehr & Proeschild, see Ohrdruf (1).

Bagnolet (1) (France, Au Port de Paris). A laboratory for porcelain experiments was active here around the middle of the 18th c. in the service of Duke Louis of Orléans.

Bagnolet (2) (France, Au Port de Paris). Abel Monvoisin produced here c. 1867 statuettes and devotional objects in biscuit porcelain. The products carried no marks.

Baguley, see Swinton.

Baignal, see Creil et Montereau and Passage.

Baignol, see La Seynie (1).

Baillieux, see Paris (6).

Ballardini, Dr. Gaetano, see Faenza.

Balle, Ignaz, see Schelten.

Balley, see Paris (7).

Balleroy, H. A., Frères, see Limoges (3).

Balleroy, Julien & Cie., see Limoges (4).

Baranger, Salomon et Cie., see Limoges (5).

Baranowka (Russia, Gouv. Nowgorod). Michel Mezer and his brother f. a factory here in 1801. The products were equal to those of the Imperial Works. The factory gained the right to use the Imperial crest as a mark. After the death of Michel Mezer in 1820, the quality declined rapidly. The business was leased out in 1845 and continued to produce utility porcelain until 1895.

Barasze (Poland). A porcelain factory existed here (according to Swinarski/Chrościcki (Posen 1949)), which used the following mark.

Barbe and Poncet, see Limoges (85).

Barbeaux. Term for a cornflower pattern, which was apparently designed by Hettlinger (Sèvres) for Queen Marie Antoinette of France. This pattern is frequently found on porcelain of Niderviller, Paris and other factories of the late 18th and early 19th c.

Barbesso, Odoardo. In a travel report about China, 1516, he recorded that porcelain was made of grounded seashells and eggshells which had been buried until decomposition.

Barbin, François (d. 1765), see Mennecy-Villeroy.

Barbin, Jean Baptiste (d. 1765), son of François, see Mennecy-Villeroy.

Barbotine. Ceramic slip of various consistencies, which acted as an adhesive for the modeller. Barbotine was also used as a medium for decoration (see pastiche).

Barcelona (1) (Spain). Manufacturas Cerámicas, S.A., f. 1894. Utility ware for restaurants, crockery, coffee and tea services, with fine decoration. The title of this factory was: from 1894: Berenguer y Canals and from 1897: Luis Berenguer en Cta.: from 1921 Manufacturas Cerámicas S.A.

Barcelona (2) (Spain). Hosta porcelain factory operated here.

Barcelona (3) (Spain, Castellbisbal). Poligono Industrial Santa Rita, porcelain factory.

Bardon, see Coussac-Bonneval.

Bareuther & Co. AG, see Waldsassen (3).

Barjaud & Lafon, see Limoges (6).

Barlois et Dabot, see Orléans (1).

Barlow, Thomas, see Longton (10).

Barmin Bros., see Frjasino.

Barny Rigoni & Langle, see Limoges (7).

Baron frères, see Mehun-sur-Yèvre (1).

Baroni, Giovanni, see Nove.

Barr, Martin, see Worcester (1).

Barrachin, see Paris (69).

Barré-Russin, M., see Orchamps.

Bartelmei, Dr. Physician of Boettgers and active as arcanist in Meissen at the time of the Böttger-period (1708–12).

Basalt ware. Black, basalt like stoneware of Josiah Wedgwood and other factories, also copied on the continent.

Basdorf nr. Berlin (Germany). The brothers Schackert founded a small porcelain factory here in 1751, but only frit porcelain was produced. The few

remaining pieces bear the signature of Basdorff.
Bastener & Daudenart, see Saint-Amand-les-Eaux (3).
Bastien et Bugeard, see Paris (8).
Batenin, Sergej, see St. Petersburg (2).
Battersea (England, London). Famous workshop here produced 'Battersea Enamels' (enamel on metal), 1753–6.
Battersea-enamel, see Battersea.
Baudour (1) (Belgium). Société Belge de Céramique, société anonyme Cérabel f. by Franz Declercq in 1842. In 1849 Nicolas de Fuisseaux, a solicitor from Mons, took over the factory. After his death his widow began to widen the scope of porcelain production which continued under her son, Léon de Fuisseaux, as a joint stock company under the name: 'Anciennes Usines de Fuisseaux'. In 1927 the firm was acquired by 'SA des Pavillons' and in 1934 the Belgium Keramikgesellschaft Cerabel annexed it. Hotel and luxury porcelain, original ornaments, figures, etc.
Baudour (2) (Belgium). Produits Céramiques de Baudour; production programme included fireproof porcelain.
Bauer & Lehmann, see Kahla (2).
Bauer, Rosenthal & Co., see Kronach (4), Ph. Rosenthal AG.
Bauer, Adam (b. c. 1743). Pupil of Lejeune's, court sculptor to the Duke of Württemberg 1770–5 and also in the Ludwigsburg porcelain factory. Master modeller in Frankenthal 1777–9. After 1779 worked at Wilhelm Beyer in Vienna and later at Sterzing am Brenner.
Baumeister, Samuel, miniaturist. Painted Nymphenburg porcelain as independent decorator in 1763.
Baumgart, Emile, see Sèvres (1).
Bäuml, Albert, see Nymphenburgh.
Baury, Charles, modeller, see Paris (60).
Bauscher Bros., see Selb (4) and Weiden (1).
Bautzen (Germany, Saxony). Schneider, J. G., porcelain painters. c. 1930.

Bavaria. Often affixed in addition to modern, Bavarian porcelain.
Bavaria AG, see Ullersricht.
'Bavaria', porcelain factory, see Waldershof (2).
Bawo & Dotter, see Fischern, Limoges (6) and (8).
Baxter Snr., see Coalport.
Baxter, Thomas (1782–1821), painter, see Swansea.
Bayer, Johann Christoph (1738 Nuremberg–1812 Copenhagen). Descended from a family of faience painters, he came to the Copenhagen works in 1768 where he remained active up to 1812. He became known for the painting of the 'Flora Danica Service', which he began in 1790 *(q.v.)*.

Bayeux (France). Anc. Ets. J. P. Morlent et G. Saintville S.A., last name of firm of porcelain makers since 1945, which in 1810 was transferred by Joachim Langlois of Valognes *(q.v.)* to Bayeux. The ownership changed frequently. After Langlois' death 1830 his widow became proprietress until 1847, then her daughter until 1849. Françoise Gosse became owner in 1870, his widow in 1873 and Jules Morlent in 1878. Imitations were designed from a Chinese prototype. Factory closed 1951. The marks are mentioned separately in Cushion and 'Tardy 75'.

1 1878–1945 – 2 – 3 1849–78 – 4 – 5 1849–78 blue underglaze – 6 1878–1945 black – 7 1830–49 green – 8–11 1830–49 blue underglaze and red – 12–13 1812–30 red – 14–17 1830–49 blue underglaze and red – 18–21 1812–30 blue underglaze

Bayreuth (1) (Germany). In St. Georgen am See near Bayreuth, a faience factory was f. in 1719, allegedly with help of the Meissen worker Samuel Kempe (who had organised the stoneware factory at Plaue a.d.H.). It is most likely that stoneware in the manner of Böttger ware was produced before 1726. Production of hard paste porcelain cannot be established by documentary evidence before 1767, but is certain from 1750 on. There must have been production on a larger scale between 1776–88. Apart from St. Georgen, another porcelain factory is mentioned in 1837, in Bayreuth itself.

Bayreuth (2) (Germany). First Bayreuth porcelain factory 'Walküre', Siegm. Paul Meyer, GmbH, f. 1900. Household, hotel and restaurant ware, fireproof porcelain cooking pots, coffee machines.

Bayreuth (3) (Germany). Anton Weidl porcelain works, 'Gloria', f. 1920. Services, wallplates. Styles: Old Vienna, Fond, Meissen, Rembrandt, flowers and roses.

Bayreuth, see also Jucht, J. and Löwenfinck, A. F.
Bayswater (England, London). Site of porcelain painting workshop for Chinese and European porcelain.

$$Bayswater$$

Beaugrand & Nöel, see Villenauxe-La-Grande (2).
Beaumarchais, Sieur de. The first known 'armorial' table service decorated in China was made for Beaumarchais during the reign of Henry IV of France (1589–1610). The commission was placed through the 'Compagnie des Indes'.
Beaupoil, Marquis de, de St. Aulaire, see La Seynie.
Bechdolff, Johann Andreas. Arcanist and decorator in Ellwangen, who usually painted on faience, but also on porcelain jugs, c. 1760–70.
Bechel, Johann Philipp Magnus (b. 1726 Fulda). He was active in 1748 and 1749 as a colourist in Höchst, and 1759–66 in Ludwigsburg. His connection with another Bechel, whose activity in Höchst in 1771 and again in 1774 is documented, is uncertain.
Becher, Alfred and Malvine, see Merkelsgrün (1).
Becher, F. & A. Stark, see Merkelsgrün (2).
Becher, Joh. Joachim (1665 Mainz–1682 London). His ceramic experiments did not go further than bone china.
Beck, Adalbert, see Königsee (1).
Beck & Glaser, see Königsee (1), Adalbert Beck.
Beddow, George, painter, see Swansea.
Bell & Co. J. & M. P., see Glasgow.

Beleek (Ireland). A porcelain factory named 'D. McBirney & Co.' was f. here in 1863 by David McBirnay and R. W. Armstrong. Around 1880 nearly 200 workers were employed. The special merit of the products was a particularly thin body, which was somewhat yellowish in the mass, and an iridescent glaze. In general, table services were made but figures, animals and candlesticks were also produced.

FERMANAGH
POTTERY

Beltrandi, Lorenzo, see Mondovi Breo.

Belville and Gherardini. Jesuit priests, who came to Peking in 1699 to bring new European artistic influence to the Imperial Factory Jingdezhen.

Benckgraff, Johannes (1708–53). Famous arcanist of 18th c. Arrived from Vienna 1747 to work in the Künersberg faience factory; 1748 to Munich; 1750–3 to Höchst. 1752 worked in Berlin with Wegely and d. 1753, some weeks after he had been called to Fürstenberg, where he had intended to make the production of porcelain possible. .

Benedikt Bros., see Meierhofen (2).

Benjamin and Fauvel, see Paris (69).

Benoist-Lebrun, see Orleans (1).

Bensinger, Fritz, GmbH, see Mannheim (3).

Bentley, G. L. & Co. Ltd., see Longton (11).

Berain Grotesques. Style of ornamentation as used by Jean Bérain (1637–1711). French architect and drawing master who had trained under the influence of Italian and French examples of the Renaissance. Bérain-grotesques patterns are found engraved or painted as decoration on Böttger stoneware.

Berchtesgaden (Germany, Bavaria). Adler, Woldemar, porcelain painting c. 1930.

Porzellankunst
Berchtesgaden

Berenger, Luis, en Cta, see Barcelona (1).

Berenguer y Canals, see Barcelona (1).

Bergdoll, Adam (d. 1797). Pupil of Benckgraff whose formulae he had recorded. Later became book keeper in Höchst and was director of the Frankenthal works from 1762–75 and 1795–96. For marks, see Frankenthal (1).

Berger, Ruth, see Schwetzingen.

Bergsee, C. W., see Copenhagen (1).

Berlin (1), *Wegely factory*. In 1751, the Berlin woollen manufacturer Wilhelm Caspar Wegely set up the first Berlin factory. 'Manufacture de Porcelaine de Berlin' under Royal Prussian patronage. The workers and technicians were recruited from Höchst and Meissen. The factory produced mainly utility ware. In the plastic production the models of Meissen and Vienna were the prototypes. But an independent style was formed very early on, which remained untouched by the courtly atmosphere. The motifs, mostly representing folk-life, were rather coarse in concept, but were inspired by a refreshing naïveté. Apart from the pale pink and violet pure colours were used: black, dark brown, iron red, chrome yellow, blue and gold. An unfired porcelain body, which was found during the building of the Berlin tramcarline c. 1900, on the original site of Wegely's factory, revealed through analysis 82–85 per cent. kaolin and 15–18 per cent. feldspar and quartz. The remarkably meagre content of river materials does explain the weak transparency of the body of Wegely porcelain. A collection of 50 pieces of this costly Wegely porcelain was in the possession of the Traugott family in Stockholm. It was transferred to the National Museum in Stockholm after the Second World War. Further pieces were kept in the former Berlin Schlossmuseum; after destruction of the castle in 1951, these pieces turned up again in the Kunstgewerbe Museum, East Berlin (Schloss Berlin-Köpenick), and in the Kunstgewerbe Museum in West Berlin, which is situated in the Schloss Berlin-Charlottenburg (Prussian Art Collection). Insolvency forced Wegely to close the factory in 1757.

Wegely factory 1751–7: all marks blue underglaze, 1, 4 and 5 each with 3 superimposed, impressed, alternate numbers

Berlin (2), *Gotzkowsky factory*. In 1761 Friedrich the Great managed to coerce the merchant Johann Ernst Gotzkowsky, who had bought the secret of porcelain making from Richard, Wegely's modeller, to set up a new porcelain factory. Attempts to secure the co-operation of Kändler failed, and so in 1761 Friedrich Elias Meyer was summoned to Berlin as modelling-master. The landscape painters Wilhelm Böhme and Johann Balthasar Borrmann, both from Meissen, were also contracted at this time. The appointment of the mosaic painter Jakob Christian Klipfel followed in 1763. Gotzkowsky transferred the management to the Councillor of Commerce, J. G. Grieninger of Saxony, who held this office until his death in 1798. Porcelain from this period has barely survived. To some extent it is very difficult to differentiate between it and Wegely's porcelain. The quality improved only very slowly. Kaolin from Passau was used. The body of porcelain from this period is yellowish-grey, the glaze at times clouded and of weak lustre. In 1765 the discovery of a lean porcelain earth was made in Ströbel am Zobten in Silesia, then in 1771 a splendid kaolin was found in Brachwitz near Halle, in Sennewitz and Morl, which the Berlin factory is still using to this day. The porcelain wares produced with this kaolin, show the typical blueish-white nuance of the Berlin porcelain. The porcelain of the Gotzkowsky period was mostly smooth. The very charming 'Radierte Dessin', later called 'relief-ornamentation', was created under Gotzkowsky, as well as the popular 'Neuzierat' new-ornamentation. This business existed only until 1763 and was afterwards sold to Frederick the Great, for 225,000 Thaler.

$$\mathcal{G} \quad \mathbf{G} \quad \mathbf{\varsigma}.$$

Gotzkowsky factory 1761–3; mostly blue underglaze, rarely in colours

Berlin (3), *Royal Works.* After being taken over by Frederick the Great in 1763 the factory continued as Royal porcelain makers. The astounding success of it at this time can be attributed largely to the King himself who took an active interest in the business. The pattern 'Neuglatt' and the Japanese dinner service for Sanssouci were made at his instigation. The Berlin service is among the most attractive creations of the German rococo.The various dinner services which Frederick the Great commissioned for his castles and his generals became well known. After his death the protracted transition to classicism occurred. Artistic style in this period was also strongly influenced by Meissen. Sculptural production acquired a unity of expression through the two brothers Elias and Christian Meyer. In 1789, the deceased master modeller, Friedrich Elias Meyer, was replaced by Karl Friedrich Riese who worked in biscuit in a classical style occasionally following designs by Schadow. The architect Hans Christian Genelli can be ranked alongside Schadow as a master of neo-classicism. Johann Friedrich Riese was master modeller during that time. The objects created during the Biedermeier period to the designs of the famous Karl Friedrich Schinkel are worthy of particular praise. The portrait medallions which were used as decorations in the Berlin Empire style originated mainly from the sculptor, Leonhard Posch. After a spell of creative stagnation, the painter Alexander Kips assumed artistic leadership in 1886. He exerted enough influence during his 22 years of service, to make the Berlin factory the centre of general interest. At the turn of the century Prof. Schmuz-Baudiss took the lead in the art department, and brought underglaze painting into prominence. He also brought the sculptor Paul Scheurich to Berlin. His plastic work revived the spirit of Rococo once again. Recent efforts of the Berlin factory concentrated on the production of beautiful wares and vases, for which simple and functional shapes are preferred. The works were destroyed in 1943. However, with foresight the models, the porcelain collection and the library had been moved to safety in Selb. In the evacuation locality was the former porcelain factory of Paul Müller

35   BERLIN (3)

which had been rented in preparation as far back as 1942. It had belonged since 1917 to Lorenz Hutschenreuther. The removal was so efficient that on 25 April 1944 the first firing took place at Selb, and on 8 May 1944, the first colour firing was done at Meierhöfen near Karlsbad, where the decorating shop had found a home in the State glass factory. The library, which had been moved into the New Mint in Berlin, was burnt and Meierhöfen fell to the Allies. Other branches of the factory which were still situated in Berlin and damaged by war events, were removed in lieu of reparations. Selb alone remained intact. Owing to the occupation Berlin and Selb worked independently from 1946 and 1949 respectively until 1955–7, when both works could be reunited again (Köllmann). *See also:* Benckgraff, J., Brecheisen, J., Chodowiecki, D., Clauce, I. J., Dittmar, Klipfel, K.J.Ch., 'Kurland Muster', Meyer, W.Ch., Müller, J. G., Pedrozzi, Tittelbach, F.

Marks of the KPM Berlin, since 1918 Staatliche Porzellan-Manufactur Berlin; all marks in blue, underglaze until 1837, hand painted, never bigger than 2 cm.

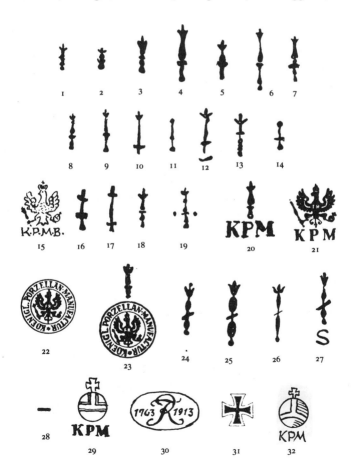

33

1–7 1763–70s – 8 c. 1780 – 9 1780s – 10–12 1790s – 13 c. 1800 – 14 c. 1810 also with cross instead of stroke under sceptre – 16 c. 1815–20 – 17–18 1820s and 1830s – 19 1837 (only in the first few months) – 20 1837–44 – 21 1844–7 also as impressed stamp without KPM since 1825, since 1837 predominantly for plates and lithophanies, also as painter's mark in red from 1823–32 – 22 1847–9 (Pfennigmarke) in two different sizes – 23 1849–70 – 24 1870–1945 – 25 1945–62 – 26 after 1962 – 27 for the production in Selb after 1945

Painters marks and commemorative marks

15 in red overglaze 1823–32 very rare, but some evidence of this – 21 also in red overglaze 1823–32 – 28 in blue or black 1803–13 in red from 1817–c. 1823 – 29 in red since 1832, also in blue underglaze for underglazed painting since 1911, and in green since 1913 but only with gold rim or simple borders on painted porcelains – 30 Jubilee mark 1913 in red overglaze for overglaze paintings, ,in blue underglaze for underglaze paintings, in green overglaze for porcelains with gold rim or coloured borders – 31 war marks 1914–18 in black overglaze for painted pieces since 21 January 1914, in blue underglaze, black underglaze, for white porcelains since 2 March 1915 – 32 today's painters' mark in red – 33 stamp in red and black overglaze was used for export c. 1890

Lithophanies from biscuit porcelain were predominantly impressed marks: sceptre over KPM or eagle without KPM. The dating of the impressed running numbers can be taken from the table:
Plate numbers according to the years:

1828–36	1–156	1847–8	352–376
1836–7	157–190	1849–50	377–410
1837–40	191–248	1850–9	411–516
1841–2	249–262	1859–60	517–535
1842–6	263–315	1861–2	536–555
1846–7	316–351	1862–5	556–580

Table showing the dating of the Berlin white porcelain after 1900.
Since the late 19th c. these products were given the year-mark (impressed mark) as well as other marks. With the aid of documented examples it is possible to reconstruct the year-marks from 1900 onwards.
A–1901, B–1902, C–1903, D–1904, E–1905, F–1906, G–1907, H–1908, I–1909, K–1910, L–1911, M–1912, N–1913, O–1914, P–1915, Q–1916, R–1917, S–1918, T–1919, U–1920, V–1921, W–1922, X–1923, Y–1924, Z–1925.
There follows the Greek alphabet in small letters (Alpha–1926 to Sigma 1943, Tau, 1949 to Omega 1954).
Since then single large capital letters have been in use. A = 1955, B = 1956, C = 1957 and so on. The dates of the object and that of the painting, are not always in the correct order.
Berlin (4). H. Richter, porcelain painters. It is neither possible to confirm the date of the firm's existence, nor whether it was ever established in Berlin at all.

R.P.M.

Berlin (5). H. Schomburg & Söhne porcelain factory, f. 1853 in Teltow. Good utility ware was produced, similar in style to that of the KPM Berlin. Already a subsidiary of the KPM Berlin in 1866. Isolators for the Reichspost were produced. In 1877 the firm established a branch in Gross-Dubrau nr. Bautzen called Margaretenhütte, which at first, produced general ware, but later only technical porcelain. 1904 the 'Porzellan Fabrik Teltow GmbH' became an independent firm. Until 1907 the concern made chinaware and art-porcelain, but production was later diverted to chemical technical porcelain. In 1929 the company was taken over by the Steatit-Magnesium AG Berlin Pankow. 1906 the art department was transferred to Dresden. At that time the firm was called Berliner Porzellan-Manufaktur Conrad Schomburg & Co., Dresden.

All marks were registered as trademarks:

M 1 on the 13.9.1904 under No. 72029
M 2 on the 13.10.1904 under No. 73022
M 3 on the 24.4.1905 under No. 78499
M 4 on the 10.5.1905 under No. 78794

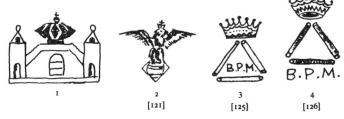

| 1 | 2
[121] | 3
[125] | 4
[126] |

Berlin (6). Vereinigung deutscher Porzellan-Fabrikanten zur Hebung der Porzellan-Industrie GmbH registered the following mark on 15 October 1908 under the No. 111474 as trademark.

[144]

Berlin (7). Vereinigte Lausitzer Glaswerke AG, porcelain, glass and pottery factory registered the following mark on 20 October 1911 under the No. 150207 as trademark. Produced porcelain wares.

[174]

Berlon & Mussier, see Vierzon (1).

Bernardand, L. & Cie., see Limoges (9).

Bernadet, Ledoux & Bailly, see Foecy.

Bernburg, Anhalt (Germany). The manufacturer Jannasch produced porcelain here c. 1870.

Bernhardt & Bauer, see Piesau.

Bernon, see Paris (9).

Berthevin, Pierre. He called himself 'chimiste et artiste en porcelaine'. His speciality was the printing from copper plates on to ceramic products. Active in Mennecy. 1766–9 head of the Swedish faience factory in Marieberg, where he was seemingly the first man to use the English printing technique. In 1769 he introduced his printing technique to Frankenthal. Credit is due to him for having made printing in underglaze on porcelain possible with cobalt blue.

Bertram, Bernhard, see Lüftelberg.

Beswick and Son, Warwick Works, see Longton (12).

Betoulet et Legrand Ets., see Limoges (45).

Bettignies, Jean Maximilian Joseph de (d. 1804), see Saint-Amand-les-Eaux (1) and Tournay.

Beulé, Reboisson et Parot, see Limoges (10).

Bever, Mme., see Boulogne-sur-Seine.

Bevington, James & Thomas, Burton Place Works, see Hanley (1).

Bevington, John, Kensington Works, see Hanley (2).

Bey, de, see Sceaux.

Beyer, Johann Christian Wilhelm (27 December 1725 Gotha–28 March 1806 Schönbrunn). Architect, painter, sculptor and porcelain modeller. After studies in Paris and Rome he was in the service of Duke Karl of Württemberg from 1759. He created numerous models in early neo-classical style for the porcelain factory of Ludwigsburg. In 1768, as court painter and sculptor in Vienna, he was entrusted with large commissions for Schönbrunn. Beyer's style is likely to have influenced the Vienna porcelain factory. See Bauer, A.

Beyer & Bock, see Rudolstadt Volkstedt (11).

Beyerlé, Jean Louis Baron de, see Niderviller.

Bibra, Heinrich VIII, von, Fürstabt zu Fulda, see Fulda (1).

Biela nr. Bodenbach (Bohemia). Julius Dressler f. a faience, majolica and porcelain factory here in 1834; produced porcelain roses, candlesticks, small wickerwork baskets, ornamental vessels. The marks on second and third marks (tower and leaves in triangle), were entered into the register of ZMA Vienna on 15 January 1900 and received numbers 2120 and 2121.

Bielotyn (Poland). A stoneware and porcelain factory was f. here in 1850 by Lewe under the protectorate of Prince Jablonowski. The management was taken over by German and Bohemian specialists. The firm was sold to Zussman in 1862. Later, the factory underwent another change of ownership and closed in 1889. The goods were of medium quality.

Billancourt (France, Seine). Porcelain painters. René Lahaussois had the following mark registered in 1895 (according to 'Tardy 75').

Billingsley, William (1758–1828). English porcelain specialist; flower painter first at Derby, then at Worcester. Later f. the Nantgarw factory. D. in Coalport. See also Paris (94).

Bing, see Charenton (1).

Bing & Grondahls porcelain factory, see Copenhagen (2).

Binns, see Worcester (1).

Biourge, see Brussels (1).

Birch, Niels. Stone quarry inspector, who discovered kaolin deposits on Bornholm. See Kaolin, sources and Copenhagen (1).

Birk, L. A. & Co., Vine Pottery, see Stoke-on-Trent (1).

Birkenhammer, see Pirkenhammer.

Birkner, Karl, see Tettau.

Birks Rawlings & Co. Ltd., see Stoke-on-Trent (1).

Birnay, D. Mc. & Co., see Beleek.

Biscuit porcelain. Unglazed porcelain. Because of its marble-like appearance it was much employed during the neo-classical period. It flourished originally in Vincennes and Sèvres.

Bishofswerda (Germany, Saxony). Paul Schreier, porcelain painters, c. 1930.

Bishop & Stonier Ltd., Waterloo Works, see Hanley (8).

Bitsch, Jeremias, see Baden-Baden.

Blackhurst & Hulme, Belgrave Works, see Longton (13).

Blairs Ltd., see Longton (13).

Blanc de Chine. Chinese porcelain, most likely from the Kangxi-period (1662–1722), so-called because of its light-yellowish tone. It consists of a transparent, glassy-white body with a velvet-soft glaze, thickly applied and closely fused to the body. Produced at the Dehua factory in the province of Fujian. Whilst the normal Chinese porcelain consists of approx. 50 per cent. of kaolin. 'Blanc de Chine' has considerably less kaolin content. This may well be the reason for its description as soft porcelain (not to be confused with frit porcelain, the composition of which is quite different). Imported into Europe in vast quantities, the Blanc de Chine figures were imitated here in the late 17th and 18th c. by faience and porcelain factories.

Blanchard, Mm., see Paris (10).

Blancheron, E., see Paris (118).

Blancheron & Neppel, see Paris (120).

Blankenhain (1) (Germany, Thuringia). VEB porcelain works, 'Weimar-Porzellan', assigned corporate body of the Blankenhainer C. & A. Carstens factory, f. 1790 by Chr. Andreas Speck, s. monogramm WS'. Very well-made porcelain but sparsely decorated at first. The later owners were, in order of succession: 1. Eduard Eichler; 2. Duxer porcelain factory AG; 3. Fasolt & Eichel; 4. C. & A. Carstens. High-quality table, coffee, tea and Mocca ware, wall plates, vases, rich gilding, transfer printing, onion pattern, cobalt decorated earthenware. Established itself internationally after the Second World War as a high-quality porcelain factory.

Blankenhain (2) (Germany, Thuringia). Edmund Krüger porcelain factory, f. 1847; utility ware. This firm no longer exists.

Blau, N. Painter in Copenhagen factory from 1791, and chief painter from 1812–20. Pieces painted by him are generally in purple.

Bleu céleste. Lustrous turquoise blue; discovered in 1752 by J. Hellot.

Bleu du Roy, descriptive term of the famous 'Royal blue' colour discovered in 1749 at Vincennes.

Bleu fouetté. Sprayed underglaze cobalt blue in Chinese porcelain.

Bleu mourant, discovered in 1782 by Prof. Achard and a chemist of the KPM, Berlin. This light blue colour was the favourite colour of Frederick II.

Blin, Amédée, Ets., see Vierzon (12).

Blin, Jaques, Ets., see Vierzon (13).

Bloch, see Luxemburg.

Bloch, see Paris (11).

Bloch & Co., see Eichwald.

Bloor, Robert, see Derby (1).

Blot, Albert & Cie., see Mehun-sur-Yèvre (2).

Blue fluted, see Ilmenauer strawflower pattern.

Blyth Porcelain Co. Ltd., Blyth Works, see Longton (15).

Boccaro, also Buccaro. Customary Portuguese description of 18th c. and earlier, for the red stoneware imported from the Province of Guangxu (from the town of Yixing), which is still produced today, and often decorated with modelling. It was already being imported into Europe in the late 17th c. in great quantities and was imitated in Holland, in Meissen under Böttger, and other manufacturing centres.

Böck, Joseph, see Vienna (4).

Bock-Wallendorf (Germany, Thuringia). Fasold & Stauch porcelain factory, f. 1903; production included ornamental porcelain of middle range.

[195]

Bodenbach (Bohemia). In 1820 a stoneware factory was managed here by Schiller & Gerbing, which later became F. Gerbing and then W. Schiller & Sons. Production also included white porcelain which was mostly exported. The wares of Shore & Co., Isleworth Pottery, Middlesex bear the Schiller & Gerbing marks.

S&G   F.G   WS&S

Bodley, E. J. D., see Burslem (1).

Bodzechów (Poland). According to Swinarski/Chrościcki (Posen 1949) a porcelain factory existed here for a short while in the second half of the 19th c.

The owner Weiss was the former Director of the Cmielów factory. The goods produced are said to have been of outstanding quality and are now very rare.
Boerner, Prof. Paul, see Meissen (1).

BODZECHOW

Böhme, Karl Wilhelm (1720–95). Employed at Meissen from 1736–61 as a landscape and figure painter. Persuaded by Frederick the Great to come to Berlin in 1761, and remained there as chief painter to the Prussian Court until 1789.
Bohne, Ernst & Sons, see Rudolstedt Volkstedt (12).
Boileau (d. 1772), see Vincennes (1) and Sèvres (1).
Boin, see Paris (38).
Boisbertrand & Theilloud, see Limoges (11).
Boisette Près Melun (France). A porcelain factory was founded here by Jacques Vermonet, in 1778. Father and son produced good frit porcelain in Paris in contemporary taste.

$$\mathcal{B} \qquad \mathcal{B} \qquad \mathcal{B}.. \qquad \underset{\mathcal{B}}{L\ P}$$

1   2   3   4

1 black or blue – 2 blue underglaze – 3 underglaze c. 1778

Boissonnet, Revol Frères, see Saint-Vallier (1).
Boizot, Louis Simon (1743 Paris–1809). Sculptor and porcelain modeller. Active at Sèvres from 1771. In 1773 he was appointed master modeller. Pupil of the sculptor Slodtz. He particularly favoured the portraiture which had previously been neglected at Sèvres. In 1781 he created the equestrian portrait of Frederick the Great. He remained the master of plastic figure work at the factory until his death in 1809.
Bojadhieff, see Radomir.
Bolognese Earth. Kaoline-containing clay from near Bologna, with which, in 1470, a Venetian alchemist is reputed to have produced porcelain.
Bolus, see Böttger stoneware.
Bondeux, see Paris (12).
Bone, Henry (1755–1834), painter, see Bristol (2).
Bone china. Bone china, technically speaking, differs radically from all other porcelains. In contrast to porcelain, but in common with earthenware, it has a lead glaze and for this reason must first be fired at a high temperature, and then at a lower temperature when the glaze has been applied. The temperature of the first firing lies far below that of hard paste porcelain. It differs chemically from porcelain and earthenware in its content of bone ash, which gives it its name. It fuses at a lower heat than porcelain, since its raw materials are similar to those found in earthenware. On the surface however, it has more of the appearance of hard porcelain than earthenware, in particular a very translucent body, and a

pure whiteness which surpasses all other porcelains. But, like earthenware it is highly sensitive to changes of temperature and breaks easily.

The raw materials used are kaolin – china clay, ball-clay – blue clay, quartz – flint, Pegmatite – Cornish stone and bone ash. This last material is obtained by burning bones which have been previously freed from fat and lime through high pressurised steam. Only pure white bones may be used, and for this reason only certain beef bones are suitable, since these contain the lowest iron content. Today the natural occurring phosphor – calcium-apatit – is used. The true inventor remains obscure since new formulae have continually been recorded as far back as 1750.

Boni, A. & Co., see Milan (1).

Bonn (1) (Germany, Rhineland). Franz Anton Mehlem f. stoneware factory here in 1755, which transferred to Pazaurek in 1836, and operated until 1903 (?). The marks are included here only because they sometimes appear under the moulds of Höchst models. After the failure of the stoneware factory at Damm in 1884, they were sold to Mehlem and used there until 1903 as earthenware moulds (see Damm). In 1903 the original moulds were sold to the Passau porcelain factory (see Passau (3)).

BONN

Bonn (2) (Germany, Rhineland). Ludwig Wessel f. a porcelain and stoneware factory here in 1775; produced utility and fancy goods of all kinds. The firm today makes only ceramic sanitary wares.

Bonnefoy's factory, see Marseille (3).

Bonneval, Marquis de, see Coussac–Bonneval.

Bonnot, see Nevers.

Booths Ltd., see Tunstall (1).

Booths & Colclough Ltd., see Longton (16).

Boray, see Satu–Mare.

Borde, de la, see Vaux and Vincennes (2).

Bordeaux (1) (France). Pierre Verneuilh f. a porcelain factory here at the end of 18th c. (c. 1781–90). His successors were Michel Vanier and Alluaud. The goods reflect contemporary Parisian taste.

1–2 blue underglaze – 4–5 1784–90

Bordeaux (2) (France). Ormont, porcelain painters on goods from Limoges and Paris, c. 1800. The pieces were mainly distributed through a Parisian commercial trading company, but were also sold in Bordeaux.

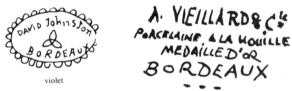

Bordeaux (3) (France). Lahens and Rateau f. a porcelain factory here in 1819. Their mark was 'LR'. The business folded after only a short while.

Bordeaux (4) (France). David Johnston f. a porcelain factory here about 1836. He was succeeded in 1845 by Vieillard, whose porcelain paste was described as very good. The mark is very rare.

violet

Bordeaux (5) (France). In 1916, according to 'Tardy 75', Julia Chevalier ran a studio here for porcelain painting. She decorated in 'façon saxe' (Meissen style).

Boreman, Zacharias (1738–1810). Active in Chelsea as a landscape painter until 1783 and in Derby from 1784–94.

Borgfeldt, Géo. & Co., see Paris (13).

Borowischtschi (Russia). A small porcelain factory was f. here in 1860 by Saitzewski, about which nothing more is known today.

Borrmann, Joh. Balthasar (1725 Dresden–1784). He was one of the best painters of battle scenes and landscapes at Meissen. In 1761 went to Berlin where he painted the main battle pictures for the Dessert Service, which was presented to Empress Katharina in 1772 by Frederick the Great. He was active in the Berlin factory until his death in 1784.

Borsdorf, Reinhold, see Teplitz–Schönau.

Boscowitz, Samuel, see Pápa.

Boseck, Carl Fr., & Co., see Haida (1).

Bossart, Adolf F., & Co., see Lübtheen.

Bossierer. In the 18th c. a 'bossierer' – called also poussierer or poussier – was the workman whose tasks were: to press out from the moulds the individual parts of the figures in porcelain paste; to combine the pieces into whole figures or groups; to decorate with small, free-worked details; and to prepare for the firing. The Boissierers cannot be said to have an independent artistic significance.

Bottengruber, Ignaz (dates unknown). Decorator in Breslau and Vienna. Married 1720. Painted Meissen and Vienna porcelain with allegorical and mythological figures between 1720 and 1730. They are surrounded by intricate leaf and ribbon designs, in monochromatic purple painting with gold highlights or also in monochromatic painting set into a contrasting multicoloured frame.

Böttger, Johann Friedrich (1682 Schleiz–13 March 1719 Dresden). Son of a cashier from Schleiz. When he was 16 years old he was apprenticed to Zorn, a pharmacist, in Berlin, where he was able to indulge his particular interest, chemistry. Like others at the time, he was convinced that he could produce gold from the three 'basic elements' of all metals: mercury, sulphur and salt, if only he could discover the correct mixture. An alternative method was said to be possible, but only with the 'stone of the wise men' (the philosopher's stone). Böttger experimented with both methods but he attracted so much attention, that he had to flee from Berlin, because Friedrich I wanted him taken into custody. Augustus the Strong of Saxony offered him protection in the hope of using Böttger's skills to his own advantage. In Dresden Böttger came into contact with von Tschirnhausen whose geological studies and invention of the 'burning glass mirror' enabled Böttger to produce porcelain by 1707. At first he only managed to produce the red Böttger stoneware. The experiments and concentrated efforts of the next two years with this red stoneware prevented Böttger, fortunately, from further search for the principle of the porcelain formula in any other sphere than ceramics. Contrary to what was thought in the past, modern research reveals that luck has played little part in the search. The outcome was not surprising in view of the tenacity with which Böttger and von Tschirnhausen investigated the clays of Saxony, in order to discover their resistance to fire. Kaolin, the essential non-melting component of porcelain was discovered during these experiments on 28 March 1709. Böttger, in a communication to the King stated that now he produced 'good white porcelain with the finest glaze and all the added decoration, which may not be above the East-Indian's but at least be equal to it'. The porcelain works of Dresden were founded by the King, Augustus the Strong, the Royal Assent being dated 23 January 1710. In 1711 Böttger was elevated to Baronial status and given the title of Oberbergrat. At the same time he became director of the 'Royal Porzellan' Factory (KPM). Böttger was determined, from the start, to decorate his porcelain with 'fired' colours. The underglaze cobalt blue decoration so valued by the King, was never achieved by him, and the sculptural productions of the 'Böttger period' are exceptionally rare. The very few pieces were mostly based on foreign models. Three years before he died Böttger made further improvements, both in the construction of the kilns and in the composition of the porcelain paste, which became a product that could hardly be faulted on any grounds. Porcelain up to Böttger's time had been mostly yellowish with a greenish, bubbly glaze, but he eventually succeeded in creating a porcelain of nearly pure white, with a thin, colourless glaze. The design of the porcelain (as of the stoneware) remained unchanged during Böttger's time, for there was a remarkable scarcity of artists. Böttger died on 13 March 1719 in Dresden.

Böttger Stoneware. Discovered 1707, this was the first positive result of the collaborative ceramic research of Böttger and E. W. von Tschirhausen. The name came into use later. It is also generally known as red stoneware (from lime and bolus). Böttger stoneware is found in both light and dark tones, according to its firing temperature. Overheating resulted in a grey or blackish colour (iron porcelain). The hard body permits grinding, engraving and polishing. Painting with lacquer, enamels, gold, silver and platinum was also used. Some of the first pieces were produced according to the designs of the court goldsmith J. J. Irminger, in a style that was a mixture of Chinese and baroque, some being mounted in silver. A particular manner of working the stoneware was the so-called 'muscheln' – a facetting of the vessels. The grinding, cutting and polishing were partly carried out in the 'grinding and polishing mill' at Dresden. In 1712 there were six persons employed in production at Dresden, three in Meissen and 10 glass cutters in Bohemia. The figures (or plastic work) which were in the antique style, cannot really be attributed to Irminger, whose best work is represented by figures of the Italian comedy (Gotha Museum). Their fresh, expressive gestures and intensity of movement bear witness to a strong artistic temperament. The first competitive commercial undertaking was founded in Plaue an der Havel by the Prussian minister von Görne.
(See also Berain Grotesques.)

Böttgerstoneware. Word used as trademark of the Saxon porcelain factory Meissen from 30 April 1919, No. 231494.

Böttger steinzeug

Botticelli. Word mark for trademark 255517 from 10 November 1920 of P. F. Rosenthal, Selb.

Bouchard, Noel (d. 1766), see La Forest.

Bouchardon, Edmé (1689–1762). Painter. Compositions of his were used by Michel le Clerc in 1737, for a series of engravings of Parisian 'Cries'. These served as sources for Kändler and his assistants.

Boucher, François (1703–70). Famous French rococo painter, he created designs for the Sèvres porcelain factory at the request of the King. These were recreated as porcelain models by the first sculptors of the time, Fernex, Suzanne, Joseph le Riche, Louis Felix de Larue and van der Voorst.

Boudon, J. F. N., see Paris (14).

Bougon, Pierre-Louis-Toussaint, see Chantilly (2).

Bouguin, see Couleuvre (1).

Boulogne (France, Pas-de-Calais). A porcelain factory f. here at the beginning of the 19th c. by Haffringue. Owners for the year 1857 were Clarté and Dunand. A beautifully white translucent porcelain was made. Haffringue employed Italian modellers. Closed in 1859.

Boulogne-sur-Mer (France). Céramique d'Art de la Madeleine produced porcelain and faience articles.

Boulonge-sur-Seine (France). Mme. Bever's porcelain factory produced artistic porcelain.

Bourbon, Louis Henri, Prince de Condé, see Chantilly (1).

Bourdon, P. H., see La Marque.

Bourdon and Son, see Orléans (1).

Bourdon des Planches, see Paris (69).

Bourdon du Susay, see Orléans (1).

Bouret Bros., see Vierzon (2).

Bourganeuf (France). Jaucourt, Filhouart et Cie started a porcelain business here in 1825. The products bear no mark.

Bourgent, see Turin (2).

Bourgeois, Emile, see Sèvres (1).

Bourgeois, Léon, see Paris (23).

Bourgeois, Page et Comp., see Salins.

Bourgion, see Lithophanes.

Bourgois, F., see Crepy-en-Valois.

Bourg-la-Reine (1) (France). The factory of Mennecy Villeroy was transferred here in 1773 by Joseph Jullien and Symphorien Jaques, under the patronage of Comte d'Eu. It is alleged that production was only of mediocre quality.

м о *Moitte* В . R .

B la R ✝ O B B R

Moitte = red, all others incised

Bourg-la-Reine (2) (France). Adrian Dalpayrat f. a studio here in 1889 where he produced, among other ceramics, porcelain with 'flambée' glazes.

Bourne, Charles, Grosvenor Works, see Fenton (2).
Boussomaert, François, see Arras.
Boutherin, Georges, see Erome.
Bouvet, see Paris (38).
Bow (England, Stratford le Bow, London). In 1744 the businessman Edward Heylin and the painter Thomas Frye gained a patent for a new method of porcelain making, but there is no evidence that a factory operated there. Possibly it began only in 1748, when Frye was given another patent for a method of porcelain production utilising a substantial amount of bone ash as an additive. In 1750 the factory was acquired by the merchants Weatherby and Crowther, though Frye remained director until 1759 (d. 1763). After his departure the artistic quality of the work declined. A year after Weatherby's death Crowther was declared bankrupt, but seems to have continued with the business till 1776. In that year William Duesbury bought the factory, terminated the work there and removed the moulds to Derby. Far Eastern porcelains were the models for productions of the first period (from 1748–55). Characteristically excellent in the quality of the colours, the paintings in the manner of famille rose and the Kakiemonware were particularly good. Porcelain figures were a significant part of the production at the London workshop. East-Asiatic porcelain, especially the Kakiemonware, also set the tone. The figures were imitative of Meissen, but in such an individual style that one could hardly call them copies. The bases were at first flat, but in 1760 these were replaced by high bases in rococo style with scroll decoration. In the third period, after 1760, the quality declined. The painting betrayed the influence of Chelsea and Worcester. Well decorated Bow porcelain from this period possibly stemmed from independent painting shops. The Bow factory produced a soft paste porcelain with added bone ash that was comparatively heavy weight. Glaze and toning were similar to the porcelain of Mennecy. See also Bacon, the Elder.

MADE AT NEW CANTON 1750

I

1–3 perhaps c. 1750 – 5–11 Bossierer marks, all blind 1750–60 – 12–17 all blue underglaze on blue decorative pieces – 18 red – 19 blue-red 1760–75 – 22–26 blue – 27 the mark by which Neuwirth refers to Jewitt (1878) and Grollier (1914), appears in Honey (1952) and Godden (1964 and not 68)

Bowers, George Frederick (& Co.), Brownhill Works, see Tunstall (2).

Bowker, Arthur, see Fenton (3).

Bowls with seven panels (à sept bords). Bowls from the period of Yongz, in eggshell porcelain; so named because of the panels arranged on the rim and enclosed by various basic patterns which are always in the most delicate tones, the main colour being pink (famille rose).

Boyer, see Paris (50).

Boyle, Zachariah (& Sons), see Hanley (3).

Brain, E. & Co. Ltd., Foley China Works, see Fenton (4).

Brambach (Germany, Saxony). Alfred Aurnhammer, Brambacher porcelain factory. Cups for export, Oriental and small fancy goods. Extant in 1910.

Brameld, John and William, founders of the 'Rockingham Factory' in Swinton (England).

Brammer, E., see Dresden (4).

Brancas-Lauraguais, Porcelain du Duc d'Orléans. The Duke of Orléans, together with Guettard and le Guay, started experiments in porcelain making in 1758. Success eluded them, until 1765, when Comte de Lauraguais (Louis-Léon-Félicité, 1733–1824), with Darcet and le Guay, developed a frit porcelain. The body was greyish and imperfect. Production was low; what was made was in the Chinese taste (Kakiemon and famille rose).

Brandenburger porcelain. Name applied to the products of a small porcelain works in Plaue and der Havel, where workers from Dresden had imported the formula for the Böttger stoneware. See Plaue.

Brandenstein, see Altbrandensteinmuster and Neubrandenstein.

Branksome Ltd., see Westbourne.

Braunschweig (Germany). Around 1870 Steinhoff maintained a small porcelain factory here.

Braunschweig, Karl I., Duke of (1713–80), see Fürstenberg.

Brecheisen, Joseph. Court painter. Born and trained in Vienna. In Berlin 1748–57, known particularly as box decorator. Active as manager of the painting department in Copenhagen, 1763. At Meissen from 1766, under the chief directorship of Dietrich.

Brehm, Johann Adam, flower painter, see Gotha (1).

Breidenbach, Emmerich Joseph, Freiherr von, Elector of Mainz, see Höchst.

Bremer & Schmidt, see Eisenberg (1).

Brenner & Liebmann, see Schney.

Breslau (Germany). According to a travel guide there was a small porcelain factory here producing 'health ware' and 'hygienic ceramics'.

Breslauer Stadtschloss service. According to Köllmann this was the most renowned service of the KPM, 'with gilded antique ornamentation and blue mosaic painted with naturalistic flowers and garlands' (1767).

Bressler, Hans Gottlieb, von (d. 1777). Independent decorator of porcelain in Breslau, pupil of Bottengruber, whose influence is evident in work made between 1732–40.

$$\mathcal{H}. \mathcal{G}.v. \mathcal{B}. \qquad\qquad \mathcal{H}.\mathcal{S}.$$
$$1739. \qquad\qquad\qquad \mathcal{B}.$$
$$\qquad\qquad\qquad\qquad 1732.$$

Brichard, d'Eloi, see Vincennes (1).

Bridgett & Bates, see Longton (12).

Bringeon, see Paris (15).

Bristol (1) (England). In 1768 W. Cookworthy received a patent for the use of Cornwall kaolin. In the same year he f. a porcelain factory in Plymouth, but moved it to Bristol in 1770. He accepted the help of Richard Champion, who became the manager and bought the business in 1773. The patent for the use of the Cornwall kaolin expired in 1775, and upon the request for renewal, Josiah Wedgwood, as well as other Staffordshire potters, were in opposition. Champion sold his right finally in 1781 to the Society of the Staffordshire Potteries. The products were in large measure executed in the style of Sèvres and Derby. Champion ordered armorial services for several of his friends but in spite of the excellent painting even these beautiful services are bereft of originality. The colours used for the painting which had been developed in Plymouth, included a lovely leaf green and a deep wine red which deserve special mention. Among the noteworthy painters were Henry Bone and William Stephens. A simply decorated ware, under the description 'cottage china', with garlands and flower patterns without gilding, was made.

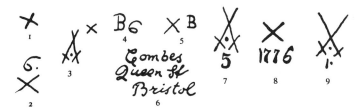

1–5 blue – 6 red – 7 blue, letter of year in gold – 8 swords blue, rest gold – 9 swords blue, number gold

Bristol (2) (England). In 1750 William Lowdin produced porcelain and porcelain-like articles (soap stone) for which he procured kaolin from Cornwall. Some pieces in the Chinese taste have survived. But by 1752 the factory was sold to Worcester.

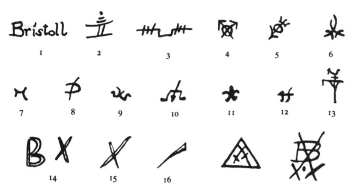

1 pressed into relief – 2–4 blue – 5 red – 6 blue or brown – 7–11 blue – 12 red – 13 blue – 14–16 incised

Bristol (3) (England). Pountney & Co. Ltd. The Bristol Pottery. Founded in 1652; produced tableware for domestic and hotel use. Originally this enterprise was known as 'Bristol Pottery'.

Britannia China Co., see Longton (17).
Britannia Porcelain Works, Moser Brothers, see Meierhöfen (1).
Brodel, Giovanni Vittorio. F. a porcelain factory in Vinovo nr. Turin in 1776. See Vinovo.
Broillet, Jaques Louis, see Paris (75).
Brongniart, Alexander (1770–1847). Geologist. Director of the Sèvres porcelain factory (1800–47). See Sèvres (1) and Elbogen (1).
Bronnitzi (Russia). A porcelain factory with the name 'Merkur' was f. here in 1884. It employed 700 people. In 1892 it was merged with the Kusnetzoff-Konzern (see Kusnetzoff). The factory still operates under the name State-Porcelain-Factory, Proletarij Bronnitzi, near Novgorod. Some pieces from 1925, marked with the last mark shown, are in the Hermitage, Leningrad. After 1925 only utility ware was produced.

Brouhaut, see Saou (1).
Brown, Robert, see Lowestoft.
Brown, Westhead & Co., see Shelton (1).
Brownfield, William (& Son), see Cobridge (2).
Bruchmühlbach (Germany, Rhinepfalz). Porcelain factory, f. 1951 and uses the following marks.

Bruckberg, see Ansbach.
Bruckmann & Son, see Deutz, nr. Cologne.
Bruère-Allichamps (France, Cher.). Manufacture de Porcelain Anc. Etts.

Avignon, f. 1877; produced porcelain ware in the style of Copenhagen, plates, vases, china containers, candlesticks, etc., fireproof kitchen ware and porcelain for sanitary and electric fitments. This firm was formerly called Ancne. Mon. Demay, Avignon and after 1945 Sté des Anciens Etablissements, Avignon. Mark: 'Porcelaine GDV à feu'.

GDV
BRUERE

Brühl, Heinrich Graf (1700–63). See Meissen (1).
Brühlsches-Allerleimuster. Meissen porcelain pattern, designed in 1742. The rim has six well-defined arches, each subdivided by an indentation. C-scrolls encircle fields of various plait and lace work, featuring a flower bouquet and a shell motif alternately.
Brûle-parfum. Name for vessels and containers which are used for burning incense.
Brunet, Cirot, & Co., see Vierzon (3).
Bruni, Baron de, see La Tour d'Aigue.
Brunin, Ferdinand, see Paris (16).
Brüning, Heinrich Christian (1797–1855). Worked as painter in Fürstenberg. He painted topographical and idealised landscapes in the English taste, as well as allegorical representations.
Brunnemann, see Meissen (1).
Brunner & Plötz, see Munich (1).
Brussels (1) (Belgium). A porcelain factory existed in Schaerbeek (nr. Brussels), 1786–90. It was f. by J. S. Vaume and known as 'Manufacture de Montplaisir' with Biourge as Director. Production was in the style of contemporary Parisian creations. Camaieu painting in sepia and green, but also in polycrome decoration.

Brussels (2) (Belgium). At Etterbek in 1787, Chrétien Kuhne from Saxony f. a porcelain factory which operated until 1803. Porcelain articles were made in the French style which did not warrant special artistic acclaim. Apart from utility ware, figures were made in biscuit and glazed porcelain.

1 red-brown – 2 red – 3 B M black, B blind impressed – 4 red

Brussels (3) (Belgium). A factory existed here from 1791–1803, ran by Louis Cretté, but there is no evidence whether porcelain was actually made there or merely painted. The painting somewhat resembles French contemporary porcelain. Products from the Parisian porcelain works, 'La Courtille' were also decorated here.

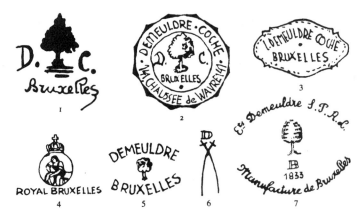

Brussels (4) (Belgium). F. 1818 by F. Faber in the Rue de Madeleine, later taken over by Capellmann.

Brussels (5) (Belgium). Christophe Windisch, the former superintendent of Faber, Brussels, f. a porcelain factory in Etterbek in 1832. Successors of his were Caillet, Vermeren–Coché, Demeuldre–Coché. This firm still works today, owned by Henri Demeuldre, and called: 'Etablissements Demeuldre S.P.R.L., Manufacture de Porcelaine de Bruxelles'. During their collaboration, Faber was painter, whilst Windisch made the moulds. After their separation, Windisch's products have, in contrast, predominantly plastic decorations, but also painting in monochrome gold, which was kept to a brownish tone (or 'bruni à l'effet'). Pieces in the manner of the Medici porcelain were also made. Multi-coloured decorations from 1852–69 (Theodore Vermeren-Coché) are extant. After 1870 the undertaking increasingly concentrated on mass-produced but good quality porcelain. Heavy losses incurred during the last war, resulting in a reduction in the capacity of the factory.

1 1920–30 on handpainted porcelain – 2 1920–41 on hotel porcelain – 3 1920–41 on tableware – 4–7 other modern marks

Brussels (6) (Belgium). Manufacture de Fleurs en Porcelaine Fernand Stoefs, f. 1900; produced porcelain flowers. This firm no longer exists.

Brüx (1) (Bohemia). Brüxer porcelain factory of the Structural Clay and Brick Association, Brüx GmbH, f. in 1924; produced utility ware.

Brüx (2) (Bohemia). Carl Spitz f. a porcelain and stoneware factory in 1896; produced utility ware and gift articles.

Buchau (Bohemia, now Bochov). Josef Pollak f. a factory here in 1902 which produced porcelain dolls heads. It was taken over by Josef Plass in 1908, and later traded as Plass & Roesner. In 1913 the factory premises were extended and enlarged. In 1933 it went out of action temporarily, but it started work again in 1937 and was reorganised for utility ware, chiefly for export. The factory was no longer being recorded in the archives of 1941.

Buchwald, Johann. Bossier and arcanist. Apart from his divers activities in stoneware and faience factories, he worked also in the porcelain factories in Höchst (1748), Fulda (1748), Rörstrands (1757) and Marieberg (1758).
Buckauer porcelain works AG, see Magdeburg-Buckau.
Bückert, Heinrich. Independent porcelain painter in Dresden, exhibited in Paris. His main work consisted of copying the paintings of the Dresden Gallery.
Budapest (1) (Hungary). Fischer'sche Keram. Factory AG, formerly Emil von Fischer, f. 1866. Utility ware, vases and bonbonnieres.

Budapest (2) (Hungary). 'Granit' porcelain and stoneware factory, f. 1922. This factory used to produce porcelain, but today is organised for faience.

Budapest (3) (Hungary). Theodor Hüttl f. a factory here in 1852, at first only for painting, but later for full porcelain production. Hüttl worked mainly upon commissions. He died in 1910 and his sons succeeded him. The factory was still in operation in 1927. That Hüttl rather than Herend supplied the Royal castle illustrates the quality of his ware – Herend had delivery problems. The mark A was registered on 24 April 1899 at the Chamber of Commerce, Budapest under No. 6029. It appeared on: porcelain ware, mainly table settings; tea and coffee china; laundry, coffeehouse and restaurant ware; presentation goods, etc.; distinguishing marks: underglaze. On 10 June 1891, mark B, which had already been in use since 1878, was registered in Fünfkirchen. This mark received the No. 6 and this was reserved for porcelain, majolica and faience products. It was underglazed or impressed. The last of the marks is used as a painter's mark on white porcelain by John Ridgway, Shelton (England). See their mark No. 17.

Budapest (4) (Hungary). M. Lang porcelain painting at the beginning of 20th c.

Budapest (5) (Hungary). Joint stock company. Porcelain, earthenware, ovenware and utility ware produced c. 1930.

Budapest (6) (Hungary). Budapest Zsolnay'sche porcelain and faience factory AG; utility ware. See also Pecs.

Budau (1) (Bohemia). Franz Lang f. a porcelain factory here in 1825, which, according to documentary evidence, he ran until 1829. His son Anton Lang continued with the business until 1880. It is recorded in other sources that it was still in production in 1894.

B: AL FL

Budau (2) (Bohemia). The Spitzl brothers f. a porcelain factory in 1914, producing household crockery. The firm was closed in 1938.

Budweis on the Moldau (1) (Bohemia). Joseph and Karl Hartmuth (father and son?) moved their porcelain business here from Vienna in 1846. Little is known about the products, although a few marks are on record. Some may date from the time when the firm was in Vienna, or they may be regarded as 'memorial marks'.

WIENER   WIEN   HARDMUTH   W

Budweis on the Moldau (2) (Bohemia). Sattler brothers were porcelain painters here c. 1930.

   KOH I NOOR

Budy nr. Charkow, see Kusnetzoff.

Buen Retiro (Spain). Country seat near Madrid. Carlos III of Spain, previously Karl IV of the two Sicilies, moved his Royal porcelain and majolica factory here from Naples (Capodimonte) in 1759, the same year as he inherited the Spanish throne. The artists and workmen from Capodimonte, were all transferred to Buen Retiro, including the arcanist Schepers and the modeller Guiseppe Gricci, who became the first directors. The factory was also called 'La China'.

Bartolome Sureda who in 1802 had been sent by Charles IV to study in Sèvres, became director in 1804, bringing with him from Sèvres the arcanist Vivien and the painter Perche. Under the direction of Sureda, instead of using the frit body, porcelain was made with kaolin which had been found in Madrid as an additive. A new complex was built for the factory in the gardens of the country palace. It is said to have cost the unbelievable sum of 11.5 million reals. During the wars of 1808–12, the factory was ransacked. The products of the first years still closely resemble the work of Capodimonte. Gricci created the décor for a porcelain room in the palace at Aranjuez, similar to that which he had made for a room in the Palace of Portici in Naples. Memorial vases were also produced. Little general ware was made, generally speaking the production of 30 years, up to the death of Charles III was for the Crown only, possibly mainly for the fittings of the Palace. During this period, except for work executed in the Chinese taste, the style of Louis XIV predominated and the influence of Sèvres was obvious.

2 fleur de lys in blue, rest gold – 3 fleur de lys and F.G. blue, rest blind impressed, F.G. = Felice Gricci – 5 blind impressed – 6 black – 7 blue – 8 blindstamp, fleur de lys blue – 9 CC = Charles III – 10 blindstamp – 11–15 blue, 1759–1803 – 16 mark of the Salvator Nofri 1718 red, 1804–8 under Soreda. This mark was also customarily in use after 'La Moncloa' under Soreda's direction ' 17–18 customarily in use after 'La Moncloa' under Soreda's direction – 19 artist's signature of either Cájetano or Carlos Fumo.

Bufe, E. and A., see Langenberg.

Buffon Service. Named after the famous zoologist. Consisted of china painted with birds from the Sèvres (1779–81) and Tournay (1787) factories.
Bühl, H. & Sons, see Grossbreitenbach (2).
Bulidon, Henri, sculptor, see Vincennes (1).
Bünde (Germany, Westphalia). Severin & Co., porcelain painting, c. 1930.

Buontalenti, Bernardo, also called: delle Girandole (1536–1608). Italian painter, sculptor, builder and engineer. Most of his works were inspired by Leonardo. Directed the production of the Medici porcelain in Florence, under the Great Duke Francesco Maria I de Medici.
Burgau-Göschwitz a.S. (Germany, Thuringia). Ferdinand Selle, Burgau a.S. porcelain works, f. 1900; utility ware, luxury and Art Nouveau porcelain. The works no longer exist.

[104]

Burggrub (Germany, Upper Frankonia); Schoenau & Hoffmeister, porcelain factory, f. 1901. Dolls' heads and dolls.

Burgstein. Word used as trademark No. 259361 from 26 January 1921 by the P. F. Thomas, Marktredwitz.
Burgsteinfurt (Germany, Westphalia). H. Pettirsch, porcelain works f. 1950. Luxury and utility porcelain, decorated with flower spriggs, relief decoration, fond and gold. Genres: Berlin, Meissen and individual development. Styles: Baroque, Empire, Modern.

Burguin, see Lurcy-Levy (1).
Burslem (1) (England). E. J. D. Bodley, Hill Pottery, 1875–92 (Crown Works since 1882), formerly Bodley & Son, 1874–5.

Burslem (2) (England). Doulton & Co. Ltd., porcelain factory, f. 1815. According to Godden the undertaking was active from 1820–1956 in Lambeth, London (1820–54 under Doulton and Watts). The first mark originates from this period but it is not a porcelain mark since porcelain was not made until the firm set up in 1882. Production included antique and modern services, figures, etc. This firm is working to this day.

Burslem (3) (England). Dale Hall Works. Operated as Bates Elliot & Co., 1870–5; Bates Walker & Co., 1875–8; Bates Gildea & Walker, 1878–81; Gildea & Walker, 1881–5; James Gildea, 1885–8. The marks often accompany variations of the No. 1 with the date '1790'.

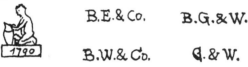

Burslem (4) (England). Thomas Hughes & Sons, Unicorn pottery, stoneware and porcelain factory, 1895–1957. Formerly Thomas Hughes, Top Bridge Works, 1860–94, no porcelain.

Burslem (5) (England). John & Richard Riley (1802–28). Two marks for porcelain were traced by Godden.

Busch, August Otto Ernst von dem (1704–79). Canon of Hildesheim, he decorated porcelain with a technique similar to etching, marking the outline and then completing the design by scratching the glaze with a diamond, afterwards filling in the lines with black colourant.

Busch, Christian Daniel (d. 1790). Porcelain painter who worked in Meissen up to 1745, then in Vienna, Munich, Künersberg, Sèvres, Kelsterbach and finally, from 1765 until his death, again in Meissen.

Buschbad, see Meissen (5).
Bushell, Stephan W., English doctor and sinologist. His book *Oriental Ceramic Art* (New York 1897) is a most valuable supplement to that of Julien.
Bustelli, Franz Anton (12 April 1723–18 April 1763 Munich). Porcelain modeller. Bustelli started employment on 3 November 1754 in Nymphenburg, as sculptor. Of his training and earlier places of work nothing is known. However, one can assume with some certainty that he came from Vienna to Munich where, as master modeller, he created numerous figures and groups of an accomplishment and elegance that represents the pinnacle of porcelain modelling of the rococo period. In particular, his comedy figures are the most enchanting objects ever created in porcelain.

Cabaret, Antoine, see Sceaux.
Cabinet service, see Petersburg (1).
Cachepots. Name for flowerpot holders.
Cäcilie. Wordmark as trademark 265979 from 25 May 1921 of the P. F. Rosenthal, Selb.
Caen (France, Calvados). A porcelain factory was run by d'Aigmont-Desmares and Ducheval, 1793–1806. The products were in the English and French taste. The decoration was applied in Paris by the enamel painters, Halley and Dastin.

'**Café-au-lait-'glaze.** Lighter coloured version of the 'capuziner-brown'.
Caffiéri, Jacques (1678–1755). Famous silversmith, who also fashioned mounts for porcelain in precious metals.
Caffiéri, Jean-Jacques (1723–92), sculptor, see Sèvres (1).
Caillat, Jean-Mathias, painter, see Sèvres (1).
Caillet, see Brussels (5).
Caillouté. A pebble shaped net pattern on a marbled ground, found on Sèvres porcelain.
Calais (France). Soft and hard paste porcelain, is said to have been produced here c. 1870, with the mark 'Calais'.
Callot, Jacques (1592–1635). French engraver and etcher. Callot figures: representations of dwarfs made by Meissen, Vienna, Venice and Chelsea after engravings from 'Il Calotto resuscitato' (newly furnished dwarf cabinet) which appeared in 1716 at Wilhelm Koning's in Amsterdam. A German version appeared in Augsburg, with engravings by Elias Baeck. The precursor of both is the dwarf series of 'Goppi' Callot's.
Camaieu decoration (monochrome decoration). Generally in green or purple.
Camelford, Lord (Thomas Pitt), see Plymouth.
Camrath, Johann. Was active as portrait painter for Copenhagen, from 1780–96. His medallions in grey porcelain are famous.

Camrath, Johannes Ludwig (1779–1849). Active as decorator at Copenhagen from 1794–1849, famous for his flowers and fruits.

Canary yellow. A particularly beautiful yellow porcelain colour of the Derby porcelain factory.

Candiana nr. Padua (Italy). A manufacturing family settled here, making something that resembled Medici porcelain. Marked with a 'G'. See 'G'.

Canneto sull'Oglio (Italy, Mantova). Ceramica Furga porcelain factory f. here in 1872; production included table services and household crockery, dolls and dolls' heads.

FURGA
Hallmark

FURGA
Hallmark

Capodimonte (Italy, a castle near Naples). The factory was f. in 1743. The inspiration behind the enterprise came from the wife of King Charles III of the two Sicilies, Princess Maria Amalia of Saxony, daughter of August III, King of Poland and Elector of Saxony, and sister of the Electoress of Bavaria, Maria-Sophia. The King bore all the initial outlay and manufacturing costs. Technical advisers were the arcanist Livio Ottavio Schepers, a modeller from Belgium, and the painter and gemcutter Giovanni Caselli. The products, which to begin with were destined for the Court, imitated the yellowish frit porcelain of Meissen. Outstandingly fine ware with antique reliefs were made, and also some large sculptural works. Their major achievement is considered to be the room in the Villa Portici, decorated in porcelain. In 1759, the factory was transferred to Buen Retiro where it was active until 1808.

See also: Gricci, G., and Restile, L.

In many variations, in blue underglaze

Capellmann, see Brussels (4).

Capellmanns Sen., see Hal et Ixelles-les Bruxelles.

Cara China Co., The, see Longton (18).

Carlsbad (1) (Bohemia). In 1930, more than 30 porcelain factory owners from the Carlsbad region collaborated in the foundation of the 'Porcella', an economic organisation subtitled 'Evidenz-Kontroll-und Incassobüro GmbH'. In character it had much in common with a syndicate.

Carlsbad (2) (Bohemia). Central administration of the ÖPIAG – Austrian porcelain industry AG (Österreichische Porzellan-Industry AG). This organisation involved the economic co-operation of Bohemian porcelain factories, the statutes of which were sanctioned in Vienna on 12 March 1918. On 3 March 1918 the International Bank of Vienna took it over. The Constitution was laid down on 30 April 1918. The Anglo–Czechoslovakian Bank assumed the patronage (in 1918).

The members were, in chronological order:
1) 1918 Pröeschold & Co., Dallwitz (*q.v.*);
2) 1918 Springer & Co., Elbogen (1) (*q.v.*);
3) 1918 O. and E. Gutherz, Altrohlau (4) (*q.v.*);
4) 1918 Fischer & Mieg, Pirkenhammer (*q.v.*);
5) 1919–20 Schamotte factory, Lickwitz;
6) 1923 Menzel & Co., Aich (*q.v.*), ceased in 1933.

After the First World War, on 30 June 1920, the name was changed into EPIAG – First Porcelain Industry (Erste Porzellan-Industrie AG). According to a letterhead dated 31 August 1918 (a copy of which is in the possession of the author), the name of the firm 'Betriebsstätte Dallwitz' already incorporated the letters 'EPIAG'. The following factories were subsequently accepted by the federation:

1) Vereinigte porcelain factory, Meierhöfen formerly Benedikt Bros. AG in Meierhöfen.
2) Porcelain factory and kaolin processing plant, 'Alp' GmbH, Lubau nr. Podersam and Lickwitz, closed in 1939.
3) Porzellan-Union Klösterle and Thurn. Closed down in 1934.
4) Brittania Porcelain Works, Moser Brothers, formerly Eberhard & Co., Meierhöfen.
5) Feldspatwerk Metzling.

Carlsbad (3) (Bohemia). Friedr. Simon porcelain decorating studio, c. 1930.

Carlstadt, Jacob and Cornelius, modellers, see Kelsterbach.

Carolsfeld, Hans Veit Schnorr von. In 1708, near Aue in Saxony, he discovered some hitherto unknown clay which was dry and white like powder. He called the pit, where he made his discovery, 'White Andreas'. At first he sold the Schnorr clay as wig-powder. In 1709 Böttger used it to replace original Colditz clay. The pit was exhausted in 1850.

Carrara and Parian. So-called after the famous Italian marble quarry and that of the Isle of Paros. Name used in England for manufactured ceramic products composed, in addition to feldspar and kaolin, of diverse ingredients in greatly varying proportions. It was the aim, in the 19th c., to change the cold, white body of biscuit porcelain into something more like marble.

Carraro, Pietro, SNC., see Nove.

Carrier Belleuse, see Sèvres (1).

Carstens, C. & A., see Blankenhain (1).

Carstens, C. and E., see Sorau (1) and Zeven.

Cartlidge, F., & Co., see Longton (19).

Cartouche. Originally a scroll, later a surround to an inscription, or a title, or a shield consisting of scroll work or leaf designs.

Cartwright & Edwards Ltd., see Longton (20).

Caselli, Giovanni. Gemcutter from Piacenza, active around the middle of the 18th c., as a porcelain painter.

Castelli (Italy). Industria Maioliche Abbruzzesi Castelli 'S.I.M.A.C.' S. A. Tableware and luxury porcelain.

Catherine Service. Biscuit service, ordered by Empress Catherine II in 1778 from Sèvres, made in the neo-classical taste with about 750 pieces. Half the staff at Sèvres was engaged in the completion of this order which took one and a half years. It served as a model for the arabesque service, (*q.v.*) (although this service is not biscuit).

Caudéran (France, Bordeaux). Céramique d'Art de Bordeaux S.A. Art and luxury porcelain.

Caughley (England). This firm was f. after 1750 and by 1754 was sold to Gallimore, whose daughter married the Worcester born Th. Turner. In 1772, he became the owner and produced porcelain in the Worcester style. A retail branch, named 'Salopian China Warehouse' was established in 1783 in Portugal St. in London. Turner associated himself with Robert Hancock in 1775, who introduced transfer printing. The business was sold in 1799 to John Rose. He still had the porcelain produced in Caughley, but glazed and painted in his factory at Coalport. The Caughley factory was closed down in 1814. The goods differ from those of the Worcester factory only in the colour of the paste.

1 blind press – 2 moon: blue; name: blind press – 3 blind press – 4–5 S = Salopian, blue underglaze – 6 all blue underglaze – 7–13 all blue underglaze – 8 printed

Caulden Potteries Ltd., china and earthenware manufacturers, see Stoke-on-Trent (2).

Cavazzale (Italian). 'del Giglio', artistic porcelain, more recently (still working) Italian porcelain factory.

"del
Giglio„

'Cawk', see Jasper ware.

Celadon. Porcelains of the Sung Dynasty (960–1280) with a watery green glazed surface. This particular watery green colour was referred to in *L'Astrée*, a fashionable pastoral romance by Honoré d'Urfé (1610–27). In the stage version, the hero of the novel (Celadon) was dressed in this colour, thus making the porcelain decorated in the 18th c. famous. The place of production was Liu-t'ien in the vicinity of Longquam in the province of Tsche-Kiang. It was therefore named Longquam yao. The beginning of Celadon production may have been even earlier than A.D. 1000. Most of the surviving pieces belong to the Ming period, yet a considerable number were made in the Sung- or Yüan-period, as evidence shows. In Egypt and the Near East Celadon is called 'Martabani' after the seaport of Martaban in the Far East. The pieces thus named, are bowls with an uncommonly thick, resonant and hard body. Celadon glazes were especially popular in the Kangxi period.

Celadon green, see Celadon.

de Cente, see Vienna Neustadt.

Centrale de Porcelaine, see Limoges (12).

Cerabel-Belgische Keramikgesellschaft, see Baudour (1).

Céralene, porcelain factory, see Paris (17).

Ceramica Furga, porcelain factory, see Canneto sull'Oglio.

Cerámica Industrial Montgatina, S.L., see Montgat.

Ceramica Lombardo & Fil., see Leghorn.

Cerámicas Hispania, S.L., Fabrica de Loza y Porcelana, see Manises (1).

Céramique d'Art de Bordeaux SA, see Caudéran.

Céramique d'Art de la Madeleine, see Boulogne-sur-Mer.

Céramique de la Gironde, see Caudéran.

Céramique Limousine, La, A. Chastagner, see Limoges (41).

Ceramique Montoise, SA, see Mons (2).

Ceres Service. Tableware of KPM Berlin by Theo Schmuz Baudiss 1910–14. A significant example of late Art Nouveau, which lapsed into obscurity after the First World War (owing to the change in style). (Köllmann)

Chabrol Frères & Poirier, see Limoges (13).

Chalot, Jacques-Louis and Louis-Isidore, see Chantilly (2).

Chambelan (also Ciamberlano), see Duplessis, C. T.

Chamberlain, Walter, see Worcester (1).

Chambrelans. French for private decorator, see 'Hausmaler'.

Chamotte and Klinkerfabrik Waldsassen AG., see Waldsassen (1).

Chamfleury, see Sèvres (1).

Champion, Richard (1743–91). Owner of the Bristol porcelain factory from 1773. See Bristol (1).

Champroux (France). Rodolphe Thuret owned a small porcelain factory in about 1867. No factory mark was used.

Chanou, Henry Florentin, see Paris (18).

Chantilly (1) (France). Louis Henri de Bourbon, Prince de Condé, f. a porcelain works here in 1725. The directors of the firm were: from 1725–51 Ciquaire Cirou; 1751–4 de Montvallier and de Roussière; 1754–60 de Montvallier; 1760–76 Pierre Peyrard; 1776–9 Louis François Gravant; 1779–81 Dame Gravant (his wife); 1781–92 Antheaume de Surval. In 1792 this factory was acquired by the Englishman, Christopher Potter (who also owned the Paris factory, Rue de Crussol). The production under Cirou was very remarkable, especially the painting after the Kakiemon porcelains. The products of this time are particularly praised because the tin glaze used on soft-paste porcelain was of a fine white colour – up until 1755 tin glaze usually had a yellowish tint. Goods produced during these years were of great artistic value. The years between 1755–80 were also an outstanding period of the manufacture, when simple but very tasteful pieces were made. Modellers were the well-known brothers Gilles and Robert Dubois (later in Vincennes) and Louis Fournier.

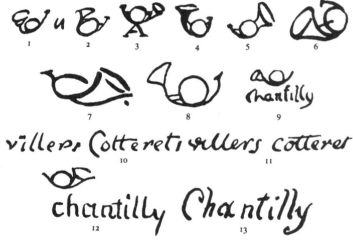

1–8 hunting horn in many variations – 9 red or gold – 10–11 incised artist's signature – 12 blue underglaze – 13 incised

Chantilly (2) (France). M. Pigorry established a porcelain factory here in 1803 after the closure of the Prince of Condé's factory. It specialised in general utility ware and tea services. His successors were Bougon & Chalot. In 1845, Michel Aaron père (Limoges) took charge of the factory, which continued to be run by his son. The 19 statuettes in biscuit porcelain, after models by Pradier, are well known. Under Aaron, father and son, the impressed hunting horn mark of the old factory, M A (the signature of the owner), or Chantilly was used.

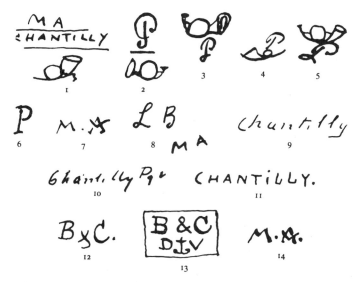

1 blue underglaze – 2 c. 1803 blue underglaze – 3–7 blue underglaze – 8 L B incised, M A
blue underglaze – 9–10 blue underglaze – 11 incised – 12–13 Bougon & Chalot 1818–45 –
14 M. J. Aaron 1845–70

Chapelle, Jaques, see Sceaux.
Chapelle-Maillard, see Paris (27).
Chaplain, see Sèvres (1).
Chapmann & Sons, see Fenton (1).
Chapmans Ltd., Albert Work, see Longton (21).
Chaponnet-Desnoyer, see Paris (19).
Chapperon, see Paris (20).
Charenton (1) (France, Seine). Porcelain was produced here in about 1870. The
manufacturers were: Leulier Fils, Bing, Diffloth et Fils, Gauthier, Gaquin,
Rollin. The products bear no marks.
Charenton (2) (France, Seine). According to 'Tardy 75' the porcelain painters,
Levy & Cie., were engaged here.

Charenton-Saint-Maurice (France, Seine). According to 'Tardy 75' the
brothers Gaultier ran a porcelain factory here in 1860. The numbers under the
marks are model numbers. Excellent dolls' heads, destined for the famous dolls
factory of Emil Jumeau Success., Paris, around 1873. 'F.G.' stands for
Ferdinand Gaultier.

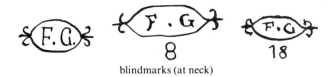

blindmarks (at neck)

Charey (also Chaurey), see Lorient.

Charlionais et Panassier, see Lyon and Toulouse,

Charlottenbrunn (Germany, Silesia). Jos. Schachtel purchased a small porcelain factory in 1859, in Sophienau, Post Charlottenbrunn (Silesia). In the beginning the production was limited to pipe bowls, as the intention was to make the south-east of Germany and districts around the border, independent in their requirements of this commodity from the 'expensive Thuringian "pipe bowls"'. After 1866 production turned exclusively to simple, white utility ware. Following a strong demand for this ware a new factory with its own painting shop was established in 1875. This was the first porcelain factory in Germany to produce electro porcelain. 1887 Jos. Schachtel took over the work with his two sons Max and Eugen. The factory was closed c. 1920.

Charlottenburg (Germany). Berlin's porcelain and chamotte factory. Alfred Bruno Schwartz registered the following mark as a trademark under the No. 14956 on 28 May 1891 and 21 March 1896. Porcelain wares.

[46]

Chatillon (France, Seine). It is reputed that a porcelain factory existed here in 1775, but little is known of it.

chatillon   **D̗t̗V**
                    Chatillon

Chartres, Louis-Philippe-Joseph, Duke of. The Duke of Chartres, later Duke of Orléans, known as Philippe Egalité, was the protector of the porcelain works both of Vincennes and of Rue Amelot in Paris.

Châtres-sur-Cher (France). Porcelain factory of Châtres-sur-Cher, formerly Gaston Sailly, f. 1918. Tableware, coffee, tea and dessert ware. Earlier the firm was known as S.A. des Ets. Gaston Sailly.

Chauffriasse, Rougérie & Co., see Limoges (14).
Chaurey (Charey), see Lorient.
Chaussard, see Paris (69).
Chaviot, see Assay-le-Chateau.
Chazal et Cie., see Courbevoie.
Chelsea (1) (England, London). Information about the beginning of this firm is very sparse. One known signature 'Chelsea 1745', as well as some goblets or cups marked with a triangle, provide some evidence that this was the date the factory was founded. The first products have a milky white glaze with diverse small blemishes, among them pin-sized holes and spots, the so-called 'pin-holes'. Flower reliefs, grooved rims on plates, corals and shellwork are typical decorations. The order of succession of Nicholas Sprimont, a silversmith of Lüttich, and Charles Gouyn, a later owner of the factory is not clear. One of the first proprietors was Sir Everard Fawkener under whom Sprimont directed the factory from 1749–58, after which it was closed for two years. At what date Sprimont became the owner cannot be ascertained; in any event, he sold the factory in 1769 to James Cox, who, a year later, passed it on to William Duesbury and John Heath. From that time on, the production was limited almost exclusively to tableware. The factory closed down in 1784. The products of the last period (Chelsea Derby Period 1770–84), are more in the Derby than in the Chelsea tradition. The first of the marks, a plain red anchor, is sometimes painted overglaze, usually very small, at other times it is embossed in relief on a raised oval. Much praise is given to the quality of the cool, soft glazes on the products around 1755. The Meissen influence is striking. The works in the Far Eastern styles are often mere copies of Meissen pieces in the Chinese taste. Some remarkable unpainted busts of members of the Royal Family, which are ascribed to the sculptor Roubiliac, are signed with the red anchor mark. Specific mention should be made of the so-called 'Chelsea toys', painted scent bottles, snuff boxes, cases and bonbonniers, as well as other small objects, which created the firm's world reputation. During Sprimont's sole direction of the works after Fawkener's death, changes appeared in the quality of the body (paste) as well as in the artistic style. Rich gilding and decoration, on some parts rather overdone, but reminiscent of Meissen, and the engraved marks, are characteristics of the 'Gold Anchor Period'. An outstandingly beautiful Chelsea product is the service commissioned in 1762 by George III for the Duke of Mecklenburg-Strelitz. It is decorated with pictures of exotic birds and has borders in deep (mazarin) blue. The most outstanding artists of the works were the two sculptors from Tournay, Joseph Willems and Gauron.

Chelsea 1745   R   (anchor mark)   N 198
                                   *
1   2   3   TTL
                                   4

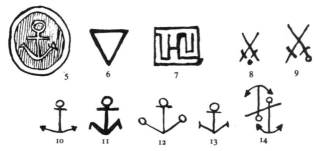

1 blind impressed – 2 blind impressed signature of the sculptor Roubiliac – 3 blue underglaze 1745–50 – 4 blind impressed – 5 relief impressed 1750–3 – 6 blind impressed – 7 blind impressed in Chinese copies – 8–9 blue underglaze (Meissen) – 10–14 red or gold (Gold Anchor)

Chelsea (2) (England, London). In 1769 Duesbury (Derby) bought this factory, but did not amalgamate it with his own firm until 1784. The so-called Chelsea Derby Marks, according to Godden are:

1 red or gold 1770–84 – 2 gold 1770–80

Chelsea Toys, see Toys.

Chemnitz (Germany, Saxony). Alfred Löffler, porcelain painter, had the following mark entered on 28 June 1920, under No. 249336, as the trademark. Production involved porcelain painting only.

[235]

Cheron, E., see Paris (21).

Chessington (England). Heatherley Fine China Ltd. In 1961 bone china was being gilded and painted here.

Chevalier, Julia, see Bordeaux (5).

Chicaneau, Louis Dominic François, see Paris (107).

Chicaneau, Pierre. Owner of a faience factory in St. Cloud nr. Paris, where frit porcelain was made in 1677. His widow married Charles Trou, who continued directing the factory under the patronage of the Duke of Orléans and raised its standards. See St. Cloud.

'China-Clay'. English for kaolin. See 'Porcelain'.

China vases. Vases of the 18th c., with capucine-brown or coffee-coloured glaze on which a design was cut to reveal the white porcelain beneath (mostly Dresden). This was called 'Schnittdecor'; 'Schnitt' can mean equally cut or incised.

Chinesse. This is the term used for porcelain decoration, which reproduced fabric patterns.

Chinoiseries (French). Chinese paintings, also called Chineseries. Freely adapted, oriental style representations of Chinese scenes were popular during the baroque and the rococo and persisted into the 19th c. These themes were favourites in the applied arts, especially for the decoration and modelling of porcelain and faience.

Chin-te-cheen, Imperial factory in Peking. See Belville and Gherardini.

Chodau (1) nr. Carlsbad (Bohemia, now Chodov). In 1811 the coalmine owner, Franz Miessl, was given permission to open a porcelain factory, which, however, produced only stoneware at first. In 1830–4 F. Weis was the leaseholder. On 1 July 1834 Miessl sold the factory to Johann Dietl from Einsiedl and his associates Johann Hüttner and Johann Schreyer. The firm's name was 'Hüttner & Co.' and it gained the Regional Licence for porcelain production in 1835. Before 1842, a Dr. Geitner from Saxony was the owner, but he sold the business in 1842 to Moses Porges von Portheim, whose sons, Ignaz and Gustav supervised it efficiently. Besides utility porcelain the products were also: painted cups, figurative work, candlesticks, vases, writing implements, and drinking glasses. Biscuit was also produced. In October 1872 the Portheims sold the whole of their estate (above all the browncoal interests) to the 'Falkonia AG' which at once resold the porcelain factory to Haas & Czjzek of Schlaggenwald. The latter owner finally led the undertaking to success. In about 1928 there were 25 people in administration and 500–600 workmen. Production consisted of utility porcelain for household, hotels and restaurants. The export went mainly into the Royal Kingdom of Austria–Hungary and the successive states, Balkan, the Near Orient, Egypt, the Northern Countries, Holland and colonies, England and the U.S.A. The owners in 1928 were Olga Baroness Haas-Hasenfels and Herr Felix Czjzek, Edler von Smidaich (the families were ennobled in the K. K. Monarchie, at the end of the 19th c.). There is evidence from 1835–40 that Hüttner and Dietl made lithophanes for light shades, although no surviving piece is known.

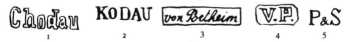

1 oldest impressed picture mark from 1810 – 2 impressed stamp, can also be incised – 3 impressed stamp, under v. Portheim and Portheim and Son – 4 VP = v. Portheim – 5 P & S = Portheim and Son

C

H & C

Chodau (2) near Carlsbad (Bohemia, now Chodov). Richter, Fenkl and Hahn f. a porcelain factory here in 1883, which was called the 'New Factory' in contrast to the one already established. In 1885 Alois Hahn died and Albert Richter endowed his son-in-law, Anton Langner, with his share. Langner, together with Karl Fenkl, built considerable extensions to the factory, so that by 1890 they owned the largest porcelain factory in the vicinity of Carlsbad (called also Fenkl & Langner). Products ranged from the simple to the finest execution in utility ware and were exported to Holland and its colonies, England and the U.S.A. They maintained several warehouses abroad with stocks of samples. By 1928 there were 40 administrative staff and up to 8,000 workmen. The factory was closed down in 1947–8.

Chodowiecki, Daniel-Nikolaus (1726–1801). Famous Berlin copper engraver and etcher who also tried his skills as a painter at the Berlin porcelain works. Reproductions of his prints (or engravings) can be found on Berlin porcelain.
Chodziez (Poland). Fabyka Porcelany i Wyrobow Ceramicznych w Cmielowie, Spolka Akcyjna, f. 1882; produced coffee, tea, table and kitchenware.

Choisy-le-Roy (1) (France). It is reputed that a porcelain factory was f. here by M. Clement. Succeeding owners were Lefèvre and Villiers. The mark shown, which up to now has been considered of unknown provenance according to 'Tardy 75', has been assigned to this firm. However, Berling and Lange (both 1911) reported that it belonged to Desjardin, who had been forbidden its further use by virtue of an order of the KPM, which came into force before 1886.

Vion et Baury

Désiré Vion

Choisy-le-Roy (2) (France). Thomas, Girault et Clement were active here in their painting shop in 1887.

Chotain, see Paris (22).
Choudard des Forges, Edame, see Saint Cloud.
Chrapunoff, see Moscow (8) and Kusjaeff.
Christfeld, Conrad (1754–1829). Active as painter and colourist from 1796–8 in Frankenthal and from 1798–1829 in Nymphenburg. His son too was employed from 1813 onwards as painter in Nymphenburg.
Chromium green underglaze. Chromium oxide coloured yellow-green to dark green. See Meissen: vine leaf wreaths.
Chuffier and Thomas, see Sezanne.
Church, Gresley (1) (England). It is claimed that a small porcelain works was f., c. 1794, with the aid of Gresley (Sir Nigel). It closed down, however, in 1808. No piece of this production can be identified.
Church, Gresley (2) (England). The modern signature on the following mark indicates that this concern is not identical with the above.

Churfürstlich-Mainzische privilegierte porcelain factory, see Höchst.
Cie. de Baie Hudson, La, see Paris (26).
'Cintra', particularly transparent porcelain, see Gustavsberg (1).
Cirou, Ciquaire (d. 1751), see Chantilly (1).
Clain, see Paris (79).
Clain & Perrier fils, see Paris (79).
Clair, Adam (18 August 1763 Frankenthal–14 November 1829 Munich). Pupil of Melchior. From 1776–99 employed as bossierer (repairer) in Frankenthal and from then until his death he worked as bossierer in Nymphenburg. His monogram, 'AC' (see over), which can often be found on Nymphenburg pieces of this period, was the cause of the misunderstanding that he had also worked as modeller.

'**Clair de lune' glaze.** Light-blue Chinese glaze of the Sung-Dynasty (960–1279). Imitations can be found on later Chinese porcelain.

Clairvaux (France). A porcelain factory was here c. 1810.

Claret. Chelsea porcelain colour equivalent to the 'rose pompadour' of sèvres.

Clarté and Dunant, see Boulogne.

Clarus, Johann Felician, see Höchst.

Clauce, Isaac Jacques (1728–1803). Porcelain painter who came from Meissen to Berlin in 1754, and assumed supervision of painting and training of apprentices. Until 1757 he worked in Wegely's factory; from 1761–3 in Gotzkowsky's; finally he was employed in the Royal Berlin factory.

Clauss, Jean. Marx and Marc Eugen, see Paris (23) and (94).

Clement, M., see Choisy-le-Roy (1).

Clement-Massier, see Paris (24).

Clerc, Michel le (also Leclerc), engraver and modeller, see Bouchardon and Sèvres (1).

Clio, Hans (1723–c. 1786). Employed as painter and drawing master for Copenhagen, from c. 1775–86.

$$\mathcal{H}.\,\mathcal{Cio}.$$

Clodion, Claude-Michel (1745–1814). Sculptor, see Sèvres (1).

Clostermann (or Klosterman). There are various potters known under this name who may be related to one another. One 'Closterman', b. 1705, is mentioned as being a chemist in the colouring department of Vincennes in 1753. Another worked from 1784–7, also as a chemist, in the Royal factory of Limoges. In 1805 he was the owner of the La Seynie porcelain factory, and later of the Baignol's factory, again in Limoges. The name 'Klostermann' is mentioned again in Limoges in records of 1834–5. The most well-known member of this family is undoubtedly Pierre Clostermann, who was active in Alcora as an arcanist from 1787–98. His son too was working for the same factory in 1789 as a painter.

Cloud nr. Paris, see Saint Cloud.

Cluj, see Klausenburg.

Cmielow (Poland). Wyrobow Ceramiaznych w Cmielowie porcelain factory, Spolka Akcyjna, f. 1789; production included table, coffee and tea services and kitchen crockery. From 1842, porcelain was also produced here. The factory was still in production in 1930.

Coalbrook Potteries, Cleveland Works, see Shelton (2).

Coalport or Coalbrookdale (England). John Rose f. a porcelain factory here in 1796, which was absorbed into the Caughley Works in 1799. In 1819 Rose managed to secure the services of William Billingsley. In 1822–3 stocks and moulds were taken over from Nantgarw and Swansea. The early Coalport porcelain cannot be distinguished from that manufactured at Caughley. A great deal of unpainted china was sent to London where it was decorated by Baxter Sr. From 1820–50 multi-coloured painted products were made in the style of other manufacturers. John Rose died 1841 and the establishment was then directed by his nephew William. Nowadays the firm's name is: Coalport China Ltd., Stoke-on-Trent.

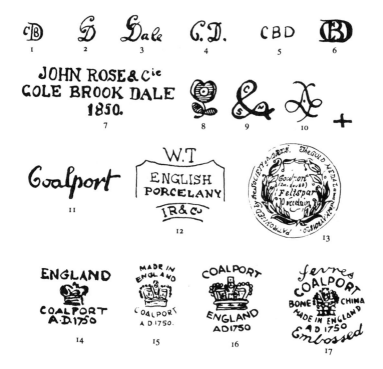

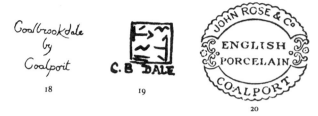

Coalbrookdale by Coalport

18

C.B DALE

19

20

1–5 mostly blue underglaze from 1780 – 6 blue or gold – 7–8 purple – 9 gold since 1861, CSN = Caughley, Swansea, Nantgarw – 10 in imitation of Sèvres – 11 blue underglaze – 12 W.T. = Will Taylor (painter's mark), IR & Co = John Rose & Co. – 13 red printed – 14–17 modern, printed – 18 c. 1820 – 19 1810–20 for 'blue printed willow pattern' (according to Godden) – 20 1830–50 also merely with initials 'J. R. & Co' and 'I. R. & Co' (according to Godden)

Cobridge (1) (England). Samuel Alcock & Co. supervised the Hill Pottery from here from 1828–53 when it was moved to Burslem. Besides stoneware, Parian porcelain, of the simplest quality to the finest, was made. Apart from the marks shown, some with a full address were in use as well. The successors were Sir James Duke & Nephews, 1860–3. The so-called Presentation-Vessels stemmed from this period. A handmark is supposed to have been used: blind-impressed.

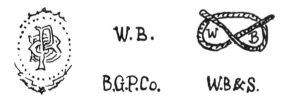

PATENT
SAM'ALCOCK&CO.

Cobridge (2) (England). William Brownfield (& Son), 1850–91. Produced good quality porcelain since 1871. By 1880 over 500 people were employed. His successor was Brownfield Guild Pottery Soc. Ltd., 1891–1900. Other marks carry the full address.

W.B.

B.G.P.Co.

W.B&S.

Cobridge (3) (England). Crystal Porcelain Pottery & Co. Ltd., 1882–6; tiles and plaques of porcelain.

C P P Co.

Cobridge (4) (England). Viking Pottery Co., f. 1936; production included household crockery and sculptural porcelain.

Coburg (1) (Germany, Upper Franconia). Albert Riemann porcelain factory GmbH, f. 1860; production included luxury porcelain and figures.

Coburg (2) (Germany, Upper Franconia). In 1870 two manufacturers, Kuhnle and Hoffmann, made porcelain here.

Cocker, George (d. 1868). Modeller for Derby and Coalport from about 1810 until 1826. As an independent producer of porcelain he devoted himself to the production of biscuit articles.

Cocots or Cocot-Töpfgen, see Pots à crème.

Coclough & Co., see Longton (76).

Coclough China Ltd., Vale Works, see Longton (23).

Coclough, H. S., Vale Works, see Longton (23).

Coeur d'Acier, see Paris (25).

Coggins & Hill, see Longton (22).

Coiffe & Co., see Limoges (15).

Coiffe jeune, see Limoges (16).

Colditz (Germany, Saxony). VEB Porzellan Combinat Colditz. One of the greatest porcelain companies of the DDR, together with VEB Porzellan-Werk Freiberg and Sintolanwerk Annaburg.

1977

Coke, John, see Pinxton.

Colenbrander, Th. A. C. (b. 1841), see Rozenburg.

Collingwood Bros. Ltd., St. George's Works, see Longton (24).

Colmar (France). It is assumed that porcelain was produced here by Anstett c. 1803.

Anstett   Colmar

Cologne (1) (Germany, Rhineland). Ducrot and Th. Olbers jr. produced porcelain here in 1867.

Cologne (2) (Germany). In Nippes, nr. Cologne, according to Berres, Engelbert

Cremer & Son f. an earthenware factory here in 1793, which also offered 'transparent porcelain in the Parisian manner' and 'all kinds of table, coffee and drinking services'. A shop in the Glockengasse sold the products with the notice 'Mauenheim im Nippes'. Some pieces of doubtful quality are known. The marks are impressed, the anchor black.

'Eng. Cremer u. Sohn . Cremer Nippes' KöLN ⚓
in Cöln a. R.'

Colonnata (Italy). Società Ceramica Richard-Ginori was f. in 1735. Production included utility crockery and Capodimonte porcelains. See Doccia.

Compagnie Anglo-Française, see Saint-Gaudens.

Compagnie des deux Indes. In 1719, Louis XV f. this company for the exclusive purpose of porcelain trading.

Compagnie des Indes. In 1602 this company was founded by Dutchmen for the promotion of trade exchanges with the Far East. It succeeded in usurping the up-to-then predominant position of Portuguese traders.

'Concordia', porcelain factory, see Lessau.

Condé, Louis-Henri de Bourbon, Prince de (1692–1740), see Chantilly (1).

Conflans (France, Seine). Julien, in association with Dupuy, ran a porcelain factory here from 1827–56. Later Delangre became the owner.

Conta & Boehme, see Pössneck.

Conventional zwiebelmuster. Traders' term for strawflower pattern. See Ilmenauer strawflower pattern.

Cook, Cyrill, see Hancock, Robert.

Cooke & Hulse, see Longton (25).

Cookworthy, William (1705–80). From 1745 he was experimenting in a quest for a satisfactory hard paste porcelain. In about 1758, after he had discovered kaolin in England, he succeeded. His role as arcanist was decisive in the establishment of the porcelain factories of Bristol (1764) and Plymouth (1768).

Co-operative Wholesale Society, Ltd., Windsor Pottery, see Longton (26).

Cope, H. J. & Co., see Longton (27).

Copeland, William (father) and William-Taylor (Son), see Stoke-on-Trent (11).

Copeland, W.-T. & Sons Ltd., see Stoke-on-Trent (3).

Copenhagen (1) (Denmark). The first unsuccessful experiments in porcelain making in Copenhagen were conducted by Elias Vater, a mirror and glass maker from Dresden, in 1731. He had already tried to produce porcelain in Munich in 1729, with similarly unsuccessful experiments. Those arranged in 1754 by Johann Gottlieb Mehlhorn and Johann Ludwig Lück were failures too. Only after the discovery, by the quarry master Niels Birch, of greater kaolin deposits on the Isle of Bornholm in 1755, was it possible to establish a porcelain factory nr. Christianshavn, which was subsequently directed by the Meissen blue decorator Johann Gottlieb Mehlhorn. This factory merged with the faience factory of Jakob Fortling at Kastrup on the Isle Amager in 1760, which led to the official name 'Factory at the blue tower' (Fabrik am blauen Turm). After Fortling's death and Mehlhorn's withdrawal in 1761, the Frenchman, L. Fournier (who had worked in Chantilly and Vincennes), became director. Various Danish artists assisted him. Fournier produced only frit porcelain, following the French example. Few pieces from this Fournier period have been preserved. Fournier returned to France in 1766 after the accession of Christian VII. His successor Franz Heinrich Müller at last met with success in the production of true porcelain in 1773. From 1755 the factory was a joint-stock company, the shares of which were mainly owned by the Royal family. In 1779 the joint-stock company was taken over by the state, and is now called the 'Royal Danish Porcelain Factory'. In 1780 a sales depot was set in Copenhagen. This was a flourishing time for the Copenhagen porcelain factory, which enjoyed the support of Queen Marie of Denmark. As a whole the artistic production could never free itself from the influence of the European factories, the sole exception being the 'Flora Danica Service'. The prominent members of the factories were:

1. The modeller Anton Karl Luplau from Fürstenberg, who worked from 1776–95 as master modeller in Copenhagen.
2. The Nuremberg flowerpainter Johann Christoph Bayer who was active in Copenhagen from 1776.

After the Battle of Copenhagen in 1801, Müller was pensioned off by the King in 1802 and his successor was I. G. L. Manthey. Under his direction the production rapidly declined, only run-of-the-mill utility products being made. In 1824 Hetsch became the director. Richly gilded ornamental vases and candelabras, as well as figures and reliefs in biscuit were then produced. In 1833 C. W. Bergsoe became director, and in 1867, the factory, which until this time had been called 'Royal', had yet another owner, A. Falck, who reserved the right to retain the old name and mark. In 1843–80 dolls' heads were produced using mark no. 2. In 1884 the factory passed into the ownership of Philipp Schou. In 1885 he engaged Arnold Krog as the artistic director, who rejected the conventional methods and centred his attention on underglaze decorations. In 1889, in Paris, the first works with underglaze decorations were shown and sold very well. Renowned decorators of this period were: F. August Hallin, Oluf Jensen, W. Th. Fischer and Gotfred Rode. In 1902, the son-in-law of Ph. Schou, Fr. Dalgas, took over the directorship of the factory. In 1923 Dr. Berg and Mathiesen produced so-called iron porcelain. It is a soft porcelain, similar to English bone china with a lead glaze; its composition does not contain bone ash however, but it differs widely from the usual material. The result is a hard body, so hard in fact that the consumers gave the product the name 'iron porcelain'. The factory has maintained its high artistic reputation up to the present day.

See also: Albert, C. C., Brecheisen, J., Camrath, J. Sr., Camrath, J., Clio, H., Faxoe, N. Ch., Gülding, J., Hald, A., Hansen, L., Holm, J., Lehmann, H. B. L., Luplau, Chr., Meyer, E., Ondrup, H., Preuss, S., Richter, J., Schmidt, J., Sciptius, G. Ch., Stanley, S., Tvede, C.

1

2

3
[179]

4

5

6

1 1775 – 2 1830–45 – 3 c. 1885 – 4 1889 – 5 1890 red or green overglaze – 6 1894 green underglaze, wavelines blue – 7 1897 green underglaze, wavelines blue – 8 Juliane Marie-porcelain, blue underglaze – 9–10 1923 green underglaze, wavelines blue – 11 since 1929

Copenhagen (2) (Denmark). Bing & Grøndahl AG 1853, f. by the M. Ludwig Bros. and Harald Bing and Frederik v. Grøndahl. Under the directorship of Harald Bing and the decorator Pietro Krohn, a new approach was adopted from c. 1880. The Reiher Heron Service was produced in 1889. 1897–1900 saw the artistic direction of the decorator J. F. Willumsen. It is due to his work that the factory had such great success at the World Exhibition in Paris. Production included artistic porcelain, domestic porcelain, and earthenware, 'Nordische Note'.

[192]

Copenhagen (3) (Denmark). Dahl-Jensens porcelain factory, f. 1925. Objets d'art, Art Nouveau.

Copenhagen (4) (Denmark), Denmark porcelain factory AS, f. 1936. Utility ware and luxury porcelain. See Kongens Lyngby.

Copenhagen (5) (Denmark). P. Ipsens Enke porcelain factory, AS, c. 1930.

Copenhagen (6) (Denmark). Den Kongelige porcelain and faience factory Aluminia AS, f. 1779. Utility porcelain and figures.

Copenhagen (7) (Denmark). Schmidt, W. J., porcelain decorating studio, c. 1930.

Copenhagen (8) (Denmark). Weidingers Glasmalerei (glass painting workshop). Produced porcelain services. Speciality was gold decoration.

Coperta. Italian term for tin glaze, see Tin glaze.

Copper glazes. In 1890, Prof. Dr. Seeger of Berlin, experimented with reduction techniques on copper which ultimately became, at the turn of the century, the famous crystalline and 'flaming glazes' used in the KPM Berlin. In advertisements for the KPM in 1906 and 1909 the text read 'vessels of Seger porcelain with "China Red" copperglaze'.

Coquerel, see Paris (141).

Coral red Porcelain. It applies in general to the background as it is often found in the 'famille verte'.

Corbin, see Saint-Denis (3).

Córdoba (Spain). Sociedad de Utensilios y Productos Esmaltados, f. 1900. Kitchen and household crockery with metallic overglaze decoration. The mark was: SUPE.

Cornwall Kaolin, see Bristol.

Cossé-Mailard, see Paris (27).

Cotta, Franz, see Kotta.

'Cottage china', see Bristol (1).

Cotteau. Worked at Sèvres from 1780–4. It is believed that in about 1782 he invented the 'jewelled' decoration. A 'jewelled' vase dated 1783 bears the signature 'Coteau'.

Couderc, see Paris (28).

'Couleurs de demi grand feu'. French term for blue overglaze as used in Chinese porcelain.

Couleuvre (1) (France, Allier). Bouguin produced porcelain here in c. 1867.

Couleuvre (2) (France, Allier). Manufacture des Porcelaines d'Art de Couleuvre, f. here in 1789. Production included decorative and utility porcelain and reproduction of old porcelain.

Courbevoie (France). Chazal et Cie., carried out porcelain painting, c. 1930.

Courtille, La, see Brussels (3) and Paris (94).

PIC

Coussac-Bonneval (France). The Marquis de Bonneval f. a porcelain factory here which made hard paste porcelain from 1819–1935. It was acquired by Bardon in 1830, who then made it over to Charpentier de Bellecourt.

Coutan, Jules Felix (b. 1848), sculptor, see Sèvres (1).

Cox, James, see Chelsea (1).

Cozzi, Geminiano. With the support of the Venetian Senate he established a porcelain factory in the district of San Giobbe in 1764. It continued in production until 1812.

Craemer & Héron, see Mengersgereuth.

Craquelé (glaze cracks), in Chinese, Tsui-khi. Accidental or intentional hair cracks in the glaze of ceramics, which develop either when body and glaze, or when two layers of glaze, are cooled under uneven tension.

Cream ware. English cream-coloured earthenware body improved and perfected by Josiah Wedgwood I. Also called Queen's ware.

Creidlitz nr. Coburg (1) (Germany, Upper Franconia). Th. Gumtau porcelain factory had the following mark registered as a trademark on 24 September 1906: No. 90942. Production was taken up with porcelain wares.

 [134]

Creidlitz nr. Coburg (2) (Germany, Franconia). Creidlitz porcelain factory GmbH, f. 1907. Produced utility ware, dinner sets and gift articles. The firm changed from a joint stock company into a GmbH (limited liability company).

Creidlitz nr. Coburg (3) (Germany, Franconia). Siebert & Hertwig, porcelain factory, registered on 22 November 1903 the following mark as a trademark: No. 63821. Produced porcelain ware.

COBURG [112]

Creil et Montereau (France). A faience factory was f. here in 1796 by Saint-Cricq-Cazeaux, which also attempted to produce porcelain. Saint-Cricq-Cazeaux later joined up with Baignal. Fine stoneware was produced c. 1840. Up until 1863 soft paste porcelain after the English manner was produced, but only by Leboeuf and Milliet.

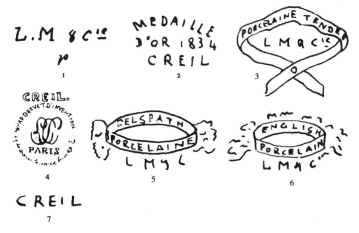

1–2 green underglaze – 3 violet – 4 sepia – 5 violet – 6 blue – 7 green underglaze

Cremer, Engelbert & Bernhard Monheim, see Cologne (2).
Cremer, Eugen, & Son, see Cologne (2).
Cremieux, see Saou (2).
Crepy-en-Valois (France). A porcelain factory was f. here in 1762 by Louis François Gaignepain, an artist from Mennecy. A historical report of 1764 highly praised the quality of the products. Gaignepain went into partnership with F. Bourgeois but the firm closed down in 1767. Snuffboxes and figures were produced in large numbers.

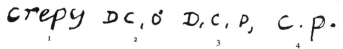

blind

Cretté, Louis, see Brussels (3).

'Cris de Vienne'. Term for the first figures, mostly groups of workmen, made at the factory at Vienna.

Cros. Painter family in Alcora, in the middle of the 18th c.

Cross hatched diaper. Customary English term for the popular trellis or lattice border of the Jiuqing Period (1522–66).

Crown China Crafts Ltd., see Stoke-on-Trent (4).

Crown Staffordshire China Co. Ltd, Minerva Works, see Fenton (5).

Crowther, John, see Bow.

Crushed strawberry. Name for the Chinese porcelain glaze which reflects the impression of crushed strawberries.

Cruz de, Gaspar. In 1569 he wrote the first detailed treatise about the factory method of Chinese porcelain: 'Tractado em que se cotam muito por estese as consas da China co suas particularides, & assi reyno dormuz'.

Crystal glaze. Glaze showing the formation of crystals. To produce this glaze zinc oxide, silicid acid and titanite acid is added to it.

Crystal Porcelain Pottery & Co. Ltd., see Cobridge (3).

Crystalline Terracotta. Josiah Wedgwood's ceramic production, made of a combination of variegated clay with strong gold relief ornamentation.

Cuccumaos, Filippo. F. the porcelain factory in Rome in 1761. See Rome (1).

Custine, Adalbert-Philibert, Comte de (1740–93). Owner of the porcelain and faience factory, Niderviller, from 1770/1 to 1793. See Niderviller.

Cutts, John, painter, see Pinxton.

Cyfflé, Paul Louis (1724–1806). From Brügge. Famous modeller who came from Lunéville to Ottweiler c. 1765 to establish a porcelain works. See Hastière.

Czartorsky, Prince Iwan, see Gorodnitza and Korzek.

Czestochowa (Poland). 'Karolida' factory.

Daeuber, F., see Oude Amstel.

Daffinger, Johann (d. 1796). Father of the famous Moritz Michael Daffinger. He worked as flower painter around the middle of the 18th c. in the Imperial porcelain factory Vienna, and from c. 1770 he worked in Zurich.

Dagoty, P. L., see Paris (30).

Dagoty, Brothers, see Paris (29).

Dagoty et Honoré, see Paris (71).

Dahl-Jensen, Jens. P. (b. 1874). Sculptor. 1893–6 Copenhagen Academy; 1897–1917 modeller for Bing and Grondahl; 1917–25 artistic director of the Norden porcelain factory; 1925 f. Dahl-Jensen porcelain factory, Copenhagen.

Dahl Jenson porcelain factory, see Copenhagen (3).

Dalgas, Fr., see Copenhagen.

Dallwitz nr. Carlsbad (Bohemia, now Dalovice). F. in 1804 by Joh. Ritter von Schönau as an earthenware factory. From 1804–18 Benedikt Haslacher (the founder of Altrohlau) was director. His son, Wolfgang Julius received the concession to produce porcelain in 1830, but by 1832 he had sold the business to Wilhelm Wenzel Lorenz. Transfer printing was carried out from 1844, and there were 100 workmen and an extensive production programme. The plaited fruit-baskets are especially famous. The firm was sold in 1850 to Franz Fischer who later collaborated with Urfuss. According to other sources, the firm still traded in 1870 as 'Fischer, Lorenz & Urfuss'. In 1872, Riedel von Riedelstein bought the factory for 600,000 Guilders. He remained owner until 1889. From 1889–91, the owner was Baron von Springer. Proeschold & Co. then became the owners (co-owners being Rudolf Gottl and Donath Zebisch). The factory merged in 1918 with ÖPIAG. Utility ware was being produced c. 1940.

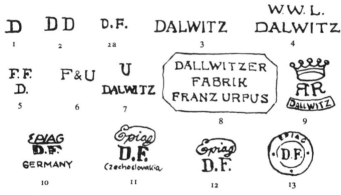

1–3 impressed printing – 4 impressed printing, still with one L – 5 impressed printing after 1832, time of Wilhelm Wenzel Lorenz – 6 F.F.D. Franz Fischer Dalwitz – 7 F & U = Fischer & Urfuss, blind stamp – 10 colour printed, time of Riedel von Riedelstein to end of 1880 – 11–13 EPIAG marks with the exception of 10, all marks were also used for stoneware

Dalpayrat, Adrian, see Bourg-la-Reine.

Damm nr. Aschaffenburg (Germany, Bavaria). A Bavarian gamekeeper, Muller, established a stoneware factory here, with von Hefner as partner and artistic director. Initially original moulds were bought from the Höchst factory after its closure and these were used for earthenware until 1856. Meanwhile porcelain production had been started but did not develop further. It ought to be mentioned here that by this time there was preference for the Melchior models, or such models as purported to be of this type. In 1860 Müller sold the factory to Marzall, who went into bankruptcy in 1874, and attempts to keep the factory going were eventually abandoned in 1884. The moulds were sold to the Mehlem stoneware factory in Bonn (see Bonn). Marks used at Damm were the Höchster wheel mark and an additional 'D' (Damm). Under Marzall the 'D' was omitted.

1 1840–5 – 2 1845–50 – 3 1850–60 – 4 1860–78 – 5 1880–4. During this time the wheel with the six spokes was still used – 6 without date – 7 stoneware mark Damm. With the exception of 7 the mark is mostly in blue overglaze

Dancegroups, the modeller of, see Ludwigsburg (1).

Danhofer (also Dannhofer, Dannhöffer), Joseph Philipp (1712 Vienna–1790 Ludwigsburg). Porcelain painter. As a young man he came to the Vienna porcelain works. In 1737 he joined the Knöller faience factory at Bayreuth, where he worked together with Adam Friedrich von Löwenfinck. Later he worked as a colourist (or painter) in Abtsbessingen, from 1749 in Höchst and from 1762 in Ludwigsburg, where he died in 1790. For mark see Höchst.

Daniel, Henry and Richard, see Stoke-on-Trent (5).

Daniel, John, see New Hall (1).

Daniell, A. B. & R. P., see London.

Danish porcelain factories, see Kongens Lyngby.

Dannecker, Johann Heinrich (15 October 1758 Stuttgart–8 December 1841 Stuttgart). A famous sculptor from Württemberg, the models for the Ludwigsburg porcelain factory were also his handywork.

Dannhauser, Leopold (d. 1786, Vienna). Porcelain modeller. Worked as a repairer before 1749, but also active as a modeller in the same factory. A group of rococo figures in Vienna is attributed to him.

Daoulas (France). R. Goubin & Co. produced porcelain here c. 1867. It bears no marks.

Darcet, Jean (1725–1801), see Brancas-Lauraguais.

D'Arclais de Montamy. In 1765 he published 'Traité des couleurs de la peinture en émail et sur porcelaine', in Paris. This work can be regarded as complementary to Guettard (*q.v.*). A German edition, 'Treatise on the colours for porcelain and enamel painting', was published in 1767 in Leipzig.

Darte Bros., see Paris (31).

Dastin, Enamel painter, see Caen and Paris (32).

Daudin & Laner, see Paris (33).

Davenport, John, see Longport.

David, Michel, see Paris (34).

Davis, William. Directed the Worcester porcelain factory 1751–83.

Decaen Bros., see Arboras, Grigny and Nantes (1).

Derclercq, Franz, see Baudour (1).

Declercq, see Mons (1).

Décor bois. A form of decoration which has a painted ground in imitation of grained wood, mostly with a suitable space left for a picture. Popular decoration for more simple crockery, used in the second half of the 18th c. See Mayer, J. G. J.

Décor de coleurs nacrées à base de Bismuth. Mother of pearl glaze. See Paris (62).

Degenring, Th., see Gehren.

Déjeuner. Common term for breakfast crockery, mostly as a set assembled on a serving tray for one person, as 'solitaire' or for two people as 'Tête-à-tête'.

Delaherche, Auguste (1857–after 1931). Potter. 1877 and 1879–83 Ecole des Arts décoratifs, Paris. 1883–6 director of the L. Pilleux factory in Goincourt (ceramic architectural decoration). 1894–1904 own pottery in Armentières. Awarded gold medal at the Paris World Exhibition of 1889. 1900 Grand Prix. Exerted great influence on the development of the whole ceramic industry of his time.

Delange, see Conflans.

Delaunay, René, Succr., see Saint-Uze.

Delemert, Dmlls., see Arras.

Delft (Holland). N.V. Koninklijke Delftsch-Aardewerkfabriek 'De Porceleyne Fles' v̈/h Joost Thofft & Labouchère, f. 1653. The name is misleading; it originated in the 17th c., when the Dutch potters copied Chinese porcelain in earthenware and majolica (see also Keizer). Until 1876 the factory was simply called 'De Porceleyne Fles'; from c. 1800 the 'Firma Piccardt & Co.' was added; and from c. 1880 it became 'Delftsch-Aardewerkfabriek De Porceleyne Fles, Fa. Joost Thooft & Labouchère'. In 1903 it became a joint stock company and the present name came into use in 1919.

Delinières & Co., see Limoges (18).

Dell, Francesco, see Naples.

Delvincourt, see Vierzon (11).

Demartine, F., & Co., see Limoges (19).

Demeuldre–Coché, see Brussels (5).

Demont, see Paris (136).

Den Haag, see The Hague.

Den Kongelige Porcelains Fabrik. Danish name for the Copenhagen porcelain factory *q.v.*

Denk, Wwe., Albine. Independent Viennese porcelain factory of considerable importance in its time (1880).

Denkendorf nr. Stuttgart (Germany, Württemberg). M. W. Reutter f. a porcelain factory here in 1948, producing dolls' sets and children's games.

Denków (Poland). Several small pottery workshops have existed here for some time. There is evidence of perhaps five workshops existing in the middle of the 19th c. The first large factory was established in 1869 by Gottfried Weiss, the former director of Cmielów, but it was closed down again in 1874. The products compare with those of the firm in Cmielów.

WEISS

25

Denk's, Ww., Albin, see Vienna (5).
Denton China Co., see Longton (28).
Denuell & Cadetole Vaux, see Paris (120).
Denuelle, Dominique, see Paris (112) and La Seynie (1).
Derby (1) (England). William Duesbury porcelain was produced here for the first time in 1750. The factory was very successful and by 1755 it was moved and enlarged. By 1769 Duesbury was already in a sufficiently strong economic position to buy the well known porcelain factory of Chelsea, which he directed independently. It did not become part of his own factory in Derby until 1784, when Chelsea production consequently ceased. In 1776 he bought the Bow porcelain factory, and its production continued in Derby. From 1773 Duesbury signed his products with the first letter of his name, 'D'. However, sometime later, following a visit of King George III, he was granted the use of a crown in his factory mark. Duesbury was succeeded by his son who associated with Michael Kean, who, after the death of the younger Duesbury in 1796, carried on the business alone until 1811, when it was bought by Robert Bloor. The factory was closed in 1847 when Bloor died. However a number of Derby potters, sculptors and painters set up a factory in King Street, which they called 'Old Crown Derby China Company'. The firm was subsequently known as Locker & Co. (1849), Stevenson & Sharpe (1859), Stevenson, Sharpe & Co. (1880) and later Hancock & Co. When in 1877 exports expanded, the little firm in King Street was no longer economically viable and therefore formed a closer association with the Royal Crown Derby Porcelain Co. Ltd. The companies did not merge completely, however, until 1935, when they became the 'Royal Crown Derby Porcelain Co. Derby'. Today the firm still produces tea and coffee services and sculptural porcelain.
See also: Boreman, Z., Bacon d. Ä., Cocker, G., Deys, S., Pardoe, Th., Spangler, J., Stephan, P.

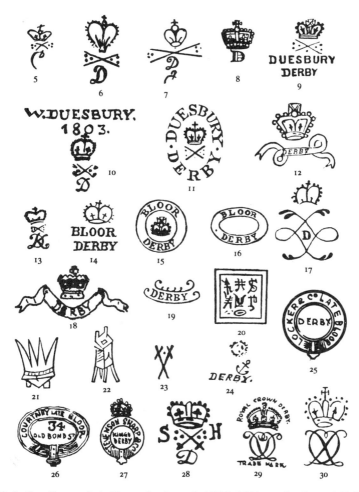

1 1750–5 – 2 earliest marks in blue underglaze – 3–4 1773–84 blue underglaze – 5–7 also in red after 1784 – 8–12 predominantly red – 13 Duesbury & Cean c. 1795–1809 – 14–17 Bloor marks 1811–49 – 18 1848 – 19–22 China marks – 23 Meissen marks on figures – 24 Derby from 1776, very rare – 25 Locker & Co. 1849 – 26 'Courtney' Bloors agent in London – 27 Stevenson Sharp & Co. 1859 – 28 Stevenson & Hancock 1862 – 29 mark of Derby Crown Porcelain Co. 1877–89 – 30 mark of the Royal Crown Derby Porcelain Co. from 3 January 1890

Derby (2) (England). Richard Lunn. Former artistic director of the Derby Crown Porcelain Works, f. 1889. Fine tableware and museum reproductions.

Déroche, see Paris (36).
Deruelle, Pierre. In 1771 he f. the Clignancourt porcelain factory. See Paris (37).
Desarneaux, Mm., see Paris (38).
Deschamps, René, see Limoges (20).
Desforges-Naudot, see Paris (39).
Desgouttières, see Magnac-Bourg.
Desiré, Vion, see Choisy-le-Roy (1).
Desjardin, see Choisy-le-Roy (1).
Desoches. Sculptor. From 1769–74 he worked as Feyliners' successor as master modeller at Fürstenberg, creating very lively and charming portrait busts. See Fürstenberg.
Desplaces, Louis (d. 1739). He originated the designs for the swan-service, *q.v.*
Desprez, see Paris (40).
Dessaux (or Dessaut) de Romilly, Jaques-Etienne, see Orléans (1).
Dessendorf (1) (Bohemia). According to Grollier, in 1871 a porcelain factory, owned by Schnabel & Son, was operating here and using the following mark. Utility ware and technical porcelain. Still operating 1930.
Dessendorf (2) (Bohemia) R. S. Rösler porcelain factory. Utility ware of all kinds.

 S.D.

Desvres (France). Manufacture de Fayence d'Art Gabriel Fourmaintraux was f. here in 1899. Produced utility ware and original art objects.

Deusch & Co., Friedrich Deusch, see Lorch.
Deuster, see Trier.
Deutsche Blumen (German flowers). The contemporary name for naturalistic painted flowers of the indigenous flora, in contrast to the 'Indian flowers' which had been adapted from Far Eastern art forms. Having been in use in faience painting c. 1680, they became a highly favoured decoration around the middle of the 18th c.
Deutz nr. Cologne (Germany, Rhineland). Bruckman & Son produced porcelain here c. 1870.
Devilhaut, see Aprey.
Deyander & Schmitt, Schmitt Frères, see Saarbrücken.
Dickhut, J. F., see Proskau.
Diemar & Co., see Elgersburg (2).
Dieringhausen (Germany, Rhineland). Spitzer porcelain factory GmbH, c. 1930.

Dieterle, R. and Kämpf R., see Grünlas.

Dieterle, see Sèvres (1).

Dietl, Julius, see Elbogen (3) and Kaltenhofen.

Dietrich, called Dietricy, Christian Wilhelm Ernst (1712 Weimar–1774 Dresden). Pupil of the landscape painter Johann Alexander Thiele in Dresden. In 1741 he became Court painter, and in 1748 Inspector of the Court Gallery. He was tutor at the Meissen Art School until 1765, where he directed the training of the porcelain painters 'to prevent further decline of painting in the factory'. His art was strongly influenced by Rembrandt and Ostade, and was thus truly derivative. His engravings often served as patterns for ceramic figures. In 1764 he brought the sculptor, Michel Victor Acier (a student of the Paris Academy), to the factory and granted him full independence of Kändler.

Dietrich, Philipp, see Älteste Volkstedter (4).

Diffloth et Fils, see Charenton (1).

Digeon (France). According to 'Tardy 75', S.S. Usine de la Broche, later Société Nouvelle La Broche S.A., has been in operation since 1931 and had the following mark registered in 1961.

DIGOIN

Dihl. He f. the 'Manufacture du Duc d'Angoulême' in the Rue Bondy in 1780. See Paris (41).

D.K.G. = Deutsche Keramische Gesellschaft (German Ceramic Association).

Dillwyn, Lewis Weston (1778–1855), see Swansea.

Dione, D., & Baudry, see Paris (42).

Dirks and Giersberg, see Köln-Kalk.

Discry, see Paris (25).

Ditmar-Urbach AG, see Turn (1) and Znaim.

Dittmar, Wilh., Friedr. Silhouette painter of the Königlichen Porzellan Manufactur Berlin (Royal Porcelain Factory Berlin), at about the end of the 18th c.

Doat, Taxile (b. 1851 Albi). He was at the Sèvres porcelain factory as a ceramist from 1877–1905, and from 1909 was director of the Ceramic School in St. Louis, U.S.A. He brought the 'Pâte sur Pâte' decorative technique back into favour and decorated his vessels and boxes with coloured heads from antiquity. They resemble cameos raised above the coloured ground. He produced about 2,000 ceramic works.

Doccia (Italy). The Marchese Carlo Ginori f. a porcelain factory here in 1737, with the help of the Viennese arcanist, J. Karl Wendelin Anreiter von Zirnfeld. Workers from Saxony were also recruited, who at first exerted a strong influence over the style of the products. This influence weakened rapidly, however, after the arrival of renown Italian artists, such as Antonio Smeraldi, Carlo Ristori, Giovanni Giusti, Fanciulacci, Fiaschi, Bruschi and Liri. The so-called 'masso bastardo' body originated from this time. Under the direction of Lorenco Ginori vases and statues were produced in such sizes as had never been seen in porcelain before. Present day copies of these pieces are called 'Ginori Antico'. At various times between 1811 and 1835, moulds and models were bought from Capo di Monte and Doccia was allowed to mark reproductions from these with the crowned 'N'. In 1896, the Ginori porcelain factory was incorporated with the Richard of Milan factory (see Milan San Cristoforo). Since then the name of the company has been 'Società Ceramica Richard-Ginori'. Retail branches were also set up in the large Italian cities after 1896. In 1897 the factory was bought by the ceramic factory in Mondovi, which produced chalk-rich pottery ware. In 1906 the Rifredi factory in Florence was bought up and reorganised for the production of electrical insulators. This concern was enlarged in 1936 through the acquisition of the F.J.L. factory in Leghorn (built in 1918) and the manufacturing plant 'Ortica' of the Ceramica Lombardi di Lambrate. F.J.L. produces electrical porcelain, 'Ortica' makes pottery-ware. During the last war all these factories suffered heavy losses, due partly to bombs and partly to their location in battle regions. Today, Doccia produces only artistic porcelain, while the 'Sesto Fiorentino' factory handles industrial production. Today the firm has eight factories in Lombardy, Piemonte and Tuscany.

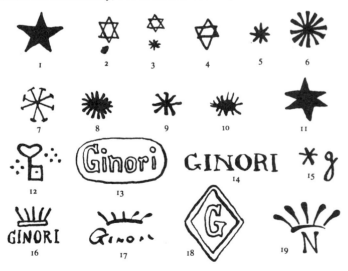

1-11 all in use between 1737-1860 – 13 1884-91 – 14 1868-1903 – 18 1874-88 – 19-20 1850-1903 – 23-24 20th c. marks

Dodé, see Fours (1).
Dommer, Georg & Co., see Niever Amstel and Oude Amstel.
Donaldson, John (1737-1810). Miniaturist and porcelain painter. According to an old tradition he is said to have worked for Chelsea (he may be the creator of the naturalistic birds and figures on the large 'gold anchor' vases produced around 1760-5). It is also said that he painted vases with mythological figures.

Donatello. Name of mark used by P. F. Rosenthal, Selb as trademark No. 255263, from 5 October 1920.
Donath & Co., see Dresden (5).
Donovan, father and son, from Dublin (Ireland) 1770-1829. Around 1800 they were decorating porcelain from Minton and other factories.

1 red and violet – 3 red – 4 blue and red overglaze

Dorez Barthélemy, see Lille (1).

Dörfl, Franz, see Vienna (6).

Dorfner & Cie., Ernst, see Hirschau.

Doric China Co., see Fenton (6).

Dorna, name of mark used as trademark No. 99701 from 17 July 1907, by the Plateel bakkerji Delft.

Dornheim, Koch & Fischer, see Gräfenroda (2).

'Dorothy Ann' Floral China, see Stoke-on-Trent (6).

Dortu, Johann Jacob (1749–1819). Dortu was descended from a French immigrant family. He worked from 1764–7 in the Royal Porcelain Factory, Berlin, as an apprentice colourist in blue and polychrome. From 1777–8 he was active as arcanist in the Marieberg factory, where, under his direction, porcelain was made for the first time. He was one of the founders of the Nyon porcelain factory at the Sea of Geneva, where he worked from 1781–1813. See Marieberg and Nyon.

Dot period (Punkt Zeit), see Meissen (1).

Doulton & Co. Ltd., see Burslem (2).

Dowbysz (Poland). A porcelain factory, possibly f. by the Count Ilinski, existed here from c. 1840. It closed down only in the first years of this century.

Drechsel & Strobel, see Marktleuthen (1).

Dresden (1) (Germany). The experiments which took place here in the beginning of 1708, seeking a recipe for 'Delft faience', helped pave the way to the discovery of porcelain in 1709.

Dresden (2) (Germany). The following mark (which up to now, has presented many problems), was entered at the Royal County Court Dresden for four different firms (with consecutive numbers), on 7 March 1883, at 5.30 p.m.

No. 116 Richard Klemm, Dresden Striesen, porcelain decorating studio – No. in the WZR 24.

No. 117 Donath & Co., Dresden, porcelain decorating studio – No. in the WZR 25.

No. 118 Oswald Lorenz, Com. Ges., Dresden – No. in the WZR 26.
No. 119 Adolf Hamann, Dresden, porcelain decorating studio – No. in the WZR 27. Probably an early syndicate!

Dresden (3) (Germany). Karl Anhäuser, who ran a porcelain decorating studio, came to the fore in 1913 owing to the injunction of the KPM, Meissen, which was introduced to prevent his unauthorised use of the sword mark. Archival evidence supports this version of events.

Dresden (4) (Germany). E. Brammer, Oppelstr. 52, Deutsche Kunst und Verlags-Anstalt for photo-ceramic painting. Their speciality was paintings of all kinds on milk glass and porcelain plates.

Dresden (5) (Germany). Donath & Co., 25 Wachsbleichstrasse, f. 1872. Porcelain decorating studio which specialised in the Dresden and Viennese style. Awarded prizes at Brussels 1888, Barcelona 1888, Chicago 1893, Dresden 1895.

Dresden (6) (Germany). Dresden porcelain factory GmbH, was in operation prior to 1910. Production included luxury porcelain, Dresden type, Old Meissen, Sèvres, Old Vienna. This firm gradually collapsed. See also Berlin (5), H. Schomberg & Sons.

DRESDEN.   DRESDEN.

Dresden (7) (Germany). Richard Eckert, well known porcelain factory in Volkstedt. On 26 November 1909 the firm had the following mark registered for the production and trading of art objects. Trademark No. 115256.

Dresden (8) (Germany). Greiner & Son, a studio for porcelain decorating, f. in 1871. Their specialities were painting on plates, vases, trays, etc., and portraits from photographs.

Dresden (9) (Germany). According to Neuwirth, Josef Günther ran a porcelain decorating studio here c. 1894.

Dresden (10) (Germany). Adolf Hamann, Serrestrasse 8. A porcelain decorating studio which was in operation from 1866, and also an art and antique business. Their speciality was painting executed in Dresden, Meissen and Viennese styles.

[115]   [27]

Dresden (11) (Germany). Heufel & Co. A porcelain decorating studio, operating c. 1900–40. Their specialities were cups, vases, and knick-knacks. Occasionally exported to the U.S.A.

Dresden (12) (Germany). Franziska Hirsch GmbH, Struwestrasse 19, in business from late 19th c. until c. 1930. The painting was in the Meissen style. In 1896 the Meissen KPM successfully contested the use of the mark of two crossed staffs with an H. Any further use was prevented and the mark was deleted in the trade register of the German Reich 1896–8.

[103]

Dresden (13) (Germany). C. M. Hutschenreuther AG porcelain factory and porcelain decorating studio. Produced luxury porcelain.

Dresden (14) (Germany). Franz Junkersdorf, Prager Str. 23, f. in 1897. Specialised in buttons, belt buckles, hat pins, armorial painting, heraldic articles, and painting in the antique style. Genre: Dresden, Meissen, Vienna. Exported to England, U.S.A. and Russia. Still working in 1934.

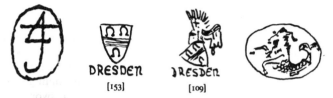

DRESDEN [153]   DRESDEN [109]

Dresden (15) (Germany). Klauber & Simon, a metal ware and button factory, registered the following mark as a trademark on 12 October 1920, under No. 253868.

[236]

Dresden (16) (Germany). Karl Richard Klemm, Vorstadt Striesen. Porcelain decorating studio f. in 1869, producing Dresden, Meissen and Vienna styles. On 29 August 1890, at the K. K. Zentral-Markenregister in Vienna, the marks 1 and 2 were recorded under Nos. 694 and 695. Klemm renewed these on 11 September 1900 under No. 13166/67. The marks are printed in black, partly fired, partly labelled. The factory was prosecuted as recently as 1940 by the KPM Meissen, for misuse of the sword mark, and ceased operating altogether in 1949.

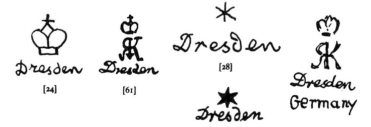

[24]   [61]   [28]

Dresden (17) (Germany). Louis Knöller, Bismarkplatz 1. Porcelain decorating studio.

Dresden (18) (Germany). Wilhelm Koch, porcelain decorating studio and saleroom c. 1928–40. Collectors items including mocha cups, cannisters, tea and coffee cups and bowls.

Dresden (19) (Germany). A. Lamm, a porcelain decorating studio, and art and antique business, f. in 1887, and still active in 1934. This firm decorated in the Meissen tradition but adopted other styles as well – the Copenhagen-type products are notable. According to the Keramadressbuch, 1906: 'Specialities: Old Dresden flowers, Watteau and mythology, decorated luxury and utility articles in the old and new style.' The products are of outstanding quality. The workshop, because of its alleged unauthorised use of the sword mark, was involved in court proceedings, instigated by the KPM Meissen, as late as 1943. Archival evidence supports this.

[162]   [88]

Dresden (20) (Germany). Adolf Leube, Waisenhausstr, porcelain decorating studio, c. 1906.

Dresden (21) (Germany). Oswald Lorenz had the following mark registered at the Königlichen Amtsgericht Dresden on 27 May 1881. Produced porcelain ware.

[26]   [17]

Dresden (22) (Germany). Meyers & Son, f. end of the 19th c., decorated in the 'Meissen-style'.

Dresden (23) (Germany, Saxony). Anton Ott, porcelain decorating studio, f. 1922, still working in 1934.

Dresden (24) (Germany). Arthur Reissig, Serrestr. Studio for porcelain and hollow glass decoration. Specialised in tombstones, door and shop signs, as well as other lettering work, armorial crests and coats of arms, emblems, etc., for students and clubs. In business since 1876.

Dresden (25) (Germany). Anton Richter, studio for porcelain decorating. Specialised in Old-Vienna, Sèvres and Dresden styles. Four of the craftsmen received silver medals in Dresden in 1891 and also in 1896. In operation since 1887.

Dresden (26) (Germany). Max Robra, ceramic workshop and porcelain decorating studio f. in 1919. Speciality was utility and luxury ware.

Dresden (27) (Germany). Oskar Gustav Schade, Schäferstrasse 42. Porcelain decorating studio, f. in 1886. Specialised in Dresden and Old Meissen styles, and still active in 1906.

Dresden (28) (Germany). Otto Schmidt, porcelain decorating studio f. in 1918. Formerly a branch of the Fraunreuth AG porcelain factory. Produced in the Berlin, Meissen, Vienna and Sèvres styles. Still active in 1934.

Dresden (29) (Germany). Strobel & Petschke, porcelain painting studio f. in 1869. The mark, according to Neuwirth, was used for 'dark-blue on glaze'.

S. u· P.

Dresden

Dresden (30) (Germany). Ella Strobel, porcelain decorating studio and shop, and Johann Strobel, Trompeterstr. 19, porcelain decorating studio, kiln and shop, f. in 1867. Both studios specialised in Viennese and Dresden decorations, and, to a lesser extent, flowers. Still working in 1934.

Dresden (31) (Germany). L. Sturm and Marie Till (whose deceased husband Franz Till had originally run the business), Pragerstrasse 1. Porcelain painting studio. Owners were Margarete Till (a widow) and Franz Sturm. Business manager was Franz Carl Sturm. Their specialities were paintings on plates, ivory miniatures, portraits, etc. Operating since 1872 and still working in 1906.

TILL
DRESDEN

Dresden (32) (Germany). Ufer, Studio for porcelain decoration. No dates have so far been confirmed.

Dresden (33) (Germany). Adolf Wache. Studio for porcelain decoration. Specialities were decorated luxury and utility ware in the manner of Dresden, Berlin and Vienna, in ancient and modern styles, Watteau and flowers and decorated cane-tops. Active since 1880.

Dresden (34) (Germany). Carl Wagner, Wettinerstrasse 49. Studio for porcelain decoration, with kiln.

Wagner

Dresden (35) (Germany). Rich. Wehsner, Zinzendorfstrass 16, studio for porcelain decoration. Specialities were finely painted decoration and Dresden type decoration for export. In operation since 1895.

Dresden (36) (Germany). Helena Wolfsohn. Studio for porcelain decoration from 1843. Wolfsohn's successors were Leopold Elb and W. E. Stephan. Exquisite decoration in Meissen-style. In 1879 the A.R. mark was applied to pieces which had already been decorated and the KPM Meissen, as is shown by archival evidence, started legal proceedings. According to Neuwirth the last shown mark, 'Augustus Rex', possibly belongs among the marks misused by Wolfsohn.

[40]

Dresden (37) (Germany). L. Wünsche, Marienbergerstrasse 81. Ceramic workshops in business from 1930. Produced porcelain in the Dresden, Meissen and modern styles, and used applied flowers and peasant-type decorations.

Dresden (38) (Germany). Mark of unknown decorator.

Dresden Floral Porcelain Co., see Longton (29).
Dresden Porcelain Co., see Longton (15).
Dresden porcelain factory GmbH, see Dresden (6).
Dressel, Cuno and Otto, see Sonneberg.
Dressel, Kister & Co. AG, see Älteste Volkstedter (4).

Dresser, Matthäus. In 1597 he wrote 'Histories and reports of the recently discovered Kingdom of China'. He refers to Martinus de Herrada in general and gives a detailed account of porcelain making.

Drimmer, L., see Rodez.

Dryander, L. W., see Niderviller.

Duban, see Paris (43).

Du Bellier, Karl, see Schwabach.

Dubois & Cie., see Mons (3).

Dubois and Jamet, see Vierzon (11).

Dubois, Brothers, see Dubois, Robert and Dubois, Gilles, see also Vincennes (1) and Sèvres (1).

Dubois, Gilles (b. 1713). Active as potter and decorator in Chantilly in 1731 and in Vincennes in 1738.

Dubois, Jerôme-Vincent, see Paris (44).

Dubois, Leopold, see Limoges (45).

Dubois, Robert (b. 1709). Active at Chantilly as potter and arcanist, from 1725–38, at Vincennes from 1738–41, and at Tournay in 1753.

Dubois, see Orléans (1).

Dubois, see Paris (45).

Duchatelet, see Limoges (6).

Ducheval, see Caen.

Ducrot, see Cologne (1).

Duesbury, William Sr. (1725–86). In the beginning of his career in London, he decorated porcelain of various factories, from 1751–3. Became the owner of Derby in 1756, of Chelsea in 1770, and he is reputed to have been the owner of Longton Hall c. 1760.

Duesbury, William Jr. (1763–96 or 97). Son of William Duesbury Sr. He was the owner of the Derby porcelain factory from 1786 until his death.

Duhamel, see Paris (46).

Duisdorf nr. Bonn (Germany, Rhineland). Rhenania porcelain factory GmbH, Duisdorf-Bonn, f. in 1904. Produced utility and decorative porcelain. Now known as the Westdeutsche Porzellanfabrik GmbH.

Duljewo (Russia). In 1832 T. J. Kusnetzoff f. the porcelain factory which operates to this day under the title 'Prawda Porzellan-Fabrik Duljewo'. The mark shown was in use c. 1930. Some bowls, painted in polychrome, are in the Hermitage.

See also Kusnetzoff.

Dulongmuster. A Meissen porcelain relief pattern of rococo scrolls enclosing panels. The border is enclosed by four large arches between each of which are three smaller ones. The arch's radial grate divides it into three areas, each of which, without any subdivision, is given a rocaille. A flower is placed in the outermost section, and a pendant, or shell, in the inner partitions. It was designed in 1743.

Dunaschoff, see Moscow (2).

Duplessis, Claude-Thomas, actually Chambelan (d. 1774). Pupil of the sculptors Oppenort and Meissonnier. In 1745 he was instructed to work in Vincennes and remained there and in Sèvres until his death in 1774. Produced designs for tableware, vases and presentation pieces.

Dupuy, see Conflans.

Dupuy, E., see Sauviat.

Dupuy, Georges, see Limoges (21).

Dura Co. Ltd., Empress pottery, see Hanley (4).

Durham China Co. Ltd., see Gateshead-on-Tyne.

Dürrbeck & Ruckdäschel, see Weissenstadt.

Düssel & Co., see Rehau (3).

Dutertre, Bros., see Paris (47).

Duval, see Paris (48).

Duve, J. F., painter in Copenhagen (1782–3) and decorator.

Duvivier, Henri Joseph (d. 1771), see Tournay.

Dux (1) (Bohemia). Duxer porcelain factory AG, formerly Ed. Eichler, f. 1860. Produced figures, etc. Still independent and active in 1948. See also Blankenhain (1).

[186]　

[219]

Dux (2) (Bohemia). C. Riese, porcelain terracotta, and majolica factory, f. 1883. Produced fancy and luxury items, ivory porcelain, and items for the international trade.

Ebelmann (or Ebelmen), Jacques-Joseph (1814–52), see Sèvres (1).

Eberhard & Co., see Meierhöfen (1).

Eberlein, Johann Friedrich (1696–1749). Porcelain modeller who worked from 1735–49 in the Meissen factory under Kändler.
See also Brühlsches Allerlei-Muster.

Eck, Bertold, see Unterneubrunn.

Eckert, Richard & Co. AG, see Volkstedt Rudolstadt (7) and Dresden (7).

Edelstein porcelain factory AG, see Küps (1).

Edwards and Brown, see Longton (30).

Edwards, John & Co., see Fenton (7).

Effaucure, a type of porcelain decoration. The historic tables of the 'Deutsche Keramic Gesellschaft' name Prof. F. R. H. Schlinderbusch, in Prague in 1930, as the inventor. Nothing could be discovered about the technique itself for many years – only recently did Pöttig manage to bring it to light. A notification of patent in Prague (17 May 1930), and Vienna (26 January 1931) was found. According to this Rolf Hubert Schlindenbuch of Prague registered the patent of a kind of painting decoration which fundamentally differed from any previously used in the decoration of ceramic objects. This method consisted of colouring the whole of the body with black or any dark colour and then to subject it to wiping or rubbing out, engraving, scraping, retouching and the adding of new colours. A quick glance confirms that the original aim was to produce an effect which differed completely from the conventional manner of decorating. These were the tools listed: small cedarwood sticks, flat steel pens, lilac, elderberry or mullein pith for wiping and paint brushes. The origin of the name is found in the French 'effacer', although this is not mentioned in the Austrian patent No. 127777.

Effner, Andreas (also Ettner or Oettner), see Ettner.

Egehard, C. Signature on a porcelain plate in the Stuttgarter Landesmuseum, possibly the mark of a porcelain decorator c. mid 18th c.

Egelkraut, Karl, see Kleindembach.

Eger, Hugo, formerly E. Wagner, see Geraberg (1).

Eger, Jacob F. H., painter, see Kelsterbach.

Eger & Co., see Martinroda.

Eggebrecht, Peter (d. 1738). Potter from Berlin. On 1 February 1708, he was engaged by von Tschirnhaus for the newly established faience factory in Dresden Neustadt, where red stoneware and Dutch tiles were made.
See also Petersburg (1).

Eggendobel nr. Passau (Germany, Bavaria). In 1835 a small porcelain factory was f. here, about which we know nothing else.

Egyptian Service. Sèvres table service from the time of Napoleon I, decorated with scenes from his Egyptian Campaign. Completed in 1808.

Eichhorn, Eugen, see Laucha.

Eichhorn, H. K., see Schney.

Eichhorn & Bandor, see Elgersburg (1).

Eichler, Ed. (now Durex porcelain works), see Dux (1) and Blankenhain (1).

Eichwald (Bohemia, now Duby). Dr. Widera & Co., Kdt.-Ges. factories produced ovenware and wall plaques in Eichwalder porcelain; earlier Bloch & Co. factories (f. 1871) produced utility ware and luxury articles in Eichwalder porcelain. Recent discoveries show that Bloch (who owned a licence issued by Meissen) was producing porcelain decorated with the onion pattern in the 19th c. The so-called 'Karlsbader Zwiebelmuster' (onion pattern) is produced exclusively in Duby today, and is marked with the following:

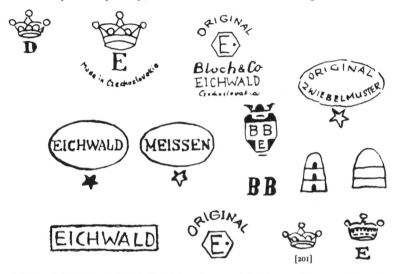

Eichwald (Bohemia) Adolf Schippel, porcelain flower factory, in business in 1894.

Eierschalen porcelain (Eggshell porcelain). Porcelain with very thin and translucent body (Chinese invention).

Eigl, Karl Heinz, see Ottensheim.

Eisele, Johannes, see Ludwigshafen.

Eisenach (Germany, Thuringia). August Sältzer, artist and potter who owned a porcelain decorating studio f. 1858. Purveyor to the royal household and still working in 1924.

Eisenberg (1) (Germany, Thuringia). Bremer & Schmidt porcelain factory, f. 1895; produced household porcelain, stapleware, Mocha services and Mocha cups (small coffee cups) for the Balkans and the Orient; used the onion pattern.

Owners were Dr. Schmidt & Knüpfer. Now named VEB Spezialporzellan Eisenberg (a subsidiary of the Porzellan Kombinat Kahla). The trademark with SPE is currently (1977) valid.

Eisenberg (2) (Germany, Thuringia). Wilhelm Jäger porcelain factory, f. 1867. Produced tea, coffee, tea and breakfast services, hotel ware; used the onion pattern. Now (1977) called: 'VEB Vereinigte Porzellanwerke Eisenberg' (previously F.A. Reinecke Eisenberg). The Fortuna mark is now used.

[178]

Eisenberg (3) (Germany, Thuringia). Kalk GmbH porcelain factory, f. 1900. Produced coffee and tableware; used onion and strawflower patterns. Previously called Geyer, Koerbitz & Co.; now (1976) 'VEB Porzellan-Fabrik Eisenberg' (belonging to the Porzellan-Kombinat Kahla). The crossed arrows are used as marks without any other additions.

Eisenberg (4) (Germany, Thuringia). F. A. Reinecke, porcelain factory, f. 1796; produced utility ware. It is of special interest that here too porcelain was decorated with the Meissen onion pattern. The crossed staves with RPME was used as a mark originally but today Fortuna is used.

Eisenberg (5) (Germany, Thuringia). Around the end of the 19th and beginning of the 20th c. porcelain may have been produced by J. Schmeisser. The first mark

was also used for Schumann, Moabit, according to Scheffler who is supported by
archival evidence.

Eisen porzellan. Böttger's stoneware, the surface of which has been coloured or
turned into black-grey by firing at a high temperature.

Eisenträger, Heinrich (b. c. 1750), porcelain decorator from Kassel. Figure,
landscape and miniature painter of the Fürstenberg factory, where he worked
from 1757–67.

H: Eisenträger. pict

1 7 8 5.

Ekberg, Josef (1877–1945). Painter and designer. Pupil of Wennerberg from
1898–1945. At Gustavsberg from 1914–17 as the leading artist of the factory
until Wilhelm Kages was appointed as artistic director.

Elbogen (Bohemia). Julius Dietl, porcelain factory of Elbogen and Kaltenhof, f.
1897. Utility services.

Elbogen (1) (Bohemia, now Loket n.O.). A porcelain factory was f. here in 1815
by the Haidinger brothers, supported by Niedermayer, who was director of the
Vienna porcelain works, from 1805–27. The firm called itself 'Wiener Porzellan-
Fabrick'. At first it made only white porcelain, using kaolin from Zettlitz. The
products of the early years were very hard and greyish in colour, and were sold
undecorated to Viennese porcelain decorating studios. Successes and ex-
hibitions came in 1831. The director of the Sèvres Works visited this factory in
1836, and took some pieces back to Paris with him, which are still there. In c.
1870 the last of the Haidinger brothers died and in 1873 the heirs sold the factory
to Springer & Oppenheimer. The amalgamation was called 'Erste Elbogner
Porzellan und Kohlen Industrie KG'. In 1885 Oppenheimer left again; from
then on the firm's title was 'Springer & Co.' and was one of the factories which in
1918 formed a confederation with the ÖPIAG. Mark No. 3 was registered on 15
August 1891 (under the No. 3) by Springer & Co. K.K., private porcelain
factory, for the K.K. trademark register in Vienna.

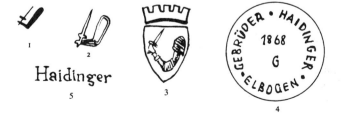

1 blue underglaze until 1833 – blind stamp 1833-60, mostly with year – 3 coloured, also underglaze – 4 jubilee 1868 – 5–7 on figures and larger pieces mostly with no. of year to first half of 19th c. – 8–12 modern marks

Elbogen (2) (Bohemia, now Loket n.O.). Johann Hoffmann directed a porcelain decorating studio here in 1927–45.

Elbogen (3) (Bohemia, now Loket n.O.). Winter & Co., f. 1880; utility and hotel ware, cosmopolitan products.

Elbogen (4) (Bohemia, now Loket n.O.). In 1887 Winter & Co. f. an earthenware factory here. Production of porcelain and earthenware had already begun in 1888. In 1891 the owners were Kretschmann & Wurda and in 1899 H. Kretschmann became the sole proprietor. Produced for a wide export field, Tunisia in particular. In October 1938 this firm was deleted from the trade-register, but was reopened later by Rokyta & Co. and then finally closed again after 1945. Simple utility ware and Turkish beakers were produced. Mark was H.K.

Elbogen (5) (Bohemia, now Loket n.O.). A porcelain factory was f. here in 1890 by Winter, Lochschmied & Co. In 1896 Karl Speck & Co. marked the products with the name 'Austria', and in 1920 the factory was taken over by the Persch Bros. of Hegewald (*q.v.*). Utility ware (strawflower pattern) was produced. According to Heimatkunde des Bezirks Falkenau (historical accounts of the districts), the firm was called Karl Speck, Benj. F. Hunt & Son in 1898. Unfavourable economic circumstances caused the factory to be closed in 1937.

Elbogen (6) (Bohemia, now Loket n.O.). Porag ran a factory here from 1937 as successor to Perch who established the business. Business directors were Josef Dengler and Arthur Dieterle. The factory was closed in 1945.
Elbogen (7) (Bohemia, now Loket n.O.). The following mark cannot be attributed to any of the porcelain factories in this locality. Sometimes it is used in combination with the so-called 'Hoheitszeichen' (national emblem) on thick walled 'Wehrmachtsgeschirr' (crockery for the Armed Forces).

Elers, David and John Philip. In c. 1693, in Fulham and later in Staffordshire, they made a product which was similar to the red Böttger stoneware, and which was known as 'Elersware'.
Elgersburg (1) (Germany, Saxony-Coburg). E. & F. C. Arnoldi porcelain factory, f. in 1808, formerly Eichhorn & Bandorf; utility ware. This concern was reorganised after the war for the production of technical porcelain.

[69]   [184]   ]185]

Elgersburg (2) (Germany, Saxony-Coburg). Diemar & Co. porcelain factory was in business in 1894.

Elkin, Knight & Bridgewook. The Foley Potteries, see Fenton (8).
Ellwangen nr. Utzmemmingen (Germany, Württemberg). The widow of A. F. Prahl, owner of the Utzmemmingen faience factory, may have produced porcelain here c.1760.
See also J. A. Bechdolff.

Else. Name of pattern for No. 280222, registered on 13 February 1922 by the P. F. Rosenthal, Selb.

Elster, Georg Heinlein, see Mühlhausen.

Emaildruckverfahren (transfer printing). An invention of Robert Hancock (1730–1817) of Battersea (England). It involves taking an impression with thin paper from a copper plate, which is prepared in the same way as for taking engravings and brushed with the desired colour, and transferring it to ceramic vessels. According to the consistency of the glaze, the impression more or less fuses with the glaze during the firing. See also Transfer printing.

Email sur biscuit. Painting with enamel colours on unglazed fired porcelain (biscuit).

Emden (Germany, Ostfriesland). Kruse, H. A., porcelain decorating studio, c. 1938.

Emeljanoff, see Morje.

Emilczyn (Russia, Gouv. Wolinsky). Duke Lubomirski f. a porcelain factory here, which was later taken over by Uwaroff, his son in law. The factory worked for c. 25 years until 1852 (?). Sets and vases, mostly for presentations, were produced.

Empire Porcelain Co., Empire Works, see Stoke-on-Trent (7).

Empire-Service. Created in Nymphenburg in 1800 by J. P. Melchior. Very severe white service, ornamented with wide gold borders.

Enamel. Consists of transparent or opaque coloured glass-flux. In ceramics these enamel colours are used under the name 'muffle-colours'.

Enamel decoration. The enamel is a compound of lead glass with tinted mineral oxides. It is applied to a glaze which has been fired, and fused or melted to it in another firing at a low temperature in a muffle kiln. First used in the early 18th c. in China and Japan only; used in Europe later.

Enamel glazes. Partly white, partly coloured, opaque glazes which contain tin

oxide as well as lead oxide. They melt easily and serve as cover for the often rather ugly colours of the layer underneath the glazes. They are used for faiences.
En camaieu. Meaning one colour only in porcelain decoration.
Engelden, M. N., see Rozenburg.
Engelhardt, O., see Gehren.
Engelhardt, Waldemar (1860–1915) worked as chemist, from 1892 until his death, for the KPM Copenhagen, where the crystalline glazes (the outcome of his research) were used in an artistic manner.
Englebienne Frères et Ch., Harweng, see Mons (1).
Englisches Service (English service). Viennese work, created for King George IV on behalf of the Court in 1821–4. Rich painting of flowers and gilt decoration with the Royal coat of arms. According to Neuwirth, the King would have preferred a case of Tokay to this service, which is hardly surprising in view of his escapades as Regent and subsequently King.
Engobe. Clay mixture. In the case of porcelain, engobe means a porcelain slip containing fireproof colouring-matters (metal oxides or oxide-mixtures). After the initial firing into biscuit stage the porcelain is dipped into this engobe and receives a thin surface of colour and is then fast-fired.
Ens. Karl, see Rudolstadt Volkstedt (13).
Ens & Greiner, see Lauscha and Rudolstadt Volkstedt (13).
d'Entrecolles. Jesuit father, active as missionary at the end of the 17th c. in China. Given the task of obtaining the porcelain recipe from converts among the workers in the Chinese porcelain factories. His very informative reports were published in 1716 in the *Journal des Cavantes* and were added to the work of the Duke Nicolas-Chrétien de Tuy Milly. The reports could not lead to any definite conclusion, because d'Entrecolle's research had no scientific basis. Incidentally, it was the greasy shine of the glazes, which gave rise to his term 'oils used as glazes', and provided the reason for the failure of experiments based on his accounts, reports and recipes.
EPIAG, see Carlsbad (2).
Epinal (France). According to 'Tardy 75' a porcelain decorating studio was active here, run by 'Les porcelaines artistiques d'Epinal' which signed with the following mark.

Epinay (France). According to 'Tardy 75' Salmon et Cie registered the following mark in 1822.

Eps, Ludwig, see Nyon.
Erbendorf (1) (Germany, Oberpfalz). Christian Seltmann porcelain factory GmbH, Werk Erbendorf was f. here in 1923 as the Erbendorf porcelain factory

GmbH and was taken over in 1940 by the Seltmann firm. Produced utility ware and sets.

Erbendorf (2) (Germany, Oberpfalz). Hans Schrembs, porcelain factory.

Erbsmehl, Johann Gottlieb (1708–41). Porcelain decorator. Worked in Meissen at the time of Höroldt.

Erdglasuren (alkaline siliceous glazes). Transparent glazes made from crushed pebbles, clay and alkaline materials requiring high firing temperatures. The glaze used on true hard paste porcelain is one of such glazes made.

Erikson, Algot (b. 1868). Ceramist and sculptor. Designer and modeller at Rörstrands, Lidköping from 1886–1916. Introduced underglaze painting on relief ground and later also used the 'pâte sur pâte' technique.

Erkersreuth (Germany, Oberfranken). Hofmann brothers, porcelain factory.

[237]

Erome (France, Drôme). Georges Boutherin f. a porcelain factory here in 1910, according to 'Tardy 75'; for which he registered the following mark in 1911.

Erotokritou, Neoptolemos, see Nicosia.

Erthal, Friedrich Karl Joseph, Freiherr von, Kurfuerst von Mainz, see Höchst.

Ess (Äss), Franz Joseph (1735–96), from Hanau. Worked as modeller in Ludwigsburg from November 1759, producing mostly flowers. From 1764, he was modeller in Nymphenburg, where his activity from 1767–75, was defined as 'Obertafel-geschirr-Possierer' (upper table service modeller').

Esser, Max (1885–1945). Sculptor, with three years apprenticeship. Attended evening school at the Königlichen Kunstgewerbe Museum, Berlin. In 1904–5, he was the sole pupil of the animal sculptor August Gaul. He sculptured animals in bronze with gold and silver inlayed 'damascened'. From 1920–6 he worked in the Staatliche porcelain works in Meissen. He became Professor and a member of the Prussian Academy of Arts in 1923.

Este (Italy). Porcelain of the 18th–19th c. See Milan San Cristoforo. The similarity of the first mark indicates that the Este business was possibly transferred to Milan San Cristoforo.

Esternay (France, Marne). Porcelainerie d'Esternay, porcelain decorating studio, c. 1930.

Etablissements Demeuldre S.P.R.L., Manufacture de Porcelaine de Bruxelles, see Brussels (5).
Etched design, see Berlin (2).
Etiolles nr. Corbeil (France). A porcelain factory was f. here before 1768 by Jean-Baptiste Monier and Dominique Pellevé; it produced work in the Parisian style.

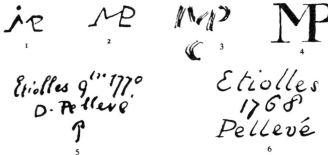

1–4 soft paste porcelain – 5–6 hard paste porcelain

Etruscan Service. The Royal Factory of Naples produced this table set c. 1775, which was adapted from Greek vases. Ferdinand IV, King of Naples, presented it as a gift to George III of England. It is still to this day in Windsor Castle (Köllmann).
Ettel, Guiseppe. Named as master in Doccia.
Etterbek, see Brussels (2) and (5).
Ettlingen (Germany, Baden). Emil Leonhardt porcelain factory, which was still in production in 1930.

Ettner (or Oettner, or Effner), Andreas. A painter who worked from 1756–7 in Vienna and Neudeck-Nymphenburg, in 1759 in Frankenthal as well as in Ludwigsburg, and in 1766 in Höchst. Andreas Philipp Etner, mentioned as a miniature painter in 1770 in Vienna, was perhaps a son of Andreas and possibly the independent painter named 'Etner' who in 1770 was also registered in Vienna.

d'Eu, Comte, see Bourg-la Reine (1).

Eulau nr. Bodenbach (Bohemia, now Lilové). Mehner Bros. porcelain decorating studio, c. 1930.

Eutrope Morin, see Saintes.

Evans and Glasson, see Swansea.

Eythra (Germany, Saxony). Ullrich, Wenzel, porcelain decorating studio, c. 1930.

Fabbrica Ceramica Vallescrivia, see Serravalle Scrivia.

Fabbrica Porcellana Luigi Fabris, see Milan (3).

Faber, F., see Brussels (4).

Fábrica de Cerámica Decorativa Jesus J. Escobar Folgado, see Manises (2).

Fabrica Gospodina Gulina, see Moskow (5).

Fabrica de Porcelana da Vista-Alegre, see Lisbon (2).

Fabrik am blauen Turm, see Copenhagen (1).

Fabrique de Monsieur, see Paris (37).

Fabrique de Porcelaines Blanches et Décorés Anciens Ets.J. Teissonnière & Cie., see Limoges (22).

Fabrique de la Reine, see Paris (84).

Fabryka Procelany i Wyrobow Ceramicznych w Cmielowie, Spolka Akcyjna, see Chodziez and Cmielów.

Facon komod. Porcelain container for writing implements, in the form of a commode.

Faenza (Italy). The International Museum for Ceramics, f. in 1908 by Dr. Gaetano Ballardini.

Falck, A., see Copenhagen (1).

Falconet, Etienne Maurice (1716–91). Sculptor and porcelain modeller. First modelling master in Sèvres from 1755, and, until 1766, artistic director of the whole of the factory. His groups and figures, mostly executed in biscuit, are under the influence of early classicism. His work at Sèvres came to an end when he was summoned by Catherine II to Russia.

Falkonia AG, see Chodau (1).

Famille noir. Name for a Chinese porcelain of the Kangxi period (1662–1722) which is of particular value to collectors. The ground of the email-sur-biscuit decoration is formed by a black enamel colour.

Famille rose. Term for an important range of Chinese porcelains of the Qianlong period (1736–96), which is remarkable for the dominance of pink or carmine enamel colours. The popularity of the colour may have had its origin in foreign influences, since the Chinese identify the porcelains of this group as being painted with 'foreign colours'. These pieces, with their daringly large forms and snow-white bodies, are amongst the most desirable pieces for European collectors.

Famille verte. Term for an important range of Chinese porcelain which is distinctive for the prominence of green enamel colours. It flourished in the Kangxi period (1662–1722).

Fanchon, Hypolyte, see Sezanne.

Fanciulacci, Giovanni, miniature painter, see Doccia.

Farge, A., see Limoges (23).

Farges-Allichamps (France). Porcelain factory of the Noyer Bros., f. 1909. Table service.

Farkashazy-Fischer, Moritz, see Herend.

'Farsta' and 'Farsta-Rust', see Gustavsberg (1).

Fasold, Ferdinand, see Liezen.

Fasold & Stauch, see Bock-Wallendorf.

Fasolt & Eichel, new title for Duxer porcelain works AG, formerly Ed. Eichler, see Blankenhain (1).

Fassonierung. This is a term used to describe the way grooves or kerbs incised at the edges of crockery, enhance the basic outline.

Fauquez, Jean Baptiste Joseph (1742–1804), see Saint-Amand-les Eaux (1) and Valenciennes.

Faure & Co., see Ponsas.

Favot, see Niderviller.

Fawkener, Sir Eberard (1684–1758), see Chelsea (1).

Faxoe, Nicolay Christian (1762–1810). From 1783–1810 was active as flower painter in Copenhagen.

Fedjaschin, see Jirowaja.

Feilner (also Feylner), J. Simon (b. 20 February 1726, Weiden–17 March 1798, Mannheim). Modeller. On his travels as a journeyman he worked in Paris as a flower painter and in 1753, together with Benckgraff and Zeschinger, he came from Höchst to Fürstenberg where, according to the archives of the factory, he was 'artistic Poussierer'. From 1770 he was inspector of the Frankenthal Works, where he managed to introduce a number of improvements. He invented a 'black underglaze colour' (underglaze which is of an extremely deep black), a royal blue, a blue celeste, a variegated gold-changeant, a relief-gilding à quatre couleurs. In 1775 he succeeded Bergdoll and became overseer of the porcelain production. He is regarded as one of the greatest colour technicians in the art of porcelain making of the 18th c.

Feldherren-Service (Field Marshal Service). This was painted in 1817–20 by the KPM Berlin by order of Friedrich Wilhelm III in the classical style, depicting battles of the Wars of Independence. The King presented this service to his generals, and also to the Duke of Wellington. This 'Wellington-Service' was further enriched by a centrepiece created after designs and models by Schadow, the most significant work in porcelain by him (1818). It was divided into 470 parts and the laurel and oakleaf garlands tied with the sashes of various orders which adorn the Field Marshal Service, were in the case of the Wellington Service, replaced with etched and engraved borders in gold.

Feldspar. Group of minerals, which represent substantial essential ingredients of crystalline rock; all contain silicic acid and aluminium oxide.

Fenkl & Langner, see Chodau (2).

Fenton (1) (England). Atlas China Co. Ltd., formerly Chapmann & Sons. 1889–1906. Porcelain factory. Two other marks display the full name.

Fenton (2) (England). Charles Bourne, Grosvenor Works, 1817–30. Produced tea services and very fine vases in the tradition of Spode-Copeland. The number of the marks is that of the present models. (Godden.)

Fenton (3) (England). Arthur Bowker porcelain factory, producing sculptured porcelain.

Fenton (4) (England). E. Brain & Co. Ltd., Foley China Works, f. in 1850. Produced tea, coffee and table services. Originally the firm called itself Robinson & Son; since the beginning of 1900 the present title has been used.

Fenton (5) (England). Crown Staffordshire China Co. Ltd., Minerva Works (since 1948). Formerly known as: Green & Richards (1801–47); Thomas Green (1847–59); M. Green & Co. (1859–76); T. A. & S. Green (1876–89); Crown Staffordshire Porcelain Co. Ltd. (1889–1948). Produced domestic crockery of all kinds and artistic porcelain.

Fenton (6) (England). Doric China Co., a porcelain factory which also produced dolls' heads. Operated from 1924–35 when it was taken over by the Royal Albion China Co. (see Longton (67)) under which name it stayed in business until 1948.

Fenton (7) (England). John Edwards (& Co.), 1847–1900. According to Godden, apart from the two marks shown, two other marks incorporate the full address.

J. E.   J. E. & Co.

Fenton (8) (England). Elkin, Knight & Bridgewood, The Foley Potteries, porcelain and earthenware factory, operating 1827–40. Neither its predecessor Elkin, Knight & Co. (1822–6), Elkin, Knight & Elkin, nor the successors, Knight, Elkin & Knight, produced porcelain.

E. K· B.

Fenton (9) (England). Porcelain factory producing floral and fancy goods. The articles are called: 'Floral Productions'.
Fenton (10) (England). E. Hughes & Co., porcelain factory, f. 1883. Produced domestic goods, tea and dinner services.

Fenton (11) (England). A. G. Harley Jones, Royal Vienna Art Pottery, earthenware, stoneware and porcelain factory, 1907–37.

Fenton (12) (England). William Kirkby & Co., Sutherland Pottery, porcelain and earthenware factory, 1879–85.

Fenton (13) (England). Samuel Radford Ltd., porcelain factory dealing in tea and dinner services.

Fenton (14) (England). Thorley China Ltd., see Longton (78).

Fenton (15) (England). J. Wilson & Sons, Park Works, porcelain factory, operating 1898–1926; formerly known as Wilson & Co.

Fenton, Alfred & Sons, see Hanley (5).

Ferdinand IV, King of Naples, see Herculaneum Service and Naples.

Ferdinand VII, King of Spain, see La Moncloa.

Ferner, F. J. c. mid 18th c. he decorated old Meissen porcelain with pastoral and market-scenes, German and Indian flowers in rather rough workmanship.

T·$ Ferner pinx   *$\mathcal{H}$*

Fernex, Jean-Baptiste de (1729–83), sculptor. See Sèvres (1) and Boucher.

Ferreira Pinto Basso, José, see Vista Alegre.

Ferretti, Domenico (1720–74), sculptor. Member of the 'Academie des Arts' Stuttgart. In 1747 came to Stuttgart from Vienna, where he created the Attika figures of the Stuttgarter Residenz-schloss from 1748–51. In 1762 he worked on the statues of the pillars. Evidence exists of his activity for the Ludwigsburg porcelain factory between 1764–5.

Ferrière, see Paris (49).

Ferté, La, see Saint-Denis (2).

Feston Rosenthal. Name for trademark 259365 of the P. F. Rosenthal, Selb from 26 January 1921.

Feuervergolding (fire gilding). Pulverised gold, mixed with bismuth trioxide and oil. The lustre is produced by burnishing afterwards.

'Feuille morte'. Iridescent red brown to light brown, used on Chinese porcelain.

Feuillet, see Paris (50).

Fèvre, Le (also Lefèvre), see Choisy-le-Roy (1).

Feylner, J. S., see Feilner and Frankenthal (1).

Fiaschi, Angelo, painter and modeller, see Doccia.

Finch, A. W., see Helsinki.

Fink. see Reval.

Finney, A. T. & Sons Ltd., Duchess China Works, see Longton (31).

Fischer, Anton, see Neumark.

Fischer, Arno, see Ilmenau (2).

Fischer, Christian. see Zwickau (1).

Fischer, Desider. see Tata.

Fischer, Franz, see Dallwitz.

Fischer, von Farkasház, Eugen, see Ungvár.

Fischer, Johann Sigismund (d. 1770). From 1751–70 principal painter in Vienna.

Fischer, Johann Sigismund, see Nove.

Fischer, W̊. Th., painter, see Copenhagen (1).

Fischer & Co. GmbH, see Oeslau (1).

Fischer, Lorenz & Urfuss, see Dallwitz.

Fischer & Mieg (formerly Fischer & Reichenbach), now: 'Epiag', see Pirkenhammer.

Fischer & Reichenbach, see Pirkenhammer.

Fischer'sche Keram, Fabrik-AG, formerly Emil v. Fischer, see Budapest (1).

Fischern nr. Carlsbad (1) (Bohemia, now Rybárě). From 1842, Carl Knoll directed an establishment here for the preparation of kaolin, which soon became a porcelain factory. After his death in 1868, his sons, Adolf, Carl and Ludwig succeeded him and produced 'porcelain and ceramic specialities for luxury and everyday use'. The firm still exists today. In 1941 it was called 'Karlsbader Porzellan Fabrik Carl Knoll'. The present name is 'Karlsbader Porzellanfabrik'. In about 1920 the 'onion pattern' was added to their stock of decorations. In Vienna, on 9 April 1883, C. Knoll registered a mark like a banded escutcheon (Reg. No. 53) which was renewed in Eger under No. 365, on 25 August 1893. However, as a result of allegations made by Carl Rädler of Vienna, concerning the sole right to use the banded escutcheon (or the 'beehive') mark, it was withdrawn in the same year. Later, the mark was recorded on 19 September 1883 at the Royal County Court, Leipzig, under No. 3133, for the purpose of inclusion in the Trademark Register of the Imperial Patent Office in Berlin; it continued to be used on export wares, which constituted the largest part of the turnover. According to unsolicited evidence of the time, considerable stock, marked with the 'banded escutcheon', was still in existence.

1 impressed mark on unpainted porcelain 1850–60 – 2 from 1868 – 3 on undecorated porcelain c. 1900 – 4–5 impressed mark or coloured, beginning of the 20th c. – 6–9 modern marks – 10 'banded escutcheon'

Fischern nr. Carlsbad (2) (Bohemia, now Rybárě). Bawo and Dotter. Apart from the two marks which Pelka identified (which could only have been used until the end of the First World War), nothing was known of this concern. It has now been established that the business must have been a sizable porcelain decorating workshop, founded as far back as 1884, and still active in 1924. The whole of the production, and some additional merchandise, was most likely exported to the USA. From 1873, a porcelain decorating studio operated alongside the workshop under the same management; according to 'Tardy 75' these were the successive addresses of this firm: 1873 – Rue de la Fonderie; 1894 – Av. de Poitiers; 1896 – Rue Grange Garat; 1898 – Rue H. Faure; 1902–20 – Rue de Ecole de Med. In 1898 the porcelain decorating studio which had been f. by Barjaud de Lafon in Limoges in 1881, was absorbed into the company. Subsequently all products from Limoges were exported to the States (until 1920). As a means of coping with the widespread business commitments, which included a glass refinery and decorating workshop in Steinschönau (Bohemia), there was a self-owned export and import business in Paris and a ceramic import business in New York. The head office of the concern was in Kötzchenbroda (Saxony).

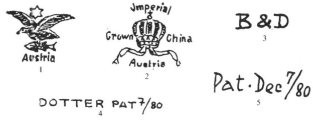

4–5 neck marks of dolls in biscuit porcelain, which had been imported to the USA

Fischhäusel nr. Frainersdorf (Czechoslovakia). Richard Schiller, porcelain decorating studio, c. 1930.

Fismes (France, Marne). Vernon f. a porcelain factory here in 1840, where he produced soft paste porcelain, similar to the English kind.

Five colour decoration (Chinese: Wucai). Term for porcelain decoration comprised of designs painted in contrasting enamel colours (e.g. blue, red, yellow, green, lilac), in which cobalt blue was frequently painted separately under the glaze. The term 'five colour painting' is also commonly used for polychrome enamelling in Chinese porcelain.

Flächenvergoldungen (the gilding of surfaces to produce a gold ground). Often goods are 'guillcched'', a method by which one engraves ornaments with a sharp agate stylus.

Flaxman, John (1755–1826). Sculptor. From 1775–87 a famous modeller for Wedgwood.

Fleurot, Franz. Master modeller, active in 1770 in the Swedish factory of Marieberg.

Fleury, see Paris (51).

Fliegel (also: Flügel), Johann Georg. Faience decorator in various factories, he also decorated porcelain independently, e.g. certain Nymphenburg products which are occasionally signed only with the name of his place of residence, such as 'Amberg', or 'Amb.'

Flight, Joseph and John (d. 1791), see Worcester (1).

Flora Service by the KPM Berlin 1768, much in the spirit of the Meissen 'Gotzkowsky erhabene Blumen' (a pattern introduced in 1744, which has four narrow panels left plain, alternating with four wide panels decorated with sculpted flowers which also appear in the centre of the plate). The Flora Service only received its name in 1860.

Flora Danica Service. This famous Copenhagen Service was made between 1790–1802 and was intended for Catherine II of Russia. In the contempory journal of the factory it was listed as 'Perle model broget malet med Flora Danica'. Originally the service was designed for 80 people and 1,835 pieces were ready in 1794. After the death of Catherine II in 1796 the service was enlarged for 100 people and it is preserved today in the Castle of Rosenberg. The characteristic border pattern is a wreath of foliage accompanied by strings of pearls, partially gilded. It was designed by the former master modeller of the factory, Anton Karl Luplau. The decoration was executed by the painter J. C. Bayer, while the botanist Theodor Holmskjold, a pupil of Linné's, assisted him in this work, which reproduced the whole of the Danish flora.

Floral production, see Newcastle.

Floral productions, see Fenton (9).

Florence (1) (Italy). During the time of the rule of the Medici, c. 1574–1620, the so-called Medici porcelain (a type of soft paste porcelain), was produced here. However, the bulk of the production took place between 1581–6. (According to records compiled by Andrea Pussonis, a Venetian ambassador, the production of porcelain took place from 1575–85, the period of the Grand Duke Francesco Maria I.) The paste was slightly yellowish and before it was decorated (usually in underglaze blue), it was given a white tin-glaze. The paste is halfway between hard and soft porcelain. After the death of Francesco Marias, Fernando I continued the production with the help of Bernado Buontalenti (1536–1608). His work was fully developed by Cosimo II in 1620. Only a few pieces, c. 30, have come down to us and these belong among the treasures of ceramic production.

1   2   3   4   5

1–3 in different variations, all blue – 4 FMMDE II = Francesco Medici, Magnus Dux Etruriae II – 5 blue

Florence (2) (Italy). Manifattura di Signa, Soc. Ind. Porcelain factory operating c. 1930.

Florence (3) (Italy). Ottorino del Vivo & C. Porcelain factory producing table services.

Florida, see La Moncloa.

Flügel, J. G., see Fliegel.

Flurl, Matthias (5 February 1756, Straubing–27 July 1823). Adviser in mining and minting matters. Munich mineralogist, and commissar of Nymphenburg 1788–1807. He published a book in 1792 entitled *An Account of the Mountains of Bavaria and the Upper Palatinate.* It was due to him that Frankenthal was united with Nymphenburg in 1800.

Foecy (1) (France, Cher). Bernardet, Ledoux & Bailly, porcelain factory produced white and decorated porcelain.

Foecy (2) (France, Cher). Klein f. a porcelain factory here c. 1800 which expanded rapidly and was owned by the Pillivuyt family. c. 1800 1,500 workers were already employed. Branches were opened in Mehun and Paris. The factory is still working and is amongst the foremost porcelain factories, producing hotel and ovenproof porcelain, with particular emphasis on the production of technical porcelain.

𝒫&F
France

C. H. PILLIVUYT
& Cie Paris.
PARIS. FOESCY. MEHUN.

A·P·
FOECY

AP&CO
FRANCE

Foecy (3) (France, Cher). Louis Lourioux, porcelain factory, f. 1898. Produced luxury and utility ware.

FRANCE

Foecy (4) (France, Cher). Ch. Pillivuyt & Co., known as Mehum & Noirlac, porcelain factory.

C P
&·Co.

Foecy (5) (France, Cher). B. Pilorget, porcelain decorating studio, since 1936; from 1942 known as Société Française de Porcelaine. According to 'Tardy 75' the following marks were used.

Foley China, see Fenton (4), Brain & Co.
Folk figures, modeller of, see Ludwigsburg.
Fomin, P., see Moscow (3).
Fond écaille. Term for a tortoise shell brown, high temperature glaze in use at Sèvres since 1775.
Fondporcelain. Porcelain with coloured ground (fond), e.g. yellow, celadon, purple, Royal blue, etc.
Fontaine, also Desfontaines (1769–1823), porcelain decorator, see Sveebac.
Fontainebleau (1) (France). Benjamin Jacob and Aaron Smoll f. a porcelain factory here in 1795. They were succeeded by Baruch Weil. In 1830 or 1834 the factory was sold to Jacob and Mardochée Petit, who managed it successfully. As for the marks, only Petit's is known, this was also used in Belleville. According to Cushion & Honey (1956), mark 5 was used by the Godebaki & Co. factory, Fontainebleau. Both Berling and Lange (1911) report that from 1886 Sluizer used mark 6 on porcelain here. In 1896 the KPM Meissen instigated proceedings to prevent any further use of the mark.

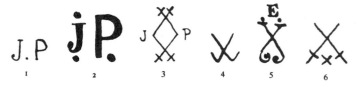

1–3 1830–62 – 4 1862 – 5 1874 – 6 from 1886

Fontainebleau (2) (France). The following marks with the names and dates of independent porcelain decorators have been recorded by 'Tardy 75'.

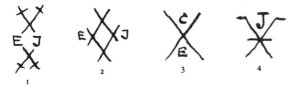

1–2 Jaquemin 1863 – 3 P. J. A. Cochard 1876 – 4 F. Febure 1877

Fontanille & Marraud, Manufacture de Porcelaines Artistiques, see Limoges (50).

Fontebasso Bros., Guiseppe and Andrea, see Treviso (1).
Fontelliau, A. Painter and colourist in Sèvres from 1747–80.
Ford, T. & C., see Hanley (6).
Ford & Pointon, see Hanley (11).
Forester, Thomas & Sons Ltd., Imperial Works, and also Phoenix Works, see Longton (32).
Förster, Alexander, see Vienna (7).
Fouque, see Saint–Gaudens.
Fouque, Arnoux & Cie., see Valentine.
Fourmaintraux, Gabriel, Manufacture de Fayence d'Art, see Desvres.
Fourmy Fils, Fournerat et de Nivas, see Nantes (2).
Fourneira, see Limoges (31).
Fourneron, Emile, see Ponsas-sur-Rhône.
Fournier, Louis, modeller, see Chantilly (1) and Copenhagen (1).
Fours (1) (France). Dodé and Frin f. a porcelain factory here c. 1825 which mainly produced works in relief.
Fours (2) (France). Lebrun & Co. ran a small factory here c. 1867 and did not mark their products.
Frachon, Paul, see Saint-Vallier (2).
François et Cie., see Limoges (24).
Francossi, Joseph François, see Paris (52).
Frank & Friedhern, see Freienorla.
Frankenthal (1) (Germany). Having been forced by Louis XV's tenure of monopoly to close his factory in Strasbourg, P. A. Hannong, an active painter himself, moved it to Frankenthal. The patent, at the time of the opening of this factory, dated from 16 May 1755. Hannong sold the flourishing factory in 1759 to his son Josef Adam and was paid 10,000 livres for the arcanum alone. In 1762 the Elector Karl Theodor von der Pfalz bought the factory which in 1775 he placed under the direction of the arcanist Adam Bergdoll from Höchst, who managed it successfully. He was succeeded by J. S. Feylner who retained the post until 1793. In 1795, on the occasion of the French occupation, the factory was declared 'French National property' and sold to Peter van Recum, who returned it to the Elector's officers when the French army withdrew. In 1797 the French troops re-occupied the left bank of the Rhine and the factory had to be returned to the lawful successor, Johann Nepomuk van Recum. After some limited production, the factory ceased working completely. The factory was closed on 27 May 1800 by the edict of the Elector, Maximilian IV.

The factory used mainly Passau kaolin. The paste, with its sand-coloured tones, sometimes bears resemblance to the French pâte tendre. Figure production was predominant. Practically no other German porcelain factory (apart from Meissen) can rival the number of models Frankenthal produced. The early figure production under Johann Wilhelm Lanz is distinguished by its faience character. Under Joseph Adam Hannong the production corresponded more to the courtly style. His general modeller was Johann Friedrich Lück. Later on, under the management of the Elector, the sculptor Konrad Linck worked in the factory. He was one of the outstanding artists in Frankenthal and one of his most enchanting creations is the Nine Muses. Karl Gottlieb Lück, master modeller c. 1767–75, specialising in small, lively, plastic figures, worked at the factory following Linck. Johann Peter Melchior retained his mature style during his stay in Frankenthal. Neither of Melchior's two pupils, Adam Clair and Landolin Ohnmacht (Ohmacht), have any independent reputation. The most distinguished figure painters of Frankenthal compare well with any Meissen painters of the Höroldt-periods, and were: Jakob Osterspey, Winterstein and Magnus. The Frankenthal factory and its superb products belong among the leading German porcelain factories of the 18th c. A reissue of Frankenthal figures was made in Grünstadt, where some of the moulds were brought by van Recum in 1801.

See also Berthevin, P., Bauer, A., Ettner, A., Fretz, J. H., Heinrici, J. M., Höflich, G., Höflich, J. J., Knipffer, J. Cht., Nierwein, Offenstein, M., Rahner, J., Riehl, P., Windschlügel, A.

1–4 Paul Hannong Frenkenthal 1755–9, blue underglaze or blind mark – 5–7 1759–62, 6–7 Monograms of Joseph Adam Hannong – 8–9 Carl Theodor mark 1762–70 under Adam Bergdoll – 10 Carl Theodor mark with year number 1770–89 – 11 1780–93 – 12–13 Peter van Recum 1795 – 14–15 Johann Nepomuk van Recum 1797–8 – 16–22 artist's mark – 16–17 Adam Clair – 18–19 Bernhard Magnus Pinxit – 20 Marx (modeller) – 21 decorator's mark 1761–6 in red – 22 blindmark LINCK – all Frankenthal marks blue underglaze

Frankenthal (2) (Germany, Palatine). Friedrich Wilhelm Wessel, porcelain factory, f. 1949. Produced figures and utility porcelain until its closure.

Frankfurt a. M. (1) (Germany). Höchst porcelain factory, f. 1965 to continue the tradition of the old Palatine Mainz Höchst porcelain factory. **Frankfurt** a. M. (2) (Germany). Höchst porcelain factory GmbH newly built 1947, producing utility porcelain and art porcelain.

HÖCHST

Franconia. Name for trademark No. 265780 from 25 May 1921, of P. F. Thomas, Marktredwitz.
Franzen, Henrik (d. 1781 or 1782). Decorator in Marieberg from 1760 until his death. His sons were all decorators in Marieberg: Johann Franzen from 1761–6, E. Franzen from 1760–3, F. H. Franzen from 1766–80.
Frauenthal zu Lassnitz (Austria). Ing. Ludwig Neumann GmbH, f. 1920, produced utility ware.

Frauenwald (Germany, Thuringia). Otto Hermann Spindler, Thüringer factory dealing in porcelain majolica, earthenware and terracotta. Produced utility porcelain.

Fraureuth (1) (Germany, Saxony). Fraureuth porcelain factory AG, f. 1866, produced good utility porcelain. The Wallendorf porcelain factory was managed as a branch factory from 1919–26. According to DKG Fraureuth it was closed in 1935.

[94]   [221]

Fraureuth (2) (Germany, Saxony). The Römer & Födisch porcelain factory was here in 1880, producing thin porcelain with good glazes which cracked easily.

Frede, Joh. Christian, see Kelsterbach.

Freiberg (1) (Germany, Saxony). VEB Freiberg porcelain works, producing domestic and decorative porcelain. It may be the successor to the

Freiberg/Sachsen porcelain factory which was f. in 1906 by the Kahla porcelain factory AG. The former was originally producing exclusively electro porcelain, but produced porcelain in 1924.

Freiberg (2) (Germany, Saxony). Branch of the Kahla porcelain factory AG, f. in 1906.

Freiburg (Germany, Breisgau). Risler, Duffay et Comp. produced porcelain buttons here c. 1870.

R & C

Freienorla nr. Orlamünde (Germany, Thuringia). Frank & Friedheim, porcelain factory, f. in 1924, formerly known as Kurt Müller & Co., dealing in general porcelain. The factory is now closed.

Freienwaldau (Germany, Silesia, County Sagan). H. Schmidt, porcelain factory. On 17 March 1922 the following mark was registered under No. 282532 as trademark for porcelain wares.

[245]

Freital-Potschappel, see Potschappel.

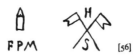

F P M   [56]

Freiwaldau (1) (Bohemia). H. Schmidt f. a small porcelain factory here in 1842 and later formed an association with Olremba. Nothing is known about the production of this firm.

Freiwaldau (2) (Bohemia). Bing, Glas & Keramik K.G.; now known as the Freiwaldau Robert Tietz porcelain factory.
Freiwaldau (3) (Bohemia). Freiwaldau Robert Tietz porcelain factory.

Frelon, Eugène, see Villedieu (2).
Fretz. Johann Heinrich. In 1756 was potter in Frankenthal, in 1765–7 decorator in Strasbourg and in 1782 in Pfalz-Zweibrücken.
Friberg, Berndt, modeller, see Gustavsberg (1).
Fricker & Co., see Heidelberg.
Friedland (Bohemia). Jos. Ed. Heintschel, porcelain factory, f. in 1869 and dealing in utility ware.

J B H
F

Friedrich II (the Great), King of Prussia, see Berlin (3), Prussian Service, Prussian musical design, Punct, K. Ch., Vestunen-Service.
Friedrichs, Baron von, see Morje.
Frin, see Fours (1).
Frit porcelain (fritten porzellan, porcelaine à fritte, porcelaine vitreuse), often described as soft porcelain 'porcelaine pâte tendre'. When Asian porcelain was introduced to Europe, it became an object for imitation. The first to be produced was the French frit porcelain which was produced by Morin in 1695 on the basis of experiments by Réaumur (Dietz). It contained hardly any clay substance and no kaolin at all. Its production is difficult and complex, more so than that of true porcelain (pâte dure). Crystallised sand, saltpetre, sea salt, soda, alum and

gypsum or alabaster chips are all mixed together and fired for approximately 50 hours to the consistency of a white frit. This is then ground to powder, mixed with clay, and after procedures involving green soap and boiling water, which last several weeks, a plastic body mass is produced. The process of making the glaze is similarly complicated. During the firing the colours fuse with the glaze which has been applied and take on a luminosity which cannot be achieved in hard paste porcelain. The low temperature of the firing permits the use of the most delicate colours. Frit porcelain can only be employed for luxury articles and figures, however, since both the body and the glaze are highly sensitive to changes of temperature and are too fragile for general use. Frit porcelain reached the height of its perfection in the mid 18th c. in Sèvres.

Fritsch, modeller, see Schlaggenwald (1).

Fritsch & Weidermann, see Altrohlau (2).

Fritsche, Rudolf, see St. Pölten.

Fritten. General term for heating a pulverised mixture until it softens and the particles superficially fuse together.

Fritz & Rosenthal, see Schauberg (3).

Fritz, Franz, Successor, see Grossbreitenbach (3).

Fritzsche, Georg. Porcelain modeller, evidence indicates that he worked in Meissen from 1712–28.

Frjasino (Russia). The Barmin brothers f. a porcelain factory here between 1810–20, which worked until 1850; its production was very diverse although the artistic standard was low.

Fröhlich, Court jester, bust of, see Kirchner, J. G.

Frugier, René, see Limoges (25).

Frye, Thomas (1710–62). Painter, see Bow.

Füger, Heinrich (1751–1818). Vice-Chancellor of the Vienna Academy, made designs for figures during the third period of the Vienna porcelain production.

Fuisseaux, Leon de, see Baudour.

Fuisseaux, Nicolas de, see Baudour.

Fulda (1) (Germany, Hessen). The Fürstlich Fuldaische Feine porcelain factory was f. in 1764 by the Prince Abbot Heinrich VIII von Bibra zu Fulda. The arcanist Nikolaus Paul, a former worker of Wegely's, was engaged. In 1767 the factory was burnt down; it was rebuilt under the direction of the second arcanist, I. Abraham Ripp. The modellers were Wenzel Neu (Ney) from Bohemia, who had been active already in the Fulda faience factory (1741–58), as well as Johann Valentin Schaum and Georg Bartholome. In 1788, Adalbert III von Harstall (Prince Bishop from 1788–1803) became the owner; the production came to an end in 1789. Figure production shows clearly a close resemblance to Frankenthal. The other wares are more reminiscent of Höchst products. The pieces are conspicuous through their shiny, polished glaze; the body is pure white. The porcelain is mostly painted in monochrome (frequently in purple or iron red), mainly in the style of Louis XV. The whole production was of extraordinary refinement, completely faultless in body and glaze. The figures produced are now considered to be among the most precious of German porcelain. See also: Buchwald, J., Schick, J. Ph.

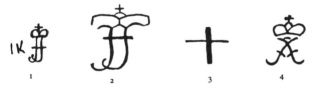

1 IK blind; FF blue underglaze – 2 FF = Fürstlich Fuldaische 1765–88 blue underglaze – 3 1765–80 – 4 1788–80 Adalbert-mark, very rare

Fulda (2) (Germany, Hessen). Fuldaer faience and porcelain factory GmbH, f. 1946. Produced coffee services and utility ware.

Fulvy, Orry de. Founder of the Vincennes porcelain factory, see Vincennes (1).

Fürsten Name of trademark No. 70704 of the Royal Saxony porcelain factory Meissen, from 1 July 1904, for high-fired tiles from true porcelain.

FÜRSTEN [118]

Fürstenberg (Germany). In 1747, under Duke Karl I of Braunschweig, von Langen (master of hounds), managed to win over the director of the Höchst porcelain factory, Johannes Benckgraff, who, with the help of his son-in-law (the painter Johannes Zechinger), and the repairer J. S. Feilner, made the Fürstenberg porcelain factory economically viable. At first kaolin was bought from Hafnerzell nr. Passau, but soon local supplies from the village Lenne nr. Fürstenberg were used, which resulted in a grey or yellowish body paste. Little can be said of the production of the 1760s. The most successful period (1770–90), is remarkable for its superb decorative painting. This compensated for the shortcomings of body and glaze. This period was a time of transition from rococo to classicism. The production of vases was of greater importance in Fürstenberg than anywhere else. Painting greatly dominated figure production. Apart from Feilner who has already been mentioned, the modellers Rombrich and Luplau must be named. In 1769 the modeller Desoches, a Frenchman, joined them and through him the contact with Sèvres and Wedgwood became closer. He also tirelessly endeavoured to improve biscuit production. After his departure (in 1775), his place was taken by Carl Gottlieb Schubert, who worked in Fürstenberg until his death. From 1807 the Royal porcelain factory experienced increasing financial difficulties. Gerverot at that time director, did, however, gain the support of King Jérome which enabled the factory to remain in production. Under Gerverot, whose best work was contemporary with the period of the Empire, the demand for the vases lessened as the Empire came to its close. The production of biscuit, however, came into prominence, and the painting of this time is of a particularly high quality. The successor of Gerverot, Prössel, proved to be inefficient; his successor Leschen, who was in charge of the factory from 1821–5, could not establish any success either. But it was Stünkel, the successor to Leschens, who skilfully guided the factory during the next 30 years, even when internal political tensions and excise problems were presenting difficulties. The Government leased out the factory in 1859 until 1876 when it became privately owned. In 1888 it became a joint stock company and from this time on up-to-date methods were introduced and machines and factory equipment modernised. Apart from the production of utility porcelain, Fürstenberg never ceased to reproduce its masterly achievements from the rococo period. In later years the products came into prominence through the excellent porcelain service which was designed by Prof. Wilhelm Wagenfeld (Köllmann).

See also: Albert, C. G., Brüning, H. C., Eisenträger, H., Geisler, G. F., Geisler, Ch. (son of G.F.), Hendler, P., Lücke, J. C. L., Weitsch, F.

1 from 1750 – 2 from 1770 – 3–4 in the 18th and 19th c. in variations – for modern utility porcelain – present day mark – all marks in blue underglaze – 7–8 according to the factory's information the small jumping horse was used as press or incise mark for busts at the end of the 18th c. The letter under the little horse, a 'W' or 'F', refers to the modeller. The oval mark (overglaze) was put on products for export, particularly to the U.S.A., since c. 1915

Füssli. Heinrich (1755–1829). Important Swiss painter and antiquarian. In 1771 he was apprenticed to the Zürich porcelain factory and remained active there until 1781.

'*G*'. Family of factory owners in Candiana nr. Padua, who marked their products, which resembled the Medici porcelain, with a 'G' from 1627–33. The body however, has more of a majolica character.

Gabel, Johann Georg, landscape and figure painter, see Gotha.

Gaboria, see Lille (2).

Gadoiun, Cirot & Co., see Vierzon (4).

Gadrooning (Gadronierung). Applied as a decorative edging to porcelain ware, it consists of convex curves or inverted fluting.

Gaebler, Otto, see Ladowitz (1).

Gaignepain, L. François (d. 1770), see Crépy-en Valois.

Gaillard, see Paris (53).

Galanterien. Name given in England to porcelain scent bottles, bonbonnières, snuff boxes, étuis and the like, made in imaginative shapes (figures, fruits, animals, etc.). They were so called because they were peculiarly suitable for a cavalier to present to his 'dame de coeur'.

Gallimore, see Caughley.

Galluba & Hofmann, see Ilmenau (3).

Galway (Ireland). Royal Tara porcelain factory, 1942. There are also different marks incorporating 'Royal China' or 'Regina'.

Gambier, see Paris (54).

Gaquin, see Charenton (1).

Gardie a Paris, L., see Paris (55).

Gardner, Francis. Founder and owner of a renowned porcelain factory in Werbiliki nr. Moscow. See Moscow (4).

ГАРДНЕРЪ

Gareis & Kasseker, see Jokes-Wickwitz.

Gareis, Kühnl & Cie. AG, see Waldsassen (2).

Garmisch-Partenkirchen (Germany, Bavaria). Porcelain decorator, Josef Sommer f. this works in 1933. Produced armorials, views, flowers and animals.

Garnituren (Garniture-de-Cheminée). A name originally given to a set of five porcelain vases, arranged symmetrically in order of size, the tallest being placed in the middle.

Gärtner, Friedrich, see Onyx Service.

Gateshead-on-Tyne (England). Durham China Co. Ltd., Team Valley Trading Estate, 1947–57. Produced utility ware.

Gatschina nr. Petersbourg (Russia). A porcelain factory was directed by Fischer here, from c. 1800–2. Neither information nor actual pieces of the production have been preserved. When it had closed the buildings were used by the Imperial factory, Gatschina, as a production-centre. According to Solodkow, this porcelain decorating studio was f. by the Zsar Paul I during his brief reign (1796–1801), as a branch of the Imperial factory St. Petersburg.

Gaucher, Edgard (later: Vve. E. Gaucher et Fils), see Vierzon (5).

Gaugain, see Paris (56).

Gaul August. Animal sculptor. Meissen bought 15 works from his estate in 1922, to be used as models for reproductions in Böttger stoneware and soft paste porcelain.

Gauldré-Boileau, see Magnac-Bourg.

Gaultier Bros., see Charenton-Saint-Maurice.

Gauron, Nicolas François. Famous modeller in Mennecy in 1753 and later in Vincennes, possibly Nic. Joseph Gauron, master modeller in Tourney from 1758–64, was the same man.

See also: Chelsea (1).

Gauthier, Jean, see Paris (57).

Gauthier, see Charenton (1).

Gävle (Sweden). Gefle Aktiebolag porcelain factory, f. 1850. Table, tea, and coffee services and articles of jewellery. The business was an earthenware factory from 1850–1910 when it switched to porcelain production.

Gefle porcelain factory, see Gävle.

Gehren (Germany, Thuringia). Günthersfeld porcelain factory AG, f. 1884, formerly named Th. Degenring with O. Engelhardt as the owner. After the Second World War it was renamed Thüringer Porzellan Werke Betrieb, Gehren. Produced utility ware, presentation articles and advertising goods.

[42]

Geiersthal (Germany, Schwarzburg-Rudolstedt). Sontag & Sons, porcelain decorating business, had the following mark registered as a trademark under No. 32080, on 25 July 1898. It was still in existence in 1930.

[89]

Geisler Georg Friedrich (1714–82). Flower painter in Fürstenberg, probably after 1759. His son Christoph worked in the same factory as a decorator.
Geitner, Dr. Ernst. He built the Geitner & Co. factory in 1809 in Lössnitz (Erzgebirge), for the production of ceramic colours. It moved in 1816 to Schneeberg. This factory, until recently in the ownership of the founder's family, is the earliest specialist factory for ceramic colours.
Gejer, Bengt Reinhold, see Lidköping (2).
Genelli, Hans Christian (1763–1823). Architect and sculptor, see Berlin.
Geneva (Switzerland). Jean Pierre Mühlhausen was active here (1805–18), as a porcelain decorator.

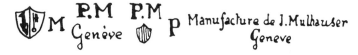

Gentile, André, see Limoges (26).
George III, King of England, see Derby (1).
Gera (Germany, Thuringia). In 1779, Johann Gottlob Ehwaldt and Johann Gottbrecht f. a small porcelain factory here under Heinrich XXX von Reuss. It was transferred to Johann Andreas and Georg Wilhelm Geier shortly afterwards and they directed it as a branch of their Volkstedter factory until 1782. Gaudily coloured figures of inferior quality and coarse modelling were produced. The porcelain has an off-white body and a grey-blue and grey-green glaze. The products are made in the classical style.

All blue underglaze

Geraberg (1) (Germany, Thuringia). Hugo Eger (formerly E. Wagner) porcelain factory, f. 1882. Since the last war it has been renamed Thüringer Porzellan Werke Betrieb, Geraberg. Produced household porcelain.
Geraberg (2) (Germany, Thuringia). C. Riemann porcelain factory, f. 1896. Produced utility porcelain.
Gera-Langenberg (Germany, Thuringia). E. and A. Bufe porcelain factory, Langenberg, f. 1902. Produced utility porcelain with one 'L' within a circle as a mark. See Langenberg.
Gerald, see Limoges (27).
Gerard, see Paris (58).
Gerard. Family of painters in Sèvres, c. 1750–1820.
Gerarer porcelain factory, see Untermhaus.
Gérault d'Areaubert, Claude-Charles, see Orléans (1).
Gerbing, F., see Bodenbach.
Gerlach, J. Karl (d. 1786). Engaged in Meissen as a porcelain decorator until 1745; active as a miniature and porcelain painter in 1746 and 1747 in the service of Frederick the Great, whose intention at that time was to establish a porcelain factory in Berlin. In 1758 he was active in Vienna, where he worked simultaneously for Neudeck. He was firmly engaged there in 1759, but he left after five months to go for two years to Ansbach, after which he returned to Meissen where he died on 7 July 1786; he was reputed to have been the 'best painter' of the factory.
Gerlach, L., porcelain decorator, see Schlaggenwald (1).
Gerold & Co., see Tettau (2).
Gerona (Spain). The assumption that some porcelain was produced here in the 19th c. has been contradicted by the theory that the porcelain was of Chinese origin and only decorated in Gerona, or that it was made and marked in China to the dictates of the German firm.

Shield of Cordova in red or blue

Gerrier Bros., Le, see Paris (59).
Gerverot, Louis Victor (1747–1829). Painter, colourist, chemist and arcanist. He furnishes us with one of the best examples of the 'Itinerant', a travelling porcelain specialist in the 18th and 19th c. There is evidence of his work from the

following establishments: Sèvres 1764–5; Weesp 1771; Oude Loosdrecht 1777–8; Wedgwood 1786; and Fürstenberg 1795–1814 where he was a director. His work is also recorded in other places – Niderviller, Fulda, Ludwigsburg, Ansbach Bruckberg, Höchst, Frankenthal, Offenbach, Lane End. A special mention should be made of his activity in Schrezheim (1773–5). According to official records, the famous 'Schrezheimer Faience Altar' could only have been accomplished with the help and co-operation of Gerverot.

Geschwenda (Germany, Thuringia). Orben, Knabe & Co., f. in 1909. Produced presentation and gift ware.

Gessner, Salomon (1730–88). Poet, painter and engraver. Co-founder of the Zurich porcelain factory (Schonen). Occasionally he also worked as a decorator dilettanté in the factory. Several pieces bear his signature.

Geyger, Johann Caspar (d. 1780), see Würzburg.

Gherardini, see Belville.

Gibus, see Limoges (34).

'Giesche' porcelain factory AG, see Katowice-Bogucice.

Giesshübel nr. Buchau (1) (Bohemia, now Stružná). A small porcelain factory operated here from 1891.

Giesshübel nr. Buchau (2) (Bohemia, now Stružná. Christian Nonne, who was also the lessee of Volkstedt and Ilmenau, f. a porcelain factory here in 1803 after his lease in Klösterle ran out (see Klösterle). It was called Nonne & Roesch like the one in Ilmenau, but was sold only seven years later in 1810 to Joh. Anton Hladik. Further tenants were: Benedikt Knaute, as sole tenant from 1815 and as joint tenant with Franz Lehnert from 1835. In 1825 W. A. Ritter von Neuberg came into the Hladik family through marriage and became the owner of the factory. Knaute withdrew from the factory in 1840 and some years later so did Lehnert, who f. a small establishment in Hirschen in 1846 (see Hirschen). Von Neuberg directed the factory himself from 1846. The ownership changed again and the factory was called Priviligierte Gräflich Czerninsche porcelain factory, until 1892. To begin with it was rented by Adalbert Schuldes and Sons (in 1892), and was then bought in 1904 by Johann Schuldes. Production included general ware, figures, vases and goods for export in the beginning of the 19th c. The concern was still active in 1941, under the name of Gieshübel/Johann Schuldes porcelain factory. According to Poche the strawflower pattern was in use c. 1800.

1 blue underglaze or coloured, mark of Christian Nonne 1803–13 – 2 older form of 1 with
an arrowhead – 3–4 since 1815, blindmark before 1835 – 6–8 NGF = Neuberg-Griesshübel
factory, in the time of Ritter von Neuberg, after 1846 Giesshübel also in flat type

Giesshübel nr. Buchau (3) (Bohemia, now Stružná). Josef Riedl, porcelain
decorating studio, c. 1930.

Giey-sur-Aujon (France). F. Guignet directed a porcelain factory here in
1809–40.

'del Giglio', see Cavazzale.

Gijon (Spain, Asturia). 'La Asturiana' porcelain factory S.A. f. 1876. Produced
tableware.

Gilding. Gold was dissolved in mercury water *(q.v.),* pounded with iron vitriol
into a brown powder which was mixed with porcelain flux, then grated and
applied as overglaze colour. In the firing the gilding took on a yellow ocre tone,
and was subsequently burnished with a blood or agate stone to a high polish. If a
matt-finish was required, it would have been treated with glass brushes. A silky
gloss could be achieved if the burnished gilding was fired once again. See Alt-
Wein-Vergoldung.

Gille, see Paris (60).

Gillet & Brianchon, see Paris (61).

Ginori, Carlo, Marchese. F. the Doccia factory in 1737 which is still working
today.

Ginori antico, see Doccia.

Gioanetti, Vittorio Amadeo, Dr., physician (1729–1815). He was dedicated to
the study of natural sciences and proved, with the aid of the 'Voltesian
Apparatus', the changeability of the most diverse kinds of soils. In the course of
these experiments he discovered a clay substance which was endowed with a
state of 'rare pérfection' and in 1780 obtained a patent for the re-opening of the
porcelain factory in Vinovo nr. Turin, which had been closed by Royal

Command. He directed this factory most successfully from the technical and economical points of view. In Italy, the porcelain from Vinovo is regarded as the best in the world.

Giovanelli-Service. Ludwigsburg 1760. This table, tea and toilet service was designed by G. F. Riedel. It is decorated in gold on blue with rocailles, flowers in relief and landscape paintings and was produced by order of the Duke Karl Eugen for his favourite, the Marchesa Giovanelli.

Girandole, delle, see Buontalenti.

Giraud, A., Brousseau, Chiry & Cie., see Limoges (28).

Giraud, André, see Limoges (29).

Gitterborte, see Cross hatched diaper.

Giusti, Giovanni. Modeller, see Doccia.

Gjelsk nr. Moscow (Russia). In 1801–12 a factory was here which was f. by Otto.

Glacières. An 18th c. name for a porcelain cooling vessel used for food.

Gladstone China, see Longton (33).

Glanzgold (liquid gold gilding). An adhesive, discovered in 1879 by the chemist Heinrich Roessler (in Frankfurt am Main). This invention began the production of ceramic colours in Roessler's firm.

Glanzvergoldung. Discovered in Meissen c. 1830 and used for simple porcelain ever since. 10–15 per cent gold is mixed with sulphuric oils into the so-called gold-balsam which is thinly applied to achieve a pink lustre. This lustre gilding, which permits alterations to be made, is considerably cheaper than true gilding because the burnishing of the gold is unnecessary, but the result is considerably harder looking.

Glas-und Porzellankunst GmbH, see Munich (2).

Glasgow (Scotland). J. & M. P. Bell & Co. f. a factory here in 1842 which specialised in earthenware and porcelain. Products were mainly vases and reliefs in frit porcelain. This factory still produces earthenware.

Glassner and Greiner, see Schmiedefeld (1).

Glaze. Although the fired body of porcelain is completely waterproof, it is usually glazed as a means of achieving a polished surface. The glazes are essentially composed of the same basic substances as the porcelain itself. They do, however, contain more fluxing agents which means that they are more fusible and glass-like. Glazing is usually achieved by immersion. On delicate or very thin pieces, the glaze is sprayed on. The glazes used in Germany during the 18th c. were cold transparent calcine glazes consisting of 50 per cent quartz crystal, 37 per cent kaolin and 12.5 per cent limestone. At the same time France preferred a cloudy but warm feldspar glaze, which consisted of 80 per cent. siliceous earth, 12 per cent. aluminium oxide and 8 per cent. potash.

Glazes, sprayed on. The liquid glaze is blown onto the object through a bamboo pipe, the end of which is covered with a fine silk gauze screen. If the process is repeated the resultant glaze is exceptionally even (known as the Chinese technique).

Glot, Richard, see Sceaux.

Gluchow (Ukraine), see Kaolin sources.

Gmunden (Austria). Johann Hufnagl, porcelain decorating studio, c. 1930.

Goblets à Vermouth. Slim beakers which are generally *en suite* with a glass for water and a sugar-bowl, combined with inserts or united on a credence of precious metals.

Godebaki & Co., see Fontainebleau (1).

Goebel, Wm., see Oeslau (2).

Goldätzdecor, see Gold brocade.

Gold anchor period, see Chelsea (1).

Gold brocade pattern. Here the ground of the design is etched into the surface of the porcelain with fluorspar acetone. The etched portions remain dull after the firing while the remainder can be burnished. In France gilding is also used under the glaze. Gilded etching on porcelain was introduced in 1862 by Hughes, a glassmaker from Stoke-on-Trent (England).

Gold chinoiseries. A popular porcelain decoration, which features the usual chinoiseries in gold silhouettes, painted on in etched drawing in reserve. The gilded chinoiseries on imported Chinese porcelain and early Meissen porcelain originate in the main from Augsburg decorators of the Auffenwerth and Seuter decorating studios. Dating is difficult because this decoration was applied to older porcelain as early as the mid 18th c. and has remained practically unchanged. This type of decoration must be regarded as a monopoly of the Augsburg workshops; it is also found with polychrome decoration on pieces painted in Meissen itself as well as with pure gold silhouettes on porcelain from other factories, e.g. Doccia and Buen Retiro.

Goldscheider Art Pottery, see Hanley (7).

Goldscheidersche Porcelain Works and Majolica factory, see Vienna (7).

Golenitscheff-Kutusoff, Duke, see Morje.

Göltz, Johann Christoph, see Höchst.

Gomon et Cie., see Saint Brice.

Gonord, see Paris (62).

Goodwin & Bullok, Dresden Works, see Longton (34).

Goodwin, John E., see Wedgwood.

Goodwin Stoddard, J., & Co., see Longton (35).

Göritzmühle nr. Steinbach (Germany, Thuringia). Albin Eichhorn. porcelain factory, f. 1838. Produced mocha cups and 'Turkish Cöppchen' (little Turkish heads).

This mark also appears without 'Made in Germany'

Görne, Friedrich von, see Plaue on the Havel.

Gorodnitza (Poland). In 1798 the burnt-out factory of Korcec was replaced by a new porcelain factory, built with the support of Prince Iwan Czartorsky. In 1814 Prince Lubormirsky became the owner. It is possible, however, that production began only after the joining of Rulikowski in 1856. Later the factory had to stop working, again through fire damage in 1870. Judging by the technique the products of the period of Rulikowski were the best.

Gorsas, see Limoges (30).
Goss, William Henry (Ltd.), Falcon Pottery, see Stoke-on-Trent (8).
Gossler, Willi, see Thiersheim.
Gotha (1) (Germany, Thuringia). Wilhelm Theodor v. Rotberg (1718–95). f. a porcelain factory here in 1757. Initially greyish, earthenware type porcelain was produced, but in 1772 translucent china with a creamy yellowish glaze appeared. Export consignments in 1775 achieved a turnover of 6,000 Thaler. In spite of this, the economic viability was too small and consequently, in 1782, the factory was leased to its workers. The 'Consortium' was made up by the painter Christian Schulz, J. A. Brehm and the composer Och. The factory was called Schulz & Co. from 1782. In spite of the right of first refusal, the widow of Rotberg sold the factory in 1802 for 13,000 Thaler to the hereditary Prince August von Sachsen-Gotha, who employed his former valet, Friedrich Aegidius Henneberg as supervisor. In 1837 there were three kilns, by 1870 this had risen to six. In about 1850, 100 people were employed there. August Henneberg, who took over the factory after the death of Joh. Christoph, died in 1833, and his heirs sold it to the Simson Brothers, owners of the well known munitions factory in Suhl. An early underglaze painting, mainly 'blade, stalk or straw-pattern', reminiscent of the Meissen strawflower pattern was used. The products retained the style of the last phase of rococo, with some likeness to the Berlin production. Good work was done in the style of Louis XVI and of the Empire period. Apart from a few dinner, coffee and tea services, memorial cups, solitaires and tête á têtes were produced, as well as relief medallions in biscuit (Liers Neumeister).

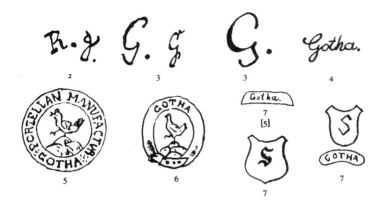

1 1757–c. 1787 and 1795 – 2 1795–1802 and 1805 – 3 c. 1802–c. 1834 – 4 1805–34 – 5 1834–c. 1860 – 6 1860–c. 1883 – 7 from 1883

Gotha (2) (Germany, Thuringia). Morgenroth & Co. porcelain factory, f. 1866, producing fancy articles, figures, etc. This factory was transferred to Friedrich Schwab & Co. in 1919 and since then it has carried his name. It produced utility and tableware, artistic and luxury articles in the genres of Meissen, Copenhagen and 'modern'.

[226]

Gotha (3) (Germany, Thuringia). E. Pfeffer, porcelain and faience factory, f. in 1892, producing figures and dolls' heads. The factory no longer exists.

Gotha (4) (Germany, Thuringia). Schützmeister & Quendt, porcelain decorating studio, 1893–1914, working with dolls and dolls' heads.

Gothic Service (Gotisches Service). Viennese work of 1824 for the K. and K. Court. The decoration depicts ruins of medieval castles and fortresses in Austria, enclosed in Gothic tracery.

Gottbrecht, Fr., see Reichmannsdorf (1).

Gottfried & Vielgut, see Klösterle (2).

Göttingen (Germany, Nether Saxony). Theodor Holborn, glass and porcelain decorating studio, f. 1889, dealing in family and college crests. Still active in 1949.

Gotzkowsky, Johann Ernst (b. 1710 Conitz). Wholesale merchant and porcelain factory owner from Berlin. The second Berlin porcelain factory belonged to him from 1761–3. In the years between 1740 and 1750 he ordered from Meissen on a large scale. In 1768 his autobiography, *The History of a Patriotic Merchant* was published (reprinted in the *Schriften des Vereins für die Geschichte Berlins,* booklet VII, p. 1).

'Gotzkowsky flower pattern' (erhabene Blumen). Popular Meissen decoration, which was designed in 1741 for the founder of the second Berlin factory, Gotzkowsky, for his own porcelain service. The rim of the plates is divided by four narrow panels alternating with four wide panels each decorated with flowers sprigs in light relief which also appear in the centre of the plate in the form of a wreath decorated with ribbons and bows.

Goubin, R. et Comp., see Daoulas.

Gournay-en-Bray (France). According to information in the *Dictionnaires des Postes aux Lettres* a porcelain factory was here in 1802.

Gout de Ville S.a.r.l., see Paris (63).

Gouyn, Charles, see Chelsea (1).

Göz, Johann. Was the Director and repairer in charge of the production of figures in Ludwigsburg from 1760–3. Christ assumes that he is the anonymous 'Master of the Apollo candlestick'.

Gräbner, Ch. Z., see Ilmenau (1).

Gräbner, Karl. In 1837, he published *The Secret of the preparation of such divers porcelain as stoneware, faience and pottery and their glazes truly revealed.*

Graf, Fritz, see Grossbreitenbach (4).

Gräf & Krippner, see Selb (1).

Gräfenhain (Germany, Thuringia). Simon & Halbig, porcelain factory 1870–1925. One of the largest German producers of biscuit dolls' heads. This mark is found internationally in connection with the most renowned doll manufacturers. In German dolls the mark is predominantly found combined with those of Kammer & Rheinhardt, Waltershausen, Thuringia. Kammer & Reinhardt also made dolls' heads themselves.

    S & H   SIMON HALBIG

Hallmark

Gräfenroda (1) (Germany, Thuringia). Chr. Carstens K.G., porcelain factory.

Gräfenroda (2) (Germany, Thuringia). Dornheim, Koch & Fischer, porcelain factory, f. 1860; production included luxury and fancy goods, dolls and dolls' heads with the following neck marks. The factory no longer operates.

Gräfenroda (3) (Germany, Thuringia). August Heissner Nachf., porcelain decorating studio c. 1930.

Gräfenroda (4) (Germany, Thuringia). Oscar Mell porcelain factory, f. 1891. Produced figures, vases, saints, busts, etc.

Gräfenroda (5) (Germany, Thuringia). Gräfenroda-Ort-Reinhold Voigt OHG, porcelain factory f. 1910. Produced utility and decorative porcelain.

Gräfenthal (1) (Germany, Thuringia). A porcelain factory was f. here in 1861, by Unger, Schneider and Hutschenreuther, by Ducal concessions. Schneider had previously been a businessman in Wallendorf and Unger was a modeller. The enterprise developed favourably; by 1865 a considerable profit had already been made. In 1885, Unger left the firm which changed its name to 'Schneider & Hutschenreuther'. Hutschenreuther also left in 1886, when the firm then assumed the name it still carries today: Carl Scheider's Heirs'. Production concentrated on figures, groups and animals, which in some instances, were life size; some fancy goods were also made.

[250]

Gräfenthal (2) (Germany, Thuringia). A. H. Pröschold, porcelain factory, f. in 1897, producing figures and other items. The firm is no longer in existence.
Gräfenthal (3) (Germany, Thuringia). Carl Schneidig, porcelain factories, f. 1906. Produced fancy porcelain and electroporcelain, using the onion pattern. Today it is called VEB Gräfenthaler Porzellan-Figuren and is the factory of the ornamental porcelain works, Lichte. The second mark is still in use.

Gräfenthal (4) (Germany, Thuringia). Weiss, Kühnert & Co., K.G., porcelain factory, f. 1891. Produced ornamental porcelain and since 1945 coffee and general children's ware (although to a lesser extent).

Gräfenthal-Meernach (Germany, Thuringia). Heinz & Co. porcelain factory, f. 1900. Produced ornamental porcelain.

Grainger, Thomas, see Worcester (1).
Grahl, Karl Gottlieb (1740–82), see Ottweiler.
Gramont (Gamont?), see Paris (64).
Granesau (Bohemia). Heinzl & Co., porcelain factory, f. 1924. Produced coffee beakers, cooking pots, cups, etc. The factory ceased production after 1945.

Granger & Co., see Limoges (54).
'Granit' porcelain and earthenware factory, see Budapest (2).
Grassi, Anton (1755 Vienna–31 December 1807 Vienna). Viennese sculptor, and Professor at the Academy from 1794. He created many statues and portrait busts for the Castle of Schönbrunn. The figurative production of the Viennese factory was greatly influenced by him; in 1784 he became Niedermayer's successor. As chief modeller he set the style of the Sorgenthal period. Until 1792 he worked in the manner of the late rococo; work in the neo-classical taste was executed almost exclusively in biscuit.

Gravant, François (d. 1765), see Vincennes (1).
Gravant, Louis François, see Chantilly (1).
Gravant, Dame, see Chantilly (1).
Greder, A., see Paris (3).
Green, Clark & Clay, see Longton (40).
Green, T. A. & S., see Fenton (5).
Greiner. A painting and potting family, members of which were employed in various porcelain factories in Thuringia, or worked independently. The head is thought to have been Gotthelf, who helped in the foundation of Wallendorf in 1764, and f. Limbach in 1762. In 1782 he became owner of Grossbreitenbach and in 1786 of Ilmenau. His five sons (Ernst, Johann Friedemann, Johann Georg Daniel, Johann Jacob Florentin and Johann Michael Gotthelf) took the ownership of Kloster Veilsdorf. Johann Georg Wilhelm and Johann Andreas, who were originally painters in Volkstedt, also later owned Gera (from 1780). Johann Friedrich, Johann Georg and Christian Daniel f. Rauenstein in 1783 and Wilhelm Heinrich was the co-owner of the Volkstedt porcelain factory in 1799. In conclusion, one may regard the Greiners as the founders of the great modern porcelain industry in Thuringia.
Greiner, Gotthelf. Reputed, like Macheleid, and independently of Böttger, to have discovered the porcelain arcanum. In 1762 he f. the small Limbach factory and in 1764 f. Wallendorf. Was the owner of Grossbreitenbach (1782) and Ilmenau (1786).
Greiner, G. & Co., see Schauberg (1).
Greiner & Herda, see Oberkotzau (2).
Greiner & Sohn, see Dresden (8).
Greiner, Stauch & Co., see Rudolstadt Volkstedt (1).
Greising (Germany, Saxony). Strnact jun., Josef, porcelain decorating studio c. 1930.

Grellet, Gebrüder, see Limoges (31).
Gresley, Sir Nigel, see Church (1).
Gricci, Guiseppe (d. 1770). Active as modeller in Capodimonte in 1744; he was transferred to Spain in 1759, when the factory moved to Buen Retiro.

Grieninger, Johann Georg (d. 1798). Director of the Gotzkowsky Berlin factory from 1761–3, and the Royal Berlin factory, from 1763–98. In 1790 he set down the history of both factories (Hohenzollernjahrbuch 1902, p. 175).

Griesbach, Julius, see Koburg Cortendorf.

Grigny (France, Rhône). The Decaen brothers, who in 1839 also directed a porcelain factory in Arboras, produced porcelain here in the 'english manner' in 1837, together with porcelain flowers. In 1844 Ardouin became the owner and appointed Mittenkoff as director. Today only white and domestic ware is produced.

Gripsholm-Service (Infodsret Service). The name for a table service which had been made and painted in China for Sweden.

Grisaille. Monochrome decoration in grey on porcelain, common in the later part of the 18th c.

Gronsveld-Diepenbrock, Count. Founder of the first Dutch porcelain factory at Weesp.

Gros bleu. A deep blue underglaze which combines readily with the glaze. Customary in Vincennes and Sèvres 1749–60, and imitated in Chelsea (Mazareen).

Gröschl & Spethmann, see Turn (2).

Gross, modeller, see Isle St. Denis.

Grossbaum, M. B., see Vienna (9).

Grossbreitenbach (1) (Germany, Thuringia). A factory f. in 1778 by Anton Friedrich Wilhelm Ernst von Hopfgarten and still existing today. In 1782 he sold it to Gotthelf Greiner, the owner of the Limbach porcelain factory. As a branch of Limbach, the mark of which it employed, the factory, under the direction of the son of G. Greiner, Friedemann, promptly grew in significance. According to records of 1812, the porcelain decoration was limited exclusively to the blue underglaze. Any precise attribution of porcelain as the products from Grossbreitenbach is impossible because since 1788 the clover leaf mark was also used by Limbach and Ilmenau. The factory remained in the hands of the Greiner family until 1869.

Grossbreitenbach (2) (Germany, Thuringia). H. Bühl & Son, porcelain factory f. 1780; production included pipe bowls, dolls and dolls' heads. The factory no longer exists.

]240]   Hallmark

Grossbreitenbach ((3) (Germany, Thuringia). Franz Fritz Nachfolger porcelain works. F. by Horst Zedler, in 1874. Produced topographical and armorial decorations, gift articles.

Grossbreitenbach (4) (Germany, Thuringia). Fritz Graf porcelain factory. Produced cheap gift articles until its closure.

Grossbreitenbach (5) (Germany, Thuringia). Grossbreitenbacher porcelain factory GmbH, f. 1861. Mass produced utility and luxury ware.

Grossbreitenbach (6) (Germany, Thuringia). Adolph Harras Nachfol., Oberende, porcelain factory, f. 1861. Mass produced cheap utility and luxury articles. This factory no longer exists.

Grossbreitenbach (7) (Germany, Thuringia). Jul. Eginh. Harras, porcelain factory f. 1886, producing souvenir articles. The firm no longer exists.

Grossbreitenbach (8) (Germany, Thuringia). Marienfeld porcelain factory, active in 1899. Produced figures and dolls' heads.

Grosse, A., & O. Feuereisen, see Töppeles.

Grossmann, Christ. Gotthelf. Meissen decorator from 1750–66; he also worked for Sèvres and Ludwigsburg.

Grosvenor China Ltd., see Longton (36).

Grünes & Co., see Horn.

Grünlas (Bohemia, now Loučki). In 1908, Benjamin Hunt took the initial steps in founding a porcelain factory, which by 1911 had already passed into the hands of R. Kämpf. This factory is said to have been called R. Dieterle & R. Kämpf GmbH at some stage. Produced table ware.

Grünstadt (Germany, The Palatinate). Figure modelling from Frankenthal moulds, brought here by van Recum, was carried out here from 1801. See Frankenthal (1).

Grusinow, see Kusnetzoff.

Guay, le, see Brancas-Lauraguais.

Gudenberg, W. van, see Rozenburg.

Guélaud, see Paris (65).

Guerhard, see Paris (41).

Guérin-Pouyat-Elite Ltd., see Limoges (32).

Guery-Delnières, see Limoges (9) and (33).

Guettard, Jean Etienne (1715–86). Doctor of medicine. A pupil of Réaumur's, he was occupied for a considerable time with investigations in minerals. In 1765 he published his major work *Histoire de la decouverte Faite en France, de matières semblables à celles dont la porcelaine de la China est composée*. See Brancas-Lauraguais.

Guibald, Barthélemy, see Hastière.

Guignet, F., see Giey-sur-Aujon.

Guillard, Claud, see Naples.

Gülding, Jürgen (Dane). Active as a decorator in the first Copenhagen period (1760–5)

Günther & Co., see Petersburg.

Günther, Josef, see Dresden (9).

Günthersfeld AG, see Gehren.

Gusi (or Chusi). Family of decorators in Strasburg and Hagenau in the 18th c.

Gustavsberg (!) (Sweden). AB Gustavsberg factory. Here, in 1822, porcelain production started in the Odelberg factory which had been working since the middle of the 17th c. The factory was a family concern until c. 1910 and it struggled hard during the second half of the 19th c. in order to survive intense European competition. Since 1866 bone china production was also undertaken. An individual style only developed in the last quarter of the 19th c., until then work mainly followed the English tradition. Gustavsberg is therefore the only European porcelain factory which has produced bone china apart from England. After 1917, under the direction and personal influence of Wilhelm Kåge, the factory produced work of a highly individual character; today it specialises in 'Modern Swedish'. Kåge invented a silver decoration called 'Argenta'. 'Cintra' is a particularly transparent porcelain, 'Farsta' shows a copper glaze and 'Farsta Rust' is the name of a surface treatment using iron oxide decorated with primitive geometric shapes which are reminiscent of Inka-pottery. Stig Lindberg created surrealistic compositions which are, generally speaking, glazed in monochrome. Berndt Friberg is the creator of excellent models and also makes up his own glazes.

1   2   3

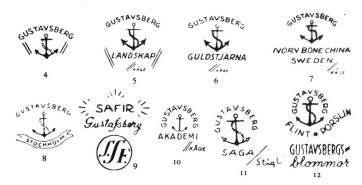

1 1810 – 2 1845 – 3 1866 – 4 1910–40 – 5–6 1924 – 7 1928 – 8–9 1930 – 10 1934 – 11–12 1940

Gustavsberg (2) (Sweden). A. B. Gustavsbergs Interessenter factories; f. 1827. Produced household china.
Gutenbrunn (Germany, Pfalz-Zweibrücken). In 1767 Duke Christian IV von Pfalz-Zweibrücken f. a 'high-quality crockery and porcelain factory' in his Gutenbrunn Castle, with the help of the arcanist and physician, Dr. Stahl (who was assisted by Laurenzius Russinger). In 1768 I. M. Höckel from Höchst was engaged to replace Russinger. In 1769 the factory was moved to Zweibrücken and had to be closed down in 1775. Apart from some presentation pieces, only simply decorated porcelain was made. One can distinguish the two types; in the case of the first, kaolin from the Passauer Becken was used; and in the second the less suitable kaolin from Nohfelden was used.

Guterbaum, J., see Paris (66).
Gutherz, Oscar & Edgar, see Altrohlau (4).
Guy, Barthélémy (d. 1798), see Paris (67).
Gysbz, see Oude Amstel.

H., GmbH, see Probstzella.
Haag, Johann Jakob Heinrich and Johann Friedrich. Thuringian decorators working independently and in factories in the second half of the 18th c., were among the artists who decorated Nymphenburg porcelain. J. Friedrich was also active in Regensburg where he decorated porcelain from Thuringia, Ansbach and Nymphenburg for export to the Near East.

Haas, see Schlaggenwald (1).

Haas & Czjzek, see Chodau (2) and Schlaggenwald (1).

Habertitzel, Franz Anton, see Rabensgrün.

Habertitzel, see Klösterle (1).

Hache & Julien, see Vierzon (11).

Hache & Pépin-le-Halleur, see Vierzon (11).

Hachez, A. & Pépin Lehalleur Frères, see Vierzon (11).

Hackefors (Sweden). Hackefors Porslin Aktiebolag J. O. F. by Nilson in 1929. Produced coffee, tea and mocha services and gift articles.

Hackenberg, Max, see Unterköditz (1).

Hackwood, William (d. 1839). Wedgwood's chief modeller from 1769–1832.

Hädrich & Son, see Reichenbach (3).

Hädrichs, Otto, Wwe. Kdt. Ges., see Reichenbach (2).

Hafringue, see Boulogne.

Haffnerzell, Donau (Germany, Bavaria). Kaolin source in the Passau vicinity which supplied the Vienna, Nymphenburg, Frankenthal and Ludwigsburg factories during the 18th c.

Hagen, Karl and Friedel, see Passau (2).

Hagenau, see Strasbourg and Hannong, K. F. and his sons and grandchildren.

Hague, The (Holland). Porcelain factory f. in 1775. It was successfully directed by Anton Leichner (also Lynker) from Vienna, until his death in 1781, when his son Johann Franz took his place. In 1790 the factory became insolvent and had to be sold. The production was in the style of the late 18th c. The decoration, particularly the Boucher style and polychrome flower paintings were highly praised. The monochrome purple decoration is also famous. One can assume that decorators of this factory sometimes also decorated frit porcelain which had been produced in Tournay.

all blue (the city coat-of-arms)

Haida (1) (Bohemia). Carl Fr. Boseck & Co., porcelain factory. Produced luxury and utility ware, handpainted Old-Vienna decoration. Still working in 1934. The notice for the mark was entered on 9 April 1892 in Reichenberg under No. 310 for publication in the K. K. Mark-Gazette and on 29 April 1892 at 11 a.m. was registered with the Kgl. Amtsgericht Leipzig under No. 5260, as WZ.

[49]

cinnabar red on the glaze

Haida (2) (Bohemia). Paepkke & Schäfer, porcelain manufacturing and decorating firm existed in 1930. Specialised in little baskets, bowls, vases, smoking garnitures, boxes of all kinds, bonbonnieres, table plates, mocha, coffee, and tea services.

Haidinger, Bros., see Elbogen (1).
Haidrich, Fr., porcelain decorator, see Prag.
Haigh Hirstwood, porcelain decorator, see York.
Haimhausen, Sigmund Graf von (1708–93), see Nymphenburg.
Haindorf (1) (Bohemia, now Heinice). Josef Kratzer & Sons, porcelain factory, f. 1880. Produced domestic goods, childrens' and dolls' services. The factory closed after 1941.

Haindorf (2) (Bohemia, now Heinice). Josef Kratzer & Son, porcelain decorating workshop, c. 1930.

Hald, Andreas, Sculptor in Copenhagen, 1781–97.

Hal et Ixelles-lez-Bruxelles (Belgium). J. B. Capellmans Sr. produced porcelain here c. 1870.

Hall Bros. Ltd., Radnor Works, see Longton (37).

Halley. Porcelain decorating studio of the early 19th c. in Paris. See Caen.

Halley-Lebon, see Paris (68).

Hallin, August, F. Decorator, see Copenhagen (1).

Halmmuster (Blade pattern). Service decoration used in the Thuringian porcelain factories from the end of the 18th c. It has much in common with the Meissen strawflower pattern of c. 1740, and is very distinctive. See also Ilmenauer Strawflower pattern.

Haly, François. Arcanist in Alcora in 1751.

Hamann, Adolf, see Dresden (10).

Hamann, J. W. (later Hertwig & Co.), see Katzhütte and Wallendorf.

Hamburg (1) (Germany). Schumacher Bros. had their products made of kalli pasta (ivory paste), and chromopasta (dyed ivory paste). The following mark was entered at the Landsgericht, Hamburg on 23 July 1884.

[33]

Hamburg (2) (Germany). Klosterthor 8. Rosenthal Works and Schauberg S. Rosenthal & Co. porcelain factory existed in 1930. There is evidence of its address and mark.

Hammersley, J. and R., see Hanley (12).

Hammersley & Co. Ltd., china manufacturers, Alsager Pottery, see Longton (38).

Hancock, Robert (1730–1817). English draughtsman and engraver, considered (according to research by Cyril Cook, London, 1955) to be the sole inventor of 'transfer printing', introduced c. 1747.

R. Hancock fecit.

Hancock & Co., see Derby (1).

Hanika, Alfred, see Rudolstadt Volkstedt (14).

Hanley (1) (England). James & Thomas Bevington directed the Burton Place Works, 1865–78; Thomas Bevington, 1877–91; Hanley porcelain Co., 1892–9; Hanley China Co., 1899–1901 (Godden).

J. & T. B.   T. B.

Hanley (2) (England). John Bevington ran the Kensington porcelain Works, 1872–92. According to Godden, Bevington presented his products as reproductions of Dresden, Derby, Chelsea and Worcester. He produced porcelain figures, vases, candelabras, candlesticks, small baskets, etc. These Bevington pieces are sometimes erroneously attributed to Coalbrookdale or Derby.

Hanley (3) (England). Zachariah Boyle (& Sons), Hanley 1823–30, Stoke 1828–50, porcelain factory.

BOYLE   Z. B.   Z. B. & S.

Hanley (4) (England). Dura Co. Ltd., produced empress pottery, 1911–21.

Hanley (5) (England). Alfred Fenton & Sons, 1887–1901.

A. F. & S.

Hanley (6) (England). T. & C. Ford, 1854–71; Thomas Ford, 1871–4; Charles Ford, 1874–1904. Sold to Robinson & Sons, Longton, in 1904.

T. & C. F.   T. F.

Hanley (7) (England). Goldscheider Art Pottery, produced artistic porcelain 1946–59. See Vienna 7.

Hanley (8) (England). Waterloo Works Livesley Powell & Co., 1851–66 (?); Powell & Bishop, 1876–8; Powell, Bishop & Stonier, 1878–91; Bishop & Stonier, 1891–1939. Produced richly decorated porcelain.

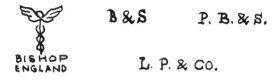

Hanley (9) (England). Mann & Co., 1858–60, porcelain and earthenware factory, later Mann, Evans & Co. The mark displays the full name and locality.
Hanley (10) (England). Pointon & Co. Ltd., porcelain factory, 1883–1916; formerly R. G. Scrivener, porcelain and earthenware factory, 1870–83.

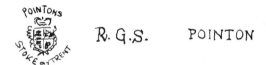

Hanley (11) (England). Ford & Pointon, porcelain factory, 1917–36; formerly Pointon & Co., 1883–1916.

Hanley (12) (England). J. and R. Hammersley, 1877–1917; R. Hammersley, 1917–20.

J. R. H

Hanley (13) (England). Sandland & Colley, porcelain and earthenware factory, 1907–10; formerly Sandlands Ltd. Directed by W. Sandland until c. 1913.

Hanley (14) (England). David Wilson (& Sons), porcelain and earthenware factory, ecclesiastical work, 1802–18. Formerly Robert Wilson, factory which handled no porcelain production.

WILSON

Hanley China Co., see Hanley (1).
Hanley Porcelain Co., see Hanley (1).
Hannong (I), Karl Franz (1669–1739). He learned the craft in Dutch potteries and pipe factories and was later active in Cologne and Maine. In 1709 he f. a pipe factory in Strasbourg and collaborated in 1721 with the porcelain maker Heinrich Wockenfeld, a faience factory owner from Strasbourg. This collaboration resulted in the founding of the famous faience factory in the Stampfgasse. It was managed by Hannong alone, from 1721; in 1724 it was enlarged by the acquisition of the Hagenau factory. In 1730 he transferred both the factories to his sons Paul Anton and Balthasar.
Hannong (II), Paul Anton (1700–60), the son of Hannong I. Under his direction both factories, Strasbourg and Hagenau, flourished: Strasbourg from 1732 and Hagenau from 1737. With the help of C. W. v. Löwenfinck and J. G. Rode, porcelain production was already high in 1751. Because of the French monopoly, which forbade any porcelain production outside Vincennes, Paul Anton transferred his factory to Frankenthal in 1755. Here he was also active as a decorator. In 1759 he sold this successful establishment to his son, Joseph Adam. See Frankenthal (1).
Hannong (III), Joseph Adam (1734–c. 1800), son of Hannong II. In his youth, he travelled as arcanist and in 1759 bought the Frankenthal factory from his father. He worked as modeller here for some considerable time. In 1762, he sold the factory to the Elector Karl Theodor; at the same time he received 10,000 Livres for the arcanum. From that time onwards he directed only the Strasbourg and Hagenau faience factories, where in 1774, he produced porcelain once again. In 1779 both factories went bankrupt. He made his home in Paris from 1787–90.

$$\dot{I} \ H$$

Hannong (IV), Peter Anton (1739–c. 1793 Paris), son of Hannong II. As a 16-year-old he worked in Frankenthal. He managed the Strasbourg and Hagenau faience factories from 1759–61. In 1761 he attempted to sell the arcanum to Sèvres and in the same year f. a small new faience factory in Hagenau which did not last more than a year. In 1769 he worked as arcanist in Paris at the porcelain factory of the Duke of Artois, Faubourg St. Denis. Some years later he f. the porcelain factory of the Duke of Chartres in Vincennes with Vittorio Brodel. After this he rented a small faience factory in Verneul.
Hannong, Balthasar (1703–53). In 1732 he succeeded his father Karl Franz as director of the Hagenau factory, which in 1737 became his brother's, Paul Anton's, property. After a fruitless attempt to gain the ownership of the Durlach faience factory he returned to Hagenau.
Hannong, Karl Franz Paul (1732–57). In 1755–7 he was director in his father's (Paul Anton Hannong II) factory in Frankenthal.

Hannong, Karl Franz (1734–88). Stanislaus Karl Konstantin (1769–1832), Louis Konstantin (1809–89) were son, grandson and great grandson of Balthasar Hannong, and all instilled new vigour into the Hagenau factory.

Hansen, Lars. Worked in Copenhagen 1777–1800. His work is regarded as some of the best in underglaze blue decorating.

'Hard paste porcelain' ('Pâte dure'). Hard paste is a contrast to 'soft paste', 'pâte tendre'. The two kinds of porcelain differ only in their composition in regard to the amount of kaolin used. Whilst 'soft paste' contains less kaolin and therefore can be fired with a lower temperature, 'hard paste', with its higher kaolin content, requires a higher firing temperature. Chinese porcelain, generally speaking, is 'hard paste', and European porcelain may be either hard or soft.

Hardmeier, J. J., see Maennedorf.

Harras. In c. 1880 he worked as an independent porcelain decorator in Grossbreitenbach. His best known works are copies of 'old masters'.

Harras, Adolph Nachf., Oberende, see Grossbreitenbach (6).

Harras, Jul. Eginh., see Grossbreitenbach (7).

Harstal, Adalbert III von, Prince Bishop of Fulda, see Fulda (1).

Härtl, Johann Georg, also Hartl (d. 21 June 1754 Munich). Court repairer and at the Nymphenburg Court porcelain factory from 1749. In 1733 he came from Passau to Munich and in 1749 he was for a short time active as modeller at the local factory in Neudeck.

Härtl, J. Paul Rupert (c. 1715 Passau–21 December 1792 Traunstein). Son of Johann Georg and a chemist, who, at the end of 1752 was ordered to join Ringler at Neudeck (Nymphenburg) as arcanist. He was porcelain factory inspector of Neudeck (Nymphenburg), 1754–61. In 1762 he became the author of a pamphlet about the making of porcelain (Staatsbibliothek Munich cod. germ. 3750).

Hartmuth, Joseph and Karl, see Budweis (1).

Harvey, Adams & Co., see Longton (39).

Harvey, C. & W. K., see Longton (40).

Haselhuhn. , E., see Aachen (1).

Hasenfell-Glasur ('Glaze like hare fur'). Name of glaze used on Chinese stoneware of the Sung Dynasty (960–1279) which resembles the fur of the hare.

Haslach (Upper Austria). Robert Riedl, former porcelain decorator of the K.K. Viennese Porcelain decorators, managed a porcelain decorating studio from 1873. Representative work was even displayed at the Vienna World Exhibition.

Haslacher, Benedikt, see Altrohlau (1).

Haslöder, Joseph. Employed as 'blue colouring decorator' in Nymphenburg from 2 September 1754. From 1757 he was employed by Ringler at Ludwigsburg.

Hastière (Belgium, Prov. de Namur). P. L. Cyfflé is supposed to have f. a factory here in 1777. A second was f. in 1785 by Barthélemy Guibal, which he later transferred to Ixelles.

Hattenberger, Franz Xavier, see Moscow (4).

Hausen nr. Lichtenfels (Germany, Bavaria). Here in 1837, the Silbermann brothers managed a porcelain factory, which at that time employed about 200 workmen and generally produced Turkish heads and pipebowls. The date of the beginning of porcelain production is unknown. In 1882 the factory received a diploma from the Bavarian King for excellent blue underglaze decoration. In 1894 the owners were: Hans, Jeanette and Anna Silbermann. In 1938 Alboth and Kaiser from Kronach (today Staffelstein) annexed the factory.

H

Hausmaler. Porcelain decorator. Other names are: Winkelmaler, Pfuschmaler or Überdecorateur (Fr. Chambrelans); as private businessmen they purchased white porcelain from various factories which they decorated with muffle enamel colours.

Haviland, Charles Field, see Limoges (2) and (34).

Haviland, David, see Limoges (35).

Haviland, Frank, see Limoges (36).

Haviland, Jean, see Limoges (37).

Haviland, Johann, see Waldersdorf (1).

Haviland, Théodore, see Limoges (38).

Healthware and hygenic ceramics, see Breslau.

Heath, John, see Chelsea (1).

Heber & Co., see Neustadt (1).

Hefner, v., see Damm.

Hegewald nr. Friedland (Bohemia). In 1850 a porcelain factory existed here under Ad. Persch, which continued under the management of his son Robert Persch in Mildeneichen and Raspenau from 1869.

See also Elbogen (5).

$$\textbf{APH} \qquad \textbf{R} \qquad \textbf{RPM} \qquad \textbf{PH}$$
$$\text{\scriptsize 1} \qquad\qquad \text{\scriptsize 2} \qquad\qquad \text{\scriptsize 3}$$

1–2 blindstamp of Ad. Persch – 3 blindstamp of Robert Persch from 1809

Hehl, J., see Xanten.

Heidelberg (Germany, Baden). Fricker & Co., produced porcelain here in 1870.

Heinecke, Dr. Albert (1854–1932). Chemist, in Berlin from 1879 and from 1885, provisional director and successor of Hermann Segers at the institute for chemical experiments. He made possible the production of a crystalline glaze which had been in use for a considerable time in Copenhagen and Sèvres,

Heinrich & Co., see Selb (2).

Heinrici, Johann Martin (1711–86). He was regarded, in his time, as the most competent portrait painter in Meissen. He rejected Höroldt's style and his paintings on porcelain were exact copies of easel paintings. From 1756–63 and again in 1775, he worked in Frankenthal.

Heintschel, Jos. Ed., see Friedland.

Heintze, Johann Georg. Landscape painter in Meissen 1720–49. One of the ablest of Höroldt's staff and possibly the founder of the Meissen landscape style, with harbour scenes and small figures. His only known signed work is an enamel plaque in the Landes Museum, Stuttgart, decorated with a view of the Albrechtsburg and dated 1734 and 46; the last number is possibly the date of the overpainting of a crack developed from an earlier firing. A cylindrical cup with the initials 'SH' (similar to 'IH') which was earlier regarded as his signature, has now been dismissed as not being his work. He was imprisoned, probably for spying in 1749. He fled to Prague, Vienna, Holitsch and was later in Berlin, but nothing is known of his work during this period.

Heintze, Dr. Julius, see Meissen (1).

Heinz, Rudolf, & Co., see Aelteste Volkstedter (3).

Heinz & Co., see Gräfenthal-Meernach.

'Heinzelmann, Frederik Liverpool 1779', see Liverpool.

Heinzl & Co., see Granesau.

Heissner, Aug., success, see Gräfenroda (3).

Helchis, Jakob. Porcelain decorator for the Vienna factory until 1747. From 1747–9 he worked as an arcanist in Nymphenburg. He employed fine drawings in black dots, landscapes with supporting figures and 'deutsche Blumen' (German flowers).

Jacobus Helchis fecit

Hellot, Jean (1685–1766). Member of the Académie de France from 1735, studied the composition of porcelain, particularly the so-called 'kunckel phosphor'. He was in Vincennes from 1745, and from 1751–66 he was technical manager of the Sèvres factory.

Hellwig, Bruno, see Stotzheim.

Helsinki (Finland). Wärtsilä-koncernen A/B Arabia, f. 1874. Produced domestic earthenware and porcelain. The influence of the Belgian, A. W. Finch, is very discernible – Finch lived in Finland from 1897 and from 1902 was teacher of ceramics at the Central Technical School for the Decorative Arts. Before the takeover by the Wärtsilä-Konzern in 1948 the factory was named: O/Y Arabia A/B.

Hendler, P. Modeller in Meissen (until 1769) Vienna and Fürstenberg (1780–5).
Henneberg (Germany, Coburg-Gotha). This factory exhibited in London in 1851. The quality of production was singled out for favourable mention. C. E. and F. Arnoldi were the owners. See Ilmenau (1).
Henneberg, Ägidius (d. 1834), Joh. Christoph and August, see Gotha (1).
Hennebont (France). According to entries in the *Dictionnaires des postes aux lettres*, a porcelain factory was here in 1802.
Hennicke Service. Made specifically by the KPM Meissen in 1739 for the Court General-Superintendent of the House of Brühl, Count Hennicke. This table service was decorated, regardless of the various shapes of the pieces, with modelled fruits, flowers and birds, scattered all over the surface (Walcha).
Hentschel, Hans Rudolf (b. 1869). Porcelain painter and engraver. Attended technical college of the Meissen works. 1889–93 Munich Academy; 1894 Julian Academy, Paris; 1895 Etaples. Instructor at the Meissen works until 1933.
Hentschel, Julius Konrad (1872–1907). Sculptor and modeller. Trained during 1890–4 at the technical school of the Meissen porcelain factory. From 1891–3 he was at the Munich Academy; 1884–97 repairer and modeller; 1899–1900 Dresden Academy. Produced 'crocus model' breakfast service and probably dinner service too in 1896, and the wing-pattern decoration in 1901.
Herculaneum Pottery, see Liverpool.
Herculaneum Service. Ferdinand IV, King of Naples (1759–1825), during whose reign the excavations of Herculaneum and Pompeii were carried out, had this service made for his father, Charles III of Spain in 1775. It was neo-classical in style and was produced in his own porcelain factory.
Herend (Hungary). Moritz Farkashazy-Fischer, whose family had long before produced tiles and faience pieces, f. in 1839 (with the help of Prince Esterhazy) a porcelain factory in Herend. Fischer discovered suitable kaolin in the Herend vicinity. In 1842, the firm took part in an exhibition for the first time. The factory particularly welcomed orders for replacements for broken pieces from famous collections. The replacement pieces were so perfect that only the factory's mark betrayed its origin. The porcelain from Herend was decorated with amalgamated colours, which made it necessary to fire it up to three times. Some special colours of this porcelain are: bleu de roi and Demidoff green, but other colours are also worth mentioning because of their vividness and depth. The great artistic quality of the porcelain from Herend declined after the death of the founder, when the factory became a company under the direction of the owner. However, after this set-back which occurred during 1875–95, there were some exceptionally good pieces produced, under the grandson of the founder, Eugen Farkashazy-Fischer. At this time there were over 400 employees in the factory. See also Victoria Service.

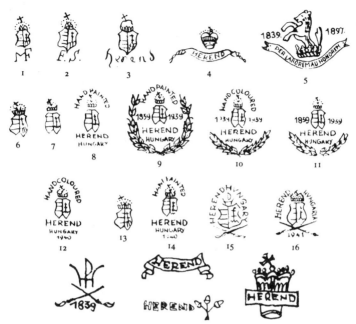

1 1875 – 2 1875–85 – 3 1885–91 – 4 1891–7 – 5 1897–1900 – 6–7 1900–34 – 8 1935–8 – 9–11
1939 – 12–14 1940 – 15 1941 – 16 1948

Hering & Son, Julius, see Köppelsdorf (1).

Herlitz, Carl Gustav, see Lidköping (2).

Hermannsdorfer. Ambros (1699–1770). First inspector of the decorators'
workshop in Nymphenburg from 1761–4. At the same time he was also active as
a fresco painter in Bavaria. One of the most prolific painters of the factory.

Hermsdorf (Germany, Thuringia). Branch of Kahla porcelain factory AGF in
1889. Porcelain services and later electro porcelain.

Herold(t), Christian Friedrich (1700–79). Decorator in Meissen from c. 1724.
Specialised in figures and gilding.

Hertel, Jakob & Co. GmbH, see Rehau (2).

Hertel, Schwab & Co. GmbH, see Stutzhaus.

Hertwig & Co., see Katzhütte.

Hervé, see Lorient.

Herzinger & Co., see Rudolstadt Volkstedt (15).

Herzogliche ächte Porcellaine Fabrique, see Ludwigsburg (1).

Herzogliche porcelain works, see Ludwigsburg (2).

Hess, Franz Joachim, repairer, see Kassel.

Hess, Georg Ignaz, decorator, see Kelsterbach.

Hessen-Darmstadt, Ludwig VIII, Count von, see Kelsterbach.

Hessen-Philippstal, Ernst Constantin, Prinz von, see Rudolstadt Volkstedt (1).

Hessische Keramik-Manufaktur GmbH, see Holzhausen.

Hetsch, Gust. Friedrich (1788–1864), see Copenhagen (1).

Hettlinger, Jean Jacques (1734–1803). Geologist and chemist from Winterthur. 'Inspector' in Sèvres in 1784 and a director, together with Meyer, until 1786.

Heubach, Ernst, Köppelsdorfer porcelain factory (now: Vereinigte Köppelsdorfer Porzellanfabriken formerly Armand Marsseille and Ernst Heubach), see Köppelsdorf (2).

Heubach, Gabriel, see Wallendorf.

Heubach, Fabrikant, see Altwasser (1).

Heubach Bros. AG, see Lichte (2).

Heufel & Co., see Dresden (11).

Hevisé et Comp., see Plombières.

Hewelke, Nathaniel Friedrich. F. Venice's third porcelain factory in 1758, but could not compete with the highly developed factory in neighbouring Nove.

Hewitt & Leadbeater, Willow Pottery, see Longton (41).

Heylin, Edward, see Bow.

Hibbert & Boughey, see Longton (42).

Highfired enamel. A thick flowing enamel decoration is painted on the glaze and then the two are fired together at a high temperature. This high-fired enamel is outstanding owing to its fabulous colour-effects and transparency.

Hijos de J. Giralt Laporta, see Madrid (2).

Hildburghausen (1) (Saxony). Weber f. a porcelain factory here in 1763 about which nothing else is known.

Hildburghausen (2) (Saxony). Wilhelm Simon, porcelain factory, registered the following mark at the Herzoglichen Kreisgericht Hildburghausen on 29 April 1875. Production included toys and porcelain.

[2]

Hildburghausen, F. W. E. Prince von (d. 1795), see Kloster Veilsdorf.

Hildesheim (Germany, Prussia). It is thought that a porcelain factory existed here from 1760 onwards. The two independent decorators Busch and Kratzberg worked in Hildesheim, and it is possible that the name of the locality, which was added to their signatures, was mistakenly interpreted as the name of a factory in which they were working.

Hilditsch & Son, see Lane End (1).

Hill & Co., St. James Works and Windsor China Works, see Longton (22).

Hill-Pottery, see Burslem (1).

Hippolythe, see Sèvres (1).

Hirsch, Franziska, GmbH, see Dresden (20).

Hirschau (Germany, Oberpfalz, Upper Palatinate). Ernst Dorfner & Cie., porcelain factory, f. before 1867; produced utility ware. The business no longer exists.

D.&C.   **E.D.&Cie.**   E. D. & Cie.
                              Hirschau.

                                                              HIRSCHAU

Hirschberg (Germany, Prussia). According to a travel account by Mentionné, a porcelain factory was here in 1826. This account was confirmed by Demmin in 1867.

Hirschen nr. Lubenz (Bohemia). H. Reinl, porcelain factory, f. 1846. Produced utility ware.

Hirtz, Samuel. Arcanist during the foundation of the Rome porcelain factory in 1761.

Hizen (Japan). Japanese province of Kiu-shiu, the most southerly of the island. Main territory of the Japanese porcelain industry during the 18th c. See Imari porcelain, Arita, Japanese porcelain.

Hochgesang, Johann, decorator, see Oxan, G.

Hochzeitszug (Wedding Procession). Art Nouveau tablecentre by Adolf Amberg of the KPM Berlin 1905. The most significant sculptural work produced before the First World War, designed for the occasion of the wedding of the German Crown Prince (but made later in 1910–11). At least as many as 20 figure groups, multi-coloured underglaze.

Hocquart, see Vaux.

Höchst (Germany, Hesse). The factory was f. on 1 March 1746 under Joh. Friedr. Karl v. Osthein Elector Kurfürst von Mainz, and privileges were granted for 50 years to the two managers of the Electoral mirror factory in Lohr, Johann Christoph Göltz and Johann Felician Clarus. The factory was under the technical direction of Adam Friedrich Löwenfinck until 1749, when Johannes Benckgraff became his successor until 1753. It is suggested that Löwenfinck may have produced only faience, as he did in Bayreuth, Ansbach and Fulda, and that the true porcelain was made later by his successor Benckgraff who went to Fürstenburg in 1753 with Feilner and Zeschinger. The financial difficulties of the factory resulted in it becoming a joint-stock company in 1765, and as such the name of it was 'Churfürstlich-Mainzische privilegierte Porcellaine-Fabrique' from 1765–78. The Elector, now Emmerich Joseph Freiherr von Breidenbach was main shareholder, and invested 5,000 Fl. in the factory, which became the sole property of his successor, the Elector Friedrich Karl Joseph Freiherr von Erthal in 1778. This was a period of high artistic acclaim for the factory, but it closed, nonetheless, in 1796. General porcelain production was of secondary importance to the figure modelling. The moulds were sold in 1840 to the earthenware factory in Damm, nr. Aschaffenburg, where the models of Melchior in particular were produced from these moulds, first in earthenware, later also in porcelain. See Damm.

First period 1746–9 Faience production under Löwenfinck only.
Second period 1749–53 Production strongly reminiscent of Meissen.
Third period 1753–6 Rococo period.
Fourth period 1756–9 In the hands of the receiver; perhaps only figure production from existing models.
Fifth period 1759–64 Naturalistic modelling of figures by Russinger.
Sixth period 1765–78 Under Johann Peter Melchior: transition to neo-classicism.

See also: Bechel, J. Ph. M., Buchwald, J., Danhofer, J. Ph., Ettner, A., Höckel, Brüder, Kilber, J. Ch., Kuntze, A., Ludwig, A., Lück, J. F., Löwenfinck, Ch. W. von Melchior, J. P., Nierwein, Richter, J. G., Ries, K., Usinger, J., Wohlfahrt, K.

1–2 blindstamp or incised, also painted in overglaze colours until 1763 – 3 from 1763 blue underglaze – 4 probably owner's mark of the Elector Emmerich Joseph v. Breidbach, until 1774 – 5 artist's mark of J. P. Danhofer – 6 marks of I. P. Melchior – 8–11 painter's mark of Joh. Zechinger

Höchster Porcelain Works GmbH, see Frankfurt (2).

Höckel, Bros. Jakob Melchior was a porcelain decorator and arcanist, his brother whose Christian name is unknown, was a repairer. Both were in Höchst until 1767 when they moved to Gutenbrunn (Palatinate-Zwei-Brücken). Jakob Melchior returned to Höchst in 1774 and was still there in 1782. His brother had left Gutenbrunn in 1775 and was sculptor in the Divenstein faience factory until 1788. In 1789 both were active in Kelsterbach.

Hoffmann, see Coburg (2) and Ohrdorf.

Hoffmann, Adolf, see Osnabrück (1).

Hoffmann, Franz, see Osnabrück (2).

Hoffmann, Georg von, see Ludwigsburg (3).
Hoffmann, Johann, see Elbogen (2).
Hoffmann, Rudolf, see Asch.
Hoffmann & Laluette, see Paris (70).
Höflich, Gottfried. Decorator in Frankenthal (1765–6). His son Johann Jakob
was also working there in 1760, as a decorator. He left for Ludwigsburg, where
he worked until 1769.
Höflinger, Christian Jakob. Colour chemist in Ludwigsburg from 1783–1802
and first decorator from 1791.
Hofman Bros., see Erkersreuth.
Hof-Moschendorf (Germany, Bavaria). Otto Reinecke f. the Moschendorf
porcelain factory in 1878; in 1894 the owners were Kühnert & Tischer. Produced
utility porcelain.

No. 1 also appears without 'Maschendorf Bavaria'

Hohenberg a.d. Eger (Germany, Bavaria). Carl Magnus Hutschenreuther,
porcelain decorator from Wallendorf, f. a porcelain factory here between 1814
and 1822. After his death in 1845 it was managed by his son Lorenz. The factory
was damaged by fire in 1884, but progressed steadily. Lorenz Hutschenreuther
withdrew from his father's factory in 1857 and with his inheritance f. the well
known porcelain factory in Selb. Hohenberg produced on a wide industrial
basis, and in 1890 employed about 400 workers. In 1904 the factory became a
joint stock company, and bought the M. Zdekauer porcelain factory in Alt-
Rohlau nr. Carlsbad in 1909. This factory turned out mass produced goods. In
1918 the Arzberg factory, which was f. in 1839 by Äcker, was incorporated into
Hutschenreuther AG Hohenberg, together with the C. Thielsch & Co. porcelain
factory in Altwasser. Hohenberg also ran a porcelain factory in Dresden which
was destroyed during the Second World War. This concern, which is among the
largest German porcelain factories, employed c. 2,300 people in 1939. The
factories in Alt-Rohlau as well as in Altwasser were lost owing to the
consequences of the last war. The factory is still among the foremost German
factories. In 1969 Lorenz Hutschenreuther acquired the majority of shares, see
Selb.

Höhr-Grenzhausen (Germany, Rhenish Palatinate). Klaus & Peter Müller, porcelain factory, f. in 1950; production of porcelain figures.

Holborn, Theodor, see Göttingen.
Holdship, Richard, Stecher, see Worcester (1).
Hölke, Friedrich, see Pirkenhammer.
Holland & Green, see Longton (40).
Hollingworth, see Saint-Gaudens.
Hollins & Wartburton, see New Hall (1).
Holloházá (Hungary). This stoneware factory, which was f. in 1830 produced the five or six pieces which are the only ones in the Budapester Kunstgewerbe Museum collection. In 1894 the owners were Istvany & Co. and at that time the blind mark 'Hollohaza' was used. It is assumed that after 1954 the factory took up porcelain production also, since the author has knowledge of porcelain services with decoration in a folklore edition. It is marked with the following marks.

· HOLLOHAZA·

H
O
LLOHAZA

Handpaintet
Moole in Ungaria
1851

Holm, Jesper Johannsen (b. 1747). Modeller and member of the Royal Academy. From 1780–1802 he was active in the Copenhagen factory, as chief modeller.

Holmskjold (Holm), Theodor (1732–94). Danish botanist, pupil of Linnés. His name was Holm but when elevated into the nobility, he assumed the name Holmskjold. Prof. of Medicine and natural sciences, he was one of the directors of the Copenhagen porcelain factory. In his capacity as botanist he supervised the decoration of the 'Flora Danica Service'.

Hölterhoff & Exner. Renowned independent porcelain decorators in Cologne c. 1880.

Holzapfel, Karl, see Rudolstadt Volkstedt (1).

Holzhausen, Gladenbach (Germany, Hessia). Hessian ceramic factory GmbH, f. in 1946. Ceramic and porcelain services.

Honoré, F. M. (d. 1855), see Paris (71) and La Seynie (1).

Hopfgarten, Anton Friedrich Wilhelm Ernst von, see Grossbreitenbach (1).

Hoop, C. van der, see Oude Amstel.

Horn nr. Elbogen (Bohemia, Hory). Grünes & Co. f. a porcelain factory and

decorating workshop here in 1903. It was taken over in 1905 by Heinrich Wehinger. In 1921 the factory was called 'Wehinger & Co., producing utility ware for export. There was a branch factory in Janessen, nr. Meierhöfen.

Horn, Joh. Christoph (b. 1698), decorator in Meissen, c. 1720–60.

Hornberg (Germany). Porcelain and stoneware factory f. in 1832, was still here in 1880. Its products were marked with the blindstamp, Hornberg. Production was in utility ware.

HORNBERG

Höroldt, Christian Friedrich (1700–79), decorator (apparently a relative of J. C. Höroldt), see Meissen (1).

Höroldt, Johann Gregor (6 August 1696 Jena–26 January 1775 Meissen). Probably trained in miniatures and enamel-painting and worked from 1719–20 in the newly founded Vienna porcelain factory, from where he moved to Meissen. There he became the manager of the decorators' workshop, Court-decorator in 1723 and overseer of the factory in 1723. During the seven year war (1756–63), he fled to Frankfurt, but returned to Meissen in 1763 and retired in 1765, after Christian W. Dietrich was made the overseer of the factory. As a colour technician Höroldt developed the pigments which had already been used by Böttger and enriched the range of the palette. As an artist, he set the style of decoration of the Meissen porcelain up to the middle of the 18th c. His influence upon practically all other porcelain and faience factories in Europe is inestimable. He created a special type of chinoiseries, introduced the decoration of European landscapes, harbour and battle scenes, deutsche blumen and birds; he was also particularly famous for the development of the enamel ground colours. He also exerted his influence over the shape of porcelain in that he clearly rejected the shapes of silver table services and turned to forms which were more suitable to the nature of porcelain.

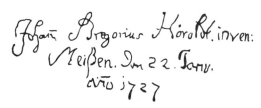

Höroldt'sche Zeit, the period of Höroldt (1720–35), called also the 'painterly period'. The time during which the Viennese decorator Johann Gregor Höroldt was the artistic director of the Meissen porcelain factory.

Hortense. Name used as trademark 260889 from 4 March 1921 by the P. F. Rosenthal factory, Selb.

Hosta, see Barcelona (2).

Houry, J. Charles. Independent Parisian porcelain decorator c. 1875.

Houry, J., see Paris (72).

Housel and Guy, see Paris (67) and (84).

Housset, see Paris (73).

Huart, see Longwy.

Hubatsch, Hermann Hugo (1878–1940). Sculptor and ceramist, pupil of Manzel and Haverkamp at the Berlin Academy (KPM Berlin since 1903). Awarded Brussels gold medal in 1910. Produced about 50 models for Berlin.

Hubbe Bros., see Neuhaldensleben (1).

Huber, Johann Adam. Gilder at the Nymphenburg factory. His primitive, independently decorated work, produced between 1762–79, is also known.

Hudson & Middleton Ltd., China factories, Sutherland Pottery, see Longton (43).

Hufnagl, Johann, see Gmunden.

Hughes, E. & Co., see Fenton (10).

Hughes, Thomas, & Sons, see Burslem (4).

Huilier, see Port carafe.

Hulme & Massey, see Longton (2).

Hulse & Adderley, see Longton (2).

Hunger, Christoph Conrad. Gilder and enamel decorator from Weissensee (Thuringia). Hunger worked together with Böttger in Meissen and fled in 1717 to Vienna, where in partnership with S. Stölzel, he f. the Vienna factory (in 1719). Two years later he established a porcelain factory in Venice, experimenting there with clay from Saxony in a quest for porcelain. In 1725, Hunger appears again in Meissen as gilder. In 1729–33 he worked in Stockholm and in Lidköpinğ/Rörstrands, in 1737 at the Danish Court. In 1741 he was given permission to establish a factory 'making sugar moulds and apothecary vessels'. These items must have been made of red Böttger stoneware. In 1742, Hunger was again in Vienna, from where he moved to Petersburg for the years 1744–8, where he co-operated in the foundation of the local factory. He is credited with the discovery of kaolin deposits in the Passau catchment. His main achievement, however, was his introduction of Höroldt, in the years 1719–20, to the porcelain decorating profession. Hunger's manner of decorating, which was copied by others, was to apply relief gilding and also to use transparent enamel colours. His most famous work is the so-called 'Emperor Beaker'.

Hunt, Benjamin, see Grünlas.
Huth, Louis, see Pössneck (2).
Hutschenreuther, C. M., AG, see Arzberg (1), Hohenberg and Dresden (13).
Hutschenreuther, Fr. Chr., see Wallendorf.
Hutschenreuther, Lorenz, AG, see Selb and Hohenberg.
Hüttensteinach (Germany, Thuringia). Schoenau Bros., porcelain factories (originally two), f. 1865. Utility ware. The KPM Meissen registered protest, prior to 1896, over the use of the mark in the second factory (crossed staves with H), which resulted in the prohibition of the further use of the mark and its removal from the trademark register of the German Reich (1896–8). At the present time the name of the factory is: Porzellan-Fabriken Gebr. Schoenau, Swaine & Co., o. H. G. Köppelsdorf-Nord-Thüringen, see Köppelsdorf-Nord.
Hüttl, Tivador, see Budapest (3).
Hüttner & Co., see Chodau (1).

Igló (Hungary, Comitat Zips). Weiser & Löwinger, porcelain, majolica and faience factory, f. 1888; produced vases, jardiniers, palm pots, pitchers; rich gold damascene.

Ikonnokoff, see Moscow (12).
Ile St.-Denis, (France, Seine). Laferté f. a porcelain factory here in 1778. For a factory mark the Sèvres mark was copied. In addition to this sign the modeller Gross signed with the dates 1779 and 1780, and these signed pieces provide proof of their source.

Illinger & Co., see Krummenaab (1).
Ilmenau (1) (Germany, Thuringia). In 1777, Ch. Z. Gräbner f. a small porcelain factory here, which was taken over by Duke Karl August von Sachsen-Weimar in 1872, who later, in 1784, appointed Franz Joseph Weber as director. In 1786 it was leased to Gotthelf Greiner and then in 1792 to Christian Nonne. He introduced the mark 'I', before that the products had no marks. In 1808 Nonne, together with his son-in-law Roesch, bought the factory and the mark consequently changed to 'N&R' = 'Nonne & Roesch. In 1871, the company was taken over by a limited liability company. The Ilmenau porcelain factory existed until the end of the Second World War under the name 'Ilmenauer Porzellanfabrik Graf von Henneberg AG'. The present (1977) name is: 'VEB Henneberg Porzellan Ilmenau'. This honoured and much esteemed factory became the most modern of porcelain works and has been located in a new establishment for some years now. Mark no. 13 (right), has been in use since 1977. In 1782 Goethe said of Ilmenau's porcelain 'I wish the body was of better quality'. In its early years this factory imitated the products of Meissen. The years 1792–1808, a very prosperous time for the factory, saw the production of white on blue ground in the style of Wedgwood 'Jasper ware'. Of all the artists employed there, the modeller Johann Lorenz Rienck from Eisfeld, employed in 1781, and Senff, the modeller of classical plaques, (also Senfft) deserve particular mention.
See also Strawflower pattern.

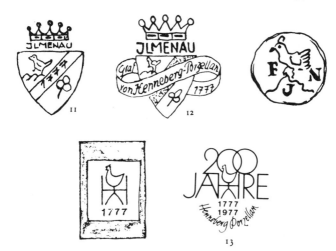

1–2 1786 and 1788 and 1788 and 1792, very dubious evidence only – 3 hastily painted 'i' always underglaze – 4 beginning of the 19th c. – 5 Nonne & Roesch from 1808 – 6–12 newer marks – 13 1977

Ilmenau (2) (Germany, Thuringia). Arno Fischer, porcelain factory, f. 1907. Fancyware.

Ilmenau (3) (Germany, Thuringia). Galluba & Hofmann, porcelain factory, f. 1888. Luxury articles, figures and similar. The establishment no longer exists.

[63]   [168]   [129]

Ilmenau (4) (Germany, Thuringia). Küchler & Co., porcelain factory, c. 1900.

Ilmenau (5) (Germany, Thuringia). Metzler Bros. & Ortloff, porcelain factory, f. 1875. Produced artistic and gift porcelain, small utility ware.

Ilmenau (6) (Germany, Thuringia). August Schmidt, porcelain decorating studio, c. 1930.

Ilmenau (7) (Germany, Thuringia). Schumann & Klett, porcelain decorating studio c. 1920.

Ilmenauer Strawflower pattern. The origin of patterns with this name goes back to the Meissen Strohblumenmuster (strawflower pattern) of c. 1740, which was not only in use in Ilmenau from 1745, but also in most of the Thuringian forest factories which produced simple porcelain with underglaze decoration, from the end of the 18th c. and right through the 19th. The Bohemian factories around Carlsbad also adopted the pattern. In Copenhagen it was refined and is called 'Muselmalede Moster' there today, or 'Blue fluted', if it is for the international market. In 1900 it was called by the trade-name 'conventional onion pattern' and was the most popular domestic porcelain. At that time it was used as a standard decoration by numerous factories and today it enjoys renewed popularity. In 1957, according to Leistikow, Copenhagen (*q.v.*) expanded the Muselmalede Moster according to contemporary requirements.
Imari decoration. Name for the decoration on the Imari porcelain in the 18th c., which had also been copied by European faience and porcelain factories. The typical Imari pattern has Japanese decorations in underglaze blue, and red and gold in muffle colours.
Imari porcelain. Japanese porcelain from the factories of Arita in the province of Hizen. It was exported from the port of Imari which gave its name to the porcelain in Europe (which can also be called Arita porcelain).
'Indianische Blumen' ('Indian' flowers). In contrast to the 'Deutsche Blumen' (German flowers) these flowers were freely adapted from East Asian designs, first by Höroldt, who decorated Meissen porcelain and figures with this pattern, and soon after by other porcelain factories.
Indra. Trademark 280221 of the P. F. Rosenthal, Selb, from 13 February 1922.
Industria Maioliche Abbruzzesi Castelli, Soc. A., see Castelli.

International Museum for Ceramics, see Faenca.
Iridescent colours, see Meissen (1) and Rose lustre.
'Iris', Soc. An. Rom. pentru Industria Ceramica, see Klausenburg (Cluj) (3).
Irminger, Johann Jakob. A Court goldsmith in Dresden who, during the Böttger period, designed models for the Meissen porcelain factory. See Böttger stoneware.
Iron red. Porcelain colour for underglaze decoration based on iron-oxide. Without doubt its discovery is due to the fact that traces of iron-oxide which are found in kaolin are the cause of unsightly red-brown speckles under the glaze.
Irún (Spain). Luso Espanola de Porcelanas, S.A., Fabrica de Bidosa, f. in 1935. Utility porcelain and artistic porcelain. Mark: 'PB'.

Isberner, Wilhelm, & Co., see Oeslau (3).
Isenbart, see Paris (73).
Isigny (France, Calvados). A porcelain factory existed here from 1840–6. It was f. by Royville and its director was F. Langlois from Bayeux. Langlois was later (after 1846) active in Moncloa (Spain).

Isleworth Middlesex (England). J. Shore, Shore & Co. and Shore & Goulding, Isleworth Pottery, 1760–1825, stoneware and porcelain factory (although the production of porcelain is questionable). The marks are said to have been partly those of the firm of Schiller & Gerbing, Bodenbach (*q.v.*), which delivered undecorated products (including porcelain) to Shore.

S. & CO.   **S. & G.**   **S. & G.**
                                           ISLEWORTH

Isolde. Trademark 255261 of the P. F. Rosenthal, Selb from 5 October 1920.
Ixelles, see Hastière.

Jackson & Gosling Ltd., see Longton (44).
Jacquemart, see Paris (75).
Jacquemin, Etienne , see Paris (76).
Jacques, Symphorien (d. 1798). See Bourg-la-Reine, Mennecy-Villeroy and Sceaux.
Jacques & Boyer, see Paris (50).
Jaeger & Co., see Marktredwitz (2).
Jagdservice (Hunting Service). Service from the St. Petersburg factory, see Petersburg (1).
Jäger, Wilhelm, see Eisenberg (2).
Jaget et Pinon, see Tours (2).

Jannasch, see Bernburg.

'Japanese work'. One of the names which were used during the 18th c. for chinoiseries.

Japanese porcelain. The manufacture of porcelain in Japan was begun as late as 1520, by Gorodaya Schonsui, who had learnt the art of the making of porcelain in Chinese factories. The earliest factories were built in the Province of Hizen (Arita), which to this day remains the centre of the Japanese porcelain industry. In the early years porcelain was made solely in the Chinese manner but by the 17th c. some originality had been achieved by the Japanese factories. The considerable export of porcelain with the patterns of Kakiemon and Imari to Europe, influenced the decoration and polychromy of European ceramics. Certain Japanese sources record the production of porcelain in Japan as being started early in the time of the Mikado 'Seiwa', who reigned from 856–876. However, this information has been proved to be without foundation.

Jaquin, L. & Cie., see Vierzon (6).

Jaronek, Alois, see Roznan.

'jasper dip', see Jasperware.

Jasperware. This name was given by Wedgwood to his hard, fine grained, slightly translucent stoneware, perfected in 1775 and containing a novel ingredient: 'sulphate of barium', which was obtained in the form of a mineral, known as 'cawk'. The jasperware can either be white or stained with metallic oxides, producing coloured bodies. The best-known is the pale blue jasper, but lilac pink, sage green, yellow and black are also used. The coloured ground was often decorated with white relief figures in classical style. 'Jasper dip' was a surface wash of the coloured body only.

Jaspis porcelain. Marbled ware. A name given by Böttger to his newly invented red stoneware.

Jaucourt, Filhouart et Cie., see Bourganeuf.

'Jaune clair'. A porcelain colour also known as 'Jonquil yellow', only rarely used on Sèvres porcelain, owing to its prohibitive cost.

Jean, see Vierzon (7).

Jeanne, see Paris (77).

Jensen, Oluf (b. 1871), decorator, see Copenhagen (1).

Jérome Bonaparte, King of Westphalia, see Fürstenberg.

Jessen, J. C., see Milgravi.

'jewelled' decoration, see Jewelled Porcelain and Cotteau.

Jewelled porcelain. The term usually employed to refer to a type of porcelain decoration in which pearls, precious or semi-precious stones are set in the surface. It was used, e.g. in the late 18th c. in Sèvres, and was particularly popular in the 19th c. 'Jewelled porcelain' also refers to a type of decoration which uses translucent enamel colours, as used by Hunger.

Jirowaja (Russia). Fedjaschin began to produce porcelain here in 1840. This factory is reputed to have existed until recent times. Nothing is known about the style and quality of the products.

Jokes-Wickwitz (Bohemia). Gareis & Kasseker f. this factory in 1880. It became Gareis & Mader in 1895. Later, in 1904, the factory came into the possession of Jos. Tw. Menzl. His mark is the only one we know of today and is found on porcelain services.

Jolly, René François, see Ottweiler.
Jones, A.-B. & Sons, see Longton (45).
Jones, George (& Sons Ltd.), Trent Pottery and Crescent Pottery, see Stoke-on-Trent (9).
Jones, A. G. Harley, Royal Vienna Pottery, see Fenton (11).
Jonquil yellow, see 'jaune clair'.
Jossé, see Paris (69) and (98).
Jouhanneaud, Hippolyte, see Limoges (40).
Jucht, Johann Christoph. Decorator, active from 1736–46 in the Bayreuth faience factory. He worked later as an independent decorator.

B.H.

Jofann Furfoef Jüft.

Jüchtzer, Christoph-Gottfried (1752–1812 Meissen). In 1769 he had come to Meissen in order to work as an apprentice, and became, as a modeller, a fellow worker of Kändler. After Acier had been pensioned off, he rose to become the most important sculptor of the factory and was promoted to 'Obergestaltungsvorsteher' (art director).
Juliane Marie von Dänemark, see Copenhagen (1).
Julien, Stanislas Aignan. French sinologist. In 1856 he published his *Histoire et Fabrication de la porcelaine chinoise.* Generally speaking, this work represents a translation of the most important Chinese source, *The book of Tscheng-T'ing Kuei,* written in 1815, about the porcelains of 'Jing dezhen'. Julien, furthermore, proved that the earliest inscriptions on Chinese ceramic were poetic quotations, which had been composed between 702 and 795.
Julien, see Conflans.
Julienne, see Paris (79) and (83).
Julienne-Moreau, see Paris (79) and (84).
Jullien, see Saint-Léonhard.
Jullien, Joseph (d. 1774), see Bourg-la-Reine (1), Mennecy-Villeroy and Sceaux.
Jullien, S. P., see Paris (78).
Jünger, Christoph. Viennese decorator in the second half of the 18th c.
Junkersdorf, Franz, see Dresden (14).
Jussupow Service. In St. Petersburg at the end of the 18th c., a table service consisting of 659 parts was made in classical taste, with cobalt blue ribbons and an acanthus pattern.

KPM (Berlin). Königliche Porzellan Manufaktur (Imperial Porcelain Works). Renamed Staatliche Porzellan Manufaktur in 1918. See Berlin (3).

Kaestner, Friedrich, GmbH, see Oberhohndorf and Zwickau-Oberhohndorf.

Käge, Wilhelm, see Gustavsberg (1).

Kahl (also Kuhl), decorator, see Ansbach.

Kahla (1) (Germany, Thuringia). Kahla porcelain factory, f. 1844. Utility ware and hotel porcelain.

Kahla (2) (Germany, Thuringia). Bauer & Lehmann, porcelain decorating studio, f. in 1885. Porcelain of better quality, heraldic patterns and landscapes. Still in existence in 1949.

Kahla (3) (Germany, Thuringia). Julius Lange porcelain factory, owned by Paul Seiler.

[159]

Kahla (4) (Germany, Thuringia). C. A. Lehmann & Son, porcelain factory, f. 1895. Utility ware. This concern no longer exists.

Kahla-Könitz (Germany, Thuringia). 'VEB Porzellankombinat Kahla', formerly Kahla porcelain factory and Könitz porcelain works. From 1 February 1964 known as 'VEB Vereinigte Porzellan-Werke'. Produced domestic and hotel porcelain. The second mark is now (1977) in use.

Kaiserbecher, see Hunger, Ch. C.

Kaiserliche Manufaktur, see Petersburg (1) and Vienna.

Kaiser Porzellan. Words used as trademark 154300 from 30 January 1912 by P. F. Heinrich & Co., Selb.

Kaiserlieblingsblumen decoration. The Emperor's favourite flower pattern. Name used as trademark 192330 of the P. F. Fraureuth AG, Fraureuth, from 23 April 1914.

Kaja. Japanese province, where the porcelain to which it gave its name is produced; its ostentatious decoration covers the whole of its surface.

Kakiemon Sakaida (1596–1666). Renowned Japanese ceramist, born in the province of Hizen as the son of the potter, Ensai. The name Kakiemon, it is said, was given to him on account of his having a particularly decorative piece of porcelain in the form of a Kaki (Japanese persimmon). In 1643 he began his experiments in decorating porcelain with enamel colours and met with success soon afterwards. He thus created favourable conditions for the rapidly flourishing porcelain industry of Japan. His name is connected with a multi-coloured decoration, related to the Kano style, in which, in contrast to the red blue gold decoration of the later imari porcelains which covers the entire body surface, the undecorated space plays its part in the design. The decoration of these Kakiemon porcelains, which in old reference books have the name 'première qualité coloriée de Japan', were first copied in the Meissen factory for the Japanese Palais, and subsequently imitated by many European porcelain and faience factories.

Kalk, suburb of Cologne (Germany, Rhineland). According to reliable sources, the Kalk porcelain factory AG Seifert existed here in 1895. It specialised in the production of coffee, table and toilet services. It is assumed that the firm was f. in 1863 and used two crossed arrows as marks. The similarity in name and mark to the Eisenberg porcelain factory Kalk GmbH forces one to suggest that Eisenberg can be regarded as the successor to Kalk, particularly since the Eisenberg was only f. in 1900.

Kalk GmbH, see Eisenberg (3).

Kaltenhofen nr. Elbogen (Bohemia). F. by Franz Peter as an earthenware factory in 1867. From 1890 the owner was Hugo Winter (Columbia), and from 1900 Julius Dietl. Porcelain production was begun here c. 1890. Utility ware.

Kaltenlengsfeld (Germany, Thuringia). VEB porcelain decorating studio, producing utility, fancy and luxury porcelain.

Kammer & Reinhardt, see Waltershausen (1).
Kämmner, Rudolf, see Rudolstadt Volkstedt (16).
Kampe, factory owner, see Altwasser (1).

Kämpf, R., see Grünlas.
Kämpfe, Friedrich, see Wallendorf.
Kändler, Johann Friedrich. A cousin of the Meissen chief modeller. He directed the artistic productions of the Ansbach-Brückberg porcelain factory (c. 1758).
Kändler, Johann Joachim (1706–75 Fischbach, nr. Dresden). Pupil of the Court sculptor Benjamin Thomae in Dresden from 1723. In 1730 he was engaged on the 'Grünen Gewölbe' where the King became acquainted with his work. On 22 June 1731 he was appointed 'overseer of figure production' at the factory, and in 1733, after the departure of Kirchner, he became chief modeller. He was still, however, subordinate to Höroldt's direction and this caused problems in their collaboration. They most likely separated in 1740 when Kändler assumed control over the moulders, modellers and turners. His first designs after the dismissal of Kirchner were many models for the Japanese Palais. The Sulkowski and the Swan services are his primary works of 1735–38 (possibly 1737–41). The difference in style between these successive works is obvious. Also at this time he made an altar-set for the Empress Amalie of Austria, mother-in-law of August III, after the designs of various artists from the circle of Bernini. In 1744 together with Peter Reinicke, he modelled a number of busts of Hapsburg emperors, measuring 33 cm high, perhaps presents for the Viennese Court. His hand-span high figures and groups which earned Meissen its worldwide reputation, were created (or at least some of them were) in 1737–41. In these small figures his mastery is revealed at its purest, and full justice is done to the material. He influenced the whole of European porcelain figure production. The number of figures runs into c. 900. The life size equestrian statue of King August III, which took years to produce, was not finally completed to his satisfaction. He died while at work at the age of 69 on 18 May 1775.

J. J Kaendler.

Kanton. Main export harbour of China in the 18th c. Used for porcelain, tea, silk, lacquer work and paper.
Kaolin. Mineral found in white earthy mass of fine triclinic crystals, mostly little hexagonal plates; in chemical terms hydrated aluminium silicate, $H_4 Al_2 Si_2 O_9$. It is the main substance used for the production of porcelain (porcelain clay). The Chinese name must have derived from one of the main places of discovery,

the mountain Kao-Ling. In the 18th c. the terms Marga Porcellana or Terra Porcellana, were used.

Kaolin sources of the 18th c. Kaolin takes its name from the first Chinese source, and its place of discovery – the 'high pass' (Kao-Ling).

Germany
1. Aue nr. Schneeberg, one of the largest kaolin deposits in Europe. This kaolin was also called 'Schnorrsche Erde' (Schnorrsche earth), after Veit Hans Schnorr von Carolsfeld, who found kaolin in his iron mine in 1698. The export was explicitly forbidden by law from 13 July 1728.
2. In the Lower Passauer Forest, discovered through the persistence of the arcanist Hunger (1718), who was engaged upon the search for kaolin to be used exclusively by the Vienna porcelain factory, it was also called 'Passau earth' (Passauer Erde).

Denmark
In 1755 Niels Birch, the stone quarry inspector uncovered large kaolin deposits in Bornholm, and from there the Copenhagen porcelain factory received its supplies.

Italy
There were supplies in the middle of the 18th c. in Tretto, nr. Vincenza. Earlier, Ginori had imported his raw materials from China.

Spain
Buon Retiro made use of magnesia silicate from the pits of Vallecas nr. Madrid.

France
In 1768 vast kaolin deposits in Saint-Yriex-la-Perche nr. Limoges were discovered. In 1769 the State secured these pits to supply Sèvres. In Germany it was called 'Limoger Stein' (Limoges stone). Apart from Sèvres, the pits also supplied Strasbourg (Hannong), Frankenthal, Nymphenburg and Copenhagen.

England
In the middle of the 18th c. the pharmacist William Cookworthy found extensive kaolin pits in Cornwall, which enabled him to establish the Plymouth porcelain factory.

Russia
In the 18th c. kaolin was discovered in several places such as Moscow, Kiev, Cherson; the pits of Tschebarkul in the Ural yielded the most, together with those nr. Gluchow in the Ukraine.

'Kapuzinerbraune' glaze. Often used on Chinese porcelain when underglaze cobalt blue has already been applied.

Karlowsky. Assumed to have come from Meissen. From the beginning of the reign of Catherine II (1762–96), he was the first exponent of modelling in the Petersburg Imperial factory.

Karlsbader Kaolin Industrie Gesellschaft in Vienna, see Merkelsgrün (1).

Karlsbader porcelain factory, see Fischern (1).

Karlskrona (Sweden). Aktiebolaget Karlskrona porcelain factory, f. 1918. Utility porcelain, hotel porcelain. This factory was taken over (in 1942) by the Upsala-Ekeby Aktiebolag and now has the following name: 'Upsala-Ekeby AB Karlskronafabrik.

Karlskrona

Kasel, W., see Amberg.

Kasseker, Hirschen Bros., see Lubenz (1).

Kassel (Germany, Hessia). In the Hessen-Kassel faience factory which existed since 1680, porcelain was made from 1766–88, although it did not reach the artistic level of other factories. The arcanist Nicholaus Paul came from Fulda, as did the repairer Franz Joachim Hess. The chief modeller and head turner J. G. Pahland and the repairer Friedrich Künckler, came from Fürstenberg.

Katowice-Bogucice (Poland). Giesche porcelain factory AG, f. 1922. Utility ware.

Katzhütte (Germany, Thuringia). J. W. Hamann f. a porcelain factory here in 1762, but since he obtained no privilege in Schwarzburg, he transferred his concern to Wallendorf (1764). This factory was still working in 1945 and was called Hertwig & Co. (the owners were Ernst and Hans Hertwig). The production at this time was limited to fancy and utility stoneware and dolls' heads.

[191]   [197]

Kaufbeuren (Germany, Allgäu). Südkeramik, Gebr. Sauermann o.H.G. Utility and luxury porcelain and polychrome services.

Kawan, Josef, see Vienna (10).

Kean, Michael (d. 1823). Miniature painter, see Derby (1).

Keelin, A. and E., see Tunstall (3).

Keizer, Aelbregt de. Factory owner in Delft. By the mid 17th c. he was already engaged in experiments in the search for 'Japanese porcelain'.

Kelsterbach (Germany, Hessen-Darmstadt). Wilhelm Cron and Johann Christian Frede f. a faience factory here in 1758, which in 1761 came into the possession of Landgrave Ludwig VIII von Hessen-Darmstadt. The landgrave engaged the Meissen arcanist C. D. Busch as manager of the factory and porcelain production began in the same year. Busch remained until 1764. E. D. Pfaff succeeded him as director. In 1766 a new factory complex had been built, but the production ceased in 1768 after the death of the Landgrave. For the next 20 years only faience was made, but in 1789, the director (J. J. Lay since 1773) resumed porcelain production with the help of the arcanist, I. M. Höckel from Höchst. Ten years later Lay bought the factory for himself but discontinued porcelain production in 1802. During the Landgrave period the porcelain was of a high quality. Under the direction of Busch (1761–4) Vogelmann and Carlstadt were active as modellers and the decorators were F. I. Weber, Georg Ignaz Hess and Jacob Eger. The factory was economically doomed however, since the unfashionable models produced (particularly Vogelmann's) could not compete with the neighbouring Höchst and Frankenthal. Under the direction of Pfaff, Vogelmann was replaced by the Nymphenburg modeller, P. A. Seefried, who made figures after models of Bustelli during his stay. When the factory was re-opened in 1789, models of Meissen and Höchst were copied. The services were made in the neo-classical taste of the time.

Until 1765 without mark – 1 1765–6 blue underglaze – 2 blindstamp 1765–8 – 3 1789–92 blue underglaze – 4 1799–1802 blue underglaze – HD = Hessen-Darmstadt

Kempe, Samuel, arcanist, see Bayreuth (1) and Plaue on the Havel.
Kent, James (Ltd.), see Longton (45).
Keramische Fabrik München-Schwaben AG, see Marktschwaben.
Keramischer Druck Transfer-printing or atmography. Pictures taken from lithographed stones painted with enamels, transferred to porcelain then fired. See also Enamel printing and Transfer printing.
Keramische Werke Zehnder & Co., see Tirschenreuth (2).
Keramos Wiener Kunst-Keramik and porcelain works AG, see Vienna (11).
Kerkow, C. F., see Nauen.
Kerr, see Worcester (1).
Kestner & Comp., see Ohrdruf (2).
Kestner, J. D., see Ohrdruf (2).

Keys, Samuel (1771–1850). Active as gilder and porcelain decorator in Derby (1760–70). He generally adapted Meissen motifs.

Kiesling, decorator, see Schlaggenwald (1).

Kiev (1) (Russia). The kaolin rich surroundings of this city were the main sources of the raw material for the Russian porcelain factories. In the town itself, the 'Miklaschevski' factory was granted a licence for production only from 1851–62. Georgeous table services and expensive luxury items were produced. Also famous are the Ukrainian folk figures. The factory was regarded as the most important in Southern Russia during the 19th c.

Kiev (2) (Russia). The Mejigorje faience factory nr. Kiev is supposed to have also produced small quantities of porcelain in the early 19th c. The marks reproduced below, are said to have been used for faience as well as porcelain.

Kilber, J. Christoph. From 1 July 1763 he worked as chief turner in Nymphenburg and came later to Höchst. He introduced the 'cobaltblue underglaze' to Nymphenburg. During the period of the recession at Höchst, in 1767, he was dismissed and later re-employed as modeller.

Kindler, Rudolf. Porcelain, stoneware and earthenware factory, see Aussig.

Kioto (Japan). Picturesque landscape which gave its name to the porcelain produced there.

Kips, Alexander (1858–1910). Decorator. Deputy of the artistic director

Sussmann-Hellborn at the KPM Berlin, from 1886. 1888–1908 he was artistic director proper, and in 1885 Professor. He specialised in porcelain tiles and wall-decorating.

Kirchenlaibach (Bavaria). Thomas am Kulm, Speichersdorf-Plössen porcelain factory. Subsidiary of the Rosenthal Porzellan AG, f. 1959. Utility porcelain. The themes of the decoration show considerable influence by Rosenthal.

Kirchenlamitz (Germany, Bavaria). Oscar Schaller & Co. Successor, porcelain factory, f. 1921. Utility ware, and gift articles.

Bavaria

Kirchenlamitz (Germany, Oberfranken). Rudolf Wächter, porcelain decorating studio c. 1930.

BAVARIA

Kirchner, Franz R., see Stützerbach.
Kirchner, Johann Gottlieb (b. 1706 Merseburg). Sculptor. On 29 April 1727 he took employment in the Meissen porcelain factory, where he was initially active for only one year. After his dismissal he was re-instated on 20 January 1730 as modeller to become chief modeller in 1731. He worked mainly on the decoration of the Japanese Palais. In 1733 he resigned to work exclusively as a sculptor. After his stay in Heinecken, he spent the last years of his life in Berlin, where he created clay models. His major work from his first spell at Meissen is considered to be the wall fountains, several examples of which still survive together with some watch cases. The bust of Fröhlich, the Court jester, long thought to be a work of Lücke, may be Kirchner's. According to his own records of work, in 1731–3 he made an elephant, a bison, a leopard, a tiger, a lynx, a rhinoceros, a forest devil, a bear, a fox and a white wagtail. First rate works are, among others, his Pietà and the Apostle Peter. He is known as the 'Master of Large figures'.
Kiriakoff, see Moscow (7).
Kirkby, William, & Co., Sutherland Pottery, see Fenton (12).
Kirsch, Hugo F., see Vienna (12).
Kirsch & Hertwig, see Lengries.
Kirschner, Friedrich (1748–89). From Bayreuth. A pupil of Riedel and a virtuoso flower painter in Ludwigsburg.

Kirchner.

Kiseleff, see Retschina.

Kister, A. W. Fr., GmbH, see Scheibe-Alsbach.

Kitchen porcelain. Kitchen and domestic porcelain ware was made from about 1800.

Klablena, E., Langenzersdorfer Keramik, see Vienna (13).

Klauber & Simon, see Dresden (15).

Klaus, Ferdinand, see Tettau (1).

Klausenburg (1) (Rumania, now Cluj). At the end of the 19th c. there were several porcelain decorators active here working in the Chinese as well as in the Herend style.

Klausenburg (2) (Rumania, now Cluj). Manufactura Nationalé de Portelan, Turda, S.A.R., f. 1935. Utility and hotel porcelain.

Klausenburg (3) (Rumania, now Cluj). 'Iris', Soc. An Rom. pentru Industria Ceramica, f. 1922. Utility ware.

Klee, Fritz, see Königliche Fachschule of the porcelain industry.

Klein, see Foecy (2).

Klein, Johannes (b. 1750). Active as decorator in the Nymphenburg factory (1765–71) and later as an independent decorator, working on Nymphenburg porcelain.

Kleindembach nr. Pössneck (Germany, Thuringia). 'Union' Quist & Kowalski porcelain factory, f. 1905. Utility ware. This factory no longer exists.

[229]   [229]   [135]   [208]

Kleindembach (Germany, Thuringia). Karl Egelkraut, porcelain factory, f. 1910; after the Second World War the factory became 'Property of the People' Utility ware.

Klein-Schadowitz (Bohemia). Adolf Prouza, porcelain factory, f. 1908. Groups, figures and similar.

Klemm, Karl Richard, see Dresden (16).

Klentsch (1) (Bohemia). Jos. Mayer f. a small porcelain factory here in 1835 which was finally owned by Anton Schmidt. The factory was closed in 1889.

Klentsch

Klentsch (2) (Bohemia). J. Milotz, porcelain, stoneware and earthenware factory. Kitchen and toilet garnitures.

Klentsch

Klimsch, Fritz (1870–1960). Sculptor. With Max Liebermann, he f. the Berlin Secession in 1898/99. Main theme was idealised female figures. Models for KPM Berlin and other porcelain factories.
Kling & Co., see Ohrdruf (3).
Klinger, Johann Gottfried (c. 1701–81). From Meissen.
Klingler, H., see Landstuhl (2).
Klipfel, Karl Jacob Christian (1727–1802). Was initially a porcelain decorator at Meissen. In 1763 became 'mosaic painter' at Berlin and took over the management, in partnership with Grieninger, until 1801.
Klösterle (1) (Bohemia, now Klašterec n.O.). In 1794, by order of the Count F. J. Thun, the forestry superintendent, Nicolaus Weber and the arcanist, J. G. Sonntag, f. a porcelain factory. From 1797–1803 this was leased to Christian Nonne (*q.v.*), and then from 1803–20 to Habertitzel. Count Mathias Thun then took the factory over. Until the 20th c. it was called 'Gräflich Thun'sche Porzellan Fabrik Klösterle'. The following decorators were active there: Vollrath, Santvoort (from Brussels), Schlott (from Ilmenau) and Rösch (from Thuringia). The director Karl Venier, active from 1848, exerted decisive influence. Besides good creative work, the 'onion-pattern', Ilmenauer straw-flower pattern (*q.v.*), and bird and rockery patterns were used. More details: A. Bergmann, *Egerländer Porzellan* (bibliography p. 14). This production is still maintained at the factory and the Ducal castle has a porcelain museum. According to legal documents, the Thun factory produced lithographies from 1850–60, and light and lampshades were also produced. The signature 'Sikora' occurs.

1 1794–1803 – 2 1804–30 – 3 1808–30 (all three blue underglaze) – 4 blindstamp c. 1830 – 5 blindstamp in variations 1839–70 – 6 1839–70 blindstamp in various sizes often with year – 7 chromegreen underglaze printed from 1895 – 8–9 modern marks

Klösterle (2) (Bohemia, now Klašterec n.O.). 'Porcelain Union' Vereinigte porcelain factory AG f. as counterweight to the ÖPIAG, on 26 November 1921.
1) Vernier & Co., factory for ceramic products, Meretitz nr. Klösterle since 1901;
2) Tuma & Vielgut porcelain factory in Meretitz;
3) Gottfried & Vielgut porcelain factory in Meretitz;
4) Ernst Wahliss in Turn nr. Teplitz;
5) Julius Neumann, porcelain factory, Bhf. Klösterle.
The Porcelain Union was eventually absorbed into the EPIAG in the 1920s. In 1934 it spasmodically ceased production and stopped altogether in 1939.

Kloster Veilsdorf (Germany, Thuringia). The most important Thuringian porcelain factory of the 18th c. It was f. in 1760 by Prince F. W. E. von Hildburghausen with the help of the arcanist Meyer. The arcanist Nikolaus Paul was active here from 1766–8. After the death of the Prince in 1795 the next owner was Duke Friedrich von Sachsen-Altenburg, who sold the factory to the sons of Gotthelf Greiner of Limbach and to the firm Friedrich Christian Greiner of Rauenstein. The factory remained in the possession of the Greiner family until 1822. The early products made under the management of Nikolaus Paul, were of good quality, with a milky-white paste and blemish free. The figurative and decorative work in this period reflected the rococo style. The services are reminiscent of Meissen – the Neu-Brandenstein pattern was imitated – and the edges of the pieces were mostly shell patterned. A clear yellow, a fresh brick red, dark brown, purple and turquoise were used in overglaze painting. Monochrome decoration was occasionally used. The porcelain is often decorated with scenes after Watteau and Teniers. The figures rarely have marks; their quality is superb and they rank among the best products of the Thuringian factories. Dolls and dolls' heads were also produced. The neo-classical decoration was inspired by Sèvres. The factory still works today.

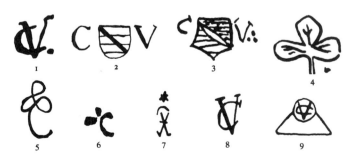

10   11

1 general mark in many variations, blue underglaze – 2–3 underglaze until 1765 – 4–6 on general porcelain ware since 1797 – possibly an intended forgery of the swords mark – 8–10 modern – 11 neck mark dolls' heads

Kloster Vessra (Germany, Saxony). Vessra porcelain factory, f. 1892. Utility porcelain of all kinds. This factory no longer exists.

Klum (Bohemia). Feresch produced porcelain here, 1800–50.

KLUM   **J. Jerefch**   **T.PERESCH**

Knaute, Benedikt, see Giesshübl (2).
Knipffer (also Knüpfer), Johann Christian. Decorator in Frankenthal in 1759 and active as arcanist and decorator in the porcelain factory of the Count Aranda in Alcora from 1764. In his later years he worked in Ludwigsburg.
Knoch, Bros., see Neustadt (2).
Knoll, Carl (now Carlsbader porcelain factory Carl Knoll), see Fischern (1).
Knöller, Louis, see Dresden (17).
Knöller, faience factory, Bayreuth, see Danhofer, J. Ph.
Koburg Cortendorf (Germany, Upper Frankonia). Cortendorf Julius Griesbach porcelain factory. This factory, which was f. in 1890, produced (according to their own records) 'Feinsteingut' – fine earthenware – exclusively. Porcelain figures, which had the mark shown below, were only produced c. 1958–60. When the production of porcelain stopped, the overglaze production of fine earthenware and faience continued.

Friedrichsburg

Koch, Wilhelm, see Dresden (18).
Königsee (1) (Germany, Thuringia). Adelbert Beck, porcelain factory, f. in 1911; known as Beck & Glaser in 1929. Household porcelain, children's toy services and dolls for dolls' houses. The factory did not use any mark. The first picture mark, a nursery with children playing, surrounded by a chain pattern, was entered on 5 June 1913 under No. 176409.

Königsee (2) (Germany, Thuringia). VEB (B) Porzellanwerke Königsee and Garsitz. The concern bought the earlier Porzellanfabrik Adelbert Beck (see above) and a second concern, which was previously owned by a Dr. Roehler. The Garsitz factory, recently unknown as a porcelain producer, is supposed to have been founded in about 1892.

Königszelt (Germany, Silesia). Königszelt porcelain factory, f. 1860. Table, hotel porcelain and gift items. The factory is reputed to have been founded owing to the efforts of the businessman and builder Silber, who exploited the rich source of raw material, clay and coal. In the beginning he decorated the basic ware in 'Indian blue' strawflower and 'onion' patterns. In 1872 the factory was called 'Heckmann and Rappsilber' and in 1886 it was turned into an AG company (shareholders company). The 1890 edition of the Ceramic Industry Directory lists the original name as the Königszelt porcelain factory AG, formerly August Rappsilber. The letters A.R., found beneath the familiar mark depicting an eagle can be explained as the owner's initials. The factory is now in Polish possession. The eagle mark with AR also appears c. 1870–80, without AR.

P.K.
SILESIA·

A.R.
[15]

SILESIA
[193]

[247]

Koetting, Friedrich August, see Ultramarine.

Köhler, David (d. 1725). Arcanist and chief manager in Meissen. In Meissen in 1720, he succeeded in decorating porcelain with underglaze cobalt blue, which was much admired by the King, and made the imitation of the blue and white decoration of Chinese porcelain and Delft faiences possible. Köhler, who died in 1725, passed on his secret to Höroldt.

Kok, J. Jurrian (1861–1919), ceramist, and architect. Director of the Haagsche Plateelbakkerij Rozenburg 1895–1913. The products of Rozenburg which today are known and sought after the world over, were often created from Kok's designs. He and his co-workers introduced the waferthin frit porcelain and established the reputation of the factory.

See also Rozenburg.

Kolmar (Germany, Prussia). Kolmar porcelain factory GmbH, f. 1897, became a joint-stock company in 1900. Coffee services, cups, mugs and saltcellars, often using onion pattern.

Köln-Kalk, see Kalk.

Köln-Kalk (Germany, Rhineland). Dirks & Giersberg, f. 1904. Figure modelling in terracotta. Distillers and porcelain decorators.

Kolo (Poland). Czestlaw Freudenreich, porcelain factory c. 1925.

Kolosvar (Hungary, now Cluj). Several porcelain decorators were active, here at the end of the 19th c., working in the Chinese as well as the Herend styles.
Kominik & Son, see Turn (9).
Kongelige porcelain and faience factory Aluminia AS, see Copenhagen (6).

Kongens Lyngby (Denmark), Porcelain factory AS, f. in 1936. Utility ware.
Königliche Fachschule of the porcelain industry (in Bavaria). Architect and craftsman Fritz Klee, later Professor, from Munich, became director of the Royal Technical School of the porcelain industry on 15 May 1908, where he remained until 1 May 1938. As a technical adviser he had to select Selb, Hof, or Munich as the site of the school. He settled on Selb and provisionally started an

interim course in the Town Hall of Selb. On 1 April 1909, the 'Royal Technical College for the Porcelain Industry, Selb' moved into a former primary school which the City had put at the disposal of the College.

Königliche Meisterschule for Ceramics, see Landshut.

Königliche Porzellan Manufaktur, (KPM), see Berlin (3).

Königsbauer, Alfons and Ernst, see Munich (3).

Koninklijke Delftsch-Aardewerkfabriek De Porceleyne Fles, see Delft.

Könitz (Germany, Thuringia). The Metzel Bros. f. a porcelain factory here in 1909. In 1948 it was administered by a trust company and in 1950, under expropriation, was annexed into the SAG Hescho/Hermsdorf. Produced porcelain services and used the onion pattern since c. 1930.

Konjaschino (Russia). A certain Markoff is said to have produced porcelain here in 1830–40, about which nothing else is known. Accompanying mark (overglaze blue) was found on a coffeepot in the Hermitage in Leningrad, in the late 19th c.

Konstanz (1) (Germany, Baden). Porcelain works GmbH, c. 1930.

Konstanz (2) (Germany, Baden). J. A. Pecht, Steingut-Fabrik, possibly a porcelain decorating studio c. 1924.

Köppelsdorf (1) (Germany, Thuringia). Julius Hering & Son, porcelain factory f. 1893. Coffee and tea services, figures and others. Since 1945 the factory has been called: 'VEB Hochvolt-Porzellan, formerly Julius Hering & Son porcelain factory'.

[157]

Köppelsdorf (2) (Germany, Thuringia). Ernst Heubach, Köppelsdorfer porcelain factory, f. 1887. Biscuit dolls' heads. Heubach became a partner with Armand Marsaille (*q.v.*) in 1919. The horseshoe mark is used also without the monogram. Both these marks are said to have been discontinued in 1930. The horseshoe as a neck mark on dolls' heads appears in connection with many European and U.S. doll manufacturers.

Köppelsdorf (3) (Germany, Thuringia). Armand Marsaille factory, f. in 1885, after he had purchased the Liebermann & Wegescher porcelain factory, which, until this time, had produced only pipebowls and tankards for military reservists. Of all the anchor marks only No. 6 was in use after 1930. The ring mark had already appeared in 1834. Mark No. 3 was notified as W.Z. on 17 May 1910. His neck mark for dolls' heads, the full name, occurs in connection with all renowned international dollmakers.

Köppelsdorf (4) (Germany, Thuringia). Vereinigte Köppelsdorfer porcelain factory, formerly Armand Marsaille and Ernst Heubach, f. 1885 and 1887. Technical and electro porcelain and dolls' heads (biscuit) were produced from 1919. The factory was still working in 1949 and was then called Thüringer porcelain factory VEB. It is not known for how long after the merger the horseshoe mark, the little flag pennant, and marks 5 and 6 of Armand Marsaille were used.

Used in 1930

Köppelsdorf Nord (Germany, Thuringia). Porcelain factories of the Schoenau Swaine Bros. & Co. o.HG. (name of the firm after the census of 1949) were f. in

1864. Originally there were two firms which, according to the marks used, were both working in Hüttensteinach. The merger must also have taken place there but it is difficult to establish the date. The marks are only partly separated. The earliest are probably the crossed staves with the intermittently placed 'H' (Hüttensteinach). Apart from luxury and utility porcelain in the styles of 'Berlin', 'Dresden' and 'Meissen' baroque, Biedermeier and modern, it can be said that the factories, even before their amalgamation, produced a very fine onion pattern. Schmuz-Baudiss was active here in 1901–2, producing the Pensée Service. In addition electro and laboratory porcelain were produced.

Körber, Paul, see Mosaics in porcelain.

Korea. A porcelain, resembling Chinese porcelain, but more granular was produced here up to the 17th c. It was a popular import into Holland. The trading arrangements with Europe were generally made through the 'Compagnie des Indes'.

Kornhas, Carl, see Weingarten.

Korniloff, Sawin Wassiljewitsch, see Petersburg (4).

Korzec (Poland), Prince Iwan Czartorsky f. a porcelain factory here, which was active from 1790–7. The direction was by Michael Mezer. When the factory burnt down in 1798, the production continued in Gorodnitza. In 1803 Mérault

from Sèvres managed the factory and engaged the chemist Pétion as his
assistant. Under his direction very beautiful porcelain was produced.

Koscherowo, Gjelsk (Russia). Samsonoff f. a new porcelain factory here in
1819. It worked until 1875. Production consisted of large amounts of utility
ware.

Kosloff, P., see Moscow (6).

Kostial & Co., see Leer.

Kotta (Cotta), Franz, decorator and modeller in Cloister Veilsdorf 1778,
Grossbreitenbach 1778–80 and Volkstedt 1783–97.

Kranichfeld (Germany, Saxony-Meiningen). Kranichfelder porcelain works
Reinhard Rothe, f. 1903. Vases, jardiniers, Christ figures (after Thorwaldsen)
and ancient figures after the Old Masters (no crockery).

Kratzberg, Johann Gottfried. A canon in Hildesheim (c. 1773), who, like
Canon v.d. Busch, incised (with a diamond point) contours and drawings into
the glaze, and later rubbed black colour into them.

Kratzer, Jos., & Sons, see Haindorf (1) and (2).

Krause, R. M., see Schweidnitz.

Krautheim & Adelberg GmbH, see Selb (5).

Krautzberger, Mayer & Purkert GmbH, see Wistritz.

Kretschmann, Heinrich, see Elbogen (4).

Kretschmann & Wurda, see Elbogen (4).

Kretschmar, Johann. Blue-painter from Meissen whose work, until the middle of the 18th c., was marked with the swords and a 'K' in underglaze blue.

Kriebern (Bohemia). Steinberger & Co., porcelain decorating studio, c. 1930.

Kriegel & Co., see Prag.

Krister, Carl Franz, see Waldenburg (2).

Krister, name of mark used as trademark 1359 from 6 February 1896, and trademark 292212 from 12 October 1922 of P. F. Waldenburg.

Krister porcelain works (Rosenthal Porzellan AG), see Landstuhl (2), Selb and Waldenburg (2).

Krog, Arnold Emil (1856–1931). Architect, painter, ceramicist and craftsman. 1874–80 studied architecture at the Copenhagen Academy 1881–2 ceramic studies in Italy; 1885 appointed by Ph. Schou as artistic director of the KPM Copenhagen; 1889 World Exhibition Paris where he had great success and renewed the world-wide reputation of the KPM. From 1891–1916 he was director of the factory, and a member of the council of the academy from 1911–19. Krog introduced underglaze painting to Copenhagen and appointed numerous outstanding artists; he created c. 200 models for Copenhagen.

Krohn, Pietro Kobke (1840–1905). Ceramicist and decorator. Studied under Marstrand and Skovgaard. Genre painter from 1872–8. From 1885–90 he was artistic director of Bing and Grondahl. From 1890 onwards, he was director of the Kunst-industriemuseet, Copenhagen, and produced the 'Heron Service'. He initiated the development of a new style in Bing and Grondahl as well as in the KPM Copenhagen.

Kronach (1) (Germany, Oberfranken). Kühnlenz Bros., porcelain factory, f. in 1884. Pipebowls and technical porcelain.

$$ \text{ⒸⒾⓀ} $$

Kronach (2) (Germany, Oberfranken). OCA Oechsler & Andexer porcelain factory; f. 1950. Coffee, tea and mocha services, refined gift-items.

Kronach (3) (Germany, Oberfranken). R. & E. Pech, porcelain factory f. about 1830. Porcelain figures.

Kronach (4) (Germany, Oberfranken). Ph. Rosenthal & Co. AG porcelain factory, Filiale Kronach, f. in 1897; formerly Bauer, Rosenthal & Co. Com. Ges. Utility and artistic porcelain. The parent company is Rosenthal Porzellan Aktiengesellschaft, Selb.

1 1897 Bauer Rosenthal & Co. chromegreen underglaze – 2 1898 F. artistic porcelain (in gold) – 3 1901–27 – 4 1928–35 – 5 1935–53 – 6 since 1953

Kronach, G. G., see Küps.
Kronenburg. Term for Ludwigsburg porcelain. The crown in the mark was the reason for this name.
Kronester, J, & Co. GmbH, see Schwarzenbach (1).
Kronstadt-Brasov (Roumania, Siebenbürgen). Schmidt Bros., porcelain decorators, c. 1930.

Krug, Fritz, see Lauf.
Krüger, Edmund, see Blankenhain (2).
Krummennaab (1) (Germany, Oberpfalz). Krummennaab, Illinger & Co. porcelain factory, f. in 1931. See Krummennaab (4).
Krummennaab (2) (Germany, Oberpfalz). Hermann Lange GmbH, porcelain factory, f. in 1934. Utility ware. See Krummennaab (4).

Krummennaab (3) (Germany, Oberpfalz). W. Mannl, porcelain factory and decorating studio, f. in 1892. Utility ware. See Krummennaab (4).

[207]

Krummennaab (4) (Germany, Oberpfalz). Christian Seltmann GmbH porcelain factory, f. in 1897. Coffee and table services, gift items and utility ware. At first the firm's name was: W. Mannl porcelain factory, Krummennaab, and later Illinger & Co. porcelain factory Krummennaab. From 1934–9 it was Hermann Lange porcelain factory Krummennaab and from 1939 Christian Seltmann GmbH porcelain factory. The mark is Seltmann Weiden.

Kruse, H. A., see Emden.

Kuba, Josef, see Wiesau (1).

Kügemann, Heinrich. Independent porcelain decorator from Nuremberg, c. 1800.

Kuhl, see Kahl.

Kühlgefässe. Porcelain cooling vessels, see Glacieres.

Kühn, Heinich Gottlieb (d. 1870), see Meissen (1).

Kuhne, Chrétien, see Brussels (2).

Kühnel, Christian Friedrich (1719–92). Polychrome decorator in Meissen who painted landscapes and battlescenes. Manager of the porcelain decorating studio under Dietrich.

C.F.Kühnel.

Kühnert & Tischer, see Hof-Moschendorf.

Kuhnle, see Coburg (2) and Ohrdorf.

Kühnlenz Bros., see Kronach (1).

Kumpf, Johann Georg (1769–1835). In 1787 he worked in Nymphenburg, at first as a white turner, later as model turner. From c. 1802 he was manager of the white-turning department in the factory of Vienna. From December 1810 he again worked in Nymphenburg where he replaced Seefried as chief repairer. In 1823 he assumed the directorship of the earthenware factory in Regensburg. In 1833 he acquired a small porcelain factory in Passau.

Künckler, Friedrich, repairer, see Kassel.

Kunstadt (Bohemia). Franz Schamschula, porcelain decorating studio, c. 1930.

Künstner, Wilhelm, see Pfullingen.

Kuntze, Andreas (1729–70). He was active in various faience factories as a decorator; according to certain evidence he was in Höchst in 1765 as colour chemist and flower painter.

Künzel, L., see Schlottenhof.

Kün-yao (also Kuan Yao), 'Government porcelain'.

See also Aubergine glaze.

Küps (Germany, Bavaria). A certain G. G. Krinach managed a small porcelain factory here in 1837.

Küps (1) (Germany, Bavaria). Precious stone porcelain factory. Joint stock-company, f. in 1932. Utility ware and gift articles.

BAVARIA   BAVARIA

Küps (2) (Germany, Bavaria). Lindner porcelain factory KG, f. in 1931. Gift articles, coffee and mocha services (richly decorated).

KUEPS BAVARIA

Küps (3) (Germany, Bavaria). Ohnemüller & Ulrich Oberfrankish porcelain factory. Appeared for the first time in 1899 and was still active in 1906. Utility porcelain, figures, vases, watch cases, clock cases.

 K

Küps (4) (Germany, Bavaria). Wilhelm Rittirsch, porcelain factory, f. in 1950. Porcelain figures.

Küps (5) (Germany, Bavaria). Wenck & Zitzmann porcelain factory, f. in 1882 and still in existence in 1890. Utility ware, predominantly for export.

Kurfürsten Service (Elector Service or Clement August Service). It was ordered as a coffee, tea and chocolate service from the KPM Meissen for the Elector Clemens August von Cologne. It was decorated with cartouches containing the monogram 'C.A.' This extravagant decoration also incorporated painted and modelled flowers. Sculptured putties were used as handles on lids. In 1741 the complementary dinner service was ordered (Walcha).

Kurland-Muster. Empire Service from the Berlin factory, made in 1774. The

rims of the plates were decorated with a broad gold stripe interwoven by festooned green bands. According to Köllmann this pattern was fully developed as late as 1790–6. Is still used even today on white porcelain.
Kusjaeff nr. Moscow (Russia). Nikita Chrapunoff was in charge of a porcelain factory here from 1820–40. This factory produced mainly figures. Today there are only some examples left; any other achievements of this factory are unknown.
See also Moscow (8).

HX   HX

Kusnetzoff. T. J. Kusnetzoff was the senior member of a family of porcelain factory owners, who managed to run large factories in Russia with extraordinary success throughout the 19th c., and remain in command of the industrial production of porcelain up to the present day. Since their production concentrated on utility ware, there follows a purely chronological account of the most important dates for this great European porcelain business. At the start of the 19th c. T. J. Kusnetzoff f. a porcelain factory in Novocharitonowa which existed until 1870. In 1832 the factory was established in Duljewo, which after Kusnetzoff's death went to S. T. Kusnetzoff and in 1864 passed in turn to his son. In 1842 M. S. Kusnetzoff f. a porcelain factory in Riga which employed c. 2,000 workers at the end of the 19th c., and was part of the M. S. Kusnetzoff also acquired the Auerbach faience factory in Kusnezowo in 1870, which employed c. 800 workers in 1884. In 1878 I. E. Kusnetzoff built the Wolchow factory and employed 1,100 workers; in 1887 M. S. Kusnetzoff founded the Budy porcelain factory nr. Charkow, employing c. 2,000 people in 1889. M. S. Kusnetzoff turned the family business into a company which absorbed very many small Russian porcelain factories, among them the famous factory of Gardner in Werbiliki (Twer), in 1891, which at that date employed 1,000 workers. In 1892 the factory in Slawjansk was built, giving work to 800 people. This factory burnt down in 1900. In 1900, I. E. Kusnetzoff took charge of the Merkur factory in Bronitzi and established the works in Grusinow in the same year with 500 workers.

Kyoto (Japan). The name for this porcelain derives from the place of production.

La Broche S.A., see Molinet.
Labrut Frère et Soeurs, see Vierzon (8).
La Cartuja, see Seville.
Lace. An imitation of lace made in porcelain. This was the method by which it was achieved: fabric lace was dipped into porcelain slip, dried and fired in such a way that the textile web was burned away, leaving the laceform in solid porcelain. This method had been introduced at Meissen c. 1770. In Strasbourg, at approximately the same time, J. A. Hannong is said to have invented a similar technique to produce his own version of lace porcelain. This type of decoration is found a great deal on French and German porcelain. In the early 19th c. it was also used by the Derby factory.
La Celle-Bruère (France, Cher). Avignon porcelain factory. Produced fancy goods.

PORCELAINE
G.D.V.

A FEU

La Ceramique, see Limoges (71).
La Ceramique Limousine, A. Chastagner, see Limoges (41).
'La China', see Buen Retiro.
'La Courtille', see Brussels (3) and Paris (94).
Ladowitz nr. Dux (1) (Bohemia). Gaebler & Gröschl, porcelain and earthenware factory f. in 1893. Fancy and luxury ware in ivory-porcelain.

Ladowitz nr. Dux (2) (Bohemia). Robert Hanke, porcelain factory, f. 1882. Fancy and luxury production, made of transparent ivory coloured porcelain. Specialised in vases, jardiniers and bowls.

R.H.

Ladowitz nr. Dux (3) (Bohemia). Pietzner & Co., Plastographische Gesellschaft; porcelain and earthenware factory, f. 1893 by Otto Gaebler, still in existence c. 1900. Luxury goods. This concern had a branch in Vienna, Vl Mariahilferstr. under the name Photographische Gesellschaft Pietzner & Co. The mark PLASTO without the wreath was registered with the K.K. Zentralmarkenregister, Vienna, on 27 May 1899 under Nos. 10877 and 10876.

[258]

Laferté, see Ile St.-Denis.
Lafond A. & Co., see Amsterdam.
La Forest (France). Noel Bouchard f. a porcelain factory here c. 1768, the products of which are unknown.
Lagrenée. see Paris (80).
Lahaussais, see Paris (81).
Lahaussois, René, see Billancourt.
Lahens et Rateau, see Bordeaux (3).
Lahoche, see Paris (38).
Lahoche-Pannier, see Paris (38).
Laillet, Marcell, see Vierzon (9).
Lallemant de Villehaut, Joseph, see Aprey.
Lalouette, M., see Villedieu (1).
Lamare, see Paris (1).
La Marque (France, Lot-et-Garonne). P. H. Bourdon worked here as an independent factory owner c. 1848, prior to which he had been active in Creil and Sèvres (1824–7). Later he collaborated with Johnston and together they directed a factory in Bordeaux.
Lamm, A., see Dresden (19).
La Moncloa (also Florida), nr. Madrid (Spain). Ferdinand VII f. a small porcelain factory here, which was active from 1817–50. Remaining stocks and tools from the factory of Buen Retiro which had been plundered by French soldiers in 1808 and 1812, were acquired and put to use. Under the direction of Bartolomé Sureda the porcelain production was of French taste of the period without any individual characteristics.

Lamoniary, see Valenciennes.

Lamotte-Beuvron (France). 'La porcelainerie Nouvelle S.A.' decorative table and hotel porcelain from 1931 (according to 'Tardy 75') using the following marks.

Lamprecht, Georg (d. 1828). Painter in Vienna 1772–84, in Sèvres 1784–7, later again in Vienna 1788, in Paris Clignancourt 1793, and once again in Vienna 1797–1825, when he died.

Landshut (Germany, Bavaria). In 1873 the Bavarian Government f. the 'Royal Masterschool for Ceramics' here as the first ceramic technical college.

Landstuhl (1) (Germany, Rhinepfalz). H. Klingler, porcelain decorating studio, c. 1930.

Landstuhl (2) (Germany, Rhinepfalz). Krister porcelain works of the Rosenthal Porzellan AG was in Waldenburg (Silesia) until 1945 and was moved to Landstuhl in 1952. See Waldenburg (2).

Lane Delph (England). Miles Mason, together with his sons, f. the 'Minerva' porcelain factory here c. 1800. The factory adopted the 'New Hall' style. In 1813, ironstone china was patented. Blue transfer printed Japanese style decorations are known.

Lane End (1) (England). Hilditsch & Son f. a porcelain factory here c. 1830 which produced mainly utility ware.

Lane End (2) (England). Mayer and Newbold; according to Godden porcelain was made here between 1817–33, but rarely marked. (Mark depicts a hand.)

Lane End (3) (England). William Ratcliffe, as quoted by Godden, produced porcelain here from 1813–40.

Lane End (4) (England). John Turner (1762–1806) produced porcelain (amongst other things), bearing the marks 'Turner', c. 1770, 'Turner & Co.', c. 1780–6 and an impressed mark 1803–6.

Lanfrey, Claude François. Director in Niderviller, 1802–27.

Lang, Franz and Anton, see Budau (1).

Lang, Jean, see Villedieu-sur-Indre (1).

Lang, M., see Budapest (4).

Lange, Hermann GmbH, see Krummennaab (2).

Langen, Johann Georg von (1699–1776), see Fürstenberg (1).

Langenberg (Germany, Thuringia). E. and A. Bufe K.G., porcelain factory, f. 1902. Kitchenware. A stamped 'L' was usually used, but no other special mark is recorded.

See also Gera-Langenberg.

Langenthal, Bern (Switzerland). Langenthal porcelain factory AG, f. 1906. Tableware, hotel and fancy ware.

Langenwiesen (Germany, Thuringia). Oscar Schlegelmilch porcelain factory Langenwiesen, f. 1892. Utility and fancy ware.

Langlois, F., see Isigny.
Langlois, Joachim, see Valognes (1) and Bayeux.
Lanz, Johann Wilhelm. Modeller. He worked in Strasbourg in 1748 under Hannong and moved with him to Frankenthal, where he was chief modeller 1755–61. A group in Ludwigsburger porcelain, attributed to the 'Master of the Apollo candlestick', seem to be very similar to the Frankenthal figures, modelled by Lanz, but there is no evidence to suggest that he was connected with this factory also.
La Porcelaine artistique, see Le Coteau.
La Porcelaine Limousine, see Limoges (42).
La Porcelainerie Nouvelle S.A., see Lamotte-Beuvron.
Larue (also La Rue), Louis Felix de (1731–65), sculptor, see Sèvres and Boucher.
La Seynie (1) (France, Saint-Yrieix). The Marquis de Beaupoil de St. Aulaire f. a porcelain factory here in 1774, which was taken over in 1789 by Baignol from Limoges. He left in 1794. In 1810 Honoré from Paris bought the factory and sold it in 1822 to Denuelle. The factory existed until 1856; the production had little artistic merit.

BAICNOL
Fabricant
à S'Yrieix

La Seynie (2) (France, Saint-Yrieix). Porcelaines Industrielles du Limousin, S.à.r.l. Domestic porcelain.
Lassia, Jean Joseph, see Paris (82).
La Tour d'Aigue (France). Baron de Bruni, who directed a faience factory here from c. 1753, obtained a licence from the state in 1773 for the manufacture of porcelain. At the same time he was obliged to limit the decoration of his products to merely one colour and the use of gold was forbidden to him and other manufacturers. The pieces which have been attributed to him and which bear the following mark, most likely came from Tournay.

Laub and Bandelwerk (leaf and ribbon work). A widely applied ornamentation, used in Germany c. 1715–40. Composed of tendrils and geometrically arranged ribbons. This decoration was often used on porcelain in the first half of the 18th c.

Laucha (Germany, Prussia). Eugen Eichhorn produced porcelain globes here in 1877.

Lauche. Decorator of Meissen porcelain, of whom nothing further is known.

Lauenstein (Germany, Oberfranken). Keramika Arno Apel, porcelain factory, f. 1954; decorative ware.

Lauf nr. Nuremberg (Germany, Frankonia). Fritz Krug K.G., porcelain and terracotta factory f. 1871; until 1939 produced tomb decorations made of porcelain and terracotta, and from 1950 also produced porcelain dolls sets.

[106]

Laufer, Adolf, see Turn (3).

Laulau, Anton Karl, see Flora Danica Service.

Lauraguais-Brancas, Louis Léon Félicité Graf (1733–1824). Member of the Académie de France. He occupied himself in his castle at Lassay with ceramic experiments. In 1766 he presented some trial pieces of hard porcelain, marked 'L.B.', to the Académie but without any formula. This was the first hard porcelain produced in France.

Laurer, Rudolf, see Lubenz (2).

Lauscha (Germany, Sachsen-Meiningen). Ens & Greiner, porcelain decorating studio, f. 1837, had the following mark registered at the Herzogliches Amtsgericht Steinach on 14 December 1885. It was transferred to Volkstedt (Rudolstadt) in 1897.

[37]

Lauth, Charles, see Sèvres (1).
Laveno (Italy). Società Ceramica Italiana. Table services, vases and luxury porcelain.

Lavergne, Gaston, et Cie, see Limoges (43).
La Villette (France). Morel owned a porcelain factory here c. 1819.
Lay, Joh. Jakob (1734 Frankfurt–26 November 1807). Active from 1766 in the factory in Kelsterbach. In 1772 he became the director of the local faience factory. In 1788 he became the co-owner and introduced porcelain production again in 1789. After having been forced to close the factory, he managed to re-open it and remained the director until 1802. When the factory collapsed again he still remained the lease-holder of the estate of the faience factory.
Lazeyras, Th. & Fils, see Limoges (44).
Leadbeater, Edwin, see Longton (47).
'Le Bassin de Neptune'. Ludwigsburg table centre, which had been made by order of Duke Carl Eugen of Württemberg, in 1763–4. It represented a great ballet of the period.
Leboeuf, André-Marie f. a porcelain factory in the Rue Thiroux, Paris in 1776. See Paris (83).
Leboeuf et Milliet, see Creil et Montereau.
Lebon and Lebon-Halley, see Paris (68).
Lebourg, see Paris (85).
Le Brun, see Orléans (1).
Lebrun et Co., see Fours (2).
Le Cateau (France). Simon & Cie., porcelain decorating studio, c. 1930.

Lechevallier-Chevignard, see Sèvres (1).
Lechthaller, Taddäus, independent decorator, working with Nymphenburg porcelain; at the end of the 18th c. he was active in Passau.
Leclerc, Michel, see Clerc.
Leclerc, Nikolas, see Ottweiler.
Le Coteau (France). According to 'Tardy 75' the firm 'la Porcelaine artistique', has the following mark registered in 1928.

Leder, Heinrich, see Lichte (2).
Ledgar, Thomas P., see Longton (48).
Leer (Germany, Ostfriesland). Kostial & Co., porcelain factory. Utility ware of all kinds.
Lefèvre, see Choisy-le Roy (1).
Lefèvre, Bildhauer, see Magnac-Bourg.
Lefèvre, Caron, see Paris (98).
Le Gerriez, Bros., see Paris (59).
Leghorn (Italy). Ceramica Lombarda & Son, porcelain factory, f. 1922. Hotel porcelain. See Doccia.
Legrand, Gabriel, see Paris (85).
Legrand et Cie, see Limoges (45).
Legros, d'Anisy, François Antoine (1772–1849), see Paris (74).
Lehmann, H. B. L. From Hamburg. He came to Copenhagen from Berlin in 1780 as a decorator and remained active there until his death in 1800. His specialities were landscapes, figures and birds.
Lehmann, Theodor, see Arzberg (3).
Lehmann & Son, C. A., see Kahla (4).
Lehnert, Franz, see Lubenz (1).
Le Hujeur, Balthasar Augustin, see Paris (74).
Leichner (also Lynker), Anton (1718–81). F. the porcelain factory in The Hague in 1775, see The Hague and Ansbach.
Leichner (also Lynker), Johann Franz. See The Hague.
Leipzig (Germany). Oscar Zenari, porcelain decorator c. 1910. Specialities: mocha cups and tea services.

Leithner, Joseph. Famous decorator at the Vienna porcelain factory c. 1800. He was general manager and arcanist and particularly active as colour technician. The 'Leithner blue', a royal blue of outstanding brilliancy, was named after him. He also introduced beautiful, metallic lustred grounds, ranging from the deepest violet to a pale lilac and copper red. He shared with Perl the acclaim for the creation of the antique style peculiar to the Vienna porcelain factory. He also is known for his copies of paintings on porcelain.
'Le jeu de l'écharpe'. Table centre-piece. Created at Sèvres, 1900 after designs of Léonard-Agathon van Weydeveldt, Paris (called Agathon Léonard). The figures are in biscuit, each 42 cm high. This design had previously been made in bronze.
Lejeune, Pierre François (1721–90). Sculptor from Brussels. He studied in Brussels and Rome and was active as Court sculptor for Duke Karl Eugen in Stuttgart from 1753–78. From 1761, he was also a teacher at the local Academy. From 1771–2 he worked as sculptor and superintendent at the Ludwigsburg porcelain factory.
Le Juste, see Paris (86).

Lemaire, see Paris (98) and Vincennes (2).
Le Marois & Co., see Valognes (2).
Le Masson, see Valognes (1).
Lemberg (Poland). The factory owners Lewicki, R. Schwurz and B. Stilber produced porcelain here in 1867.
Lemire, Charles-Gabriel Sauvage, called Lemire (1741-1827). Modeller in Niderviller, from c. 1759-1808. His early works were influenced by Cyfflé. He later used a classical style, and worked mostly in biscuit, sometimes using 'Lemire père' as a mark.
Lenglern (Germany, Hannover). Meissen-Burg-Porzellan, GmbH, porcelain factory, f. 1948. Utility porcelain.
Lengries (Germany, Oberbayern). Kirsch & Hertwig, porcelain factory, f. 1955. Lamps, bowls, candlesticks with modelled roses and fancy figures.

Lenharts, Josef, Heirs. See Altrohlau (6).
Leningrad (Russia). The factory called 'Kaiserliche Porcelain Works, St. Petersburg' (*q.v.*) was here until the Russian Revolution (1917). It subsequently became known as 'Staatliche porcelain works, Petrograd' (St. Petersburg was renamed Petrograd in 1914 and it retained this name until 1924). This last name appeared as a mark in 1922, on a serving dish in the Hermitage. Only after 1924 was the factory given the name which it retains to this day: 'Staatliche porcelain factory M. W. Lomonossow Leningrad'. The artistic decline of the last decades before the First World War, were brought to an end by new developments which began after the Revolution of 1917, when the factory became Property of the People. Renowned artists were employed. The factory, after years of stagnation, found a new style, which, in 1924 the connoisseurs recognised as an artistic achievement. The name of famous modellers have been recorded in an inventory (produced after 1920) in the Hermitage: 1918 V. Kutznetzoff; 1920 N. Danko; 1926 A. Matveyev; 1931 Z. Kulbach.
Recorded as decorators were the following: 1931 Z. Kobyletzkaya, V. Rukavishnikova; 1930 N. Suetin, L. Protopopova; 1920 A. Schtschekatiknina-Pototskaya; 1929 M. Mokn.

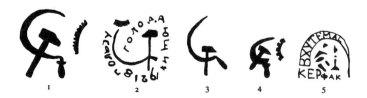

1–5 State factory Petrograd 1917–24; translation of 2 is 'for the sake of the starving' – 6–7 present day marks of the State factory Leningrad. The LFS in Russian letters from these marks stands for 'Leningradskij Faforowyj Savod' = 'Leningrad porcelain factory

Lenk, see Passau (3).
Lenox, Walter Scott, see Trenton.
Lenoxchina, see Trenton.
Lenz, J. F., see Zell.
Leofold, J., see Paris (87).
Léonard, Agathon, see 'Le jeu de l'écharpe'.
Leonhardt, Emil, see Ettlingen.
Leperre-Durot, see Lille (2).
Leplé, see Paris (88).
Le Puy (France). According to 'Tardy 75', Marie Raynaud registered the following trademark in 1955.

BERRY LIMOGES
PORCELAINE

Lerch, Joseph. Active in Nymphenburg as decorator specialising in flowers, birds, insects and fruits 1764–70.
Le Riche, Josse-François-Joseph (b. 1739). Sculptor. Pupil of Falconet. He worked in Sèvres from 1757–1801 as modeller, from 1780–1801 as chief modeller. Among his original models, which date from 1767 onwards, are several groups of contemporary themes, figures after Boucher models, busts of Maria Theresia and Stanislas, King of Poland. The mark 'L.R.' can be found on models which could not possibly have been made by him, although they may have been made by others under his supervision.
Lerosey, M., see Paris (89).
Lerosey, see Paris (123).
Le Roy, Louis-François, see Orléans (1).
Leschen, see Fürstenberg.
Les Établissements Gustave Revol Père & Fils, see Saint-Uze (2).

Les porcelaines artistiques d'Epinal, see Epinal.

Les Porcelaines Industrielles du Limousin, see Saint-Yrieix (2).

Lessau (Bohemia, now Lesov). The K.K. porcelain factory, 'Concordia', was f. in 1888 (by permission of the provincial authority). From 1904 onwards the owners were Kühnel & Co. In 1913 it was taken over by Tichy from Schönfeld who transferred it later to Paris from Oberköditz (Thuringia). Following this, the owners were (in 1919) the brothers Löw and subsequently Winterling & Co., Oberköditz, became leaseholders. Produced Turkish coffee cups and chocolate cups (for Dutch East India); specialised in coffee pots. After 1945 it belonged to the 'nar. podnik Thunska', was burned to the ground in 1946, but was rebuilt in 1947. In 1923–30 lithophanes were produced here. J. A. Wolff, who has been mentioned under Pirkenhammer, was active there from 1923–30 as modeller. Among his work was a transparency of the President Masaryk.

Le Tallec, C., see Paris (90).

Lettin (Germany, Saxony). Lettin AG porcelain factory, f. 1858. Renamed in 1945, VVB-Keramik-Zweigbetrieb porcelain factory Lettin. Utility and ornamental porcelain.

'Lettres edifiantes et curieuses'. This collection of letters, published in 1717 and 1724 are communications of the Jesuit father d'Entrecolles, concerning the secret of porcelain making. The report of d'Entrecolles had appeared in the *Journal de Scavant* as early as 1716. See d'Entrecolles.

Letu, see Villenauxe (1).

Leube, Adolf, see Dresden (20).

Leube & Co., see Reichmannsdorf (2).

Leulier, Fils, see Charenton (1).

Leutre, de, see Paris (69).

Léveillé, see Paris (84).

Le Villain, see Paris (91).

Levensohn, Louis, see Tiefenfurt.

Levy, Charles and Henry, see Maisons Alfort.

Levy, L., see Paris (92).

Levy et Cie., see Charenton (2).

Lewicki, see Lemberg.

Ley & Weidermann, see Neuhaldensleben (2).

Lichte (1) (Germany, Thuringia). Today the 'Kombinat VEB Zierporzellan-werke Lichte'. This is an association of the former most important factories: Lichte; Piesau; Wallendorf; Unterweissbach; Rudolstadt. The marks which were in use in 1976, were placed below the individual subject word. Below is the mark of the Lichte porcelain factory.

Lichte (2) (Germany, Thuringia). Heubach Brothers AG. F. 1822 by Johann Heinrich Leder with the privilege of the Ducal Schwarzburg Government. According to his will of 1824, Lichte endowed the factory to his cousins Wilhelm and Heinrich Liebmann. From 1830, Wilhelm Liebmann was the sole owner. In 1840 Christoph and Philipp Heubach bought the ownership with all privileges and rights. They changed the name to 'Heubach Bros'., and became a joint stock company in 1904. Until c. 1850 utility ware, then toys and divers small articles such as 'ornamental porcelain', porcelain trinkets and portraiture decorations. In 1898 the factory was modernised and the artistic department created models by famous artists. The technical and artistic quality of the products around 1900 is due to the efforts of Richard Heubach. The creations in the field of animal-modelling are compared favourably by Pelka, with those of Nymphenburg. Models by H. Krebs, Chr. Metzger, Wilhelm Neuheuser and Paul Zeiler were produced. The Heubach Bros. AG is one of the largest producers of dolls and dolls' heads. The mark with the WZR-No. 161 occurs as neck-mark in connection with all the renowned international dolls' factories. Electro-porcelain has also been made since 1910. After 1945 it was known as VEB Keramik-Zweigbetrieb Porcelain Works Lichte (Thuringia). Production has remained the same and since 1976 the firm has been called VEB Zierporzellanwerke Lichte (Thuringia).

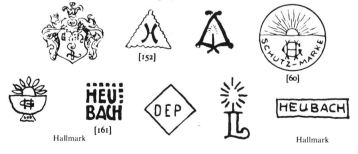

Lichte (3) (Germany, Thuringia). Zehender & Grosswald, porcelain decorating studio, c. 1930.

Lidköping (1) (Sweden). A factory using the following marks, produced porcelain from 1910–39. After this, it was taken over by Rörstrand.

Lidköping (2) (Sweden). Porslin Fabriker Rörstrands. In 1726 a faience factory was f. here, in which Chr. Konrad Hunger had worked for some years (1729–33). The production of porcelain began only after 1797 when Bengt Reinhold Gejer bought the factory. The earliest pieces were made in the English taste which is also clearly recognisable in the faience products which had been made up to that period. Services and general porcelain ware were produced. Towards the end of the last century these were recognisable by their distinctive characteristics. In 1874 the O./Y. Arabia porcelain factory in Helsinki (Finland) was built to produce goods for the Russian market. Thirty specialists and 150 workmen were originally employed. At the time of the Art-Nouveau movement Alf Wallander *(q.v.)* was the artistic director, himself creating many models. He and his co-worker Erkikson and the two Linströms made excellent models and underglaze colours. In 1916 the factory was incorporated with the large Finnish concern Wärtsila (see Helsinki). Gustav Herlitz, Councillor of Mining, managed the factory from 1906–47. During this period the factory developed into a major industrial concern, which had a labour force of c. 2,000 workers. The products have a strong 'nordic' appearance and became world famous.

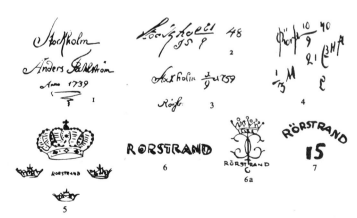

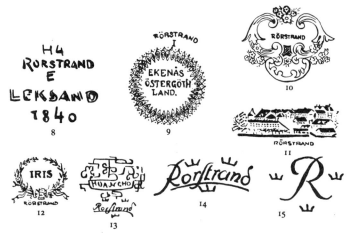

1 decorator's mark – 2 signature 1740–50; IG = decorator's mark – 3 signature on a service with stag and wild pig motifs from 1759 – 4 signature from 1770–5 blindstamp of name, crowns blue underglaze, for the porcelain ware of the Royal castle in the early 19th c. – 6 blindstamp, early 19th c. – 6a monogram Herzog Karl until his coronation in 1809 as Karl XIII, for palace porcelain, early 19th c. – 7 blindstamp 1830–40 – 8 Rörstrands: blind incised. Remaining: black-grey printed c. 1850 – 10 blue underglaze, 1852 – 11 brown 1857–60 – 12 coloured c. 1870 – 13 from c. 1884 – 14–15 modern marks

Liebermann, Math., see Schmiedefeld (1).
Liebmann, Eduard, see Schney.
Liegl, Elisabeth, see Munich (4).
Liersmühle nr. Stotzheim (Germany, Rhineland). Fr. C. Schmeisser. Ivory porcelain and porcelain flowers, f. 1882.

Liezen (Austria, Steiermark). Ferdinand Fasold (b. 1919 Cili, Yugoslavia). Apart from other ceramic products also decorated porcelain. Forced to close in 1963.

Lijsberg, Carl Frederick (1860–1909). Sculptor and painter. Active 1885–1909 for the KPM Copenhagen. Many of the animal models and underglaze decorations are his. In 1892 he informed the KPM in St. Petersburg of the technique of underglaze painting.
Lilian porcelain, Lilly porcelain, see Vienna (14).

Lille (1) (France). Barthélemy Dorez from Douai f. a faience factory here in 1711. He was in partnership with his son-in-law Pelissier and passed his share in the factory to his son François. Until 1730 a soft porcelain was produced which is extremely difficult to differentiate from the products of the St.-Cloud works. The mark 'L' may possibly stand for Lille, the mark 'D' for Dorez.

all marks in blue – 6 D = Dorez – 7 JB = Joseph François Boussemart

Lille (2) (France). A soft porcelain factory existed here during the first half of the 18th c. and in 1784 Leperre-Durot, under the protection of the Dauphin, f. a hard porcelain factory here, which received concessions through a decree of 13 January 1784. The factory was called 'Manufacture Royale de Monseigneur le Dauphin' and used a dolphin (Dauphin) as a mark. In 1790 a new company took the business over and appointed Gaboria as director. He was succeeded, as director or owner, by Roger, Graindorge et Cie. and lastly Renault, who closed the factory down in 1817. Products were in contemporary Parisian style.

fait par
Lebrun à Lille   *a Lille*   *a . lille*

1–3 stencilled – 5 blue underglaze – 6 gold

Lilly, John, see Worcester (1).

Limbach (1) (Germany, Thuringia). In 1762 Gotthelf Greiner f. a porcelain factory here with the concession of the Duke of Meiningen, which was renewed in 1772. The production consisted of simple porcelain ware for wholesale, decorated with coarse modelling. But the figures were of a much higher quality. At the end of the 18th c. Greiner and his five sons acquired the following factories, in this order: Ilmenau (1786?), Grossbreitenbach (1788?) and Veilsdorf (1797). Since that time all the factories have had use of the clover leaf as a mark. The quality of the products improved considerably in the 19th c., under the direction of Greiner's sons. The mark, two 'L's with a star, which could easily be mistaken for the mark of the Meissen Marcolini period, had to be given up after a difference of opinion with Meissen in 1787. The production stopped in the middle of the 19th c.

Ŗ	L	X	Ꮿ	⌘	♣
1	2	3	4	5	6

1–2 LB or L = Limbach – 3 apparently copy of the Marcolini mark of Meissen – 5–6 after 1788

Limbach (2) (Germany, Thuringia). Limbach porcelain factory AG. Artistic porcelain and gift-items, dolls and dolls' heads. The factory, now closed, considered itself the successor to the old Limbach porcelain works of 1772. It closed in 1944.

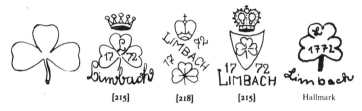

[215]   [218]   [215]   Hallmark

Limoges (1) (France). Charles Ahrenfeld, porcelain factory, f. 1894. Utility ware of all kinds.

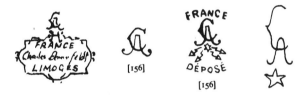

[156]   [156]

Limoges (2) (France). François Alluaud, director of the Royal porcelain factory, 1788–93, and co-owner with Michel Vanier of the Bordeaux porcelain factory. In 1798 he established himself in the Rue des Anglais. His products were pure white biscuit, luxury porcelain and his services were much admired. His son, François Jr., who owned kaolin quarries in Saint-Yrieix, moved the factory in 1816 to the Faubourg des Casseaux, after he had bought the Monnerie et Joubert factory in 1808. The factory remained in the possession of the Alluaud family until 1878, when it was owned by Ch. F. Haviland. See also Limoges (34).

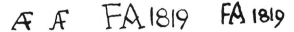

Limoges (3) (France). H.-A. Balleroy Brothers, porcelain factory, f. 1889.

Limoges (4) (France). Julien Balleroy & Cie., porcelain factory, f. 1914. Luxury porcelain.

Limoges (5) (France). According to 'Tardy 75', in 1943 Salomon Baranger et Cie started a porcelain decorating studio which marked their products with the following:

DRB
LIMOGES
FRANCE

DRB
LIMOGES
FRANCE

Limoges (6) (France). Barjaud & Lafon. Several dates have been suggested for the year of the founding, the earliest being 1871, and naming the factory as a successor to Duchatelet, which existed as a porcelain decorating studio since 1862. Bawo & Dotter bought it c. 1896–7 and directed it until 1920. The products were generally exported to the U.S.A., where Bawo & Dotter managed their own import house.

Limoges (7) (France). According to 'Tardy 75' a porcelain decorating studio was run here by Barny, Rigoni & Langle from 1894–1902, which had the following mark registered in 1894.

BARNY & RIGONI

M. REJON
BARNY & RIGONI
LIMOGES

LIMOGES
FRANCE

Limoges (8) (France). Bawo & Dotter, see Limoges (6) and Fischern (2).
Limoges (9) (France). Bernardaud, L. & Cie. f. a factory in 1905 which succeeded the Delinières & Cie. factory (see Limoges 33). The following marks were registered in 1912. This factory still exists and has maintained a branch factory in Paris, Rue de Paradis since 1925. The mark, which has remained valid from this time, is the last one shown.

Limoges (10) (France). Beulé Reboisson et Parot, porcelain factory. White and decorated porcelain.

Limoges (11) (France). Porcelain factory, f. 1884 by Boisbertrand & Theilloud. In 1896 the co-owner was Dorat. From 1903– c. 1938 Boisbertrand & Dorat were joint owners.

Limoges (12) (France). According to 'Tardy 75' the following mark was entered in the 'Centrale de Porcelaine', 1951.

Limoges (13) (France). Chabrol Frères & Poirier. Successor to Perigord & Fils porcelain decorating studio, f. in 1917. Mark was registered in 1920.

Limoges (14) (France). Cushion identifies Chauffriasse, Rougérie & Co. with the following mark. F. 1926 (according to 'Tardy 75').

Limoges (15) (France). Porcelain factory f. 1873 by Coiffe & Co. Known by the following names: Emile Coiffe & Co. (1877–9); Coiffe, Touron & Simon (1880); Coiffe & Touron (1888); Coiffe (1892); Coiffe & Laviolette (1895); Laviolette (1896). Products: very beautiful tableware with good glaze.

Limoges (16) (France). Coiffe jeune, porcelain decorating studio, from 1887. Later known as: Coiffe & Mathieu (1908); Coiffe (until 1914); Coiffe & Runaud & Co. (until 1924) (according to 'Tardy 75').

Limoges (17) (France). A small porcelain factory may have been here c. 1875, which used the following mark.

Limoges (18) (France). There is evidence that Delinières & Co. were active here as porcelain decorators in 1829 (according to 'Tardy 75').

Limoges (19) (France). G. Demartine & Co. had the following mark registered in 1890, according to 'Tardy 75'.

Limoges (20) (France). René Deschamps porcelain factory f. 1884, known as Deschamps & Massaloux from 1915. Mark registered 1898, according to 'Tardy 75'.

Limoges (21) (France). Georges Dupuy f. a porcelain decorating studio here in 1944 and registered the following mark at the same time.

Limoges (22) (France). Fabrique de Porcelaines blanches et décorées Anciens Ets. J. Teissonnière Cie., f. 1908. Miniatures and fancy porcelain.

Limoges (23) (France). A. Farge, porcelain decorating studio, 1867–87 according to 'Tardy 75'. Service with monogram.

Limoges (24) (France). According to 'Tardy 75' François et Cie. f. a porcelain decorating studio here in 1924 and registered the following mark.

LIMOGES
A. F.
FRANCE

LIMOGES
A.F
FRANCE

Limoges (25) (France). According to 'Tardy 75' René Frugier f. a porcelain decorating studio here in 1900 and registered 2 marks at the same time.

F.R.G.

LIMOGES
FRANCE

Limoges (26) (France). André Gentile had the following mark registered in 1889 (according to 'Tardy 75').

LIMOGES

Limoges (27) (France). Gerald f. a porcelain factory here in 1881 which continued to produce porcelain under his widow's management from 1899 to 1902. The fine quality of the products is highly praised.

J B G
L

Limoges (28) (France). A. Giraud, Brousseau, Chiry & Cie., porcelain factory, f. 1870. Table, tea and coffee services and luxury porcelain. Bleu de Sèvres.

A.GIRAUD
& BROUSSEAU
LIMOGES
Made in France

Limoges (29) (France). André Giraud f. a porcelain decorating studio here c. 1925 and had the following mark registered (according to 'Tardy 75').

Limoges (30), Fg. des Casseux, Fg. Montjovis (France). Gorsas, Montastiers and Perier f. a porcelain factory here c. 1842 which soon became the property of Cibus & Redon. The decoration is much acclaimed.

M R

Limoges (31) (France). The Grellet Bros., together with Massié and Fourneira, f. a porcelain factory here under the protectorate of the Comte d'Artois. The concern became the property of the Crown in 1784. From 1788–93 the director was Alluaud. This factory was in constant economic difficulties and finally closed in 1796. White porcelain made in Limoges was painted in Sèvres.

Limoges (32) (France). Guérin-Pouyat-Elite Ltd., porcelain factory. This business did not survive.

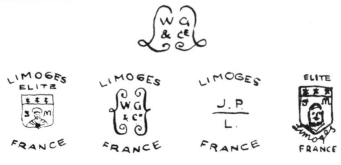

Limoges (33) (France). Guery-Delnières f. a porcelain factory at the Chemin de la Borie in 1863 (according to 'Grollier' 1922). It used the following mark.

$$\underline{D \& C^o}$$
$$FRANCE$$

According to Chaffers, this factory showed a breakfast set at the Exhibition of 1867. The previous concern had ceased production 1879. 'Tardy 75', however, ascribes the mark to Dellinières & Cie. which had already exhibited a remarkable dessert service in 1829, at the Exposition-Universelle. L. Bernardaud & Cie., f. in 1905, presented themselves as successors to the decorating studio, f. in 1829 – but using the same address as Grollier (Chemin de la Borie). The firm is still active and also states the year of their foundation as 1863. Their branch is in Paris. This contradictory information is yet to be clarified by future researchers.

Limoges (34) (France). Charles Field Haviland acquired an export business in 1875 which had been directed by a certain Rees since 1854, on behalf of Alluaud. In 1878, on the death of the last Alluaud, Ch. F. Haviland took over the concern, but in 1883 he passed it to Gerard Morel & Duffraisseix, who closed it in 1901. The products are much acclaimed. High firing and muffle colours were used in the decoration.

Limoges (35) (France). David Haviland f. an important factory here in 1842. Apart from his own products, porcelain from other factories was decorated. His sons Charles and Théodore became owners in 1879. In 1873–85 they ran a subsidiary firm in Auteuil, where ceramic wares were decorated in impressionistic style, causing quite a stir. His Tang shell motifs, created from c. 1870, owe much to Far Eastern and English sources.

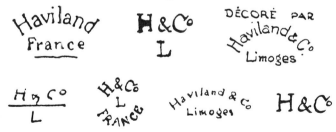

Limoges (36) (France). Frank Haviland 1910–39 (he operated under this name from 1924), had the following marks registered.

Limoges (37) (France). According to 'Tardy 75' Jean Haviland registered the following mark in various forms in 1957.

Limoges (38), Avenue de Poitiers (France). Théodore Haviland f. his porcelain factory in 1893. Table services and luxury ware. Renowned artists were employed as decorators: Bracquemond, Palladre, Jean Dufy, Susanne Lalique and Solange Patry-Bie.

Limoges (39) (France). It is assumed that a small porcelain factory was here c. 1880 and used the following mark.

Limoges (40) (France). Hippolyte Jouhanneaud f. a porcelain factory here c. 1843 and collaborated in 1845 with Leopold Dubois, who continued alone from 1866 onwards. The mark 'HJ' appears as blindstamp, 'L. Dubois' in various colours overglaze.

HJ   L Dubois

Limoges (41) (France). La Céramique Limousine, A. Chastagner, 1946–58. Luxury porcelain and fancy ware, hotel porcelain. The mark was registered in 1952 (see 'Tardy 75').

LIMOGES

Limoges (42) (France). La Porcelaine Limousin S.A. 1905–39 successor to Redon, anc. associé de Gibus of 1854. Later (from 1903–5) known as 'Redon, Barny & Rigoni'. Marks are shown in chronological order.

Limoges (43) (France). According to 'Tardy 75' Gaston Lavergne et Cie registered the following mark.

Limoges (44) (France). Th. Lazeyras & Fils, f. in 1906. The factory works exclusively on porcelain decorating; in 1906 the workshop was called Th. Lazeyras and from 1929 Th. Lazeyras & Fils SARL.

Limoges (45) (France). According to 'Tardy 75' Betoule & Legrand Ets existed here in 1910; in 1920 known as Betoule & Cie. and in 1923–6 Legrand & Cie.

Limoges (46) (France). 'Limousine de Porcelaine', f. 1947, signed, according to 'Tardy 75' as follows:

Limoges (47) (France). Londe (1866–1915), porcelain decorator and engraver. The following mark was already registered in 1880 (according to 'Tardy 75').

PORCELAINE LONDE VERRERIE
à LIMOGES

Limoges (48) (France). Sigismond Maas (1891–1935), signed his products with a mark which had been registered since 1898. Table, coffee, dessert and cooking porcelain.

Limoges (49) (France). Madesclaire jeune, porcelain factory, f. in 1959. Coffee and tea services, advertising articles.

Limoges (50) (France). Manufacture de Porcelaines Artistiques Fontanille & Marraud, f. in 1925. Fancy goods, miniatures, coffee, tea and mocha services. The factory was a partnership combining Anciennes Maisons Pillivuyt & Fils, and Anciennes Maisons Chauffriasse.

Limoges (51) (France). Manufacture de Porcelaines Robert Haviland & C. Parlon, f. in 1924. Tableware. The factory was named Robert Haviland & le Tanneur from 1924–49, and Robert Haviland & C. Parlon from 1949 onwards.

Limoges (52) (France). Manufacture de Porcelaines A. Lanternier & Cie., f. in 1855. Table, tea, and coffee ware, and also produced for the export market. Producer of the famous Bébé – dolls' heads after M. Lejeune.

ALC
LiMOGES

Hallmark

Limoges (53) (France). Manufacture de Porcelaines A. Vignaud, f. in 1911. Table porcelain. The firm was named Vignaud Brothers until 1937.

Limoges (54) (France). Charles Martin porcelain factory f. by Michel Nivet in 1875. In the past the factory has been known as Martin Freres (1880); Charles Martin (1895); Martin and Nephew (1903); Ch. M. (1906); Martin & Ducher (1925–35). Mark No. 1 has been in use since 1912.

Limoges (55) (France). Mavaleix & Co., porcelain factory 1908–14. Also known as: Mavaleix & Granger (1920); I. Granger & Co. (1922–7); Granger & Co. (1944–50).

Limoges (56) (France). Merlin-Lemas, porcelain factory, f. 1926. White and decorated porcelain.

P M L

LIMOGES

(FRANCE)

Limoges (57) (France). Miautre, Raynand & Cie. (1924–34 according to 'Tardy 75') was traced by Cushion through the following mark.

M. R. Cie
LIMOGES

Limoges (58) (France). Moreau ainé et Cie., 1880–2, had the following mark entered in 1880, according to 'Tardy 75'.

Limoges (59) (France). Nardon et Lafarge 'Limoges Porcelaine', f. 1937. According to 'Tardy 75' the following mark was registered in 1951.

Limoges (60) (France). G. Papault, porcelain decorating studio, 1933–7.

Limoges (61) (France). Paul E. Pastaud operated between 1923–36. According to 'Tardy 75' the following mark was registered in 1926.

Limoges (62) (France). Plainemaison Frères, 1889–1909. According to 'Tardy 75' the following mark was registered in 1895.

Limoges (63) (France). Porcelaine Georges Boyer, f. 1934. Utility porcelain.

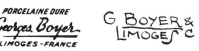

Limoges (64) (France). 'Porcelaine de Limoges Bourganeuf', 1904–14. The following mark was registered in 1909.

Limoges (65) (France). Porcelaine Pallas S.A., porcelain factory, f. 1927. The mark was registered in the same year (1927).

Limoges (66) (France). Porcelaine Ch. Reboisson, f. in 1942; since then the following mark has been used.

Limoges (67) (France). Porcelaines Singer, 1950. Ornamental and utility porcelain.

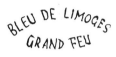

Limoges (68) (France). Porcelaines 'Elté' Léon Texeraud, f. 1923. Tea and coffee services, utility porcelain and fancy goods.

  L. T.
            LIMOGES
            France

Limoges (69) (France). Porcelaines GDA, ancienne Maison Gérard, f. in 1798. Table porcelain.

FRANCE

Limoges (70) (France). Porcelaines Limoges Castel, formerly J. Chateau. Ornamental porcelain.

A⌐ ⌐hateau

Limoges (71) (France). The owner of the stone quarries of St.-Yrieix, J. Pouyat, f. a porcelain factory here in 1842 and associated with Russinger. His successors retained the mark 'J. Pouyat' in green underglaze and added, if for export, 'France'. According to 'Tardy 75', 'La Céramique' was established as the succeeding factory in 1905. Apart from the old mark the following was also registered.

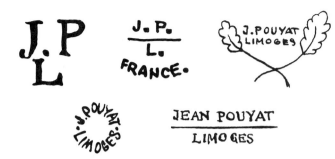

JEAN POUYAT

LIMOGES

Limoges (72) (France). In the 19th c., according to some reports, a small porcelain factory was active here and used the following mark.

Limoges (73) (France). M. Raynaud, porcelain factory, f. 1911. Tableware in classical and modern taste. Associated with Porcelaine Gustave Vogt from 1920 and from then on known as 'Porcelaines Raynaud & Cie.

1   1911   2   1912   3   1928   4-5   1943   6   1961

Limoges (74) (France). Reboisson, Baranger & Cie., porcelain factory f. 1923. Coffee, tea and table services. According to 'Tardy 75' it operated from 1927–40.

R B & C

Limoges (75) (France). Sophie Redon decorated porcelain here in the style of Louis XV. According to 'Tardy 75' the following mark was registered in 1891.

Limoges (76) (France). Rousset & Co., porcelain decorating studio, f. 1923. Later known as Rousset & Guillebot (1924); Rousset & Feuillerat (1927); Rousset, Guillerot & Dessagne (according to 'Tardy 75') (1936).

Limoges (77) (France). Ruaud f. a porcelain factory here in 1829 which was active until 1869. He was the first factory owner in Limoges to decorate his porcelain with underglaze colours. His successors, Jules Parant and later Pinot & Barboud closed the factory in 1879.

Limoges (78) (France). Léon Sazerat f. a porcelain factory here in 1852, which was active until 1890.

Limoges (79) (France). Léon Sazerat, Blondeau & Co. managed a porcelain decorating studio here from 1884–93.

Limoges (80) (France). Serpaut (nothing is known about him apart from his name). Cushion identifies the following mark as his. (According to 'Tardy 75' f. c. 1905.)

Limoges (81) (France). Société Porcelainière de Limoges, f. 1926. Fine table service and hotel ware.

Limoges (82) (France). Soudana & Touze managed a porcelain decorating studio here from c. 1863, which Touze directed by himself from 1869. In 1878–96 the firm was called Ws. Touze, Marty & Theilloud; 1901–13 Touze & Co., and from 1920–42 Touze, Lemaître Frères et Blancher.

Limoges (83) (France). C. Tharaud, f. 1919. Porcelain production and execution of decorations.

Limoges (84), Route de Paris (France). P. Tharaud f. a porcelain factory here in 1817, which he sold in 1819 to Barbe & Poncet. In 1854 Poncet became a partner with Henry Ardant and in 1859 with Raymond Laporte. In 1883 the factory belonged to the Noussat brothers, and in 1892 to Lanternier.

Limoges (85), Place Tourny (France). P. Tharaud. After the sale of the factory in the route de Paris to Barne & Poncet in 1819, Tharaud (called Tharaudmainville) established himself in the Place Tourny. In 1821 Charles X conferred the title 'Royal Works' upon the factory. After Tharaud's death in 1843, his widow managed the factory until she sold it in 1864. Pierre Tharaud did not mark his products. Another Tharaud opened a factory in 1851 which had a new owner in 1874, and was known as Bac & Périgault. Its mark is the following.

Limoges (86), 16 C. Jourdan (France). Tressemann & Vogt, c. 1883, possibly exporters. Known as 'Porcelaine Vogt' (Vogt & Dohse) from 1909–10. Associated with Raynaud from 1920, see Limoges (73).

Limoges (87) (France). Union Céramique, porcelain factory, f. 1900 (Maurel, Chapeau, Charles & Veyrier).

Limoges (88) (France). Union Limousine, porcelain factory, f. 1908. Services of all kinds.

U L
LIMOGES
FRANCE

Limoges (89) (France). Villegoureix, Noël & Co., f. 1922. Later known as Villegoureix & Cie (1924–6); S.A. Porcelaine Villegoureix (1928–9).

Limoges stone, see Kaolin sources (France).
Limoges Unic, see Paris (93).
Limousine de Porcelaine, see Limoges (46).
Linck, Konrad (1732–93). Sculptor and porcelain modeller. He studied at the Kunstakademie in Vienna and worked in Berlin and Potsdam as sculptor. He was master modeller from 1762–6 at the Frankenthal factory. Even after he was called to Mannheim as Court sculptor, he still provided the factory with models. His elegant, courtly style, in the manner of the late rococo had a far-reaching effect on the rich figure production of Frankenthal.

LINCK

Lincke, Prof., see Lustre glaze.
Lindberg, Stig. Modeller of surrealistic compositions, see Gustavsberg (1).
Lindemann, Georg Christoph, porcelain decorator from Saxony. He was chief decorator in Nymphenburg from 1758–60. At times he signed his work with 'L'. He was the son of the Meissen painter Christian Philipp Lindemann, who had also worked as miniature painter in Nüremberg, Regensburg and Italy.

C. G. LINDEMA

Linschoten, Jan Huygen van. In 1595, he reported on his travels in *Iterneratio, Voyage if te Schipvaert ect,* which contained a lucid description of the making of porcelain.

Linström, see Lidköping (2).

Lippelsdorf nr. Gräfenthal (Germany, Thuringia). Wagner & Apel, porcelain factory, f. 1877. Porcelain figures of animals, children, boxes, vases, gift articles, technical porcelain.

Bertram

Lippert & Haas see Schlaggenwald (1).

Lisbon (1) (Portugal). J. J. Paszoa produced porcelain here c. 1870. According to Burton and Hobson the following mark was used from 1833.

|IAC|

Lisbon (2) (Portugal). Fabrica de Porcelana da Vista-Alegre, f. in 1824. Beautiful table and hotel services. This firm is still active today, see Vista-Alegre.

List, C., see Neuhaus (1).

List, J. G., see Pirkenhammer.

Lithophanes. Lightscreens of biscuit porcelain exploiting the transparency of thin porcelain plates into which relief moulds are pressed. After the firing the decoration is evident. The thicker parts make up the shadows, the thinner parts supply the light in the pictures. These lithophanes were mounted into cheap lead frames, suspended from thin chains, and hung against windows. The size of the plates, which occurred in irregular shapes, ranged from 10 × 15 cm to 15 × 20 cm. Lithophanes were particularly popular in Bohemia where they formed the decoration on the bottom of porcelain cups and plates. Views of Carslbad were typical decorations. According to DKG, lithophanes were invented in Paris by Bourgion in 1927, but the KPM Berlin was the first to manufacture them and soon became the leading factory in this field. 136,730 pieces were produced within the space of 30 years. Paris, Meissen and other well-known porcelain factories in Thuringia and Bohemia were also engaged in lithophany. In Berlin Frick developed a formula which led to the production of a particularly transparent body. As well as Berlin Palaces and other famous buildings, portraits (mostly of the Royal family), lithophanes were decorated with, or after, Teniers, Rembrandt, Rubens and Ruisdael, or modern painters like Begas, von Cornelius, Krüger, von Kaulbach, Meyerheim, Overbeck, L. Richter, Magnus, W. v. Schadow, von Carolsfeld and Stieler. In 1850 there are reports of painted lithophanes. These lithophanes are very rare and are hardly seen even in specialist auctions. However there follows a table of Berlin dates and numbers.

Plate-numbers belonging to the year

1828–36	1–156	1847/8	352–376
1836/7	157–190	1848/50	377–410
1837–40	191–248	1850–9	411–516
1840/1	249–262	1859/60	517–535
1842–6	263–315	1861/2	536–555
1846/7	316–351	1862–5	556–580

Literature: Hans Leichter, *Berliner Lithophanien* (1974).

Littler, William, see Longton Hall.

Littler's Blue. A deep blue, which was invented by Littler, the founder of Longton Hall (1750), in his stoneware factory even before porcelain was produced there.

Liverpool (England). The extent to which porcelain had been produced in the 18th c. remains largely a matter of conjecture. It is certain that some potters (Chaffers, Podmore, Ph. Christian Gilbody, Reid & Co., Barnes) had produced porcelain and it is possible that true, hard porcelain had even been made by some. Many products of this time which had been described as porcelain, were in fact frit porcelain (soft paste), and the characteristically English 'bone and soap stone' porcelain. An important documentary piece is a porcelain jug, now in the British Museum, which is inscribed 'Frederik Heinzelmann, Liverpool 1779'. It is said to have come from the factory of Barnes.

1–3 1796–c. 1833, blind or printed

How accurately Herculaneum pottery can be identified cannot yet be established, but the factory existed under various owners from 1793–1841. Godden identified the following marks.

Lladro SA, see Tabernes.

Lloyd, John, see Shelton (3).

Lochotin nr. Pilsen (Bohemia). Lochotin porcelain factory, f. 1881. Mocha cups, Turkish beakers.

F.S.
P.

Locker & Co., see Derby (1).

Locket, Baguley & Cooper, Victoria Works, see Shelton (4).

Locré, Jean Baptiste, see Paris (94).

Lodz (Poland). According to Demmin porcelain is reputed to have been made here in 1867.

Loehnig, Johann Georg (1743–1803). He was the most significant porcelain decorator of the Punkt (Dot) and Marcolini period in Meissen. He was called the first German 'Louis XVI painter'. He was a virtuoso in portraits, pastorals, mythological scenes and landscapes with figures.

Löffler, Alfred, see Chemnitz.

Lomello, Giovanni, see Vinovo.

Londe, see Limoges (47).

London (England). A. B. & R. P. Daniell were retailers here from 1825–1917. The mark appears on Coalport and other porcelain and ceramic products which were especially made for the firm.

Longport (England). Davenport f. a ceramic factory here in 1793 which operated until 1882. Certain marked pieces from the first half of the 19th c. are still extant. The Derby style predominated, with richly gilded rims and naturalistic flowers and fruits being characteristic. According to Godden, the standard mark, number 3 below, was in use from 1870–87.

Longton (1) (England). Adams & Cooper, porcelain factory, 1850–77.

A. & C.

Longton (2) (England). Adderley Floral & Figurine China Co. Ltd., f. 1945. Tea services, figures and statuettes, flower groups.

Longton (3) (England). Adderleys Ltd., f. 1906 by G. E. Wotherspoon, formerly known as Willina Alsager Adderley (1876–1905); and Hulse & Adderley (1869–75). Tea, table services and porcelain figures.

Longton (4) (England). Charles Allerton & Sons, porcelain factory, 1859–1942. All other marks show the full name.

C. A. & SONS

Longton (5) (England). Alton China Co. Ltd. porcelain factory, 1950–7.

ALTON
BONE
CHINA

Longton (6) (England). C. Amison & Co. Ltd., China Manufacturers, Stanley China Works, f. 1875. Tea, coffee and fancy ware.

Longton (7) (England). Anchor Porcelain Co. Ltd., porcelain factory, worked from 1901–18 (according to Godden).

A. P. CO.

Longton (8) (England). Aristocrat Florals & Fancies, porcelain factory, f. 1958.

ENGLISH *Aristocrat Florals* BONE CHINA

Longton (9) (England). Aynsley china, John Aynsley & Sons Ltd., f. 1864. Table services.

Longton (10) (England). Thomas Barlow produced stoneware and porcelain here from 1849–82. The impressed B is interchangable.

B

Longton (11) (England). G. L. Bentley & Co. (Ltd.), Old cyples pottery, porcelain factory, operating 1889–1912 (according to Godden).

G. L. B. & Co.

Longton (12) (England). Beswick & Son, Warwick Works, porcelain factory 1916–30. Acording to Godden it was formerly known as Bridgett & Bates (1882–1915); Bridgett, Bates & Beech (1875–82).

B & S   B & B

Longton (13) (England). Blackhurst and Hulme Belgrave Works, porcelain factory, 1890–1932.

B. & H.

Longton (14) (England). Blairs Ltd., porcelain factory, 1880–1930. Tableware.

Longton (15) (England). Blyth Porcelain Co. Ltd., Blyth Works, 1905–35; formerly Dresden Porcelain Co. (1896–1904). Coffee, tea and dinner services. Blyth was taken over by Finney in 1935. See Longton (31).

1 1880 – 2 1900 – 3 1914–1930

Longton (16) (England). Booths & Colcloughs Ltd. (Hanley), 1948–54. In 1948 two firms, Booths Ltd. Tunstall (f. 1891) and Colcloughs China Ltd., Longton (1937–48) (formerly known as H. J. Colclough Ltd., Vale Works, 1897–1937, *q.v.*), were amalgamated. Booths was a stoneware factory while Colclough and his predecessors had produced porcelain which has often been praised since 1897, mostly table and tea services. In 1948 the business was taken over by a group of ceramic factories which did not produce porcelain.

Longton (17) (England). Britannia China Company, 1895–1906. Other marks show the full name.

B.C. Co.

Longton (18)(England). The Cara China Co., porcelain factory, f. 1945, produced figures, flowergroups, etc. The products show the mark 'Mayflower'.

MAYFLOWER   CARA CHINA

Longton (19) (England). F. Cartlidge & Co., 1889–1904. China.

F. C.   F. C. & CO.

Longton (20) (England). Cartwright & Edwards Ltd., f. 1858. Tableware, mark: 'Victoria'.

C&E·
1

2

C & E. Lᵗᵒ
"BORONIAN"
WARE
3

BORONIAN
WARE
MADE IN
ENGLAND
C&E Lᵗᵒ
4

WARE
C&E LIMITED
ENGLAND
5

VICTORIA CHINA
ENGLAND

1 1880 – 2 1912 – 3 1926 – 4 1929 – 5 1936

Longton (21) (England) Chapmans Ltd., Albert Works porcelain factory, f. 1916. Utility ware.

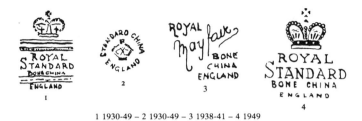

1 1930-49 – 2 1930-49 – 3 1938-41 – 4 1949

Longton (22) (England). Coggins & Hill (1892–8), became Hill & Co., St. James Works (1898–1907) and then Windsor China Works (1907–20).

C & H   H. & CO.

Longton (23) (England). H. J. Colclough, Vale Works, 1897–1937. Porcelain and stoneware factory. Active as 'Colclough China Ltd.' until 1938 and was eventually incorporated into Booths & Colclough Ltd., Hanley in 1948.

Longton (24) (England). Collingwood & Greatbatsch, Crown Works (1870–7), later Collingwood Bros. Ltd., St. George's Works (1887–1957). Porcelain factory. Dessert, breakfast, tea and drinking services.

Longton (25) (England). Cooke & Hulse, porcelains, 1835–55.

COOKE & HULSE   « Alma Japan »

Longton (26) (England). Co-operative Wholesale Society Ltd., Windsor pottery, f. 1922. Tea, coffee and breakfast services.

Longton (27) (England). H. J. Cope & Co., porcelain factory, taken over by the Booths & Colcloughs Ltd. factory in Hanley, Stoke-on-Trent.

Longton (28) (England). Denton China Co., porcelain factory f. 1945, producing artistic porcelain.

Longton (29) (England). Dresden Floral Porcelain Co., f. 1945, producing artistic porcelain. Closed in 1956.

Longton (30) (England). Edwards & Brown, porcelain factory, 1882–1933. Tea and dinner services.

Longton (31) (England). A. T. Finney & Sons Ltd., Duchess China Works, f. 1947, produced tea services.

Longton (32) (England). Thomas Forester & Sons (Ltd). Imperial Works (also Phoenix Works), 1884–1959; formerly (1880–4) Thomas Forester Son & Co.

Longton (33) (England). Gladstone China, 1952 onwards; formerly Th. Poole & Gladstone China Ltd., 1939–52.

1 1946–61 – 2 and 3 from 1961

Longton (34) (England). Goodwin & Bullock, Dresden Works, 1852–8.

Longton (35) (England). J. Goodwin Stoddard & Co., porcelain factory, 1898–1940 (according to Godden).

Longton (36) (England). Grosvenor China Ltd., porcelain factory, f. 1961.

Longton (37) (England). Hall Bros. Ltd., Radnor Works, f. 1947. Figures and similar ornaments.

Longton (38) (England). Hammersley & Co. Ltd., china manufacturers, Alsager pottery, f. between 1860–70. Tea, coffee and dinner services. The factory was originally in the hands of Messrs. Harvey Adams & Co. Closed in 1932.

Longton (39) (England). Harvey, Adams & Co., porcelain factory, 1870–85; ownership later passed to Hammersley (see Longton (38)).

Longton (40) (England). According to Godden a factory operated under the following names: C. & W. K. Harvey (1835–53); Holland & Green (1853–82); Green, Clark & Clay (1882–91). Other marks show full names.

H. & G.
LATE HARVEY

C. & W. K. H.

Longton (41) (England). Hewitt & Landbeater, Willow Pottery, 1907–19. Dolls' heads were also produced (1914–18).

Longton (42) (England). Hibbert & Boughey, stoneware and porcelain factory, 1889.

Longton (43) (England). Hudson and Middleton Ltd., china manufacturers, Sutherland pottery, 1889–1941. Tea, coffee and breakfast services.

Longton (44) (England). Jackson & Gosling Ltd., porcelain factory, f. 1886. Coffee, tea and breakfast services.

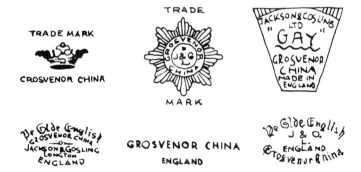

Longton (45) (England). A.-B. Jones & Sons, porcelain factory. Tea and breakfast services, luxury porcelain articles.

Longton (46) (England). James Kent (Ltd.), porcelain and stoneware factory, f. 1897.

Longton (47) (England). Edwin Leadbeater, 1920–4. Most likely a porcelain decorator.

Longton (48) (England). Thomas P. Ledgar. Stoneware factory, 1900–5, formerly Wildbloos & Ledgar, 1896–1900. No porcelain was produced.

TPL

Longton (49) (England). Longton Porcelain Co. (Ltd.), Victoria Works, porcelain factory, 1892–1908.

Longton (50) (England). William Lowe, Sydney Works, 1874–1930. The first mark was used 1874–1912.

Longton (51) (England). Andrew Mackee, Foley Works, porcelain and stoneware factory, 1892–1906.

$$A.M.$$
$$L.$$

Longton (52) (England). Mason, Holt & Co., Dresden Works, porcelain factory, 1875–84.

$$M.H.\& Co.$$

Longton (53) (England). Mayer & Sherratt, porcelain factory, 1906–41. Utility porcelain and then from 1914–18 excellent dolls' heads, marked 'Melba' on the shoulderblade.

Longton (54) (England). Moore Bros. produced decorative porcelain, 1872–1905. Operated as Bernard Moore until 1915.

1 printed, rare from 1902–5 – 2 printed 1880–1902 – 3 by hand or stippled on Moore's 'Chinese-style glaze effects' products 1905–15 – 4 1868–75, blind stamp or printed – 5 blind stamp 1872–1905

Longton (55) (England). Thomas Morris, porcelain factory, 1892–1941.

Longton (56) (England). Thomas Morris, Anchor Works, porcelain factory, 1897–1901.

Longton (57) (England). New Chelsea China Co. Ltd., 1951–61; formerly New Chelsea Porcelain Co. Ltd. (1912–51). Coffee, tea and tableware. Part of the Grosvenor China Ltd. (Longton (36)) since 1961.

1 1912 – 2 1919 – 3 1936 – 4 1943 – 5 1951-61

Longton (58) (England). Osborne China Co., porcelain factory, 1909–40; during this time it was already part of Booths & Colcloughs Ltd. (Hanley) (see Longton (17)).

Longton (59) (England). Paragon China Ltd., f. 1897; table services. Until 1919 this firm was called Star China Co., from 1919 it was known as Paragon China Ltd., and is now called 'Paragon China Ltd., Atlas Works'.

last row of marks show the Star China Co., Atlas Works mark, 1901–19

Longton (60) (England). George Procter & Co. (Ltd.), Gladstone pottery, 1891–1940.

Longton (61) (England). Redfern & Drakeford (Ltd.), Chatfield Works, 1892–1902; Balmoral Works, 1902–33. Taken over in 1933 by Royal Albion China Co. (see Longton (67)) who ran the business until 1948.

Longton (62) (England). Regency China Ltd., porcelain factory, f. 1953.

Longton (63) (England). Reid & Colk Park Place Works, porcelain factory, 1913–46; Roslyn China, 1946–63.

1 1913 – 2 1924 – 3 1937-1946

Longton (64) (England). Rosina China Co. Ltd., Queen's Pottery, f. 1887. Utility ware and fancy articles.

Longton (65) (England). Roslyn China, Park Place Works, f. 1911. Tea, coffee and breakfast services.

Longton (66) (England). Thos. C. Wild & Sons Ltd., f. 1894. Tea, coffee and table services in Royal Albert Bone China.

Longton (67) (England). Royal Albion China Co., 1921–48. Incorporating the Redfern & Drakeford Co. Ltd. from 1933 (see Longton (61)) and the Doric China Co. from 1935 (see Fenton (6)).

Longton (68) (England). Thomas Poole & Gladstone China Ltd., f. 1845. Royal Stafford China. Utility ware.

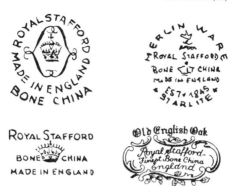

Longton (69) (England). Salisbury China Co. Ltd., 1927–61. Household and hotel services.

Longton (70) (England). Salt & Nixon Ltd., porcelain factory, 1901–34. Coffee and tea cups, plates.

Longton (71) (England). Sampson Smith Ltd., porcelain factory, Sutherland Works, 1846–1963. Tea and breakfast services, 1914–18 dolls and dolls' heads.

Hallmark

Longton (72) (England). John Shaw & Sons Ltd., Willow Pottery & Warwick Works, 1931–63. Household and artistic porcelain.

Longton (73) (England). Shelley Potteries Ltd. F. 1892 (according to Godden), called 'Wileman & Co., Foley Works' until 1925. The name 'Shelley Potteries' was adopted in 1925, and changed to 'Shelley China Ltd.' in 1965.

engraved around 1892   engraved around 1911

Longton (74) (England). Shore & Coggins Ltd., f. 1911 (?). Formerly known as: J. Shore & Co. (1887–1905); Shore, Coggins & Holt, Edensor Works (1905–10). Tea, coffee and breakfast services.

Longton (75) (England). Spencer Stevenson & Co. Ltd., 1948–60. Household and hotel ware. The products bear the name: 'Spencer Stevenson'. Other marks show the full name.

Longton (76) (England). Stanley Pottery Ltd., stoneware and porcelain factory, 1928–31; formerly Colclough & Co., 1887–1928. The marks were retained.

Longton (77) (England). Taylor & Kent, Ltd., Florence Works, f. 1967. Tea and coffee services.

Longton (78) (England). Taylor Tunniclif (Refractories) Ltd., Albion Works, f. 1868. From 1898 only technical and fireproof goods were produced. The last mark shown was entered on 13 February 1920 in the DRWZV, under No. 242542.

[228]

Longton (79) (England). Thorley China Ltd., f. 1940. Fancy porcelain ware, bearing the name 'Thorley'.

THORLEY CHINA
LTD.
MADE IN
ENGLAND

Longton (80) (England). Trentham Bone China Ltd., 1952–7. Tea services.

Longton (81) (England). Tuscan China R. H. & S. L. Plant Ltd., 1881–98. Tea, coffee and tableware. Until 1913 the firm was called R. H. Plant & Co.

Longton (82) (England). Charles Waine (& Co.) (Ltd.), Derby Works, 1891–1920; formerly Waine & Bates.

C. W.

Longton (83) (England). J. H. Walton, Baltimore or Albion China Works, 1912–21; formerly Walton & Co.

Longton (84) (England). G. Warrilow & Sons Ltd., porcelain factory, f. 1875. Tea and breakfast services.

G.W.   G. W. &S.   G.W. & SONS

Longton (85) (England). Wild Bros., Edensor Crown China Works, porcelain factory, 1904–27.

Longton (86) (England). Wildblood, Heath & Sons (Ltd.), Peel Works, porcelain factory, 1899–1927. Originally known as Hulme & Massey, then Massey, Wildblood & Co. (1897–9).

M.W. & CO.

Longton (87) (England)., H. M. Williamson & Sons, 1879–1941. Breakfast and tea services.

Longton Hall (England). The earliest porcelain factory in Staffordshire existed here between 1751 (possibly even earlier) and 1760. F. by William Littler, who, together with various partners, formed an association which disbanded in 1760; the factory was consequently put up for sale. Very little else is known about the undertaking. The mark used by Littler, a crossed 'L', was also used to mark the saltglazed stoneware. The products were simple, not unlike those of Chelsea. Blue underglaze colours were used; the finer pieces being decorated in the style of Meissen. Evidence shows that gilded decoration was sparingly used between 1758 and 1760. It has been assumed that a small porcelain factory was active in Newcastle-under-Lyme as early as 1750. This may have been the predecessor of Longton Hall.

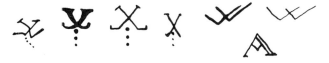

Longton Porcelain Co. (Ltd.), Victoria Works, see Longton (49).
Longwy (France). Huart f. a small porcelain factory here in 1828. The products were sold in Paris, 42 rue de Paradis.

Lorch (Germany, Württemberg). Deusch & Co., metal porcelain factory f. 1898. Utility ware and luxury porcelains. Friedrich Deusch, Schwäb. Gmünd, a master of engraving, developed the modern technique of metal porcelain in 1898. A layer of metal is fused to the porcelain by galvanisation. This work is very time consuming since the metal layer takes from 16 to 30 hours before it reaches a required thickness which can be fused indivisibly with the porcelain. The metal decoration is executed in 'fine silver' (assayed 1000/000) or 'silver-plated copper' (less expensive); the decorations are either highly polished or matt white. A special type of metal porcelain are the so-called 'silver porcelains' which are completely metalised. This means that the unfired porcelain article has its surface completely covered with a galvanised silver coating, which is then polished.

Lorenci, Pietro, see Nove.
Lorenz, Oswald, see Dresden (21).
Lorenz, Wilh. Wenzel, see Dallwitz.
Lorenz & Trabe, see Selb (6).
Lorient (France, Morbihan). A porcelain factory was active here in the late 18th, early 19th c. It was successively directed by Charey, Sauvageau and Hervé. The mark 'PL' stands for 'porcelaine Lorientaise'. The products are very rare but of little artistic value. A vase in the Sèvres Museum displays the following inscription at its base: 'Fabrikqué dans le Dept. du Morbihan par Sauvageau à Lorient'.

FABRIQUE DANS LE Dept du MORBIHAN
PAR SAUVAGENU A LORIENT   PL T

Louault, M., see Villedieu (1).
Louis, Jean–Jacques. From Namur. Chief repairer in Ludwigsburg, 1762–72. His forte was the modelling of animals in naturalistic settings but he also produced figures in contemporary costume.

Lourioux, Louis, see Foecy (3).

Lowdin, William, see Bristol (2).

Lowe, William, Sidney Works, see Longton (50).

Löwenfinck, Adam Friedrich von (1714–54). Porcelain and faience decorator. Active in Meissen 1727–36 as decorator of figures and particularly of 'Indian Blumen'. Afterwards he worked in the Bayreuth faience factory, following a short spell in Ansbach, and in 1741 he worked as 'Court enamel painter' in Fulda. In 1746 he f. a porcelain factory in the Speicherhof in Höchst, with the help of the Frankfurt businessmen, Gölz and Glarus. Nowadays it is doubted whether he really produced genuine porcelain. Later Löwenfinck was director in the faience factory of Hannong in Hagenau from 1749 where he died in 1754. His brothers Christian Wilhelm and Karl Heinrich were also porcelain decorators; evidence shows Christian Wilhelm working in Meissen, Fulda and Strasbourg. His wife, Maria Scraphia, whom he married in 1747, was also a porcelain decorator; her father was the Fulda painter I. P. Schick. After Löenfinck's death she became director in Hagenau, and when her second husband, de Becke, died, she directed the Ludwigsburg faience factory from 1763–95.

Löwenfinck, Christian Wilhelm von (d. 1753). Younger brother of A. F. von Löwenfinck decorator in Meissen from 1726, in Höchst in 1747 and in Strasbourg from 1748.

Löwenfinck, Karl Heinrich von (1718–54). Younger brother of A. F. von Löwenfinck and C. W. von Löwenfinck. Worked in Meissen as decorator and Court enamel painter from 1730, in Fulda from 1741–3 and in Strasbourg from 1748.

Löwenfinck, Maria Seraphia (1741–1805), porcelain decorator, see Löwenfinck, A. F. von.

Lowestoft (England). A small soft paste porcelain factory was f. here in 1757. The earliest experiments were conducted without success by Hewlin Luson, but this did not prevent further work being done by Robert Brown and his partners Walker, Brown, Aldred and Richman. Brown died in 1761, when the management of the factory was taken over by Walker, one of his partners. At first the production was generally limited to table services with modest decorations. The body is soft and light, with a matt glaze, similar to the products of Bow. Both have an additive of bone-ash in common. Dark blue underglaze decoration is the main theme of the first period. Many pieces have a lively similarity to the products of Worcester. The decorations and rims of the services are sometimes very simple, while at other times they display charming Chinese patterns. Chinese export porcelain was in any case copied to a large extent.

Large punch bowls with blue decoration are regarded as the finest pieces. After the closure of the factory in 1802, the director, Robert Allen (who held the position from 1780), ordered that the left-over porcelain be decorated in London at his own expense. These products have the inscription 'A trifle from Lowestoft'.

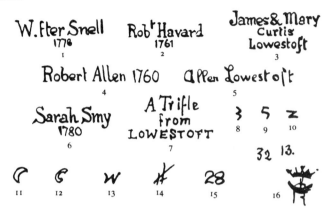

1 violet – 2 blue – 3 black – 4–7 blue – 8–10 on the inner side of foot flange of service – 11–13 on Worcester copies – 14 swords mark

Lubartow (Russia). Count P. Lubjansk directed a factory here from 1840–50, which produced earthenware as well as porcelain. These pieces, produced in the classical taste, are notable for their clean execution and good decoration.

Lubau (Bohemia). The 'Porzellan Fabrik and Kaolinschlämmerei Alp GmbH' evolved from the porcelain factory which had been f. by the Martin Bros. in 1874. It was annexed in 1939 by the EPIAG and was subsequently closed.

Lubenz (1) (Bohemia, now Lubenec). Franz Lehnert f. 'Am Hirschen' porcelain factory here in 1846. His successors were Schwab, followed by the Kasseker Bros., who traded as 'K u. K private Porzellan-Fabrik Gebr. Kasseker, Hirschen'. Their successor, the porcelain manufacturer H. Reinl of Hirschen, turned the business into an exemplary factory.

Lubenz (2) (Bohemia, now Lubenec). In 1848 Rudolf Laurer f. a porcelain factory in Hirschen. Utility ware and English mugs.

Lubjansk, Graf P., see Lubartow.
Lubormirsky, Duke, see Emilczyn and Gorodnitza.
Lübtheen (Germany, Mecklenburg). Adolf F. Bossart porcelain factory. The firm is now closed.
Lück, Johann Christian Ludwig, see Lücke.
Lück, Johann Friedrich (1727–97). Active as a repairer in Meissen. Worked in 1757 in Höchst and from 1758–64 as master modeller in Frankenthal. In 1764 he was in Meissen again as 'manager of white production' where he remained until his death. The greater part of his work consisted of costume figures.
Lück, Karl Gottlieb (1730 Freiberg in Saxony–1775). Brother of Johann Friedrich; active from 1767 until his death as master modeller in Frankenthal, where he was known as early as 1760 as 'experienced in the art of a repairer' (evidence is available to support this). Due to his technical competence, he was called to Meissen as technical adviser when the life-sized statue of King Augustus III was planned in 1760.
An unusual situation occurred in which both factories used the same marks in part (Terre de Lorraine). Produced table services and figures, mainly in biscuit.
Lücke, Johann Christian Ludwig (d. 1780). Ivory sculptor. After Kirchner's dismissal from Meissen in 1728, Lücke was engaged as a modelling master, but his work was not satisfactory and he was dismissed in 1729. Later, in 1752, he worked in Vienna as 'first master modeller', but moved to Fürstenberg in the same year. He was in England in 1760, and later in Dresden again. He was a typical representative of the wandering artist and arcanist of the 18th c. and died after much wandering about in Danzig in 1780.
Ludwig, Adam. From Saxony. Active as decorator in Höchst, c. 1750–8, specialising in 'Indian flowers'. His signature 'AL' was erroneously attributed to Löwenfinck.
Ludwigsburg (1) (Germany, Württemberg). In 1758 the 'Herzoglich ächte

Porcellaine Fabrique' was f. by decree of Duke Karl Eugen von Württemberg, as a 'necessary attribute of splendour and dignity'. Johann Gottlieb Trothe was appointed as the first director. The factory was initially installed in a barracks but in 1760 it was moved into the small ducal castle 'Jägerhaus'. The factory flourished under the arcanist Josef Ringler (from 1760–7), and also under the master modeller, I. W. Chr. Beyer. Viewed in its entirety the figure production reflected the transition from rococo to classicism in its style. As is the case with all south German porcelain producers the manufacture of services and tablewares was of secondary importance. Kaolin from Hafnerzell nr. Passau was used. The colour of the body ranges from a light grey to a dingy grey. After 1767 the artistic quality steadily declined. Duke Friedrich von Württemberg assumed the administration of the factory in May 1802, but despite this, it was leased out once more in 1817. In 1819 it began to manage itself again until a decree of King William I of Württemberg finally closed the business in 1824.

From its primitive beginnings Ludwigsburg developed a figure-style of expressive individuality surprisingly quickly. A painterly style, typical of the rococo, was most likely established by Gottlieb Friedrich Riedel (1759–79), but was fully developed after 1762 by Beyer, Ferretti and Lejeune, who replaced the original style with an emphasis of the human figure. Ludwigsburg, as the foremost German porcelain factory, adopted the classical style under Wilhelm Beyer. The unsatisfactory nature of the research pertaining to Ludwigsburg porcelain, is illustrated by the fact that a large number of models are still attributed to three anonymous masters who are named after their characteristic works: modeller of the Apollo candlestick, modeller of the dance groups and modeller of the folk characters.

See also: Bauer, A., Bechel, J. Ph. M., Danhofer, J. Ph., Dannecker, J. H. Ess (Äss), F. J., Göz, J., Grossmann, Ch. G., Haslöder, J., Höflich, J. J., Höflinger, Ch. J., Kirschner, Fr., Knipffer, J. Ch., Louis, J.-J., Oest, J. A., Pernoux, J., Sausenhofer, D. Ch., Scheffauer, Ph. J., Schmidt, J. H., Sperl, J.-U., Steinkopf, J. F., Weber, F. J.

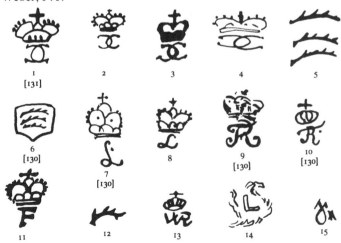

1 [131]	2	3	4	5
6 [130]	7 [130]	8	9 [130]	10 [130]
11	12	13	14	15

1–4 blue underglaze 1758–93, monogram of Duke Carl Eugen of Württemberg; marks also appear without crown – 5–6 blue underglaze, heraldic shield of Württemberg, 1770–5 – 7–8 blue underglaze, monogram of Duke Ludwig 1793–5 – 9–11 F.R. = Friedrich Rex. F. = monogram of King Friedrich. 9 and 10 red or gold, also blind-impressed. 11 black, 1806–16 – 12 blue underglaze usually 1810–16 – 13 red or gold, also impressed, W.R. = Wilhelm Rex 1816–24 – 14 Signum Jean Jacob Louis 1762–72 – 15 Signum D.C. Sausenhofer 1760–1802 – Although the factory closed in 1824, Nos. 1, 6, 7, 10 and 13 were registered again in the trademark-register of the German Reich on 13 June 1906, by the administration of His Majesty King Wilhelm II of Württemberg's private estate. A possible reason for this was to prevent further unauthorised use (see Passau)

Ludwigsburg (2) (Germany, Württemberg). Formerly Herzogliche porcelain works, Ludwigsburg, f. 1948; produce included utility and art porcelain.

marks 2–4 should all be accompanied by the signature 'Ludwigsburg'

Ludwigsburg (3) (Germany, Württemberg). Georg von Hoffmann, refinement of porcelain, glass and earthenware. Produced services, tableware, mocha-cups in Carlsbad, baroque and modern styles. Schlackenwerth has been the local factory since 1873.

Ludwigshafen (Germany, Baden). Johannes Eisele, porcelain decorating studio, c. 1930.

Ludwigstadt (Germany, Oberfranken). Ludwigstadt porcelain factory GmbH, Wiegel & Co., f. 1907. Services and luxury porcelain. This factory is now closed.

Lüftelberg, Post Meckenheim (Germany, Rhineland). Bernhard Bertram, porcelain decorating studio, c. 1930.

Luisenburg. Name of mark used as trademark No. 251851, from 4 February 1921, of P. F. Thomas, Marktredwitz.

Lunéville (France). Cwhen Cyfflé directed a porcelain factory here between 1769–80, about which there is little reliable information. However, it is known that moulds as well as recipes were sold to Niderviller, so that it is difficult to separate the work of Lunéville from that of Niderviller.

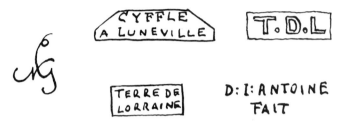

Lunn, Richard, see Derby (2).

Luplau, Anton Karl (d. 1795). From Blankenburg. From 1765–76 he worked in Fürstenberg, first as a moulder, then repairer, and finally as independant modeller. After his departure to Copenhagen he worked in the factory there as modelling master and arcanist (1776–95).

$$\mathcal{L}uplan\ fec.$$
$$1781$$

Luplau, Christian. Brother of the Fürstenberg master modeller; worked for some time as decorator in Fürstenberg and later he and his brother travelled to Copenhagen.

Lurcy-Lévy (1) (France). Burguin f. a porcelain factory here in 1819. Its method of production (pouring porcelain slip into moulds) was patented.

Lurcy-Lévy (2) (France). A porcelain factory owned by the Marquis of Sinety was here in 1819.

Luso-Espagnola de Porcelanas S.A., see Madrid (1).

Luso Espanola de Porcelanas S.A., Fabrica de Bisoda, see Irún.

Lustre glaze. In 1901, the two Professors Dr. Lincke and Dr. E. Adams, developed a lustre for easily melting glazes which was a direct result of the presence of very delicate, transparent metal laminae. In the reducing firing it is possible to obtain glass-clear tones which range from yellow and ocre through to dark brown, depending on the composition of the glaze, firing temperature and firing time.

Lutz, Robert, see Albersweiler.

Luxemburg (Luxemburg). It is claimed that in the Bloch Sept Fontaine factory here, only faiences were produced. Porcelains do exist, however, bearing the mark LB, which are decorated in a style which belongs to the Luxemburg factory and cannot be attributed to the factory which usually employed the mark.

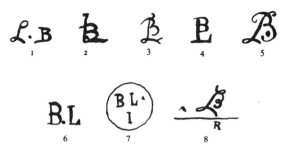

1–3 blue – 4 in different colours – 5 blue – 7 blind-stamped – 8 blue

Lyon (France). Charlionais et Panassier (Etablissements), porcelain factory.

Maas, Sigismond, see Limoges (49).
Maastricht (Holland). N. V. Porselein-en Tegelfabriek Mosa, f. 1883. Household ware and hotel porcelain. At its foundation the factory was called: Louis Regout & Zonen; later C. V. Porselein-en Muurtegelfabriek Mosa; now N. V. Porselein-en Tegelfabriek Mosa.

Mäbendorf (Germany, Saxony). Matthes & Ebel, Mäbendorfer porcelain factory.

Mabille, see Paris (95).
Macao nr. Kanton (China). The factory which was founded here in 1557 by the Portuguese, was of crucial importance to the development of the porcelain trade between China and Europe.
Macheleid, Georg Heinrich (b. 1723). From Schwarzenberg. c. 1750 he discovered, quite independently of Böttger, how to make a porcelain, which, after initial difficulties, was similar to Meissen hard paste porcelain. It was due to

him that the factory Rudolstadt-Volkstedt was founded c. 1760. See Sitzerode and Rudolstadt Volkstedt (1).

Machelein, Triebner & Co., see Volkstedt Rudolstadt (1) and (6).

Mackee, Andrew, Foley Works, see Longton (51).

Macquer, Pierre-Joseph (1718–84). Chemist, who worked intermittently as arcanist of the French State Works, and continued experiments with bone-ash in accordance with the groundwork done by Réaumurs and was the first to exploit, scientifically speaking, the kaolin sources of Limoges. In 1768 he had already presented a paper about French hard paste porcelain to the Academie.

Madelaine. Name of trademark No. 256174 from 24 November 1920 of the firm P. F. Rosenthal, Selb.

Madeley (1) (England, Shropshire). A factory was here from 1825–40 which produced soft paste porcelain. It is possible that the founder was Billingsley. T. M. Randall was in charge of the production which mainly specialised in Sèvres imitations.

Madeley (2) (England, Shropshire). Madeley Works (Thomas M. Randall), porcelain factory, 1825–40.

Madesclaire jeune, see Limoges (50).

Madrid (1) (Spain). Luso-Espagnola de Porcelanas S.A., association of several Spanish porcelain factories.

Madrid (2) (Spain). Hijos de J. Giralt Laporta, f. 1887; marks used were 'Trebol' and 'Valma'.

Madrid, see also Buen Retiro and La Moncloa.

Maennedorf (Switzerland). The factory owner, J. J. Hardmeier is said to have produced porcelain here c. 1967.

Maffersdorf (Bohemia). Eduard Stiassny, porcelain factory, f. 1896. Powder boxes, bonbonnieres, apothecary vessels.

Magdeburg-Buckau(Germany, Prussia). Buckaauer porcelain works AG, f. 1823. Utility and hotel porcelain. This factory has now closed.

1   BPM   BPM
             2   3

Magdeburg-Neustadt (1) (Germany, Prussia). F. Mesch & Co., porcelain decorating studio, c. 1930.

Magdeburg-Neustadt (2) (Germany, Prussia). Reps & Tinte, porcelain decorating studio, c. 1930.

Magnac-Bourg (France). A porcelain firm, f. by Gauldré-Boileau existed here from 1824–60: Desgouttières, Thomas and Moussnier. The sculptor Lefèvre is mentioned. He usually signed his works with his personal device.

Magnus, Johann Bernhard (d. 1798). A Frankenthal decorator who was known as master of 'multi-coloured children, figures inspired by Ovid and Watteau, landscapes on services, vases and boxes'.

Mahler and Weber, see Villingen.

Maier & Comp., see Poschetzau.

Maisel, L., see Tettau (1).

Maisons Alfort (France). Charles Levy f. a porcelain factory in Charenton in 1875, which was moved here by Henry Levy in 1881. Produced biscuit and painted statuettes after models by Gille, Vion, Baury, Sluizer, Letu, Manger and Jacob Petit. According to 'Tardy 75' only the mark of the above mentioned Baury is well known.

Malzeff, see Pesotschnaja.

Mandarin-porcelain. Purely a trading description, referring to the decoration of export porcelain of the 18th c. with elegant Chinese costume figures, which were thought to be Mandarins. This name was also used to increase the value of this ware in the eyes of the European customers, since it implied that these pieces were made exclusively for the Mandarins. The form and decoration of this type of porcelain was subjected to European influence.

Manifattura di Signa. see Florence (2).

Manises (1) Valencia (Spain). Cerámicas Hispania S.L., Fabrica de Loza y Porcelana, f. 1941. Art objects and utility ware and majolica.

Manises (2) Valencia (Spain). Fábrica de Cerámica Decorativa Jesus J. Escobar Folgado, f. 1909. Artistic porcelain and ceramic. The factory is called 'La Espanola'.

Manka, Franz, see Altrohlau (7).
Mann & Co., see Hanley (9).
Mann & Porzelius AG, see Unterweissbach.
Mannheim (1) (Germany). Rheinische porcelain factory, Mannheim GmbH, f. c. 1900. Utility ware of all kinds. This factory no longer exists. Some of the models from the Frankenthal porcelain factory (which was closed in 1800 by the Elector Maximilian IV) came into the possession of this factory in the early 20th c. They were used immediately and the copies sold as fakes with the C.T. (Carl Theodor) mark. However, the Mannheimer Altertumsverein succeeded in buying these models from the Rheinische factory.

[151]   [98]

Mannheim (2) (Germany). M. Sterner, porcelain works, had the following mark registered on 9 December 1896 under the No. 20946 as trademark. Porcelain and stoneware.

[74]

Mannheim (3) (Germany). Fritz Bensinger GmbH, porcelain decorating studio, c. 1930.

Mannl, W., see Krummenaab (3).
Mansard, see Paris (96).
Manteau, see Paris (97).
Manthey, I. G. Ludwig, see Copenhagen (1).
Manufactura Nationalá de Portelan, Turda, S.A.R., see Klausenburg (2).
Manufacturas Cerámicas, S.A., see Barcelona (1).
Manufacture du Duc'd'Angoulême, see Paris (41).
Manufacture de Madame la Duchesse d'Angoulême, Dagoty E. Honoré Paris, see Paris (71).
Manufacture D.S.M. L'Empératrice, P. L. Dagoty à Paris, see Paris (30).
Manufacture de Fleurs en Porcelaine Fernand Stoefs, see Brussels (6).
Manufacture de Montplaisir, see Brussels (1).
Manufacture de Porcelain de Berlin, see Berlin (1).
Manufacture de Porcelaine Marcel Guillard, see Asnières.
Manufacture de Porcelaines Artistiques Fontanille & Marroud, see Limoges (50).
Manufacture de Porcelaines Anc. Etts Avignon, see Bruère-Allichamps.
Manufacture de Porcelaines de Chatres sur Cher, see Chatres sur Cher.
Manufacture de Porcelaines Robert Haviland & C. Parlon, see Limoges (51).
Manufacture de Porcelaines A. Lanternier & Cie., see Limoges (52).
Manufacture de Porcelaines A. Vignaud, see Limoges (53).
Manufacture du Prince de Galles, see Paris (120).
Manufacture de la Reine, see Paris (84).
Manufacture Royale de Monseigneur le Dauphin, see Lille (2).
Manufacture Royale de la Porcelaine de France, see Vincennes (1).
Manufacture Royale de porcelayne d'Orléans, see Orléans (1).
Manufactures de Faiences du Moulin des Loups, see Saint-Amand-les-Eaux (2).
Marburg (Germany, Hessia). Ludwig Schneider, generally assumed to be a porcelain decorating studio, c. 1924.

Marc-Lozelet, see Vendrennes.
Marcolini, Camillo Graf (1739 Fano (Kirchenstaat)–1814 Prag). He was the chief director (from 1774–1814, the Marcolini-period) of the Meissen factory. His actions were motivated solely by a wish to prevent the collapse of the factory, but owing to the competition of other porcelain and stoneware factories, and the difficulties caused by the war years, the decline of the factory was inevitable.
Marco Polo (1254–1323). He gave a comparatively accurate description of the making of Chinese porcelain in one of his travel accounts of the 13th c.

Marelli & Cie., see Villedieu-sur-Indre (2).
Marga Porcellana (porcelain clay), see Kaolin.
Margarethenhütte nr. Bautzen (Germany, Saxony). Branch of the H.
Schomburg porcelain factory, Moabit nr. Berlin, which produced domestic
porcelain ware (mainly electro porcelain) until 1894.

Maria. Name of the mark used as trademark No. 259852 from 4 February 1921
of the P. F. Rosenthal, Selb.
Maria Theresia, Empress, see Tournay.
Mariaschein (Bohemia). Schneider Brothers, porcelain and faience factory, f.
1889 in Probstau. Flowers and luxury objects.

Marie Antoinette, Queen of France, see Paris (83).
Marieberg (Sweden). A faience factory existed here from 1758 and provided a
small department for porcelain production under the direction of Pierre
Berthevin. Between 1766–9, he produced frit porcelain in the manner of
Mennecy. Under the direction of Stein, the porcelain was very white and well-
glazed but not particularly transparent; it was, however, very brittle. These
pieces were marked with MB, or with three pointed crowns with the initials (see
marks 1 and 2). True hard porcelain was perhaps only produced during the time
when Jakob Dortu worked in Marieberg (between 1777–8). The decorations
were carefully executed, often in monochrome. Despite a distinct originality, the
influence of Copenhagen is clearly evident.
See also: Buchwald, J., Fleurot, F., Franzen, H.

1 below Berthevin M.B. = Marieberg not Marieberg Berthevin – 2–4 below Stein Dortu –
3–4 heraldic arms of the Wasa – 4 red, three dots in blue

Markoff, see Konjaschino.
Marktleuthen (1) (Germany, Bavaria). Drechsel & Strobel registered the first
mark illustrated as trademark No. 34281 on 21 September 1898. In August 1900
they registered the second mark under No. 45675 as a trademark. Produced
porcelain wares.

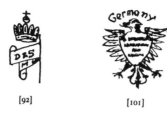

[92]   [101]

Marktleuthen (2) (Germany, Bavaria). Heinrich Winterling, porcelain factory, f. 1903. Table, coffee and tea services, mocha coffee cups and gift items.

Marktredwitz (1) (Germany, Bavaria). Kerafina GmbH, porcelain factory. Gift articles.

Marktredwitz (2) (Germany, Bavaria). Marktredwitz Jaeger & Co. porcelain factory, f. 1872. Table, coffee, tea services, gift articles.

[90]   [183]

the last mark illustrated appears with the title 'Queen Louise' RWZR No. (169)

Marktredwitz (3) (Germany, Bavaria). Franz Neukirchner, porcelain works, f. 1916. Travel souvenirs, hotel and domestic porcelain ware, gift items.

the last mark illustrated also appears without FN and without GERMANY

Marktredwitz (4) (Germany, Bavaria). F. Thomas porcelain factory, f. 1903. Gift articles were a particular speciality: hunting and fish services were also popular and porcelains for chemical uses were produced. This factory has been incorporated in the Rosenthal-Porzellan Aktiengesellschaft, Selb since 1908.

[119]   [146]

the last mark illustrated also appears without Thomas and without Bavaria

Marktschwaben (Germany, Upper Bavaria). Keramische Fabrik München-Schwaben AG. Porcelain of all kinds, practical and decorative. This concern no longer exists.

Marre de Villiers, Honoré de la, see Paris (98).
Marsaille, Armand, see Köppelsdorf (3).
Marseille (1). There is evidence that all faiences factories in Marseilles were endeavouring to produce porcelain as well. Joseph-Gaspard Robert alone succeeded, in 1777, with the help of the Berlin arcanist Jacob Dortu (who later worked in Marieberg and Nyon), but the results of his porcelain production were not significant. The products remained very similar to faience, and the factory closed down in 1793.

$$\dot{R} \quad R \quad \dot{R} \quad \overline{R} \quad \mathcal{R}$$

Marseille (2) (France). J. B. Pons & Cie. porcelain works. Utility ware. This concern no longer exists.
Marseille (3). Cushion mentions yet another porcelain factory here: Bonnefoy's factory, which was active from 1762–1827 and produced porcelain from 1803. At about the same time there was an artist of the same name working in Chantilly.

$$\mathbf{B} \quad B$$

Marseille Pattern. Form of decoration used on Meissen services in 1739, consisting of incised divisions of the rim, making six sections. Between each of these incisions is an arrangement of a large arch between two smaller ones, and three rococo cartouches in light relief which spread on to the centre of the plate. This design has its origin in a Marseilles pattern.

Marsault, Louis-Athanase, see Sceaux.
Martin, see Saint-Genou (1).
Martin, Charles, see Limoges (54).
Martin, François (d. 1786), see Alcora.
Martin, Brothers, see Lubau.
Martinroda (Germany, Thuringia). Martinroda, Eger & Co. porcelain factory,
f. 1901. Souvenir articles, useful and fancy porcelain in cobalt overglaze
decoration. At present (1977) known as: VEB Porzellanwerk Martinroda.

Marzall, see Damm.
Marzolf & Cie., see Montreuil (1).
Mascaron. Masks or grotesque sculptured ornaments which were popular in
the rococo period. The identical decoration was also applied to porcelain.
Mason, Holt & Co., Dresden Works, see Longton (52).
Massé et Surget, see Mehun-sur-Yèvre (3).
Massey, Wildblood & Co., see Longton (86).
Massié, André, see Limoges (31).
'*Masso bastardo*', see Doccia.
Masson et Auriac, see Montreuil (2).
Mathieu, Jean Adam. Royal Court Enameler. At the f. of the Vincennes
porcelain factory in 1745, he was appointed as the first manager of the
decorating department.
Matthäi, Johann Gottlieb (1753–1832). During the time of Acier, was the most
successful exponent of the ever flourishing neo-classical development. He was
active in Meissen from 1773 and in 1776 he worked for one year in Copenhagen
after which he returned to the KPM. Matthäi, Jüchtzer and Schönheit, were the
three successors of Acier.
Matthes & Ebel, see Mäbendorf.
Maubrée, Joseph, see Paris (120).
Mauge & Pézé. see Paris (99).
Mauger, see Villenauxe (1).
Mauksch, Johann Karl (d. 1821). Arrived at Meissen when Dietrich was
director, as a painter of landscapes and battle scenes.

Maurel, Chapeau, Charles & Veyrier, see Limoges (84).
Maurer, C., repairer, see Nyon.
Maurer, J. G. decorator, see Nyon.
Mavaleix & Co., Limoges (55).
Max III, Joseph (1727–77), Elector of Bavaria, see Nymphenburg.
Mayer Bros., owner Ernst Mayer, see Wiesau (2).

Mayer, Franz Ferdinand. Private decorator in Pressnitz, where he painted mostly on early Meissen porcelain with genre-scenes of all kinds, perhaps between 1745–70. He appears to have managed a large workshop. It is possible that he was the originator of the particularly rich, gold calligraphic ornamentations on Meissen porcelain which were executed outside the factory.

Mayer, Jean-Ghislain-Joseph (1754–1825). Porcelain and faience decorator in Tournay. Private decorator from 1774–1815. His brother, Adrien-Dominique-Joseph Mayer and his son J.-A. Mayer were also painters. Claims have been made that all three of the Mayer family decorated porcelain with wood graining.

J. Mayer

Mayer, Stephan and Son, see Amberg.
Mayer & Newbold, see Lane End (2).
Mayer & Sherratt, see Longton (53).
Mayerhofer von Grünhübel, Karl Franz Xavier. Director of the Vienna factory, 1744–52.
Mazarin blue. Ground blue colour of the Chelsea porcelain factory, the colour which invoked envy all over Europe.
Mazeaud, see Sèvres (2).
Mazurin, see Paris (100).
Mecklenburg Strelitz Service. A porcelain service from Chelsea in the 'gold-anchor-period' which had been made in 1763 for George III and Queen Sophie Charlotte, to be presented to the Queen's brother, the Duke of Mecklenburg Strelitz. Now deposited in Windsor Castle. The decoration consists mainly of exotic birds and flower paintings in 'mazarin blue' and the rims are gilded. There are copies of this service in Berlin, Hamburg and in the Victoria and Albert Museum.
Mecklenburg-S.. ɛiitz, Karl, Herzog von, see Chelsea (1).
Medallion or Peking bowls. Small bowls of Chinese porcelain of the Qianlong Period, on which the decoration consists mostly of four reserved medallions, painted with landscapes or flowers.
Medici, Francesco Maria I, Ferdinando I, Cosimo II, Grand Dukes of Tuscany, see Florence (1).
Medici porcelain, see Florence (1).
Meeheim, see Potsdam.
Mehlem, Franz Anton, see Bonn (1).
Mehlhorn, Johann Georg (d. 1735). Worked under Böttger at the Meissen

factory. In 1720 he improved the body of the porcelain; in the same year his son
was a decorator in the factory.

Mehlhorn, Johann Georg (son of Johann Georg), decorator in blue enamel. See
Copenhagen (1).

Mehner brothers, see Eulau.

Mehun-sur-Yèvre (1) (France). Baron brothers porcelain decorating studio, f.
1942. The following mark was registered, according to 'Tardy 75', in 1948.

Mehun-sur-Yèvre (2) (France). Albert Blot Cie., porcelain factory. Household
ware.

La Mehunite

Mehun-sur-Yèvre (3) (France). Massé et Surget, porcelain factory. Table,
coffee and tea services.

Mehun-sur-Yèvre (4) (France). Pigois & Jaquet, porcelain factory. Hotel and
catering porcelain ware and crockery.

Mehun-sur-Yèvre (5) (France). Pillivuyt et Cie., la Porcelaine de France, f.
1853. Fireproof porcelain and hotel ware.

Meierhöfen (1) (Bohemia. now Dvory). Britannia Porcelain Works, Moser
Brothers, f. 1890; formerly Eberhard & Co. Utility and luxury porcelain. The

second mark was entered in Eger (on 9 March 1898) under the No. 591, for notification in the Zentralmarkenanzeiger, Vienna.

Meierhöfen (2) (Bohemia, now Dvory). The Benedikt brothers f. a factory here in 1883, which made white and decorated porcelain. In 1918 the Britannia Porcelain Works, Moser Brothers (f. 1890 or 1898 in the same locality), was acquired. From this time on the factory was named: 'Vereinigte Porzellan-Fabrik Meierhöfen, vorm. Gebr. Benedikt'. Useful and luxury porcelain. In 1918 it was absorbed by the EPIAG. The factory burnt down several times which explains the colloquialism of the name: 'Brennedikt'.

Meissen (1) (Germany, Saxony). The first German porcelain factory was f. on 23 January 1710 in Dresden by Royal decree, as a result of the work of Friedrich Wilhelm Böttger, and named the Kursächsische Manufactur. The first factory was housed in the Laboratory on the Venusbastei which was suitably equipped for experiments in transmutting base metals into gold and for porcelain. A short time later it was found to be inadequate for the red stoneware production (Böttger Stoneware) which was also carried on, and for this reason the Wettiner Castle, in the Albrechtsburg nr. Meissen, became the new workshop by Royal decree of 7 March 1710. The management consisted of a board of directors. The organisation of the workshop was left to Böttger himself, while the technical direction was assigned to the two arcanists, Nehmitz and Barthelmi. In the first years of the Böttger period (1710–19), the works was mainly concerned with the production of red stoneware, which was decorated by Bohemian glass cutters, although polishing, lacquering and gilding were also used. From 1713 the production of true porcelain superseded the making of stoneware. The colour of the porcelain body at that time was still fairly yellowish. In the early period, 1713–20, Böttger's lack of organisation resulted in several crises for the young factory. Only after the death of Böttger on 13 March 1719, and the appointment of Steinbrücks as administrator, did the spectacular rise of Meissen begin. The appointment of the Viennese decorator Johann Gregor Höroldt, proved to be particularly successful. By this time the porcelain paste was of an outstanding pure whiteness. Höroldt, who is reputed to be the greatest colour technician of the 18th c., achieved the truest luminosity in the Böttger colours. In 1725 he discovered new ground colours. During his time at Meissen European colour decoration came to its first splendid realisation. The decorators Heintze, Horn and Christian Friedrich Höroldt, and the modeller I. G. Kirchner (from 1727 onwards), worked under Höroldt. The Höroldt period lasted from 1719–31. From then on the concern was directed by a treasury board, under the presidency of the King, August the Strong, who retained this position to the time of his death in 1733. His successor, August III, appointed his Cabinet Minister, the Count of Brühl to this position. He exerted a decisive influence, in artistic as well as in commercial considerations. When in 1731 the sculptor Johann Friedrich Kändler was engaged, the emphasis in production moved slowly to the plastic execution of porcelain. Kändler, the creator of the European porcelain figure production, set the pattern for the plastic style of Meissen up to the present day. The decorations of the Höroldt-Kändler period (Plastic Period), which is thought to be from 1731–63, present us with creations in the style of the French rococo painters, battle and hunting scenes after Ridinger and others. The 'Deutsche Blumen' are another creation of this period. From 1740 the 'Zwiebelmuster' (onion-pattern) was used in the underglaze blue decoration which has retained its fame to the present. The renowned sculptors Johann Friedrich Eberlein and Friedrich Elias Meyer worked alongside Kändler at this time. In the final years of the 'plastic' period mounting difficulties can be seen in the growing number of competitive factories and in the disastrous effects of both the Second Silesian War and the Seven Years War. In fact, from this time on the factory was run at an annual deficit of c. 50,000 Talers. During the period 1763–74, Meissen porcelain was marked with the crossed palatine swords, with a dot between the cross pieces. Consequently this period is known as the dot period. It began with a reorganisation, in the course of which an art school was set up within the factory. In 1764 the French sculptor, Michael Victor Acier was placed on an equal footing with Kändler, which may have been the cause of Kändler's dismissal in 1765. Under Acier, the transition from Baroque to the style of Louis XVI was swiftly accomplished. From 20 August 1774 the direction of the factory passed into the hands of Count Camillo Marcolini, the favourite of King Friedrich August III since 1768. His reforms created only a temporary easing of the general economic situation; and when Acier relinquished the artistic management the decline could be postponed no longer. Marcolini requested his retirement in 1799, but it was only granted to him in 1814. The factory's debts at that time had increased to over 410,000 Taler. Pieces from the Marcolini period (1774–1813) are marked with a six-pointed star which is placed between the cross pieces of the swords. Acier's successors, the sculptors Schönheit, Jüchtzer and Matthäi, launched the figure production into the period of Neo-classicism. The rocaille-forms now turn into more undefined curves. White relief decoration is found on pastel coloured ground, and portraits and copper engravings in the English taste were introduced. In the period which follows (1814–33), the Napoleonic Wars worsened the financial crisis. In 1815 King Friedrich August set up a commission to attempt to improve the by now outdated artistic, technical and administrative methods, but the results were insignificant. Some Wedgwood copies result from this period as well as pieces which were produced with the use of moulds devised for pressed glass. In 1827

Kühn invented the gold foil technique. Copper engravings were used for underglaze decorations, from 1814 until the 1870s. From 1817 chrome green was increasingly used; the 'Weinkranz muster' painted in this green is popular even today. From 1833–70 the director of the factory was Heinrich Gottlieb Kühn. In 1833 he wrote about 'a new technical innovation in the form of a decoration, in the Old German-Greek style and "en bas relief", which is to take advantage of the unique gilding method of the Royal Works as well as the increasing application of paintings'. Copies of famous paintings in the Dresden galleries were at that time very popular. Iridescent colours, 'Schillerfarben' Kühn's discovery, were used from 1852. In figure production the style of earlier models was adopted. In 1870–94, under Raithel's direction, blue underglaze decoration flourished once more. Export to America began in 1878 and increased steadily from then on. New buildings were put up and modern interiors created. Successful experiments led to the following: production of thin-bodied porcelain ('muslin porcelain'); a wider choice of high temperature colours for enamels; and perfection of the 'pâte sur pâte', technique which had been introduced in 1874 at the Sèvres porcelain factory. This last was achieved at Meissen in 1878 by the work of Dr. Julius Heintze. Brunnemann directed the factory from 1895–1901. Meissen left it rather late before deciding to work in the style of the turn of the century. Art Nouveau pieces are therefore comparatively rare, but the figures that do exist are in a clear naturalistic style. In the years after the First World War Meissen made no attempt to produce pieces in the style of the New Sachlichkeit; instead the production of this period was limited almost exclusively to the forms of the famous services of the 18th c. Only the figure production presented innovative work, amongst which the work of Paul Scheurich deserves the highest praise. In 1921, Prof. Paul Boerner of the Staatlichen porcelain works, Meissen, began the production of monumental porcelain figures, for the decoration of the Nikolaikirche in the Stadtpark of Meissen and the war memorial to the Dead of the First World War. These works were completed in 1928. Prof. Boerner also cast small bells. This factory is now the oldest European porcelain works still in existence and its mark is: Staatl. Porzellanmanufaktur Meissen VEB.

Chronological chart:

Böttger period (1710–19).

Höroldt period (painterly period) (1719–31).

Höroldt-Kändler'sche period (figure period) (1731–63).

Dot period (1763–74).

Marcolini period (1774–1814).

See also: Adam, E., Adelmann, Ch., Borrmann, J. B., Bottengruber, I., Brecheisen, J., Busch, Ch. D., Erbsmehl, J. G., Ferner, F. J., Fritsche, G., Gerlach, K., Grossmann, Ch. G., Heinrici, H. M., Hendler, P., Hunger, Ch. C., Klipfel, K. J. Ch., Köhler, D., Kretschmar, J., Kühnel, Ch. Fr., Loehning, J. G., Löwenfinck, A. F., Löwenfinck, Ch. W. von, Löwenfinck, K. H. von, Lück, J. F., Lücke, J. Ch. L., Mauksch, J. K., Mehlhorn, J. G., Punct, K. Ch., Reinicke, P., Richter, Ch. S. H., Riedel, G. F., Schäffler, J. Ch., Schenau (Schönau), J. E., Schlimper, J. G., Schubert, J. D., Stadler, J. E., Stölzel, S., Teichert, F. F.,

Wagner, J. J., Wegner, A. F., Zeissig, J. E.
Some background knowledge is useful when studying the Meissen marks. The custom of marking with many swords placed side by side, and of dating with great precision, which has been practised for many decades, has now, finally, come to an end. In *Meissen Porzellan* (1973), by Walcha, he concludes, 'The unsteadiness of the line drawings illustrates the fact that "swording" had been relegated to the youngest and most unskilled apprentices'. Now it is known that the practice of 'swording' was intended to give the apprentices to the blue decorators (those working in the onion pattern for example), the opportunity to gain a firm brush stroke. We know that the sword marks on white porcelain (that which was decorated after the high firing) which, of course, are under the glaze, were put on by the workers in charge of the glazing. Accordingly, the following guideline, from a publication, *Meissen 1975,* should be borne in mind: 'The trademark (cobalt blue), is to be applied by hand. Its form is entirely dependent on the hand of the individual decorator, and therefore embraces changes in form and colour tone'. More explicit guidelines are concerned with marks added to the swords. However, it is not certain that a dot always appeared in the so-called 'dot period' 1763–73, or that use of the dot was confined to these years (some were used as early as 1756). Its significance is unknown. The same applies to the star used in the Marcolini mark (1774–1814). Many pieces do not show the star. Walcha says simply: 'The whole of the 18th and the first quarter of the 19th c. made use of the swords in a steep, dagger-like curved form, with the points of the crossing blades at a high level. The hilts are frequently much emphasised right into the 1860s.' One can safely deduce from this that many kinds of variations were possible within this enormous span of time.

Meissen model numbers of the figure production:

1744   Kändler initiated the organisation of the moulds.
       The registration was entrusted to his brother, Christian Heinrich Kändler (1711–66). The increase in the number of different forms soon demanded a system of running numbers.

1763   This office was given to the newly appointed controller of models, Joh. Jac. Petri. How far Ch. H. Kändler had progressed in the registration is not known. Neither does one know whether Petri continued where Ch. H. Kändler left off as was intended, or whether he worked over the previous dates.

1764   (19 July), having numbered consecutively to No. 3051, it was decided to begin at 1 again with an additional letter as a prefix (i.e. A1).

up to 1774   A1–100, B1–100, etc., up to E60.

up to 1813   E61–M100.

up to 1833   N1–T183 (T101–T183) were later used once again for other porcelain.

up to 1870   Ua–Y57 and A101–200, B101–200, etc., up to H181.

after 1870   The number system no longer continued chronologically. Various old numbers were discarded for aesthetic reasons and so that they could be re-used for new porcelain.

from 1973   Five digit numbers impressed, incised or stamped in green
             underglaze.

Supposing that model No. 1 had in fact been made in 1731, and given that No.
3051 had been reached by 19 July 1764, it stands to reason that subsequent
numbers were assigned at a later date. They could only have been given to pieces
which were made from moulds which remained in stock after 1764, and were
thus available for numbering. Only in the case of models made after July 1764
may the date of their production coincide with the initial casting date.

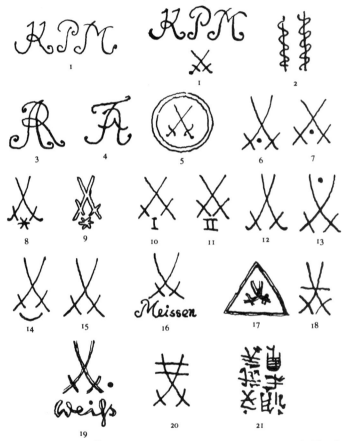

1 1722–5 – 2 1722–80 the Äsculap stave in combination with the AR mark. The significance
is still obscure, possibly for Turkish exports until 1780 – 3 1725–40 Augustus ·Rex
Monogram – 4 1733 (from 1 February 1733 – 5 October 1733) Friedrich August's
Monogram before he had been crowned as King of Poland. Rarely decipherable
(according to Walcha) – 5 1725–32 also without ring – 6–7 dot mark 1763–73, although it
appears as early as 1756 according to Walcha (dot has unknown significance) – 8
Marcolini mark 1774–1814 – 9 1774 blindstamp of the Marcolini mark for biscuit – 10
1814–15 special mark for shards of pastes of individual composition (according to
'Meissen 75') – 11 as 10, from 1820 – 12 the whole of the 19th and first quarter of the 20th c.,
with emphasised hilts until 1860 (according to Walcha) – 13 1924–34 under the direction of

Pfeiffer – 14 1945–7 – 15 1947–73 also 1935–45 – 16 since 1974 – 17 after 1814 blindstamp for biscuit (according to 'Meissen 75') – 18 until 1850 brush stroke across the point where the swords cross for white porcelain of all qualities (according to 'Meissen 75') – 19 blindstamp for white porcelain from the beginning of the 20th c. – 20 from 16 November 1850 two brush strokes, at first only for decorative porcelain, later as a mark to indicate imperfections of which the customer may be unaware but which exist nevertheless – 21 1780–1830 pseudo-Chinese marks for exports to Turkey – All in blue underglaze, with the exceptions of 17 and 19. The marks cannot be reproduced in their actual sizes. The following additional marks have not been considered: decorators, modellers, casters, turners, property or inventory marks.

The Meissen marks Nos. 1, 2, 5, 6, 7, 8, 11 were entered into the AMA at the K.K. Patentamt Vienna as early as 15 November 1876. The A.R. mark however, was only registered on 26 November 1892

Among the marks which were registered with the trademark offices were those of the KPM Meissen (from 20 May 1875), see Nos. 1 and 2 below, which have not been used at all – A doll's head with the sword mark in overglaze pink, and made in 1825, fetched $650 at an auction in New York in 1973 (mark No. 3)

1
[4]

2
[4]

3

Meissen (2) (Germany, Saxony). Oven and porcelain factory, formerly Teichert, f. 1864. Produced porcelain utility ware with Meissen onion pattern. The Staatliche Porcelain Works Meissen granted a licence to the firm of Teichert in the beginning of this century to use the forms and decorations of the famous onion pattern. Teichert stopped their porcelain production in 1930. Their executive rights, as well as the original models for the 'Blue Onion Pattern Service' passed in April 1930 to the Lorenz Hutschenreuther porcelain factory AG in Selb.

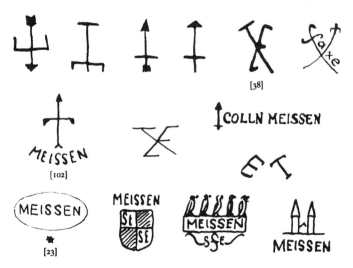

[38]

COLLN MEISSEN

MEISSEN
[102]

MEISSEN
[23]

MEISSEN

MEISSEN

MEISSEN

Meissen (3) (Germany, Saxony). Keramische Werkstätte Arthur Rohleder & Son, f. 1934. Style: Old Meissen and modern. Still active in 1949.

Meissen (4) (Germany, Saxony). Saxony Porcelain Works. Nothing is known about its dates. 'Tardy 75' remarks 'Marque en imitation moderne de vieux Saxe'. This mark occurs frequently.

Meissen (5) (Germany, Saxony). L. Schleich. decorating studio. The meaning of the term 'Buschbad' which appears in Graesse applied to the products of this period, is still unknown. There is no locality with this name. According to Lange, Meissen 1911, the town of Meissen was raised to the status of a Spa in 1797, through the establishment of a mineral watering place, the 'Buschbad'. This may suggest that the decorating studio was an early one.

Meissen (6) (Germany, Saxony). VVB-Keramik, porcelain factory, f. 1948. Porcelain utility ware, gift articles and decorative items.
Meissen Burg Porzellan GmbH, see Lenglern.
Mejigorje nr. Kiev, see Kiev (2).
Melchior, Johann Peter (1742–1825). From Lintorf nr. Düsseldorf. He was apprenticed to sculptors in Düsseldorf and in Aachen. His journeying led him to Lüttich, Döln and Koblenz. He settled in Mainz. There is no proof that he stayed in Paris, but his knowledge of French art of the period is remarkable. In 1767 he became master modeller of the Höchst porcelain factory. Melchior is regarded as the foremost master of this factory and raised the artistic level to a considerable height. In 1770 he was appointed to the post of 'Court sculptor to the Elector of Mainz'. In 1779 Melchior moved to Frankenthal where he worked as master modeller in the porcelain factory until 1793. From 1797, until he was pensioned off in 1822, Melchior was active, as master modeller and inspector in Nymphenburg. His Nymphenburg work was in the neo-classical style. His main works here were small portrait reliefs and busts, which were generally made in biscuit. In 1784 he published *On the visible and the sublime in Art.*

Joan Petr
Melchior F

II 7 6 8

Mell, Oscar, see Gräfenroda (4).
Menard, see Paris (26).
Mengersgereuth nr. Sonneberg (Germany, Thuringia). Mengersgereuth-Sonneberg S. C. Craemer & Héron porcelain factory, f. 1909. Fancy goods, cups. This factory is no longer active.
Menissier et Galatry, see Saint-Pierre-le-Moutier.

Mennecy-Villeroy (France). In 1734 François Barbin f. a ceramic factory in the Rue de Charonne, where he obviously experimented with porcelain making. In 1748 he applied for a licence to produce porcelain, which was not granted. Soon after, the Duke of Villeroy granted permission to Barbin to build a factory on his estate. Jean Baptiste Barbin succeeded his father in 1750 and ran the factory until 1765. His successors were Joseph Jullien and Symphorien Jacques. The small statuettes from the first period, characterised by a charming simplicity, later became more refined. The biscuit products are finely modelled, yet they cannot compete with Sèvres in surface quality. Apart from these, the production included flowers and multi-coloured table and toilet services. Utility ware is more rare.
See also Bourg-la-Reine (1).

1 in different colours – 2 red – 3–4 blindstamp

Menzel & Co., see Aich.
Menzl, Jos. Te., see Jokes-Wickwitz.
Mérault (the Younger), see Korzec.
Meretitz nr. Klösterle (Bohemia). Christian and Franz Vernier, probably descendants of Karl Vernier, director at Klösterle (f. 1794), from 1848, f. a porcelain factory and decorating studio here in 1901. Porcelain ware with lead free glaze. The marks have not yet been traced.

Merkelsgrün (1) (Bohemia). Karlsbader Kaolin-Industry-Gesellschaft, Vienna, f. 1881, with a ceramic-school. The porcelain factory had already been f. in 1870 by Alfred and Malvine Becher, but after successive ownerships it passed to the Zettlitzer Kaolin Werke AG as late as 1912. Until 1926 the production was solely utility ware but after that it switched to electro porcelain. The letter heading dated 15 October 1918 shows the size of the undertaking:

> Zettlitzer Kaolin Werke – AG
> Abteilung: Porzellanfabrik Merkelsgrün
> Kaolin and Kohlengruben, Kaolinschlämmereien (Kaolin and coalmines, kaolin processing)
> Zettlitz und anschliessende Umgebung (Zettlitz and surrounding areas), Altrohau, Dallwitz, Fischern, Ottowitz, Schlackau, Sodau, Wickwitz.

Productions: Isolators and isolator accessories, utility ware in hard paste porcelain.

Merkelsgrün (2) (Bohemia). It is assumed that at the end of the 19th c. a small porcelain factory was active here which may have been directed by Bruder & Schwab. According to latest research, porcelain produced by the F. Becher & Stark factory, was already being exhibited in 1871. Which of these two factories used the mark, B&S, remains uncertain.

$$B\&S$$
$$M$$

Merkur porcelain factory, see Bronnitzki.
Merlin-Lemas, see Limoges (56).
Mesch & Co., see Magdeburg-Neustadt (1).
Meslier, see Paris (101).
Metallic lustre. Produced by adding carbolic acid to gold, silver, platinum, or bronze.
Metzel Bros., (now belonging to the SAG Hescho/Hermsdorf), see Könitz.
Metzer & Ortloff Bros., see Ilmenau (5).
Metzsch (also Metsch), Johann Friedrich (d. 1766). Independent decorator in Bayreuth 1735–51, where he painted on Chinese, Viennese and early Meissen porcelain.

F. M.
Bäyreuth
1744
n· 24

Metzsch.
· 1·49.
Sbye

Metzsch.
· 1748
Bayr.

Metzsch Bros., Selb, see Plate drying installation.

Meuselwitz (Germany, Thuringia). Hentscheil & Müller, porcelain factory, c.1910. Owned by the Kloster Veilsdorf porcelain factory in 1930.

Meyer, Arcanist, see Kloster Veilsdorf.

Meyer, Elias (Danish). Apprenticed in Dresden, active in Copenhagen as flower and landscape decorator from 1785–1809. A member of the Dresden Academie.

Meyer, François, director in Sèvres, see Sèvres (1).

Meyer, Friedrich Elias (1723–85). Sculptor. In 1732, in Gotha, he became a pupil of the Court sculptor Grünebek and worked at various Ducal Courts until 1748. From 1748–61 he was Kändler's assistant in Meissen. He did not have a happy relationship with him and must have been grateful for the chance to work in the Gotzkowsky porcelain factory, after Kändler declined the position in Berlin.

Meyer, Moise, see Paris (112).

Meyer, M. Von. Active as designer in Copenhagen from 1784–92.

Meyer, Siegm. Paul. The earliest porcelain factory in Bayreuth, 'Walküre', see Bayreuth (2).

Meyer, Wilhelm Christian (1726–86). Sculptor. Pupil of his brother, Friedrich Elias Meyer, he later continued his education in Leipzig, Berlin and Halle. He was appointed to Düsseldorf in 1757, and later moved to Bonn. In 1766 his activity in the Berlin factory began. He had a considerable influence upon his brother Friedrich Elias Meyer, the master modeller of the factory. In 1783 he became a member of the Royal Academy of Arts, and in 1786 was appointed Chancellor. His best known works are eight groups which were transferred from the Berliner Opernbrücke to the Leipziger Platz in 1824.

Meyers & Son, see Dresden (22).

Meyze, see Solignac.

Mezer, Michel (d. c. 1825), see Baranowka, Korzec and Tomaszow.

Miautre, Raynand & Cie., see Limoges (57).

Michel, David, see Paris (102).

Michel, see Paris (103).

Middlesborough (England). In 1880 J. Wilson & Co. managed a ceramic factory here which had been f. in 1831. It also produced porcelain. The services are interesting because of the decorated edges, and the landscapes in blue transfer-painting.

Mignon, see Paris (104).

'Miklaschevsky', see Kiev (1).

MIDDLESBRO
POTTERY CO.

Milan (1) (Italy). A. Boni & Co., produced porcelain here c. 1850.
Milan (2) (Italy), Ceramica Briantea, f. 1947. Utility ware.

Milan (3) (Italy). Luigi Fabris porcelain factory. Porcelain figures. This concern has closed down.
Milan (4) (Italy). Societa Ceramica di Bollate, Anon., f. 1919. Hotel ware.

Milan- San Cristoforo (Italy). Luigi Tinelli f. a factory here in 1833, which made porcelain and faience ware. Wedgwood pieces were copied, but signed with their own mark. Carlo Tinelli took over the factory from his brother and went into partnership with Giulio Richard from Turin (an experienced ceramist) in 1841. Richard became the sole owner in 1870 and in 1873 renamed the factory 'Societá Ceramica Richard'. In 1887 he bought two other ceramic factories from Palme in Pisa: St. Marta and St. Michele, but he did not produce any porcelain there. The St. Michele factory is still active and produces, as it has always done, earthenwares with brilliant glazes. In 1896 the amalgamation with Ginori of Doccia took place *(q.v.)*.

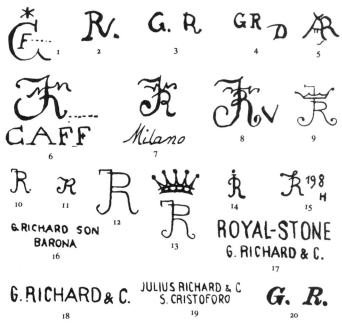

ITALY
New Stone
G. RICHARD & C.

21

RICHARD
24

SCR
25

S.C. RICHARD
31

1	1830–3	16	1847	23	1875–85
2–4	1842	17	1870–3	24	1885
5	1850	18	1860–70	25	1874
6–8	1842–60	19	1850–60	26	1880
9	1870	20	1860	27–28	1883
10–12	1860–70	21	1870–3	29–30	1903
13–15	c. 1870	22	1868–81	31–35	modern marks

Milde, Ary de (1634–1708). Dutch potter. Produced mainly teapots of red stoneware after Chinese models. Pieces with his marks do not differ much from Böttger stoneware. De Milde, however, could never have produced the high temperature needed for Böttger stoneware. It is therefore assumed that Meissen copied some pieces of de Milde complete with his mark.

Mildeneichen (Austria). Austrian porcelain factories at Mildeneichen and Raspenau, G. Robrecht, f. 1850. Utility ware and technical porcelain items.
Mildeneichen. see Hegewald nr. Friedland.
Milet, Paul, & Fils, see Sèvres (4).

Milgravi (Mühlgraben) nr. Riga (Lettland). J. C. Jessen, porcelain factory, f. 1886. Porcelain and faience ware.

Miller (Müller), Ferdinand. From Mannheim. Arcanist in St. Petersburg, later in Milan and Naples. He f. the Nyon porcelain factory in 1780.
Millet, Optat, see Sèvres (3).
Milliet, see Creil et Montereau.
Milly, Nicolas-Chrétien de Tuy, Comte de (1728-84). In 1759 he entered the service of Duke Karl Eugen of Würtemberg, the founder of the Ludwigsburg factory, where he acquired the technical knowledge of porcelain manufacture. In 1766 he returned to France, where he continued with his chemistry studies. He is the author of the most important and extensive (illustrated) work about the technology of porcelain in the 18th c. *L'art de la Porcelain.* This work, published in 1765 within the *Encyclopédie des sciences, des arts et des métiers,* appears in a German translation in 1775, in *Schauplatz der Künste und Handwerke,* Vol. 13.
Minerva, porcelain factory, see Lane Delph.
Minton, Herbert (1792-1858). See Stoke-on-Trent (10).
Minton, Thomas (1765-1836). Pupil of Thomas Turner. In 1796 he created the famous factory in Stoke-on-Trent, see Stoke-on-Trent (10).
Minton porcelain factory, see Donovan.
Miskolcz (Hungary). Max Koos, porcelain and stoneware factory, f. 1882. Utility ware.

Mitterteich (1) (Germany, Bavaria). Josef Rieber & Co. porcelain factory AG, f. 1868. Production: utility ware, coffee and tea services. This concern traded under the following names: 1. Joseph Rieber porcelain works, Selb; 2. Julius Rother & Co., porcelain factory and decorating studio in Mitterteich; 3. Joseph Rieber, Selb; 4. Josef Rieber & Co., Mitterteich with the branch works at Thiersheim; 5. Josef Rieber & Co. porcelain factories AG, Selb-Thiersheim-Mitterteich; 6. Josef Rieber & Co. porcelain factories AG, Mitterteich, with branch factory at Thiersheim.

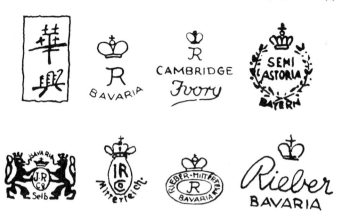

Mitterteich (2) (Germany, Bavaria). Mosaic Pottery (Mitterteich porcelain factory), Max Emanuel & Co. utility ware. This undertaking no longer exists.

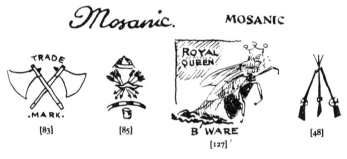

Mitterteich (3) (Germany, Bavaria). Porcelain factory AG, f. 1917. Utility ware, services, gift articles.

Mladenof, G. & Co., see Widin.

Moabit, Berlin (Germany). M. Schuman and Son produced porcelain here from 1835. These products were much praised. It is alleged that Schomburg & Son were producing porcelain in Moabit at the same time and that Ludloff & Co.

also did so from 1880. The marks with the caption '1844–7' is also used for Eisenberg.

1844–7	c.1850	Friedrich
blue underglaze	blue underglaze	Adolph Schuhmann
		d. 1851

Moehling, J., see Aich.

Moerobergen, see Schaala (1).

Mohammedan Blue. European term for underglaze blue which had been in use in China from 1368–98 (Emperor Hongwu).

Mohn, Samuel (1762–1815). Private decorator in Berlin, Dresden, Leipzig, and Vienna (?), working on porcelain and glass. Renowned for his silhouette portraits.

Moitte, see Paris (37).

Mol, Johannes de (d. in 1782). F. Oude Loosdrecht porcelain factory in 1771 *(q.v.)*.

Molier-Bardin, see Orléans (2).

Molinet (France). La Broche S.A. Further particulars are not available. According to 'Tardy 75' the following marks were registered in 1961.

Möllendorf, General von, see Prussian Service.

Möller & Dippe, see Unterköditz (2).

Momparler, Tomás, see Valencia.

Mondovi Breo (Italian). Lorenzo Beltrandi, porcelain factory, f. 1880. Vases and table services.

Mondovi-Carassone (Italian). Società Ceramica Richard Ginori (see also Doccia).

Monier, Jean Baptiste, see Etoilles.

Monnerie et Joubert, see Limoges (2).

Mons (1) (Belgium). A modern factory firing in coal kilns was already established in 1867 under the directorship of Declercq. Porcelain was also produced by Englebienne Bros. et Ch. de Harweng.

Mons (2) (Belgium). Céramique Montoise, Soc. Anon. Dinner services.

Mons (3) (Belgium). Dubois & Cie., porcelain factory. Fancy articles.

Montamy, d'Arclais de. Author of *Dissertation concerning the colours used in the enamelling and decoration of porcelain* (from the French), Leipzig 1767.

Montarcy, Jean Baptiste Augustin de, see Paris (98).

Montastiers, see Limoges (30).

Montereau, see Creil et Montereau.

Montgat, Barcelona (Spain). Céramica Industrial Montgatina, S.L., f. 1935. Table services.

Montginot, see Paris (105).

Montreuil (1) (France, Seine). Marzolf & Cie. porcelain works, f. 1885. Artistic porcelain (such as copies from Chinese, Saxony and modern porcelain), also earthenware and stoneware. This factory's earlier name was Marzolf, L.

Montreuil (2) (France, Seine). Masson et Auriac decorated door knobs here from 1921 which are still popular even today. The following marks are registered:

MC   AM   ALM

Montreuil (3) (France, Seine). Alfred Patte, porcelain decorating workshop, registered the following mark in 1905 (according to 'Tardy 75').

Montreuil (4) France, Seine). François Thomaret, porcelain decorators. According to 'Tardy 75' the following mark was registered.

PORCELAINE
THOMARET
Déposé

Montreuil-sous-Bois (France, Seine). Tinet f. a porcelain factory here in 1815 which copied Chinese and Japanese models.

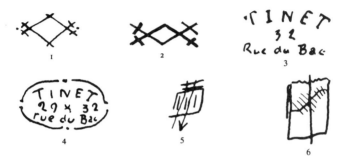

1–2 underglaze – 3–4 red – 5–6 blue underglaze

Montvallier, Buquet, de, see Chantilly (1).
Montvoisin, Abel, see Bagnolet (2).
Moore Bros., see Longton (54).
Moreau, Constant, see Paris (106).
Moreau, Marie, see Paris (107).
Moreau (or Merault), see Vaux.
Moreau ainé et Cie., see Limoges (58).
Morel, see La Vilette.
Morel, Gerard, & Duffraisseix, see Limoges (34).
Morelle, see Paris (108).
Morgenroth & Co., see Gotha (2).
Morin, François de (d. 1710). Director of St.-Cloud. Wrote *Mémoire sur la Fabrication de al Porcelaine* in 1692.
See also Frit porcelain.
Moriot, N., see Sèvres (5).
Moritz, Carl, see Taubenbach.
Morje, Schlüsselburg (Russia). At the beginning of the 19th c., Baron Friedrichs f. a porcelain factory here, which had the following successive owners: C. J. Postkotschin from 1817–47; Count Golenitscheff-Kutusoff from 1847–87; and finally Emeljanoff, from 1887 on. The products were beautiful services and utility ware for restaurant catering. The best pieces of this factory were made in the Postkotschin period, 1817–47, but by and large there is no artistic merit in the production.

Morlent, J. P., and G. Saintville, J.P., see Bayeux.
Morris, Henry (1799–1880), decorator, see Swansea.
Morris, Thomas, see Longton (54).
Morris, Thomas, Anchor Works, see Longton (55).
Mosa, V. V., see Maastricht.
Mosaic Pottery, Max Emanuel & Co., see Mitterteich (2).
Mosaics in porcelain. In 1923 Paul Körber, Bad Homburg vdH, worked out a technique for the making of mosaics or mosaic imitations. Small tesseraes (20 mm × 20 mm), which had been produced through pouring, stamping, punching or pressing techniques, could be assembled to produce different mosaic patterns.
Moscow (1) (Russia). In 1860 Anochin f. a small porcelain factory in the near Karpowo, which produced mainly unpainted statuettes.

Moscow (2) (Russia). Porcelain had been produced by Dunaschoff in Turygino nr. Moscow since 1830.

Moscow (3) (Russia). P. Fomin produced porcelain here from 1806 onwards with the mark as shown. The factory worked until 1883 although it came to a stand-still in the 1850s. Parts of the production were of exceptional quality.

Moscow (4) (Russia). An Englishman, Francis Gardner, f. a porcelain factory in 1765 in Werbiliki nr. Moscow, which was not only of local importance, it became one of the most renowned Russian factories of the 18th c., second only to Petersburg. He was helped by F. X. Hattenberger, who later worked in the Imperial factory in Petersburg. Gardner's business was so successful that it soon became a serious rival of the Imperial factory. Many figures are famous, particularly the ones which recreate Russian folk-types. A simple grace is combined with a naive colourism. The pale blue glossy glaze which was used in the beginning of the 19th c. deserves mention. The factory produced some renowned services, which were made by order of the Emperor. Whilst the factory produced mainly figures in its early years, in the 19th c. it concentrated on the production of utility ware. The factory remained in the possession of the Gardner family until 1891, when Kusnetzoff became the owner, under whose name porcelain factories are working to this day.

Moscow (5) (Russia). A porcelain factory worked under the name of 'Fabrica Gospodina Gulina' in Rjasan, south-east of Moscow, from 1830–50.

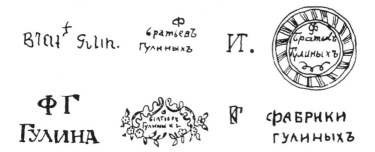

Moscow (6) (Russia). Between 1820 and 1856 a ceramicist, P. Kosloff, directed a porcelain factory here; its biscuit figures are often surprisingly delicately modelled. The products are valued and sought after by collectors.

Moscow (7) (Russia). Nasonoff produced porcelain nr. Spassk (Moscow district) and sold the factory to Kiriakoff in 1813; some years later it was closed. The products were of good quality.

Moscow (8) (Russia). The Novyki Brothers f. a porcelain factory in 1820 which was amalgamated with Chrapunoff in 1840. Some significant works of this production have been preserved: beautiful cups with portrait decoration and black flower services; both are representative of the factory.

Moscow (9) (Russia). Alexander Popoff f. a porcelain factory in Gorbunovo, a village in the vicinity of Moscow in the beginning of the 19th c. The figure production was similar to that of Gardner's factory. The products were of excellent quality and testify to great artistry. During this period of the highest achievements (1810–30), the products show rich gilding and brilliant decoration. Popoff invented a beautiful chestnut brown colour and a luminous blue. Of all the factories f. in the beginning of the 19th c., this one deserves the greatest attention. It was closed in 1872.

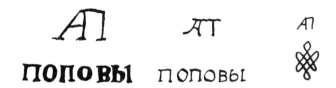

Moscow (10) (Russia). The Ratchkin Brothers directed a porcelain factory here from 1820–70.

Moscow (11) (Russia). In the village of Narotkaja (within the jurisdiction of Moscow) from 1830–40, Safronoff directed one of the most famous porcelain factories to be established under Nikolaus I. This factory was, at one time, leased out to S. T. Kusnetzoff. The most beautiful pieces of the production are without blemish in form or colour, and can be favourably compared with the products of the foremost Russian porcelain factories. However, the value of the products varies considerably.

Moscow (12) (Russia). Vsevolojsky and Polivanoff managed a porcelain factory in the village of Elisawietino (within the jurisdiction of Moscow) from 1813–55. In the beginning the products were of high quality; however, after Polivanoff left to establish his own factory in Aschuat, this high standard fell rapidly. In 1820 the factory came into the possession of Sipiagin, the son-in-law of Vsevolojsky, and was soon closed down. It resumed production again in 1850–5 and was sold to Ikonikoff. The products from the later periods were regarded as the best. Particularly beautiful figures were also made.

Mother of pearl glaze (Perlmutterglaze). Iridescent porcelain glaze which was already being used on Meissen porcelain of the Böttger period (first period). This glaze had been used before by the Chinese.

Mouchard, see Angoulême.

Moulin, see Sinceny.

Moulins-sur-Allier (France). According to an entry in the *Dictionnaires des Postes aux lettres* there was a porcelain factory here.

Mousnier, see Magnac-Bourg.

MPM. This mark which was unknown until recently, was used for porcelain made in the second half of the 19th c. which was similar in form and decoration to the Waldenburger products of the same time. Use of the onion pattern can also be seen.

MPM

Muffle or muffel kiln, is a double-walled firing kiln made of bricks in which the products are protected from direct contact with the fire during firing by the inner wall.

Muffle colours, see Enamel glazes.

Muffle decoration, see Overglaze decoration.

Mühlgraben nr. Riga (Lettland), see Milgravi.

Mühlhausen nr. Bad Elster (Germany, Saxony). Elster porcelain factory, Georg Heinlein. Utility ware. This factory no longer exists. On the basis of the following mark which was used, it can be established that the Elsterwerke owned the well-known porcelain factory, Zeh, Scherzer & Co., AG, Rehau, during the period 1924–6. It has been confirmed that the mark, taken over at the same time, continued to be used for some months after the take-over.

Mühlhauser, Jean Pierre (1779–1838), decorator, see Geneva.

Mühlheim am Rhine (Germany, now a suburb of Cologne). Josef Heck factory, f. in 1906, produced decorated porcelain.

Müller, August and Son, see Unterköditz (3).

Müller, E. & A., AG, see Schönwald (1) and Schwarza-Saalbahn.

Müller, Ferdinand, decorator, see Nyon.

Müller, Franz Heinrich (1732–1820). Apprenticed to a pharmacist in Copenhagen, and also studied chemistry, botany, minerology and metallurgy by himself. From 1760–7 he was active as assay master at the Bank of Copenhagen. After this he undertook a three-year journey through the Continent, under an assumed name. He was the first to produce hard paste porcelain successfully for the Copenhagen factory. The factory flourished and under his management renowned European artists were employed there.

Müller, Johann Georg. Modeller in Berlin from 1763. Master modeller 1785–9.

Müller, Johann Gottfried. Arcanist from Meissen. In 1759 he designed and planned the lay-out of the Petersburg porcelain factory which he built on the Neva embankment.

Müller, Kurt, & Co., see Freienorla.

Müller, Förster, see Damm.

Müller, Paul, see Selb (7).

Müller and Co., Volkstedt-Rudolstadt, see Rudolstadt Volkstedt (17).

München-Allach (Germany). Allach-München GmbH porcelain factory, f. 1935. Porcelain figures. The firm no longer exists.

Münchhof nr. Chodau (Bohemia). Münchhofener porcelain and stoneware factory, f. 1879. Utility ware. This factory had its own kaolin pit.

Münden (Germany, Prussia). A. Wurstenfeld directed a small porcelain factory here in 1867.

Munich, see Nymphenburg (Neudeck).

Munich (1) (Germany). Brunner & Plötz, porcelain decorating studio from 1924.

Munich (2) (Germany). Glass and porcelain studio GmbH, decorating studio from 1930.

Munich (3) (Germany). Alfons und Ernst Königsbauer, porcelain decorating studio, c. 1930.

Munich (4) (Germany). Elisabeth Liegl, Kunsthandwerkliche Erzeugnisse and porcelain decorators, f. 1945. Exclusively designed pieces after famous artists.

" **L** "

Munich (5) (Germany). Karl Rau, porcelain and glass decorators, f. 1857, formerly in Schönfeld nr. Carlsbad. Dinner and coffee services, ornamental porcelain, cabinet cups, vases, presentation bowls, all with gold etching decorations.

Munich (6) (Germany). Rosenthal hand-painting department. The owner was: Rosenthal-Porzellan AG, Selb.
Munich (7) (Germany). Tannhauser Bros., factory for tin glazed ware and porcelain decorating studio, c. 1910.

Munich (8) (Germany). Martin Wiegnad, porcelain decorator, registered the following mark as a trademark on 6 July 1918, under No. 225106. Porcelain decorations only.

[209]

Munich (9) (Germany). G. Wieninger, porcelain decorators, f. 1879. Drinking vessels, views, heraldic shields, photographs on porcelain.

Münster (Germany, Westphalia). August Roloff porcelain works, c. 1930.

Murko, M. J., see Nová Bana.

Muselmalede moster, see Ilmenauer Strawflower pattern.

Musselin porcelain. Particularly thin-walled porcelain which the director Raithel produced in Meissen (1870–94) in imitation of Chinese products. See Meissen (1).

Nabeschima porcelain, see Okawaji porcelain.

Nägeli, Hans Jacob. In the beginning of the 19th c. he was one of the owners of the porcelain factory in Zurich.

Naestved (Denmark). Hermann Kähler, A., A.-S., porcelain decorating studio. c. 1930.

Nantes (1) (France). Decaen directed a small porcelain factory here in the years 1800–8.

$$\mathcal{J}_o$$

Nantes (2) (France). In 1780 the faience factory owner Fourmy f. a factory here which was later called 'Fourmy Fils, Fournerat et de Nivas'; it closed however in 1790.

Nantgarw Glamorgan (England, Wales). William Billingsley and Samuel Walker f. a porcelain factory here in 1813, which, after a short time, was transferred to Swansea for one or two years but appears to have returned to Nantgarw once again. Perhaps it may have been that the Swansea products were only decorated in Nantgarw. In 1820, Billingsley moved to Coalport; his successor was William Weston Young. The products, according to Billingsley, were of the standard of Sèvres. They were of immaculate white paste and very translucent. They were inclined to lose their shape in the high-firing, however. The chief product was general porcelain ware, its decoration, painting and gilding, was applied in the French manner. Billingsley's individual flower-decoration is very rare. The decorations were partly made in London.

NANT-GARW   *Nantgarw*   C.W.
C.W.   NANGAROW
                                                   C.W

Naples (Italy). The Capo-di-Monte porcelain factory existed near Naples from 1743–59. In Naples itself Ferdinand IV, son of Charles III, established a porcelain factory in the Royal Villa of Portici in 1771. In 1773 it was moved into the Royal palace, where it flourished until 1806. The artistic production was dominated by neo-classical research. Antique marble and bronze were copied and made in biscuit. From 1772-81 the directors were Tommaso Perez, a Spaniard, and after his death, Domenico Veduti. In 1806, owing to the French occupation of Naples, the production came to a temporary halt. In 1807, after frequent changes of ownership, the factory and all its tools became the possession of the French firm Giovanni Poulard Prad in Doccia, where one half of it was sold to Claud Guillard and Giovanni Tourné and the remaining part to Francesco Paolo Dell. Later it changed hands again and was closed down in 1834. In the last period the artistic production was of little value. See Doccia.

1–4 impressed – 5–8 blue underglaze – 9–13 R.F. = Ferdinand IV Rex – 9 blue – 10–11 red – 12–13 blue underglaze

Nardon & Lafarge 'Limoges Porcelaine', see Limoges (59).
Nasonoff, see Moscow (7).
Nassau-Saarbrücken, Wilhelm Heinrich (1718–68) Fürst von, Duke, see Ottweiler.
Nast, J. N. H. (1754–1817). Founder of the porcelain factory in Rue Popincourt, 1782. See Paris (109).
Nathusius, Gottlob, see Alt-Haldensleben.
Naudot, Camille, & Co., see Paris (110).
Nauen (Germany, Mark nr. Berlin). C. F. Kerkow. Porcelain decorating studio, c. 1910.

Nauendorf (Germany, Thuringia). Alt, Beck & Gottschalck GmbH, porcelain factory, f. 1854. Figurative porcelain dolls and dolls' heads.

Nehmitz, arcanist, see Meissen (1).
Nehracher, Matthias (d. 1800). In 1793 he bought the Zurich porcelain factory.
Nemours (France). According to the *Dictionnaires des Postes aux lettres,* there was a porcelain factory here in 1817.

Nenert, Guéry and Latrille, see Solignac.

Neppel (or Neppele), Jean-Louis. Decorator in St.-Cloud, 1740–50, and Mennecy, 1753. See Nevers.

Neu, Wenzel (c. 1708–74), modeller, see Fulda (1).

Neuberg, W., Ritter von, see Giesshübel (2).

Neubrandensteinmuster, Meissen porcelain pattern. An adaption of the Oldbrandensteinmuster. Only two-thirds of the outer edge is decorated with a grid and basket-weave pattern. The divisions are 's'-shaped ribs in bas relief which extend to the face of the plate, following the curvature of the rim in light relief.

Neudeck, see Nymphenburg.

Neudulang pattern. Meissen porcelain decoration. The radial grate of this pattern is 's'-shaped and curved.

Neuerer, K. G., see Oberkotzau (1).

Neuglatt. Pattern of the Royal porcelain factory, Berlin, 1769, see Berlin (3).

Neuhaldensleben (1) (Germany, Saxony). Hubbe Bros. porcelain factory, had the following mark registered as a trademark under No. 14596 on 7 March 1896. Produced white and decorated artistic and utility ware.

[71]

Neuhaldensleben (2) (Germany, Saxony). Ley & Weidermann, porcelain factory, c. 1924–30.

Neuhaldensleben (3) (Germany, Saxony). Hugo Lonitz & Co., porcelain, stoneware, earthenware and terracotta factory, f. 1868. Utility and luxury articles of high standard.

[6]

Neuhaldensleben (4) (Germany, Saxony). Saxony porcelain and ceramic art factory which, according to Pelka, used the following mark c. 1924.

Neuhaldensleben (5) (Germany, Saxony). Saxon porcelain factory, c. 1930.

Neuhaldensleben (6) (Germany, Saxony). Sauer & Roloff, porcelain factory, c. turn of the century. Still active in 1924.

[148]

Neuhaldensleben (7) (Germany, Saxony). J. Uffrecht & Co. porcelain factory, had the following mark registered on 15 February 1895. Still active in 1924.

J.U.&C.

Neuhaus am Rennweg (1) (Germany, Thuringia). C. List f. a factory here in 1831, which is probably identical to the Kämpfe & List porcelain factory (c. 1900). Fancy goods and toys.

1

2

3

1 from 1831 – 2 1894 – 3 c. 1900

Neuhaus am Rennweg (2) (Germany, Thuringia). Rudolph Heinz & Co., porcelain and faience factory and decorating studio, f. c. 1859. A decorating shop since 1859, and a porcelain factory since 1885. Luxury products (no utility ware). Styles: Copenhagen, Sèvres, Delft, Worcester and 'Modern'.

Neuhofen an der Krems (Austria). Otto Kunz, porcelain factory. Household and hotel porcelain, gift articles. After the death of Kurz in 1965, the factory was closed.

Neuilly (France, Seine). Thesmar directed a porcelain factory here in 1892.

Neukirchner, Franz, see Marktredwitz (3).
Neumann, Julius, see Klösterle (2).
Neumann, Ludwig, Ing., GmbH, see Frauenthal zu Lassnitz.
Neumark (Bohemia). In 1832 Anton Fischer f. a porcelain factory here which was later taken over by his son.

Neumark

Neumünster (Germany, Schleswig-Holstein). Neumünster porcelain factory, GmbH, f. 1897. Utility ware. This factory does not work any longer.

PN

Neureuther, Christian (1868–1921). Ceramicist. Student at the ceramic school in Lichte, the Kunstgewerbe School in Munich and pupil of the painter, L. Hutschenreuther (1855–1915). Director of the Lichte-Wallendorf drawing school. Produced models for a number of porcelain factories.
Neurohlau (Bohemia). 'Bohemia', ceramic works AG, f. 1921. Table, coffee, tea services, hotel porcelain and luxury articles; onion pattern 1976.

Neu-Schmiedefeld (Germany, Thuringia). A porcelain factory which used the following mark, may have worked here c. 1900.

Neuses über Kronach (Germany, Bavaria). Adolf Schedel, porcelain factory f. 1958. Produced mocha services and collecting cups until 1964 when production included gift articles with town views and cartouches.

Neusiss (Germany, Thuringia). Neusiss porcelain factory AG, f. 1922. Produced gift articles, coffee and tea services. This firm has closed down.
Neustadt (1) (Germany, Gotha). Heber & Co., porcelain factory, f. 1900. Utility items, figures and others.

Neustadt (2) (Germany, Coburg). Knoch Bros., porcelain factory, f. 1887. Figures and similar, dolls and dolls' heads.

Neustrelitz (Germany, Mecklenburg). Albert Schulze, porcelain decorating studio, c. 1930.

Neuzierat, Berlin porcelain pattern which, according to Köllmann writing in 1767, was adopted by the KPM Berlin (Gotzkowsky 1762). Rocaille in relief with painted twigs, branches and leaves.
Nevers (France). Neppel and Bonnet directed a small factory here which produced porcelain. Decorations were applied, and produced by a stamping device for which a patent was granted on 10 March 1809. The sucessors of Neppel were Bonnot and Pillivuyt.

J. Reppel

Newcastle (England). Floral production, 1952–62. Fancy wares in porcelain.

FLORAL
PRODUCTIONS
BONE CHINA
ENGLAND

Newcastle-under-Lyme (England). Dr. Pococke mentioned in one of his travel reports, that a porcelain factory was here in 1750. This is the only source of information regarding it.

New Chelsea China Co. Ltd., see Longton (57).

New Chelsea Porcelain Co. Ltd., see Longton (57).

New decoration (Neuzierat). Meissen pattern of 1742, an adaption of the Old pattern. The bas relief basket-weave pattern covers two-thirds of the rim which is deeper and everted. The number of the moulded ribs is now increased to 16, and are grouped closer together in fours, They are 's'-shaped and extend to the face of the plate where they follow the curvature of the rim.

New Hall (1) (England, Shelton). In the factories which were f. by Hollins & Warburton in Shelton in 1781–2, utility ware was produced in a kind of hard paste porcelain until 1801, when John Daniel became the co-owner and added bone china to the production. Production of the hard paste porcelain ceased in c. 1815, the bone china in 1831. In the early period of the factory, the decoration was in imitation of Chinese export porcelain. From about 1800, there were festoon patterns and wave motifs as well as work which was similar to Sèvres. During the last 20 years porcelain was also decorated with landscapes, etc., in purple and gilded over-print.

red 1810–35 only on bone china

New Hall (2) (England, Shelton). Rarely found. Godden records the following mark as being used on porcelain during the period 1810–12.

WARBURTON'S
PATENT

New-Palais-Service, 'the first Potsdam table service 1765' (Friedrich Elias Meyer). The first porcelain service of the KPM Berlin after the take-over by the

King in 1763. Relief ornamentation, gilded garlands and naturalistic flowers and gold mosaic. The second Potsdam service differs only in its use of green mosaic in its spandrels. It was delivered in 1767. 'In spite of many shortcomings in body and glaze, this service of the KPM Berlin is artistically the most accomplished German rococo table service; it has not been equalled by Meissen or any other German factory' (Köllmann).

New York (USA). C. Arenfeld & Son. *A Book of Pottery Marks* by Parcival Jervis, states that the following mark was used for the year 1887. Since the known pieces are of European pedigree it may be assumed that the mark was used exclusively for the imported European ware of the Árenfeld firm.

Nicolet, see Paris (111).
Nicolle, Joseph, see Sèvres (1).
Nicosia (Cyprus). Neoptolemos Erotokritou. Produced porcelain, ceramic and stoneware, utility ware and crockery.
Niderviller (France). The old faience factory of 1735 was bought by Jean Louis Baron de Beyerlé in 1742. The technical knowledge of how to make porcelain had been passed on to de Beyerlé by a former worker of the Vienna factory. Porcelain production was begun immediately and by 1766 it had gradually replaced the faience production. The kaolin required was obtained from Passau until 1765, when de Beyerlé acquired a kaolin deposit in Saint-Yrieix. From 1754 the artistic and technical management was in the care of the painter and chemist François-Antoine Anstett, a former pupil of Paul Hannong. In 1770, Count Philibert de Custine, General of the Royal Army, became the owner; Anstett remained in charge of the factory until 1779. In 1802 Claude-François Lanfrey became director and remained until his death in 1827. It is reputed that the porcelain from his time was particularly fine. L. W. Dryander was the owner from 1827; he chose not to exploit the factory's own deposit of raw material in Saint-Yrieix, thus stopping the porcelain production. He preferred to produce ceramics in the English taste. He also industrialised the factory which later was taken over by his two sons. From 1886 the firm called itself: S.A. Fayencerie de Niderviller, and is still active today.

1–6 Beyerle marks until 1770 mostly underglaze blue – 7–14 Custine marks 1774–89 –
15–17 1789–93 mostly in underglaze blue, also in brown, green and gold – 18–21 Lanfrey
marks in blue underglaze, red, gold, 1802–27, mostly stippled shading – 22–26 other
artists' marks – 27–32 Niderviller in various forms, mostly in black

Niderviller, see also Barbeaux (cornflower pattern).
Niedermayer, see Elbogen (1).
Niedermeyer, F. Ignaz (d. 1710), see Nymphenburg.
Niedermeyer, Johann Josef (d. 1784). Probably a pupil of Raphael Donner.
Niedermeyer was originally a drawing master at the Vienna Academy and later
became master modeller at the Vienna porcelain factory where he remained until
the appointment of Anton Grassi, the chief modeller of the third period under
Sorgenthal. Under Niedermeyer's direction a great number of figures in rococo
style were made.

Nieder-Salzbrunn (Germany, Silesia). Franz Prause, porcelain factory GmbH,
f. 1849. Table, coffee and tea services with onion and strawflower pattern. This
factory has now closed.

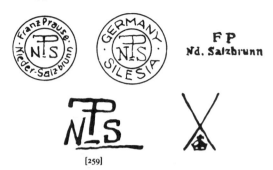

[259]

Niedersalzbrunn (1) (Germany, Silesia). Hermann Ohme, porcelain factory, f. 1882. Household and hotel porcelain. Onion and strawflower pattern. This concern no longer exists.

[142]

[29]

Niedersalzbrunn (2) (Germany, Silesia). Niederschlesische porcelain factory GmbH, c. 1910.

Niederschlesische Porcelain Works GmbH, see Niedersalzbrunn (2).

Niemeyer, Adalbert (1867–1922). Painter, architect, designer for arts and crafts. Co-founder of the local Werkbund and the Deutsche Werkstätten in Munich in 1880. He produced porcelain designs for the factories of Nymphenburg, Berlin, Meissen, Heubach Bros. and Schwarzenberger Werkstätten.

Nierwein. Decorator in Frankenthal in 1768, and again from 1772. In the period in between he was also active as a decorator in Pfalz-Zweibrücken. In 1782 he was employed at Höchst.

Nieuhoff, Johann. In his report to the Emperor of China about the Embassy of the East-India Company (1655–7), he writes in detail about porcelain (published in Leyden 1665).

Niever Amstel (Holland). Georg Dommer & Co. f. a porcelain factory here in 1808, which received the patronage of the Queen of Holland. Despite the Crown's annual subsidy of 20,000 Dutch guilders the factory had to be closed in 1810. The mark can be differentiated from the other similar marks by the horizontal stroke in the 'A'. Very little is known about the quality of the products. The factory received a 'distinction' award in the world exhibition in Utrecht in 1808.

Nilson, J. O., Hackefors Porslin Aktiebolag, see Hackefors.

Nimy (Belgium). Seat of the 'Master school for ceramics' where the main aim is individual artistic expression in ceramic art. Production concentrates on individual pieces which are signed by the artist. Models which are sold to industry, however, are not allowed to bear an artist's signature. The school is also involved in the furthering of ceramic techniques.

Nivet, Michel, see Limoges (54).

Noirlac (France). A porcelain factory directed by Vital-Roux and Merkens may have functioned here in 1846. A retail outlet may have been active in Paris, Rue Poissonière.

Nonne, Christian. The Volkstedt-Rudolstadt factory flourished under his directorship. See Rudolstadt Volkstedt (1), Ilmenau (1) (after 1792), Klösterle (1) (after 1797) and Giesshübel (2) (after 1830).

Nonne & Roesch, see Giesshübel (2).

Norden (Denmark). Norden porcelain factory AS. Under Dahl-Jensen's direction this factory produced artistic porcelain only. In December 1975 the Keramadressbuch listed only electro porcelain.

'Normande' La Céramique, S.á.r.l., see Oissel.

Nová Bana (Slovakia). Murko, M. J., porcelain decorating studio, ceased to exist in 1930.

Nove (Italy, Bassano). The faience factory owned by Pasquale Antonibon, began to produce porcelain in 1752, with the aid of the Saxon arcanist Johann Sigismund Fischer. Pietro Lorenci succeeded him. The owner took his son as a partner in 1781, and in the same year associated with Paroline. In 1802, they both withdrew in favour of Giovanni Baroni. Baroni could not increase the profits of the factory and gave it up in 1825, but Antonibon's successors resumed porcelain production again in 1832, just before the factory was finally closed. The best products were made in the period between 1760–80 and are characterised by their individual style. The paste is at times a little grey and not particularly transparent; however, shining glazes and deep colour tones compensate for the technical shortcomings. The gold-edged pieces of the late 18th c. and the decorations in light colours are outstanding, and those in purple deserve a special mention.

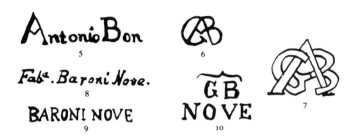

Antonio Bon
5

Fab^a. Baroni Nove.
8

BARONI NOVE
9

6

GB
NOVE
10

7

1–3 red or coloured – 4 in different variations, gold – 5 1762–1802 – 6–7 monogram of Giovanni Battista Antonibon 1762–1802 – 8–10 Baroni-marks 1802–25 – 9 impressed signed – 10 red

Nove (1) (Italy, Vincenza). 'Sele Arte', present-day porcelain factory.

Nove (2) (Italy, Vincenza). Pietro Carraro S.N.C., recently built factory for porcelain and other ceramic products.
Novisad (Yugoslavia). Fabrika Porculana i Majolike d.d., f. 1922. Utility ware.

Novy Dwor (Poland, Warsaw). Fabryka Faiansu i Porcelany A. Winogradow.

Novyki Bros., see Moscow (8).
Nowocharitonowo, see Kusnetzoff.
Noyer Bros., see Farges-Allichamps.
Nymphenburg (Germany). The pottery master Ignaz Niedermeyer, f. a porcelain factory in Neudeck, a suburb of Munich, on the meadowland beside Paulanerkloster. He was sponsored by the Elector Max III Joseph of Bavaria. It

was named 'Churfürstl. Porcelaine Factory', but only produced porcelain after the arrival of the Vienna arcanist Joseph Jacob Ringler. The director was Count Sigismund of Haimhausen, director of the College of the Mint and Mines. Ringler remained only a few months, but during his stay it quickly became apparent that he added nothing of relevance to the porcelain production, and his services could be dispensed with. In 1761 the factory moved to specially built premises in the Castle Rondell at Nymphenburg, where it still stands. Although the artistic aspect of production flourished, the financial rewards were so inadequate that the Elector was forced to increase his subsidy. He died in 1770 to be succeeded by Karl Theodor of the Palatinate, who was already occupied with his factory at Frankenthal. He relegated Nymphenburg to second place until the Frankenthal factory closed in 1799 and the situation altered. I. P. Melchior who had already gone to Nymphenburg in 1797, was now followed by some other industrious Frankenthal workers. After the unification of the Principality of Passau with Bavaria, Nymphenburg came into the enviable situation of having direct access to the kaolin deposits near Passau. The factory met with further good fortune when, in 1754, they engaged the most prominent rococo-figure modeller, Franz Anton Bustelli, born in 1723 in Locarno. He worked in Nymphenburg until his premature death in 1763. His main works are the 16 figures of the Italian Comedia dell Arte which rank among the choicest porcelain figure creations of the 18th c. His successor was Dominikus Auliczek, whose performance was not comparable with that of Bustelli. Auliczek was pensioned when J. P. Melchior was appointed chief modeller in 1797. Melchior (see Frankenthal) created, among other things, portrait busts of members of the Bavarian Royal Family. Bustelli's achievements must not blind us to the high-quality general porcelain ware that Nymphenburg also produced. The factory remained a possession of the State until 1862, when it was leased to a private company, Arendts and Scotzniovsky. Arendt withdrew in the same year, leaving Scotzniovsky to manage by himself until 1888, when Albert Bäuml, Counsellor of Commerce, became the director. His sons are still the leaseholders. Since 1900 the factory has gone from strength to strength both artistically and economically. Besides upholding the great rococo tradition, the production strives for modern forms and decorations. From 1862–1925 biscuit dolls' heads were also produced, with mark No. 4 (below) as a neck mark.
See also: Adler, Ch., Auer, A. U. M. J., Baumeister, S., Benckgraff, J., Christfeld, C., Clair, A., Ess (Àss), F. J., Ettner, A., Härtl, J. G., Härtl, J. T. R., Haslöder, J., Helchis, Hermannsdorfer, A., Huber, J. A., Kilber, J. Ch., Klein, J., Kumpf, J. G., Lerch, J., Lindemann, G. Chr., Octtner, A. Ph., Pletzger, J. A., Purtscher, K., Rauffer, F. K., Schwanthaler, L., Seefried (Seyfried), P. A., Walcher, B., Weiss, J., Zächenberger, J.

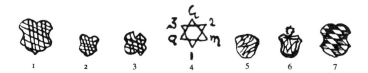

1   2   3   4   5   6   7

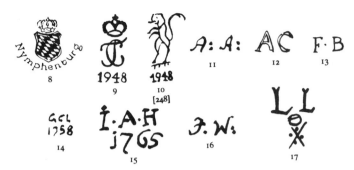

8   9   10
[248]

14   15   16   17

11   12   13

1 impressed mark 1755–65 – 2 impressed mark 1760–70 – 3 impressed mark 1780–90 – 4 hexagram, mark blue underglaze 1763–5 – 5 impressed mark 1810–50 – 6 impressed signed with star 1850–62 – 7 impressed signed from 1862 – 8 modern mark on ware and on a large number of figures – 9–10 for models of old Frankenthal moulds. The year under the mark stands for the year of production – 11 signature of the painters and the decorator Anton Auer 1795–1814 – 12 Adam Clair – 13 Franz Bustelli – 14 Georg Christian Lindemann 1758–60 – 15 I. A. Huber – 16 Johann Wielland – 17 almost certainly used exclusively on Turkish mugs, but according to the factory it should always occur in combination with the Rautenschild mark (the Bavarian shield with oblique lozenges)

Nyon (Switzerland). Swiss porcelain factory, f. 1781 in the Canton Waadt, on the Lake of Geneva. This factory was established by the Frankenthal decorator, Ferdinand Müller, and his son-in-law, Johann Jakob of Berlin; in 1813 it ceased to operate. Dortu was the driving force, being involved with both the technical and artistic management. The partners separated after a quarrel in 1786. Dortu then took charge of the concern which became a joint stock company in 1809. Porcelain production was halted in 1813 after which only products of pipeclay were made. The artistic style leant heavily towards the French. The artists active in the factory were: J. G. Maurer from Zurich, painter, Joseph Revelot from Luneville, painter, Joseph Pernoux from Ludwigsburg, painter, W. Chr. Rath from Stuttgart, painter, Ludwig Eps from Öttingen/Sa., repairer, C. Maurer from Zurich, repairer. They drew inspiration from the renowned European porcelain factories. The tableware was made in the style of Louis XVI and the Empire period. Nyon figures are very rare. The last mark shown, 'CM', may belong to the aforementioned J. G. Maurer, as well as to C. Maurer, both from Zurich.

Obelisk. Trademark No. 60161 from 11 May 1903 of the P. F. Waldenburg.

Oberhohndorf nr. Zwickau (Germany, Saxony), Friedrich Kaestner, porcelain factory, f. 1883. Table, coffee and tea services and utility ware. The use of the third mark shown below (crossed swords with FKZ), was successfully challenged and its use forbidden by the KPM Meissen (before 1896). The mark was removed from the trademark register of the German Reich of 1896–8.

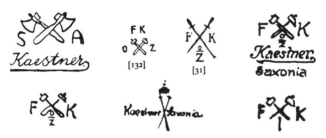

Oberkassel nr. Düsseldorf (Germany, Rhineland). Rheinische porcelain factory, L. Hermann, f. 1861. Utility ware and lithophanes, lighting appliances and fittings. Decorations in high temperature colours and glazes; this factory no longer exists.

Oberklingensporn (Germany, Upper Frankonia). Bernhardschütte porcelain factory, GmbH, c. 1910.

Oberköditz (Germany, Thuringia). Paris Bros., porcelain factory. Small coffee cups and children's services.

Oberkotzau (1) (Germany, Upper Frankonia). Neuerer porcelain factory KG, f. 1898; see Oberkotzau (2).

Oberkotzau (2) (Germany, Bavaria). Greiner & Herda, porcelain factory, f. 1898; became 'Neuerer porcelain factory KG' in 1943. Utility ware.

Oberkotzau (3) (Germany, Upper Franconia). Leni Parbus, porcelain decorating studio, f. 1904; ornamental and utility porcelain. Still operating in 1955.

OCA-Porzellan-Fabrik Oechsler & Andechser, see Kronach (2).
Och, see Gotha (1).
Oechsler & Andexer, OCA Porzellan Fabrik, see Kronach (2).
Oegstgeest (Holland). Amphora. This ceramic business, which seems to have produced chiefly earthenware, is mentioned here only because it shares its name with the P.F. Amphora, Riessner & Kessel in Turn nr. Teplitz. The pieces, perhaps from the same period, are very similar in decoration. Designers were C. J. van der Hoef, R. Sterken and J. Schelling.
'Oeil-de-Perdrix', flowered, dotted circles on a coloured background, introduced by Sèvres around 1760.
Oelze nr. Grossbreitenbach (Germany, Thuringia). A Voigt, porcelain factory, Marienfeld, f. 1892. Fancy goods, dolls, and goods for the international market.

Oeslau (1) (Germany, Upper Frankonia). Fischer & Co., GmbH, porcelain factory and decorating studio, f. 1950.

Oeslau (2) (Germany, Upper Frankonia). Oeslauer porcelain works W. Goebel KG, formerly the Oeslau and Wilhelmsfeld porcelain factory, f. 1871. Wide

range of production, such as ornaments of porcelain, fine earthenware and
terracotta.

[143]

[224]   [224]   [224]

Oeslau (3) (Germany, Upper Frankonia). Wilhelm Isberner & Co. GmbH,
porcelain factory, f. 1946. Utility ware and figure porcelain.

Oeslau (4) (Germany, Upper Frankonia). J. Walther & Son, porcelain factory.
Luxury porcelain and dolls' heads.

Oest, Johann Andreas. From Kassel. He joined the porcelain factory in
Ludwigsburg as a decorator when it was f. in 1753. He was a member of the
academy of painters in Braunschweig and was also Ducal Court painter,
creating in particular portraits and children caught 'eating sweets on the sly', etc.

Oettner, Andreas Philipp. Porcelain decorator from Vienna. He may originally
have worked in the factory in Vienna. From May 1756 to December 1757, he
worked in Neudeck, as a 'common fire-decorator'; in 1759 he worked in both
Frankenthal and Ludwigsburg and was employed in Höchst in 1766. He was
regarded as the first competent porcelain decorator of the Nymphenburg
factory.
See also Ettner.

Offenstein, Michael (d. 1767). Master modeller in Frankenthal 1794–7.

Ohme, Hermann, see Niedersalzbrunn (1).

Ohnmacht (Ohmacht), Landolin (1760–1834). A pupil of Melchior and
'repairer' in Frankenthal, creating mostly portrait medallions.

Ohrdorf (Germany, Saxony–Coburg–Gotha). The factory owners Kugnle and
Hoffmann maintained a small porcelain factory here in 1867.

Ohrdruf (1) (Germany, Thuringia). Baehr and Proeschild, porcelain factory, f.
1871. Utility ware, Holy images, dolls and dolls' heads.

[251]   Hallmark   Hallmark

Ohrdruf (2) (Germany, Thuringia). Kestner & Co., porcelain factory; formerly J. D. Kestner Jr., f. in the beginning of the 19th c. Fancy ware, dolls' services, dolls' heads, etc.

Ohrdruf (3) (Germany, Thuringia). Kling & Co. porcelain factory, f. 1836. Fancy porcelain goods, gift items, dolls and dolls' heads. The factory closed in 1941.

Oissel (France). La Céramique 'Normande', Sàrl. Ornamental porcelain, ovenware and fire-proof products for laboratories.

Okawaji porcelain (or Nabeschima porcelain). Named after the village of Okawaji in Hizen, or after the Prince of Nabeschima, for whom the Okawaji porcelain was produced in the 18th c. It is among the best Japanese porcelain, decorated in cobalt blue underglaze, and then fired with enamels in overglaze. The Okawaji porcelain products are marked on the under side with the 'comb pattern'.

Olbers, Th., see Cologne (1).

Old Crown Derby China Company, see Derby (1).

Old decoration (Altoziermuster). Meissen pattern from 1730. The brim of the plate, sectioned off by 12 arches, is outlined with a cord and divided into 12 segments by 12 radially arranged sticks, ornamented with a regular, fine plaiting in light relief. See New decoration.

Old Viennese Gilding, see Alt-Wein-Vergoldung.

Olsufjeff, see Petersburg (1).

Olympia, Mario Tosin & Co., see Vicenza (2).

Omi (Japan). Japanese province, where, according to legend, porcelain was being made in 27 B.C., by a Korean King's son.

Ondrup, Hans Christopher. Worked as decorator in Copenhagen 1779–89. His speciality was landscapes.

Onion pattern, see Zweibelmuster.

Onyx Service. Produced in Nymphenburg in 1822 by Friedrich Gärtner, successor of Melchior, for King Max I. It comprises semi-precious cut stones in neo-classical style, intricate, rich decorations and gilding. It was the most extravagant order placed during this period and consisted of more than 700 individual pieces.

'Opaque china'. The name used by the English factory at Swansea for its stoneware products, 1815–40.

ÖPIAG, see Carlsbad (2).

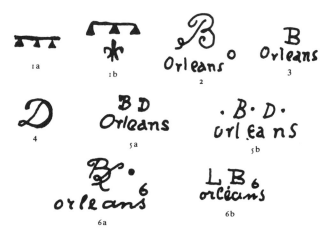

Orben, Knabe & Co., see Geschwenda.

Orchamps (France). According to M. Brongniart, a porcelain factory owned by M. Barré-Russin was here from 1829–56.

'Orica' (works of the Ceramica Lombarda di Lambrate), see Doccia.

Orléans (1) (France). In 1753 Jacques-Etienne Dessaux de Romilly obtained permission to found a faience factory, which was directed by Louis François Le Roy. Claude-Charles Gérault·d'Areaubert took over this concern in 1760 and began the production of porcelain in 1767 under the name 'Manufacture Royal de porcelayne Orleans'. Gérault died in 1782; his widow continued to manage the factory for a limited time. The following were later owners:

1767–88	Gérault	M 1 a and b	blue underglaze
from 1788	Bourdon du Susay	M 2	gold
from 1795	Bourdon and Son	M 3	gold
from 1797	Piedor-Dumuys and Dubois	M 4	red
about 1800	Barlois & Dabot	M 5 a and b	gold
1806–12	Benoist–Lebrun or le Brun	M 6 a and b	red

Good quality utility ware, decorated statuettes in biscuit, very fine decoration and gilding.

Orléans (2) (France). About 1793 there was a small porcelain factory here run by Molier & Bardin of which nothing is known apart from the marks. The factory stopped working before the end of the 18th c.

Orléans, Louis, Duke of (1703–52), see Bagnolet (1).
Orléans, Louis-Philippe Joseph, Duke of (1747–93), see Paris (98).
Ormont, see Bordeaux (2).
Orry de Fulvy, Jean-Louis-Henry (1703–51). Founder of the French porcelain factory in Vincennes, in 1738.
Ortmans, Justin, see Saint Gervais.
Ortolani, Lodovico. According to marks found on certain pieces, he was active as decorator in the porcelain factory in Venice.

Osborne China Company, see Longton (58).
Osnabrück (1) (Germany, Westphalia). Adolf Hoffmann, porcelain decorating studio. Services, tableware, biscuit tins, vases. Styles: Dresden, Meissen, Delft, Baroque, rococo, Biedermeier, modern. Was still active in 1949.

Osnabrück (2) (Germany, Westphalia). Franz Hoffmann, porcelain decorating studio, c. 1930.

ÖSPAG, see Vienna (14).
Osterspei, Jacob (1730–82). He joined the decorating workshop at the porcelain factory in Frankenthal when he was still a young man, but he was nevertheless regarded as the best decorator. Pieces with his signature justify his fame. He was active in Frankenthal until his death.

Osthein, Johann Friedrich Karl von, Elector of Mainz, 1743–63, see Höchst.
Ostrich egg glaze. A surface which is similar to that of the Chinese porcelain of the Ming Dynasty, 1368–1643.
Ott, Anton, see Dresden (23).
Ottensheim (Upper Austria). Karl Heinz Eigl porcelain factory, f. 1953 in Vienna. Specialises in domestic porcelain ware and gift articles.

Ottorino del Vivo & Co, see Florence (3).
Ottweiler on the Saar (Germany). Etienne-Domonoque Pellevé, from Sinceny, founded a porcelain factory here in 1763. He was sponsored by Prince Wilhelm Heinrich von Nassau-Saarbrücken. In 1764 Pellevé associated with the merchant Georg Heinrich Jeremias Wagner and in 1765 another partner joined, the merchant Isaak Wille. In the same year the modeller Paul Louis Cyfflé from Bruges was employed but Pellevé could not get on with him and he was replaced by the modeller Tentz. In the same year Karl Gottlieb Grahl and J. Ph. Wagner shared the management of the business which was leased to two Frenchmen, René François Jolly and Nicolas Leclerc in 1769. Through these two, French artists were engaged. Porcelain production ceased in 1770, however. The products are of varying quality, the porcelain is seldom pure white. The output consisted mainly of tableware in rococo style, including jugs and terrines. The beautiful decoration depicts mythological scenes in monochrome painting in purple and underglaze blue. The porcelain decorator, Friedrich Karl Wohlfahrt was active in Ottweiler from 1769–70, and perhaps in 1771.

1–2 NS = Nassau-Saarbrücken, date in blue or gold, also incised – 3 property mark of Prince Wilhelm Heinrich Nassau-Saarbrücken

Oude Amstel (Holland). The Oude Loosdrecht porcelain factory was transferred here in 1784, without any changes in ownership. A German, F. Daeuber, became the director. The factory developed well but was unable to withstand the English competition and consequently passed to new owners, the gentlemen J. Reudorp, C. van der Hoop and Gysbz. Daeuber remained as director. In 1799, Dommer & Co. became the owners; in 1809 they combined the factory with their chemical plant in Nieuve Amstel, but in 1820 production ceased. The products were of indifferent quality and drew much from the production of the previous factory, but they also produced in the neo-classical style.

Amstel
M. O. L

Oude Loosdrecht (Holland). Johannes de Mol ('the preacher') f. a new porcelain factory here in 1771. He used the remainder of the inheritance from the Weesp porcelain factory. With the help of the arcanist, L. V. Gerverot, the business prospered rapidly. On the death of de Mol in 1782, the factory became the property of a Limited Company, and in 1784 it was transferred to Oude-Amstel; it produced porcelain of outstanding quality in the styles of the leading European factories such as Meissen and Sèvres. Tableware with gilded-rocailles rims and colourful decoration are the most popular. A noticeable peculiarity is the use of a predominant brown colour in the decorations.

1 incised – 2 blue or red underglaze – 3 purple or mixed colours – 4 black or multi-coloured – 5 violet – 7–8 on one piece, 7 blue, 8 incised – 9 gold or violet – 10–11 on one piece, 10 blue, 11 incised – M:OL = Moll Oude Loosdrecht; M.O.L. = Oude Loosdrecht factory

Ouwens, B., see Untermhaus.

Overglaze decoration, also muffle kiln decoration or enamelling. By far the majority of porcelain is decorated with overglaze enamels. These consist of colour-bound metals or oxides, in short a dye and a flux-substance which combines the colouring ingredients with the glaze, fixing the colours and adding a shine. Combinations of uranium, copper, iridium, iron, tin, zinc, lead, mangnese, chromium, and cobalt can be used as metal colourants. As a flux medium one generally uses mixtures of quartz, fire stone, red lead, bismuth oxide, saltpetre, borax, natron, and calcium carbonate. These substances are finely grounded, made fluid with lavender oil and flexible with thickened and filtered turpentine, and are then ready to be used. These enamels are painted onto ready fired and glazed porcelain which is afterwards fired in a muffle kiln at a moderate temperature of c. 750–900°.

Owari (Japan). Ancient Japanese province which gave its name to the porcelain made there.

Oxan, Giovanni. Porcelain decorator. Originally his name was Hohann Hochgesang and he was from Bayreuth where he was active in the faience factory. He painted in the Vinovo porcelain factory nr. Turin, 'Hocseauch pittore'. He was last active in the Amberg faience factory.

Ozier pattern, see Old decoration and New decoration.

Paepke & Schäfer, see Haida (2).

Pagodas. Buddha-like porcelain figures, which were copies of Chinese figures, produced during the Böttger period, and later at Meissen and other factories.

Pahland, J. G., master modeller and turner, see Kassel.

Pajou, Augustin (1730–1809). French sculptor whose works were copied in biscuit at Sèvres.

Pakaniewo. According to Swinarski/Chrościcki (Posen 1949), an earthenware and porcelain factory existed here from 1879, the products of which were signed with the following mark.

Palme, Josef, see Schelten.

Pápa (Hungary). Samuel Boscowitz, porcelain decorating studio, c. 1930.

Papault, G., see Limoges (60).

Paquier, Claudius Innocenzius du (d. 1751). In 1719 he founded, with the aid of the Meissen arcanist Stölzel and the decorator Christoph Conrad Hunger, the Vienna porcelain factory which he sold in 1744 to the State. See Vienna (1).

Paragon China Ltd, see Longton (59).

Parant, Jules, see Limoges (77).

Parbus, Leni, see Oberkotzau (3).

Pardoe, Thomas (1770–1823). Porcelain decorator in Derby, Worcester and Swansea factories, and an independent decorator from 1797–1821.

Pardoe, Fecit Bristol.

Parent, see Sèvres (1).

Parian and Carrara. A highly feldspathic porcelain named after the famous marble quarry at Carrara (Italy), and the Greek quarry on the Isle of Paros. The ceramic products were made in England and contained several other ingredients, apart from feldspar and kaolin, which were added in greatly varying proportions. The aim was to imitate marble with the cold white biscuit porcelain. 19th c.

Parian, see Stoke-on-Trent (11).

Paris (1) Gros Caillou II (France). Advenier and Lamare f. a porcelain factory here in 1773, about which little is known. It is important to mention that the factory belonged to the nine Parisian studios which were granted a licence to decorate porcelain on 16 May 1784. Before this time they, like all other porcelain decorating factories, were only permitted to paint in a single colour and gilding was forbidden. Polychrome decoration and gilding were the prerogative of Sèvres.

Paris (2), Rue du Jour (France). Allard founded a small porcelain factory here between 1825 and 1828.

rot

Paris (3) (France). Anciens Etablissements Noublanche, porcelain factory.

Paris (4), Rue N.-D.-de-Nazareth (France). André directed a small porcelain factory here between 1810 and 1840.

Paris (5). 5 Passage Violet (France). André & Cottier managed the small selling agency of Foescy (later Luis André & Co.) here in 1834.

Manufacture de Foëscy
Passage Violet, No. 5.
R. Poissonnière, à Paris.
Paris. A. Cottier

Manut-de Foessy
Passage Violet n°5
R Poissonniere a Paris

Paris (6), 27 Rue de Filles de Calvaire (France). Baillieux directed a porcelain decorating studio here from 1839 (according to 'Tardy 75').

Paris (7) (France). It was here that Balley introduced the use of stencils during work at the potter's wheel in 1855 (DKG).

Paris (8), Rue de Paradis (France). Bastien & Bugeard managed a porcelain decorating shop here from 1830–50. The white porcelain was bought from Limoges (according to 'Tardy 75').

Paris (9), Rue de L'Arbre Sec (France). Bernon maintained a porcelain decorating studio here from 1845 until the time of the second Empire.

Paris (10), Rue des Vieux-Augustins (France). In 1830 a Mme. Blanchard was active here as a porcelain decorator.

Paris (11), Rue de Paradis (France). In 1922 Bloch used the following mark for porcelain (according to 'Tardy 75').

Paris (12), Cour des Fontaines (France). Bondeux maintained a porcelain decorating studio here 1800–40.

Paris (13), 43 Rue de Paradis (France), Géo Borgfeldt & Co, had the following mark entered in 1906 (according to 'Tardy 75'). The New York branch (1881–1914) was called George Borgfeldt & Co., and produced dolls' heads.

Paris (14), 14 Rue de la Fidélité (France). J. F. N. Boudon, Faincerie et porcelaine.

Paris (15), Rue Vivienne (France). Bringeon f. a porcelain decorating shop here c. 1850.

Paris (16), 18 Rue de la Paix (France). In 1818, Ferdinand Brunin directed a workshop for porcelain decoration and gilding here.

Paris (17) (France). Céralene, porcelain factory, since 1960. Luxury wares.

Paris (18), Barrière de Reuilly (France). Henri Florentin Chanon et Comp. from Sèvres, directed a porcelain factory here whose production was decorated in polychrome. It must be mentioned that this factory belonged to the nine Parisian decorating studios which were permitted, according to a decree of 16 May 1784, to practise polychrome decorating on porcelain. Prior to this, they, like all other porcelain factories, were only allowed to use one colour, and no gilding. Polychrome decoration and gilding were the privilege of Sèvres.

1   2   3

2 and 3 red

Paris (19) (France). Chaponnet-Desnoyer produced Sèvres imitations of very good quality here in 1823. Besides the Sèvres mark the following mark was used (according to 'Tardy 75').

$$D \quad C$$
$$M$$
$$23$$

Paris (20), Rue de Dragon (France). Chapperon, porcelain decorator, managed a retail shop for luxury porcelain here from 1815–30, according to 'Tardy 75'.

Paris (21), 15 Boulevard Montmartre (France). The dealer E. Cheron registered the following mark in 1905.

```
┌─────────────────────┐
│         AU           │
│  VASE de SEVRES      │
└─────────────────────┘
```

Paris (22), Rue des Marais-du-Temple (France). Chotain, the decorator and gilder, was active here c. 1830 (according to 'Tardy 75').

Paris (23), Rue de la Pierre-Levée (France). Jean Marx Clauss, who already worked as an independent porcelain decorator in 1822, transferred his studio in 1829 to the Rue de la Pierre-Levée with the intention of continuing Locre's tradition. After his death in 1846, his son Alphonse took over the studio and conducted the business until his death in 1868. His son Marc Eugen was solely in charge until 1887, when he made Achille Bloch and Leon Bourgeois his partners. M. E. Clauss withdrew in 1890 and Leon Bourgeois followed in 1900. From this time on the factory remained in the possession of the Bloch family. Achille Bloch's son Robert and his grandson Michel Bloit are still directing the factory to date (1976). The three Clausses produced luxury porcelain exclusively, expensive table services, vases, groups and statuettes. Chardin, Watteau and

Boucher were the prototypes for the decoration. The firm continues to produce in this tradition without neglecting modern ideas. In 1948 it officially accepted the title: 'Porcelaine de Paris', which had been in use for many years before. Household and sanitary ware was added to the products in 1949. There was already worldwide export during the time of the Clausses. According to Berling and Lange, both 1911, the KPM Meissen successfully prosecuted their use of the sword mark No. 1, before 1896.

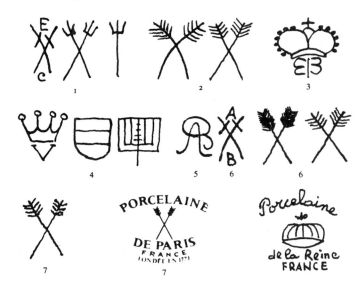

1 Mare Eugen Bloch 1868–87 – 2 Bloch & Cie. 1887–1900 – 3 Bourdois & Bloch 1890–1900 – 4 Bourdois & Bloch c. 1899 – 5 Achille Bloch 1900–20 – 6 marks since 1920 – additional mark c. 1963 – All marks in blue, partly under, partly overglaze

Paris (24) (France). Clement-Massier in Golfe-Juan (Alpes Maritimes) produced lustred ware at the end of the 19th c. They were sold in his Parisian shop in the Rue de Rivoli.

$$Clement\text{-}Massier$$
$$Golfe\text{-}Juan . A.M$$
$$L \ Levy.$$

Paris (25), Rue Popincourt (France). The Coeur d'Acier f. a small porcelain factory here c. 1797. A further establishment was situated in the Rue Saint-Honoré, but this was already in the hands of Discry by 1842. Chief products were Chinese porcelain copies. Menard became the successor to Discrys.

C. H. MENARD
Paris
72 Rue de Popincourt.

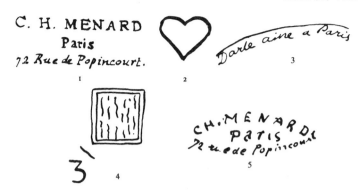

1   2

3

4

5

Paris (26), 129 Rue de Fgb. Poissonière (France). 'La Cie, de la Baie de Hudson' had the following mark entered in 1931 (according to 'Tardy 75').

Paris (27), Boulevard des Italiens (France). Cossé-Maillard managed a porcelain decorating studio c. 1830, which Chapelle-Maillard took over in 1845.

·Chapelle
19 B^des Italiens
Médaille Exp.^m 1844
1

Cosse Maillord
B^o italiern 71-19
2

Chapelle/Maillad
paris.
3

1 purple – 2 red – 3 gold

Paris (28), Boulevard Montmartre (France). Couderc directed a porcelain decorating studio here c. 1840.

Paris (29), Rue N.-D.-des-Champs (France). According to the Yearly Commercial Register, the Dagoty Bros. directed a small porcelain factory at the Boulevard Poissonnière c. 1800. A second business is mentioned in the year 1810 in the Rue N.-D.-de-Chevreuse, which was also the property of Dagoty.

Dayoly freru

gold

Paris (30), Boulevard Poissonnière (France). P. L. Dagoty f. a porcelain factory here at the end of the 18th c., which was called (after 1804) 'Manufacture D.S.M.l'Emperatrice P.L. Dagoty à Paris'. Porcelain was made in the Chinese and neo-classical taste.

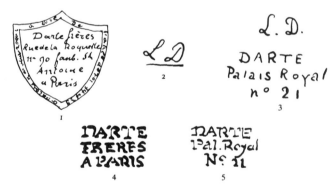

P. L · DAGOTY de S.M.L'Imperatrice   Manufacture   *Dagoty*
A PARIS   P.L DAGOTY   à Paris.   *à paris*

1 red – 2 red shaded – 3 gold

Paris (31), Rue de Charonne (France). The Darte Bros. f. a porcelain factory here in 1795, which was transferred to the Rue de la Roquette in the beginning of the 19th c., and subsequently into the Rue Popincourt. In addition they managed a porcelain decorating studio in the Palais Royal.

Darte frères
Rue de la Roquette
11° 90 faub. St
Antoine
à Paris
1

LD
2

L. D.
DARTE
Palais Royal
n° 21
3

DARTE
FRERES
A PARIS
4

DARTE
Pal.Royal
N° 11
5

2 incised – 3 blue underglaze and red – 4 red – 5 red

Paris (32), Rue de Bondy (France). Dastin f. a porcelain factory here c. 1810, where Aaron executed the decorations.

Dastin   *Dastin r Du. ban*   DASTIN
1   2   3

1 gold – 2 gold – 3 red

Paris (33), 46, Rue de Paradis (France). According to 'Tardy 75' Daudin & Laner had the following mark registered in 1911.

Paris (34) (France). Michel David, porcelain decorating studio.

Paris (35) (France). Théodore Deck, director of the Sèvres porcelain factory from 1887–91, f. a workshop for artistic faiences in 1859. His influence on the entire ceramic industry during this period, is clearly evident.

$$.D \qquad \mathcal{A}.DECK$$

Paris (36), 12 Rue Coquillère (France). Déroche owned a porcelain factory here c. 1812, where he mainly produced and decorated vessels for pharmacies. He later moved his factory into the Rue J.-J.-Rousseau. His successors were: Pochet-Deroche, Vignier and H. Pochet.

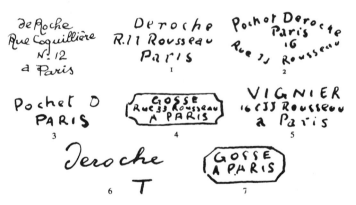

1 red – 2–3 black – 4 blind stamped – 5 black – 6 gold – 7 black

Paris (37), Clignancourt (Parisian suburb nr. Montmartre) (France). Pierre Deruelle f. a porcelain factory here in 1771, which came under the protection of the brother of King Louis XV. It was called 'Fabrique de Monsieur'. Deruelle's son-in-law, Moitte, succeeded him and directed the factory until at least 1798 (possibly later). The porcelain was of exceptionally good quality during the period of Royal patronage. Artists of calibre were employed, coming mostly from Vienna and Sèvres. It should be mentioned that the factory belonged to the nine Parisian decorating studios, which were permitted, by a decree of 16 May 1784, to decorate porcelain. Prior to this decree, they, like all other decorating studios, were not allowed to decorate in more than one colour and gilding was forbidden. Polychrome decoration and gilding were the privilege of Sèvres.

1–2 red – 3 gold – 4–5 red – 8–9 red – 11–12 red – 14 blue underglaze – 15 blue – 16 red – 17 gold or red

Paris (38), Palais Royal. L'Escalier de Cristal (France). Madame Desarneaux (or Desarnaux) directed a porcelain decorating studio here from 1802, as well as retailing crystal ware. The succeeding owners were: Boin (1828), Bouvet (1837), Lahoche-Pannier (1854–1900). In about 1874, the business was moved to the Rue Scribe, later it was transferred to the Rue Auber.

Marks in black, red or gold

Paris (39) (France). Desforges-Naudot, porcelain factory. Table service and luxury porcelain.

Paris (40), Rue des Recollets (France). A porcelain factory worked here between 1793 and 1825 whose founder was Desprez. His son established himself in the Rue des Morts, dealing in portrait medals.

DESPREZ   DESPREZ   DESPREZ
Rue des Ricollets   Rue ue. Recolets
a Paris   u°.2-a Paris

Paris (41), Rue de Bondy (France). Dihl f. a porcelain factory here in 1780 which enjoyed the protection of the Duke of Angoulême and was styled 'Manufacture du Duc d'Angoulême'. Dihl possibly associated with Guerhard before 1786 and was still connected with him in 1817. In 1795 the factory moved to the Rue de Temple and later, in 1825, to the Boulevard St. Martin. It closed in 1829. Porcelain ware with simple decoration, particularly the so-called 'Angoulême' pattern, a cornflower design, is well known but some richly decorated pieces were also made. It should be noted that this factory was among the nine Parisian decorating studios which were permitted, by a decree of 16 May 1784, to decorate porcelain. Prior to this, they, like all the other porcelain factories, were only allowed one colour, and gilding was forbidden. Polychrome decoration and gilding were the privilege of Sèvres.

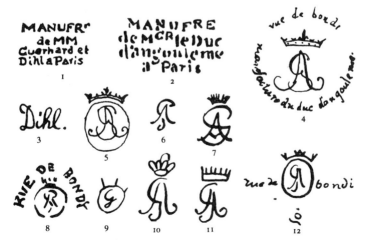

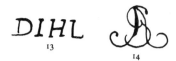

DIHL
13

14

1 red – 2 red shaded – 3 red or incised – 4–5 red – 6 gold – 10 blue – 11–12 gold – 13 incised – 14 blue – 15–21 in red after the French Revolution

After the French Revolution the following marks were produced in red (according to 'Tardy 75').

MANUF^re
DE DIHL
ET GUERHARD

GUERHARD
ET DIHL
A PARIS

M· de
Guerhard
et Dihl

DIHL ET
GUERHARD
A PARIS.

Rue de Bondy

Dihl

M^r de
Guerhard
et Dihl
a Paris

Paris (42), 45 Rue de Paradis-Poissonnière (France). D. Dione & Baudry used the following mark in 1876, according to 'Tardy 75'.

Paris (43), Rue Coquillère (France). Duban produced porcelain here which was marked with his name, c. 1800.

Duban

Paris (44), Rue de la Roquette (Faubourg St. Antoine) (France). Jerôme-Vincent Dubois f. a porcelain factory here in 1774; beautiful pieces in the Empire style are known. The factory was called 'Drei Windhündmnen' (Three Greyhounds) and since it was based in the 'Hôtel des Arbalétriers' (cross-bow-soldiers) the mark used depicted two crossed arrows in blue. It is possible to confuse them with the torches of 'La Courtille', although the products of Locrés are considerably more refined. Existed until 1790.

all blue

Paris (45), 66 Rue de la Roquette (France). Dubois created statuettes from biscuit porcelain here in 1816. Together with his son he produced figures 42 cm high (crucifixes) in c. 1830.

Dubois.ft   Dubois.f.   VDubois

Paris (46), Quai de la Cité (France). Duhamel owned a porcelain factory here from c. 1790–1827.

Duhamel

gold

Paris (47), 15 Passage du Jeu-de-Boule (France). The Duterte Bros. managed a porcelain decorating studio here c. 1847. In 1849 they acquired the method for high gloss gilding from Meissen.

   Dutertre.fres   D.F

Paris (48), 3 Rue des Augustins (France). Here, c. 1809, Duval signed any porcelain he decorated with his name (according to 'Tardy 75').

Duval

Paris (49), 77 Rue Basse du Temple (France). Ferrière was active here as a porcelain decorator in 1830, according to 'Tardy 75'.

Ferrière.
a Paris

Paris (50). Rue de la Paix (France). Feuillet introduced a porcelain decorating studio here c. 1820. Since his decorations are found only on hard paste porcelain, it is feasible that these products were chiefly from the Royal factory Sèvres. His successors were Boyer (1845), Jacques & Boyer, Paul Blot and Hebert.

Feuillet
rue de la Pau
– n° 20

1   2   3

4

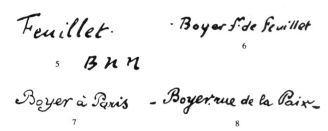

1 green or gold – 4 green – 5 gold – 6–8 red

Paris (51) (France). Fleury directed a porcelain factory in the Rue de Faubourg-St.-Lazare in 1803, which was seemingly managed until 1835 by Flamen Fleury in the Rue de Faubourg-St.-Denis. His products are very well known. In 1847 Fleury is still found as a producer of figures (in the Rue des Trois Couronnes).

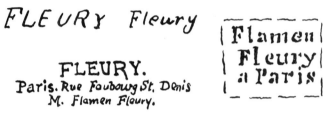

all in gold or red

Paris (52), 6 Rue de Crussol (France). Joseph François Francossi managed a porcelain decorating studio here in 1825–40.

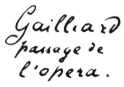

Paris (53), Passage de l'Opéra (France). Gaillard maintained a porcelain decorating studio here in 1840.

Gaillard
passage de
l'opera.

gold

Paris (54), Rue de L'Arbre Sec. (France), Gambier managed a porcelain decorating studio here c. 1812–30.

Gambier

Paris (55) (France). L. Gardie, porcelain decorating studio, c. 1850–1900. Decoration is in the style of Sèvres. According to Chaffers the goods were of mediocre quality.

*L Gardie,
a Paris*

Paris (56), Rue de Grenelle-Saint-Germain (France). Gaugain managed a porcelain decorating studio here c. 1815.

Gaugain

Paris (57), 13 Rue de Paradis (France). According to 'Tardy 75' Jean Gauthier had the following mark registered for porcelain in 1913.

Paris (58), 83 Rue St.-Honoré (France). Gerard, porcelain decorator since 1802 (according to 'Tardy 75'), signed with his name.

*Gérard .
à Paris*

Paris (59), 20 Rue de la Harpe (France). The Le Gerriez Bros. managed a porcelain decorating studio here in the mid-19th c., which changed addresses several times after 1870 (according to 'Tardy 75').

LE GERRIEZ
20 R! DE LA HARPE
paris

Paris (60), Rue de Paradis-Poissonnière (France). Gille f. a porcelain factory here in 1845. The bulk of the production was made up of biscuit busts, statuettes and groups, in the realist style. The modeller was Charles Baury, who later, together with Vion, became the owner.

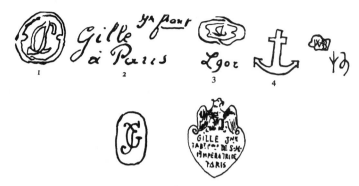

1-3 incised – 4 green

Paris (61), Rue de Lafayette (France). In 1857 Gillet & Brianchon received a patent for glazing porcelain with a mother-of-pearl lustre, 'décor de couleur nacrées à base de bismuth'. The porcelain products were decorated in their own studio. This patent also existed in England. When the patent expired, the technique was adopted by Beleek.

Paris (62), Rue de Courty (France). Gonord directed a porcelain decorating studio here from 1806–45, which was later taken over by Perenot.

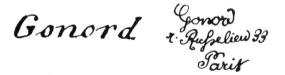

Paris (63), Place des Vosges (France). Gout de Ville S.à.r.l., porcelain decorating studio which also had a branch in Limoges.

Paris (64), Boulevard de la rue de Gramont (France). In 1778 it is said that Gramont (Gamont?) f. a small porcelain factory here.

Paris (65) (France). Guélaud, a liqueur manufacturer had his porcelain bottles signed with the following mark (from after the French Revolution until the Empire period).

Paris (66), 170 Rue de Temple (France). According to 'Tardy 75' J. Guterbaum had the following mark registered in 1853.

Paris (67), Rue du Petit-Carrousel (France). A small porcelain decorating studio worked here from 1775–1800. The owner was the businessman Barthélémy, who later, with Housel, also directed the factory in the Rue Thiroux.

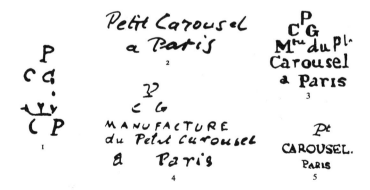

1 red – 2 gold – 3 red shaded – 4 red and black

Paris (68) (France). In 1800 Halley was active as a porcelain decorator, Boulv. Montmatre. Lebon directed his studio in the Rue Neuve of Petits-Champs. In 1812 Lebon-Halley, son-in-law and successor to Halley, in the Rue Montmatre.

all in gold

Paris (69), Faubourg St.-Denis (France). In 1771 Peter Anton Hannong f. a porcelain factory here, for which the mark 'H' had been entered. The directors were Barrachin, Chausard and de Leutre. The owner was the Marquis de Usson; Stahn was his successor. The factory worked under the protection of Charles Philippe Comte d'Artois. In 1783 Bourdon des Planches became the owner and Josse was director in 1787. The factory was successful from the beginning and managed to keep up production alongside the Royal factory, through which the products were sold. The factory survived the Revolution. Two new factories were active in 1798 under the direction of Benjamin and Fauvel. In 1828 Schoelcher owned a business which operated under the same name, which remained his until 1828. The products are praised for their outstanding translucency as well as their excellent glaze. It should be noted that this factory was one of the nine Parisian decorating studios which, by a decree of 16 May 1784, were permitted to decorate their porcelain. Before this date they, like all other porcelain factories, were limited to the use of monochrome decoration and gilding was forbidden. Polychrome and gilding were the privilege of Sèvres.

1 gold – 2 gold or red – 3–8 blue underglaze – 10 gold – 11 blue underglaze

Paris (70), 71 Fbg.St.-Denis (France). Hoffmann & Laluette ran a porcelain factory and retail business here. It was active in 1793.

Paris (71), Boulevard St. Antoine (France). F. M. Honoré f. a porcelain factory here in 1785 and in 1812 his two sons, Edward and Theodore, entered into partnership with him. They in turn collaborated with Dagoty and opened a second business in the Rue Chevreuse. The name of the firm from this time on was 'Dagoty et Honoré'. In 1820, the partners separated and the factories were divided between them. Dagoty retained the factory in Seynie. The Honoré Bros. kept the Parisian business which they moved to Champroux. Its products were marked with 'Mture de Madame Duchesse d'Angoulême Dagoty E. Honoré Paris'.

F. M. HONORÉ.

ED. HONORE
B oulevard Poissonniere à
A. PARIS

R. F. DAGOTY.

Mᵁʳᵉ de MADAME
Duchesse d' Angoulême
Dagoty E. Honoré
PARIS.

F. D. HONORÉ
à Paris.

Ed HONORE
à PARIS
Bou lera cd Poisson

P. L. Dagoty
&
E. Honoré
à Paris.

Paris (72), Cité du Thrône (France). J. Houry had his porcelain decorating studio here from 1863. The marks are interchangeable with those of Hannong.

Paris (73), Rue du Faubourg St.-Honoré (France). Housset managed a porcelain decorating studio here in 1845. In 1874 it was passed on to Isenbart.

red

Paris (74), Rue de Fbg. Joint-Martin (France). Balthasar Augustin Le Hujeur had a studio here c. 1870, where he mostly copied old styles. According to 'Tardy 75' the following mark was registered in 1889. Neither the mark nor the products bear comparison with Samson, Paris.

Paris (75), Gros Caillou I (France). In 1765 Jaquemart f. a factory here for porcelain production, but it seems that during his management only experimental pieces were produced. The factory was called Jacques Louis Broillet, and its initials were used as a mark in 1762. There is no evidence of any pieces.

Paris (76), 17 Rue de Paradis-Poissonnière (France). Etienne Jacquemin is mentioned here only because his mark is interchangable with that of Fontainebleau.

Paris (77), Rue St.-Louis (France). A porcelain decorating workshop was established here in 1827 by order of the Duke of Angoulême and was managed by Jeanne. It is possible that this is the Jeanne who managed the studio in the Rue de Nazareth, under Louis Philippe (1830–48).

   gold

Paris (78), Rue de Grésillons (France). S. P. Jullien, successor of Ww. Lalouette, directed a porcelain decorating studio here from 1819–27. His successor was Margaine.

Paris (79), Rue de Bac (France). Julienne managed a studio for decorating porcelain here c. 1830.

Jullienne   gold

Paris (80), Galéries du Louvre (France). Lagrenée from Sèvres managed a porcelain decorating shop here in 1793. His successors were Julienne-Moureau (1845), Perrier (1859), Clain (1879) and Clain & Perrier fils.

Lagrenée/fils

brown

Paris (81), Pont de Sèvres (France). Lahaussais directed a porcelain decorating shop here in 1896.

PT SEVRES
R.L & Cie

Paris (82), Rue de Reuilly (Faubourg St. Antoine) (France). Jean-Joseph Lassia f. a porcelain factory here in 1774. Little information about the products is available.

1 red – 3 gold – 4 red – 5 black

Paris (83), Rue Thiroux (France). André Marie Leboeuf f. the 'Fabrique de la Reine', also called 'Manufacture de la Reine' here. This establishment enjoyed the patronage of Queen Marie Antoinette and flourished. The mark 'A' was registered in 1776. Leboeuf's successors were Housel and Guy. The owners were Julienne in 1816, Léveillé in 1832, Pullain in 1850 and Léveillé again in 1869. Production was in the style of the Sèvres and Meissen factories. The quality of the products is praised. It must be noted here that this factory was among the nine Parisian decorating workshops which were permitted to decorate porcelain by a decree of 16 May 1784. Before this date they, like all other porcelain factories, were limited to painting in only one colour, and gilding was forbidden; polychrome decoration and gilding were the privilege of Sèvres.

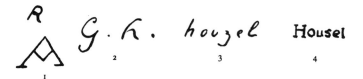

Housel

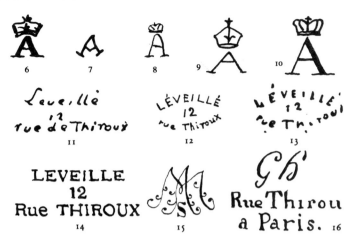

1 blue underglaze – 2 red – 3 gold – 4 red – 6–7 gold – 9 red – 10 blue underglaze – 11 gold and blue underglaze – 12–13 red

Paris (84), Rue du Corbeau (France). Lebourg produced painted porcelain flowers here c. 1844.

Paris (85), 28 Rue de la Fontaine-au-Roi (France). Gabriel Legrand directed a porcelain decorating studio here.

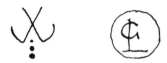

Paris (86) (France). According to 'Tardy 75' Le Juste directed a porcelain decorating studio here. Some pieces from c. 1820–50 are still in existence.

Paris (87) (France). J. Leofold, porcelain factory.

Paris (88). 19 Rue du Bac (France). Leplé directed a porcelain decorating studio here c. 1808. His signature follows, the other two marks are those of his son (Leplé jeune).

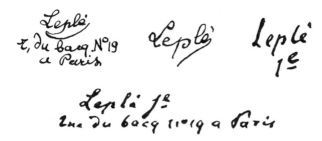

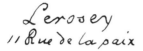

Paris (89) (France). Porcelain decorating studio f. here by M. Lerosey c. 1880.

Paris (90), Villa Faucheur (France). C. Le Tallec, porcelain decorator 1928–40, worked in the style of the 19th c. and produced mostly polychrome decoration on impressed 'pure gilding'. According to 'Tardy 75' the mark shown here was used from 1928–40. The roman numeral showing the year applies only to half a year. The letters below the mark are the initials of the decorators and pupils.

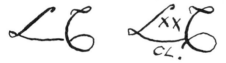

Paris (91) (France). Le Villain, porcelain decorator who is known only through his signature. He decorated in the manner of 'Porcelaine de la Reine' (according to 'Tardy 75').

Paris (92), 5 Rue de Charonne (France). L. Levy, porcelain decorator at the end of the 18th c. (according to 'Tardy 75').

L · LEvy.

Paris (93), Rue de Paradis (France). In 1953 the 'Limoges Unic' was f. here and used the following mark.

LIMOGES UNIC

Paris (94). Rue Fontaine-au-Roi (France). In 1771 Jean Baptiste Locré f. a porcelain factory here, which was known as 'La Courtille'. He was granted the two crossed torches as marks in 1793. In 1774 Locré chose the German porcelain modeller Laurentius Russinger *(q.v.)* as his partner. Russinger became the sole owner from 1787–97. At about this time he was forced to sell shares to Francois Pouyat, whose sons became the owners from 1808–c. 1825 (some sources say until 1840). The younger Pouyats moved one part of the factory to Fours (Nièvre) c. 1825. The Parisian section became the property of Jean Marx Clauss *(q.v.)* c. 1829. The factory produced outstanding porcelain in Meissen style and supplied all Europe. For example, the white porcelain which was sold to England, was decorated to a certain extent by Billingsley *(q.v.)*. Very beautiful biscuit figures from the hands of Russinger, are still in existence; they are mostly marked with the impressed torches. It is important to mention that this factory belonged to the nine Parisian decorating studios which were given permission to decorate porcelain by a decree of 16 May 1784. Before that date they, together with all other factories, were permitted only to use a single colour and gilding was forbidden. Polychrome decoration and gilding were the privilege of Sèvres.

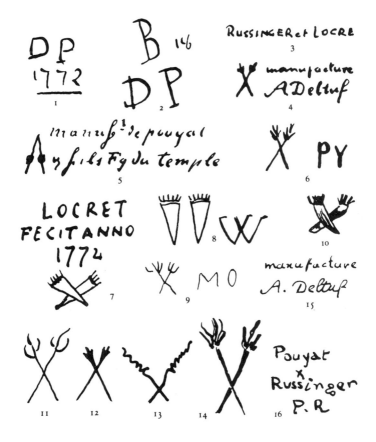

1 violet – 2 blind – 4–5 blue underglaze and gold – 6 violet and blue – 8–9 blind – 10–14 blue underglaze – 15 blue-gold – 16 red – 17 red

Paris (95), Boulevard des Italiens (France). During the first Empire Mabille managed a retail business for faience and porcelain here. After the return of the Bourbons he became supplier to the Court.

Paris (96), Rue de Paradis-Poissonnière (France). Mansard ran a porcelain decorating studio here c. 1830.

Paris (98), Rue Amelot (France). Louis Honoré de la Marre de Villiers and Montarcy f. a porcelain factory on 22 April 1784 in the Rue des Boulets (Faubourg St. Antoine). It is said that the factory was first active in the Rue Amelot and later in the Rue Pont-aux-Choux. Louis-Philippe-Joseph, Duke of Orléans, appointed himself as protector and the factory took his name. From then on the mark was the monogram of the Duke (until 1789). Werstock, Lemaire and Josse (1798), Caron Lefèvre and others were said to have been the owners. The products have little artistic merit. It is important to mention that this factory belonged to the nine Parisian decorating studios which, by a decree of 16 May 1784, were allowed to decorate porcelain. Before that date they, like all other factories, were only permitted to use a single colour and gilding was forbidden. Gilding and polychrome decoration were the privilege of Sèvres.

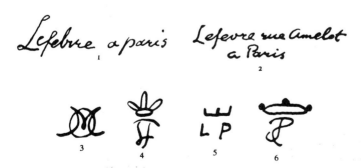

3 red – 4 blue underglaze – 5 red – 7 blue underglaze – 8 gold – 13 red – 14–16 blue underglaze

Paris (99), 15 Rue de Paradis (France). Mauge & Pézé had the following mark entered in 1889.

Paris (100), 13 Rue Montmartre (France). According to 'Tardy 75' Mazurin was active as a porcelain decorator here.

Paris (101), Rue de l'Arbre Sec (France). Meslier was active here as a porcelain decorator and gilder from 1820. His studio was taken over by his son and was still in existence in 1863.

Paris (102), 5 Rue Martel (France). David Michel had the following mark registered in 1927 (according to 'Tardy 75').

Paris (103), 243 Rue Neuve de Harlay (France). The merchant Michel had the following mark used for porcelain in 1798, according to 'Tardy 75'.

Paris (104), Pont-aux-Choux (France). Mignon owned a small factory here from 1774–84. The fleur de Lys mark was registered on 10 March 1777. It produced soft paste porcelain in the English style which was marketed under the name 'Terres d'Angleterre'. The factory was called 'Fayencerie Anglaise'. It must be mentioned that this factory belonged to the nine Parisian decorating studios which were permitted to decorate porcelain by a decree of 16 May 1784. Before that date, this factory, like all other porcelain factories, was allowed to decorate only in a single colour and gilding was forbidden. Polychrome work and gilding were the privilege of Sèvres.

both blue underglaze

Paris (105), Boulevard des Italiens (France). Montginot maintained a porcelain decorating studio here c. 1830 and carried stocks for retail.

Monginot
{o Boulevart
des Italiens

1

ｃＭｏｎｇｉｎｏｔ
ｇｏｕ ｔｅｖａｒｔ ｄｅｓ ｉｔａ ｌｉｅｎｓ
Ｎｏ ２０ ａ. ｐａｒｉｓ

2

1 incised – 2 gold

Paris (106), 37 Rue de Paradis (France). Constant Moreau had the following mark registered in 1907, according to 'Tardy 75'.

Paris (107), Fbg. St.-Honoré, Rue de le Ville l'Evêque (France). Marie Moreau established a branch of the St.-Cloud factory here, which she managed independently from 1722–43, transferring the directorship to her nephew, L. D. F. Chicaneau. After her death in 1743 the business was bought back by St.-Cloud until 1766. The production was in the style of St.-Cloud. The marks stand for Chicaneau–Moreau.

blue

Paris (108), Rue de la Roquette (Faubourg St.-Antoine) (France). Morelle f. a porcelain factory here in 1773. His mark 'MAP' means 'Morelle à Paris'.

Paris (109), Rue Popincourt (France). I. N. H. Nast f. a porcelain factory in 1782 which was still flourishing in 1748 in the Rue Amandiers Popincourt. Artistically, however, the production was insignificant. His sons directed the factory until 1835. In 1789 Jullien named this factory as one of the four largest in Paris. Nast improved his products with the use of figurative decoration 'a la molette', which was patented by him in 1810. Vases and decoratively gilded pieces, also porcelain figures in biscuit.

NAST a PARIS [1]

NAST. [2]

N... à: Paris [3]

Nast a Paris [4]

NAST a Paris [5]

nast a Paris par brevet d'invention [6]

Nast a paris par brevet d'invention [7]

Manu fre de Porcelaine du (en Nast) 7 ue des Amandiers D°u Popincourt [8]

[9]

MANUF^RE DE PORCELAINE DU (E^N NAST A PARIS [10]

J Lucablé [11]

1 gold – 2 impressed printing – 4 red – 5–7 gold – 8 incised – 9 red – 10–11 impressed printing

Paris (110), 7 Rue de Petites Ecuries (France). Camille Naudot & Cie., f. 1900. In 1904 the first mark shown was used. The factory was closed intermittently but continued to use this mark until 1919. Soft paste porcelain with perforated sides which were filled with coloured enamel. Gold leaf decoration under transparent enamel.

Paris (111), Rue du Rocher (France). A porcelain factory may have worked here in about 1799, called 'à la Pologne' and the owners were Nicolet and A. Greder.

Peres. 1814.

Paris (112), Rue de Crussol (France). The foundation of this little factory may have taken place in 1800. A certain Patrault is mentioned at about this time and two years later there are reports about a factory owner, Moise Meyer. In 1810 the name of Constant is mentioned and in 1919 a published report names the owners as Vaux and Denuelle. Nothing is known about the quality of the products.

DENUELLE
Rue de Crussol a Paris
1

DENUE LLE
A PARIS
4

PATRAULT

MAN^re de PORCELAINE
DE S A.R. M···e
"D^ss de BERRY
DENUELLE
Rue de Crussol a Paris
2

Denuelle
Boulevard S'Denis
a Paris
3

1 red/brown – 2 red – 3 red – 4 red/brown

Paris (113) (France). Perche, a Parisian porcelain decorator from 1795–1825, worked chiefly for the factory in the Rue du Petit Carrousel, but also decorated products from other factories; he signed either with his name or the fish mark (perche).

Schalcher
1

2

PERCHE
3

1 red/brown – 2 blue – 3 red

Paris (114), Boulevard Montmartre (France). Person directed a porcelain factory here.

Person
gold

Paris (115) (France). E. Personne directed a porcelain decorating studio here at the end of the 19th c., marking the goods with his address.

Produits de Serres
Ed. Personne
8 Rue Royale Paris.

Paris (116), Belleville (France). Jacob Petit produced porcelain here from c. 1790. The products have been highly praised and show an individual style. But porcelain was also made in the style of Meissen; these pieces were marked with the Elector's swords. Patents dealing with improvements to the formula of the porcelain paste and surface techniques were given notice of in England in 1853. In 1834 the factory incorporated the Fontainebleau porcelain factory (see Fontainebleau).

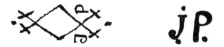

Paris (117), 20 Rue de Paradis (France). Pillivuyt Jr. had the following mark entered here in 1931, according to 'Tardy 75'.

A.H & C⁰
V
FRANCE

SOCIETE
DES
ANCIENS
ETABLISSEMENTS
A.HACHE & C·
PARIS
VIERZON

Paris (118), 30 Rue de Paradis (France). Pillivuyt & Co. entered 'Apilco' in 1926 and 'AP + F' in 1928 (according to 'Tardy 75').

Apilco   AP & F
FRANCE

Paris (119), Rue Cambon (France). 'Porcelainerie de la Haute-Vienne' had the following mark registered in 1925 (according to 'Tardy 75').

Paris (120), Rue de Crussol (France). Ch. Potter, an Englishman, f. a porcelain factory here in 1789 which he called 'Manufacture du Prince de Galles' and its products were called 'Prince of Wales China'. In 1792 it became the property of E. Blancheron. Subsequent owners were Joseph Maubrée in 1807, Blancheron & Neppel in 1810 (it is said), Denuell & Cadet de Vaux in 1819. Her Royal Highness the Duchess of Berry favoured the factory with her patronage in 1823. The pieces were praised for their miniature decorations as well as for their fine gilding.

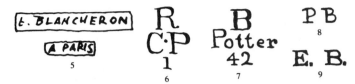

3 red – 4 gold – 5 raised – 6–9 blue underglaze

Paris (121), 22 Rue du petit Lion Saint-Sauvour (France). Quettier & Co. managed a studio for porcelain decorating here in 1815 (according to 'Tardy 75').

Paris (122), Rue Caumartin (France). A porcelain decorating studio owned by Renou existed here from 1725–1820.

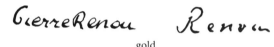

gold

Paris (123) (France). Renaud directed a porcelain decorating studio here in 1896.

Paris (124), Rue Neuve des Capucines (France). Revil was active here as a porcelain decorator from 1810.

REVIL Rue Neuve des Capucines	REVIL Rᵉ Neuve des Capucines	REVIL Rᵘᵉ Neuve des Capucines
1	2	3

1 red – 2 red shaded – 3 red

Paris (125), Rue de la Paix (France). J. Rihouet, in association with Lerosey, directed a porcelain decorating studio here in 1820.

Rihouet
1

LErosey
11 rue de la Paix
à Paris.

RIHOUET
Fbur
rue du Roi
de la Paix
2

Lerosey
7 Rue de la paix

1 gold – 2 violet

Paris (126), Boulevard St.-Martin (France). Francisque Rousseau directed a studio here which produced outstanding underglaze colours and decoration in relief. The factory frequently changed its address and may have been active until c. 1870.

```
Rousseau                    ROUSSEAU
    43                  Bould St Martin
Rue Coqvillere           49
                       Fournisseur du Roi
```

Paris (127) (France). According to Berling and Lange (both 1911), it is possible that Arnold Rub-Leprince marked their ware here at the end of the 19th c. with the first mark shown. In 1896 the KPM Meissen took out strict injunctions against the use of the mark. It has been ascertained that the mark had been registered with the Klg. Amtsgericht Leipzig as a trademark on 20 May 1892, its number being the current No. 5261.

[50]

Paris (128) (France). The following decorator's mark in gold has been found on porcelain c. 1870 (Kovel).

Paris (129) (France). Establissements Gaston Sailly (Société anonyme des), porcelain factory.

Paris (130), 43 Boulevard Voltaire (France). In 1891, Leon Saison used the following porcelain mark here.

Paris (131), Rue Béranger (France). Edm. Samson (Samson the Imitator) set up his factory here in 1873. He worked mostly for private collectors and museums producing restorations, replacements and exact copies of pieces from all European factories which were as good as, as well as similar to the originals.

Production was in series and also for export. From 1873–6 he marked with 1, and from 1876 with mark 2. His son Emile used the marks 3–7 from 1885. It is not known how long his factory existed. However, in 1941 it revived and again produced copies of famous pieces, but this time not only in porcelain. For Meissen reproductions the marks Nos. 8, 9, and 10 were used; Sèvres copies are marked with 11 and 12. Pieces which imitated Capo di Monte, Buen Retiro, St.-Cloud, Mennessy and Chantilly, were given mark 13 (from 1941). 13a was also used for products in the English style. Italian pieces and those which imitated Pallissy, had mark No. 14, from 1941. In 1957 marks 15 and 16 were removed. It is possible that the marks 9, 10 and 12 were used as early as 1875.

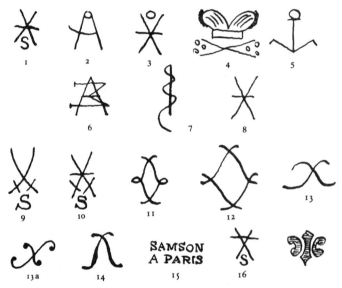

Paris (132), Boulevard de Magenta (France). According to 'Tardy 75', the following mark was registered for 'S.A.R.L., Rue de la Paix' in 1963.

Paris (133), Rue de la Folie-Méricourt (France). In 1,897 Charles Sauzin

decorated door handles and door knobs which he marked with marks 1 and 2. In 1921 V. Vandenbossche continued as director of the decorating studio.

Paris (134), Cour-Mandar (France). Scheilheimer directed a porcelain establishment here in 1799.

Scheilheimer Cours Manday
No 5

gold

Paris (135), Faubourg St.-Denis, Boulevard des Italiens (France). Marc Schoelcher was already the owner of a porcelain factory in the Rue de la Monaie, when he purchased one of the Hannong factories in the Faubourg St.-Denis. He also ran a retail shop in the Boulevard des Italiens. Schoelcher enjoyed the protection of the Duke d'Artois. His son Victor took charge of the factory in 1832, after he already had been a partner for four years. Although the production of porcelain had already ceased in 1810, the decorating studio remained active until 1834.

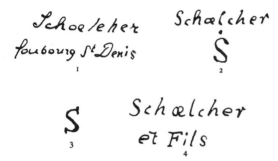

1 gold – impressed mark blue or violet – 3 blue underglaze – 4 violet

Paris (136), Rue Taranne (France). In 1802 a porcelain decorating studio was active here, f. by Séjourneau and directed at one time by Demont.

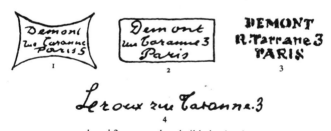

1 and 2 engraved and gilded – 4 red

Paris (137) (France). Victor Sigel, porcelain factory, 1918–24.

Paris (138) (France). 'Société de la Rue Chaptal', the Parisian association of

amateur decorators, who painted faience and porcelain. Beside their own name, they added the ensign of their society.

Paris (139), 46 Rue de Paradis (France). 'Société Française de porcelaine', f. 1946 (according to 'Tardy 75').

Paris (140), Rue de la Roquette (France). In 1773 Souroux f. a porcelain factory here of which we know nothing except the registration of the mark.

1 red – 2–3 blue underglaze – 4 red

Paris (141), Rue St.-Merry (France). Stone, Coquerel and Legros directed a factory here from 1807–49, which was transferred in 1825 to the Rue Charlot and later into the Rue de Poitou. Nothing is known of the products as regards quality. In 1803 Legros d'Ansy discovered a printing process which was patented in 1808. The undecorated porcelain came mainly from the Sèvres factory. The factory existed until 1849. The lettering encircling the marks says: Manufacture d'Impression sur Faience Porcelaine & c PAR BREVET D'INVENTION', printed in black or sepia on transfer printing, 1808–49.

Paris (142), Cité de Paradis (France). Stocklin & Co., porcelain merchants, had the following mark registered in 1939 (according to 'Tardy 75').

Paris (143), Boulevard des Capucines (France). On 18 July 1811 W. Story received a patent for his invention of the 'bleu Imperial', a sky blue, which he sold to other porcelain decorating studios. For packaging this material he used cylindrical containers of porcelain, with a blue network decoration, the lid being topped with a golden button. According to 'Tardy 75' these containers were marked with the following mark in black.

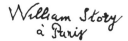

Paris (144), 40 Rue du Fbg. Poissonnière (France). Taverne & Co., porcelain merchants, had the following mark entered in 1893 (according to 'Tardy 75').

Paris (145), Rue de Trevise (France). P. Thiacourt, decorator and modeller, ran a studio and workshop here for the restoration of porcelain and faiences. He wrote a treatise on this subject which was published in 1868. Thiaucourt also produced copies of old porcelain, which were decorated by his daughter Adrienne. Her signature appears in 'Tardy 75'.

Paris (146) (France). J. Tiélès, porcelain factory.

Paris (147), 12 Rue la Michodière (France). Touchard directed a porcelain decorating studio here in 1839.

Paris (148), Rue de la Chausée-d'Antin (France). It is reported that a porcelain factory whose owner was W. E. Toy may have worked here.

violet

Paris (149), 27 Rue Montmartre (France). Vallée directed a porcelain decorating studio here in 1815 (according to 'Tardy 75').

Paris (150), 4 Rue de la Boule rouge (France). Jules Viallate, porcelain decorator, had the following mark entered in 1876, according to 'Tardy 75'.

Paris (151), 19 Rue E. Varlin (France). Pierre Vignaud (Jamault & V.). Artistic porcelain since 1963 (according to 'Tardy 75').

Paris (152), Rue de Lancre (France). In 1900 Vilterd & Collet produced perforated porcelain here which was decorated with translucent enamel colours. See Naudot, Paris (110).

gold

Paris (153) (France). Several French porcelain decorating studios used the following mark. Only numbers 3 and 4 have any connection with each other (the names are similar and the year is the same).
1   1870 Balth. Aug. Le Hujeur
2   1889 Abel François Le Fèvre
3   1889 Philippe Levy
4   1889 Charles Levy, Choisy-le-Roi
5   1927 Samson f. Sèvres Reproductions (1941).

Passage (Spain). According to Demmin the Baignal Bros. produced porcelain here.

Passau (1) (Germany, Bavaria). In 1766 the arcanist Nikolaus Paul (under the patronage of the Bishop of Passau), made one unsuccessful attempt at producing porcelain.

Passau (2) (Germany, Bavaria). In 1799 Karl Hagen and Friedel f. a porcelain factory here which produced only mediocre porcelain. They were nevertheless commercially successful owing to their decorations of Nymphenburger and Wallendorfer products which were exported to Turkey.

Passau (3) (Germany, Bavaria). Dressel, Kister & Co., f. 1840. The factory belonged to the Lenck family from the second half of 19th c. until 1937, when it was taken over by the Philipp Dietrich porcelain factory of Passau, which closed in 1942. It produced artistic porcelain. Dressel, Kister & Co. marked the products which were made from moulds from the Höchst factory (and which had been acquired by the Mehlem factory, Bonn, in 1903), with the old Höchst mark of the bishop's crocier (according to Esser/Reber). After the closure of the factory the widely travelled moulds from Höchst disappeared. It is possible that pieces from moulds of other old porcelain factories were also marked with the corresponding old marks. It cannot be ascertained when the factory started to call itself: Aelteste (the oldest) Volkstedter Porzellan-Fabrik AG. The 'L' with a crown and traces of a bishop's crozier mark, which until recently has been untraced, has been found marking a saucer.

[108]   [141]   [111]

[107]

Passauer Erde, see Kaolin sources (Germany).

Passau-Innstadt, porcelain factory, see Aelteste (oldest) Volkstedter (4).

Pastaud, Paul E., see Limoges (61).

Pastiche. Free-worked or pre-cast ornamentations which the modeller used when assembling figures or other pieces of porcelain which are composed of small parts.

Pastor, Christobal, see Alcora.

Paszoa, J. J., see Lisbon (1).

Pâte dure, see Hard paste porcelain.

Pâte Dure Nouvelle, see Seger porcelain.

'Pâte sur Pâte' decoration. Discovered by Robert in Sèvres 1849. This 'paste upon paste' decoration consists of applying white porcelain reliefs to coloured porcelain ground. A particularly striking effect can be achieved by letting the ground appear through translucent layers of the reliefs.

'Pâte tendre', see Frit porcelain.

Patrault, see Paris (112).

Patte, Alfred, see Montreuil (3).

Paul, Nikolaus, arcanist. According to his own writings, he 'helped to establish the factories of Berlin, Fürstenberg and Höchst'. After this he moved to Weesp in Holland, and in September 1764 went to Fulda to found a porcelain factory for Prince-Abbot Heinrich III of Bibra. Paul is subsequently referred to as being in Passau, Kassel and Kloster Veilsdorf, and once more in Fürstenberg after 1770.

Paulus, Georg, see Schlaggenwald (1).

'Peach-bloom' glaze. Peach-bloom coloured glaze on porcelain of the Kangxi period. The Chinese term 'apple-red' is, however, a more accurate description of the colour.

Peacock feather pattern (Pfauenfedernmuster), already used on majolica as decoration in the 15th and 16th c. Delft later adopted it for its earthernware decoration and later still Meissen, Chelsea and other factories used it.

Pea green. Chelsea discovered this effective green in 1759.

Pearl Service. Commissioned by Frederick II in 1784, and the very last service to be produced by the KPM Berlin. The king, who was fond of the rococo style, disregarded this preference and encouraged his factory to keep in step with modern styles. The relief decoration on this service consists of semi-spherical beads around the rim.

Pearl-Service. Nymphenburg 1792. Designed by Dominicus Auliczek. Strings of pearls and oval medallions. Apart from the Electoral service by the KPM Berlin, it is the purest example of neo-classicism.

Pech, R. & E., see Kronach (3).

Pecht, J. A., see Konstanz (2).

Pécs (Hungary). Zsolnay'sche Ceramic factories, originally an earthenware factory, f. by Ignaz Zsolnay in 1862. By 1865 it had been taken over by Vilmos (Wilhelm) Zsolnay, who rapidly led the factory into prosperity. His son Nicolaus (who had joined the factory in 1878) succeeded him in 1900 and introduced the production of porcelain (according to Csany, Budapest 1954). In addition to general ware, the factory made small figures of artistic merit. It is now a wholesale concern and state property.

Pedrozzi. Modeller for Berlin, 1765-7. Figures, birds and mythological reliefs for large vases were made by him.

Pegmatite (74 per cent., silica). Used in France and England for porcelain production instead of the scarce feldspar.

Peichon, B., see Saint-Vallier (4).

Peignot, Emily, see Rioz.

Peking-bowls, see Medallion bowls.

Pelissier, Pierre, see Lille (1).

Pellevé, Dominique. Porcelain factory owner from Rouen. On 29 December 1763 Duke Henry Willliam of Nassau Saarbrücken employed Pellevé to establish his porcelain factory in Ottweiler (see also Etoilles).

Peltier and Mailly, see Saint-Denis (3).

Pennewitz, David. Director c. 1713 of the factory in Plaue on the Havel.

Pensée-Service. By Schmuz-Baudiss *(q.v.)* during his work at Swaine & Co, Köppelsdorf Nord *(q.v.)*.

Perche, decorator, see Buen Retiro and Paris (113).

Perenot, see Paris (62).

Perez, Tommaso (d. 1781), see Naples.

Perier, see Limoges (3).

Peringer, Leonardo. He claimed to have discovered the secret of making porcelain in 1518. See 'Vetro di latte'.

Perl, Georg (d. 1807). He and Leithner are regarded as the creators of the Viennese services made during the third period in the neo-classical style.

Pernoux, Josef (b. 1772). Decorator in Ludwigsburg and Nyon in the late 18th c.

Perrier, see Paris (79).

Perrot, see Vierzon (11).

Persch, Ad., and Robert, see Elbogen (6) and Hegewald.

Person, see Paris (115).

Pesaro (Italy). L. Sebellini maintained a small porcelain factory here in 1876.

Pesotschnaja (Russia). Malzeff f. an industrial co-operative here in the middle of the 19th c. which employed c. 500 workers in 1900, producing general porcelain ware.

Peter, Franz, see Kaltenhofen.

Peterinck, F. J., see Tournay.

Petersburg (1) (Russia). In 1718 Peter I sent the Dutchman Eggebrecht, who had a small stoneware factory in Dresden, to Petersburg to produce porcelain in the Delft style. Eggebrecht's stay was brief and his presence in Petersburg left no discernible evidence of his skill. Peter I then tried to learn the secret of porcelain-making by sending a spy, Jurij Kologriwij. to the Court of Meissen. In 1740 however, Peter I managed to buy the formula for porcelain-making from a porcelain master of the Emperor of China, but the recipe proved too difficult to use. Hunger came to Petersburg in 1744, and was forced to leave the country in 1748. At this time Winogradow, who had studied metallurgy in Freiberg and was Inspector of mining, was called to join the cabinet of His Imperial Majesty and assigned the task of studying porcelain production. According to G. Lukomskij, he rediscovered porcelain-making after 13 years of research. Winogradow died c. 1760, aged 40. His death posed no threat to the existence of the factory, his former workmen knew the formula, and in addition the Saxon arcanist Gottfried Müller had been appointed in the same year after he had passed the relevant examination. From July 1763 Catherine II supported the firm with annual subsidies of 15,000 roubles. The lieutenant of the Imperial Guard, was made the director. He appointed the Viennese arcanist Regensburger and the modeller from Meissen, Karlowsky. Olsufjeff, and later

Teploff, were supervisors, and the foreman was Josef Regensburger who had worked earlier in Vienna. After the death of Tschepotieff in 1773, Prince W. W. Wjalemsky directed the factory and enlarged it considerably; in fact the factory owes its spectacular rise to him. In this period the decorator Sacharoff and the Frenchman Rachette exerted great influence. From 1792 the factory was guided by Prince N. B. Yussupoff, an outstanding connoisseur and remarkable organiser. Towards the end of Catherine's reign the factory employed about 200 people. Under Tsar Paul nothing was done to alter the factory. Until 1765 the products were kept rather simple and natural in style. Apart from the popular snuff-boxes, Winogradow only produced tea and coffee services in limited quantities. Larger pieces could only be fired after the building of a larger kiln in 1756. Figure-making was mentioned for the first time in 1752. The technique of decorating was only perfected towards the end of Elisabeth's reign. Purple, green and gold are predominant colours.In 1784 the Arabesque Service was created which consisted of 937 pieces for 60 place-settings. It was like the Catherine service from Sèvres of 1778. The Cabinet service and the Hunting service have a similar decoration to that of the Arabesque. Rachette created a number of portrait medallions and busts in biscuit porcelain. Under Tsar Paul, 1796–1801, and Alexander I the Empire style established itself. The latter, during the earlier years of his reign, reorganised the factory considerably. During the same period several artists from abroad were offered employment and protective tariffs were arranged to facilitate the export of products. This step led to the flourishing of rival factories. Nicholas I reintroduced Russian artists and craftsmen and the next generation came chiefly from the sons of the regular staff. The products gained high praise at the Great Exhibition in London in 1851. All through Nicholas's reign the production was limited to imitation Chinese vases and Greek amphorae. A great deal of attention, however, was paid to the decoration and in this way it reached the peak of perfection. The copying of 'old masters' on to porcelain was practised with unsurpassable skill. During the reign of Alexander II development was halted despite certain technical improvements, and under Alexander III and Nicolaus the II, a rapid decline occurred. As the quantity of goods produced increased, so the quality deteriorated. Lifeless repetition with no artistic sensibility characterises the pieces of the last decade of production prior to the First World War. A new development took place after the Revolution in 1917, when the Court Works became the property of the People.

See also: Adam, H. A., Miller (Müller), F., Müller, J. G.

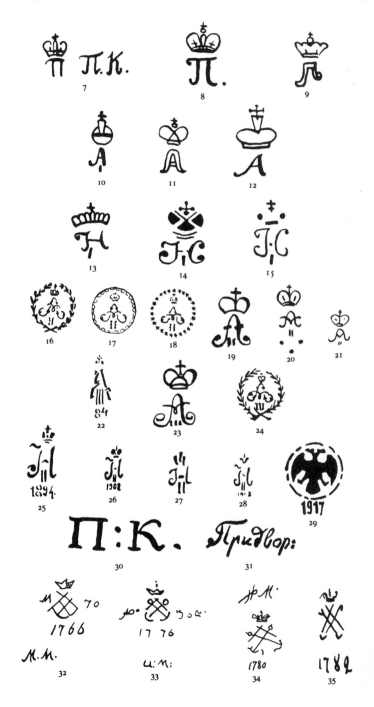

1–2 blue, 1741–62 Elisabeth – 4–6 all blue, 1762–96 Catherine II – 7–9 all blue, 1796–1801 Paul I – 10–12 all blue, 1801–25 Alexander I – 14–15 all blue, 1825–55 Nicholas I – 16–19 all blue – 20–21 green, 1855–81 Alexander II – 22–24 1881–94 Alexander III – 25–29 1894–1917 Nicholas II – 30–31 P:K Pridvornaia Kontora (Court inventory). These marks were also used in underglaze by other European porcelain factories for goods intended for the Court (No. 31 under Catherine II) – 32–35 anchor marks 1766–82

Petersburg (2) (Russia). Sergej Batenin f. a porcelain factory in 1812 in the Wiborskaja Storona, which was still working in 1839. It produced services decorated with very fine views of Leningrad after drawings by Machajew and Sergej. The pieces are distinguished by their very rich gilding.

Petersburg (3) (Russia). Günther & Co. managed a faience factory here from 1818–76, which may have also produced porcelain on a small scale.

Petersburg (4) (Russia). Sawin Wassiljewitsch Korniloff f. a porcelain factory here and attracted the services of toprank Russian and foreign artists. The products are on the same level as Gardener's (see Moscow). The factory was still working in 1885 and during its later years it produced well-made porcelain ware.

Petion, see Korzec.
Petit. Name of a painter family in Chantilly from 1756.
Petit, J., see Sèvres (5).

Petit, Jacob (b. 1796) and Mardochée, see Fontainebleau (1) and Paris (116).

Petit-feu, small fire, see 'verglühen' (red-hot) under porcelain, see also Muffle colours and Enamel glazes.

Petri, Trude, see Arcadian Service and Urbino Service.

Pettrisch, H., see Burgsteinfurt.

'Petuntse'. Term used by d'Entrecolles *(q.v.)* for feldspar. From the original Chinese 'Pai-tun', meaning 'white clay', and referring to the scoured porcelain clay.

Peyrard, Pierre, see Chantilly (1).

Pfaff, E. D., see Kelsterbach.

Pfalz, Karl Theodor and Maximilian IV, Elector of the Palatinate, see Frankenthal.

Pfalz-Zweibrücken, see Gutenbrunn.

Pfalz-Zweibrücken, Christian IV, Duke of, see Gutenbrunn.

Pfalzer, Zacharias, see Baden-Baden.

Pfauenfedernmuster, see Peacock feather pattern.

Pfeffer, F., see Gotha (3).

Pfeiffer, Max Adolf, see Unterweissbach.

Pfeiffer & Löwenstein, see Schlackenwerth.

Pfullingen (Germany, Wurtemberg). Wilhelm Künstner, porcelain decorator c. 1920.

Piccardt & Co., see Delft.

Pickmann & Co., see Seville.

Picot, see Weesp.

Piedor-Dumuys and Dubois, see Orléans (1).

Piesau (Germany, Thuringia). Bernhardt & Bauer, porcelain factory, f. 1886. Production: figures and others, used zwiebelmuster (onion pattern). Today's legal successor to the VEB Porzellanfabrik, Piesau. Its products are marked with the following.

Pigalle, Jean Pierre (1725–96). French sculptor, whose sculptures were models for the Sèvres biscuit figures.

Pigois & Jacquet, see Mehun-sur-Yèvre (4).

Pigorry, M., see Chantilly (2).

Pillivuyt, Jr., see Paris (117)
Pillivuyt et Cie., la Porcelaine de France, see Mehun-sur-Yèvre (5).
Pillivuyt & Co., see Paris (118).
Pillivuyt, Ch., & Co., see Foecy (4).
Pilsen (Bohemia). Fr. Schertler, porcelain factory, f. 1881. Utility porcelain.

Pinon et Heuzé, see Tours (3).
Pinot & Barboud, see Limoges (77).
Pinxton (England). William Billingsley f. a small porcelain factory here in 1796 jointly with John Coke. It produced a good bone china until 1801. The production modelled itself on Derby. In 1801 Billingsley moved to Mansfield; three years later John Cutts became the owner. The later products with their opaque bodies and rough glazes were made until 1813. There are, however, some pieces of very fine quality and in brilliant white.

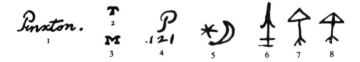

1 very rare in gold – 2–3 impress-printing – 4 red – 5 purple – 6–8 red – 9 in various colours

Pirkenhammer (Bohemia, now: Březová, Plan). Fr. Hoeke from Bullstedt (Saxony-Weimar) f. this factory c. 1803 together with Greiners from Thuringia. In c. 1810 Fischer & Reichenbach became the owners; from 1845 Fischer was the sole owner. From 1853 he associated with his son-in-law, Ludwig von Mieg, and called the factory: 'Fischer & Mieg'. His products were being praised as the 'best in Bohemia' as early as 1824. The source for the kaolin was in Zettlitz. In 1839 the factory was awarded a gold medal in Vienna. Until 1840 the products were mainly crockery ware, using in particular the so-called Ilmenauer strawflower pattern on a smooth or ribbed hard body. After 1840 figures and relief decorations were produced. The outstanding decorator was Joh. Zacharias Quast, b. 1813. The factory was fundamentally rennovated in the second half of the 19th c. and is active to this day. In 1918 it was annexed into the EPIAG *(q.v.)*. Mark No. 11 was registered for porcelain ware on 23 September 1887 in the Chamber of Commerce in Eger, under No. 98. The second registration, under No. 556, was made on 18 June 1897. The notification was given in both instances by Fischer & Mieg, K.K., private porcelain factory. It can be proved that between 1908–15 the production included lithophanes. Johann Adalbert Wolff (1867–1948), who had also worked in Elbogen and Lessau, was the modeller; his works: Franz Josef I, Holy Night, as well as 12 different models for bottoms of beer mugs; some pieces are signed 'J. WOLFF'.

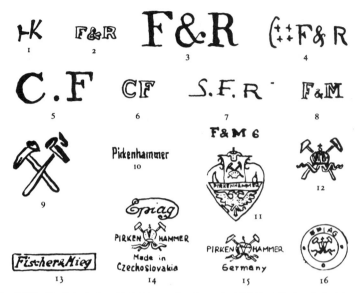

1 HK = Hölke Karlsbad after 1830, blue underglaze – 2–4 F&R = Fischer & Reichenbach, 1810–16, blind impress – 5–6 CF = Christian Fischer, 1846–57. These marks were also used by Fischer in Zwickau – 8 F & M = Fischer & Mieg, since 1857 – 9 green underglaze 1876–87 – 10 1910 – 11 green underglaze or red, since 23 September 1887 – 12 red, since 4 June 1890, also in chrome green underglaze – 14–16 modern mark

Pitt, Thomas, see Plymouth.
Place, Francis (b. 1650 London, Fulham – 1728). Engraver, pupil of Hollar (Wenzel). He occupied himself with ceramic experiments from c. 1680. He discovered a kind of clay near York, which, so it is said, he fired to porcelain. Because his work did not prove to be economically viable, he finally abandoned it.
Plainemaison Frères, see Limoges (62).
Plankenhammer (Germany, Upper Palatine). Plankenhammer porcelain factory GmbH, f. c. 1908. Household and hotel ware, gift articles.

[233] [165] [234]

Plant, James. Decorated porcelain figures in Worcester in the early 19th c. Later he worked for Nantgarw and other porcelain factories.
Plant, R. H. Ltd., Tuscan Works, see Longton (39).
Plass & Roesner, see Buchau.

Plat-de-menage. Term also used in Germany in the 18th c. for a table-stand upon which an assortment of spices in containers were arranged.

Plate drying installation. An automatic drying chamber for plates was developed by the Metzsch Bros. factory in Selb, in 1929. It dried 19,000 plates of 24 cm diameter in 24 hours.

Platterinen formerei. The potter's skill in throwing flat plates and similar items free-handed.

Plaue on the Havel (Germany, Prussia). The Prussian Minister of State, Friedrich von Görne f. a factory here in 1713, with the aid of the Meissen runaway worker Samuel Kempe, which succeeded in imitating red Böttger stoneware. The factory was managed by the decorator and lacquerer David Pennewitz, who was also a partner, and it was active until 1730. The largest collection of Plaue stoneware was in the Berlin Castle Museum. No evidence is available to suggest that figures were ever made in Plaue. The products never reached the quality of the 'Böttger stoneware'; they are called 'Brandenburgen Porzellan'.

Plaue (Germany, Thuringia). VEB Porcelain Works Plaue; also legal successor to the Schierholzsche Porcelain Works Plaue GmbH, f. 1817. Despite the comparatively late foundation of the factory, one can trace its rich tradition of distinctive features within the Thuringian factories. Plaue has been one of the few makers of lithophanes in the world from c. 1890 (and possibly earlier) until the present day (1977). (From 1870 'PMP' is impressed on lithophanes.) Besides these the factory concentrated on ceramic specialities, such as porcelain candlesticks, chandeliers, tables, as well as other luxury porcelain ware of a wider field. Painted decoration was in the style of Berlin, Dresden, Meissen, Vienna, Copenhagen, Capo di Monte underglaze decorations, lace-figures.

1–2 c. 1890 a double-cross mark which could too easily be mistaken for the Meissen swords and which had to be discontinued upon Meissen's objection – 3 from 1900 – 4 from 1910 – 5 from 1930 with the addition v. Schierholzsche – 6 1967 jubilee mark, raised addition 1817 – 7 present mark

Pletzger, Josef Anton. From Berchtesgaden. Active as a decorator in Neudeck from mid-1760, but he had designed some altar pieces before this. Pletzger used good quality colours and was a specialist in figure decorating. He survived the great Recession of 1767; the date of his departute is unknown.

Plock (Poland). A small porcelain factory was here in 1867.

Plombières (France). Hevisé et Comp. f. a porcelain factory here, which was directed by Troté.

Plymouth (England). The first English hard paste porcelain factory, f. by William Cookworthy, worked here 1768–70. According to DKG, an earlier hard paste porcelain factory was active here in 1740–74. In 1768 Cookworthy received a patent for exclusive use of kaolin deposits discovered some years earlier. He directed the factory jointly with Thomas Pitt (later Lord Camelford) and members of the Quaker society. In 1770 the factory was moved to Bristol. The products are still technically imperfect, smokey and spotted. Fire cracks are often present in the figures. However, there are some pieces (from this earlier period) of outstanding quality. The decoration shows no particular originality. The underglazed blue colour is nearly black. Coffee and tea services, as well as vases, were painted in the Worcester Style. A beautiful leaf green and a deep wine-red colour were achieved. These characteristic colours, which were later used on Bristol porcelain, were without doubt developed in Plymouth first.

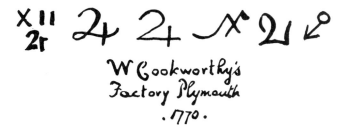

The chemical sign for tin, in several colours, also in gold, as a factory mark

Pochet, H., see Paris (36).
Pochet-Deroche, see Paris (36).
Pochler, Carl Anton, from Nuremberg. In 1871 he introduced the use of transfer prints which could be high-fired (transfer of lithography on porcelain) and used as decoration on porcelain.
Pohl, Bros., see Schmiedeberg.
Pohle, Fr. W., see Taschwitz.
Pointon & Co., Ltd, see Hanley (10).
Polivanoff, see Aschuat.
Poll, Joh. Heinrich Dr. This chemist is said to have been given an order by

Frederick the Great to produce porcelain, and may have done so in Potsdam in 1742.

Pollak, Josef, see Buchau.

Pollard, William (1803–54), decorator, see Swansea.

Pöllwitz (Germany, Thuringia). Pöllwitz porcelain factory, GmbH, c. 1920.

'à la Pologne', see Paris (109).

Poltár (Bohemia). Dr. Norbert Baratta, porcelain factory c. 1930.

Pommier, see Saint-Genou (1).

Pomona. Name used as trademark 267060 from 11 June 1921 of the P.F. Rosenthal, Selb.

Pons & Cie., see Marseille (2).

Ponsas (France). Faure et Comp., Adolphe Regal père et Fils, Reymond Sorel Fils made here in 1867 attempts to produce porcelain. No mark was used.

Ponsas-sur-Rhône (1) (France). Emile Fourneron porcelain factory. Produced fireproof crockery, domestic goods and luxury articles.

Ponsas-sur-Rhône (2) (France). A. Sorrel, porcelain factory.

Pontenx-les-Forges (France, Landes). De Rosly managed a small porcelain factory here which was active c. 1779–90. The mark has been found on a piece in the Grollier collection and on biscuit busts of the Four Seasons.

Poole, Th., & Gladstone China Ltd., see Longton (33).

G
pontenx

Poppelsdorf nr. Bonn (Germany, Rhineland). Ludwig Wessel, Actien Gesellschaft für Porzellan – and Steingutfabrikation, f. 1755. Utility porcelain articles and luxury porcelain of all kinds. Specialities were artistic faiences with underglaze decorations, toilet services, vases and flowerpots. See Bonn (2).

[52]

Popoff, Alexander. Founder and owner of the porcelain factory in Gorbunowo. See Moscow (9) and Tambow.

ПОПОВЫ

Porag, see Elbogen (6).

Porcelain, its origins. Reliable information about the earliest production of porcelain can be found in the annals of the Sui 581–671 and T'ang 618–905 dynasties. By the mid-8th c. the porcelain of the Yüeh-Yao and Ting Yao was preferable to any other. The former was compared with jade or ice, and the latter with silver and snow. The translucency of the porcelain, which makes it distinctive from all the other ceramic products, was described in the first instance, by the Arab, Saleyman or Soliman, in mid-8th c.

Porcelain

1. Definition

Porcelain is a ceramic product made from kaolin, quartz and feldspar. The constituents of European hard paste porcelain are, generally speaking, used in the following proportions: 40–65 per cent kaolin, 12–30 per cent quartz and 15–35 per cent feldspar. The plasticity of the kaolin gives the mass malleability and resistance to a high firing temperature. Feldspar and quartz are the so-called shortening, meaning that they reduce the plasticity as well as the firing and drying shrinkage, and act as medium of flux.

2. Production

a) Raw materials. All raw materials must be pure, and particularly iron-free. Very good, meaning pure and white-burning, kaolins can be found in Czechoslovakia (Zettlitz, Carlsbad, Chodau), in Germany, e.g. in the vicinities of Halle a.d.S., Meissen, Kemmlitz, Mügeln, Börtewitz in Saxony and Passau. There are also some excellent kaolins in England (Cornwall), which are sold as China-clay (scoured condition). For feldspar one generally uses orthoklas. The most important feldspar deposits for the production of porcelain are in Norway (Oslo, Bergen, Arendal) and on the East and South coast of Sweden. Quartz of great purity is found in Germany, e.g. near Hohenbocka (Lausitz), Dörentrup (Lippe) and Herzogenrath nr. Aachen.

b) Preparation of the raw materials. The brittle, earthy and easily crumbling raw kaolin is scoured with much water in a churning apparatus and coarse particles are sieved off. The well-stirred slip is dehydrated in filter presses, leaving the small particles of kaolin to settle. Feldspar and quartz are broken down in stone-crushers, crushing-rollers and drum mills filled with flint churned to dust, or, if mixed with water, milled to pulp.

c) Preparation of the body. The kaolin which has been prepared by washing and dredging, and the ground feldspar and quartz are mixed together in accurately measured proportions, and stirred to form a stiff mixture in a large, vat-like vessel with an agitator, the so-called mass stirrer. This mass, however, still contains too much water for the next process and is therefore pressed through filters. The resultant mass, still containing c. 20–30 per cent water, is stored in a damp cellar, the so-called mass-cellar, to impart plasticity to the mass. When it is needed for production the stored mass is kneaded through once again, by beating and pressing thoroughly in the so-called mass beating machine, which also rids it of air bubbles.

d) The Forming. The porcelain pieces are shaped by modelling, casting and turning. Turning is used for round, flat objects, e.g. plates; this is done on the potter's wheel. Casting is used for a variety of objects, e.g. figures, but now also for vases, tureens and bowls. To begin with, the desired article is modelled in clay. From this model a cast is taken which forms the mould. The mould is made in sections to facilitate the removal of the finished model. The porcelain mass, which is mixed with water and some soda, is now poured into the plaster mould. The plaster mould extracts the water from the mass while it is drying, causing it to shrink a few millimetres from the sides of the mould, and the object is thus created. After a certain time any superfluous mass is poured off, the form is opened and the object is taken out. Production of pieces by the method of pressing with metal moulds is used particularly for mass production and under accurately controlled conditions, such as always using constant quantities as in e.g. the case of insulators for electrical uses.

e) Drying, firing, glazing. After the casting the pieces are slowly dehydrated in carefully aired drying-rooms. This process of drying is very tedious and must take place under carefully established conditions so that no shrink cracks occur. After this the pieces are fired at a temperature of c. 800° in order to strengthen their structure and prepare them for glazing. In addition to this they gain a certain porosity and the capacity to readily absorb the fluid. This peculiarity is important for the application of the glaze. The glaze is applied by immersing the piece into the viscous glaze gruel, which consists essentially of the same materials as the basic mass, but it does contain more fluxing agents and is therefore easier to melt and is more glass-like. A satisfactory glaze must flow well at the relevant temperature, meaning it should form a resilient skin without running down the vertical walls of the object to be glazed. Furthermore, it must possess the same ratio of expansion as the shard, otherwise cracks will develop and hair-cracks of the glaze will flake off. The surplus glaze (e.g. at the bottom edges of cups and plates) has then to be removed from the finished pieces.

f) The firing. The porcelain is given its characteristic properties during the second firing. The glazed objects are put into the seggars (round boxes of fireproof clay), so that the ware is protected from direct contact with fire and smoke. These seggars are stacked in layers, in the kiln. The firing takes place in circular kilns, gas chambers or tunnel kilns (ceramic ovens), at a temperature of 1,300–1,400°. The actual procedure of the firing is not yet fully explained, but one may assume that it takes this course: The clay breaks up at a temperature of c. 500–600° through the loss of the water bound chemically in the clay earth and silicid acid. These combine again at c. 900° to a certain extent, to form the so-called mullit, a crystallised silicate of the chemical formula $3AL_2O_3 \cdot 2SiO_2$. At about 1,200° and above, the feldspar begins to melt into a tough, glass-like mass, which fills all pores and gaps in the basic fireproof clay. Finally, the feldspar is still capable of dissolving large quantities of quartz, whereby the minute quantities of silicid acid are also dispersed. The mullit, which formed initially, is likewise dissolved. Since, however, the powers of dissolution of the developed mullit is limited, a large quantity is expelled in the form of large or small, crystalline needles. A microscopic section of a porcelain shard displays a basic milky, glassy amorphic mass, in which, besides a great number of quartz splinters, mullit needles, both large and small, are embedded. Generally speaking, during the firing the glaze melts a little later than the feldspar, but much more vehemently, covering the whole of the object with a shiny, steel hard glass coating. The pieces must not be glazed where they touch the sagger, otherwise they will stick to it. Furthermore, the pieces must be supported in a suitable manner (e.g. cups at the upper rim through insertion of tension rings) since the mass becomes soft.

Porcelain coins. In Siam porcelain discs serve as gaming chips in the casinos. The first porcelain factory producing K.K. emergency or token-money was Aich nr. Carlsbad in 1850. In Germany, the Staatliche porcelain works in Meissen minted porcelain coins from after the First World War until 1923; nevertheless, they were not introduced officially. The only other minting was that of porcelain medalions and commemorative coins.

See also Köllmann *Berliner Porzellan 1966*, Vol. 1.

Porcelain Fabriken, Norden SA, see Norden.

Porcelain pagoda. This describes a tower, 80 metres high with nine floors, made of porcelain bricks. It was erected in the reign of Yong-ho in Peking in 1421. It was damaged at various times and rebuilt again, but finally destroyed during the capture of Peking in 1862.

Porcelain Union, Vereinigte porcelain factory AG, see Klösterle (2).

Porcelain Works Dresden, see Meissen (1).

Porcelain Works August Roloff, see Münster.

Porcelaine Georges Boyer, see Limoges (63).

Porcelaine du Duc d'Orléans, see Brancas-Lauraguais.

Porcelaine à fritte, see Frit porcelain.

Porcelaine de Limoges Bourganeuf, see Limoges (64).

Porcelaine Pallas (SA), see Limoges (64).

Porcelaine Ch. Reboisson, see Limoges (66).

Porcelaine de la Reine, see Paris (83).

Porcelaine Singer, see Limoges (67).

Porcelaine de Sologne Lamotte O L & V, see Vierzon (10).

Porcelaine vitreuse, see Frit porcelain.

Porcelaine Gustav Vogt, see Limoges (73).

Porcelaine Vogt (Vogt & Dohse), see Limoges (86).

Porcelainerie d'Esternay, see Esternay.

Porcelainerie de la Haute-Vienne, see Paris (119).

Porcelaines 'Elté', Léon Texeraud, see Limoges (68).

Porcelaines GDA, ancienne Maison Gérard, see Limoges (69).

Porcelaines Industrielles du Limousin, S.à.r.l., see La Seynie (2).

Porcelaines Limoges Castel, see Limoges (70).

Porcelaines Raynaud & Cie., see Limoges (73).

Porcelainière de la Haute-Vienne, see Saint-Léonard-de-Noblat.

'Porcelana contrahecha'. A term used in Spain c. 1570 for imitation porcelain.

'Porcella', see Carlsbad (1).

'Porcellana contrafatta'. A Venetian term for imitation porcelain already in use in 1508.

Porselein–en Tegelfabriek Mosa, see Maastricht.

Porsgrunn (Norway). Porsgrunds porcelain factory, f. 1887; porcelain services.

Portadown (Ireland). Wade (Ulster) Ltd., porcelain factory.

Port-caraffe. Generally an oval stand with a lining which takes two small cans or 'corvines', similar to the later invention 'Huilier'.

Portheim, Moses Porges von, see Chodau (1).

Portici, Villa (nr. Naples), see Buen Retiro and Capodimonte.

Posch, Leonhard (1750–1831 Berlin), sculptor, see Berlin (3).

Poschetzau (Bohemia). W. S. Mayer & Co. porcelain factory, f. 1890. From c. 1900, owners were J. S. Meyer Karlsbad and Phil. Schreyer, both in Chodau. The production was mainly utility ware for export to England, France, the Orient, North/South America. Closed in 1968 (according to Pöttig).

MADE IN
CZECHOSLOVAKIA

Pössneck (Germany, Thuringia). Conta & Boehme, porcelain factory, f. 1790. Luxury and fancy articles, dolls, dolls' heads and dolls which could be bathed. Exported particularly to England. This factory no longer exists.

Pössneck (Germany, Thuringia). Louis Huth, porcelain decorating studio, f. 1894 (according to Neuwirth), purveyor to the Court Saxony-Meiningen. Active until c. 1920.

Postkotschin, D. J., see Morje.

Poterat, Louis (1641–96). From Rouen. In 1673 he received a patent from Louis XIV for the making of porcelain 'after the style of Chinese porcelain'. He produced high quality frit porcelain in Rouen until his death in 1696.

$$ \text{Ж}_{\text{P}} $$

Potpourri vase. A vase or pot decorated with landscapes, flowers and portraits, strictly speaking 'pots-pour-ri'. In fact they served as scented vases because of their contents. The sole means by which they are recognisable is in the perforated body of the vase and the lid.

Pots à crème. Also called cocots or cocot-pots. Small containers with lids, often with two handles for serving all kinds of crème dishes.

Pots de chambre. In the references and price lists of the porcelain factories they were called 'galanteries'. There are some elaborately decorated examples.

Potschappel (Freital-Potschappel) (Germany, Saxony). Carl Thieme f. the Saxon porcelain factory at Potschappel in 1872. The present name (1977) is 'VEB Sächsische Porzellan-Manufaktur Dresden'. As in the past, the production consists exclusively of handpainted fancy and luxury porcelain.

Potsdam. A certain Meeheim (from Meissen) attempted to establish a porcelain factory here in 1735.

Pott, Johann Heinrich (1692–1777). Alchemist from Berlin. In 1720 he gained a doctorate and in 1737 received a professorship in chemistry at the Berlin University. In 1738 he published *Exerditationes chimicae de sulphuribus metallorum.* Frederick the Great encouraged him to investigate, like Tschirnhaus – geology, with particular reference to the production of porcelain. Pott made ceaseless efforts to emulate the Meissen porcelain formula. He did not get any further than the making of white frit porcelain. His fame rests solely on his success in establishing the temperature at which certain minerals remain unaffected by temperature changes.

Potter, Christopher, see Chantilly (1) and Paris (120).

Potter. Englishman, who in 1809 at Sèvres, produced porcelain buttons with the use of moulds.

Poulard Prad, Giovanni, see Naples.

Pountney & Co. Ltd., The Bristol Pottery, see Bristol (3).

Poussierer or Poussier, see Bossierer.

Pouyat, François. One of the owners of 'La Courtille' porcelain factory. See Paris (94).

Pouyat & Russinger, see Limoges (71).

Powder blue (or powdered blue). A blue ground which is produced by blowing powdered pigment through a bamboo tube with gauze stretched across one end. A Chinese invention.

Powell & Bishop, see Hanley (8).

Powell, Lively & Co., Waterloo Works, see Hanley (8).

Pradier, James (Jean-Jacques) (1792–1862). French sculptor, pupil of Lemot Gerard and the Ecole des beaux-arts. Generally busts and groups, also monuments, models for statuettes in biscuit. See Chantilly (2).

Prag (Bohemia). The Kunerle brothers, Josef Emanuel Hübel and J. J. Lange f. the oldest Bohemian stoneware factory in 1793 (according to some sources in 1791). It was not until the time of Hübel's death (1835) when K. L. Kriegel became the director, that porcelain production was begun (1837). Soon after this (in 1837–41), Kriegel and K. Wolf became the leaseholders of the factory. During this time the letters 'K&WP' or 'K&W Prag' were used as a mark. Kriegel and E. Hofmann von Hofmannsthal became the owners in 1882. From 1842–54 the marks 'Prag' and 'K & Co. Prag' were in use. From 1845 it became a joint stock company which marked with the years 1854–1894 and with a blindpress of 'Prag-Smichow'. Figure production overshadowed the production of general porcelain ware. The grace and naivity of these figures is enchanting; they are the 'most beautiful porcelain figures which have ever been created on Bohemian soil' (Poche). From 1845 the factory was under the artistic direction of the sculptor Ernst Popp, pupil of Ludwig Schwanthaler.

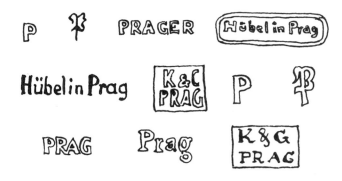

1–5 1793–1837 blind stamped on stoneware only – 6–10 1837–41 blind stamped – 11 on fakes only, mid.-19th c., perhaps from Saxony

Prager, see Prague.

Prager porcelain factory, see Smichov.

Prague (Czechoslovakia). Prof. F. R. H. Schlinderbusch developed the Effaucure technique for porcelain decorating here in 1930. This was still being praised as late as 1932 as an epoch-making invention. Nothing else is known however. Even the most well informed people from Bohemia did not know any details in 1977. See Effaucure decorating.

Prahl, A. F., widow, see Ellwangen.
Prause, Franz, see Nieder-Salzbrunn.
Prawda Porzellanfabrik Duljewo, see Duljewo.
Pressig (Germany, Bavaria, Upper Frankonia). Pressig porcelain factory.
Artistic porcelain and figures with lace.

Preuss, Sören. Modeller in Copenhagen from 1784 onwards. He created
outstanding works in refined flowers, garlands and ornaments.
Preussler (Preissler, Preisler). Silesia–Bohemian independent decorator who
painted on Chinese, Meissen and Viennese porcelain in black, grey-iron, red,
purple-camaieu and gold. His motifs were chinoiseries, hunting, battle and
harbour scenes and mythological events. He started earlier than Bottengruber
and was active until c. 1740. His works which, in part, are of outstanding quality,
also influenced the Viennese factory and other independent decorators, such as
J. Helchis. From the large number of pieces decorated by him which are still in
existence, it is clear that the studio was of considerable size.
Prince of Wales China, see Paris (118).
Privileged Ducal Czernische porcelain factory, see Giesshübel (2).
Probstzella (Germany, Thuringia). H. Hutschenreuther, GmbH, porcelain
factory, f. 1886. Utility and luxury articles.

Procter, George, & Co. (Ltd.), Gladstone Pottery, see Longton (60).
Proeschold & Co., see Dallwitz.
Pröschold, A. H., see Gräfethnal (2).
Proskau (Germany, Silesia). According to a travel report by Mentienné, a
porcelain factory worked here in 1826. It is assumed to be the same faience
factory which was in the possession of Count Leopold von Proskau in 1783. In
1783 the new owner was Friederick II; it changed to the production of stoneware
in 1788 and gave up making faiences in 1793. In 1832 the factory changed hands
and F. Dickhut became the owner. The factory remained in the Dickhut family
until it closed in 1850 (DKG).
Prössel, see Fürstenberg.
Prouza, Adolf, see Klein-Schadowitz.
Provza, Wenzel, see Satalitz.
Prussian musical designs. An excellently designed Meissen border-pattern in
relief, with musical instruments. Assumed to have been created in 1761 by K. J.
C. Klipfel for Frederic the Great.

Prussian Service. Porcelain table service produced by Meissen in mid-18th c. by order of Frederic the Great, for his General von Möllendorf. The decoration consisted of musical emblems set into medallions with iron-red mosaic patterns. This service was in the hands of fine art dealers in 1926.

Prussian Service. Dinner and dessert service of the KPM Berlin. Neo-classical in style with opulent decoration and gilding; it differs from the Feldherren service *(q.v.)* only in as far as the decorative motifs which have been used, and it has one additional piece in the form of a table centrepiece by Schadow. It was presented on behalf of the Prussian King, Frederic Wilhelm III, to the Duke of Wellington in 1819 in London. It consists of 470 pieces (28,452 Thaler). See Wellington Service.

Pullain, see Paris (84).

Punct, Karl Christoph (d. 1765). Became Court sculptor in 1763 and created models for Meissen, in particular arcadian groups and allegorical figures. Also produced other commissions from King Frederick II. He was one of the most talented co-workers of Kändler.

Punktzeit (Dot period) (1763–74), see Meissen (1).

Purtscher, Kajetan (1740–1813 Munich). In 1730 he became the pupil of Lindemann, the chief painter in Neudeck, so that 'a Bavarian too might have the benefit of tuition in the art of colour usage'. In 1760 he became Lindemann's successor as a decorator of landscapes, figures, animal and pastoral pieces, and was given a pension in 1810.

Quality control. It is claimed that as early as 1730, Meissen was marking its inferior undecorated porcelain by incising into the glaze and across the mark with the aid of the engraver's wheel. It is certain that this method has been used since 1766.

Quast, Zacharias, see Pirkenhammer.

Queen Elizabeth's Training College for the Disabled, see Surrey.

Queen's ware, see Cream ware.

Quettier & Co., see Paris (121).

Quimper (France). Jules Verlingue 1915–21, Kaolins de Cornouailles, produced dolls' heads in biscuit porcelain from 1915–21; he used the following mark on the neck of the doll's head.

Quodlibet. The term used in Copenhagen for the type of decoration which consisted of motifs such as playing-cards, artist's materials, instruments, etc. The Meissen term for this was 'Allerlei' (miscellany, hotchpotch).

Rabensgrün (Bohemia). Frank Anton Habertitzel and the porcelain dealer Jacob Just (from Thuringia) f. a porcelain factory here in 1789. The manufacturing difficulties were so great that the company soon broke up.

Rachette (French). Became successor to Karlowsky, the master modeller of the St. Petersburg Imperial factory in 1790. He had already been appointed to St. Petersburg in 1779 while he was working in Copenhagen. He quickly and energetically replaced the Meissen style with that of the Sèvres factory.

Radford. Samuel Ltd., see Fenton (13).

Rädler & Pilz, see Vienna (15).

Radomir nr. Sofia (Bulgaria). Bulgarian porcelain factory AG; later called: Bojadjieff porcelain factory, f. 1921. Utility porcelain.

Rahner, Joh. Georg Konrad, flower and fruit painter in Kelsterbach and Frankenthal between 1766 and 1785.

Raithel, see Meissen (1).

Randall, Thomas Martin (1786–1859). Decorator and potter who had been apprenticed in Coalport and had worked in Derby and Pinxton. As a partner of Richard Robins in a decorating workshop in Spa Fields in London, he imitated and copied Sèvres and decorated other porcelain of the early 19th c. In 1825 he f. a factory for soft paste porcelain in Madeley.

Ransonette. He illustrated Milly's work *Art de la Porcelaine* (1771) with excellent engravings.

Raspenau (Bohemia), see Hegewald nr. Friedland.

Rappsilber, see Köningszelt.

Ratchkin Bros., see Moscow 10.

Ratcliffe, William, see Lane End (3).

Rath, W. Chr., painter, see Nyon.

Ratkowo (Russia). Wawili Sabanin produced porcelain here in 1845–90, which was renowned for the quality of its gilding.

  Bc BC

Rau, Karl, see Munich (5).

Rauenstein (Germany, Thuringia). Duke Georg von Saxony-Meiningen granted a licence for porcelain production to three members of the Greiner family, namely Johann Georg, Johann Friedrich and Christian Daniel Siegmund. At the same time he put the Castle Rauenstein at their disposal. From the very beginning the establishment produced services in the Meissen style. The strawflower pattern (see Ilmenau) with underglaze blue and mulberry purple was used, faithfully reproduced on to the ribbed porcelain decoration, as it is used today in Copenhagen. Overglaze decoration in rustic manner and some simple views were also used. Figures are rare and somewhat coarse. The pieces, mostly with marks 3 and 4, are much sought after nowadays. Dolls and dolls' heads. Rauenstein was active until c. 1870 and employed over 100 workers. The KPM Meissen took successful legal action in 1896 against the use of mark 6 by the Fr. Chr. Greiner factory. (It had been entered on 6 December 1895 into the RWZR-Register under No. 11749.) The mark was consequently removed from the trademark register of the German Reich, 1896–8.

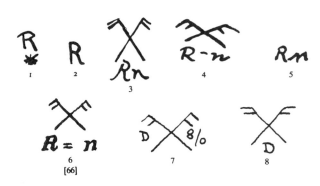

1–2 early marks from 1783 – 3–5 mid-19th c. – 6 end of the 19th c. – 7–8 neck marks – all predominantly in blue underglaze, at times in red

Rauffer, Franz Karl (1727–1802), miniature painter in Nymphenburg 1755–8, decorated many snuff boxes.

Rauh, Karl, see Schönfeld (2).

Raynaud, Marie, see Le Puy.

Raynaud, M., see Limoges (73).

Réaumur porcelain. Derives from the name of René Antoine Ferchault de Réaumur (1683–1757), French physiologist and zoologist, who also pursued ceramic studies and discovered this frit porcelain *(q.v.).* He also compared, by chemical analysis, the various kinds of porcelain.

Rebhuhn glaze. Its colour is similar to that of the partridge (rebhuhn) and is found on porcelain of the Sung Dynasty 960–1279. Taillandier of Sèvres adapted the glaze in 1760 and it became known there as 'Oeil de Perdix'.

Reboisson, Baranger & Cie., see Limoges (74).

Recknagel, Th., see Alexandrinenthal (2).

Recum, Peter and Johann Nepomuk, see Frankenthal (1).

Red stoneware, see Böttger stoneware.

Redfern & Drakeford (Ltd.), Chatfield Works and Balmoral Works, see Longton (61).

Redon, Sophie, see Limoges (75).

Redon, see Limoges (42).

Redon, Barny et Rigoni, see Limoges (42).

Rees (Germany, Lower Rhine). Jasba Baukeramik GmbH, KG. This factory also produced porcelain until 1959. The mark shown was used during this period.

Regal, Adolphe, see Ponsas.

Regéc (Hungary). The products which were marked as shown below, were regarded as earthenware until 1913. The factory was directed by Ferdinand Brezenheim from 1920. Regéc is the style and title of the Brezenheim family. The first number of the year is left out in the mark. Luxury porcelain ware and fine utility porcelain were made and the decoration is famous. The earliest piece is a vase which is dated 1831.

Regency China Ltd., see Longton (62).
Regensburg (1) Ratisbone (Germany, Bavaria). It is claimed that a porcelain factory worked here in 1829, which may have been owned by Dominikus Auliczek Jr. A cup from 1830, which is in the Bavarian National Museum in Regensburg, is ascribed to him.
Regensburg (2) (Germany, Bavaria). In 1837 Joh. Ant. Schwertner managed a factory here which had been granted a Royal patent; it had a work force of 150. Service and general porcelain ware.

R   𝕽egensburg

Regensburger, Johann Georg. From Vienna. Arcanist in St. Petersburg from 1765.
Regina, see Galway.
Regnault, Victor, director of Sèvres, 1852–71, see Sèvres (1).
Regnier, director of Sèvres, 1778–83.
Regnier & Cie. (now Ets. Jacques Blin), see Vierzon (13).
Rehau (1) (Germany, Bavaria). Zeh, Scherzer & Co. porcelain factory, AG, f. 1880. Commercial councillor Zeh suggested the establishing of a technical college for the Fine Ceramic industry as early as 1906. From 1924–6 the company owned the Elsterwerke, Mühlhausen; produced coffee and tea services and gift items.

Rehau (3) (Germany, Bavaria). Düssel & Co., porcelain production and decorating studio since 1945. Table, coffee, tea and mocha services. Silvered porcelain, gilded etching. Factory originally called Düssel, Roth & Co., f. in 1923.

Rehau (2) (Germany, Bavaria). Hertel, Jakob & Co. GmbH, porcelain factory, f. 1906. Porcelain gift articles, vases, boxes, table pieces, and table and coffee services.

Reichard, Ernst Heinrich (d. 1764). The first and only master modeller under Wegely (Berlin). He too was employed by Gotzkowsky in the new factory belonging to Frederick the Great. It is assumed that at one time he worked independently with Behling in Braunschweig.

X̄ᵀ

Carl Thieme   1872
factory at Potschappel

T

Carl Thieme   1872

Factory at Potschappel

Reichenbach (1) (Germany, Thuringia). Reichenbacher porcelain factory C. & E. Carstens, f. 1900. Better quality utility porcelain. Called in 1977: 'VEB Porzellanwerk Reichenbach', responsible to the VEB Porzellan Kombinat Kahla. The mark on the right is now in use (1977).

Carstens
Porzellan

Reichenbach (2) (Germany, Thuringia). Otto Hädrich's widow Kdt. Ges., f. a factory 1886. Table and coffee services, also executed in polished gold. Stapleware for export. Still working in 1949.

Reichenbach (3) (Germany, Thuringia). Hädrich ı Son, owner Kurt Hädrich. Porcelain decorating studio f. 1903. Fine table, coffee, tea and mocha services. Styles: baroque, Empire, modern. Still active in 1949.

Reichenstein (Germany, Prussia). A small porcelain factory was possibly f. in 1835, which may have used the following marks.

R.P

BL.P.

Reichmannsdorf (1) (Germany, Thuringia). This factory, belonging to Fr. Gottbrecht, employed c. 200 workers for porcelain production in 1833. In 1837 there were only 21 workers left. 'Turks heads' and pipe bowls were chiefly produced.
Reichmannsdorf (2) (Germany, Thuringia). Leube & Co., porcelain factory, f. 1881. Luxury porcelain, figures and similar.

Reichmannsdorf (3) (Germany, Thuringia). Carl Scheidig porcelain factory, Reichmannsdorf, f. 1864. Utility, decorative and electro technical porcelain.
Reid & Co., Park Place Works, see Longton (63).
Reinecke, F. A., see Eisenberg (4).
Reinecke, Otto, see Hof-Moschendorf.
Reinhold-Vogt, see Gräfenroda (5).
Reinicke, Peter (1715–68). Modeller and co-worker of Kändler from 1743.
Reinl, H., see Lublenz (1).
Reissig, Arthur, see Dresden (24).
Relief decoration. Originally the etched design of the Gotzkowsky factory, Berlin, from c. 1762. After the takeover by the King, this decoration was artistically worked over as 'relief decoration', an original moulding which made the 'Neue Palais Service' famous *(q.v.).*
Relief gilding. Figures and ornaments, in bas-relief, fixed to the porcelain surface and richly gilded. The technique was adapted from that of enamelling. The process was introduced by C. F. Herold from Meissen.
Renard, Camille and Winand, see Andenne.
Renaud, see Paris (123).
Renault, see Lille (2).
Renault, A., see Siereck.
Renoir, Auguste (1841–1919). French Impressionist. After leaving school he learned porcelain decorating in Paris. At first he made ornamental and flower decoration, but soon he began to copy famous paintings from the Louvre on to porcelain. One of his ambitions was to become porcelain decorator for the Sèvres factory. After five years, Renoir gave up porcelain decorating because the demand for it was diminishing owing to the growing practice of printing pictures on porcelain.
Renou, see Paris (122).
Reps & Trinte, see Magdeburg-Neustadt (2).
Restile, Luigi. Worked in Capodimonte in the mid-18th c. as decorator.
Retsch & Cie, see Wunsiedel.
Retschina (Russia). From 1830–65 Terichoff and Kiseleff produced beautifully modelled porcelain which was less well decorated.

1–2 marks of Pierre Terikoff

Reudorp, J., see Oude Amstel.

Reuss, Heinrich XXX, Prince von, see Gera.

Reutter, M. W., see Denkendorf.

Reval (Russia). A porcelain factory called Fink worked here at the end of the 18th c., producing, apart from faience, tableware, vases, figures and animals from porcelain. These were beautifully 'painted' but their forms were rather stolid; in addition the pieces broke easily. Only a few examples have survived. The factory was active for about 12 years.

Revelot, Joseph, decorator, see Nyon.

Reverend, Claude. In 1664 he received the Royal Privilege to produce porcelain in Paris, but he made only faience pieces which he sold as porcelain. See frit porcelain.

Revil, decorator, see Paris (124).

Reymond, see Ponsas.

Rheinische porcelain factory GmbH, Max Andresen, see Urbar.

Rheinische porcelain factory Mannheim GmbH, see Mannheim (1).

Rhenania, porcelain factory GmbH, see Duisdorf-Bonn.

Rhodes David (d. 1777), porcelain painter and decorator, for potteries. It is feasible that he is the same Rhodes who, in 1760, was partner to a Robinson in Leeds, where among other works, they enamelled salt glazed stoneware which they may have acquired from Staffordshire. It is possible that the polychrome decoration on early cream-coloured Staffordshire and Leeds ware is their work. Rhodes was enameller in the Wedgwood decorating studio in Chelsea, London from 1768 until he died in 1777. The painted name 'Rhodes pinxit' on an early Worcester porcelain service may have come from his hand.

Richard, Giulio, see Milan San Cristoforo.

Richard-Ginori, see Doccia.

Richman, see Lowestoft.

Richter, Anton, see Dresden (25).

Richter, Christian Samuel Hieronymus (d. 1776). From Freiberg/Sa. Worked as miniature painter in the mid-18th c. in Meissen.

Richter, Gustav H., see Warnsdorf.

Richter, H., see Berlin (4).

Richter, Johann-Georg. From Saxony. Flower decorator in Höchst c. 1748, later active in Strasbourg, and subsequently as one of the first German technicians in Copenhagen.

Richter, Fenkl & Hahn, see Chodau (2).
Ridgway, J. & W., see Shelton (1).
Rieber, see Selb (8).
Rieber, Josef & Co., see Mitterteich (1).
Riedel, Gottlieb Friedrich (1724–84). From 1743–56 in Meissen, from 1756–9 in Höchst and Frankenthal and from 1759–79 as chief decorator in the Ludwigsburg porcelain factory. Later as an engraver he published transfer patterns for porcelain decorators. In general, Riedel painted landscapes, birds and ornaments and he also provided designs for services and figures.

$$\mathcal{R}.$$

Riedel, G. F., see Giovanelli-Service.
Riedel von Riedelstein, see Dallwitz.
Riedl, Josef, see Giesshübel (3).
Riedl, Robert, see Haslach.
Riehl, P. (b. 1738). Flower painter. He worked as decorator c. 1755 in the Frankenthal factory.
Riemann, Albert, GmbH, see Coburg (1).
Riemann, C., see Geraberg (2).
Rienck, Johann Lorenz, modeller, see Ilmenau (1).
Ries, Karl (d. 2 July 1794). Mentioned in Höchst as a bossier, and later active as master modeller. Became Melchior's successor. His style of work is based closely on Melchior's.
Riese, C., see Dux (2).
Riese, Karl Friedrich (1759–1834). In 1789, in the Berlin porcelain factory, he became the successor to the master modeller, Friedrich Elias Meyer (d. 1785). Here he created models in neo-classical style influenced by the works of Schadow and Genelli.
Riessner, Stellmacher & Kessel, 'Amphora', see Turn (5).
Rifredi factory, Florence, see Doccia.
Riga, see Kusnetzoff.
Rihouet, J., see Paris (125).
Riley, John & Richard, see Burslem (5).
Ringler, Joseph Jakob (1730–1804). Worked from 1744 onwards in the Imperial factory in Vienna, where he learnt the secret of making porcelain as well as acquiring extensive knowledge about the building of kilns. Following this, he was active in Künersberg (1747–51), in Höchst and Strasbourg, and was arcanist in Neudeck and Nymphenburg from 1753–7. He was also in Ellwangen from 1758–9 when he moved to Ludwigsburg. Here he was active for over 40 years until his death in 1804. Without doubt, Ringler was one of the most influential and interesting personalities in the history of porcelain of the 18th c.
Rinsing machines. In 1930 E. Kilias examined the effect of washing agents (soda, soap and special agents under various trademarks), in hot and cold

387 RINSING MACHINES-RODEZ

conditions, upon porcelain ware with polychrome decoration, sprayed colour grounds and coral red. The result was that washing with hot solutions quite unexpectedly affected the colour-fastness and resistance of the decoration, particularly when hot washing-up agents (as used in rinsing machines) were used.

Rioz (France). Emile Peignot maintained a porcelain factory here in 1867.

Ripp, Abraham, arcanist in the Fulda porcelain factory c. 1767. Risler, Duffay & Co., see Freiburg.

Ristori, Carlo, see Doccia.

Riva, L., de la et Comp., see Sargadelos.

Rjasan, see Moscow (5). Fabrica Gospodina Gulina.

Robert, Jos. Gaspard, see Marseille (1).

Robert, Louis, manager of Sèvres from 1871–9, see Sèvres (1).

Robins, Richard. English decorator (independent), c. 1800, later partner of Th. M. Randall.

Robinson & Son, see Fenton (4).

Robra, Max, see Dresden (26).

Rocaille (French). The important shell-like ornament of the rococo.

Rockingham factory, Swinton, see Brameld, J. and W.

Rodach (Germany, Saxony–Coburg–Gotha). Max Roesler, porcelain factory, had the following mark registered on 15 October 1894 at the law courts of Saxony–Coburg–Gotha, Rodach. Produced porcelain, stoneware and fine earthenware.

[59]

Rode, Gotfred (b. 1862), decorator, see Copenhagen (1).

Rode, J. G., decorator, see Roth, Johann-Gottlieb and Hannong (II), Paul Anton.

Rodez (France, Aveyron). L. Drimmer registered his porcelain products in 1960 with the following mark, according to 'Tardy 75'.

Roesch, see Ilmenau.
Roesler, Max, see Rodach.
Roessler, Heinrich, see Glanzgold.
Roger, Graindorge et Cie., see Lille (2).
Rohleder, Arthur & Son, see Meissen (3).
Rollin, see Charenton (1).
Romanów (Poland). According to Swinarski/Chrościcki (Posen 1949) a porcelain factory worked here producing ware of very poor quality; its attempts to imitate Baranówka had little success.

Rombrich, Johann Christoph (d. 1794). Sculptor. In 1758 he worked as a master modeller in Fürstenberg, gaining the title of 'inspector at the porcelain factory' (1762). He was a master of particularly charming relief portraits and busts for the Fürstenberg works.
Rome (1) (Italy). In 1761 Filippo Cuccumos f. a porcelain factory here with the help of the Saxon arcanist Samuel Hirtz, which worked until 1784. The mark is questionable.

Rome (2) (Italy). Giovanni Trevisan, called Volpato, f. a porcelain factory here in 1785. In 1803 he was succeeded by his son Guiseppe, but he died after only a few months. His widow married the master modeller Francesco Tinucci. He was the creator of some fine reproductions of the works of Canova in biscuit. The factory closed in 1831.

G.VOLPATO ROMA

Römer & Födisch, see Fraureuth (2).
Romilly, see Dessaux.
Rondeleux et Cie., see Vierzon (14).
Rörstrands, see Lidköping (2).
Roschütz (Germany, Thuringia). Roschützer porcelain factory Unger and Schilde GmbH, f. 1811. Utility ware and services, vases, ornamental plates.

[133]

Rose, John (1772–1841). Founder of the Coalport porcelain factory. Apprenticed to Turner in Caughley and in 1793 he f. his own pottery in Jackfield (Shropshire). Some years later he returned to Coalport, where he took over the factory of his earlier master, Turner, by buying it in 1799.

Rose, William, see Coalport.

Rose du Barry. Misapplied use of name for 'Rose pompadour'.

Rose lustre, see Glanzvergoldung.

Rose pompadour. Delicate, rose red glaze of Sèvres porcelain. It is said to have been discovered in 1757 by the porcelain decorator Xrowet (Xhrouet).

Rosenburg, see Rozenburg.

Rosenkavalier. Word used as trademark No. 259363 from 26 January 1921 by P. F. Rosenthal, Selb.

Rosenthal. Word used as trademark No. 280224 from 13 February 1922 by P. F. Rosenthal, Selb.

Rosenthal Porzellan. Word used as trademark No. 280223 from 13 February 1922 by P. F. Rosenthal, Selb.

Rosenthal Porzellan Aktiengesellschaft, see Selb (9).

Rosenthal, Ph. & Co. porcelain factory AG, Filiale Kronach, see Kronach (4).

Rosenthal Handmalerei, see Munich (6).

Rosenthalrot. Word used as trademark No. 280225 from 13 February 1922 by P. F. Rosenthal, Selb.

Rosetti, Jacinto. He experimented as an arcanist in the search for porcelain in 1737 in Turin.

Rosina China Co. Ltd., Queen's Pottery, see Longton (65).

Röslau (Germany, Bavaria). Winterling Bros., porcelain factory, f. 1906.

Rösler, Richard S., see Dessendorf (2) and Schauberg (2).

Rosly, de, see Pontenx.

Roslyn China, Park Place Works, see Longton (65).

Rosoli-Becherin. Small cup like vessels, the smallest of which hardly exceeded the size of a thimble. Used for the decanting of Rosoli liqueur.

Ross, James (1745–1821), engraver, see Worcester (1).

Rosslau (Germany, Anhalt). H. Schomburg & Son, branch of the Kahla porcelain factory. This factory is closed.

Rotberg, Privy councillor Wilhelm Theodor von (d. 1769). Founder of the oldest Thuringian porcelain factory in Gotha in 1757. See Gotha (1).

Rotes steinzeug, see Böttger-stoneware.

Roth, Johann-Gottlieb (d. 1753). Painter in Strasbourg c. 1750, he may be one and the same with J. G. Rode, who was with A. F. von Löweninck in Meissen and Höchst from 1747–8. They left Strasbourg together in 1748.

Rotterdam (Holland). The blue mark 'F. L. S. A. Rotterdam 1812' show a painter's initials. There is no evidence of a porcelain factory working in Rotterdam in 1812.

Roubiliac, Louis François (1695–1762). His work as a modeller in Chelsea's first period was of outstanding merit.

Rouen (France). Louis Poterat, son of the famous faience maker Edme Poterat, was granted a Privilege in 1673 by Louis XIV for the production of porcelain, after the Chinese pattern'. Poterat discovered a formula for making frit porcelain and was thus the first porcelain producer in France. The extent of his production was limited however, because he insisted on working by himself, without even an unskilled worker to assist him, so that the secret, or the 'arcanum', would remain with him alone. His secret died with him in 1696. The best known products are in the style of the royal faiences, mostly in underglaze blue, rarely in polychrome. When the mark AP with a star was issued and by whom is still a matter of conjecture.

Rouge d'or. French term for the pinkish tint produced by the porcelain of the famille rose.

Rouge haricot. Copper oxide red found in Chinese porcelain.

Rousseau, Francisque, see Paris (76).

Rousset & Co., see Limoges (76).

Roussière, de, see Chantilly (1).

Royal Albert Bone China, Thos. Wild & Sons Ltd., see Longton (66).

Royal Albion China Co., see Fenton (6).

Royal Albion China Co., see Longton (67).

Royal Bruxelles, see Brussels (5).

Royal Bruxonia Austria, see Brüx (2).

Royal Copenhagen. Frequently used term for the porcelain of the Royal Works in Copenhagen.

Royal Crown Derby Porcelain Co. (later Limited Derby), see Derby (1).

Royal Danish Porcelain Factory, see Copenhagen (1).

Royal French Service. Sèvres Service in the style of the 18th c. Louis XVIII ordered it as a presentation to the Duke of Wellington who received it in London on 1 September 1822. See Wellington Service.

Royal Rockingham Works, see Swinton.

Royal Stafford China, Thomas Poole & Gladstone China Ltd., see Longton (68).

Royal Tara, see Galway.

Royal Worcester Porcelain Company, see Worcester (1).

Royville, see Isigny.

Rozenburg (Holland). W. van Gudenberg f. the 'Haagsche Plateelbakkerij' in 1883–4. In the beginning the ceramic products were made in the style of Delft. By 1884 Gudenberg had already secured the co-operation of one of the leading members of the 'Neuwe Kunst' (Art Nouveau Movement), Th. Colenbrander, who influenced form and decoration of the products until the 1889s. The truly characteristic Rozenburg style, however, formed later under his successor, Jurrian Kok, 1894–1913. This development was welcomed by one of the chemists of the factory, M. N. Engelden who in 1899 had discovered a formulae for making a frit-like porcelain which could have a very thin body (eggshell porcelain). This meant that porcelains were created which differed significantly from other ceramic products of the time. The pieces shown at the Paris World Exhibition 1900 had sensational success. Today 'Rozenburg' is one of the most valuable ceramic creations of the Art Nouveau. It is not known why Kok left in 1913, nor who his successor was, nor the reason for the surprising closure of the factory in 1914 or 1916. Renowned painters and designers such as J. Schellink, J. M. v. Rossum, R. Sterken and W. P. Hartgring produced signed pieces. Besides these, the following artists are also mentioned: Brouwer, Frauenberger, Hakker, Harking, Heijtze, Manfield, de Ruyter, van der Ver and Verhoog. When in 1899 the porcelain production began, the year-marks were used. The factory mark is a crown with 'Rozenburg' beneath a stork (from the city's coat-of-arms) and 'Den Haag' in black. The artist, number of model, year mark and a quartered square are also marked in black.

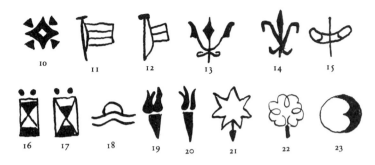

1 1900 – 2 1899 – 3 1900 – 4 1901 – 5–7 1902 – 8–10 1903 – 11–12 1904 – 13–14 1905 – 15 1906 – 16–17 1907 – 18 1908 – 19–20 1909–12 – 21–22 1913 – 23 1914

Roznan (Czechoslovakia). Alois Jaronek, porcelain decorating studio, from c. 1920–30.

Ruaud, see Limoges (77).

Rubens. Mark used as trademark No. 261466 from 8 March 1921 by the P. F. Rosenthal Selb.

Rub-Laprince, Arnold, see Paris (127).

Rudolstadt Volkstedt (Introduction). The custom of the factories in this locality to use the name and mark of 'Älteste Volkstedter', has already been discussed under 'Älteste'. This, together with the frequent name changes of the producers, gave rise to much confusion which could not have been clarified without the extensive help of the appropriate specialists of the DDR (German Democratic Republic). The factories and producers which followed one another chronologically as well as those which provide clues to any possible connections, have been arranged under the numbers 1–8; all others follow from numbers 9–24 in alphabetical order.

Rudolstadt Volkstedt (1) (Germany, Thuringia). F. 1762 by G. H. Macheleid, under the patronage of Prince J. Fr. von Schwarzberg Rudolstadt. In 1767 Macheleid leased the factory to Christian Nonne from Erfurt. In 1797 the owner was Prince Ernst Constantin von Hessen Philippstal, who sold it in 1799 to the businessmen Wilhelm Greiner and Karl Holzapfel of Rudolstadt. During the 19th c. ownership changed several times: 1815–60 Greiner, Stauch & Co.; 1816–75 Macheleid, Triebner & Co. At the present time the factory is still working under the name 'Staatl. Thüringer Porzellanmanufactur', formerly 'Älteste Volkstedter GmbH': 1977 VEB Älteste Volkstedter Porcelain Works, factory of the 'VEB Zierporzellanwerke Lichte'. The early products were somewhat grey and spotted in parts. Under Christian Nonne, during their time of greatest prosperity, they produced beautiful porcelain services with delicate decoration. They decorated plates in the style of wall paintings and neo-classical motifs and biscuit busts were also made. Some known pieces reproduce engravings by Daniel Chodowiecki in iron red enamel.

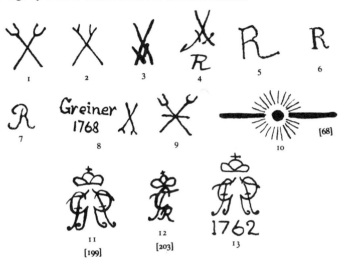

hayforks from the Schwarzenberg Royal coat of arms: 1–2 underglazed c. 1760 – 3–4 overglazed, becoming so like the Meissen swords, that Meissen protested in 1772. From c. 1787 it was decided to cross the forks with a horizontal stroke (No. 9), but this was not always done – 5–7 blue underglaze since the beginning of the 19th c. – 8 underglaze – 10–13 modern marks

Rudolstadt Volkstedt (2) (Germany, Thuringia). Triebner, Ens & Ekkert, 1876–94. The following marks were entered in 1877-86.

Rudolstadt Volkstedt (3) (Germany, Thuringia). Clemens Triebner had the following marks entered on 29 September 1894.

Rudolstadt Volkstedt (4) (Germany, Thuringia). Triebner, Ens &Co, porcelain factory, 1895–8. The following marks were registered in 1894 and 1895.

Rudolstadt Volkstedt (5) (Germany, Thuringia). Älteste Volkstedter porcelain factory, 1899–1936 and Unterweissbach, Mann & Porzelius porcelain factory. The following marks were registered in 1915 and 1916.

[199]   [203]   [200]

Rudolstadt Volkstedt (6) (Germany, Thuringia). Karl Ens porcelain factory, f. 1898, formerly: Macheleid, Triebner & Co. arts and crafts porcelain. Still active in 1949, when the owners were Paul, Anna and Augusta Ens. Now (1977) 'Unterglasurporzellan Rudolstadt', factory of the 'VEB Sitzendorfer porcelain works'. Mark No. 4 was still in use at this time.

[99]   [100]   [220]

Rudolstadt Volkstedt (7) (Germany, Thuringia). Richard Eckert & Co. AG, luxury porcelain, f. 1895. Luxury articles and figurative ornaments. This concern must have been incorporated into the 'Älteste Volkstedt porcelain factory AG' in 1930. The last three marks reproduced, were reported by Lange and Berling (both 1911), the use of which was contested by Meissen before 1896. Their use ceased and they no longer appeared in the trademark register of the German Reich of 1896–8.

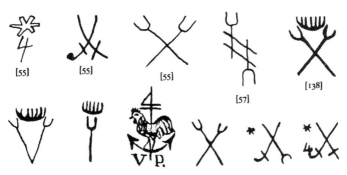

[55]   [55]   [55]   [57]   [138]

Rudolstedt Volkstedt (8) (Germany, Thuringia). Älteste Volkestedter porcelain factory AG, Abteilung Eckert. In 1930 the following mark was confirmed for this factory.

[200]

Rudolstadt Volkstedt (9) (Germany, Thuringia). Ackermann & Fritze factory, f. 1908, producing the finest artistic porcelain. Produced luxury goods and particularly well modelled figures.

Rudolstadt Volkstedt (10) (Germany, Thuringia). Rudolstadt porcelain factory AG. Still in business 1930.

Rudolstadt Volkstedt (11) (Germany, Thuringia). Beyer & Bock porcelain factory, f. 1890. Utility porcelain; according to Cushion, it is assumed that the factory began as a porcelain decorating workshop in 1853. The production of porcelain began in 1890. Today the factory is called VEB (K) Porzellanfabrik Rudolstadt-Volkstedt. The year of the foundation is given as 1853 below mark no. 3.

[128]

Rudolstadt Volkstedt (12) (Germany, Thuringia). Ernst Bohne Söhne, porcelain factory f. 1854; after 1945 became Albert Stahl & Co. Luxury and fancy articles.

[13]

Rudolstadt Volkstedt (13) (Germany, Thuringia). In 1897 the Ens & Greiner porcelain factory, Lauschau *(q.v.)*, was moved here.

Rudolstadt Volkstedt (14) (Germany, Thuringia). Alfred Hanika porcelain works, f. 1932. Porcelain jewellery, table flowers, all kinds of porcelain ornaments. Their speciality was gold etching decoration still working in 1949.

Rudolstadt Volkstedt (15) (Germany, Thuringia). Herzinger & Co., porcelain decorating studio. c. 1925.

Rudolstadt Volkstedt (16) (Germany, Thuringia). Rudolf Kämmner. The factory was f. at the end of 1945 and produced ornamental earthenware until 1953. After this date the factory was transferred to Volkstedt and produced ornamental porcelain only in the 'Dresden genre'. Decorations are embellished with porcelain flowers.

Rudolstadt Volkstedt (17) (Germany, Thuringia). Müller & Co., luxury porcelain factory, f. 1907. Luxury articles of all kinds. This factory was completely destroyed in the Second World War, but was already rebuilt by 1949 and ready to produce and deliver orders. The former owners opened a new factory in Seedorf/Württ. in 1950 which was named 'Volkstedter porcelain works'. Produced well-made figures and luxury porcelain. This factory was no longer listed in the Keramadressbuch of 1964.

Rudolstadt Volkstedt (18) (Germany, Thuringia). Schäfer & Vater, porcelain factory and decorating studio, f. 1890. Utility and luxury articles, dolls' heads.

Rudolstadt Volkstedt (19) (Germany, Thuringia). Strauch Bros., porcelain factory.

Rudolstadt Volkstedt (20) (Germany, Thuringia). L. Strauss & Sons, porcelain factory, f. 1882. Luxury and fancy articles. This factory no longer exists; in 1894 it was called New York and Rudolstadt Pottery Co. (AG). Under this name the following marks were registered on 2 May 1896 and 30 September 1904 with the WZR-Nos. 72 and 120.

[72]   [120]

Rudolstadt Volkstedt (21) (Germany, Thuringia). Volkstedter porcelain works Reinhold Richter GmbH, later Hans Richter, f. 1906. Still working in 1949. Arts and crafts porcelain.

[139]

Rudolstadt Volkstedt (22). Seedorf porcelain works (formerly Müller & Co.), see Rudolstadt Volkstedt (16).
Rudolstadt Volkstedt (23) (Germany, Thuringia). C. K. Weithase, ceramic decorating studio; views, armorials and lettering on individual orders. Still operating in 1949.

Rudolstadt Volkstedt (24) (Germany, Thuringia). Pelka showed the following mark in 1924 which up until now has not been attributed to any of the existing factories. (There may be some connection with Rudolstadt (12)).

Rulikowski, see Gorodnitza.
Russ, Willy, see Schönfeld (1).
Russia, Peter I, Elisabeth, Catherine II, Paul I, Alexander I, Nicholas I, Alexander II, Alexander III, Nicholas II, Tzars of, see Petersburg (1).
Russinger, Laurentius (c. 1740 Höchst–after 1807 Paris). Porcelain modeller. After having worked in Höchst from 1758 as a figure modeller, he was appointed master modeller in 1762. In 1767 he became technical and artistic director of the newly founded factory of Pfalz-Zweibrücken in Gutenbrunn which he left for an unknown destination, after having applied by letter for positions in Kassel, Fulda and Durlach. In 1774 he became joint owner and first director of the Allemande de la Courtille porcelain factory, f. by J. B. Locré; from 1787 on he was sole owner but financial difficulties forced him to take Pouyat as partner from 1800–7. Knowledge of his activities between 1768–74 is of decisive importance in making any assessment of Russinger's significance. The many connections which exist between the models of Fulda and Höchst in the Russinger period, almost forces one to the conclusion that Russinger was master modeller in Fulda. It is therefore also feasible that the many Höchst figures attributed to Melchior, were in fact modelled by Russinger.

Saalfeld (Germany, Thuringia). Hugo Scharf, porcelain decorating studio c. 1920–30.

Saarbrücken (Germany, Saarland). Deyander & Schmitt and Schmitt Bros. f. two porcelain factories here in 1802; these were still in production in 1867.
Saarburg (France). According to the *Dictionnaires des Postes aux Lettres* porcelain must have been produced here c. 1802–17.
Saargemünd (Lothringen). Utzschneider & Co., porcelain, stoneware and majolica factory, f. 1775. Utility porcelain; this factory no longer exists.

Sabanin, Wawili, see Ratkowo.
Sacharoff, painter, see Petersburg (1).
Safronoff, see Moscow (11).
Sailly, Gaston, see Châtres s. Cher. and Paris (129).
Sailly and Son, see Tours (1).
Saint-Amand-les-Eaux (1) (France). This faience factory, working since 1718 also produced soft paste porcelain under Fauquez between 1771–87. In 1800, Maximilian-Joseph de Bettiguies made the factory financially viable once again and it remained in his family until 1880. The production was in the style of Tournay and copies of Sèvres decorations were also made.

all marks in underglaze blue – 5–6 end of 19th c.

Saint-Amand-les-Eaux (2) (France). Manufactures de Faiences du Moulin des Loups, f. 1880. Tableware.
Saint-Amand-les-Eaux (3) (France). Bastener & Daudenart. Statuettes in porcelain and faience, c. 1896.

Saint-Brice (France). In 1784 Gomon and Croasmen f. a porcelain factory here which was called 'Gomon et Cie'. This undertaking was of very short duration; nothing is known of its products.
Saint-Cloud (France). Saint-Cloud is the second oldest French factory, and may have produced soft paste porcelain since 1693. To begin with the owners were the family of Pierre Chicaneau who died in 1678. In 1679, his widow Berthe Coudray married Henri Charles Trou, to whom the factory is indebted for the patronage of the Duke of Orléans. According to the DKG production of frit

porcelains had already begun in 1702. In 1722 a patent was granted; this was possibly after the death of Berthe Trou since her sons are referred to in connection with it. Two other members of the Chicaneau family built a branch of the factory in the Rue de la Ville L'Evèque in Paris which later became an independent concern. Both factories were combined again, however, by Henri Trou in 1742–3. The next owner was his son Henri Francois Trou, who went into partnership with Edme Choudard des Forges in 1764. In 1766 production ceased. The early Saint-Cloud porcelain is heavy, has a slightly yellow, irregular, matt looking glaze. Metal vessels, oriental porcelain with branches of blossoms in relief and later Meissen porcelain too provided examples to follow. Snuffboxes were popular, made in the shape of animals, together with jugs in the form of human figures or birds. The figures were probably not marked or decorated. The services are often blue and decorated with festoons. A limited number of pieces, e.g. snuffboxes are decorated with gilding in relief and a transparent enamel of the kind which decorates the work of Hunger.

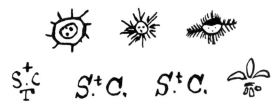

all marks in blue

Saint-Cricq-Cazeaux, see Creil et Montereau.

Saint-Denis (1), Rue Neuve (France). At the end of the 18th c. the Marquis of Torcy f. a porcelain factory here. The products do not deserve particular attention.

*rue
neuve St
Denis*

Saint-Denis (2) (France). La Ferté f. a porcelain factory here in 1778 which worked only for a limited period.

*Grosse l'isle St De
1780*

Saint-Denis (3), Rue du Fbg. (France). In 1844 Corbin managed a porcelain decorating studio here. His successors were Peltier and Mailly.

Saint-Gaudens (France). In 1829 Fouquet f. a factory here producing soft paste porcelain. In 1862 he sold the factory to some English factory owners. Hollingworth directed it from 1867 onwards and it was known by the name 'Compagnie Anglo-Française'.

Saint-Genou (1) (France). Martin and Pommier managed two porcelain factories here in 1867. Their products had no marks.
St. Genou (2) (France). 'L'Union Française' porcelain works, f. 1930. Tableware, smoking services, gift articles.

St. Georgen, Bayreuth (Germany, Oberfranken, Upper Frankonia). A small porcelain factory existed here c. 1837.
Saint-Gervais (France). It is alleged that porcelain was produced here in 1867 from the nearby Justin Ortmans and Louis Zoude factories.
St. Ives (England). Leach Pottery, porcelain factory f. 1921. Tea, coffee and table services, vases and jugs. Also ceramic studio.

Saint-Léonard (France). Jullien from Conflans f. a porcelain factory here in 1840 which worked until 1889; it produced only undecorated porcelain.
Saint-Léonard-de-Noblat (France). Porcelainière de la Haute-Vienne; ornamental porcelain and perfume flasks, containers and bottles.
St. Martin nr. Trier (Germany, Rhine Palatinate), see Trier.
St. Petersburg (Russia), see Petersburg.
Saint-Pierre-le-Moutier (France). Menissier et Galatry managed a small porcelain factory here in 1867. Its products were not marked.
St. Pölten (Nether-Austria). Rudolf Fritsche, porcelain decorating studio. F. 1924. Hand decorated table services, vases and boxes. Pure gold.

Saint-Uze (1) (France). René Delaunay, Succr., porcelain factory. Ovenproof porcelain, cooking utensils, ornamental and luxury porcelain.
Saint-Uze (2) (France). Les Etablissements Gustave Revol Père & Fils, f. 1789. Ovenproof kitchenware and advertising gifts.

Saint-Vallier (1) (France). Boissonet , Revol Frères, Siguret & Co. signed for the factory at the end of the 19th c. The following marks were used. As early as the beginning of the 20th c. the main products were ovenproof and electro porcelain.

PRECIEUX

Saint-Vallier (2) (France). Paul Frachon, porcelain factory, f. 1833. Household ware.

Saint-Vallier (3) (France). Manufacture de Porcelaine & Grès à Feu H. Montagne, f. 1830. Ovenproof kitchenware, special coffee filters, known under the name: 'Filtre Siguret'. The factory was originally called Vve. Siguret & Guichard, and later took the name Manufacture de Porcelaine H. Montagne until 1950.

Saint-Vallier (4) (France). B. Peichon, porcelain factory. Cooking recepticles.
Saint-Yrieix (1) (France). Faye & Fils, porcelain factory, utility porcelain ware.

Saint-Yrieix (2) (France). Les Porcelaines Industrielles du Limousin, f. 1774. Fancy articles, hotel ware. This factory had no marks. The current name was adopted in 1935.
Saint-Yrieix la Perche, kaolin deposit, see Sèvres (1).

Saintes (France). According to the *Dictionaires des Postes aux Lettres* (issued 1802 and 1817), there may have been a porcelain factory here at the beginning of the 19th c. Honey mentions a porcelain factory which had been active from 1779 (and possibly earlier) until 1790. The owner was perhaps Eutrope Morin.

Saison, Leon, see Paris (130).
Saitzewski, see Borowischtschi.
Salabast. Name used as trademark No. 71689 from 29 August 1904 (Hertie Berlin).
Salins (France). Bourgeois, Page et Comp. produced porcelain here in 1867. The products are not marked. The succeeding factory 'Societe de Faiencerie de Salins' marked the porcelain products (according to 'Tardy 75') with the following mark.
Salisbury China Co. Ltd., see Longton (69).
Salmon, Jean François Hylaire (1746–1803), see Sèvres.
Salmon et Cie., see Epinay.
'Salopian China Warehouse', see Caughley.
Salt & Nixon Ltd., see Longton (70).
Saltglaze. An extremely thin glassy coating on stoneware which is created by throwing common salt into the oven at the end of the firing. The salt combines with the steam and the gas produced by the firing transforms itself into natrium oxide and hydrochloric acid. The latter escapes while the natrium oxide combines with the silicic acid to form a glaze.
Sältzer, August, see Eisenach.
Sampson & Bridgwood, see York.
Sampson Smith Ltd., Sutherland Works, see Longton (71).
Samson, Edm., see Paris (131).
Samsonoff, see Koscherowo.
San Cristoforo, see Milan.
Sandier, Alexandre, see Sèvres (1).
Sandizell (Germany, Upper Bavaria). Höfner & Co., Sandizell porcelain factory, f. 1951. Fine quality figures.

Sandland & Colley, see Hanley (13).
'Sang-de-boeuf' glaze. Blood-red glaze on Chinese porcelain of the T'sing Dynasty 1644–1912; used extensively at the time of the Emperor K'ang-hi, 1662–1722.

Saou (1) (France, Drôme). Aliver & Brouhaut produced some porcelain here in 1814.

Saou (2) (France, Drôme). Cremieux produced porcelain here from 1856. The products bear no marks.

Saqui, decorator. Painted exotic birds in the Sèvres style on porcelain from the Plymouth, Bristol and Worcester factories.

Sargadelos (Spain). L. de la Riva et Comp. produced porcelain here in 1867.

S.A.R.L. rue de la Paix, see Paris (132).

Sartel, du. Important French collector who published an illustrated volume about his own collection in 1861.

Satalitz (Bohemia). Wenzel Provza, porcelain factory. Articulated porcelain dolls, figures, etc.

Sattler Bros., see Budweis (2).

Satu-Mare (Rumania). Dr. Boray, porcelain decorating studio, c. 1925.

Sausenhofer, Dominikus Christoph (1727–1802). From Vienna. In Ludwigsburg from 1760 until 1802; appointed as chief colour technician in 1776 and chief decorator in 1780.

Sauvage, Charles-Gabriel, see Lemire.

Sauvageau, see Lorient.

Sauviat (France). E. Dupuy, porcelain factory. Artistic porcelain, luxury articles.

Sauzin, Charles, see Paris (133).

Savoyen, Carl Emanuel II, see Vinovo.

Saxe ombré. Name for the Meissen insect and flower decoration in which the falling shadows of the subjects are also painted. This fact leads one to suppose that this type of decoration is inspired by engravings.

Saxon Service. Dessert service from the KPM Meissen, produced in 1818, giving 'the impression of a hesitant adaptation of the Empire style'. Made by order of the Saxon king Friederich August III as a gift for the Duke of Wellington. Consists of 134 pieces. See Wellington Service (Köllmann).

Saxony, August II (the Strong) and August III, Elector of, see Meissen (1).

Saxony–Meiningen, Georg, Duke of, see Rauenstein.

Saxony-Weimar, Karl August, Duke of, see Ilmenau (1).

Saxony porcelain and ceramic art factory, see Neuhaldensleben.

Saxony Porcelain works, see Meissen (4)

Sazerat, Léon, see Limoges (78).

Sazerat. Léon, Blondeau & Co., see Limoges (79).

Sceaux (France, Seine). The faience factory f. here in 1748 (or earlier) by von de Bey and Jacques Chapelle, perhaps began to produce soft paste porcelain in 1763, when Joseph Jullien and Charles-Symphorien Jacques bought the factory and the Duke of Penthièvre became the patron. The successive owners were as follows: Richard Glot from 1772; Antoine Cabaret from 1796; and Marsault from 1810. But the production of porcelain seems to have stopped towards the end of the 18th c. In contrast to the high quality of faiences from Sceaux, the porcelain was only average. Mennecy, Chantilly and Sèvres served as models.

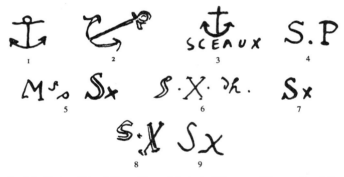

1–3 mark of the Duke of Penthièvre, Great Admiral of France – 4 Sceaux Penthièvre – 5–9 Glot's marks

Sceaux. Name for a porcelain bottle cooler of the 18th c.

Schaala nr. Rudolstadt (1) (Germany, Thuringia). Moerobergen produced porcelain here in 1867.

Schaala nr. Rudolstadt (2) (Germany, Thuringia). Herrmann Voigt porcelain factory, f. 1872. Figures and other objects. The factory no longer exists.

[16]

Schachtel, Joseph, see Charlottenbrunn.

Schade, Oskar Gustav, see Dresden (27).

Schadow, Gottfried. Modelled the biscuit statuettes 'Crown Princess Louise and Princess Frederike' for the KPM Berlin in 1796. In 1820 he created the Fieldmarshall Service *(q.v.).*
See also Prussian service.

Schaerbeek nr. Brussels, see Brussels (1).

Schäfer & Vater, see Rudolstadt Volkstedt (18)

Schäffler, Johann Christoph. By 1712 he was being hailed (together with Stechmann and Bader) as 'The illuminator of good porcelain'. Belongs to the earliest group of three decorators about whom we have more detailed knowledge.

Schaller, Oscar & Co., see Schwarzenbach (2).

Schaller, Oscar & Co., successor, see Kirchenlamitz (1) and Windische-schenbach.

Schamschula, Franz, see Kunstadt.

Schaper, Johann (1621–70), Independent decorator in Nuremberg, see Schwarzlot.

Scharf, Hugo, see Saalfeld.

Schatzlar (Bohemia). Schatzlar porcelain factory, f. by Theodor Pohl, 1878. Commemoratives and advertising articles, figures, etc.

Schaubach, Heinz, see Unterweissbach and Wallendorf.

Schauberg (1) (Germany, Upper Frankonia). G. Greiner & Co., porcelain factory, f. 1807. Utility and luxury articles. This factory is now closed.

Schauberg (2) (Germany, Upper Frankonia). Richard S. Rösler porcelain factory has been active here since 1948; it was originally f. in 1933 in Dessendorf. It produces table and utility porcelain as well as varied technical porcelain.

Schauberg (3) (Germany, Upper Frankonia). Schauberg, Fritz and Rosenthal porcelain factory. Gift articles and services.

Schaum, Johann Valentin (b. 1714), modeller, see Fulda (1).

Schedel, Adolf, see Neuses.

Schedewitz. Unger may have produced hard porcelain here at the end of the 19th c.

Scheffauer, Philipp Jacob (1756–1808). Pupil of Lejeunes, worked in Ludwigsburg as a modeller at the end of the 18th c.

Scheibe-Alsbach. 'VEB Scheibe Alsbach porcelain factory', f. 1836; formerly A. W. Fr. Kister GmbH. This factory's production of porcelain figures gave it an international reputation. First class artists and sculptors were involved. Produced high class figures in the Meissen genre, excellent works after old Masters and busts of poets and composers, as well as tomb ornaments, dolls' heads, dolls which could be immersed in water, jointed dolls and other toys. Won many international prizes between c. 1870–1914.

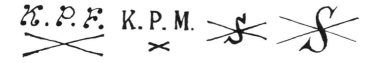

Scheidig, Carl, see Gräfenthal (3).

Scheilheimer, see Paris (134).

Schelten (Bohemia). Josef Palme f. a small porcelain factory here in 1829 which came into the possession of Ignaz Balle in 1851. In 1860 the factory was closed.

Schenau (Schönau), Johann Eleazar (b. in 1737). Studied in Dresden and Paris. He was a pupil of Louis Silvestre and from 1773–96 manager of the decorating-department of the Meissen factory. There he also produced figures and groups.

Schepers, Cajetano and Sons, see Capodimonte, Buen-Retiro and La Moncloa.

Schertler, Fr., see Pilsen.

Scheurich. Paul (b. 1883, New York, d. 1945, Brandenburg). About 1920 the directors of Meissen under Max Pfeiffer (*q.v.*), were successful in winning Paul Scheurich as freelance-artist. Over several years he created the astonishing number of 102 models. Without doubt, these, together with other work of Scheurich, represent the most exceptional work which has been produced so far in the 20th c. Walcha elevates Scheurich to the heights reached by Kändler and Bustelli. Other models also for Berlin, Nymphenburg and Schwarzburg.

Schick, Johann Philipp (d. in 1768). Co-founder of the Fulda porcelain factory. Adam Friedrich von Löwenfinck married the daughter of Schick Maria-Seraphia. See Löwenfinck.

Schierholz'sche Porzellanmanufaktur Plaue GmbH., see Plaue.

Schiller, Richard, see Fischhäusel.

Schiller, W., and Sons, see Bodenbach.

Schiller & Gerbing, see Bodenbach.

Schindler, A., see Schönfeld.

Schindler, Philipp Ernst (1723–93). The most important figure decorator of the Imperial porcelain factory Vienna, in the second half of the 18th c. His Watteau scenes are particularly well-known. His equestrian groups after Rugendas, shepherds and peasants' rustic scenes, hunting pictures and lovers are also famous. Before he was active in Vienna, he worked, as his father had done before him, in Meissen.

Philipp Ernst Schindler
M·DCCXLVI

Schinkel, Karl Friedrich (1781–1841), architect, see Berlin (3).

Schippel, Adolf, see Eichwald.

Schirnding (Germany, Bavaria). Schirnding porcelain factory AG, f. 1902. Utility services.

Schlackenwerth (Bohemia). Pfeiffer & Löwenstein, porcelain factory, f. 1873. Coffee and tea services, hotel and domestic ware. This factory ceased working in 1945.

Schlaggenwald (1) (Bohemia, now Horni Slavkov). Georg Paulus f. this factory in 1793 after various experiments. From 1800, Louise Sophie Greiner from Gera was the owner, and from 1808, it was owned by Georg Lippert and Wenzel Haas K. K. Bergmeister and known as 'Lippert & Haas'. The quality of the products was already being praised in 1828. Porcelain workers from Meissen were engaged. Lithophanes were produced in 1830. In 1831, the Imperial and Royal Ministry of Finance stated that the Schlaggenwalder products were of superior quality than those of the Vienna factory. At about this period, the concern had branches in Vienna, Prague, Brunn and Budapest. In 1836 the factory already had c. 110 co-workers and in 1847 there were 206 porcelain workers. In 1867 the factory had developed into the largest porcelain production of Bohemia. During these years, Georg Haas accepted Johann Czjzek as partner. The factory was enlarged once more, in 1872 the 'Falkonia AG' was acquired from the Chodau porcelain factory. The production covered a wide range from simple domestic ware to the choicest porcelain. A gold medal was awarded in Vienna in 1845. The Radetzki service was produced in 1848–64. In the course of the following years it received a number of international recognitions. From 1847 Haas became the sole owner (Lippert died in 1843). Renowned decorators: L. Gerlach 1814; Hürrer 1834; Kiesling 1839; modeller: Fritsch.

Haas & Czjzek were the first in Bohemia to introduce pension schemes for invalids, widows and orphans. Both owners were knighted by the Imperial and Royal monarchies. Strawflower pattern, blue and purple underglaze used since c. 1800. Mark No. 13 was registered on 14 June 1889 under No. 134 in Eger, for the entry in the K.K. trademark register in Vienna, by Haas & Czjzek.

Archival evidence shows that Lippert & Haas produced lithophanes between 1831–43, lightshades and cups with lithophane bottoms.

1 blue underglaze or red before 1800, Paulus porcelain – 2 blue underglaze under Lippert and Haas, in addition to the year-marks 1817–30, impressed – 3 gold or multi-coloured, until 1830 – 4 blindstamp from 1830–70 – 5 L + H = Lippert and Haas, occurs until 1847 beside 4, and in front of blindstamp 6 – 7–8 blindstamp, also cursive in use since 1830 – 9 in different borders, black or chrome green, 1830–88 – 13 green 1888–96, from 1896 without any marks – 14–19 modern marks – 20 for export to USA 1939 – 21 jubilee mark

Schlaggenwald (2) (Bohemia, now Horni Slavkov). F. by Anton Waldman in 1901, this porcelain factory was taken over in 1904 by Sommer & Matschak. Tableware.

Schlegel milch, Erhard, see Tillowitz (1).

Schlegelmilch, Erdmann, see Suhl.

Schlegelmilch, Oscar, see Langewiesen.

Schlegelmilch, Reinhold, see Tillowitz (2).

Schleich, L., see Meissen (5).

Schleusingen (Germany, Saxony). Carl Schmidt, porcelain factory, f. 1863. Figures and other wares.

Schlierbach (Germany, Hessen-Nassau). Wächtersbacher Steingutfabrik, porcelain, stoneware and ceramic products. The following mark was registered on 20 November 1884, at the Königliches Amtsgericht Wächtersbach.

[35]

Schlimper, Johann Gottlob, porcelain decorator who worked in Meissen during the Höroldt period.

Schlitz-Magnus, see Strasbourg (2).
Schlottenhof nr. Arzberg (Germany, Upper Frankonia). Schlottenhof
porcelain factory GmbH, f. 1895 by Dünzel. Utility ware and gift articles.

SchlottenhofArzberg

Schlottenhof (Germany, Upper Frankonia). Hans Worms porcelain works and
ceramic factory, porcelain decorating studio, f. 1935.

Schmeisser, Fr. C., see Liersmühle.
Schmelzer & Gerike, see Althaldensleben.
Schmetz, Ferdinand, see Aachen (2).
Schmider, Georg, Vereinigte Zeller keramische Fabriken, see Zell-
Harmersbach.
Schmidt, August, see Ilmenau (6).
Schmidt, Brüder, see Kronstadt-Brasov.
Schmidt, Carl, see Schleusingen.
Schmidt, Friedrich Gottlob. Independent decorator in Meissen c. 1762.
Schmidt, H., see Freienwaldau.
Schmidt, H., (and Olremba), see Freiewaldau.
Schmidt, Jacob. Sculptor and modeller in Copenhagen, 1779–1807.
Schmidt, Johann Heinrich (d. 1821). Moulds designer and 'chief-designer' in
Ludwigsburg, 1774–91.
Schmidt, Johann Jakob (1787–1862), see Ulm.
Schmidt, Otto, see Dresden (28).
Schmidt, Sebastian, see Schmiedefeld (2).
Schmidt, W. J., see Copenhagen (7).
Schmidt. Active as an independent painter in Bamberg c. 1880. His main task
was to paint copies of Old Masters.
Schmidt & Co., see Altrohlau (3).
Schmiedeberg (Germany, Thuringia). Pohl Bros., porcelain factory, f. 1871.

[249]

Schmiedefeld (1) (Germany, Thuringia). Glasser & Greiner, porcelain factory and decorating studio, f. 1816. In 1894, Math. Liebermann was the owner. Produced copies for replacements of damaged articles, biscuit, figures, vases with applied decorations, pipe-heads. This factory no longer works.

Schmiedefeld (2) (Germany, Thuringia). Sebastian Schmidt, f. 1857, luxury porcelain and figures.

[53]

Schmieger & Sons, see Schönfeld (2).

Schmuz Baudiss, Theodor Hermann (1859–1942); decorator and ceramicist. Studied in Munich 1879–90, trained as potter under Ganser, Diessen/Ammersee. In 1897 he was co-proprietor of the Vereinigten Werkstatten, Munich. Active for the VWM in Swaine & Co. in Huttensteinach from 1901–2, when he moved to KPM Berlin. In 1904 he became a professor and in 1908–26 he was artistic director of the KPM Berlin and teacher at the ceramics department at the Handwerks-Schule (Craftman's College), Berlin.

Schnabel, J. & Sohn, see Tiefenbach.
Schnabel & Sohn, see Dessendorf.
Schneeballenbelege. Plastic decoration in the form of snowballs, developed by Kändler in Meissen in 1740. Also popular in later periods.
Schneider Bros., see Mariaschein.
Schneider, J. G., aee Bautzen.
Schneider, Ludwig, see Marburg.
Schneider & Co., see Altrohlau (6).
Schneiders, Carl, Heir (formerly Schneider & Hutschenreuther), see Gräfenthal (1).
Schney nr. Lichtenfels (Germany, Bavaria). H. K. Eichhorn maintained a porcelain factory here in 1837 which employed over 100 workers.
Schney (Germany, Bavaria). Eduard Liebmann, porcelain factory, f. 1780. According to Neuwirth, the factory was known as 'Brenner & Liebmann' in 1896. Utility ware. The factory no longer exists.

Schnorrsche Soil (after Veit Hans Schnorr von Carolsfeld), see Kaolin sources.

Schoelcher, Marc, see Paris (69) and (135).

Schoenau, Bros., Swaine & Co., see Köppelsdorf-Nord.

Schöllhammer, Johann Melchior. One of the best decorators of the Ansbach-Bruckberg porcelain factory, where he worked from 1758. Colour technician and inspector from 1785, became a director in 1799. Pieces still exist which bear marks proving that they came from his own hand.

Scholz Nachf., Hermann, see Tiefenbach.

Schomburg, H. & Sons, see Berlin (5) and Rosslau.

Schönau, Joh. Ritter von, see Dallwitz.

Schönbach, Christian Gottlob. Private decorator in Meissen from 1762.

Schönbornlust, Koblenz (Germany, Rhineland). From c. 1757–9 Stadelmayer produced ceramic ware here which was described as 'porcelain'. He worked under the patronage of the Archbishop of Trier, Johann, Philipp von Waldendorf.

Schönfeld nr. Carlsbad (1) (Bohemia, now Krasno n. T.). Willy Russ, porcelain decorating studio, c. 1930.

Schönfeld nr. Carlsbad (2) (Bohemia, now Krasno n. T.). Schmieger & Sons, porcelain decorating studio, f. 1857. Owner Karl Rauh. Speciality was fine hand decorations.

Schönfeld nr. Carlsbad (3) (Bohemia, now Krasno n. T.). F. 1883 by Jos. Spinner, this porcelain factory joined with the porcelain decorating studio which had been f. by J. Spinner in 1867. According to archival evidence from 1902, the factory was named A. Schindler. Milk-jugs and childrens' beakers.

Schönheit, Johann Karl (1730–1805). Active as modeller in Meissen from 1754, and also employed for a long time as assistant to Acier. Together with Jüchtzer and Matthäi, became the artistic successor of Acier, whose style influenced him strongly.

Schonsui, Gorodaya. First producer of porcelain in Japan. See Japanese porcelain.

Schönwald (1) (Germany, Upper Frankonia). E. & A. Müller porcelain factory, joint-stock company, f. 1904. Utility and hotel porcelain.

[181]   [160]

Schönwald (2) (Germany, Upper Frankonia). Schönwald porcelain factory, branch of the Kahla porcelain factory, f. 1879. The firm was named: 'J. N. Müller porcelain factory' until 1898 when it became a joint-stock company, known as Schönwald porcelain factory, Schönwald/Oberfranken'. In 1927 this factory joined with the Kahla porcelain factory and received its present name. Hotel and utility services. Since Lorenz Hutschenreuther Selb and C. M. Hutschenreuther Hohenberg were amalgamated, the Schönwald porcelain factory uses the last mark.

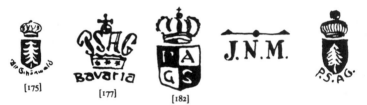

[175]   [177]   [182]

Schorndorf (Germany, Wurtemberg). Würtembergische porcelain works, C. M. Bauer & Pfeiffer, f. 1904. Table, coffee, tea services and hotel porcelain. This factory is now closed.

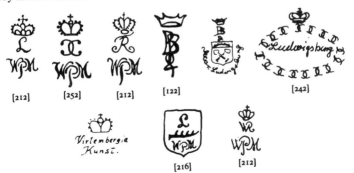

[212]   [252]   [212]   [122]   [242]

[216]   [212]

Schou, Philipp, see Copenhagen (1).

Schramberg (1) (Germany, Württemberg). Villeroy & Boch, porcelain, stoneware and majolica factory, f. 1820 and taken over by Villeroy & Boch in 1883. Utility ware. The factory no longer works.

Schramberg (2) (Germany, Württemberg). Schramberger majolica factory GmbH, had the following mark registered as a trademark under No. 226288 on 20 September 1918. Produced stoneware, porcelain and fluorescent ware.

SCHRAMBERG [210]

Schreier, Paul, see Bischofswerda.

Schreimüller (Schreitmüller), decorator, see Ansbach.

Schrezheimer Fayencealtar, see Gerverot.

Schubert, Carl Gottlieb (d. 1804). Modeller. In 1775 he replaced the Frenchman Desoches (who had left the year before) in Fürstenberg, where he remained until his death in 1804.

Schubert, Johann David (1761-1822 Dresden). Painter and engraver, successor of Zeissig at the Meissen porcelain factory.

Schuldes, Adalbert and Johann, see Giesshübel (2).

Schultz, Chr., modeller and decorator, see Gotha (1).

Schulz, Anton F. J. Porcelain decorator at the Vienna factory and also freelance decorator. Mentioned in connection with his marriage and with being a decorator of the factory in 1768. He is recorded in 1741 and 1768 as an independent enameller.

Schulze, Albert, see Neustrelitz.

Schulze, Successor, Albert, see Velten.

Schumacher Bros., see Hamburg (1).

Schumann, Carl, AG, see Arzberg (4).

Schumann, M. and Son, see Moabit.

Schumann & Klett, see Ilmenau (7).

Schumann & Schreide, GmbH, see Schwarzenhammer.

Schütz, Siegmund, see Arcadian Service.

Schütze, Johann Carl, Independent decorator c. 1762.

Schützmeister & Quendt, see Gotha (4).

Schwabach nr. Nuremberg (Germany, Frankonia). Du Bellier, Karl, porcelain decorating studio, c. 1930.

Schwaben nr. Munich (Germany, Bavaria). Schwaben porcelain factory active c. 1910.

Schwanthaler, Franz (1760–1820). He and his son were modellers in Nymphenburg in the first half of the 19th c.

Schwarza on Saale (Germany, Thuringia). Josef Franz Sieber, luxury porcelain, flowers and porcelain lace-work.

Schwarza-Saalbahn (Germany, Thuringia). E. & A. Müller, porcelain factory, f. 1890. Luxury porcelain. This factory is now closed.

[257]

Schwarzburg Rudolstadt, J. Fr. Prince von, see Rudolstadt Volkstedt (1).
Schwarzburger Werkstätten for artistic porcelain, GmbH, see Unterweissbach.
Schwarzenbach on Saale (1) (Germany, Upper Frankonia). J. Kronester & Co. GmbH, porcelain factory and decorating studio, f. 1904. Utility ware.

Schwarzenbach on Saale (2) (Germany, Upper Frankonia). Oscar Schaller & Co., porcelain factory, f. 1882. Taken over in 1917 by Winterling. Utility ware of all kinds, also the 'onion' pattern.

[149]

[198]

[51]

Schwarzenberg (Germany, Saxonia). Schwarzenberger porcelain factory. Fr. Wilhelm Kutzscher & Co., f. 1909. Miniature ivory articles. The factory is now closed.

Schwarzenfeld (Thuringia). H. Waffler, porcelain decorating studio, c. 1924.

Schwarzenhammer nr. Selb (Germany). Schumann & Schreider porcelain factory, Schwarzenhammer GmbH, f. 1905. Utility ware and, as a speciality, fretted patterns in porcelain.

Schwarzkostelez (Bohemia). Alois Vondrácek & Co., porcelain decorating studio, c. 1930.

Schwarzlot (method of decorating). Black enamel colour which had been used by the independent Nürnberger decorator, J. Schaper, in 1660, originally only for decorating faiences. Its use on porcelain was particularly popular at Vienna during the Du Pacquier-period, and was also used at Meissen and by freelance decorators in Bohemia and Augsburg.

Schweidnitz (Germany, Silesia). R. M. Krause, porcelain decorating studio, c. 1930.

Schweig, August GmbH, see Weisswasser.

Schwerdtner, see Amberg.

Schwetzingen (Wurtemberg). In 1946 Ruth Berger f. a studio for ceramic and porcelain decoration, using her own designs. Marked with own name.

Schwurz, T., see Lemberg.

Sciptius, Georg Christian. Chief decorator in the first periods (1760–5) of the Copenhagen factory.

Sebellini, L., see Pesaro.

Seedorf (Germany, Wurtemberg). Volkstedter porcelain works, f. 1950. High-class figures and other luxury porcelain. This factory is no longer listed in the Keramadressbuch 1964.

See also Rudolstadt Volkstedt (17).

Seefried (Seyfried), Peter Anton (d. 1812). He worked as a modeller in Nymphenburg from 1756–67. After a short time in Ludwigsburg he became a modeller in Kelsterbach, where he is reputed to have been the best modeller. His work is strongly influenced by Bustelli. In 1770 he returned to Nymphenburg, where he became the chief bossierer in 1786. In 1794 he became an administrator of the factory and received a pension in 1810.

Seger, Hermann (1839–93), chemist. Studied in Berlin from 1859 and became a Doctor of Philosophy in Rostock in 1868. Studied and travelled until 1870, and was editor of the ceramic technical journal 'Notizblatt' from 1872–6. In 1876 he became the publisher of the Thonindustrie-Zeitung (newspaper for the clay industry), and worked in a laboratory in Berlin at the same time. He was manager of the newly founded experimental institute, 'Versuchsanstalt der KPM Berlin', from 1878–90. In 1885 he became a Professor and in 1886 invented the 'Seger cone', a pyrometer for measuring temperatures *(q.v.).*

Seger cones. Abbreviation: SC. Named after their inventor, Hermann Seger *(q.v.).* These were small ceramic melting blocks which were introduced to the trade in the form of slim, three-sided pyramids. The different melting points of these SC served to set high temperatures in the firing kilns. Seger himself developed SCs for temperatures of 1,150–1,850°, with cones available at approximately 20° intervals. Seger's pupils, Kramer and Hecht widened the scale for lower and higher temperatures so that it ranged from 600° to 2,000°.

Seger porcelain. In the second half of the 19th c., there was a desire in the porcelain industries for strong, vibrant colours in keeping with the general fashion of the time. The high firing temperature of 1,450° made the use of such colours impossible. In 1880 Hermann Seger *(q.v.)* developed so-called Seger porcelain, a soft paste porcelain, with certain Far Eastern formulae. This porcelain had a considerably lower kaolin content than had been usual in hard paste European porcelain. This therefore made the reduction of temperature (to

c. 1,300°) possible. Seger's aim to produce artistic porcelain with over-running, crystallising, flambé and oxblood glazes, was realised in Seger porcelain. However, since its value as utility porcelain (able to withstand knocks and changes of temperatures) was considerably reduced, the Seger porcelain is best suited more to fancy articles. Seger himself is of this opinion. The KPM Berlin was still advertising 'vessels of Seger porcelain, with copperglaze China red' in 1910. Since the Sèvres factory in France had to contend with the same requests as those which stimulated Seger's work, a similar recipe for soft paste porcelain was produced a year later (1881), by Lauth and Vogt. The French name for this product is, technically speaking, a misnomer: 'Paté dure nouvelle'. The mark was registered on 8 March 1882 with the royal County Court, Berlin, under the No. 637.

[19]

Ségourneau, see Paris (136).
Segovia (Spain). According to Demmin a porcelain factory was here in 1867.

Séguin, see Vincennes (2).
Seigle, see Assay-le-Chateau.
Seinsheim, Adam Friedrich von, Archbishop of Wurtemberg, see Wurtemberg.
Selb (1) (Germany, Bavaria). Gräf & Krippner, porcelain factory; branch of Heinrich & Co., poecelain factory, Selb, since 1929.
Selb (2) (Germany, Bavaria). Heinrich & Co. The porcelain decorator Franz Heinrich set up his porcelain decorating studio in 1896, by installing a muffle kiln with a capacity of 0.75 m³ in his parent's house (he demolished the parental baking oven for this purpose!). His sole helper was a female worker. He decorated the porcelain, which he bought from other factories, himself. Later, he started his own porcelain production and the earliest Heinrich porcelain reached the trade in 1901. In 1945, after the Second World War, this firm was the first porcelain factory in West Germany to resume production.

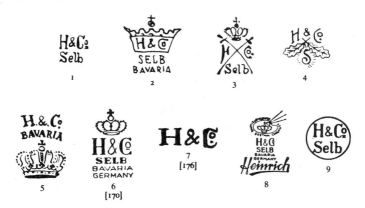

Selb (3) (Germany, Bavaria). Jager, Werner & Co., porcelain factory, c. 1910–20.

J. W
&
Co.

Selb (4) (Germany, Bavaria). Lorenz Hutschenreuther f. his own factory in Selb in 1856; his father, Karl Magnus had directed a porcelain factory in Hohenberg-upon-Eger since 1814. His first site of production was at the Ludwigsmühle in Selb. Work at the factory, which was specially built, only began in 1859, and by 1864 the premises were already being extended. Although at first the production concentrated on white utility ware, in the 1880s it switched to finely decorated table services and hotel porcelain. This was followed by the installation of a studio for artistic production. In 1902 the concern became a joint stock company and in 1906 a second factory was built in Selb which had the name: 'Abteilung B'. In 1917 the porcelain factory f. by Paul Müller in Selb in 1890, was taken over. But the most significant expansion of the Lorenz Hutschenreuther joint stock company occured in 1927 through the acquisition of the Bauscher Bros. porcelain factory in Weiden, which had been f. 1838, and was the largest speciality factory for hotel porcelain. Today it employs c. 3,000 workers. This concern is one of the leading German porcelain factories. Production: table, coffee, tea and mocha services, ranging in execution from the simplest to the most elaborate, also services in series, household ware, hotel and restaurant porcelain wares, gift articles and ovenproof cooking ware, figures and busts. In 1969 the Lorenz Hutschenreuther AG gained the majority of the shares of the C. M. Hutschenreuther AG in Hohenberg. Since 1970 the combine operates as above. Foreign holdings in the 'Coimbra Portugal', together with 'Vista Alegre' were obtained in 1970. In 1972 the company fused with Kahla AG (Schönwald), which brought them the Arzberg and Schönwald factories. New developments since 1975 are 'Hutschenreuther France' and a branch company in North-

Branford (Conneticut, USA). Hutschenreuther AG uses the lion-mark which had been registered in 1919 under No. 229582 with the trademark register of the Reich, by Lorenz Hutschenreuther, Selb. In the place of 'L.H.S.' the original year of the foundation, 1814, appears in addition to the script 'Hutschenreuther Germany'. The Hutschenreuther works uses the round mark for their hand decorated goods.

Selb (5) (Germany, Bavaria). Krautheim and Adelberg. Christoph Krautheim f. a porcelain decorating studio in Selb in 1884 and began producing porcelain in 1912. The Krautheim & Adelberg porcelain factory, Selb, developed from this concern. Table and coffee services, mass-produced services, gift articles and hotel porcelain.

Selb (6) (Germany, Bavaria). Lorenz & Trabe, porcelain decorating studio, c. 1924.

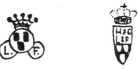

Selb (7) (Germany, Bavaria). Paul Müller, porcelain factory, f. 1890, was incorporated into the L. Hutschenreuther AG, Selb, in 1917. Household and hotel ware.

[230]

Selb (8) (Germany, Bavaria). In about 1910 Rieber managed a decorating studio here which used the following mark.

Selb (9) (Germany, Bavaria). Rosenthal Porcelain Aktiengesellschaft, f. 1879. Produced luxury and household ware of all kinds as well as porcelain products for industrial and technical uses. For many years the factory has taken care to create beautiful and timeless designs which deserve particular attention. There is hardly anyone among the European (or even American) designers who has not been under contract with Rosenthal at some stage, particularly during the post-War years. The success of such single-minded direction is patently obvious, to say nothing of the influence exerted on the porcelain industry as a whole. Some results, however, should be viewed with some caution. The first mark shown, which was introduced in 1910, has been verified by Berling as well as by Lange (in 1911 in both cases). It has been registered, several times, with the Warenzeichenregister trademark register of the German Reich: on 17 November 1891, 1 October 1894 and 4 March 1895. The following factories belong to Rosenthal Porcelain Aktiengesellschaft: Rosenthal Selb-Plössberg porcelain factory, formerly Selb-Bahnhof; Rosenthal handpainters, Munich Department; Rosenthal Porcelain Works Aktiengesellschaft Kronach. Annexed to the Rosenthal Porcelain Aktiengesellschaft are the following factories: F. Thomas porcelain factory, owner Marktredwitz; Rosenthal Porcelain AG; Thomas & Co. porcelain factory, Sophienthal (nr. Bayreuth); Waldershof porcelain factory Aktiengesellschaft, formerly Johann Haviland, Waldershof; Krister porcelain works Landstuhl (Rheinpfalz) (since 1923).

[47]   [136]

Selb (10) Staatliche porcelain works. From 1944–55/57, the Staatliche porcelain works, Berlin produced on the premises of the Paul Müller porcelain factory, which had been the property of L. Hutschenreuther since 1917. (See Berlin (3).)

S

Selb-Bahnhof (Germany, Bavaria). Jacob Zeidler & Co., porcelain factory, f. 1866. Household domestic and hotel ware. This factory no longer exists.

J Z & Co.
[166]

Selb-Plössberg, formerly Selb-Bahnhof (Germany, Bavaria). Rosenthal porcelain factory, f. 1867. Table and coffee services, ranging from the simplest to the very ornate, containers, vases, bowls, antique and modern forms, figures, animal figures in over and underglaze decoration, candelabra, lamps, table decorations. Their specialities were silver galvanised porcelain decorations, coffee, tea sets with exquisite silver decoration. Owned by Rosenthal Porcelain Aktiengesellschaft, Selb.

[214]   [225]

Sele Arte, see Nove.
Selle, Ferdinand, see Burgau-Göschwitz.
Seltmann, Christian, GmbH, see Erbendorf (1), Krummennaab (4) and Weiden (2).
Seltmann, Johann GmbH, see Vohenstrauss.
Semeida, Alvaro. He was the first to mention in his Chinese history of the 17th c., that the production of porcelain was dependent on the use of the correct clay.
Semlin nr. Belgrade (Yugoslavia). Porcelain was produced here in 1867.
Senff (also Senfft). Modeller, see Ilmenau (1).
Senlis (France). According to entries in the *Dictionnaires des Postes aux Lettres'* a porcelain factory worked here in 1802 and 1817.
Senter, see Seuter, B.
Serpaut, see Limoges (80).
Serravalle Scrivia (Italy). Vellescrivia ceramic factory. Vases, coffee and tea services and advertising items.
Service. A collection of objects more or less inclusive, bearing matching decoration and created from standardised moulds, intended for use with particular foods and drinks. The ornate forms and numbers of pieces making up such a set reached a pinnacle during the rococo period, with its many differentiations of meal courses. Services which had been ordered from the large factories by celebrities or which had been made for the famous, were given their

names, or the name of the particular pattern used in the decoration. The designs created for them were often adopted for use on more general porcelain ware.

Service with the Red Dragon. In 1730 the KPM Meissen introduced this pattern from Japan where it dated from 1700. It displays two fighting cocks in the centre of the plate. This design was used exclusively for the Saxon Court until 1918; since the middle of the 20th c. it was released for general sale. The colours used are green, yellow, blue, violet, brown and black.

Service with the Yellow Lion. KPM Meissen 1728; incorporated into their repetoire of patterns. The lion on the flat of the plate is surrounded with irregularly scattered little motives (butterflies and flowers). These were either positioned in a deliberate manner by the decorator or they were placed to cover iron spots (Walcha).

Sesto Fiorentino, see Doccia.

Seto (Japan). Japanese landscape after which the porcelain produced there is named.

Settela, Manfredo (1600–80). Canon in Milano, famous in Europe as a mathematician and copperplate engraver. He fired fragments of porcelain with the aid of a burning mirror. He marked them with a particular sign in order to differentiate them from Chinese porcelain. He became acquainted with Tschirnhausen in 1676.

Seuter (also Senter), Bartholomäus (1678–1754). Goldsmith, copper-engraver and private decorator in Augsburg. As well as other work he decorated Meissen porcelain, polychrome and monochrome, favouring purple, brown and yellow, dark flowers and Watteau-scenes in strap work-cartouches. He and his pupils also gilded underglaze blue decorated Meissen porcelain, whereby the white ground was covered with gold (see 'Gold chinoiseries').

B.S.

Severin & Co., see Bünde.

Seville (Spain). The owners of the 'La Cartuja' factory, Francisco de Aponte and Pickmann & Co., produced porcelain here in 1867.

Sèvres (1) (France). The Vincennes porcelain factory was moved to Sèvres in 1756. It was still owned by the joint stock company (with about 25 per cent Royal shares), which had been founded in 1753. The eight leaseholders, with c. 30,000 Francs each, received a Royal privilege for 30 years under the guidance of the Royal Commissioner Charles Adam. After considerable differences of opinion between himself and the other shareholders, the King took over the factory personally in 1759. The directors were: Boileau, 1753–72, Parent,

1773–8, Regnier with Salmon, 1778–83, J. J. Hettlinger and Meyer, 1784–96. Caillat bought the formula for the colour combination, and the gilding process was sold by Hippolyte to the joint stock company. The Dubois brothers were soon dismissed. Master modellers were Falconet (1757–66), Bachelier (1766–74) and finally Boizot (1774–1809). The best masters of the period put their efforts at the disposal of the factory – amongst others were Pajou Pigalle, Clodion, Leclerc, Caffièri and Le Riche. Hard paste porcelain production began only in 1768 when La Perche discovered the large kaolin deposit in St. Yrieix, but frit porcelain production was not stopped immediately. At first Chinese and Japanese examples were copied, but later pastoral scenes, generally in the spirit of Watteau, Bouchers and Fragonard formed the bulk of the decoration. In 1780 the effects of a recession began to make themselves felt and it was impossible to retain the state monopoly. A new boon began in 1800, however, when the famous ceramist and geologist Alexandre Brongniart became the manager. Right at the start he sold off the considerable amount of old stock and retained only the best workers, so that he could continue production without a state subsidy. Regular financial support came when the factory was elevated to an Imperial porcelain factory in 1804; from then on Brongniart devoted most of his energies to meeting orders for the Emperor. This is the period in which gigantic presentation vases with strong bodies were produced. Also during this time several formulae were altered and new ones introduced. From 1804 the factory made hard paste porcelain exclusively. Brongniart concluded his achievements with a very detailed publication, the *Treatise on the Ceramic Arts,* which was published in 1834. Difficulties arose when in 1815 allied troops occupied the factory and put forward their intention to sell all the products amd also the moulds; fortunately this disaster was averted by Brongniart. In 1847, after Brongniart's death, Ebelmann became the director and revived the frit porcelain production immediately. The untimely death in 1852 of this able engineer, is to be much regretted. Regnault, a member of the Academy, was his successor, from 1852–71. Under him worked such artistic managers as Dieterle, who was succeeded by Nicolle. He was also responsible for initiating faience production and introduced enamel-work on copper. Robert became the next director, retaining the position from 1871–9. He had already worked in the factory for over 40 years, at the end of which he was in charge of the decorating department. The artistic direction during this period was the responsibility of Carrier Belleuse, until his death in 1887. Charles Lauth administered the factory from 1879–87. Under him some formulaes were altered slightly, and he discovered a combination which resembled the formulae of Chinese porcelain to an astounding degree. Since this paste was particularly suitable for coloured enamel decoration, it was retained in Sèvres from this time on. During the period of 1887–91, the factory was directed by the great ceramist, Théodore Deck; the author Champleury and M. Emile Baumgart were enlisted as his aides one after the other. In 1891 an alteration was made in the staffing of the management which affected both these new appointments: Emile Baumgart became administrator, Georges Vogt director of the technical and artistic production, and Coutan, Chaplain and Alexandre Sandier became directors of the artistic aspects. In 1909 it was decided to appoint Prof. M. Emile Bourgeois, of the University of Paris, who was greatly in favour of research and development. The successor of Bourgeois in 1920 was M. Lechevallier-Chevignard, who had been employed in the factory since 1903. As author of several important works about the factory, he was a suitable choice for instigating the required re-organisation of the factory. During the 19th c. some of the pieces were marked only by the decorators of Sèvres; this porcelain came originally from Limoges and is mostly marked in underglaze, with 'Limoges'. 'Tardy 75' has given a very extensive dating of the porcelain of the 19th and 20th c. Decorators marks are found in the appendix, p. 507.

See also: Fernex, Gerard, Hellot, J., Larue, L. F. de, Macquer, P. J., Susanne, Voorst.

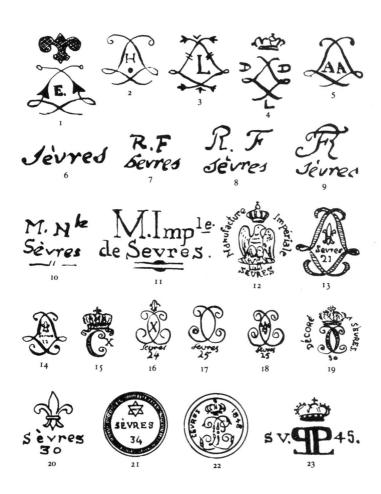

Louis XV and XVI 1756–92: 1 1757 blue underglaze – 2 1760 blue underglaze – 3 1764 blue underglaze, occasionally red – 5 1778 blue underglaze

I. Republic 1793–1803: 6 gold or coloured – 7–9 blue underglaze consulate 1803–4 – 10 blue

I. Empire 1804–14: 11 red mottled shaded – 12 red printed

Louis XVIII 1814–24 – 13–14 both blue underglaze

Charles X 1824–30: all blue underglaze

Louis-Philippe 1830–48: 20 blue underglaze 1830 – 21 blue or gold 1831–4 – 22 blue or gold 1834–45 – chrome green underglaze 1845 – 24 blue or gold 1848 – 25–27 Palast marks 1845–8

II. Republic 1848–52: 28 chrome green 1851, this mark was used from 1833–99 for white porcelain and biscuit – 29 1848–9 – 30 1849 red – 31 1850 red

II. Empire 1850–70: 32–34 all in red

III. Republic: the round mark 35 (1872–99), 35a (1900–2), 35b (1903–41) and the round mark 36 (1872–99), 36a (1900–2), 36b (1903–41) red and red brown overglaze – 37 blindstamp – 38 red – 39 1900 and later – 40 1871 underglaze brown – 41 1926 – 42 1928–40

– 43 from 1941 – 44 1971 – 45 The blindstamp DN, which occurs c. 1923, stands for 'pâte dure nouvelle' (see Seger porcelain)
From 1753–93 the following letters were added to the Sèvres marks (instead of the year numbers):

A	1753	O	1767	DD	1781
B	1754	P	1768	EE	1782
C	1755	Q	1769	FF	1783
D	1756	R	1770	GG	1784
E	1757	S	1771	HH	1785
F	1758	T	1772	II	1786
G	1759	U	1773	JJ	1787
H	1760	V	1774	KK	1788
I	1761	X	1775	LL	1789
J	1762	Y	1776	MM	1790
K	1763	Z	1777	NN	1791
L	1764	AA	1778	OO	1792
M	1765	BB	1779	PP	1793
N	1766	CC	1780		

This arrangement had already been used in Vincennes in 1753–5.
Sèvres (2) (France). In 1946 Mazeaud had the following mark entered for his decorating studio here.

Sèvres (3) (France). Optat Millet produced porcelain here in 1877.

Sèvres (4) (France). Soc. Paul Milet & Fils, f. 1866. Artistic ceramics. The factory was called: Céramique d'Art Milet until 1941.

Sèvres (5) (France). In the years between 1844 and 1852, N. Moriot (previously a decorator at the Royal factory Sèvres) f. a porcelain decorating studio. He collaborated with J. Petit from Fountainbleau.

Sèvres (6) (France). Vinsare registered the following mark for his decorating studio in 1936.

Sezanne (France, Marne). Hypoyte Fanchon directed a porcelain decorating studio here from 1897. The following mark was registered in 1912.

Shaw, John & Sons Ltd., Willow Pottery & Warwick Works, see Longton (72).
Shell decoration, faceting of the vessels. See Böttger-stoneware.
Shelley China Ltd., see Longton (73).
Shelley Potteries Ltd., see Longton (73)

Shelton (1) (England). John Ridgeway f. a stoneware factory here in 1802, which his sons continued to direct, introducing porcelain production from c. 1830. In 1850 Queen Victoria gave permission for the crown to be added to the factory's mark. The successive changes of ownership can be seen in the following table. Besides utility ware, porcelain of high quality was produced and from c. 1875 luxury services gained international acclaim. The Prussian Court and the King of Morocco were among the customers.

1	Job Ridgeway	1802–8
2	Job Ridgeway & Sons	1808–14
3	John & William Ridgeway	1814–30
	During this period porcelain production began	
4	John Ridgeway (& Co.)	1830–55
5	John Ridgeway, Bates & Co.	1856–8
6	Bates, Brown-Westhead & Moore	1859–61
7	Brown-Westhead, Moore & Co.	1862–1904
8	Cauldon Ltd.	1905–20
9	Cauldon Potteries Ltd.	1920–62

1–2 1802–8 – 3–4 1808–14 – 5–6 1814–30 – 7–8 1850–5 – 9 1850–8 – 10 1856–8 – 11 1859–61 – 12–14 1862–1904 – 16 c. 1891 – 17 1905–20 – 18–19 1950 – 20–21 1962. Marks 9 and 16 were marked with the word 'Cauldon' and the date '1905–20'. Mark 17 was still used from 1905–20, together with the lettering 'Cauldon England' on white porcelain. It appears underglaze together with the decorating stamp of Hüttl, Budapest. See Budapest (3)

Shelton (2). Coalbrook Potteries, Cleveland Works. Porcelain ornaments.

Shelton (3) (England). John Lloyd produced porcelain figures here from 1834–50, according to Godden.

LLOYD
SHELTON

Shelton (4) (England). Locket, Baguley & Cooper, Victoria Works, 1855–60. Mark appears with full address.

Shore & Co., Middlesex, see Bodenbach.

Shore & Coggins Ltd., see Longton (74).

Shrink measures. During the course of production, porcelain undergoes two shrinkage procedures. 'Dry shrinkage' is the reduction in the size of the body after the moulding and takes place as the porcelain is drying in the air. 'Fire shrinkage' is the contraction of the body during the firing. This shrinkage generally reduces the porcelain by about 20 per cent. This reason alone makes any forgeries of well-known figures and other pieces quite impossible.

Sieber, Josef Franz, see Schwarza.

Siebert & Hertwig, see Creidlitz (3).

Siereck (France). In 1867 A. Renault directed a small porcelain factory here; it did not mark its products.

Sigel, Victor, see Paris (137).

Siguret, Vve. & Guichard, Manufacture de Porcelaine H. Montagne, see Saint-Vallier (3).

Silber, see Königszelt.

Silbermann Bros., see Hausen nr. Lichtenfels.

Silesian porcelain factory P. Donath GmbH, see Tiefenfurt (1).

Simon, Friedr., see Carlsbad (3).

Simon, Wilhelm, see Hildburghhausen (2).

Simon & Halbig, see Gräfenhain.

Simons et Cie, see Le Cateau.

Simson Bros., see Gotha (1).

Sinceny (France). Moulin, an accomplished ceramist from Sèvres, f. a small porcelain factory here in 1854.

Sinety, Marquis de, see Lurcy-Lévy (2).

Sipiagin, see Moscow (12).

Sisti, Nicolo. Worked in Pisa until 1620, continuing the production of Medici porcelain. The products were somewhat less accomplished than the originals.

Sitzendorf (Germany, Thuringia). The Voigt Bros. owned a porcelain factory here which specialised in producing copies of Meissen porcelain. The factory was f. in 1850 and was later called Sitzendorfer porcelain works, formerly Alfred Voigt AG. Present name (1977) is 'VEB Sitzendorfer porcelain works', producing, as in the past, luxury porcelain and specialising in high quality porcelain. The third mark shown is still used (1977). A cartouche mark with the letters 'Sitzendorf' was entered under No. 210321 in the Waren Trademark register of the German Reich on 17 May 1916.

Sitzerode, also Selzerode (Germany, Thuringia). Macheleid f. a porcelain factory here c. 1759, which was soon transferred (1760) to Volkstedt.

Slama & Co., see Vienna (16).
Slawjansk, see Kusnetzoff.
Slodtz, sculptor, see Boizot, L. S.
Sluizer, see Fountainbleau (1).
Smeraldi, Antonio, modeller, see Doccia.
Smichov (Bohemia). Porcelain factory in Prague since 1825.

PRAG
SMICHOW

Smith, Joachim, modeller. During the period 1773–4 he worked at the Wedgwood factory making portrait reliefs. One medallion which depicts Wedgwood himself in light colours on brown enamel ground, is signed with 'Jo Smith fecit'.
Smith, Sampson. Potter in Longton, Staffordshire, who produced white earthenware and porcelain figures, in very striking colours from c. 1851.
Smoll, Benjamin Jacob and Aaron, see Fountainbleau (1).
Sociedad de Utensilios y Productos Esmaltados, see Córdoba.
Società Ceramica di Bollate, Anon, see Milan (4).
Società Ceramica Italiana, see Laveno.
Società Ceramica Richard, see Malan San Cristoforo.
Società Ceramica Richard-Ginori, see Colonnata, Doccia, Malan San Cristoforo and Mondovi-Carassone.
Société des Anciens Etabilissements Avignon, see Bruère-Allichamps.
Société Anonyme des Pavillons, see Baudour.
Société Belge de Céramique Société anonyme 'Cerabel', see Baudour (1).
Société de la Rue Chaptal, see Paris (138).
Société d'Exploitation des Etablissements Larchevêque, see Vierzon (15).
Société Française de porcelaine, see Paris (139).
Société Nouvelle La Broche SA, see Digeon.
Société Porcelainière de Limoges, see Limoges (81).
Soft paste porcelain ('Pâte tendre'). Differs from hard paste porcelain only in that it contains less kaolin; see hard paste porcelain.
Solagna (Italy). Cesare Villari, artistic porcelain and other cermaic products. A new porcelain factory is now working.

Solignac (France). In 1824 Meyze f. a porcelain factory here which was later enlarged by Nenert, Guéry and Latrille.

Soliman. Arabian merchant. In 1951 he reported (perhaps the first to do so) on the white, translucent potteries of East Asia.

Solitaire. Ceramic coffee, tea or chocolate service, for one person, generally with a porcelain tray.

Soliva, Miguel. One of the best decorators of the Alcora porcelain factory between 1727 and 1750.

Sommer, Josef, see Garmisch-Partenkirchen.

Sommer & Matschak, see Schlaggenwald (2).

Sonneberg (Germany, Thuringia). Cuno and Otto Dressel, 1873–1925. Successors of Ernst Dressel in the doll factory which produced the porcelain dolls' heads in biscuit which were marked with the following:

Sonnenschein, Johann Valentin (22 May 1749 Ludwigsburg–1828). Pupil of the Court stuccoist Luigi Bossi, then of Beyer and possibly also active in the Ludwigsburg porcelain factory. In 1775 he himself became Court stuccoist; in 1773 professor at the academy; 1775–9 master modeller at the Zürich porcelain factory in Schonen; he lived as a sculptor in Berne until his death in 1828.

Sonntag, J. G., see Klösterle (1).

Sonntag, see Altwasser (1).

Sonntag & Son GmbH, see Tettau (1).

Sonntag & Son, see Geiersthal.

Sonthofen (Germany, Bavaria). Allgäu porcelain decorating studio, f. 1952. Dinner and coffee services, vases, pitchers, ornamental flowers, heraldic decorations. This studio was closed in 1962.

APOMA

Sophienau, see Charlottenbrunn.

Sophienthal nr. Bayreuth (Germany). Thomas & Co. porcelain factory, Sophienthal, f. 1928. Utility porcelain, gift articles and advertising items. The factory is part of the Rosenthal Porzellan Aktienbesellschaft, Selb.

Sorau (1) (Germany, Brandenburg). C. and E. Carstens, porcelain factory Sorau, f. 1918. Refined utility porcelain ware.

Sorau (2) (Germany, Brandenburg). Sorau porcelain factory GmbH, f. 1888. Utility ware. This factory no longer exists.

[87]   [56]

Sorel Fils, see Ponsas.

Sorgenthal, Konrad Baron von (d. 1805). Directed the Imperial porcelain factory at Vienna from 1784. His leadership was responsible for the artistic and economic prosperity of the factory.

Sorrel, A., see Ponsas-sur-Rhône.

Soudana & Touze, see Limoges (82).

Souroux, see Paris (140).

Spangler (Spengler). John James. Went to Chelsea in 1790. Inspiration for his modelling derives from Francesco Bartolozzi and Angelica Kauffmann. He was also active from 1790–5 as modeller in Derby.

Spechtsbrunn (Germany, Thuringia Forest). Spechtsbrunn porcelain factory GmbH, f. 1911. Utility and decorative porcelain.

Speck, Chr. Andreas Wilhelm, see Blankenhain (1).

Speck, Karl & Co., see Elbogen (5).

Spencer, Stevenson & Co. Ltd., see Longton (75).

435 SPENGLER-STADTLENGSFELD

Spengler, Adam (d. 1790). Father of John James Spangler and the first director of the Zurich porcelain factory in 1763.
Sperl, Johann Ulrich (1718–96). From Öttingen. Chief blue decorator of the Ludwigsburg porcelain factory from 1759–96. Also an inspector of faiences.
Sperl, Susanna, see Baden-Baden.
Spindler, Otto Hermann, Thuringian porcelain, majolica, earthenware and terracotta factory, see Frauenwald.
Spinner, Jos., see Schönfeld nr. Carlsbad (3).
Spitz, Carl, see Brüx (2).
Spitzer GmbH, see Dieringhausen.
Spitzl Bros., see Budau (1).
Spode, Josiah (father and son), see Stoke-on-Trent (11).
Sprimont, Nicholas (1716–71). Goldsmith from Lüttich. From 1749–58 he was director and from 1758–69 owner of the Chelsea factory.
Springer & Co., see Elbogen (2).
Springer & Oppenheimer, see Elbogen (2).
Staatlich porcelain works Berlin, Werk Selb, see Selb (10).
Staatliche porcelain works Meissen VEB (present name of the firm), see Meissen (1).
Staatl. Thüringer porcelain works, formerly Älteste Volkstedter GmbH, see Rudolstadt Volkstedt (1).
Stadler, Johann Ehrenfried, porcelain decorator, worked at Meissen during the Höchst period.
Stadtilm (Germany, Thuringia). Stadtilmer porcelain factory GmbH, f. 1894. Utility ware.

Stadtlengsfeld (Germany, Thuringia). Stadtlengsfeld AG porcelain factory, f. 1889. Utility ware, table and coffee services. Name used now is: VVB-Keramik-Zweigbetrieg Porzellanfabrik Stadtlengsfeld-Rhön.

Staffelstein (Germany, Bavaria). alka-Porzellanfabriken, Alboth & Kaiser KG, f. 1923. In 1938 the Silbermann factory in Hausen was taken over. Firm remained in Kronach until c. 1956. Decorative, ornamental and utility porcelain, figures in Dresden and Meissen style.

Staffierer (decorator). This was the name given to decorators who did not work on services and vessels, but specialised in applying coloured ornamentation to figures.

Staffordshire Pottery, the Society of, see Bristol (1).

Stahl, Dr. Physiologist and arcanist. Duke Christian IV of Pfalz-Zweibrücken appointed him as an adviser, when the Gutenbrunn porcelain factory was f. in 1767.

Stahl, Albert & Co., see Rudolstadt Volkstedt (12).

Stahn, see Paris (69).

Stanislaw, Aignan Julien (1799–1873). French sinologist, author of the work (which was translated into German in 1837), *Histoire et Fabrication de la Porcelaine Chinoise.*

Stanley, Simon Carl (d. c. 1761). Modeller in Copenhagen under Kastrup and Fournier.

Stanley Pottery Ltd., see Longton (76).

Stanowitz (Germany, Silesia). Striegauer porcelain factory AG, formerly C. Walter & Comp., f. 1873. Table, coffee and washing services. This factory does not exist any more.

Star China Ltd., see Longton (59).

Staral, Robert Franz, see Vienna (17).

Starorolský porcelán národni podnik Stará Role. Altrohlau porcelain factories AG, formerly Moritz Zdekauer, see Altrohlau (1).

Stauch Bros., see Rudolstadt Volkstedt (19).

Stechmann, see Schäffler, J. Ch.

Stein (Sten), Henrik (1730–97), see Marieberg.

Stein, see Tellwitz.

Steinbach nr. Sonneberg (Germany, Thuringia). First Steinbach porcelain factory was Wiefel & Co., KG, f. 1923. Dolls' heads, mocha cups, vases, used 'onion' pattern decoration. In 1949 it became the first Steinbacher P. F. Gustav Heubach KG.

Steinberger, Emanuel, see Vienna (18).
Steinberger & Co., see Kriebern.
Steinhoff, see Braunschweig.
Steinkopf, Johann Friedrich (1737–1825). From Frankenthal. Active as animal and landscape painter in Ludwigsburg, from August 1759. Previously active in Frankenthal.
Steinmann, K., GmbH, see Tiefenfurt (2).
Steinzeugfabrik Plaue a.d.H., see Bayreuth (1) and Plaue.
Stenciled patterns and marks. Metal or paper stencils are used for applying patterns and marks. It is possible to transfer contours as guidelines to the ground with charcoal-dust, applied through pin pricks on paper; this was a method which had been used much earlier in the art of faience decoration. In another technique, similar to the batik method, the object is covered with melted wax or any other opaque, water-resistant material, or with paper cut into a pattern, then dipped into a coloured glaze. Thus treated, the object is fired in a kiln and subsequently a pattern in white or the colour of the body is left against the coloured ground. Porcelain marks were being transferred with stencils as late as the end of the 18th c. A number of examples from the small porcelain factories in Paris illusatrated this.
Stencilling. When faiences and porcelain were decorated by a high-firing method, pulverised charcoal was tapped with a cushion through pricked paper, thus producing outlines for the desired reproduction.
Stenglein, Johann (d. 1803). He was trained in France and became one of the outstanding landscape painters at the Ansbach porcelain factory, c. 1760.
Stephan, Pierre. Modeller at Derby, Etruria and Coalport between 1770 and 1795.
Stephens, William, decorator, see Bristol (1).
Stern porcelain works E. Leber & Son, see Tiefenfurt (3).
Sterner, M., see Mannheim (2).
Steubler, Karl, OHG, see Zwickau (2).
Stevenson, Sharpe & Co., see Derby (1).
Stiassny, Eduard, see Maffersdorf.
Stiller, B., see Lemberg.
Stoclin & Co., see Paris (142).
Stoefs, Fernand, porcelain flower producer, see Brussels (6).

Stoke-on-Trent (1) (England). L. A. Birk & Co., Vine Pottery, 1896–1900; Birks, Rawlings & Co. (Ltd), 1900–33. Two further marks, including the full address, can be found in Godden.

B & Co.

Stoke-on-Trent (2) (England). Cauldon Potteries Ltd., China & Earthenware Manufactures, f. 1774. Table services. At first the firm operated under the following names: John Ridgway & Co., Brown, Westhead, Moore & Co.

Stoke-on-Trent (3) (England). W. T. Copeland & Sons, Ltd., porcelain factory, f. 1770. Dinner, tea, coffee and breakfast services. See Josiah Spode, Stoke-on-Trent (11).

Stoke-on-Trent (4) (England). Crown China Crafts Ltd., f. 1946. Utility ware and artistic porcelain. Existed until 1958. Marked with full name.

Stoke-on-Trent (5) (England). Henry and Richard Daniel, porcelain and pottery of exceptionally good quality, 1820–41. See also London.

DANIEL & SON

2

H. & R. DANIEL

3

H. DANIEL & SONS

4

1

1 very rare, printed c. 1826–9 – 2 very rare 1822–6 – 3 rare, by hand or printed c. 1826–9 – 4 rare 1829–41

Stoke-on-Trent (6) (England). 'Dorothy Ann' Floral china. Artistic porcelain.

Stoke-on-Trent (7) (England). Empire Co., Empire Works, f. 1896. Also produced dolls' heads from 1914–18; this factory no longer produces porcelain.

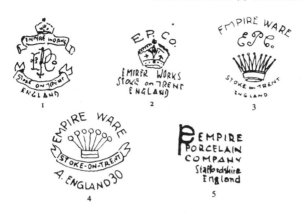

1 1896–1912 – 2 1912–28 – 3 1928–39 – 4 1940–50 – 5 from 1960

Stoke-on-Trent (8) (England). William Henry Goss (Ltd.), Falcon Pottery, f. 1858 or 1862, taken over in 1934 by Cauldon Potteries. From 1914–18 the production also included dolls' heads. Even today 'Goss' dolls are much sought after. Production ceased in 1944. The eagle-mark was registered with the German trademark register under No. 133667 on 29 August 1910.

W H G

[167]

GOSS
2o

Hallmark

Stoke-on-Trent (9) (England). Georges Jones (& Sons Ltd.) f. 1961; Trent Pottery 1864–1907; Crescent Pottery 1907–57. Porcelain since 1872.

Stoke-on-Trent (10) (England). Thomas Minton, an engraver, f. a ceramic factory here in 1793. At first it produced earthenware exclusively, but attempts were very soon made to produce porcelain as well. There is evidence that porcelain was made in the periods from 1798–1811 and 1821–5. The range is mostly limited to cream coloured and blue decorated porcelain ware. The products are widely known for their decoration, produced from copper plate engravings via the process of 'transfer printing'. The marks and the name of the firm changes frequently. Although it cannot be proved beyond doubt, research indicates that the individual names from 1793 were these: 1793–6 Thomas Minton; 1796–1800 Minton and Poulson; 1801–2 Minton, Poulson and

Pownall; 1803–22 Thomas Minton and Sons; 1823–36 Thomas Minton; 1836–41 Minton and Boyle; 1841–6 Herbert Minton & Co., Minton & Co, Minton & Co.; 1846–68 Mintons and Hollins; 1869–83 Herbert Minton & Co.; 1883–1952 Mintons Limited (Private Company). The manufacture of earthenware was halted in 1941 for an indefinite period. Since this time only porcelain of a particular quality, form and decoration, has been produced in Stoke-on-Trent.

1–2 first mark, always present until 1835, in polychrome or gold – 3 gold or blue – 4 1803 – 5 1830–40 – 6 Minton & Boyle 1836–41 – 7 1841–73 – 8 Minton & Hollins 1846–68 – 9 1851 – 10–11 1860 – 12 1863–72 – 13 1867 – 14 1868–88, after this a globe with crown – 15 since 1911 – 16 since 1951

Stoke-on-Trent (11) (England). Josiah Spode acquired John Turner's work in 1770 and experimented for a considerable time until he succeeded in transferring copper engravings to porcelain in underglaze with perfect results. In 1795 the production of transparent bone porcelain (called bone china) began. At about the same time Spode associated with William Copeland and together they produced a porcelain which was supposedly like the Chinese type. 'Felspar porcelain' was produced by Josiah Spode Jr. only after the death of his father. In 1805 Spode succeeded in producing a mixture which resembled hard paste porcelain very closely. These products he called 'stone china'. In 1829 Copeland's son, William Taylor Copeland became the sole owner. In the years after 1840, 'Parian' was the major product, with an unglazed, hard creamy white body which resembled marble and was used in the production of figures. Today the Copeland works makes earthenware and porcelain. Since 1932 the name of the factory has been 'W. T. Copeland & Sons, Ltd.' On 5 January 1895, W. T. Copeland & Sons had the following mark registered with the Chamber of Commerce in Vienna. It was given the No. 4928 and is found in black underglaze on porcelain and earthenware.

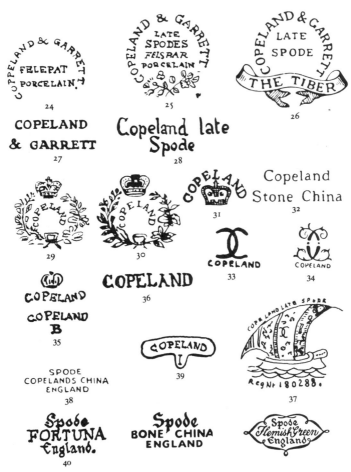

24 25 26

COPELAND & GARRETT
27

Copeland late Spode
28

29 30 31

Copeland Stone China
32

33 34

COPELAND
36

COPELAND
COPELAND B
35

SPODE COPELANDS CHINA ENGLAND
38

COPELAND
39

37

Spode FORTUNA England.
40

Spode BONE CHINA ENGLAND

Spode Flemish Green England

1–2 blindpress 1770 – 3–5 1790 – 6 blue 1795–1805 – 7 1800–20 – 8–9 blue c. 1805 – 10 blind impressed 1810–15 – 11–14 blue, 1800–33 – 15 blue c. 1810 – 16–18 c. 1815 – 19–27 1833–46 – 28 blue, 1847–67 – 29–30 blue – 31 blindpress – 32 blue – 33–34 green, late 19th c. – 35–36 late 19th c. – 37 1894–1910 – 38–40 modern marks, the last in combination of the earlier print type

Stoke-on-Trent (12) (England). Wiltshaw & Robinson Ltd., Carlton works, stoneware and porcelain factory, f. 1890. Operated under the altered name of 'Carlton Ware Ltd.' from 1958.

Stölzel, Samuel (d. 1737). Kiln master with Böttger at Meissen 1713–19, arcanist at Vienna 1719–20. From 1720 until his death he was again active at Meissen as a potter and colour chemist.

Stone, see Paris (141).

Stornay, see Villenauxe-La-Grande (3).

Story, W., see Paris (143).

Stotzheim nr. Euskirchen (Germany, Rhineland). Bruno Hellwig, porcelain factory, f. 1896. Utility ware. This factory no longer exists.

Strasbourg (1) (France). Karl Hannong f. a faience factory here in 1721, together with Wackenfeld. Wackenfeld left after only a short time, leaving Hannong as the sole owner. After having established a second faience factory, now in Hagenau, Hannong left both factories to his two sons, Paul Anton and Balthasar in 1732. Paul Anton Hannong took over Strasbourg and went into partnership with Ringler in 1751; soon after this the production of porcelain began, and before long they were in competition with the royal factory at Vincennes. The result was that the royal decree of 1754, which forbade the use of polychrome decoration to any other factory but Vincennes, forced the factory to close. Hannong transferred his factory to Frankenthal. It is therefore difficult to distinguish the porcelain of the Strasbourg factory from the Frankenthal production.

See also: Freat, H. H., Lanz, W., Löwenfinck, Ch. W. von, Löwenfinck, K. H. von.

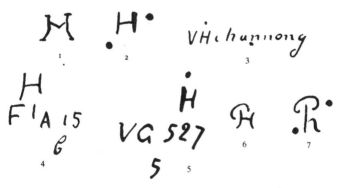

1–2 blindpress – 3 blue – 5–6 blue underglaze

Strasbourg (2) (France). A porcelain factory called Schlitz-Magnus was active here in 1880. Its faience production was of better quality than its porcelain goods.

Strasbourg (3) (France). Stulz AG, porcelain decorating studio, c. 1925.

Straus, L., & Sons, see Rudolstadt Volkstedt (20).

Strebel, see Arzberg (5).
Striegauer porcelain factory AG, formerly C. Walter & Co., see Stanowitz.
Strnackt Jr., Josef, see Greising and Turn (7).
Strobel, Ella, see Dresden (30).
Strobel & Petschke, see Dresden (29).
Stubbs, George (1724–1806). Portrait and animal painter and a friend of Wedgwood, for whom he modelled some horse-bas-reliefs.
Stulz AG, see Strasbourg (3).
Stünkel, see Fürstenberg.
Sturm, L., and Marie, widow of Till, see Dresden (31).
Stützerbach (Germany, Saxony). Franz R. Kirchner, formerly Manebacher, porcelain factory, still active in 1930.

Stutzhaus (Germany, Thuringia). Hertel, Schwab & Co. GmbH, porcelain factory f. 1910. Household porcelain, vases, etc. This concern has now closed.
Südkeramik Sauermann Bros. oHG, see Kaufbeuren.
Suhl (Germany, Prussia). Erdmann Schlegelmilch, porcelain factory, f. 1861. Utility porcelain ware and luxury articles. This factory no longer exists.

Sulkowski pattern. A pattern in imitation of a woven basket used in Meissen, designed by Kändler in 1735–7 for a service for a minister, Alexander Josef Graf von Sulkowski and subsequently used for porcelain decoration. The pattern is confined to the rim of the plates, which are divided into 12 equal parts by 12 double-arches, outlined with a rope pattern. The 12 sections contain a coarse basket work in light relief.
Sureda, Bartolomé. Director in Buen Retiro from 1804–8 and in La Moncloa, 1817–29.
Surrey (England). Queen Elizabeth's Training College for the Disabled, Leatherhead court. Artistic porcelain. The products are named: 'Tom Quec'.
Surval, Antheaume de, see Chantilly (1).
Susay, see Orleans (1).

Suzanne (Susanne), Claude (or Charles) Louis. Modeller in Sèvres. His works (in biscuit) are chiefly studies of children after Boucher.

Sveebac (also Swebach). Jacques François José (1769 Metz–1823). Originally Johann Jakob Schwebach, called 'Fountaine' of 'Des Fontaines'. He trained in Ludwigsburg as a porcelain decorator. He moved to Sèvres in 1788 where he worked for some time, decorating mostly in the Egyptian style. Later he was called to Petersburg by Alexander I where he decorated a service with battle scenes. The Tsar intended to present this service to his sister, the Queen of Würtemberg. After having spent two years in Petersburg, he returned to Sèvres, where he died in 1823. His range of works also included many engravings; among his possessions was an *Encyclopédie pittoresque*, in four volumes with 468 pages of illustrations.

Swaine & Co. (Schoenau Bros., Swaine & Co.) see Köppelsdorf-Nord.

Swan pattern. Meissen service pattern which had been designed in 1737–41 by Kändler for Count Brühl. The rims are divided into 30 parts by round arches and waving lines. The base is decorated with swans and herons in shallow relief.

Swan Service. Kändler modelled this service in Meissen, from 1737–41, with the aid of Eberlein, for Count Brühl. Its rich plastic forms incorporate reliefs in various depths, from the most delicate of shallow reliefs, to the fully rounded figures. All decorations are based on the theme of 'water' which is interpreted in constantly changing variations of wave-lines, plants and creatures found in water, Nereids and Tritons. It is thought that this service comprised over 2,000 parts. It was held in trust as an heirloom by the Brühl family, at Castle Pförten until the end of the Second World War. In 1939, there were still 1,400 pieces and parts of the service had been lent to the art and crafts Museums of Berlin, Hamburg, Dresden and Cologne (Köllmann).

Swansea (England). The 'Cambria Pottery' which had been f. in 1765, produced porcelain from 1814–22. The owner, L. W. Dillwyn, secured the services of William Billingsley from Nantgarw. In 1817 the factory was leased to Bevington, but in 1822 it was again taken over by Dillwyn. In 1831 his son Lewis Llewellyn became the director. In 1850 the concern was sold to David Evans and Glasson but was closed in 1870. The quality of the products is very similar to those of Nantgarw, and therefore cannot receive full recognition as separate products. The porcelain production was sold in London, some of it undecorated, so that the buyer's taste decided the kind of decoration used by the London porcelain decorators. Generally the articles are produced in neo-classical style; Morris and Pollard painted flowers, Beddow and Baxter figures. The very naturalistic flowers were executed by the painter Pardoe.

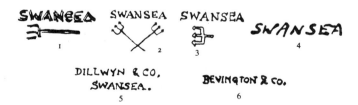

1–3 blind impress – 4 1814–17 – 5 blind impress, after 1817

Swinton (England). A factory known as 'The Pottery', existed here from 1745 to 1842 and produced porcelain from 1820. It belonged to the Rockingham works, about which little is known. From 1830 it was called 'Royal Rockingham Works', and the title 'Manufacturer to the King' was in use from 1830–7. According to Godden, Baguley and his sons had been employed here and in Mexborough as porcelain decorators. They sometimes marked their works with the well-known mark (No. 1, below) substituting their own name for 'Brameld'. Apart from some surviving pieces in English museums, some very interesting pieces have been discovered in a collection owned by D. G. Rise, who described these himself in *Treasures of the World,* (Macdonald and Jane's, London 1970).

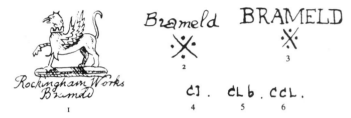

1 in red, less often in blue underglaze – 4–6 1826–40, by hand, printed or in gold

Sylvia. Mark as trademark No. 277055 from 13 December 1921 of the P. F. Rosenthal, Selb.
Szopienice Górny Slask (Poland). Porcelain figures were produced here from 1945.

Tabernes (Spain), Lladro SA, porcelain and stoneware factory, f. 1952. Porcelain figures of a high quality were produced for international markets.

Taglieb, Georg. Decorator in Ansbach, 1720–5, and later, from 1739–41, as a director in Lidköping nr. Rörstrands. His sister Appolonia was also a decorator in Ansbach.
Taglioni, Filippo. Sculptor at the Vienna factory, called to the newly founded factory of Napoli in 1781. Worked in neo-classical style.
Taillemite, Lucien, see Vierzon (16).

Tambow (Russia). Popoff managed a porcelain factory here in the 19th c. as well as in Gorbunovo.

Tännich, Joh. Sam. Friedr. (1728–85). Worked as decorator in Meissen from c. 1750, in Strasbourg from c. 1755 and in Frankenthal from 1757–9, where he spent the last years of his life as a kiln builder.
Tannova (Bohemia). A porcelain factory was f. here in 1813 which used the following mark. Utility ware, and goods for export to the Turkish market.

1 blue underglaze – 2 and 3 blindpress, Franz Joseph Mayer

Taschwitz nr. Buchau (Bohemia, now Tasovice). In 1860 Fr. W. Pohle f. a porcelain works here which produced porcelain dolls' heads. Besides fine coffee, tea and dinner services, his sons, Rudolf and Friedrich, produced hotel and utility porcelain around the turn of the century. The 'onion' pattern was used. In 1889 the factory was badly damaged by fire. Mainly export to the USA. It closed down in 1930.

MADE
IN
GERMANY
1

«CZECHOSLOWAKIA»
2

1 until 1918 – 2 after 1918

Tassie, James (1735–99). Modeller at Wedgwood from 1769–80. He was one of the modellers for the famous portrait reliefs.
Tata (Hungary). Desider Fischer directed a factory here c. 1890, where chiefly Herendem, but also Czechoslovakian porcelain, was decorated. Decorations in the style of Herend were also produced and the connection was made obvious in the use of the Herendem mark.

Taubenbach (Germany, Thuringia). Carl Moritz, porcelain factory, f. 1848. Services and figures. This factory closed.

Taverne & Co., see Paris (144).

Taylor & Kent Ltd., Florence Works, see Longton (77).

Taylor Tunnicliff (Refractories) Ltd., Albion Works, see Longton (78).

Tea sets. In the 18th c. this name did not only include the teapot and tea cups, but also the tea container which in South Germany and Austria is called 'theefläschl' (little tea bottle) and the rinsing pot.

Tebo. Apparently a Frenchman, employed as a modeller by Josiah Wedgwood who found his work unsatisfactory. It has been assumed that a T-mark, which occurs on figures from Bow, Plymouth, Bristol and Worcester, belonged to Tebo, and he has consequently been considered as the modeller of these figures. Godden (1968), gives the following, more precise, dates for his activities: Bow 1750–60; Worcester 1760–9; Plymouth 1769–70; Bristol 1770–3; Wedgwood 1774. The marks are also found occasionally on Caughley porcelain. These dates however are at variance with those given by Honey (1952).

'Teestaub' glaze. Stained, turquoise blue to greenish glaze of Chinese porcelain, in use c. 1730–40.

Teichert, Joh. Ferd. (d. 1789). Landscape painter at Meissen from c. 1780.

Teichert. Original name of Meissen kiln and porcelain factory, see Meissen (2).

Teichfeld & Asterblum, see Wloclawek.

Tellier de la Bertinière, Le, see Valognes (1).

Tellwitz (Bohemia). According to Ware (c. 1960) it is possible that Stein directed a porcelain factory, or maybe only a decorating studio, here from the beginning of the 20th c. until some time after 1918.

Tentz, modeller, see Ottweiler.

Teplitz Schönau (Czechoslovakia, now Teplice-Sanov). Reinhold Borsdorf, porcelain decorating studio, c. 1930.

Teploff, see Petersburg (1).

Terichow, see Retschina.

Terracotta ('fired clay' in Italian). A generic description for all artistic pottery pieces created with fired clay.

Terra porcellana, porcelain earth, see Kaolin.

'terre de Lorraine', see Lunneville.

Teres d'Angleterre, see Paris (104).

Terrine. A generic term for a tablepiece in a porcelain table service. Also called 'pot à soupe' ('potaile' in Nymphenburg) or 'bouillon pot'.

Tessier & Cie., see Villenauxe-la-Grande (4).

'Tête à Tête'. General term for a breakfast service on a serving tray for two people.

Tettau (1) (Germany, Upper Frankonia). The Tettau porcelain factory was f. in 1794 by Georg Christian Friedmann Greiner from Kloster Veilsdorf, with the support of a Royal Prussian privilege. In the beginning the most important products were utility ware. The body of these services is generally white with a grey cast, turning into greenish-yellow. Coffee, tea and chocolate services and also complete table services were made. The services made in the popular style in the early 19th c. deserved special mention because of their careful execution. The quality of this factory's production varies throughout the century. As well as some products of excellent quality, some rather inferior ware was turned out. Flower decoration predominated. From about 1852 the factory was owned by Ferdinand Klaus, who employed 70 people. These were the successive owners: 1866–79 Wilhelm Sontag and Karl Birkner; 1879–1902 Karl Birkner and L. Maisel. A fire destroyed the whole of the factory in 1897, but a new one was soon built on the same site, and much larger than the original. Until 1915 the factory produced under the name Sontag & Sons GmbH. In 1915 it was changed to 'Porzellan-fabrik Tettau AG'. This factory is still active and it is one of the most outstanding German porcelain factories.

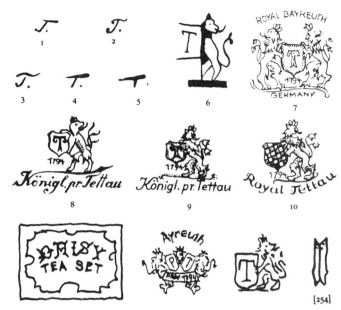

1–5 blue marks – 6 gold – 7–10 in various colours

Tettau (2) (Germany, Upper Frankonia); Neue Porzellanfabrik Tettau Gerold & Co., f. in 1904. Figures, in particular lace figures, animal groups, vases and porcelain implements.

Teutscher, Ferdinand. Private decorator in Bayreuth and Vienna around the middle of the 18th c.

Thallmayer, F. X. Independent porcelain decorator in Munich around 1800.

Thanhauser Bros., see Munich (7).

Tharaud, C., see Limoges (83).

Tharaud, P., see Limoges (84) and (85).

Theresienthal (Germany, Bavaria). The Theresienthaler crystal glass and porcelain works, transferred in 1975/76, with 50 per cent to the Hutschenreuther AG Selb, no longer produces porcelain according to their own information.

Thesmar, see Neuilly.

Thiaucourt, P., see Paris (145).

Thielsch, C., & Co., see Hohenberg.

Thielsch, C. and Egmont von, see Altwasser (2).
Thieme, Carl, Saxony porcelain factory at Potschappel, see Potschappel.
Thiersheim (Germany, Upper Frankonia). Willi Gossler, porcelain decorating studio, c. 1920.

Thomas. Mark as trademark No. 282654 from 18 March 1922, of P. F. Thomas, Marktredwitz.
Thomas, see Magnac-Bourg.
Thomas, F. (Rosenthal AG), see Marktredwitz (4) and Selb (9).
Thomas & Co. (Rosenthal AG), see Sophienthal and Selb (9).
Thomas, Girault et Clement, see Choisy-le-Roy (2).
Thomas am Kulm, porcelain factory, see Kirchenlaibach.
Thomaschefsky, Carl-Friedrich. From Berlin. From 1780 worked for a short time for the Copenhagen factory as a decorator.
Thomin, Friedrich, independent decorator, see Würzburg.
Thooft, Joost & Labouchère, see Delft.
Thorley China Ltd., see Longton (79).
Thun, Graf F. J., see Klösterle (1).
Thun'sche porcelain factory, see Klösterle (1).
Thuret, Rodolphe, see Champroux.
Thuringia porcelain works, Gehren factory (formerly Gunthersfeld porcelain factory AG), see Gehren.
Thuringian porcelain works, Geraberg factory (formerly H. Eger), see Geraberg (1).
Tiefenbach a.d. Desse (Bohemia). Herm. Scholz, successor to the Camill Seidl porcelain decorating studio f. 1840, formerly J. Schnabel & Son. Fancy items. Still active in 1930.

Tiefenfurt (1) (Germany, Silesia). Silesian porcelain factory P. Donath GmbH, formerly Louis Levensohn, f. 1883. Representatives in New York were Bawo & Dotter, Fischern. Table services. This factory is now closed. The first mark shown had to be discontinued from 1896–8 owing to the injunction against its use by the KPM Meissen; it was also removed from the trademark register of the German Reich, 1896–8 (according to Lange 1911). The eagle mark with the letters 'TPM' underneath was, according to Scheffler (1840), the accepted mark for Tuppack.

[39]   [164]   [78]

T.P.M.

[79]

Tiefenfurt (2) (Germany, Silesia). K. Steinmann GmbH, porcelain factories, f. 1883. Household and hotel services. This factory was closed in 1932. The letters 'KS' appear beneath the eagle, c. 1840, which either means that the pieces cannot be attributed to Steinmann, or that the Steinmann factory was founded earlier than 1883.

[202]

Tiefenfurt (3) (Germany, Silesia). Stern porcelain works, E. Leber & Son, c. 1920–30.

Tiefenfurt (4) (Germany, Silesia). Carl Hans Tuppack GmbH, f. 1808. Household services. This factory does not work any longer.

[223]   [241]

Tiélés, J., see Paris (146).

Till, Franz, see Dresden (31).

Tillowitz (1) (Germany, Silesia). Graf Frankenberg'sche porcelain works, f. 1852. In 1894 the owner and business manager was Erhard Schlegelmilch. In 1919, the following marks were listed.

Tillowitz (2) (Germany, Silesia). Reinhold Schlegelmilch, f. 1869. Utility and luxury porcelain. This factory is closed.

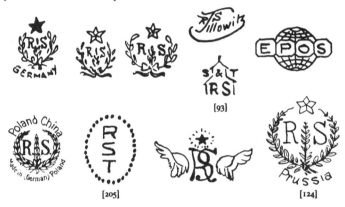

[93]

[205]   [124]

Tinglaze. An opaque glaze containing tin, used on earthenware fired at low temperature. Also used as an additional glaze on faience (Dutch: Kwaart, Italian: coperta) and as a glaze of stoneware.

Tinelli, Carlo and Luigi, see Milan San Cristoforo.

Tinet, see Montreuil-sous-Bois.

Tirschenreuth (1) (Germany, Bavaria). Tirschenreuth porcelain factory, f. 1838. Table and ornamental porcelain. In 1927 this factory was annexed to Lorenz Hutschenreuther AG Selb. Since the subsequent annexation of Lorenz Hutschenreuther, Selb to the C. M. Hutschenreuther, Hohenberg, the Tirschenreuth porcelain factory has used the last mark shown.

HUTSCHENREUTHER
GRUPPE
GERMANY

Tirschenreuth (2) (Bavaria). Zehnder & Co. ceramic factories, f. 1870.
Household porcelain, both white and decorated, and ornamental pieces.

Titanium-oxide. Used for colouring porcelain yellow, as used by Klaproth in
1794.
Titov Veles (Yugoslavia, Macedonia). Boris Kidric porcelain factory. Utility
porcelain.

Tittelbach, Franz (b. 1722). From the school of the Dresden court painter
Manyoki. Portrait decorator from 1766–89, at the Prussian factory in Berlin.
His antique busts 'en grisaille' are known, and he may have discovered new
colours.
Tizian. Mark as Trademark No. 255262 from 5 November 1920 of the P. F.
Rosenthal, Selb.
Tognana-porcellana d'Italia, see Treviso (2).
Tomaszow (Russia). The well-known Mezers (Baranowka and Korsec)
produced porcelain here between 1805–10.

Töppeles nr. Petschau (Bohemia). Porcelain factory f. 1901 by A. Grosse & O.
Feuereisen. From 1930 Reinl from Lubenz became the owner, succeeded by
Grosse & Co., and finally by Fiedler & Körper, Prague.

Torcy, Marquis of, see Saint-Denis (1).

Touchard, see Paris (147).

Toulouse (France). Charlionais et Panassier, porcelain factory.

Tournay (Belgium). F. J. Peterinck, f. a soft paste porcelain factory here in 1751; he received the patronage of the Empress Maria Teresa and was supported in his venture by the citizens. His arcanist was Robert Dubois. In 1751 Peterinck made his son the owner who in 1800 gave up the factory in favour of a newly established earthenware factory. Under the new owner, de Bettignies, the factory lost its good reputation. It remained in the de Bettignies family until 1850. The soft paste porcelain of Tournay imitated Meissen and Sèvres. At first the paste was grey but it was soon improved. Of the decorators the following require special mention: Henri-Joseph Duvivier, who was the chief decorator from 1763–71, and who worked in the Sèvres style; and his successor Jean-Ghislain-Joseph Mayer, who painted birds after illustrations in Buffon's *Natural History.* The use of the 'décor bois', a decoration imitating wood graining, within small landscapes and set in relief, was also popular in Tournay.

1–2 polychrome – 3 red – 4–5 gold – 10 tower: blue, the rest: gold – 11–14 sword mark in many variations, mostly in gold – 15 gold

Tourné, Giovanni, see Naples.

Tours (1) (France). It is possible that Sailly and his son may have produced hard paste porcelain only between 1776–83. The surviving pieces (which are signed) are mostly biscuit. There are some medallions and a few vases in neo-classical style with garlands in relief. Apart from these a single putto is extant which is marked with an incised inscription 'A tours 1782'.

Tours (2) France. Jagetet Pinon, porcelain factory. Art objects and ornaments.

Tours (3) (France). Pinon et Heuzé, porcelain decorating studio, c. 1900–30.

Touze, Marty & Theilloud, see Limoges (82).

Toy, W. E., see Paris (148).

Toys (in French: galanteries). Perfume flasks, bonbonnieres, snuff boxes and trinket boxes, which were produced during the rococo period in fanciful shapes (figures, fruits, animals, etc.), were all described as 'toys'. The Chelsea Toys have gained world fame, but those produced in the factory at Mennecy have also become famous. According to Honey, the original pattern for these pieces came from the porcelain factory at Meissen.

Trademark protection. First introduced in France in 1789; in Austria in 1858; in England 1862; in USA 1870/71; in Germany as late as 1874.

Transfer printing. This is an international term for a method of duplicating a design (see also enamel printing process.) For a long time it remained debatable whose invention this was. John Brooks (1720–60), John Sadler (1720–89) and Guy Green (1730—1800), have all been named either individually or collectively. More recent research, particularly the very detailed and penetrating investigation by Cyril Cook, London, 1955, has proved that the engraver and designer Robert Hancock (1730–1817), has the rightful claim for the invention (Kronberger-Frentzen).

Transmutation glazes. Flamed enamel coloured glazes, produced through a certain scale of reduction at various high temperatures, with oxygen added during the course of the firing.

Traugott. Family in Stockholm in possession of a famous collection of Wegely porcelain. See Berlin (1).

Trembleuse. Name for a chocolate cup, which generally has two handles. It rests in a little basket-like hollow in the saucer, which prevents it slipping even when held by a hand which may be trembling (from the French, *trembler,* to shake).

Trentham Bone China Ltd., see Longton (80).

Trenton (England). Walter Scott Lenox produced a particularly thin porcelain, the so-called 'Lenoxchina' in 1879. It resembles the products of Beleek *(q.v.)* and was also called Bellek porcelain.

Tressemann & Vogt, see Limoges (86).

Tretto nr. Vicenca (Italy). Kaolin deposits, see Kaolin sources.

Trevisan, Giovanni, called Volpato, see Rome (2).

Treviso (1) (Italy). Soft paste porcelain was produced here at the end of the 18th and beginning of the 19th c. by the brothers Guiseppe and Andre Fontebasso.

With only a few exceptions these products are of little interest and quality. The grey body is decorated with badly fused decoration. The Societa Ceramica Andrea Fontebasso (SCAFT) has apparently assumed the succession of the old factory.

1 FF Fratelli Fontebasso – 2 GAFF = Guiseppe and Andrea Fratelli Fontebasso

Treviso (2) (Italy). Tognana porcellana d'Italia, table and utility ware. One of the newer (active) porcelain factories.

Triebner, Clemens, see Rudolstadt Volkstedt (3).
Triebner, Ens and Co., see Rudolstadt Volkstedt (4).
Trier (Germany). Deuster f. a porcelain factory here in 1807 in the cloisters of the Old Abbey of St. Martin. During the French period (until 1813), kaolin was obtained from Limoges. Other raw materials were supplied by some actioneers and according to reports in the *Chronicle of Trier,* the production seems to have reached a 'glittering height'. The products were compared favourably with those of the best-known factories. One service with views of the Trier deserves particular mention. The factory obviously followed an export policy since the records of the old factory contain the phrase 'for the foreigners who are concerned with elegance'. This factory declined rapidly after 1813 but was revived in 1816 when it again employed 50 workers. An official mark was not in use, there are merely some incised marks of decorators and other specialists of the firm. It is thought that the factory closed down c. 1820.
Triple colour painting (Chinese: Sancai). Painting on porcelain with three colours, mainly green, yellow and aubergine, although the green is often replaced by a light turquoise.
Triptis (Germany, Thuringia). Triptis AG porcelain factory, f. 1891, formerly Unger and Gretschel. Coffee and tea services. Present name is VEB-Keramin – branch factory of the Triptis porcelain factory.

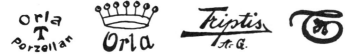

Tristan. Trademark No. 259363 of the P. F. Rosenthal, Selb from 26 January 1921.

Troté, see Plombières.

Trothe. Joh. Gottfried. First director of the Ludwigsburg porcelain factory from 1758.

Trou, Henri, see St.-Cloud.

Tscheparkul on the Ural, see Kaolin sources.

Tschepotieff, see Petersburg (1).

Tschirnhausen (Tschirnhaus). Ehrenfried Walter Graf von (1651–1708). Physicist, mathematician and philosopher. He studied in Leiden from 1668–75, and also in London and Paris. During this period he made the acquaintance of Leibnitz which later led to a correspondence between them. Towards the end of 1676 Tschirnhausen travelled to Lyon, Turin and Milan, and in 1678 to Venice and Rome. From 1679 he lived on his estate in Kieslingswalde in the Lausitz where he devoted himself to research into constructing burning mirrors made of polished copper and crystalline lenses. He ran glass-houses and a mill for cutting these burning lenses which he used in experiments such as firing the various Saxony soils. In 1687 he succeeded in producing a porcelain-like body with the aid of a burning mirror (of 1.625 m$\emptyset$) by firing a mixture of aluminium and magnesia-silicat. In order to study new kilns he stayed in Delft from 1701, moved on to Paris and occupied himself with ceramic works in St.-Cloud. In the same year he submitted a paper to the Saxon King (August the Strong), which gave an account of his studies as porcelain arcanist. Since the King did not respond, Tschirnhausen continued with his experiments in Kieslingswalde and it is claimed that in 1704 he had arrived at the point where he could actually produce a ceramic body which, in its consistency, was very close to true Chinese porcelain. After Johann Friedrich Böttger's initial work in Dresden, the King brought he and Tschirnhausen together. Tschirnhausen's geological experiences not only assisted the discovery of porcelain but may have provided the basis for the formula for making porcelain.

Tsui-khi. Chinese term for Craquelé, *q.v.*

Tui Milly, Nicholas-Chrétien, Graf de, see d'Entrecolles.

Tünnich, H., decorator, see Würzburg.

Tuma & Vielgut, see Klösterle (2).

Tunstall (1) (England, Staffordshire). Booths Ltd., porcelain factory. This factory was taken over by Booths & Colclough Ltd., Hanley. See Longton (15).

Tunstall (2) (England, Staffordshire). George Frederick Bowers (& Co.), Brownhill Works, 1842–68.

G.F.B.   G.F. B.B.T.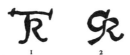

Tunstall (3) (England, Staffordshire). A. and E. Keeling, stoneware and porcelain factory, from 1795–1811.

A. E. KEELING

Tunstall (4) (England, Staffordshire). Old Boston China Ltd., porcelain factory.

ENGLAND

WEETMAN FIGURES
SANDYFORD

WEETMAN
SANDYFORD

Tuppack, Carl Hans GmbH, see Tiefenfurt (4).
Turin (1) (Italy). Giorgio Giacinto Rossetti experimented here from 1737 in search of the formula for transparent porcelain. It is claimed that the council of Turin had been presented with trial pieces in 1743. Apart from some undistinguished pieces, porcelain from his production has not been found, even to this day. The marks shown here are present on two white glazed busts in the Museo Civico, Turin.

$\overset{\text{1}}{\mathcal{R}}$ $\overset{\text{2}}{\mathcal{R}}$

1 TR = Turino Rossetti – 2 GR = Giorgio Rossetti

Turin (2) (Italy). Bourgent directed a small porcelain factory here in 1770.

Turkish Cups. Small cups without handles, which at the end of the 18th c. were produced in great quantities for export to Turkey, and chiefly decorated by independent decorators.

Turn nr. Teplitz (1) (Bohemia). Ditmar-Urbach AG, porcelain factories. See also Znaim.

Turn nr. Teplitz (2) (Bohemia). Gröschl & Spethmann, f. 1899. Ivory porcelain and luxury articles.

Turn nr. Teplitz (3) (Bohemia). Adolf Laufer, porcelain decorating studio, c. 1930.

Turn nr. Teplitz (4) (Bohemia). Melkus & Moest, porcelain factory, f. 1892. Porcelain flowers, toys and fancy and luxury articles with hand decoration. Closed before 1914.

Turn nr. Teplitz (5) (Bohemia). Riessner, Stellmacher & Kessel, porcelain factory, f. 1892. Porcelain figures. Known as 'Amphora' porcelain factory, Riessner & Kessel from 1903 and 'Amphorawerke Riessner' from 1910. In 1945 it was annexed to the CSR. No longer exists (Pöttig).

Turn nr. Teplitz (6) (Bohemia). Alfred Stellmacher K.K. priv. porcelain factory. In 1859, Stellmacher, nearly destitute, began to produce 'ornamental gadgets for rooms and salons, flower baskets, vases and fancy receptacles of all kinds'. For his famous porcelain roses he developed an individual formula in 1862, which enabled him to produce extremely thin, delicate petals (egg shell porcelain), decorated with the most exquisite enamel colours. The porcelain required a temperature as low as 1250–80°C (Seger cone (SK) 8–9). The similarity of this formula to that used in producing the famous 'Rozenburg' products from c. 1900, is surprising. In 1876 Stellmacher established a larger factory where he produced luxury and utility porcelain, ivory porcelain, figures and decorative vessels, and services with high firing enamel decorations. This concern was taken over in 1897 by Ernst Wahliss (Zimmermann). The first mark shown was entered on 29 August 1884 in Reichenberg under No. 389, for the subsequent entry in the K.K. trademark register Vienna.

Turn nr. Teplitz (7) (Bohemia). Josef Strnact Jr., porcelain decorating studio, still active in 1930.

Turn nr. Teplitz (8) (Bohemia). Turn porcelain factory, Adolf Laufer, f. 1919. Utility porcelain. Speciality: thin cups. Closed in 1936.

Turn nr. Teplitz (9) (Bohemia). Vinzenz Unger, porcelain and terracotta factory, f. 1906. Produced utility porcelain and incorporated a porcelain decorating studio. Successors were Kominik & Son, Stgt. 'Terra' factory was annexed by the CSR in 1945.

V.U.

Turn nr. Teplitz (10) (Bohemia). Ernst Wahliss already owned porcelain premises in London and Vienna, when he took over the Stellmacher'sche porcelain factory in Turn nr. Teplitz in 1897. He wanted to produce porcelain as well as deal in it.

The period between 1900 and 1910 is documented by existing porcelain decoration with designs after Viennese artists. Wahliss participated in the winter exhibition of the Museum for Art and Industry in Vienna with works in the Copenhagen style of the time as early as 1899/1900. During this period Ernst Wahliss became aware of the 600 or so original models of the Vienna factory which had closed in 1864; these he bought from De Cente for the purpose of making moulds to be used in his factory in Turn. He died in 1900, but his sons, Hans and Erich, took over at once. They produced under the trademark of 'Alexandra Porzellan Works' Ernst Wahliss, Artistic porcelain and faience factory. In 1902-3, high fire enamelling on white or coloured porcelain was introduced. Production of porcelain flowers in the Stellmacher style was begun in the early 20th c. The whole of the production was created under the theme of 'luxury porcelain'. From about 1910, porcelain was replaced by the so-called 'Serapis Faiences' (Neuwirth). The first mark shown was used in three sizes and entered on 10 June 1896 under No. 1460 at the Chamber of Commerce in Reichenberg, the second mark, under No. 5432, on 24 March 1909, likewise entered in Reichenberg, the fourth mark was entered under No. 41412 in Vienna on 24 February 1910.

Turn nr. Teplitz (11) (Bohemia). Willner Bros, porcelain and faience factory, f. 1884. Luxury goods and articles for mounting.

BW

Turquoise colour. Since 1760, Chelsea used the Turkish red of brilliant luminosity.

Turygino, see Moscow (2).

Tuscan China R. H. & S. L. Plant Ltd. see Longton (81).

Tvede, Claus. Active from 1775–83 as modeller and sculptor in Copenhagen.

Ufer, see Dresden (32).

Uffrecht, J., & Co., see Neuhaldensleben (7).

Uhlstädt (Germany, Thuringia). Carl Alberti, porcelain factory Uhlstädt, f. 1837. Utility porcelain. The VEB (B) P. F. Uhlstädt of today is possibly the legal successor of Alberti, and signs its products with the first mark shown.

Ullersricht (Germany, Upper Palatine). Bavaria AG porcelain factory. The similarity of the second mark shown, to that of Schlottenhof, is the ground for certain speculations, which cannot, however, be clarified.

Ullrich, Wenzel, see Eythra.

Ulm (Germany, Würtemberg). Johann Jacob Smith (1787–1862), son of the 'Chief bossiere', Johann Heinrich Schmidt, of the Ludwigsburg factory (which was closed in 1824). He f. a porcelain factory here in 1827 which ceased to operate in 1833. Production consisted of figures, mostly free adaptions from Ludwigsburg models, and porcelain ware in the style of early Biedermeier.

Ultramarine. In 1828 the factory inspector of the KPM Meissen, Friedrich

August Koetting, discovered the Meissen ultramarine or lasur stone blue. The KPM Meissen established a factory producing ultramarine which was a considerable asset to the factory's economy.

Underglaze blue, see Mohammedan blue and Underglaze decoration.

Underglaze decoration. The palette for underglaze decoration is more limited than that for overglaze enamels, since underglaze must withstand the full heat of the kiln. Cobalt blue, in all its shades, is the main colour (and used for the onion pattern). Chrome oxide, nickel oxide, iron oxide, some brown magenta shades, as well as copper oxide red (which had been used by the Chinese but was not discovered in Europe until the end of the 18th c.) are all suitable colours for underglaze decoration. After the firing to biscuit the porcelain ware is decorated with the underglaze colours, followed by glazing and firing at high temperatures.

Underglaze porcelain Rudolstadt, see Rudolstadt Volkstedt (6).

Underglaze print, see Berthevin, Pierre.

Unger, modeller, see Gräfenthal (1).

Unger & Gretschel, see Triptis.

Ungvár (Hungary). 'Ungvárer Porzellan- and Tonwaren AG' (until 1898). Under the direction of Eugen Fischer-Farkashazy, the production included porcelains with flowers, fruits and insect decorations.

Union Céramique, see Limoges (87).

L'Union Française, porcelain factory, see Saint-Genou (2).

Union Limousine, see Limoges (88).

'Union' Quist & Kowalski, see Kleindembach.

Unterköditz (1) (Germany, Thuringia). Max Hackenberg, porcelain factory, closed after 1941.

Unterköditz (2) (Germany, Thuringia). Möller and Dippe, porcelain and earthenware factory, f. 1846. Dolls and porcelain figures. This factory is now closed.

Unterköditz (3) (Germany, Thuringia). August Müller & Sohn, porcelain factory. Luxury porcelain figures. This factory is closed.

Untermhaus (Germany, Thuringia). In 1787 a small porcelain factory was f.

which was called 'Gerarer Porzellanfabrik'. In 1894 the owner was B. Ouwens. Utility services with the 'onion' pattern.

Unterneubrunn (Germany, Thuringia). Bertold Eck, porcelain factory, had the following mark registered with the Eisfeld County Court on 28 August 1876. Produced dolls which could be bathed.

[10]

Unterweissbach (Germany, Thuringia). Unterweissbach porcelain factory, formerly Mann & Porzelius AG (in the past it had been known as Älteste Volkstedter porcelain factory, formerly Triebner), f. 1880, produced art and luxury porcelain. Taken over in 1908 by Max Adolf Pfeiffer, and renamed 'Schwarzenburger Werkstätten für Porzellan kunst' (Schwarzenburg Workshops for Artistic Porcelain). Outstanding figures were created and the most renowned artists of the period were commissioned: Ernst Barlach, Adolf Bütt, Max Esser, Gerhard Marcks, Wilhelm Neuhäuser, Otto Pilz, Anton Puchegger, Richard Scheibe, Paul Scheurich and Otto Thiem. Pfeiffer made utility porcelain articles as did Adelbert Niemeyer. Following the appointment of Pfeiffer to Meissen in 1918, Heinz Schaubach became the lessee (in 1926?) and in 1940 the owner; he upheld the tradition of the factory. Since the end of the Second World War, the factory's name has been 'VEB Unterweissbacher Werkstätten für Porzellan Kunst' (VEB Unterweissbacher Workshops for Artistic Porcelain) and is subordinate to the Kombinat 'Zierporzellanwerke Lichte'. Now, as before, the products reach the highest level of craftsmanship. Lace ornamentation, decorating in filigree and painting are all specialities.

[150]

Upsala (Sweden). Upsala-Ekeby Aktiebolag, f. 1918. Table and coffee services. In 1942 the factory took over the AB Karlskrona porcelain factory, which now operates under its name.

   Hallmark

neck mark

Upsala-Ekeby AB Karlskrona factory, see Karlskrona.
Urbar nr. Koblenz (Germany, Rhineland). Max Anders Rhineland porcelain factory GmbH. Utility porcelain ware.
Urbino Service of the Berlin State porcelain factory, c. 1930–2, after designs of Trude Petri. Its return to the simplest basic forms earned it the title of 'the classical service of the present time' (Köllmann).
Usine de la Broche SA, see Digeon.
Usinger, Heinrich. Chief decorator of the Louis XVI period. He used his full signature (shown below) in Höchst between 1774–84.

Usson, Marquis de, see Paris (69).
Utzmemmingen (Würtemberg), see Ellwangen.
Utzschneider & Co., see Saargemünd.
Uwaroff, Emilczyn.

Valdemorillo (Spain). Otto Funke, porcelain factory, f. 1914. Plates and cups.

Valencia (1) (Spain). Tomás Momparler. Porcelain factory and import business, f. 1870. Ornamental porcelain, vases, figures and table centres.

Tomás Momparler   **Tomas Momparler**

Valencia (2) (Spain). Victor de Nalda, porcelain factory.

Valenciennes (France). Fauquez and Lamoniary f. a porcelain factory here in 1785, which was active until 1795 when there was a break in production until 1800–10. The director was Vanier for a short time. Compared with Paris and Lille, the products were not remarkable.

Valentine (France, Haute Garonne). Fouque, Arnoux & Cie., 1823–60, followed by English ownership until 1890. Porcelain and faience. The products have been favourably mentioned by Brogniart (1844).

Vallée, see Paris (149).

Valognes (1) (France). In 1793 Le Tellier de la Bertinière f. a porcelain factory here which belonged to Le Masson in 1795. The next owner was D. L. Pelduze, from 1797–1802. Joachim Longlons took over in 1802 and moved the factory to Bayeux in 1812 *(q.v.)*. The marks shown have been taken partly from Cushion and partly from 'Tardy 75'.

Valognes (2) (France). Le Marois & Co., active since 1814, in the course of which time Langlois moved it to Bayeux (in 1812). It is feasible that the marks of 'Valognes 1793' continued to be used (according to 'Tardy 75'), particularly since replacement marks cannot be found.

Vandenbossche, V., see Paris (133).

Vanier, Michel (1747–90), see Bordeaux (1), Limoges (2) and Valenciennes.

Varion, Jean-Pierre, French master sculptor who worked in the Nove porcelain factory until 1780.

Varoslöd (Hungary). It is claimed that this stoneware factory which was f. in 1845, had also produced porcelain from c. 1847–52 (perhaps even longer). The following cartouche was used as a mark during this period, when the owners were either Desider Zichy or Bishop Dominicus Zichy.

Vater, Elias, mirror and glass maker, see Copenhagen (1).

Vater, Josef, see Vienna (19).

Vaume, Jean Sebastion, see Brussels (1).

Vaux nr. Meulan (France). La Borde and Hocquart produced hard paste porcelain here in 1769 (although it may have been only for a short while), under the direction of Moreau (or Merault). It has been assumed that the mark with the crossed 'V's' derives from this factory, but it is more likely that it belongs to Bordeaux. The mark 'HL', which is frequently interpreted as 'Hannong and Laborde', is thought to have been used by the owners of Vaux. The products are made in the style of Paris and Bordeaux.

Vaux, see Paris (112).

VEB porcelain decorating studio, see Kaltnelnegsfeld.

Veduti, Domenico, see Naples.

Veilsdorf, see Kloster Veilsdorf.

Velten (Germany, Brandenburg). Albert, Schulze successor, porcelain decorating studio, c. 1930.

Vendrennes (France). Marc-Lozelet f. a porcelain factory here c. 1800; its mark was the same as that of La Seynie.

Venice (1) (Italy). It is claimed that the alchemist 'Maestro Antonio di San Simone' had already produced porcelain here in 1470 by using earth from Bologna. The quality of this porcelain was similar to that of the 'barbarians'. The secret was lost once again. In 1518, again in Venice, a German born mirror maker, Leonardo Peringer, produced a ceramic substance which may have been a milk glass made opaque with tin oxide, in other words, the so-called-'vetro di latte', 'vetro lattimo', also 'verre de Venise'. As early as 1508 these experimental pieces were given the name 'Porcellana contrafatta', which means counterfeited porcelain. There are a few surviving pieces in the Hermitage in Leningrad, as well as in the British Museum, London.

Venice (2) (Italy). The multi-talented Christoph Conrad Hunger began porcelain production here in the beginning of the 18th c. However, he did not succeed and returned to Meissen in 1725. Vezzi, Francesco and Guiseppe (goldsmiths), who had perhaps received the arcanum from Hunger, started porcelain production c. 1719–20. The kaolin they required came from Aue (Saxony). The factory was active until 1740. The quality of the porcelain wares received varied assessments. Partial mention is made of an outstanding very hard glaze; the body was often yellow or greyish. The heraldic decoration on the earliest pieces must be considered as the best work from the production by Vezzi. According to Francesco Stazzi (1964), the Vezzi porcelains of the 18th c. were the only ones to contain kaolin. According to present day opinion therefore, the other products were not technically porcelain at all.

Nath. Friedrich Hewelcke and his wife Maria-Dorothea, left Saxony during the Seven-year-war and in 1757–8, in Venice, and after great efforts, they gained a 20-year licence for the production of porcelain. It was granted with the condition that their mark would be a 'V' (for Venice). In 1763, Hewelcke associated himself with Geminiano Cozzi, but withdrew in the same year in order to resume his activities in Saxony. The products have a unique simple charm. The body, in grey tones, is not without technical blemish. Figures and puttis were produced and landscape-painted decorations are the main motifs. Geminiano Cozzi, established his own porcelain factory in 1765 with aid from the Venetian Senate. He produced soft paste porcelain decorated in the Japanese manner 'ad uso del Giappone'. However these products are not of proper porcelain. The body is often light-grey in tone. Watery glazes are generally used. The anchor mark was the one most often used. Services, figures and vases were made in the style of Meissen, but the work of other European factories was also copied. Pieces of lower artistic quality are not uncommon. If, however, the pieces were decorated with particular care they rank among the famous porcelain of the 18th c.

VEZZI: 1 red – 2 impressed mark – 3 in many variations – 4 violet – 5 redbrown – 6 blue underglaze – HELWELKE: 1 blind – 2–3 red – COZZI: 2 I.G. black, anchor red – 3 F gold; rest red – 4 red – 5 signature of decorator – 6 gold – 7 red

Venier, Christian and Franz, see Meretitz.

Venier, Karl, see Klösterle (1).

Venier & Co., see Klösterle (1).

Vereinigte Lausitzer Glaswerke AG, see Berlin (7).

Vereinigte porcelain factory Meierhöfen, formerly Gebrüder Benedikt, see Meierhöfen (2).

Verlingue, Jules, see Quimper.

Vermeren-Coché. see Brussels (5).

Vermonet, Jacques (father and son), see Boisette près Melun.

Verneuilh, Pierre (d. 1787), see Bordeaux (1).

Vernon, see Fismes.

'Verriers'. Tall oval bowls with a number of holders extending from the rim, into which glasses could be set, the contents of which were kept cool by the ice which filled the bowl. The size of the bowl was suitable either for 'vins de table' or 'vins de liqueurs'.

'Vert pomme', apple green and **'Vert pré',** English green. Two porcelain colours of the Sèvres factory which, like 'jaune clair', were seldom used because of their rarity.

Vessra, see Kloster Vessra.

Vestunen Service. During the Seven-year-war, Friedrich II ordered six services from Meissen; their designs had been created by him personally and consisted of a pierced rim with shallow flower reliefs, ribbons and bows.

Vetro di latte, or vetro lattino, or verre de Venise. Milkglass made opaque with tin oxide, which bore some resemblance to porcelain. See Venice.

Vezzi, Francesco (d. 1740) and Guiseppe, see Venice.

Viallate, Jutes, see Paris (150).

Vicenza (1) (Italy). Certain pieces of porcelain have been ascribed to this city. Their bodies resemble Medici porcelain.

Vicenza (2) (Italy). Olympia, Mario Tosin & Co., artistic porcelain and other ceramic productions; this factory is still active.

OLYMPIA

'Victoria' AG porcelain factory, see Altrohlau (3).

Victoria Louise. Mark used as trademark No. 265980 of the P. F. Rosenthal, Selb, from 26 May 1921.

Victoria Service. The Hungarian factory owner Herend produced a porcelain service, decorated with butterflies and flowers, by order of Queen Victoria on the occasion of a London exhibition of Hungarian porcelain. Since then it has retained the above name and is still produced today.

Vieillard, see Bordeaux (4).

Vienna (1) (Austria). The Vienna porcelain factory was f. in 1718 by the Austrian War Commissioner Claudius du Paquier from Trier; he had already attempted porcelain making in 1716, but had not arrived at any satisfactory conclusion. In 1717 he persuaded the Meissen enameller and gilder, Christoph Konrad Hunger, to assist him in establishing a porcelain factory. Two years later he succeeded in his quest, with the help of the arcanist and foreman, Samuel Stölzel from Meissen. The miserable financial conditions caused both men to abscond, without ever revealing the arcanum of porcelain in detail. Du Paquier however, was able to continue to manage the factory through his chemical knowledge together with his vast experience. In 1744, the city of Vienna, by Imperial instigation, provided a loan which was to save the factory from closing down. Since Du Paquier's financial situation did not improve, he offered the factory for sale to the state in 1744. He remained as director after the sale had been concluded, although he retired later in the year on a pension and died in 1751. The porcelain designs of the Du Paquier period (1717–44) are to a large extent imitations of silver ware of the time. The character of the paste and the forms themselves take up a peculiar middle position between faience and hard paste porcelain, or it reflects the influence of Meissen. Figure production is used only in combination with porcelain ware, as was customary. The chinoiseries which played a leading role up until the middle of the century, may well have been introduced by Höroldt before his departure for Meissen. The main colours of the first period are strong iron red, light violet, copper green, cobalt blue, chrome yellow and gold. These colours were also used in conjunction with 'underglaze blue'. The characteristics of the Viennese Baroque can be clearly seen in the porcelain ware of the thirties. The painterly decoration of this time may have derived, generally speaking, from the hand of J. Ph. Danhofer. About the middle of the century one of the best painters at Vienna was Jakob Helchis whose specialities were figures and landscape in Schwarzlot. The second period, that of the State ownership, dates from 1744–84. It exemplifies the native rococo, until in the 1760s when the influence of Sèvres gradually filters through. The kaolin deposits which were discovered in 1749 in Schmölnitz in Hungary, and which were far superior in quality to the kaolin of the Passau Basin, made the factory independent as far as raw materials were concerned.

It was decided to mark all pieces made with the newly found kaolin with the banded shield in underglaze blue to contrast with the blindstamp of the first period. The changing trends demanded new artists. Johann Gottfried Klinger, a few of the Meissen decorators (who only remained for short spells, however), as well as the chief decorator, Johann Siegmund Fischer, were engaged. The competent decorator Philipp Ernst Schindler also started work at the factory during this time. From 1747 the master modeller was Johann Josef Niedermeyer. After the mid-18th c. the services developed characteristic relief decorations. The economic difficulties of the Vienna factory increased despite the high, artistic output, and it was consequently put up for sale in 1784. Since no one wished to buy it, the directorship was transferred to Konrad Sorgenthal, a woollen-textile-manufacturer from Linz. Thus the third period of the Vienna factory which was dominated by neo-classicism, began. The factory was led into a new period of high achievement, and more workers had to be employed. Neo-classical services made up the bulk of the production while rococo figures made the reputation of the factory. The decorators in this neo-classical style were Georg Perl and Joseph Leithner. The sculptor Anton Grassi dictated the modelling style which was executed, after the French example, mainly in biscuit. Towards 1820 the factory declined slowly, but without any chance of recovery. In 1864 the Emperor gave his consent for the closure of the factory which had

already been decided by an Act of Parliament. Subsequently 600 service and figure moulds of the factory came into the possession of de Cente in Vienna Neustadt and from there they were sold to Ernst Wahliss in 1900. Another group of moulds was passed on to the Herend (Hungary) porcelain factory, according to reliable sources of information. Mark 14 shown below has not yet, even to this day, been used as a porcelain mark, according to Neuwirth; although it had been recorded by the 'K. K. Aerarial Porzellan-Manufaktur in Vienna', on 9 July 1859, under postal no. 169 and was published in the same year in the Monthly Addition No. 6 of the weekly journal, *Austria,* issue 1859.
See also: Beyer, C. F. W., Benckgraff, J., Bottengruber, I., Daffinger, J., Dannhauser, L., Ettner, A., Gerlach, K., Hendler, P., Lamprecht, G., Kumpf, Lücke, J. Ch. L., Mayerhofer von Grünhübel, K. F. X., Schulz, A. F. J., Taglioni, F., Weinmüller, J.

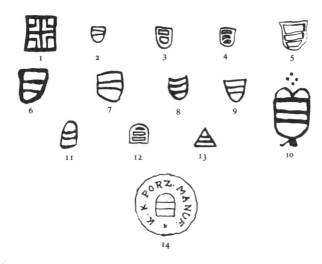

1 1720–30 among products in the Chinese style – 2 1744–9 red – 3–4 1744–9 impressed printing – 5 1744–9 incised – 6 1749–70 blue underglaze – 7–9 1770–1810 blue underglaze – 11 1820–7 blue underglaze – 12 blindstamped – 13 1850–64 blue underglaze

Vienna (2) (Austria). Ph. Aigner produced utility porcelain with impressionist decorations here in 1900.

Vienna (3) (Austria). Wiener porcelain factory Augarten, Aktiengesellschaft zur Erneuerung and Fortsetzung, formerly the Staatlichen (Aerarial-) porcelain works Wien, Vienna 11/27, Schloss Augarten, f. 1922. Joint stock company devoted to the renewal and continuation of the former state-owned Vienna porcelain factory. Figures, ornamental and luxury porcelain after both historical and modern artistic designs. The banded shield, already the mark of the Vienna porcelain factory which was closed in 1864, is marked or stamped, and, apart from the crowns, the star and the W, has the word Wien or Augarten placed above or below. 'Augarten' also occurs on its own. Elsewhere the mark may appear within a laurel wreath with encircling letters naming the factory in full.

Vienna (4) (Austria). J. Böck, porcelain factory. The ceramic concern, which was f. by Kutterwatz in 1828, came into the possession of the Böck family in 1879. As early as 1893, Joseph Böck established a porcelain decorating studio on a grand scale. In c. 1900 the finest artists of the Art Nouveau period created designs for it. Böck's porcelain designs, which in their form had much in common with Förster and Goldscheider, were reproduced in Schlackenwerth by Pfeiffer and Löwenstein, in Pirkenhammer by Haas & Czjzek and in Marktredwitz, by Thomas. The decoration was done in Vienna. The production consisted almost exclusively of table, coffee and tea services; porcelain figures were not produced. The factory was active until 1933. The last mark shown was registered for porcelain ware on 12 March 1900, in Vienna, and received the No. 11984; the mark is found either in underglaze or overglaze.

Vienna (5) (Austria). Albin Denk's Ww., porcelain decorating studio. Presented an assortment of table, coffee and tea services in the Vienna Exhibition of 1866, and received a prize. Like all Viennese porcelain decorating studios, this firm bought the white-porcelain from home and abroad. Their products were much praised at the World Exhibition 1873.

Vienna (6) (Austria). Franz Dörfl, porcelain decorating studio, f. c. 1880. In the same year it exhibited 'Viennese wares in antique and modern style' in the Vienna crafts exhibition. It received international recognition and was still working in 1923; some sources say even as late as 1930.

Vienna (7) (Austria). Alexander Förster (1861). Sculptor of the Vienna Academy, directed the Vienna Kunstkeramische (artistic ceramic) factory of Förster & Co. from 1899–1906. Apart from many other art and crafts products, this factory also dealt in porcelain which may have been produced in Bohemia after models by Förster, and decorated afterwards in Vienna. Famous artists contributed to the designs. The forms have much in common with the work of Goldschneider and Böck. Much pioneer work was carried out in the field of porcelain and biscuit figure production, and Förster also developed crystalline glazes from his own recipes, particularly successfully after the triumphs he met with in Berlin (Seger), at the World Exhibition 1900. Old Vienna statuettes and figures.

Vienna (8) (Austria). Goldscheder, f. 1885 as 'Goldscheidersche porcelain works and majolica factory'. This world famous factory, which existed until the Second World War, was originally involved with porcelain and ran its own porcelain factory in Pilsen (?), with porcelain decorating studios in Carlsbad and Vienna. The major concern centred increasingly on other ceramic fields. Particularly terracotta (metallised); besides this marble, artistic stone, even bronze were produced. From 1910 faiences were made exclusively. The stock of moulds and shapes comprised nearly 900 designs in 1954, when the factory closed. The history of the Goldscheder factory can be found in a detailed account by Neuwirth, *Wiener Keramic*.

Vienna (9) (Austria). In 1889 M. B. Grossbaum imitated porcelain products from the Sorgenthal period (Vienna). He also used the Vienna mark.

Vienna (10) (Austria). Josef Kawan, porcelain decorating studio, f. 1886 (according to some sources, 1907). Decorated in brocade, Indian blue, cobalt, using high temperature glazes and lustre. Worked until 1971.

Vienna (11) (Austria). Keramos Wiener artistic ceramic and porcelain works AG, porcelain decorating studio, c. 1920–36.

Vienna (12) (Austria). Hugo F. Kirsch (b. 1873), f. an artistic ceramic workshop in Vienna in 1906, where he produced stoneware but also porcelain. He marked his products in blue underglaze with a circular stamp 'Wiener Porz.H.Kirsch'. He also permitted other ceramists to make use of his facilities. After 1914 no porcelain is recorded. A more detailed account can be found in *Porzellan aus Wien*, by Neuwirth.

Vienna (13) (Austria). Langenzersdorfer Keramik E. Klablena, porcelain decorating studio, c. 1930.

Vienna (14) (Austria). ÖSPAG, Osterreichische Porzellan-Industrie AG (since 1945), formerly Wilhelmsburger Earthenware and porcelain factory Richard Lichtenstern & Co., Wilhelmsburg, f. 1882. Table, hotel and restaurant porcelain, also sanitary porcelain. 'Lilian-porcelain' since c. 1922.

Vienna (15) (Austria). Rädler & Pilz, 'Artistic studio for porcelain decorating'. F. after 1864. According to Neuwirth, it was the most important decorating studio of the period. Specialities were 'Portraits after photographs and after nature'. Also services in the style of Old Vienna and presentation pieces in the style of Makart's. Claimed to have been the sole owner of the Alt Vienna K.K. porcelain factory mark, from 1877; the studio used the mark, the beehive, upside down, however. Represented in London, Paris, Leipzig and Frankfurt am Main. Received the highest international recommendations.

Vienna (16) (Austria). Slama & Co. f. 1868. Porcelain decorating workshop (glass, crystal and artistic handicrafts). First mark shown below was used after 1930 for all products; second mark since 1859 and only for porcelain.

Vienna (17) (Austria). Robert Franz Staral, Old Vienna porcelain decorating studio, f. 1886. Luxury items, photographs on porcelain. Used cobalt, indian blue. Still producing in 1943. The mark was registered in the Vienna trademark-advertiser of 1923 and 1943; (according to Neuwirth).

Vienna (18) (Austria). Emanuel Steinberger porcelain factory, f. 1950. Pieces with gold etching, vases, bonbonnieres, Dejeuners services and luxury items. Style: rococo and ornamental.

Vienna (19) (Austria). Josef Vater. Porcelain decorating studio, from 1894. Vases, dejeuners, bowls, jewellery. Photo-gravures on porcelain.

Vienna (20) (Austria). Wahliss, see Turn (6).
Vienna (21) (Austria). Josef Zasche. Porcelain decorating studio f. 1854. Specialist in producing porcelain and enamel pictures from Old and New Masters of the Viennese Galleries. Also rococo services. Participated in the Vienna World Exhibition of 1873 where Zasche excelled particularly as miniaturist. He received international acclaim until the end of the 19th c.

J. Z.
Wien.

Vienna Neustadt (Austria). de Cente, factory for tile stoves and fire-proof products. In 1864, when the famous Old Vienna porcelain factory had to close, this factory bought up c. 600 moulds for figures and other articles, and sold the resultant products in large quantities. de Cente's production was in earthenware and not in porcelain. Unlike factories which adopted the banded shield of the Old Vienna factory, de Cente marked the products with his own name. When there was no further use for the moulds by de Centes, they fell into disuse. However, in 1900, Ernst Wahliss, of Vienna and Turn nr. Teplitz, acquired the whole stock of moulds, and the figures of Old Vienna were revived a second time (Neuwirth).
Vierzon (1) (France). Berlot & Mussier had the following mark registered in 1959 (see 'Tardy 75').

B.M.
VIERZON.

Vierzon (2) (France). The Bouret Bros. had the following mark registered in 1900 ('Tardy 75').

Vierzon (3) (France). Cirot Brunet & Co. had the following mark registered in 1933.

Vierzon (4) (France). Cirot Gadoiun & Co., had the following mark registered in 1951 (according to 'Tardy 75').

Vierzon (5) (France). Edgar Gaucher, porcelain factory; later named: Vve. E. Gaucher et Fils. Utility porcelain, hotel and table porcelain.

Vierzon (6) (France). L. Jaquin et Cie., porcelain factory.

Vierzon (7) (France). Jean, an experienced 'Faiencier' f. a small porcelain factory here in 1885.

Vierzon (8) (France). Porcelaines Labrut, Labrut Brother and Sisters, f. 1850. Table services, coffee and tea services, etc. The factory used no mark. The name changed to Bouchard in 1905 and again to Hubert Bouchard in 1938. It closed but was re-opened in 1945 by Labrut.

Vierzon (9) (France). Marcell Laillet had the following mark registered in 1929.

Vierzon (10) (France). Sologne Lamotte O. L. & V., f. 1850. Utility porcelain ware.

Vierzon (11) (France). Perrot and Delvincourt f. a porcelain factory here in 1815, which was taken over in 1825 by Dubois and Jamet and later changed its owner frequently. Mark No. 1 was used by Hache & Pépin-le-Halleur, mark No. 2 was used by Hache & Julien. In 1879 this factory was typical of the modern French porcelain industry. At this time the factory was called 'A. Hachez & Pépin Lehalleur Frères'. The products resembled those of the English factories and copies are made in the style of Sèvres. The technical achievement was much praised; white and patterned porcelain ware was produced. The factory is now closed.

Vierzon (12) (France). A. Vincent Fils porcelain factory was taken over in 1937 by the Ets. Blin and its name is now: 'Ets Amédée Blin'. Produced articles in thin porcelain.

Vierzon (13) (France). Regnier & Cie., porcelain works, taken over in 1941 by the Ets. Blin and since known as 'Ets. Jacques Blin'. Table, coffee and cake porcelain ware. The factory uses no mark.

Vierzon (14) (France). Rondeleux et Cie., f. 1902. Porcelain for hotels and restaurants, table services, ovenproof porcelain.

Vierzon (15) (France). Société d'Exploitation des Etablissements Larchevêque, porcelain factory, f. 1850. Hotel and table services.

Vierzon (16) (France). Lucien Taillemite, porcelain factory. Cooking implements, services, table services.

Vignaud, Pierre, see Paris (151).
Vignier, see Paris (36).
Vigo (Spain). Manuel Alvarez e Hijos, SA, porcelain factory, f. 1927.
Viking Pottery Co., see Cobridge (4).

Villari, Caesare, see Solagna.
Villedieu (1) (France). According to Brongniart, M. Louault f. a porcelain factory here which was directed by M. Lalouette in 1823.

Villedieu (2) (France). Eugène Frelon, f. 1878; later Frelon Bros.

Villedieu-sur-Indre (1) (France). Jean Lang, porcelain factory, f. 1882, table, coffee and tea services.

Villedieu-sur-Indre (2) (France). Marelli & Cie., porcelain factory, f. 1862. Table services, kitchen platters, trays, coffee and tea services.

Villegoureix, Noel & Co., see Limoges (89).

Villenauxe-la-Grande (1) (France). Autriau. Gérard, Letu et Mauger produced porcelain in their factory here in 1867. The products have no marks.

Villenauxe-la-Grande (2) (France). Beaugrand f. a porcelain factory here in 1885 called 'Beaugrand & Noël'.

Villenauxe-la-Grande (3) (France). In 1895, Stornay had the following mark entered ('Tardy 75').

Villenauxe-la-Grande (4) (France). Tessier & Cie., porcelain factory; biscuit ard artistic porcelain.

Villeroy, Louis François, Duke of, see Bourg-la-Reine and Mennecy-Villeroy.

Villeroy & Boch, see Schramberg (1).

Villiers, see Choisy-le-Roy (1).

Villingen (Germany, Baden). Mahler and Weber produced hard paste porcelain here in 1867.

Viltard & Collet, see Paris (152).

Vincennes (1) (France). From 1738–56. In 1738 Louis XV granted a privilege 'for producing porcelain in the Saxon style', to the brother of his Minister of finance, le Marquis d'Orry de Fulvy. Experiments began in 1740 in the Castle at Vincennes. The arcanists were the Dubois brothers from Chantilly who worked unsuccessfully for a period of four years. The sculptor Bulidon joined them. Subsequently the former assistant, Gravant, directed further developments and in 1745 achieved the required composition which could be fired to produce a frit porcelain of outstanding quality. In the same year a joint stock-company was formed under the name of Charles Adam, which received a privilege for 20 years from Louis XV. In 1745 Jean Hellot, the chemist from the Paris Academy, together with the royal goldsmith, Duplessis, and the enameller Mathieu, were in charge of figure-production and decoration. Boileau was the director. After the death of d'Orry de Fulvys, in 1751, d'Elois Brichard f. a new company which took the name 'Manufacture Royale de la Porcelaine de France' and adopted the royal crest as a mark. The crown held 25 per cent of the shares in this enterprise. Vincennes enjoyed the privilege of being the only French porcelain factory which could decorate in 'polychrome' and apply gilding; all other factories had to limit their decorating to monochrome. The factory was transferred to Sèvres in 1756, see Sèvres (1).

1–5 blue underglaze, all before 1753 – 6 1753 – 7 1754 – 8 1755

Vincennes (2) (France). In 1765 Peter Anton Hannong f. a faience factory here which was supported by royal patronage. Soon Hannong cunningly added a porcelain production alongside the making of faience, aided by Maurice des Aubiez and later (1769) de la Borde, a member of the court of Louis XV. Hannong was dismissed in 1770; the factory was subsequently bought by Seguin in 1774 whose mark was registered (see mark No. 7). This factory received the protection of Louis Philippe, the Duc de Chartres. Lemaire became director in 1788. From this time on there are no records available.

1–4 HL = Hannong & La Borde – 5–6 monogram of Louis Philippe, Duc de Chartres – 7
1777 registered by Seguin, blue underglaze

Vincennes (3) (France). Sté Brosset & Hutteau, Porcelaines d'art de Vincennes,
artistic porcelain.

Vincent, A. Fils, see Vierzon (12).
Vine wreath. Meissen porcelain pattern, after designs of Johann Samuel
Arnold, which have survived to this day. Introduced in 1817, following the
discovery of 'chrome green underglaze'.
Vinovo nr. Turin (Italy). In 1776 Giovanni Vittorio Brodel, from Turin, f. a
porcelain factory together with P. A. Hannong (who had held a patent from the
King of Savoy since 2 August 1765). However it was forcibly closed again in
1780 on the order of the King. Dr. Gioanetti transferred his experimental
workshop in 1780 from Vische to Vinovo, to the Royal castle, where it flourished
as a well-run factory. According to a surviving advertisement from 1784, it
invited customers to see their products, advertising 2,000 pieces for 24 Lire. The
factory was working until 1820; the owner for the last five years was Giovanni
Lomello.

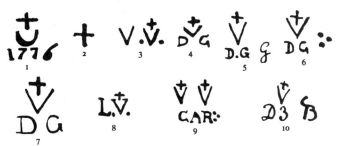

1 blue – 2 black – 3 blue – 4–7 D.G. = Dr. Gioanetti – 8 Lomello, 1815–20 – 9 CAR
Carasso, decorator's mark – 10 mark of Giorgio Balbo, red and green

Vinsare, see Sèvres (6).
'Violet pensée'. Porcelain colour of the Sèvres factory, which, like 'jaune clair',
'vert pomme' and 'vert pré' was used only rarely owing to its high cost.

Vion, see Paris (60).
Vion & Baury, see Choisy-le-Roi (1).
Vista Alegre (Portugal). José Ferreira Pinto Basto f. a porcelain factory here in 1824 which enjoyed royal patronage until 1840. During this period the mark 'VA' was topped by a crown. After 1840 the crown was omitted. The quality of

these products was much praised. This factory is still working today and is still in the possession of the founder's family. It is the only establishment in Portugal which produces services and luxury porcelain. The factory issued a detailed and chronologically ordered inventory of their porcelain marks. This list has been adopted completely, without reference to the marks which have already been mentioned above.

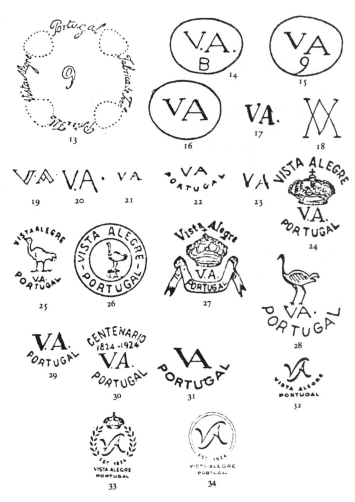

1st–2nd periods 1824–35 – 1 incised – 2 gold (1826–35); – 3rd period 1836–51 – 3 predominantly gold – 4 red or green – 5 violet; – 4th period 1862–9 – 6–7 gold – 8 blue – 9 red – 10 gold – 11 blue – 12 gold – 13 grey – 14–15 incised – 16 blind impressed; – 5th period 1870–80 – 17 underglaze blue or gold – 18 blue – 19 blind impressed – 20 blue underglaze; – 6th period 1881–1921 – 21 green underglaze – 22–27 stamp green underglaze – 28 incised; – 7th period 1922–47 – 29–30 stamp green underglaze; – 8th period 1947–68 – 31 stamp green underglaze; – 9th period from 1969 – 32 stamp blue underglaze – 33–34 blue

Vital-Roux, see Noirlac.

Vivien, arcanist, see Buen Retiro.

Vogelmann, Carl. Modeller, arcanist and ceramist in Kelsterbach 1764–6, later active in faience factories.

Vogt, Georges, see Sèvres(1).

Vogt & Dohse, see Limoges (86).

Vohenstrauss (Germany, Upper Palatine). Johann Seltmann GmbH porcelain factory, f. 1901. Table, coffee and Mocha services, gift items.

[206]   [256]

Voigt, A., see Oelze.

Voigt, Herrmann, see Schaala (2).

Volkstedt, see Rudolstadt Volkstedt.

Volkstedter porcelain works, Seedorf/Württemberg, see Seedorf and Rudolstadt Volkstedt (17).

Volkstedter porcelain factory, Reinhold Richter GmbH, see Rudolstadt Volkstedt (21).

Vondracek, Alois, & Co., see Schwarzkostelez.

Voorst, van der modeller, see Sèvres (1) and Boucher.

Vsevolojsky & Polivanoff, see Aschuat and Moscow (12).

Wache, Adolf, see Dresden (33).

Wachtersbacher Steingutfabrik (stoneware factory), see Schlierbach.

Wackenfeld (Wachenfeld, also Wockenfeld), J. Heinrich (d. 1725), see Strasbourg (1) and Hannong, K. F.

Wackerle, Josef (1880–1959). Sculptor, ceramist, designer. Attended technical school for woodcarving, Partenkirchen, Munich Academy, won the Rome prize in 1904, was artistic director in Nymphenburg from 1906–9. 1909–17 teacher at the Institute for Instruction of the Berlin Museum for arts and crafts, 1917–22 teacher at the school for arts and crafts in Munich. Created models for the KPM Berlin. In 1922 he became professor and teacher at the Munich academy (Treskow).

WACKERLE.

Wächter, Rudolf, see Kirchenlamitz (2).

Wärtsilä-koncernen, see Helsinki.

Waffenbruder. Trademark No. 206618 from 27 October 1915 of the P. F. J. Haviland, Waldershof.

Waffler, H., see Schwarzenfeld.

Wagenfeld, Wilhelm, see Fürstenberg.

Wagner, Carl, see Dresden (34).

Wagner, Georg Heinrich Jeremias. One of the owners of the Ottweiler porcelain factory, c. 1764–5.

Wagner, Johann Jakob (1710–97). Brother-in-law of Dietrich Wendl, who introduced him to the Meissen factory where he worked as a porcelain decorator, specialising in historical paintings.

Wagner, Johann Philipp, see Ottweiler.

Wagner & Apel, see Lippelsdorf.
Wahliss, Ernst, see Turn (6).
Waine & Bates, see Longton (82).
Waine, Charles (& Co.) (Ltd.), Derby Works, see Longton (82).
Walbryzych (Altwasser) (Poland). Jan Kachniewicz took over the C. Tielsch & Co. porcelain factory in 1945. Since then the following mark has been used. See Altwasser (2).

Walcher, Bonaventura (1723–96). A brother-in-law of Ringler, and chief kiln master in Nymphenburg from 1759–87.
Wald, Anna Elisabeth, née Auffenwerth. Decorated Kunersberg faiences and possibly some Meissen porcelain at the middle of the 18th c.
Waldenburg (1) (Saxony). A pottery factory was established here as early as 1388.
Waldenburg (2) (Saxony). Carl Franz Krister (1802–67). Came from Thuringia in 1823 as a blue decorator and worked in a small porcelain factory which was owned by Rausch, the linen weaver. In 1829 he f. a new factory in collaboration with Hayn and in 1833, bought the above mentioned factory from Rausch for 15,500 Taler. He owned a kaolin quarry near Meissen, and a quartz source near Schreiberkau. His products were transported 'by horse and waggon' to the Leipzig Fair for sale. After his death the 'Haenschke heirs' became owners, and in 1920 turned the factory into a joint stock-company. In 1921 they amalgamated with Ph. Rosenthal & Co. AG Selb. The 'onion pattern' was used. The mark WPM ('Waldenburger Porzellan Manufaktur') was traced to c. 1850, is found in blue underglaze, and also appears without any addition. The mark most frequently used before 1900, is the first mark shown below.

Waldendorf, Johann Philipp von, Archbishop of Trier, see Schönbornlust.
Waldershof (1) (Germany, Upper Frankonia). Waldershof porcelain factory AG, formerly Johann Haviland, f. 1907. Utility porcelain ware. The factory had the name of Johann Haviland Waldershof from 1907–24 and that of Waldershof porcelain factory AG thereafter. In 1936 the factory was annexed to the Rosenthal-Porzellan Aktiengesellschaft, Selb.

Waldershoff (2) (Germany, Upper Frankonia). 'Bavaria' porcelain factory, f. 1925. Owner: Franz Neukirchner. Silver porcelain, gold etchings, hotel and utility porcelain ware, also jewellery.

Waldmann, Anton, see Schlaggenwald (2).
Waldsassen (1) (Germany, Upper Palatinate). Waldsassen Chamotte and Klinker factory AG, f. 1882. Porcelain department since 1923. Utility porcelain.

Waldsassen (2) (Germany, Upper Palatinate). Gareis, Kühnl & Cie. porcelain factory AG, f. 1899. Household porcelain, vases, basic porcelain ware. Until 31 December 1949 the concern was called Gareis, Kühnl & Co. porcelain factory, and from 1 January 1950 it became a joint stock company.

Waldsassen (3) (Germany, Upper Palatinate). Waldsassen Bareuther & Co. porcelain factory AG, f. 1866. Utility porcelain ware and services.

 [232] [231]

Walker, Philipp (d. 1803), see Lowestoft.
Walker, Samuel, (b. c. 1785), see Nantgarw and Swansea.
'Walküre'. First Bayreuther 'Walküre' porcelain factory, Siegm. Paul Meyer GmbH, see Bayreuth (2).
Wall, John Dr. (1708 Powick–1776 Bath). Studied in Oxford and engaged in ceramic studies for a considerable time before the founding of the Worcester porcelain factory in 1751. It is assumed that he followed recipes devised by the chemist, William Davis. The production concentrated on soft paste porcelain and made use of steatite. See Worcester (1).
Wallander, Alf (1862–1914). Designer in the arts and crafts movement. Skilled craftsman, decorator, illustrator, modeller. Attended technical college 1877–8 and the academy in Stockholm 1880–5. After this, he worked as a painter in Paris from 1895–1914. He became artistic director of the Rörstrands porcelain works, where, in association with Wennerberg, he made major contributions to the development of the style of the factory until c. 1910.
Wallendorf (Germany, Thuringia). A small porcelain factory was f. here in 1763, as a private enterprise by J. W. Hamman and his partners Johann Gottfried and Gotthelf Greiner. At first certain difficulties prevented the introduction of a clear, unclouded glaze but these were overcome by the pottery master Dümmler, from Coburg. The porcelain factory remained in the family's possession until 1833. It was subsequently sold to Fr. Chr. Hutschenreuther (who had been the leaseholder for a number of years), Friedrich Kämpfe and Gabriel Heubach, who continued to direct the factory as a joint stock company. Coffee and tea services in the style of Meissen, with underglaze blue (blue black) or purple, strawflower and onion patterns. The Meissen shape of service 'broken staves' (fluted) was used with the strawflower pattern. Strong body in the early products, as in nearly all Thuringian factories. No pure white body. The more refined work was made to resemble that of Meissen and Nymphenburg. Fond porcelain. The figures with their naive charm were reminiscent of the Limbach factory. The factory closed in 1919, but re-opened between 1919–25 as the art department of the Fraureuth porcelain factory, and was then re-opened completely by Schaubach. Since 1953 it has been a Property of the People, called

'VEB Wallendorfer Porzellanfabrik' the factory of the 'VEB Zierporzellan-werke Lichte'. Since 1960 it has employed c. 1,000 workers. After the Second World War the mark used displayed the date 1764 for some time.

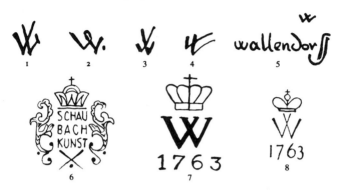

all blue underglaze – 1–4 in use until 1780. The mark W shown below is hastily applied, frequently (perhaps intentionally), confused with the Meissen swords – 6–7 Schaubach marks – 8 mark used until 1977

Walterhausen (1) (Germany, Thuringia). Kammer & Reinhardt, doll factory. Dolls' heads by Simon & Halbig, Gräfenhain were used. When this happened the products were marked on the neck with the marks of the two firms. The star however, is used alone (from c. 1902), and also appears on dolls' heads which were produced by Kammer and Reinhardt.

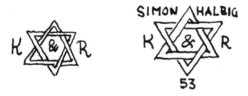

Waltershausen (2) (Germany, Thuringia). A. Schmidt, porcelain factory, c. 1900.

Walther, J. & Son, see Oeslau (4).
Walton, J. H., Baltimore or Albion China Works, see Longton (83).
Warnsdorf. Gustav H. Richter, f. 1882. Porcelain flower factory.

Warrilow, G. & Sons Ltd., see Longton (84).

Warsaw (Poland). According to Demmin, a porcelain factory was here in 1867.

Water crystal (Wasserquarz). The general 18th c. name for feldspar in Germany.

Waterloo Works, Livesley Powell & Co., see Hanley (8).

Weatherby, see Bow.

Weber, Franz Joseph. Active as a miniature painter in Ludwigsburg and before that in Kelsterbach. In Frankenthal c. 1770, later in Höchst as Controller, c. 1778. From c. 1798 he directed the Ilmenau porcelain factory. In 1798 he published a quarto volume in Hannover, *The art of producing true porcelain.* The chapter headed 'The epoche of the great porcelain factories of the past' is still valuable, particularly for the historical and biographical information contained in it.

Wedgwood. The works f. in 1769 by Josiah Wedgwood in Etruria, Staffordshire, are of the greatest importance to the history of stoneware and earthenware production. Porcelain was produced as 'bone china' under Josiah Wedgwood Jr., between 1795 (the year of his father's death) and c. 1815. In 1887, bone china production was started once again and gained considerable momentum under the artistic direction of John E. Goodwin, who amongst other innovations, introduced the Wedgwood powder blue and developed matt glazes. The 'bone china' is marked with the second mark shown from 1878, and with the third from 1900, together with the words 'England' or 'Made in England'. From about 1920 the words 'Bone China' were added to the marks.

See also: Bacon the Elder, J., Flaxman, J., Hackwood, W., Smith, J., Tassie, J.

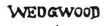
1

2

3

1 1812–16 in red rarely in blue or gold

Wedgwood, Josiah (1730–95). Founder of the Wedgwood works in Etruria, Staffordshire, England. He strongly influenced the techniques and modelling, not only of the English, but also of the continental ceramic production. His marbled earthenware, the black basalt and the particularly fine stoneware of the Jasper were so much in the neo-classical style, that soon even porcelain factories were attempting to follow his lead. Porcelain itself was never produced in Wedgwood's factories during his lifetime.

Wedgwood Dinner Service, of cream-coloured earthenware, created for Catherine II and delivered in 1774. His decorations show English landscapes painted in a mulberry, purple colour, after old engravings which depict well-known views and castles. It consists of 950 pieces, some of which were exhibited, by Wedgwood & Sons, in London in about 1900, with the permission of the Tsar.

Wedgwood-relief. A bas-relief which stands out from a coloured ground. Often white on light blue; mostly used on plaques and vessels (Pâte sur Pâte).
Weesp (Holland). The first porcelain factory in Holland was f. here in 1764 by Count Gronsveldt-Diepenbroek. He used the expertise of German specialists who worked under the leadership of the arcanist Nikolaus Paul. The machinery from the Overtoom (Amsterdam) faience factory was taken over for the new factory. In 1765, when the arcanist Paul left for Fulda, Picot became the technical manager. He attempted in vain to sell the factory to Sèvres. In 1771 Johannes de Moll took possession of the factory which he transferred to Oude Loosdrecht. The porcelain is of a good, white quality. The form and decorations have certain similarities with the products of the leading German factories. The output included pieces with good decorations in the style of Watteau. The modeller Nikolas Gauron was chief modeller c. 1765.

All blue underglaze

Wegely, Wilhelm Caspar. He established the first porcelain factory in Berlin with a privilege granted by Frederik II 1752–7. See Berlin (1).
Wegner, Andreas Franz. Modeller in Meissen 1802–8 and later, his fame rests particularly on his fine busts (of Napoleon).
Wehinger, H. & Co., see Horn nr. Elbogen.
Wehsner, Rich., see Dresden (35).
Weiden (1) (Germany, Upper Palatine). Weiden porcelain factory, Bauscher Bros., f. 1881. Hotel porcelain, porcelain for railway and maritime companies, hospitals, ovenproof cooking ware ('Luzifer'), technical porcelains, coffee and tea pots. In 1927 this factory was affiliated with Lorenz Hutschenreuther AG, Selb. The last mark shown was entered in the trademark publication of the Imperial patent office Berlin, on the 13 January 1910 (No. 125483). After the merger of Lorenz Hutschenreuther, Selb and C. M. Hutschenreuther, Hohenberg, the Bauscher porcelain factory used its internationally registered oval mark (see penultimate mark), which had been entered in the Reich trademark register in 1921, without any particular addition.

[21]

[173]

[211]

[238]

[158]

Weiden (2) (Germany, Upper Palatinate). Christian Seltmann porcelain factory GmbH, f. 1911. Utility porcelain, hotel porcelain, gift articles, ovenproof cooking vessels. Mark: 'Marie-Luise'.

WEIDEN

[172]

Weidenhammer, Peter. From Schneeberg, Bohemia. Discovered the colouring effect of cobalt ore in 1510.

Weidinger's glass painting, see Copenhagen (8).

Weidl, Anton, see Bayreuth (3).

Weil, Baruch, see Fontainebleau (1).

Weingarten (Germany, Baden). Weingarten, R. Wolfinger porcelain factory, f. 1882. Utility ware and luxury articles. According to archival records the first owner, from 1890, was Adolf Baumgarten, who signed with his monogram (see first mark, below). The sculptor and ceramist Carl Kornhas produced vases with crystalline glazes c. 1900. This factory is no longer active.

   PW

Weinmüller, Joseph (1743–1812). Pupil of Johann Baptist Straub in Munich and supplied, at the same period as Beyer, models of figures for the Ludwigsburg porcelain factory. He followed Beyer to Vienna, where he worked with him on decorations for the statues in Schönbrunn.

Weiss, Joseph (1699–1770), miniature painter. Pupil of Desmarée (1764), decorator at the Nymphenburg factory, and successor of Hermannsdorfer. Specialist in flowers, animals and landscapes. As a teacher, he exerted great influence. His period of employment there coincided with the period of the highest quality production.

Weiss, Kühnert & Co. K.G., see Gräfenthal (4).

Weissenstadt (Germany, Upper Frankonia). Weissenstadt Dürrbeck & Ruckdäschel porcelain factory, f. 1920. Utility porcelain and gift articles.

Weisswasser (Germany, Silesia). August Schweig porcelain factory GmbH, f. 1895. Utility porcelain. Name in use at present is the VEB-branch factory Weisswasser, formerly the Oberlausitzer porcelain factory August Schweig & Co.

Weithase, C. K., see Rudolstádt Volkstedt (23).

Weitsch, Johann Friedrich (called 'Pascha') Weitsch (1723–1803). From Halberstadt. Originally a soldier, but was ordered by his captain 'to be a painter'. He left military service in 1758 and entered the Fürstenberg factory, as a decorator, where he taught himself the art of oil painting. His activities, between 1762–74, are recorded in the archives. In 1778 he received the honorary diploma of a professor of the academy in Düsseldorf. In 1788 he attained the position of the inspector at the Fürstenberg porcelain factory and in the Galerie in Salzdahlum, where he died in 1803. He was a specialist for portraits, landscapes and pastoral scenes. He was also successful as a teacher and is one of the most important decorators at Fürstenberg.

Wellington Service. After the final defeat of Napoleon I and the subsequent Congress of Vienna (1814–5), each of the European Heads of state concerned, commissioned (perhaps by agreement) the most precious service from their factories as a gift to the victorious military leader, the Duke of Wellington. The four most prominent factories, Berlin, Meissen, Sèvres and Vienna, produced works of the highest quality during this 'competition'. Here they are listed under the English names which were given them: Prussian Service – Saxon Service – Royal French Service and Austrian Service. All of these services, or at least the greater parts with the most representative pieces, have been kept since that time in the palace of the Duke, in Aspley House at Hyde Park Corner in London, where they are still on view.

See also Feldherren Service.

Wenk & Zitzmann, see Küps (5).

Wennerberg, Gunnar Gunnarsen (1883–1914). Ceramist, decorator, designer. Studied in Paris and Sèvres. Artistic director in Gustavsberg from 1897–1908; in Paris, between 1908–14 where he was also active for Sèvres. He made a major contribution to the Scandinavian Art Nouveau movement.

Werbiliki, see Moscow (4).

Werstock, see Paris (98).

Wessel, Ludwig, AG, porcelain and pottery factory, see Bonn (2).

Westbourne (England). E. Baggaley Ltd., porcelain factory, f. 1945; formerly Branksome Ltd. until 1956.

INLAY COLOURS

Weston Young, William, see Nantgarw.

Weydeveldt, van, Léonard-Agathon called Agathon Léonard (b. 1841 Lille). According to Bott he was active in Sèvres in 1900. Sculptor and designer in ceramics. Studied at the Lille Academy and with D. Delaplanche, Paris (Art Nouveau). His major work, the table centre piece of 15 parts, 'jeu d' l'Echarpe', originally of bronze, was made by Sèvres in biscuit, for the World Exhibition of 1900. Taken over at a later stage by the Heubach Bros. in Lichte.

Widera, Dr. & Co. Kdt. Ges., oven and wall plates factory, see Eichwald.

Widin (Bulgaria). Georg Mladenoff & Co., c. 1930, described as porcelain factory.

Weidewelt, Johannes. Danish sculptor, fellow worker of Fournier, the director of the Copenhagen factory (during the Fournier periods 1760–66).

Wiefel & Co. GmbH, see Ludwigstadt.

Wiegand, Martin, see Munich (8).

Wiener Vienna (Hartmuth), see Budweis (1).

Wieninger G., see Munich (9).

Wiesau (1) (Germany, Bavaria). Josef Kuba porcelain factory, f. 1930, originally from Bohemia. Decorative and luxury porcelain. Decorated in styles of Old Vienna, Rembrandt, neo-classical and with gold etched edges.

Wiesau (2) (Germany, Upper Palatinate). Mayer Bros. porcelain factory, owned by Ernst Mayer, f. 1840 in Carlsbad-Fischern. Operated in Wiesau from 1947. Utility and decorative porcelain.

Wiesau (3) (Germany, Upper Palatinate). Richard Wolfram, porcelain factory, f. 1898. Utility china.

Wild Bros., Edensor Crown, China Works, see Longton (85).

Wildblood, Heath & Sons (Ltd.), Peel Works, see Longton (86).

Wildblood & Ledgar, see Longton (48).

Wileman & Co., Foley works, see Longton (73).

Wilhelmine. Trademark No. 274142 from 25 October 1921 of P. F. Rosenthal, Selb.

Wilhelmsburger Earthenware and porcelain Industry AG, see Vienna (13).

Willand, Johann. He and his son, Franz Mathias, were active as independent decorators in Regensburg, from c. 1780–93. They decorated porcelain from various factories for export, particularly to Asia Minor.

Wille, Isaak, see Ottweiler.

Willems, Joseph (d. 1766), sculptor, see Chelsea (1).

Williamson, H. M. & Sons, see Longton (87).

Willner Bros., see Turn (11).

Willumsen, J. F., see Copenhagen (2).

Wilson, David (& Sons), Church Work, see Hanley (14).

Wilson, J., & Co., see Middlesborough.

Wilson, J. & Sons, Park Works, see Fenton (15).

Wiltshaw & Robinson Ltd., Carlton Works, see Stoke-on-Trent (12).

Winckelmann, Joh. Joachim (1717–68). Famous archaeologist and art historian of the 18th c. whose theory of art was of decisive importance to the creation of porcelain, and biscuit figures in particular.

Windisch, Christophe, see Brussels (5).

Windischeschenbach (Germany, Upper Palatinate). Haberländer porcelain factory, now Oskar Schaller & Co., f. 1913. Services, series of services, gift articles as well as artistic porcelain.

Windschügel, Andreas. Arcanist and painter in Frankenthal 1770–4 and in Palatinate-Zweibrücken 1784, as well as in different faience and stoneware factories.

Winogradow, A., see Novy Dwor.

Winogradow, Dimitri (d. 1758), Inspector of Mines, see Petersburg (1).

Winter, Hugo, see Kaltenhofen.

Winter & Co., see Elbogen (3).

Winter, Lochschmied & Co., see Elbogen (5).

Winterling Bros., see Röslau.

Winterling, Heinrich, see Marktleuthen (2).

Winterling, see Schwarzenbach a.d. Saale (2).

Winterstein. Historical painter. Came in 1758 from Höchst to Frankenthal, where he has been acclaimed as the best painter after Osterspei.

Winterstein pinx.

Wistritz (Bohemia). Krautzberger, Mayer & Purkert GmbH, f. 1911. Utility ware and similar.

Wjalemsky, A. A., Prinz, see Petersburg (1).

Wloclawek (Poland Warszawskie). Teichfeld & Asterblum, porcelain decorating studio, c. 1930.

Wohlfahrt, Karl. Active as a decorator in Höchst from c. 1770. He previously worked in Frankenthal, Zweibrücken and Ottweiler.

Wolchow, see Kusnetzoff.

Wolff, Johann Adalbert, see Pirkenhammer.

Wolfinger, R., see Weingarten.

Wolfram, Richard, see Wiesau (3).

Wolfsburg, Carl Ferdinand (1692–1764). Independent porcelain decorator and enamel painter in Breslau and Vienna, a pupil of Bottengruber. His earlier works remind one of the style of his teacher, and he later influenced the style of decorations of the Vienna porcelain factory.

C.J.D. Waffsbourg
pinxit 1729

Charles Ferdinand de
Wffsbourg et Hallsdorf Eques
Fecit 1732

Carolus Ferdinandus
De Wolfsbourg. et Wals.
dorf; Eques Silesice
Jgne confecit
1733.

Wolfsohn, Helena, successor to Leopold Elb and W. E. Stephan, see Dresden (36).

Worcester (1) (England). This English porcelain factory of the 18th c. earned its place among the important factories by virtue of its large output; it was f. in 1751. The first period of the factory is known as Dr. John Wall's period, after one of the founders (1751–83), although perhaps another founder, William Davis, exerted the greater influence. In 1783 Joseph and John Flight became the owners of the factory and in 1792, a year after the death of John, Martin Barr became a part owner. In the following period the partnership accepted further members of both families. In 1840 the factory of Flight and Barr incorporated the factory which was founded by Robert Chamberlain, also in Worcester, in 1783 (originally as a porcelain decorating studio). Subsequent owners were Walter Chamberlain and John Lilly in 1848, and Kerr and Binns in 1852. Since 1852 the factory has been called 'Royal Worcester Porcelain Co.' In 1889 this company took over a competitor, the factory which had been f. in 1801 by Thomas Grainger in Worcester, and in 1905 it also acquired the Hadley Works, which were f. in 1896. Early Worcester porcelain is relatively hard, with a grey-white body and thinly glazed. The production of services was extensive, and the decoration mainly executed in underglaze blue. As early as c. 1756, overglaze decorations were introduced and engravings by Robert Hancock, Richard Holdship and later James Ross were used as designs. The models were Chinese and Japanese patterns and later included imitations of Sèvres and Chelsea, particularly the dark coloured ground. The gilding of richly modelled lace or tendrils was of outstanding quality. The most beautiful decoration is seen in the Wall period, and depicts exotic birds, reserved on coloured grounds and framed with gold ornamentation. The second period, from 1783–1840, was influenced by neo-classicism and the Empire style. The Japanese pattern remained a favourite decoration for services. In the second half of the 19th c. the factory was more orientated towards mass production. Before the beginning of the First World War the production of technical and laboratory porcelain ware was introduced, but the War interrupted this and limited the output considerably. From 1931 ovenproof porcelain was also made. During the Second World War 75 per cent of the production was technical and laboratory ware. Only a small proportion of fine porcelain was produced, for export to the USA. From 1945 this fine utility porcelain was once again produced for export purposes, this time on a larger scale. Now the factory is again in demand for its figure production.

See also: Bristol (2), Pardoe, T., Plant, J.

CHAMBERLAINS 28

GRAINGER & CO
31

GraingerLee & Co
Worcester
32

George Grainger Royal China   GRAINGER. WOOD & CO.
Works Worcester   WORCESTER
33   34

GRAINGER, LEE & CO.   NEW CHINA WORKS   GRAINGER
WORCESTER   WORCESTER   37
35   36

GRAINGER & CO.   G. G. W.
WORCESTER
38   G. & Co.
                 W.
                 39   40

41

1–3 on all products from 1751–1800 – 4–5 during the same period as 1, but only on products with decoration in blue underglaze – 6–10 W in many variations, used during the first period – 11–13 rare marks, later often faked – 14–15 on transfer prints between 1756–74 – 16 impressed from 1783–91 – 17 blue underglaze 1783–91 – 18 mark on a service for the Duke of Clarence, incised, after Barr became partner, 1793–1800 – 19 1793–1807 – 20 1807–13 – 21 1813–40 – 22 1788–1808 – 23 1814 – 24 printed 1814–20 – 25–26 printed from 1820–40 – 27 printed from 1840–5 – 28 printed from 1847 – 29 used generally 1852–62, when Kerr and Binns were the owners – 30–39 marks of the firm, Grainger & Co., which was taken over in 1889 – 34 very rare, by hand 1801–12 – 35–36 rare, by hand, otherwise blindstamped or printed 1812–39 – 37 from 1839 – 38 '& Co.', added from 1850 – 39 initials from 1850 – 40 mark of the Hedley Works, taken over in 1905 – 41 mark used generally today (but in use since 1862)

Worcester (2) (England). James Hadley & Sons, porcelain factory, 1896–1903.

2 printed 1900–1902 (the monogram alone 1896–7) – 3 printed 1902–1905

Worcester (3) (England). Locke & Co. Ltd. According to Godden produced porcelain from 1895–1904. Taken over by the Royal Worcester Porcelain Co. Ltd.

1 printed 1895–1900 – 2 printed 1900–1904

Worms, Hans, see Schlottenhof.
Worthington, Humble & Holland u.a., see Liverpool.
Wucai. Chinese term for five colour decoration, see Five colour decoration.
Wünsche, L., see Dresden (37).
Wunsiedel (Germany, Bavaria). Retsch & Cie. porcelain factory, f. 1885. Utility services and other kinds of services, vases, bowls, tins and boxes.

Wurstenfeld, A., see Münden.
Württemberg, Karl Eugen, Karl and Friedrich, Dukes of, see Ludwigsburg.
Württembergische porcelain works, C. M. Bauer & Pfeiffer, see Schorndorf.
Würzburg (Germany, Lower Frankonia). In 1775, Johann Caspar Geyger, a Councillor of the Clergy, was granted permission by the Archbishop of Würzburg, Adam Friedrich von Seinsheim, to establish a faience and porcelain factory. He produced services in the rococo taste as well as in the style of Louis XIV. H. Tünnich was employed as decorator. Carmine red monochrome decoration was particularly favoured. Some services in the Empire style, with views of Würzburg and the mark 'W.B.' in black, are known. Friedrich Thomin, an independent Würzburg decorator, painted porcelain from this factory in the early 19th c. At certain times the Bishop's Mitre has been ascribed as the mark of Würzburg, but it is more likely to be the mark of the Ellwangen factory.

C · G
W

Xanten (Germany, Rhine). Hehl, J., porcelain decorator, c. 1930.

Xrowet, also Xhrouet (b. 1736), see Rose pompadour.

Yao. Chinese term for porcelain. Literally it means 'kiln', as well as 'something fired'. Translated simply it means 'pottery'.
York (England). Haigh Hirstwood, one of the most skilled flower and insect painters at Rockingham, managed a porcelain decorating workshop here from 1838–50. The porcelain was bought from Sampson and Bridgwood in Longton and was delicately and carefully decorated.
Yussupoff, Prince Nicolaus. Director of the Imperial Porcelain Factory in St. Petersburg from 1792–1802. Owner of the Archangelskoje porcelain factory from 1814–31. See Petersburg (1).

Zächenberger, Josef (1732–1802). Decorator from Munich. He joined the staff of the Neudeck porcelain factory and was active there (until 1760) as first flower painter and teacher of flower decorating. He also painted historic scenes and landscapes. He died in Munich in 1802.
Zajecar (Yugoslavia). Zajecar porcelain factory.
Zasche, Josef, see Vienna (20).
Zdekauer, Moritz (now: Altrohlauer porcelain factory AG), see Altrohlau (1).
Zechinger, Johannes, decorator, see Zeschinger, J.
Zeh, Scherzer & Co., see Rehau (1).
Zehender & Grosswald, see Lichte (3).
Zehnder & Co., ceramic works, see Tirschenreuth (2).
Zeidler, Jacob, & Co., see Selb-Bahnhof.
Zeiller, Paul (1880–1935). Animal sculptor. Munich Academy. In Berlin from 1904. Produced models for the Heubach Bros., Lichte, Wallendorf, Metzler Bros. and Ortloff, Ilmenau.

Zeissig, Johann Eleazar (7 November 1737 Gr. Schönau–23 October 1806 Dresden). After prolonged activity in Paris he arrived in Dresden in 1769 and in 1773 was put in charge of the drawing school in Meissen, with special responsibility for its future development. On 20 August 1774 he obtained the

post of resident director of the decorating studios of the factory, and became the
leading artist at Meissen. He remained in this post until as late as 1796.
Zell (Germany, Baden). From 1846–67, J. F. Lenz produced porcelain here.

ZELL

Zell-Harmersbach (Germany, Baden). Georg Schmider, Vereinigte Zeller
ceramic factory, f. 1820. According to DKG 1807, it was the first stoneware
factory f. in Baden. Simple services. The manufacture of porcelain ceased in
1940.

[82] [91]

[140]

Zenari, Oscar, see Leipzig.
Zeschinger, Johann (b. 1723 Höchst). Trained in Höchst as polychrome
decorator early in his life. In 1753 he transferred to Fürstenberg, where in 1762
he became a member of the painting academy. He remained in Fürstenberg until
his death. At Höchst he may have been a well-known artist because he signed all
his pieces with his own name.

⊕ *Zeschinger·*

Zeven (Germany, Hannover), C. & E. Carstens, porcelain decorating studio.
Closed c. 1930

Zichy, Desider, see Varoslöd.
Zichy, Dominicus, see Varoslöd.
Zirnfeld, see Anreiter von Zirnfeld, J. K. W.
Znaim (Bohemia, today Znojmo). Ditmar-Urbach AG, porcelain factories, see
also Turn (1).

Zoude, Louis, see Saint-Gervais.

Zsolnay'svhe ceramic factories, see Pécs.

Zügel, Willi (1876–1956). Animal sculptor. Son of Heinrich von Zügel. Munich Academy. From 1903 he sculpted porcelain models for Nymphenburg, Meissen and Rosenthal, Selb.

Zurich (Switzerland). In 1763 a porcelain and faience factory was f. (as a joint stock company), in Schonen nr. Bendlikon on Lake Zurich. Amongst others, the well-known painter and poet, Salomon Gessner, was a member. The director was Adam Spengler from Schaffhausen. Although every effort was made to ensure standards of high quality, sales did not meet the output. In 1793 Matthias Nehracher became the director of the factory and after his death the new owner was the President of the company, Hans Jakob Nägeli; he favoured the production of faiences and stoneware exclusively. It is assumed that the kaolin for the porcelain production came from Lothringen. During the factory's most successful period the porcelain had a yellowish tone. Salomon Gessner created drawings and designs and at times he decorated porcelain himself as well. Landscapes were produced by the painter Heinrich Füssli, active between 1771–81. The chief modeller was Valentin Sonnenschein who was employed during the 1780s. The services made in Zurich do not have particularly remarkable forms but their merit lies in their execution and the perfection of their decoration. According to Honey the onion pattern was used. A large table service which was produced as a gift of the Council of Zurich to the Monastery of Einsiedeln, was presented in 1775 after the successful conclusion of a lawsuit. A large part of this service is now in the Landesmuseum of Zurich (Köllmann). According to Gustav Weiss it was decorated by Daffinger and is mentioned by him in his list of *Famous Services.*

1–5 all blue underglaze in many variations – 6 signature of Salomon Gessner in purple, Zurich 1765 in gold

Zweibrücken (Palatinate), see Gutenbrunn.

Zwickau (1) (Germany, Saxony). From about 1845 Christian Fischer managed a small porcelain factory here which simultaneously used the identical mark of his factory in Pirkenhammer; see Pirkenhammer.

CF R T X
[8]

Zwickau (2) (Germany, Saxony). Karl Steubler OHG, porcelain and glass decorating studio, f. 1886. Services for restaurants, heraldic motifs for towns and families and vases. Still active in 1949. The mark was entered in the RWZ Register under No. 242259, on 9 February 1920.

Zwickau–Oberhohndorf (Germany, Saxony). See Oberhohndorf.

Zwiebelmuster (onion pattern). The most popular porcelain decoration, in blue underglaze used by the Meissen factory. The earliest examples are found in an imitation of 1728 of a Far Eastern prototype. Production only began in 1739 however (glaze and colour), and at about this time the original design was altered, and apart from a few slight changes, has remained the same. The present shape of the service has its origin in the early period. The decorating was executed by blue decorating apprentices, who were under the impression that the pomegranates were onions, which is how the name came about. The design was already being copied widely in the 18th c., abroad as well as in Switzerland and particularly in Thuringia and Bohemia. South German factories used the decoration, but the use of purple is rare. At the end of the 19th c. so many imitators were active that from 1893 Meissen marked its products with the crossed swords on the upper part of the service.

Catalogue of Porcelain Marks

The first part of this section can be used to help
identify the factory of manufacture of a piece of
marked porcelain, particularly where the first letter
of a porcelain mark does not necessarily correspond
with the first letter of the factory or place name (e.g.
one of the 'AF' marks on page 511 refers to 'Bow',
while other marks using the same initials in a
different design are to be found on pieces from
'Limoges'). To obtain more precise details about an
identified mark, or other marks used by the same
factory, the relevant entry in the comprehensive
Directory of Keywords should also be consulted.
Heraldic or monogram marks, together with other
marks without inscription and Russian marks
(arranged alphabetically according to location)
may also be traced in this section, in conjunction
with the Directory of Keywords.

A

Alcora   Alcora   Alcora   Ansbach

Ansbach   Ansbach   Couleuvre 2   Bow

Ansbach

Chantilly 1   Longton Hall   Anspach   Paris 83   Paris 83

Paris 83   Petersburg 1   Petersburg 1

Petersburg 1   Petersburg 1

Petersburg 1   Göritzmühle   Gorodnitza   Turn 5

Moscow 4   Moscow 9   Konjaschino   Lauenstein   Moscow 9

Sèvres 1

Arras

Nymphen-
burg

Fulda 1

Paris 23

Paris 23

MARQUE DE   DÉPOSÉE   FABRIQUE

Mehun-sur-Yèvre 2

Bottengruber
Si Pes: f Vienna 1730
Bottengruber

Mehun-
sur-Yèvre 2

Longton 45

London

Longton 45

Nauendorf

Paris 14

Weingarten

Kiev 1

Saou 1

Nymphen-
burg

Limoges 70

Châtres-sur-Cher

Arzberg 4

Limoges 31

Paris 1

Pesotschnaja

Oude Amstel

Oude Amstel

Armentières

Paris 1

Paris 1

Vienna 5

Berchtesgaden

Paris 35

Paris 35

Armentières

Longton 3

Longton 3

Longton 3

Longton 2

Longton 3

Hanley 5

A Dieu seul l'Honneur et à personne autre 1719

Vienna 1

A. E. KEELING

Tunstall 3

A.F. & S.

Hanley 5

Bow

Limoges 2

Limoges 24

LIMOGES A. F. FRANCE

Limoges 24

LIMOGES A.F FRANCE

Limoges 24

Valentine

Limoges 23

Morje

Elgersburg 1

A.GIRAUD & BROUSSEAU LIMOGES Made in France

Limoges 28

Schirnding

Schirnding

Fenton 11

A.H & Cº V. FRANCE

Vierzon 11

A.H & Cº V FRANCE

Paris 117

Gräfenroda 3

Aich

Aich

MARQUE
A 1,
DEPOSÉE

Paris 133

Altrohlau 5

Aich   Moscow 7   Keizer   Munich 3   Budau 1

  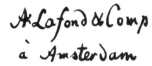

Staffelstein   Liezen   Amsterdam

Paris 120   Turn 3   Vienna 5   Turn 10

  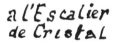

Limoges 52   Longton 12   Paris 38

Lille 2   Lille 2   Lowestoft

Paris 2

Turn 6

" Alma Japan "

Longton 25   Staffelstein   Montreuil 2

Staffelstein

Lubau

Lubau

Lidköping 1

Lidköping 1

Rosslau

Altenkunstadt

Altenkunstadt 1

Altenkunstadt 2

Altenkunstadt 1

Roschütz

Altrohlau 1

Altrohlau 1

Altrohlau 1

Altrohlau 1

Longton 5

Schönwald 2

Aich

Köppelsdorf 3

Köppelsdorf 3

Köppelsdorf 3

Montreuil 2

Frjasino

Paris 131

Kiev 1

Amberg

Paris 4

Köppelsdorf 2

Longton 51

Turn 5

Turn 5

Niever Amstel

Oude Amstel

Altrohlau 1

Limoges 81

Antᵘⁱ Anreiter VZ: 1755

Anreiter, Anton

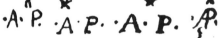

Colmar

Hegewald

Unter-
weissbach

Helsinki

Foecy 2

Hegewald

Nove

Rouen

Rouen

Rouen

Rouen

Rouen

Rouen

Rouen

Foecy 2

Paris 118

A. P. CO.

Longton 7

APOMA

Sonthofen

AR 20

Arras

Achangelskoje

Achangelskoje

A.R.

Königszelt

Münster

Dresden 36

Milan–San Cristoforo

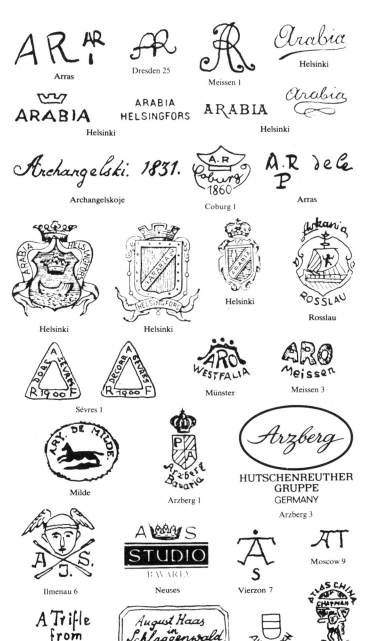

Arras

Dresden 25

Meissen 1

Helsinki

ARABIA
Helsinki

ARABIA
HELSINGFORS

ARABIA
Helsinki

Arabia
Helsinki

Archangelskoje

Coburg 1

Arras

Helsinki

Helsinki

Helsinki

Rosslau

Sèvres 1

Münster

Meissen 3

Milde

Arzberg 1

HUTSCHENREUTHER
GRUPPE
GERMANY
Arzberg 3

Ilmenau 6

Neuses

Vierzon 7

Moscow 9

A Trifle
from
LOWESTOFT
Lowestoft

Schlaggenwald 1

Vienna 3

Fenton 1

Armentières

Schlaggenwald 1

Altrohlau 1

Vienna 18

Armentières

A. & C.

Longton 1

Austria

Fischern 2

Elbogen 5

Meierhöfen 2

Elbogen

Horn

Altrohlau 1

Elbogen 5

Meierhöfen 1

Merkels-
grün 1

Paris 21

Vista Alegre

Bordeaux 4

Limoges 53

Rudolstadt
Volkstedt 5 and 8

Longton 9

Tettau 1

Novy Dwor

Longton 9

Longton 9

Aich

Acier

B

Arboras Boisette Boisette Bow Bow Longton 10

Bristol 1 Brussels 1 Brussels 1 Brussels 1

Budau 1 Korzec Paris 37 Rudolstadt Volkstedt 12 Rudolstadt Volkstedt 11 Worcester 1

Grünstadt Longton 14 Marseille 3 Baranowka Moscow 12

Satu Mare Hanley 2 Paris 11 Bristol 1 Paris 37

Mailand Milan–San Cristoforo Lettin La Seynie 1

Paris 6 Longton 26 Baranowka Baranowka

Baranowka

Poltar

Poltar

Bareuther
BAVARIA

Waldsassen 3

BARR FLIGHT & BARR
Royal Porcelain Works
WORCESTER
London House
No 1 Coventry Street
Worcester

BARNY & RIGONI

Limoges 7

BARONI NOVE

Nove

Paris 8

Paris 8

Bastien
Paris

Paris 8

Weiden 1

Weiden 1

Weiden 1

Bavaria
Kirchenlamitz

BAVARIA
Schwarzenbach 2

BAVARIA
Marktschwaben

BAVARIA
G·K·Co

Waldsassen 2

PORZELLAN.

BAVARIA
München
München 2

Bavaria
Elfenbein
Ullersricht

BAVARIA
Oberkotzau

Weissenstadt

Giesshubel 1

BAVARIA
Schwaben

Alexandri-
nenthal 2

Creidlitz 2

BAVARIA
Schauberg 3

Arzberg 4

B

Rehau 1

Planken-
hammer

Wunsiedel

Tettau 2

BAYEUX

Bayeux

Bayeux

Bayeux

BAYEUX

Bayeux

Bayeux
J.L.

Bayeux

Bayeux 1834

Bayeux

Bayswater

Bayswater

Longton 12

B B

Eichwald

B. B. W. & M.

Shelton 1

Bc   BC

Ratkowo

В.СИПЯТИНА

Moscow 12

В.Сипягина

Moscow 12

Waldsassen 3

B. C. Co.

Longton 17

Longton 17

B. D.
J

Saint-Amand-
les-Eaux 1

B D
Orleans

Orléans 1

. B· D·
υrl ea ns

BEAUGRAND
ET NoEL

Villenauxe-la-Grande 1

B 16

D P

Paris 94

BEAUGRAND
NOEL

Villenauxe-la-Grande 1

Longton 74

Longton 74

BERNARD
B/MCORE

Longton 54

Beleek

Bernon 6

Paris 9

Bernon
Rue de
l'Arbre-sec
Paris

Paris 9

Stoke on Trent 10

Bernon *JP.*
Rue de
l'Arbre sec

Paris 9

BERRY LIMOGES PORCELAINE
Le Puy

Eisenberg 1

BEST BONE Denton China ENGLAND
Longton 28

Freiwaldau 2

BEVINGTON & CO.

B.E. & Co.
Burslem 3

BIDASOA
Irún

BFB
Worcester 1

Vierzon 2

B.G.P.Co.
Cobridge 2

B.G.&W.
Burslem 3

PORCELAINE DE B H VINCENNES
Vincennes 3

BIDASOA
Irún

BIELOTYN
Bielotyn

BIELOTYN.
Bielotyn

Bielotyn 1867.
Bielotyn

B·K·
Jucht

Moscow 12

BK
Giesshubel 2

B.L
Luxemburg

BL
Saint-Ives

É. BLANCHERON
A PARIS
Paris 120

BISHOP ENGLAND
Hanley 8

B la R
Bourg-la-Reine 1

PORCELAINE VANNERIE B L LIMOGES FRANCE
Limoges 45

BLAUCHINA·DEUTSCHLAND
Schwarzenbach 2

BLEU DE LIMOGES GRAND FEU
Limoges 67

Blanchard a Paris rue des Vieux Augustins Nº 63
Paris 10

B L Leuchtenburg
Kahla 2

BLAIRS CHINA ENGLAND
Longton 14

BLAIRS CHINA
Longton 14

BLOOR DERBY
Derby 1

Luxemburg

Orléans 1

Derby 1

Derby 1

Franken-thal 1

Reichenstein

Longton 16

Vierzon 1

Vierzon 1

Bodzechów

Böttgersteinzeug

Lubau

Neurohlau

Neurohlau

Mailand 3

Paris 12

Longton 70

Longton 77

Fenton 12

Tunstall 1

Tunstall 1

Longton 38

Tunstall 1

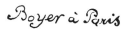

Bordeaux 1

Bordeaux 1

Orléans 1

Orléans 1

Bordeaux 2

Paris 50

Longton 20

Altrohlau 1

Epinal

BOYLE

Hanley 3

Paris 50

Paris 50

Ohrdruf 1

Ohrdruf 1

B.P. CO.LTD

Longton 15

Magdeburg-
Buckau

Longton 31

B.P.M.

Berlin 5

B.P.M.

CZECH-SLOV.

Brüx 1

BPM

BPM

Magdeburg-Buckau

B
Potter
42

Paris 120

Paris 120

Ohrdruf 1

Ohrdruf 1

Waldsassen 3

Moscow 1

Limoges 66

B . R .

Bourg-la-Reine

ВРАТЬЕВЪ
КУЗНЕЦОВЫ Ъ

Kusnetzoff 1

BRAM
MER
MALER

Dresden 3

BRAMELD

✕

Swinton

Paris 61

China
England

Westbourne

Brameld

✕

Swinton

BRC

Kronach 4

Bringeon

Paris 15

BRINGEON.

Paris 15

Bristoll

Bristol 2

Bringeon
r Vivienne

Paris 15

Bringeon
r Vivienne

BRINGEON

Paris 15

Meierhöfen 1

Bristol
Founded X in 1662
England
B

Bristol 3

BR
N

Bourg-la-Reine 1

Limoges 10

Stoke on Trent 1

Brüder Haidinger.

Elbogen 1

B.S.

Seuter

Hamburg 1

Fürstenberg

Buchau

B & B

Longton 12

B&C
FRANCE

Limoges 9

B x C.

Chantilly 2

B & CO.

Stoke on Trent 1

Stoke on Trent 1

B & C
DLV

Chantilly 2

B & D

Fischern 2

B & C°
LIMOGES
(FRANCE)

Limoges 9

B. & H.

Longton 13

B & CO
LIMOGES
FRANCE

Limoges 9

Copenhagen 2

DANISH CHINA WORKS

B & G

Copenhagen 2

MADE IN DENMARK

B & G

MADE IN
DENMARK

Danish China Works
COPENHAGEN

B.&G.

Copenhagen 2

B & S

Longton 12

B & S

Hanley 8

B. & SON

Burslem 1

Merkelsgrün 2

Buchau

Budapest 3

Longton 72

Shelton 1

CAULDON CHINA
ENGLAND

Shelton 1

LIMOGES
B & Cie
FRANCE

Limoges 3

Bayeux

Shelton 1

B. W. M. & CO.

Shelton 1

B.W.& Co.

Burslem 3

B. W. M.

Shelton 1

BW

Turn 11

Bayeux

BX

Bayeux

Bayeux

B X

Bristol 2

C

Caugley   Chodau 1   Orléans   Moscow 11   Paris 98   Chodziez

Cmielow   Sèvres 1   Derby 1   Worcester 1   C.З.К.Б   Б   Petersburg 2

Moscow 11   Chodziez   Cmielow   Uhlstädt   Clair

Arzberg 3   CAEN   Caen   caen   Caen

Frankenthal 1   Caen   CAMBRIDGE   CAOLINITE RICHARD-GINORI

Limoges 1   Ilmenau 3   Longton 6   Mitterteich 1   Milan–San Cristoforo

CARA CHINA   Carl Knoll CARLSBAD   Carolus Ferdinandus de Wolfsbourg, et Walsdorf; Eques Silesice Igne confecit 1733.

Longton 18   Fischern 1   Wolfsburg

Carl Knoll Tischern in Carlsbad   Fischern 1

Fischern 1   CARLSBAD fine PORCELAIN MADE IN CZECHO-SLOVAKIA   CARLSBAD AK CO AUSTRIA

Carlton Ware MADE IN ENGLAND "TRADE MARK"   Stoke on Trent 12

Carlsbad 3   Fischern 1

Stoke on Trent 12

Paris 98

C. A. & SONS

Longton 4

CAULDON ENGLAND

Shelton 1

CAULDON ENGLAND

Shelton 1

Uhlstädt

САФРОНОВА
2
C

Moscow 11

САФРОНОВА
C

Brancas

CB No.7

Fenton 2

Longton 20

CB 376

Fenton 2

C B

Milan 1

C.B DALE

Coalport

CBD

Coalport

C B L

Longton 20

CB&C V FRANCE

Vierzon 3

CBCie FRANCE

Vierzon 4

Buen Retiro

Buen Retiro

Buen Retiro

Niderviller

Niderviller

Niderviller

Niderviller

Schorndorf

Ludwigsburg 1

COPELAND

COPELAND

Stoke on Trent 11

Passau 3

Ludwigsburg 1

Ludwigsburg 1   Niderviller   Sèvres 1   Sèvres 1   Sèvres 1

Sèvres 1   Lidköping 2   Niderviller   Swinton   Limoges 31   Bock-Wallendorf   Shelton 1

Limoges 31   Limoges 31   Limoges 31   Coalport   Coalport

Schwabach   Sonneberg   Fontainebleau 2   Limoges 31

Hanley 7   Pirkenhammer   Pirkenhammer   Zwickau 1   Milan–San Cristoforo

Wolfsburg   Limoges 34   Limoges 34   Nauen

Kühnel   Lindemann   Creidlitz 1

Würzburg   Paris 18   Paris 18

Chamberlain & Co, Worcester

Worcester 1   Paris 18   Manises

Worcester 1

Chamberlain's
Worcester
& 63, Piccadilly,
London

Worcester 1

CHAMBERLAIN & CO
WORCESTER
155 NEW BOND STREET
& NO 1
COVENTRY ST
LONDON

Worcester 1

Chamberlains
Worcester
& 155
New Bond Street,
London

CHAMBERLAINS

Chamberlain's

Worcester 1

Chamberlains
Regent China
Worcester
& 155
New Bond Street,
London.

Worcester 1

Worcester 1

CHANTILLY.

Chantilly 2

Chantilly

Chantilly 2

chantilly

Chantilly 1

Chantilly

Chantilly 1

chantilly

Chantilly 1

Chantilly Pge

Chantilly 2

Chapelet

Bourg-la-Reine

Chapelet

Bourg-la-Reine

Chapelle/Maillard
paris.

Paris 27

Chapelle
19 Bᵈ des Italiens
medaille Expn 1864

Paris 27

chapperon

Paris 20

Chapperon à Paris

Paris 20

Hanley 1

CharlesFerdinand de
Wolfsbourg et Hallsdorf Eques
fecit 1732

Wolfsburg

CHATEAU
DE
St CLOUD

Sèvres 1

C.H
DREUX

Sèvres 1

chatillon
Chantillon

CHEOPS
LIMOGES
Limoges 9

Tournay

Chelsea 1

Limoges 34

Longton 38

Rosslau

Sarreguemines

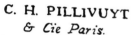
Sorau 1

Choisy-le-Roy 1

Paris 25

C. H. MENARD
Paris
72 Rue de Popincourt.
Paris 25

Chodau 1

Chodau 1

C. H. PILLIVUYT
& Cie Paris.
PARIS. FOECY. MEHUN.
Foecy 2

Mühlgraben

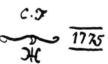
Buen Retiro

Canneto

C1 .
Swinton

C K
Kusnetzoff

Fischern 1

Fischern 1

C K W
Waldenburg 2

Waldenburg 2

Longton 26

CKW
Thuringia
Rudolstadt 23

Limoges 81

Rudolstadt
Volkstedt 23

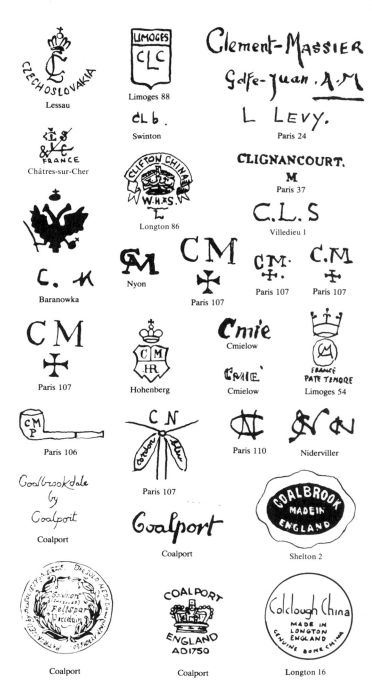

Lessau

Limoges 88

Clement-Massier

Golfe-Juan . A.M

L Levy.

Paris 24

Swinton

Châtres-sur-Cher

CLIGNANCOURT.
M
Paris 37

C.L.S
Villedieu 1

Longton 86

Baranowka

Nyon

Paris 107

Paris 107

Paris 107

Paris 107

Hohenberg

Cmielow

Cmielow

FRANCE
PATE TENDRE
Limoges 54

Paris 106

Paris 107

Paris 110

Niderviller

Coalport

Coalport

Shelton 2

Coalport

Coalport

Longton 16

BONE CHINA
A 8

Colclough

MADE IN ENGLAND
A PRODUCT OF
RIDGWAY POTTERIES LTD

Longton 16

Longton 16

Colclough
GENUINE
BONE CHINA
MADE IN ENGLAND

Longton 16

Colditz

Longton 24

Longton 23

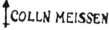

COLLN MEISSEN

Meissen

Colmar

Colmar

Combes
Queen St
Bristol

Bristol

COOKE & HULSE

Longton 25

COPELAND

Stoke on Trent 11

COPELAND

Stoke on Trent 11

Stoke on Trent 11

RegNr 180288.

Stoke on Trent 11

Copeland late
Spode

COPELAND
& GARRETT

Stoke on Trent 11

Stoke on Trent 11

Stoke on Trent 11

Stoke on Trent 11

COPELAND

SPODE

ENGLAND
New Stone

Stoke on Trent 11

Stoke on Trent 11

Stoke on Trent 11

COPELAND
SPODE
ENGLAND

Stoke on Trent 11

Copeland
Stone China

Stoke on Trent 11

Stoke on Trent 11

Corona

Schwarza-Saalbahn

Paris 27

Paris 28

Paris 28

Paris 28

Valognes

Derby

Niderviller

Paris 69

Crépy-en-Valois

Colditz

Paris 69

CPP Co.

Cobridge 3

CP
&Co.

Foecy 4

CPM

Cmielow

Purtscher

CROWN

Dresden 4

Limoges 14

CR

Dux

Cremer Nippes

Köln

crepy

Crépy-en-Valois

CROWN
CLARENCE
STAFFORDSHIRE
ENGLAND

Longton 26

Fenton 5

Longton 55

Gräfenthal 3

Brüx 2

Arzberg 4

Budapest 2

Coalport

Weiden 2

Potschappel

Nymphen-
burg

Altwasser 2

Franken-
thal 1

Altwasser 2

Franken-
thal 1

Potschappel

Frankenthal 1

Frankenthal 1

Frankenthal 1

Altwasser 2

Altwasser 2

Altwasser 2

Altwasser 2

Kusnetzoff

Kusnetzoff

Kusnetzoff

Kusnetzoff

Kusnetzoff

Kusnetzoff

C. & CO.
Longton 27

C & E. LTD
"BORONIAN"
WARE
Longton 20

C & E·
Longton 20

C & E
C
C
Sorau 1

C & Q
Longton 20

CHARLIOMAIS & TANASTIER
C & P
TOULOUSE
LYON LITHOGS

CUPROLIT

C. & W. K. H.
Longton 40

Lyon

Küps 3

Kloster Veilsdorf

Kloster Veilsdorf

CWK
Waldsassen 1

Paris 152

C V
Kloster Veilsdorf

C V
Kloster Veilsdorf

C. W.
Nantgarw

C. W.
Longton 82

C V
R
Kloster Veilsdorf

C.W. LTD
ENGLAND
Longton 82

C
Charenton 2

18 57
CZECHOSLOVAKIA
Schönfeld 2

CYFFLE
A. LUNÉVILLE
S
Cyfflé

CZECHOSLOVAKIA
CARLSBAD
Meierhöfen 2

CZECHO. SLOVAKIA
Meierhöfen 2

"CZECHOSLOWAKIA"
Taschwitz

CZECHOSLOVAKIA
Grünlas

D

Dallwitz

Derby 1   Derby 1   Derby 1

1782

Damm   Höchst   Lille 1   Nyon   Paris 37

Dresden 36   Orléans   Brussels 5

Eichwald 1   Rauenstein   Rauenstein   Chelsea 2

ORIGINAL ZWIEBELMUSTER

Damm   Damm   Donaldson   Dagoty à paris — Paris 30   Armentières

Dacca

Dagoty frere — Paris 29

Stoke on Trent 10

DALWITZ

Dallwitz

Derby 1

DAISY TEA SET

Tettau 1

DAMM

Damm

DALLWITZER FABRIK FRANZ URPUS

Dallwitz

Dallwitz

DANIEL & SON
Stoke on Trent 5

Darte fières
Rue de la Roquelle
n° 90 faub. St
Antoine
a Paris

Paris 31

DARTE
FRERES
A PARIS
Paris 31

DARTE
Pal. Royal
N.° 11
Paris 31

Darte aîné a Paris
Paris 25

DASTIN
Paris 32

Copenhagen 1

Dastin rue Du... a Paris
Paris 32

Dastin
Paris 32

Longport

Longport

DAVENPORT
LONGPORT
STAFFORDSHIRE

DAVENPORT
STONE CHINA
Longport

DAVID Johnsson
BORDEAUX
Bordeaux 4

Longport

Davenport
Longport

Davenport
LONGPORT
Longport

D.B

ESTE
G
Este

DC, ó D, C, P,
Crépy-en-Valois

D
M
23
Paris 19

C

DD
Dallwitz

D. C.
Bruxelles
Brussels 5

Biela

Delft
Köppelsdorf-
Nord

"del Giglio"
Cavazzale

D Derby
Derby 1

DELPHINE
CHINA
MADE IN
ENGLAND
Longton 43

DEKOR
KERAM SILBER
BAVARIA
Marktredwitz 3

DEMEULDRE
BRUXELLES
Brussels 5

DEMEULDRE·COCHE
D. C.
BRUXELLES
14 CHAUSSEE de WAVRE 141
Brussels 5

DEMONT R.Tarrane 3 PARIS

Paris 136

Paris 136

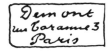

Paris 136

DEMONT R.Taranne PARIS

Paris 136

Copenhagen 1

CENMARK

Copenhagen 1

Denuelle Boulevard St Denis a Paris

Paris 120

DENUELLE Rue de Crussol a Paris

Paris 120

Déposée

Paris

Paris 39

DEP

Gross-breiten-bach 2

DEP

Lichte 2

DERBY

Derby 1

DENUELLE a PARIS

Paris 120

DERBY.

Derby 1

DERBY

Derby 1

DERBY

Derby 2

DERBY

Derby 1

de Roche Rue Coquillière N: 12 a Paris

Paris 36

Jeroche

Paris 36

T

DESPREZ

Paris 40

Deroche R.11 Rousseau Paris

Paris 36

Desarnaux à l'escalier de Cristal à paris

Paris 38

DESPREZ Rue Des Ricollets a Daris

DESPREZ Rue ne· Recolets N° 2·a Paris

Paris 40

Lorch

Deutsches=MÄRCHENPORZELLAN
München

D.F.
D.F.
Dallwitz

D.F
Paris 47

DF
Paris 47

Deutsches Victoria Porzellan
Hof-Moschendorf

DJ
COPENHAGEN
Copenhagen 3

DIAMOND CHINA
ENGLAND
Longton 14

DIAMOND CHINA B P Co Ltd ENGLAND
Longton 31

DIAMANT
J&C
Marktredwitz 2

D: I: ANTOINE FAIT
Lunéville

DIE MARK FRAUREUTH IST EINE GARANTIE
Fraureuth 1

Dihl. DIHL
Paris 41

DIHL ET GUERHARD A PARIS.
Paris 41

Dihl
Paris 41

DILLWYN & CO, SWANSEA.
Swansea

DIPPE GERMANY
Unterköditz 2

DITMAR
Znaim

DITMAR URBACH
Znaim

DITMAR
Znaim

DITMAR URBACH Z
Turn 1

DKF
DKF
Gräfenroda 2

DK
Le Coteau

DK
Derby 1

DK P
Passau 3

Do

DONAU PORZELLAN
Vienna 16

DONOVAN 481
Donovan

t DOCCIA
Doccia

Dowbysz

Dominicus Anliczek
Auliczek

Donovan's
Irish Manufactur
Donovan

DONATH
T.
Tiefenfurth 1

DORTU & Cie

Donovan
Dublin
Donovan

DORIK
CHINA
LONGTON
Fenton 6

Donovan's Irish
Manufacture
Donovan

Dortu V&B.
Dortu

DOTTER PAT 7/80
Fischern 2

DOULTON & Co.
LIMITED
LAMBETH
Burslem 2

DOULTON
BURSLEM
Burslem 2

DOULTON
BURSLEM
ENGLAND
Burslem 2

DP
1772
Paris 94

DP
V
Berlin 6

D.P. CO.
Longton 15

DRB
LIMOGES
FRANCE
Limoges 5

DRB
LIMOGES
FRANCE
Limoges 5

Dresden
Dresden 10

DRESDEN
S
GERMANY
Dresden 33

RG
Limoges 76

Dresden
Dresden 10

Dresden
Dresden 10

Dresden
Dresden 16

K
Dresden
Germany
Dresden 16

K
Dresden
Dresden 16

DRESDEN.
Dresden 6

DRESDEN.
Dresden 6

Dresden 19

Dresden 19
Saxony

Dresden 19

Dresden 12

Dresden 21

Dresden 26
DRESDEN HANDMALEREI

Dresden 5

Dresden 5

Dresden 38
DRESDEN

Dresden 16

Dresden 16

Dresden 14
DRESDEN

Dresden 2

Potschappel

Potschappel

Longton 29

Dresden 14

Paris 47

Doat

Tata

Paris 43

Paris 45

Hirschau

Limoges 33

Limoges 18

Longton 31

Longton 31

Longton 31

Rehau 3

Paris 46

Paris 47

Paris 48

Rehau

Derby 1

Derby 1

Dux 1

Chatillon

Hanley 4

Gateshead

Marktleuthen 1

Mennecy

Mennecy

Mennecy

Mennecy

E

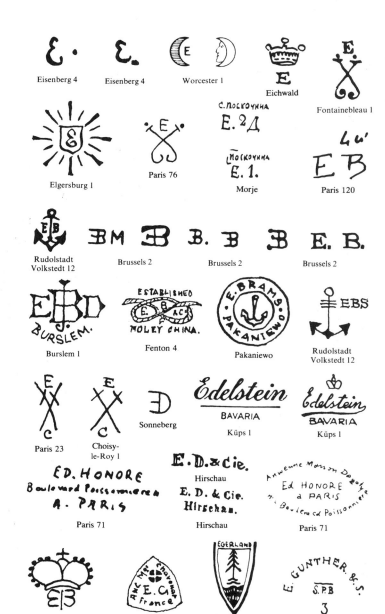

Eisenberg 4

Eisenberg 4

Worcester 1

Eichwald

Fontainebleau 1

Elgersburg 1

Paris 76

С. МОСКОVННА
E. 2 Д

МОСКОVННА
E. 1.

Morje

Paris 120

Rudolstadt
Volkstedt 12

Brussels 2

Brussels 2

Brussels 2

Brussels 2

BURSLEM.

Burslem 1

ESTABLISHED
NOLEY CHINA.

Fenton 4

E. BRAMS
PAKANIEWO

Pakaniewo

EBS

Rudolstadt
Volkstedt 12

Paris 23

Choisy-
le-Roy 1

Sonneberg

Edelstein
BAVARIA
Küps 1

Edelstein
BAVARIA
Küps 1

ED. HONORE
Boulevard Poissonnière
A. PARIS

Paris 71

E. D. & Cie.
Hirschau

E. D. & Cie.
Hirschau.

Hirschau

Ancienne Maison Dorote
Ed HONORE
à PARIS
Boulevard Poissonnier

Paris 71

Paris 23

EGERLAND

Vierzon 5

Poschetzau

E. GUNTHER & S.
S.P.B
3

St. Petersburg 3

E. Juignet Giey
Giey-sur-Aujon

St. Petersburg I

×E×H×

St. Petersburg I

EICHWALD

Eichwald

Tournay

EICHWALD

Eichwald

AUSTRIA
QUALITÄTS ERZEUGNIS
EICL
OTTENSHEIM

Ottensheim

Eirnstadt

Arnstadt 2

Eisenberg

Eisenberg 2

E J   E J

Fontainebleau 2

E. J. D. B.
Burslem 1

E. K. B.
Fenton 8

HK

Köppelsdorf 4

E
K
Krüger

Blankenhain 2

ELBOGEN
SUDETENGAU
19 39

Elbogen 7

ELGERS
ED. & CO.
BURG

Elgersburg 2

Elizabethan
FINE
BONE CHINA
BY TAYLOR&KENT
ENGLAND

Longton 76

ELITE

LIMOGES
FRANCE

Limoges 32

E.L.P.

Ettlingen

"ELSA"
GES. BESCHÜTZT

Austria

Merkelsgrün 1

"ELSA"

Austria

Merkelsgrün 1

ELTE
LIMOGES
JL
FRANCE
UNIQUE

Limoges 68

ELSTERWERKE
GERMANY

Mühlhausen

E
Made in Czechoslovakia

Eichwald

EMPIRE WARE
STOKE-ON-TRENT
A. ENGLAND 30

Stoke on Trent 7

EMPIRE WARE
E P Co.
STOKE on TRENT
ENGLAND

Stoke on Trent 7

EMPIRE
PORCELAIN
COMPANY
Staffordshire
England

Stoke on Trent 7

Emilczyn
1849

Emilczyn

'Eng. Cremer u. Sohn
in Cöln a. R.'

Cologne 2

Longton 44

Longton 78

Coalport

Longton 81

ENGLAND
Fenton 6

ENGLISH Aristocrat Florals
BONE CHINA
Longton 8

Longton 82

Fenton 5

Eichwald

Bloch & Co
EICHWALD
Czechoslovakia
Eichwald

Rudolstadt
Volkstedt 6

Rudolstadt Volkstedt 6

Stoke on Trent 7

Elbogen 1

Elbogen 1

Pirkenhammer

Elbogen 1

Elbogen 1

Pirkenhammer

Dallwitz

Dallwitz

Dallwitz

Altrohlau 4

Altrohlau 4

Altrohlau 4

Altrohlau 4

Tillowitz 2

Erbendorf 2

Mäffersdorf

Suhl

Erbendorf 1

Suhl

Suhl

Eſchenbach

Eschenbach

Windischeschenbach

ESTE

Este

Est 1792

RIDGWAY

Shelton 1

E. St.

Tellwitz

ESTABLISHED

18 R & S 50

L

FOLEY CHINA

Fenton 3

ESTABLISHED

FOLEY CHINA.

Fenton 3

E T

Meissen 2

Meissen 2

E.& B.
L.

Longton 30

Etiolles 9 1770
D. Pellevé
P

Etiolles

Etiolles
1768
Pellevé

Etiolles

E&G
L.

Lauscha

Ed Demeuldre S.T.R.C.

1833

Manufacture de Bruselles

Brussels 5

W

Windischeschenbach

W
U

Eythra

EW

Wahliss.

Turn 10

DEPOSE

EW

Turn 10

EXCELSIOR

GERMANY

Stadtlengsfeld

F

Fürstenberg Fürstenberg Fraureuth 1 Ludwigsburg 1

Frauenthal

Florence 1 Florence 1 Florence 1 Paris 50

Freiberg 2 Fürstenberg Paris 50 Limoges 2 Meissen 1

Limoges 2 Valentine Alcora

Vista Alegre

Brussels 4 Brussels 4

Nove

Moscow 12 Selb

Lorient Vista Alegre

Elgersburg 1

Fabrique de Wsevolojskoÿ
Moscow 12

fait par Lebrun à Lille
Lille 2

FAV DE BRETEUIL
Sèvres 1

FB
Grünstadt

F·B
Nymphenburg

FBB
Worcester 1

FAS
Moabit

F. C.
Longton 19

F. C. & CO.
Longton 19

F cozzi 1780
Venedig 2

F Barasze
Barasze

FD
Armentières

F X D
Choisy-le-Roy 1

F VIENNA D Austria
Vienna 6

F. D. HONORÉ à Paris.
Paris 71

FELSPATH PORCELAINE L M q L
Creil

FE
Budapest 1

Felda China AG Germany
Stadtlengsfeld

FELDA RHON
Stadtlengsfeld

FELSPAR 1803 Blue M PORCELAIN
Moscow 4

FENTONIA WARE HG ENGLAND
Fenton 11

FENIX
Barcelona 1

FERMANAGH POTTERY
Beleek

Ferdind Brunin rue de la Paix. No 18
Paris 16

FESCODA
Gijon

Feuillet rue de la Paix - No 20
Paris 50

Ferriere. a Paris
Paris 49

F. F.
Treviso 1

Feuillet.
Paris 50

Feuillet.

B N N
Paris 50

F F
Freienorla

F.F.
D.
Dallwitz

F.F.
Treviso 1799
Treviso 1

Grossbreitenbach 2

Fulda 1

Fürstenberg

F.G.
Buen Retiro

Rudolstadt
Volkstedt 5

F · G
8
Charenton–
Saint-Maurice

F.G.
St. Petersburg 3

F.G.
Vienna 8

F.G
Bodenbach

F · G
18
Charenton–
Saint-Maurice

F.G.
Charenton–
Saint-Maurice

FINE BONE CHINA
CROWN
ESTD 1801
STAFFORDSHIRE
MADE IN
ENGLAND
Fenton 4

T. J Ferner pinx
Ferner

F.H.
S.
Osnabrück 2

Filigrette
Katzhütte

FISCHER EMIL
CSASZ. BUDAPEST KIR. UDVARI SZALL.
PORCELLANGYAR
Budapest 1

FISCHER MILB BUDAPEST
Budapest 1

Fischer & Mieg
Pirkenhammer

Fischer-Vilmos
Kolozsvárt
Kolozsvar

Fischer M. A.
fia Károly
Tatán
Tata

Fischer Vilmos
Kolozsvár
Kolozsvar

K
Klösterle 1

F X K
Z
Oberhohndorf

F X K
I
Oberhohndorf

F X K
Z
Oberhohndorf

F K
O Z

F K
Z
Kaestner.
Saxonia

FL

Budau 1

FLEURY.
Paris. Rue Faubourg St. Denis
M. Flamen Fleury.

Paris 51

Flamen
Fleury
a Paris

Paris 51

FLEURY

Paris 51

Fleury

Paris 51

Paris 51

Flight

Worcester

Flight & Barr

Worcester 1

Flight

Worcester 1

Flight Barr & Barr

Worcester 1

F. L. NIDERVILLE

Niderviller

F
LONGWY

Longwy

FLIGHTS

Worcester 1

FLORAL
PRODUCTIONS
BONE CHINA
ENGLAND

Newcastle

Vienna 14

Köppelsdorf 3

LIMOGES

Limoges 63

J. L. S.
A Rotterdam
W. M.: 1812

Rotterdam

Altrohlau 6

1755

F. M.
Bäyreuth
1744
n° 24

Metzsch

BONN

Bonn 1

BONN
FRANZ ANT. MEHLEM

Bonn 1

Limoges 50

PORCELAINE ARTISTIQUE
F. M.
LIMOGES
FRANCE

Limoges 50

MADE IN
F. LIMOGES M
FRANCE

Limoges 50

FOLEY
ENGLISH BONE CHINA
PAINTED BY HAND

Fenton 3

FOLEY CHINA
F B & Co
MADE IN ENGLAND

Fenton 3

F. M. HONORÉ.

Paris 71

Fontaine F. 1770

Limoges 31

FOLEY ART CHINA
PEACOCK
POTTERY

Fenton 3

Ilmenau 1

FÖRSTER

Vienna 7

Vienna 7

FÖRSTER
Vienna 7

Fenton 3
FOLEY BONE CHINA
18 50

FORESTER'S
Longton 32

PONTE BASSO
TREVISO
Treviso 1

FORTUNA
EISENBERG
Eisenberg 4

FOROS CHINA
F&P
FORD & POINTON
ENGLAND
Hanley 11

E. L.
&
Kloster Vessra
Kloster Vessra

P
Gotha 3

FP
Pressig

E.P.C
Cmielow

F.P.C.
Cmielow

FP
K
Kaltenhofen

FPM
Freiwaldau 1

F. P. M. D. D.
NOVI SAD
Novisad

FP
Nd. Salzbrunn
Niedersalzbrunn 1

FR
Marseille 1

R
Naples

FRAC

R
Ludwigsburg 1

R
Ludwigsburg 1

R
Ludwigsburg 1

1763 R 1913
Berlin 3

RANC
Vierzon 6

FRANCE
Charles Bonnefeld
LIMOGES
Limoges 1

FRANCE
DÉPOSÉ
Limoges 1

A. LANTERNIER & Cº
FRANCE
LIMOGES.
Limoges 52

FRANK HAVILAND
LIMOGES
Limoges 36

FRANK HAVILAND
L B S
LIMOGES
Limoges 36

Franciscus Ferdi: Mayer Pinxit.
d. 15. Juny 1752.
Mayer

R
Ludwigsburg 2

R
WPM
Schorndorf

Kolozsvar

Frankenthal 2

Bonn 1

Dresden 28

handgemalt

Fraureuth 1

Freiburg 1

Villedieu 2

Villedieu 2

F.R.G.

LIMOGES
FR.INCE

Limoges 25

Friedrichsburg

Coburg 1

Mannheim 3

Herend

Pilsen

Aachen 2

Schorndorf

Bock-
Wallendorf

F.S.
P.

Lochotin

Neuilly

Fürsten

LIMOGES
F & F
FRANCE
Saint-Yrieix 1

F & M 6

Pirkenhammer

F & R

Pirkenhammer

Pirkenhammer

Bock-Wallendorf

Pirkenhammer

F & R

Pirkenhammer

Pirkenhammer

F & U
Dallwitz

FURGA

Canneto

FURGA

Canneto

F W
Moscow 12

F.VA
1865.

Vista Alegre

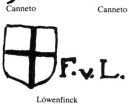

Löwenfinck

Frankenthal 2

Höchst

G

Bow　　Bow　　Paris 64　　Doccia　　Gera　　Gera　　Gera

Gehren　　Gotha 1　　Giesshüber 2　　Gräfenthal 1

Gotha 1

Giesshüber 2

Berlin 2　　Doccia　　Gotha 1　　Gross-breitenbach 1　　Moscow 4

Moscow 4　　Moscow 4　　Moscow 4

Moscow 4　　Gotha 1　　Geiersthal　　Tournay

Gehren

Paris 41

G.A.F.F.
Treviso.
Treviso 1　　Paris 41　　Paris 41　　Paris 41

Gailliard
passage de
l'opera.
Paris 53　　Limoges 75　　Gambier
Paris 54

Gaugain

Paris 56

G BAYEUX

Bayeux

GB NOVE

Nove

G. Beck auf der Porcelain Fabrik zu Blankenhain

Blankenhain

FABRIK G.B. GRÜNSTADT

Grünstadt

G B

Grünstadt

G BOYER & LIMOGES C

Limoges 63

G BK

Giesshübel 2

G.B. BREVETE PARIS

Paris 61

G B BREVETE PARIS

Paris 61

GCL 1758

Nymphen-
burg

GDA LIMOGES

Limoges 69

CEC

Katowice-
Bogucice

GDa FRANCE

Limoges 69

GD & C° LIMOGES

Limoges 19

BAVARIA

Erkersreuth

GDa FRANCE

Limoges 69

GDV BRUERE

Bruère-
Allichamps

GEBRÜDER HAIDINGER 1868 G ELBOGEN

Elbogen 1

GEBRUDER HAIDINGER ELBOGEN IN BÖHMEN

Elbogen 1

Gefle

Gävle

GEFLE-PORSLIN

Gävle

Gegr. 1817

Plaue

GEMMA

Altrohlau 3

GEORGU PAPAULT

Limoges 60

GERMANY

Rudolstadt
Volkstedt 20

Genève

Nyon

George Grainger Royal China Works Worcester

Worcester 1

PORCELAINE DURE
Georges Boyer
LIMOGES-FRANCE
Limoges 63

Zell-Hamersbach

Gera

Gérard à Paris
Paris 57

Marktleuthen 1

Germany
Kolmar

Germany
Krüger
Blankenhain 2

GERMANY
Schweig
Weisswasser

GERMANY
Rehau 1

GEROLD & CO. TETTAU
BAVARIA
Tettau 2

Gerona
Gerona

GESCHÜTZT
Elbogen 4

Desvres

Milan–San Cristoforo

Tunstall 2

G.F. B.B.T.
G.F.B.
Tunstall 2

G. F. B.
Tunstall 2

Gräfenthal–
Meernach

Oberkotzau 2

G.F.H
G.D M
Limoges 34

Paris 83

G.H.O
BAVARIA
Oberkotzau 2

Gb'
Rue Thirou
a Paris.
Paris 83

G. G. W.
Worcester 1

GHR
Warnsdorf

Lichte 2

GIEY GIEY
Giey-sur-Aujon

G & H.
MARMORZELLAN
Ilmenau 3

SCHUTZ-MARKE
Lichte 2

Giesche
Katowice-Bogucice

Gräfenthal 1

GIN

Doccia

Katowice-Bogucice

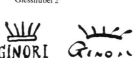

Giesshübel 2

Paris 60

Doccia

GINORI

Doccia

Paris 60

GINORI

Doccia

G I

Doccia

Dresden 9

Neu-
Schmiedefeld

Selb 1

Waldsassen 2

Kronach 1

Neustadt 2

Mitterteich

Paris 85

Longton 33

Waldsassen 2

Longton 33

Longton 60

Bayreuth 3

Longton 33

Venedig 2

G. L. B. & Co.

Longton 11

GM

Lubau

Eulau

Limoges 55

Widin

Widin

G. Nemmert
Frankenthal 1

Goebel
Oeslau 2

Goldscheider
Hanley 7

GOLDSCHEIDER
PORZELLAN
Vienna 8

Goldscheider
Wien
Vienna 8

Gonord
t. Richelieu 33
Paris
Paris 62

Gonord
Paris 62

GOSS
20
Stoke on Trent 8

GOSSE
Rue 33 Rousseau
A PARIS
Paris 36

GOSSE
A PARIS
Paris 36

GOSSE
Bayeux
Bayeux

GOSSE
BAYEUX
Bayeux

GOSSE
BAYEUX
Bayeux

GOTHA
Gotha 1

PORZELLAN MANUFACTUR
GOTHA
Gotha 1

Gotha.
Gotha 1

Gotha.
Gotha 1

pfeffer porzellan gotha

PG
Turin 1

GP
Unterm-
haus

G. P. & CO.
Longton 53

G
pontenx
Pontenx

GR
Turin 1

G. R. G. R. GR
Milan–San Cristoforo

Gräfenroda
C G
Gräfenroda 1

CK
Gräf Krippner
SELB-BAVARIA
Selb 1

Gröf Krippner
SELB-BAVARIA
Selb 1

ABJ
CRAFTON
CHINA
MADE IN
ENGLAND
Longton 45

Unterglasur
Handmalerei
Gräfenroda
Gräfenroda 3

GRAINGER, WOOD & CO.
WORCESTER

GRAINGER

GRAINGER, LEE & CO.
WORCESTER

GRAINGER & CO.
WORCESTER

Worcester 1

Worcester 1

Grainger Lee & Co
Worcester

Worcester 1

GRAINGER
& CO

Worcester 1

Longton 78

GR D

Milan–San Cristoforo

Fenton 5

Greiner
1768 X λ

Rudolstadt Volkstedt 1

G R et Cie

Limoges 31

G R et Cie

Limoges 31

G.RICHARD & C.

Milan–San Cristoforo

G.RICHARD SON
BARONA

Milan–San Cristoforo

Milan–San Cristoforo

GRIFFIN
Longton 87

GROSVENOR CHINA
ENGLAND
Longton 44

G-S

Dresden 8

G
S

Köppelsdorf-
Nord

6
H
S

Hütten-
steinach

G.S.
ZELL
BADEN

Zell-
Harmersbach

S

Zell-
Harmersbach

G. & Co.
W.

Worcester 1

Longton 34

G. & C. J. M.

Lane Delph

G & H

Longton 22

Paris 65

GUERHARD
ET DIHL
A PARIS

Paris 41

G.&.H.
J.

Ilmenau 3

Ladowitz 1

L Suignet. GIEy.

Giey-sur-Aujon

Gustavsberg 1

Gustavsberg 1

Gustavsberg 1

Gustavsberg 1

GUSTAVSBERGS-
blommor

Gustavsberg 1

GULDSTJÄRNA

Gustavsberg 1

LANDSKAP

Gustavsberg 1

IVORY BONE CHINA
SWEDEN

Gustavsberg 1

G. & W.

Burslem 3

SAGA / Stigl

Gustavsberg 1

G V
D

Paris 66

Oeslau 2

G. VOLPATO ROMA

Rome 2

G. W. & S.

Longton 84

Oeslau 2

G. W.

Longton 84

G.W. & SONS

Longton 84

G Z S
ELL

Zell-Harmersbach

H

Altrohlau 1

Hüttensteinach

Köppelsdorf-Nord

Köppelsdorf-Nord   Katzhütte

Lichte 2   Moscow 8   Morje   Paris 69   Köppels-dorf 2 and 4   Strasbourg 1

Strasbourg 1   Hausen   Fenton 10   Hermannsdorfer   Pössneck 2

Dresden 12   Ilmenau 1   Aachen 1   Granesau

Dresden 11   Altrohlau 1   Copenhagen 8   Haas & Čžjžek in Schlaggenwald

Schlaggenwald 1

St. Petersburg 2   Vierzon 11   Hackefors   Worcester 2

Worcester 2   Haidinger — Elbogen 2   Haindorf 2   Haindorf 1

Paris 68   Naestved

Longton 38

Longton 38

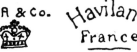
INLAY COLOURS
Westbourne

Elbogen 5

HARDMUTH
Budweis 1

H R & Co.

Longton 39

Limoges 35

DÉCORÈ PAR

Limoges 35

Limoges 38

Limoges 35

Limoges 38

Limoges 38

Kelster-
bach

Grossbreitenbach 2

Lettin

H·C.
Kassel

Neustadt

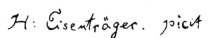
Selb 2

Clio

Kelster-
bach

Kelsterbach

H. DANIEL & SONS
H. & R. DANIEL
Stoke on Trent 5

Meinrich Maag.
Haag

Lettin

Heatherley
FINE BONE CHINA
ENGLAND
Chessington

Rudolstadt Volkstedt 15

HELIOS
ULLERSRICHT
Ullersricht

H: Eisenträger. pixit
1785.
Eisenträger

1777
1977
Ilmenau 1

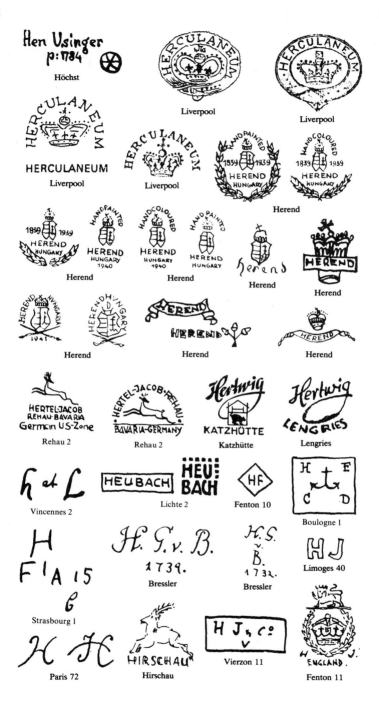

Hen Usinger p:1784
Höchst

Liverpool

Liverpool

HERCULANEUM
Liverpool

Liverpool

Herend

Herend

Herend

Herend

Herend

Herend

Herend

Herend

Herend

Herend

HERTEL-JACOB REHAU-BAVARIA Germain US-Zone
Rehau 2

Rehau 2

KATZHÜTTE
Katzhütte

Lengries

Vincennes 2

HEUBACH
Lichte 2

Fenton 10

Boulogne 1

H
F A 15
G
Strasbourg 1

Bressler

Bressler

Limoges 40

Paris 72

HIRSCHAU
Hirschau

Vierzon 11

ENGLAND
Fenton 11

Longton 23

Longton 23

H. J. C.
L.
Longton 23

Worcester 2

Emden

Rehau 2

Pirkenhammer

Klösterle 1

Landstuhl 1

Vincennes 2

Vaux

Vincennes 2

Longton 43

Lidköping 2

HÖCHST
Frankfurt 2

Tiefenfurt 2

Osnabrück 1

HOLLOHAZA
Hollaházá

Ludwigsburg 3

HOLM
1780
Holmskjöld

HORNBERG
Hornberg

Horo
Gorodnitza

Handpainted
Made in Ungaria
1851
Holloházá

Gorodnitza

Housel
Paris 84

houzel
Paris 84

Moscow 8

Burg-
steinfurt

Hohenberg

Hohenberg

Lubenz 1

Lubenz 1

Saalfeld

Freiwaldau 1

Lane End 1

Duljewo

H & C
Chodau 1

H & A
Longton 3

H&B
Longton 42

Selb 6

CORONADO
H & C
Schlaggenwald 1

H&C CHODAU
Chodau 1

Chodau 1

Schlaggenwald 1

1792
Schlaggenwald 1

Schlaggenwald 1

Rehau 2

H.&.Co BAVARIA
Selb 2

H&Co SELB BAVARIA
Selb 2

H&Co SELB BAVARIA GERMANY
Selb 2

H&Co Selb
Selb 2

H&Co Selb
Selb 2

Selb 2

H&C
Selb 2

H. & CO.
Longton 22

H & CO CHINA
Longton 38

Made in Czechoslovakia
Granesau

H&Co L FRANCE
Limoges 35

H&Co L
Limoges 35

H&Co L
Limoges 35

H&Co
Limoges 35

Hübel in Prag
Prag

Hübel in Prag
Prag

HÜTTL PORCELLÁN GYÁRA BUDAPESTEN
Budapest 3

HÜTTL TIVADAR MŰFESTÉSZETE BUDAPESTEN
Budapest 3

HÜTTL TIVADAR
Budapesten Dovottya

Budapest 3

HÜTTL·TIVADAR
BUDAPEST

Hüttl Tivador
Budapest.

Budapest 3

H&G
SELB
BAVARIA
GERMANY
Heinrich

Selb 2

HÜTTL
BUDAPEST

Budapest 3

H. & G.
LATE HARVEY

Longton 40

HUGHES
LONGPORT
MADE IN ENGLAND

Burslem 4

H U M

Meuselwitz

Hünger. F.

Hunger

P
H M M

Meuselwitz

H & P L
V

Vierzon 11

H&R DANIEL

Stoke on Trent 5

Unterweissbach

H&S

Lane End 1

H&S
3

Lane End 1

H&S
N.4

Lane End 1

H&S

Lane End 1

CM
HUTSCHENREUTHER
ARZBERG
BAVARIA · GERMANY

Arzberg 3

18 CM 14
HUTSCHENREUTHER
HOHENBERG

Hohenberg

HUTSCHENREUTHER
ARZBERG
BAVARIA
Germany

Arzberg 3

1814 CM 1914.
Hutschenreuther
Hohenberg

Hohenberg

HUTSCHENREUTHER
ALTROHLAU
HABSBURG
PORCELAIN

Altrohlau 1

1814 CM 1914.
HR
Hutschenreuther
Hohenberg
Bayern
Abteilung Dresden
Handmalerei.

Hohenberg

HUTSCHENREUTHER MANUFAKTUR
1814
HUTSCHENREUTHER
GERMANY
Handgemalt
SELB

Selb 4

Hutschenreuther
Arzberg
Bavaria

Arzberg 3

Hohenberg

Hohenberg

Hohenberg

Hohenberg

Hohenberg

Selb 7

HUTSCHENREUTHER
GERMANY
Selb 4

H
VG 527
5

Strasbourg 1

Schaala 2

HW
ML
BAVARIA
Marktleuthen 2

HX   HX
Kusjaeff

I

Ilmenau 1

Lisbon 1

Nymphenburg

Aufenwerth

Bottengruber

Bottengruber

Bottengruber

Bottengruber

St. Petersburg 1

St. Petersburg 1

Venedig 2

Hannong III

St. Petersburg 1

Schelten

Fulda

Ilmenau 1

Ilmenau 1

Fischern

Turn 5

Schlackenwerth

Shelton 1

Ilmenau 1

Shelton 1

Klausenburg 3

Klausenburg 3

IRIS

Lidköping 2

AUSTRIA
Turn 7

ISIGNY
ISIGNY
Isigny

Isigny

Isigny

ITALY
New Stone
G. RICHARD & C.

Milan–San Cristoforo

1925

Bronnitzi

Höchst

Höchst

J

J

Ilmenau 1

Fontainebleau 2

LIMOGES
J · A

Limoges 31

Longton 44

Hildesheim

Longton 44

Jacobus Helchis fecit
Helchis

Jäger

Eisenberg 2

James & Mary
Curtis
Lowestoft

Lowestoft

Lille 1

Hildesheim

Vienna 4

JB

Vienna 4

JBG
L

Limoges 27

J·B & Cⁱᵉ
FRANCE

Limoges 4

Hanley 2

J C
L

Paris 26

J. C. Bayer
Bayer

JDK
Ohrdruf 2

JDK
Ohrdruf 2

Biela

Ohrdruf 2

Manises 2

J. E.
Fenton 7

JE
Ludwigshafen

Jean
Vierzon 7

JEAN HAVILAND
Limoges 37

Jeanne

J E H
F
Friedland

J. E. & Co.
Fenton 7

Paris 77

J. Earl Wendelin Anreiter vZ
Anreiter von Zirnfeld

JFL
ZELL AM HARM. ERSBACH
Zell

J. PERESCH
Klum

J. Peresch
Klum

J. G
Wien
Vienna 8

JG
Paris 60

AND SONS
CRESCENT
Stoke on Trent 9

J.G.S & Co
FOLEY BONE CHINA
ENGLAND

J.G.S & Co
ENGLAND
Longton 35

Mannhein 1

W
J: Haag
Haag

J. H. C. & CO.
Longton 27

J.H & S
Brillant
Köppelsdorf 1

J. H. W.
LONGTON
Longton 83

JHS
Köppelsdorf 1

J.H.S.
Köppelsdorf 1

F. F. Kaendler.
Kändler

JK
BAVARIA

Kronestox
Bavaria
Schwarzenbach 1

J.H & S
KÖPPELSDORF
Köppelsdorf 1

JK
Longton 46

Longton 46

Wiesau 1

Walbryzych

J. KAWAN
Vienna 10

J L
V
France
Villedieu
sur-Indre

Paris 109

Kahla 3

Altrohlau 6

J.L.
Valognes 1

Limoges 43

J.L Bayeux
Bayeux

J. Mayer
Mayer

Paris 96

J.N.M.
Schönwald 2

Klentsch 2

Limoges 39

J. Neppel
Nevers

JOAN PETR
MELCHIOR F
1768
Melchior

JOHANN HAVILAND
BAVARIA
Waldershof 1

Waldershof 1

Höroldt

Elbogen 2

Niedermeyer

Vohenstrauss

Vohenstrauss

Coalport

Gricci

Mülheim

JOHN ROSE&Cⁱᵉ
COLE BROOK DALE
1850.

Coalport

Vienna 4

Osterspei

Fontaine-
bleau 1

Paris 116

Fontainebleau 1

Fontainebleau 1

Tours 2

Paris 116

Tours 2

Ilmenau 1

Limoges 71

Limoges 71

Limoges 32

Ilmenau 1

Höchst

JEAN POUYAT
LIMOGES
Limoges 71

J.R.   J.R.B.&CO.

Limoges 71

Shelton 1

Limoges 71

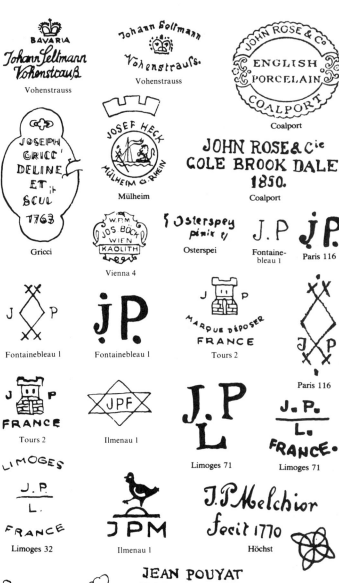

Marseille 1   Milan–San Cristoforo

Milan–San Christoforo

Milan–San Cristoforo

Milan–San Cristoforo

Shelton 1

Milan–San Cristoforo

Milan–San Cristoforo

Mitterteich 1

J. R. H
Hanley 13

Charlottenbrunn   Greising

J. S.
GERMANY

Charlottebrunn

R
BAVARIA
Mitterteich 1

J. S. & CO.
Longton 74

J. & T. B.
Hanley 1

Vohenstrauss

J. S. W.
Longton 85

J T
P
Paris
CHANÈLE
Paris 146

Bautzen

Markt-
redwitz 2

J. U. & C.
Neuhaldens-
leben 7

JULIENNE
Paris 83

JULIUS RICHARD & C
S. CRISTOFORO
Milan–San Cristoforo

Longton 44

TRADE
MARK
Longton 44

Quimper

J. W.
Nymphenburg

J. W. R.
Shelton 1

J. W
&
Co.
Selb 3

ENGLAND
J. W & S.
Fenton 15

J. Z.
Wien.
Vienna 20

J Z & Co.
Selb-Bahnhof

JZ & Cº
Selb-Bahnhof

K

Klösterle 1   Moscow 6   Klösterle 1

Küps 3

Rudolstadt
Volkstedt 16   Königsee 2   Ohrdruf 3   Ohrdruf 2

Oberhohndorf

Kahla 1   Kahla-Könitz   Kahla 1

Moscow 8

Kahla 1   Kahla-Könitz   Eisenberg 3

Kalten-
lengsfeld   Rudolstadt
Volkstedt 14   Fischern 1   Fischern 1

Czestochowa   Thuringia
Katzhütte   Moscow 6   Grossbreitenbach 1

Dresden 18   Marktredwitz 1   St. Petersburg

Vienna 11   Laveno   Vienna 16

67.

Kiev

Kiev 2   Kiev 2   Kiev 2   Kiev 2

Kiev 2   Vienna 12   Kirschner

Kiev 2   Budapest 5   Budapest 5   Vienna 1

Neuhaus 1   Klentsch 1   Klum   Chodau 1

Kusnetzoff   Köln 2   Berlin 3   Berlin 3   Kolo

Berlin 3

Königszelt   Budweis 2   Kolmar   Kolmar

Moscow 6   Korzec   Konstanz 1

St. Petersburg 4   Korzec   Korzec

Korzec
Korzec
Korzec
Korzec
Korzec

Korzec
Korzec
Korzec
Korzec

Korzec
Korzec
Korzec

Korzec
Korzec
Karlskrona
Budapest 2

Köppelsdorf 4
Scheibe-Alsbach
Eisenberg 3
Eisenberg 3

Waldenburg
Waldenburg
Waldenburg

Meissen 1
Meissen 1
Berlin 3

Berlin 3
Berlin 3
Kranichfeld
Waldenburg

Waldenburg
Waldenburg
Scheibe-Alsbach

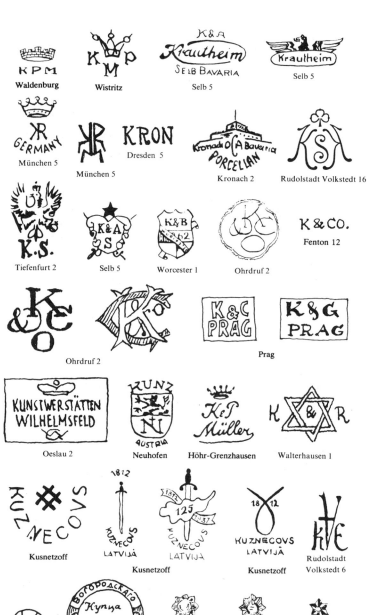

KPM
Waldenburg

Wistritz

K&A
SELB BAVARIA
Selb 5

Krautheim
Selb 5

GERMANY
München 5

München 5

KRON
Dresden 5

Kronach OC A Bavaria PORCELLAN
Kronach 2

Rudolstadt Volkstedt 16

K.S.
Tiefenfurt 2

K&A S
Selb 5

K&B
Worcester 1

Ohrdruf 2

K & CO.
Fenton 12

&KCO
Ohrdruf 2

K&C PRAG

K&G PRAG

Prag

KUNSTWERSTÄTTEN WILHELMSFELD
Oeslau 2

KUNZ NI AUSTRIA
Neuhofen

K&P Müller
Höhr-Grenzhausen

K & R
Walterhausen 1

KUZNECOVS
Kusnetzoff

1872 KUZNECOVS LATVIJA
Kusnetzoff

125 KUZNECOVS LATVIJA
Kusnetzoff

18 12 KUZNECOVS LATVIJA
Kusnetzoff

KVE
Rudolstadt Volkstedt 6

KW
Werden 1

БОГОРОДСКАГО Купца Петра Фомина
Moscow 3

КУЗНЕЦОВА
Kusnetzoff

КУЗНЕЦОВА
Kusnetzoff

И.Е. КУЗНЕЦОВА Г.Ф.
Kusnetzoff

L

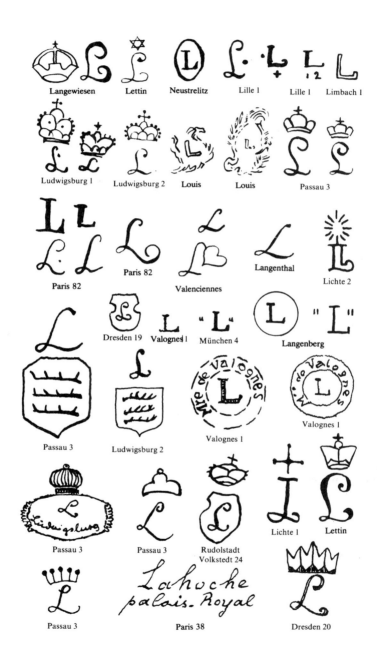

Langewiesen Lettin Neustrelitz Lille 1 Lille 1 Limbach 1

Ludwigsburg 1 Ludwigsburg 2 Louis Louis Passau 3

Paris 82

Paris 82 Paris 82 Valenciennes Langenthal Lichte 2

Dresden 19 Valognes 1 München 4 Langenberg

Passau 3 Ludwigsburg 2 Valognes 1 Valognes 1

Passau 3 Passau 3 Rudolstadt Volkstedt 24 Lichte 1 Lettin

Passau 3 Paris 38 Dresden 20

Paris 38

Paris 80

Paris 70

Paris 70

La Mehunite

Mehun-sur-Yèvre

LAMPRECT.

Vienna 1

Vierzon 10

Budapest 4

Krummennaab 2

Langenthal

Vierzon 10

Lauche

Laveno

Laveno

Lüftelberg

Limbach 1

Brancas

Brancas

Brancas

Luxemburg

Luxemburg

Luxemburg

Luxemburg

Paris 98

Paris 75

Brancas

Chantilly 2

Brancas

Orléans 1

Luxemburg

Limoges 64

Molinet

Digeon

Brussels 3

L.C.
Brussels 3

L.c
Brussels 3

*L. cretté
Brux*
Brussels 3

*L. C.
Ebenftein*
Brussels 3

*L.C
Brux*
Brussels 3

*L. cretté.
Bruxelles rue
D'Aremberg
1791*
Brussels 3

LA CÉRAMIQUE DU LIMOUSIN
LIMOGES
Limoges 41

PORCELAINE d'ART
L ⌶ D
véritable incrustation
Rodez

L. D.
D A R T E
Palais Royal
n° 21
Paris 31

LD
Paris 31

L
Bow

L DERFEULDRE COCHE
BRUXELLES
Brussels 5

Lebon - halley
Paris 68

LEADBEATER
ART
· CHINA ·
LONGTON
Longton 47

L Dubois
Limoges 40

Lefebure a paris
Paris 98

*Lafevre rue Amelot
a Paris*
Paris 98

*Le francois
à
Caen.*
Caen

LE GERRIEZ
20 R: DE LA HARPE
paris
Paris 59

Legrand
Limoges
FRANCE
Limoges 45

LE JUSTE
Breveté à Paris
Paris 86

Л 3
LENINGRAD
Leningrad

LE MiEUX
CHINA
MADE IN FRANCE
Paris 142

ZEMIRE PERE
NIDERVILLER
Niderviller

*Leplé
1ᵉ*
Paris 88

*Laplé 1ᵉ
2ue du bacq n°19 a Paris*
Paris 88

Paris 88

Paris 88

Paris 88

Paris 88

L & R
Paris 94

Lerosey
11 Rue de la paix
Paris 89

LEROSEY
11 rue de la Paix
à Paris.
Paris 125

Lerosey
7 Rue de la paix
Paris 125

l'Escalier
de Cristal
PARIS
Paris 38

Leroux rue Taranne.3
Paris 136

LETTIN
Lettin

Lettin
Lettin

Les Porcelaines d'art
MARQUE DEPOSÉE
Couleuvre 2

LEUCHTENBURG
Germany
Kahla 4

Leveillè
12
rue de Thiroux
Paris 83

LEVEILLE
12
Rue THIROUX
Paris 83

LÉVEILLÉ
12
rue Thiroux
Paris 83

LÉVEILLÉ
12
rue Thiroux
Paris 83

Le Vilain
à Paris
Paris 91

L. F.
Selb 6

L' Gardie,
a Paris
Paris 55

Lgoc
Paris 60

JR
Selb 4

L. H.
R.P.M.
Oberkassel

LIMBACH
Limbach 2

LHS
Selb 4

LILIEN
PORZELLAN
AUSTRIA
Vienna 14

Limbach 2

Limbach 2

Limbach 2

Limoges 15

Limoges 31

Limoges 16

Limoges 11

Limoges 26

Limoges 82

Limoges 52

Limoges 55

Limoges 89

Paris 137

Limoges 46

Limoges 20

Limoges 73

Limoges 79

Limoges 54

Limoges 7

Limoges 54

Limoges 73

Limoges 62

Limoges 45

Limoges 73

Limoges 70

Limoges 70

Saint-Yrieix 1

Paris 13

Limoges 29

Limoges 80

Paris 93

Linck

Küps 2

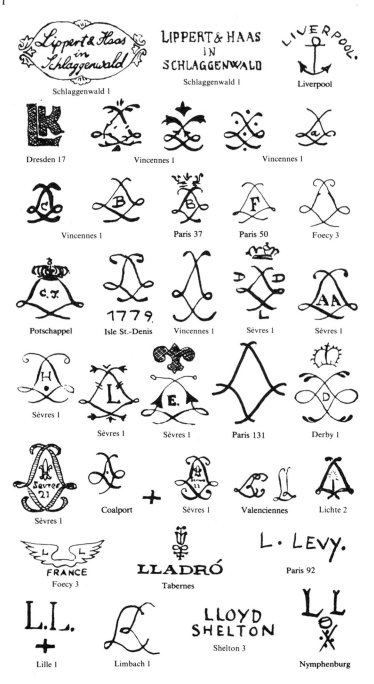

Schlaggenwald 1

LIPPERT & HAAS
IN
SCHLAGGENWALD

Schlaggenwald 1

Liverpool

Dresden 17

Vincennes 1

Vincennes 1

Vincennes 1

Paris 37

Paris 50

Foecy 3

Potschappel

Isle St.-Denis

Vincennes 1

Sèvres 1

Sèvres 1

Sèvres 1

Sèvres 1

Sèvres 1

Paris 131

Derby 1

Sèvres 1

Coalport

Sèvres 1

Valenciennes

Lichte 2

Foecy 3

LLADRÓ

Tabernes

L. LEVY.

Paris 92

Lille 1

Limbach 1

LLOYD
SHELTON

Shelton 3

Nymphenburg

PORCELAINE A FEU
L L
FOECY (FRANCE)

Foecy 3

Montreuil 1

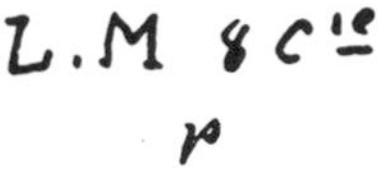

L.M & Cⁱᵉ
p

Creil

PORCELAINE TENDRE
L M a Cⁱᵉ

Creil

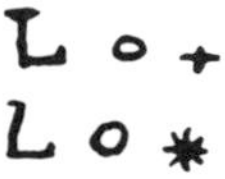

L o +
L o *

Lille 1

L M N

Paris 133

Lolim
LIMOGES FRANCE

Limoges 12

LOCKER & CO CHOCOLATE
DERBY

Derby

LOCKE & CO LTD
SHRUB HILL WORKS
WORCESTER
ENGLAND

Worcester 3

LOCKE & CO
WORCESTER
ENGLAND

Worcester 3

LOCRET
FECIT ANNO
1772

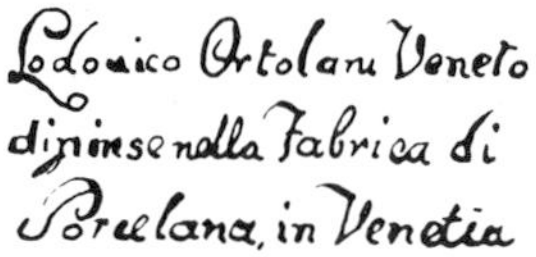

Lodovico Ortolani Veneto
dipinse nella Fabrica di
Porcelana, in Venetia

Venedig 2

IS
LONDON

Middlesborough

Paris 94

Longport

Longport

LONGPORT

Longport

L
O   S
ST KILIAN
GERMANY

Langewiesen

OSCAR SCHLEGELMILCH

Langewiesen

LOZA
ROYAL
CHINA

Vigo

R

Vincennes 2

L P

Paris 98

L.P.

L P

Paris 98

LYNGBY DANMARK

Copenhagen 3

L.P.

Vincennes 2

L P
B

Boissette

EMPIRE WORKS
STOKE ON TRENT
ENGLAND

Vierzon 10

L. P. & CO.
Hanley 8

Longton 49

Bordeaux 3

Paris 94

La Seynie 1

Vendrennes

La Seynie 1

La Seynie 1

Vierzon 16

Limoges 78

L. T.
LIMOGES
France
Limoges 68

Paris 90

Paris 90

LUBARTOW

Lubartow

Lubartow

Lubau

Dresden 37

Schorndorf

Limoges 21

Ludwigsburg 2

Schorndorf

Paris 78

Schlaggenwald 1

Luplau

L.V.LVCK
Vienna 1

L.V.
Vinovo

Poppelsdorf

Saint-Genou 2

Limoges 32

Schorndorf

Weiden 1

M

Altrohlau 1

Paris 37

Höchst

Paris 37

Paris 37

M... Paris 37

Pinxton

Sinceny

Stoke on Trent 10

Gross-breitenbach 8

Schwarza-Saalbahn

MOORE BROS. ENGLAND
Longton 54

ENGLAND BONE CHINA
M
Fenton 6

Stützerbach

Hohenberg

Oelze

SEVRES M 1880
Sèvres 3

SEVRES 1880 M A
Sèvres 3

M.
Paris 107

Dresden 22

M·M·
Chantilly 2

MA
Paris 78

MABILLE Bd des Italiens.Nº26 a Paris
Paris 95

Mäbendof
Mäbendorf

MA CHANTILLY
Chantilly 2

Mäbendorf 1882
Mäbendorf

Mäbendorf

Mada Cecho PKD Slovakia
Kaltenhofen

MADE IN HF FENTON CHINA ENGLAND
Fenton 10

MADE AT NEW CANTON 1750
Bow

MADE IN GERMANY
Brambach

MADE IN GERMANY
Taschwitz

Made KD Cecho-Slov.
Kaltenhofen

Made in Bavaria
Schauberg 2

Coalport

Helsinki

Magnus

Frankenthal 1

Longton 16

Krummennaab 3

Paris 73

MANUFACTURE
DE VALOGNES

Valognes 1

Schlottenhof

Florence

Manufacture de Foëscy
Passage Violet, No. 5.
R Poissonnière, à Paris.
Paris.   A. Cottier

Paris 5

Mengersreuth

Foecy 2

Manufacture
de S.M.L'Imperatrice
P.L DAGOTY
à Paris.

Paris 30

Manut de Foessy
Passage Violet n°5
R Poissonniere a Paris

Paris 5

MAN^{re} De PORCELAINE
DE S A R M····e
"D^{sse} de BERRY
DENUELLE
Rue deCrussol a Paris

Paris 120

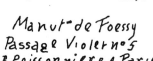

Paris 98

manufacture
du fb — St Denis
N°25   CP

Paris 69

MANUFACTURE

Langenthal

MANUFACTURE
DE VALOGNES

Valognes 1

Sèvres 1

Manufacture de J. Muihauser
Geneve
Geneva

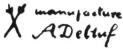

manufacture
A Delttuf

Paris 94

Sèvres 1

Sèvres

manufacture
A. Deltuf

Paris 94

Manu fre de Porcelaine
du (en Ncist)
rue des Amandiers
Dou Popincourt

Paris 109

MANUFRr
de MM
Guerhard et
Dihl a Paris

Paris 41

MANUF RE DE PORCELAINE
DU (En NAST A PARIS

Paris 109

MANUF re
DE DIHL
ET GUERHARD

Paris 41

MANUFRE
de MCRleDuc
d'angouleme
a Paris

Paris 41

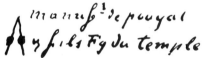

manuf de puryal
Ay fils Fg du temple

Paris 94

MAP

Paris 108

MAP

Paris 108

МАРКИ
БАРМИНА

Frjasino

Marx

Frankenthal 1

1840

Wiesau 2

MARQUE DE FABRIQUE
C.F.&P
LIMOGES

Limoges 13

Paris 84

Mauksch
Mauchsch.

Mauksch

ROYAL
Mayfair
BONE
CHINA
ENGLAND

Longton 21

MAYFLOWER

Longton 18

Mazurier
a Paris.

Paris 100

M ФB
АУНАШОВА

Moscow 2

GEBRÜDER BENEDIKT
MAYER
HÖFEN

Meierhöfen 2

Mazurier

Paris 100

MB
Marieberg

Mitterteich 3

Orléans 2

Moscow 2

MB S
Marieberg

Elgersburg 1

MC
Montreuil 2

Paris 22

M.C.КУЗНЕЦОВА
ФАБРИКИ
ТВЕР ГУБЕР.
Kusnetzoff

Kusnetzoff

Kusnetzoff

Taubenbach

Buen Retiro

La Moncloa

Buen Retiro

Poschetzau

M· de Guerhard et Dihl
Paris 41

Creil

Limoges 55

Unterköditz 2

Mehun 1

Mehun 5

Mehun 5

Kiev 2

Meissen 1

Meissen 2

Meissen 1

Meissen 2

Meissen 2

Meissen 2

Meissen 2

Höchst

Bronnitzi 1

»MELBA«
Longton 53

WARLINE WAR
ROYAL STAFFORD
BONE CHINA
MADE IN ENGLAND
EST. 1845
STARLITE
Longton 68

MELBA CHINA
ENGLAND
Longton 53

meslier.
Paris 101

MELBA BONE CHINA
MADE IN ENGLAND
Longton 53

Metzsch.
.i~49.
bayr.
Metzsch

MANUFACTURE
MESLIER AINÉ
Rue de l'Arbre sec
— Nº 37 —
de porcelaine et cristaux
Paris 101

МЕЖИГОРЬЕ
Kiev 2

МЕЖИГОРЬЕ

43
Kiev 2

MESTRE
TRE
Manises

Les ateliers de Céramiques
m f.
Sèvres
Made in France
Sèvres 2

Mf de
Guerhard
et Dihl
a Paris
Paris 41

MF
Herend

Könitz

Könitz

M G
Lubau

M.H.& co.
Longton 52

M
Gotha
Gotha 2

- *Michel* -
- A *Paris* -
Paris 103

MIDDLESBRO
POTTERY CO.
Middlesborough

MILES
Lane Delph

MINERVA
GUSTAFSBERG
Gustavsberg 1

M.Imp le.
de Sevres.
Sèvres 1

MINTON
Stoke on Trent 10

Stoke on Trent 10

Stoke on Trent 10

Stoke on Trent 10

Stoke on Trent 10

Stoke on Trent 10

Stoke on Trent 10

Stoke on Trent 10

Miskolcz

Mitterteich 1

Mitterteich 3

Mitterteich 3

Mitterteich 1

Mitterteich 3

Mitterteich 3

Schweidnitz

Schweidnitz

Paris 102

Paris 102

Paris 108

Meierhöfen 1

Paris 95

Marburg

Vierzon 9

Florence 1

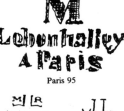

Limoges 42

Turn 4

Petersburg 1

Paris 68

M.MASON

M.MASON

Lane Delph

M^{me}Desarnaux
à l'escalier de Cristal

Paris 38

M.N^{te}
Sèvres

Sèvres 1

Paris 94

M O

Paris 98

M O

Bourg-la-Reine 1

Moitte

Moitte.

Paris 37

Ilmenau 5

Ilmenau 5

M:L

Oude Loosdrecht

M:OL.

MoL
Lm3

Oude Loosdrecht

M.ol
N°10

Oude Loosdrecht

M:ol

M:oL

Oude Loosdrecht

A

M·OL
L27

M:OL.

Oude Loosdrecht

M:o:L M:oL
87F

Oude Loosdrecht

M.O.L
*

Oude Loosdrecht

MONCLOA

Oude Loosdrecht

MONDOVI

Doccia

MONT.MERY
FRANCE

Limoges 38

MOORE

Longton 54

Monginot
loBoulevart
des Italiens

Paris 105

Monginot
boulevard des italiens
N° 20 a. paris

Paris 105

**MOORE
MOORE BROS**

ENGLAND
Longton 54

Longton 54

MOSA
MAASTRICHT
(FABRIEKSMERK)
Maastricht

Mosanic.
Mitterteich 2

Mouchard Angoulême f.ᵉᵉ

à S.ᵗᵉ Maastru

Angoulême

Le 23 aout 181

MOSANIC
Mitterteich 2

Etiolles

MP
Etiolles

Etiolles

Limoges 69

Maastricht

MPM
MPM

Plaue

Plombières

M R
Limoges 30

LIMOGES
Limoges 73

M.R.Cie
LIMOGES
Limoges 57

Voyyes
2
Plombières

Limoges 42

M. REDON
BARNY & RIGONI
LIMOGES
Limoges 7

Mʳᵉ DE
VALOGNES
Valognes 1

Schönwald 1

Mʳᵉ de Valognes
Valognes 1

Mˢⁱᵒ Sₓ
Sceaux 1

Kusnetzoff

Mᵗʳᵉ de MADAME
Duchesse d' Angoulême
Dagoly E Honoré
PARIS.
Paris 71

MᵁS
B
MADE IN
CZECHOSLOVAKIA
Poschetzau

Münchhof

Selb 7

Poschetzau

Lane End 2

M&O
Ilmenau 5

Paris 99

Longton 53

Mehun 3

Volkstedt
Rudolstadt 17

Longton 86

Altrohlau 1

Altrohlau 1

Altrohlau 1

Altrohlau 1

Altrohlau 1

Altrohlau 1

Rudolstadt
Volkstedt 17

N

Alt-
haldensleben

Doccia

Doccia

Naples

Rudolstadt
Volkstedt 12

Naples

Naples

Naples

Niderviller   Niderviller   Niderviller

Naples

New Hall

Sèvres 1   Sèvres 1   Marktredwitz 3

N.A.C.

Petersburg 3   Valencia 2

NANGAROW
C.W
Nantgarw

NANT-GARW
C.W.
Nantgarw

Nasonow

Nantgarw

N...
à
Paris
Paris 109

H
Moscow 7

NAST.
Paris 109

NAST
n
Paris
Paris 109

Nast
a
Paris
Paris 109

NAST
n
PARIS
Paris 109

nast a Paris par breved d'invention
Paris 109

nast a paris par brevet
d'invention
Paris 109

NC
Barcelona 3

N
Dresden
Sandizell

Neumark
Neumark

NEU-TETTAU
BAVARIA
Tettau 2

New Chelsea
Stuffs
MADE IN
ENGLAND
FINE BONE CHINA
Longton 57

New Chelsea
Staffs
Longton 57

NEW CHINA WORKS
WORCESTER
Worcester 1

New Hall 1

Frauenthal 1

Lunéville

N.G. **N.G.F.**

Giesshübel 2

Giesshübel 2

NIDERVILLER

Niderviller

Niedersalzbrunn 2

Frauenthal 1

Ratkowo

 79

NIDERVILLER

Niderviller

Norville

WARE

C&E LIMITED

ENGLAND

Longton 20

Nove

Nove

NOWOTNY

ALTROHLAU

Altrohlau 1

N OWOTNY IN

ALTENROHLAU

BEY KARLSBAD

Altrohlau 1

NOWOTNY IN

ALTENROLAU

BEY CARLSBAD

XX IX OV

Altrohlau 1

NOWOTNY.

Alrohlau 1

Neutettau

Tettau 2

ENGLAND

Longton 57

Niedersalzbrunn 1

Franz Prause

Nieder-Salzbrunn

Niedersalzbrunn 1

NPS

Niedersalzbrunn 1

.NS.

Ottweiler

N&R

Ilemenau 1

n·s

W·1766

Ottweiler

N 198

*

TTL

Chelsea 1

Nymphenburg

Nymphenburg

O

Bourg-la-Reine 1 Tirschenreuth 1 Vienna 14 Buen Retiro

Nieder-salzbrunn 1 Niedersalzbrunn 1 Geschwenda Oissel

Longton 71 Longton 68 Longton 71

Vicenza 2 Sèvres 3 Ondrup Milan–San Cristoforo

Oeslau 2

Triptis Triptis Klein-dembach 1 Bordeaux 2

Bordeaux Langewiesen Longton 58 Dresden 27

Orléans 2

Dresden 23 Valdemorillo Altrohlau 4

P

Probstzella

Chantilly 2

Chantilly 2

Chantilly 2

Tiefenfurt 4

Schmiedeberg

Poterat

Prag

Prag

Pinxton

Longton 14

Chantilly

Ilmenau 2

PAF

Schönwald 2

Weiden 1

Limoges 65

PALME
Schelten

Palme
Schelten

Vienna 14

PARAGON
FINE BONE CHINA

Longton 59

PARAGON
CHINA
ENGLAND
Longton 59

BY APPOINTMENT
TO HER MAJESTY THE QUEEN
CHINA POTTERS
PARAGON
ENGLAND REGD
Longton 59

PARAGON
CHINA
ENGLAND.
Longton 59

Longton 59

PARAGON
BY APPOINTMENT
FINE BONE CHINA
ENGLAND
REGD
Longton 59

PARAMOUNT
ENGLAND
Fenton 11

Pardoe, Fecit Bristol.
Pardoe

Limoges 85

Paris 52

Pat·Dec 7/80
Fischern 2

PATRAULT
Paris 112

PATENT
SAM¹ALCOCK&CO.
Cobridge 1

Selb 7

P B
Paris 120

P.B
Couleuvre 1

Paul Zeiller.
Zeiller

Longton 14

Irún

Irún

ULLERSRICHT
Ullersricht

Ullersricht

Ullersricht

P. B. & S.
Hanley 8

Burgau

Creidlitz 2

Creidlitz 2

C P G M^ru du Pl·
Carousel a Paris
Paris 67

P C C
C P
Paris 67

MANUFACTURE du Petit Carousel a Paris
Paris 67

Petit Carousel a Paris
Paris 67

Epinay

Esternay

Peres. 1814.
Paris 111

1839 1897
PER LABOREM AD HONOREM
Herend

PERCHE
Paris 113

Person
Paris 114

LIMOGES FRANCE
PD
Limoges 61

P.F.
Doccia

PF
Rudolstadt
Volkstedt 2

PF
OM
Gräfenroda 4

F.
Fraureuth 1

PFr & C
Nyon

PE
Copenhagen 5

PFS
Freiberg 2

T
F
A
Ilmenau 2

P
G
Gehren

P. G.
Trade Mark
Gehren

PG
Güntherofeld
Gehren

P
G
Florence 1

R.
Strasbourg 1

H
Strasbourg 1

PHk
Hermannsdorf

PHOENIX CHINA
Longton 32

PH
Probstzella

P H Co
Hanley 1

H
1839
Herend

PHF
Frankenthal 1

PH
Frankenthal 1

PHOENIX BONE CHINA
T. F. & S. LTD
MADE IN ENGLAND
Longton 32

PHOENIX CHINA
Longton 32

Philipp Ernst Schindler
MDCCXLVI
Schindler

PIC
Courbevoie

PICKMANN Y C
CHINA OPACA
Seville

PICKMAN
Y. CA.
CHINA OPACA
SEVILLA
Seville

PP
PORZELLAN
Piesau

PILIVITE
PORCELAINES
A FEU
PILLIVUYT&Cⁱᵉ
MEHUN
FRANCE
Mehun 5

PORCELAINES
A FEU
PILLIVUYT&Cⁱᵉ
MEHUN
FRANCE
Mehun 5

PINK
Vogue
BONE CHINA
MADE IN ENGLAND
Longton 16

Pinxton.
Pinxton

PIRKEN HAMMER
Germany
Pirkenhammer

P J S V
Vohenstrauss

Pirkenhammer
Pirkenhammer

P K BAVARIA
Krummennaab 3

Weingarten

P.K. SILESIA
P.K. SILESIA
Königszelt

P L
Stadt-lengsfeld

Paris 98

Limoges 42

P L Turn
Turn 8

PL
Lorient

FRS·NOVA SCHLACKEN WERTH
Schlacken-werth

P L FRANCE
Mehun 4

SCHLACKEN WERTH
Schlackenwerth

Planken hammer Floss Gbpf.
Plankenhammer Floss Bavaria
Plankenhammer

PLANT TUSCAN CHINA
MADE IN ENGLAND
Longton 81

PLASTO
Ladowitz 3

P. L.
LIMOGES FRANCE
Limoges 42

PLS
Schlacken-werth

PL CECHOSLOVAKIA
Lubau

P. L. Dagoty & E.Honoré a Paris.
Paris 71

P. L. DAGOTY A PARIS
Paris 30

PL S
Schlackenwerth

P L S E
Liersmühle

Schlackenwerth

P M
Geneva

P.M
Geneva

1887
Sèvres 3

Martinroda

Hof-Moschendorf

P.M
Genève
Geneva

Tschech Sl.
Merkelsgrün 1

Moschendorf
BAVARIA
Hof-
Moschendorf

P M L
LIMOGES
(FRANCE)
Limoges 56

PMR
BAVARIA
Jaegerú
Markt-
redwitz 2

P M
S
Selb 7

Tschech·Slow.
Merkelsgrün 1

PN
Neumünster

LAMOTTE
N

LAMOTTE
N
Lamotte-Beuvron

PMS
FAVORIT
BAVARIA
Selb 7

PM
SÈVRES
Sèvres 4

KG
Oberkotzau 2

Pochot Derocte
Paris
16
Rue JJ Rousseau
Paris 36

Pochet D
PARIS
Paris 36

Pöllwitz
Pöllwitz

POINTONS
STOKE a TRENT
Hanley 10

POINTON
Hanley 10

Pompa-
dour
Oeslau 2

Pöllwitz
Pöllwitz

Романовъ
Romanów

PORCELAINE A FEU
L L
FOËCY (FRANCE)
Foecy 3

PORCELAINE
DE VALOGNES
Valognes 1

PORCELAINE
DE VALOGNES
Valognes 1

Романовъ
Romanów

PORCELAINE
DE PARIS
FRANCE
FONDÉE EN 1773
Paris 23

Porcelaine
de la Reine
FRANCE
Paris 26

PORCELAINE
DE SOLOGNE
L'ARCHEVEQUE

PORCELAINE
DE SOLOGNE
LAMOTTE

Vierzon 10

PORCELAINE RESISTANT AU FEU "GEM"

Saint-Vallier 3

PORCELAINE
G.D.V.
A FEU
La Celle-Bruère

PORCELAINE LONDE VERRERIE
à LIMOGES
Limoges 47

Porcelaine Mousseline
T&H
Limoges FRANCE
Limoges 38

PORCELAINE
PATTE
garantie
déposée
Montreuil 3

PORCELAINES D'ART LIMOGES
Limoges 22

PORCELANA

Porcelana de 1850
Vista Alegre
em Portugal
Vista Alegre

MAH VIGO
Santa Clara
Vigo

Porselit Chodziez
P
Chodziez

Gräfenhain

Porzellanfabrik Arzberg
Arzberg (Bayern)
Arzberg 1

Porzellan
Kunst
Ilmenau 2

Porzellankunst
Berchtesgaden
Berchtsgaden

Pot chappel
Potschappel

Potschappel
Potschappel

potter à pau
Paris 120

Pouyat
x
Russinger
P. R
Paris 94

PORSGRUND
NORGE
P|P
Porsgrunn

Passau 3

P|P
BAVARIA
Plankenhammer

P|P
Porsgrunn

PR
Frankenthal 1

P. R
Paris 94

PRAGER
Prag

Rudolstadt Volkstedt 10

Prag

PRAG SMICHOW
Smichow

PRECIEUX

Saint-Vallier 1

Longton 74

Horn

Eisenberg 4

Suhl

Suhl

Produits de Serres
Ed . Personne
8 Rue Royale Paris.

Paris 115

Sorau 2

Sorau 2

Selb 7

Arzberg 1

Schirnding

Schönwald 2

Schönwald 2

Gorodnitza

Stadt-lengsfeld

Steinbach

Tirschenreuth 1

Schatzlar

Pt CAROUSEL.
PARIS
Paris 67

PT SEVRES
R.L & Cie
Paris 81

Schlackenwerth

P&S
Chodau 1

Schlackenwerth

Haida 2

Paris 151

Kloster Vessra

PW
Wein-
garten

Seville

Paris 94

Q

Longton 63

Longton 74

Longton 74

Longton 74

Paris 121

R

Bow

Chelsea 1

Frankenthal 1

Gotha 1

Marseille 1

Regens-
burg 2

Rauenstein

Riedel

Rudolstadt Volkstedt 1

Milan–San Cristoforo   Shelton 1   Selb 8   Gotha 1   Gotha 1

Limoges 77   Regéc   Gotha 1   Dresden 26

Roschütz   Reichenbach 1   Roznan   Lane End 3

Rudolstadt
Volkstedt 1   Dresden 36   Lidköping 2   Schmiedeberg

Haslach   Wunsiedel   Lidköping 2   Mannheim 2

Paris 83   Fenton 13   Alexandrinenthal 1

Longton 37   Teplitz   Röslau   Wunsiedel

Alexandrinenthal 1   Limoges 74   Limoges 74   Selb 9

RCK
Billancourt

Carstens
Porzellan
Reichenbach

Saint-Uze 2

Vierzon 14

Paris 120

R. C.
Rosenthal
Kronach 4

R. C.
Kronach 4

Znaim

Rudolstadt
Volkstedt 18

Stoke on Trent 10

Sargadelos

Longton 63

Dresden 24

Regéc

Regéc

REINECKE
1796
Eisenberg 4

R et C
LIMOGES
FRANCE
Limoges 73

Regensburg 2

Paris 122

Rees

Longton 62

Paris 122

REVIL
Rue Neuve
des
Capucines
Paris 124

REVIL Rue
Neuve des
Capucines
Paris 124

REVIL
R~ Neuve
des
Capucines
Paris 124

Hof-Moschendorf

Naples

Frankenthal 1

Naples

Sèvres 1

R. F. DAGOTY.
Paris 71

Sèvres 1

St. Pölten

Limoges 25

Chodau 2

Chodau 2

Rudolstadt
Volkstedt 21

La Moncloa

Sèvres 1

Sèvres 1

Sèvres 1

Sèvres 1

RF&H
Chodau 2

Marseille 1

Gotha 1

Gotha

Doccia

Limoges 76

Grünlas

Gotha

R.G.S.
Hanley 10

Gräfenroda 5

Neuhaus 2

Ladowitz 2

Worcester 1

Worcester 1

Ladowitz 2

Hancock

Bruchmühlbach

Bruchmühlbach

Limoges 51

Duisdorf

Longton 81

Worcester 1

Neuhaus 2

RICHARD
Milan-San
Cristoforo

RICHARD·GINORI
Doccia

Richard Chaffers
1769.
Liverpool

RICHARD CERAMICA
Milan–San Cristoforo

Richard Ginori
Doccia

★ RICHARD ★
GINORI ★
Doccia

PASTA
EUCLIDE
RICHARD-GINORI
Doccia

DECORAZIONE ESEGUITA DA RICHARD GINORI 26·11
Doccia

MODERN CHINA
RICHARD·GINORI
Milan–San Cristoforo

RICHARD GINORI
PITTORIA DI DOCCIA
Doccia

RICHARD-GINORI
PITTORIA
DI DOCCIA
1925
Doccia

RICHARD GINORI
MONDOVI
ITALIA
Mondovi-
Carassone

RIDGWAY
MADE IN STAFFORDSHIRE ENGLAND
EST.1792
Shelton I

RIDGWAY & SONS

RIDGWAY POTTERIES LTD
VITROCK
'STRONG AS A ROCK'
HOTELWARE
MADE IN ENGLAND
Shelton I

Rieber
BAVARIA
Mitterteich I

RIEBER-MITTERTEICH
R
BAVARIA
Mitterteich I

RIHOUET
Fdeur
rue de la Paix
Ro
Paris 125

Rihouet
Paris 125

R J L
Naples

RILEY'S
SemiChina
Burslem 5

RILEY
Burslem 5

R L
L
Limoges 72

RL
Albers-
weiler

RK
Grünlas

RK
Grünlas

R K
A
Aussig

R
KPM
Krister
GERMANY
Landstuhl 2

RMR
Mildeneichen

R-n
Rauenstein

Rn
Rauenstein

R=n
Rauenstein

Rn
Rauenstein

Rob't Havard
1761
Lowestoft

Robert Allen 1760
Lowestoft

Limoges 51

Limoges 51

Rockingham Works Branch
Swinton

RÖRSTRAND
15
Lidköping 2

RÖRSTRAND
Lidköping 2

Rörstrand
Rörstrand

RÖRSTRAND
Lidköping 2

H4,
RÖRSTRAND
E
LEKSAND
1840
Lidköping 2

Lidköping 2

NORSTRAND
Lidköping 2

RÖRSTRAND
Lidköping 2

RÖRSTRAND
I
EKENÄS
ÖSTERGÖTH
LAND.
Lidköping 2

Münster

Roloff
Münster

Rosen
WerkeThal.
Hamburg 2

Rosenthal
KRONACH-GERMANY
Kronach 4

Rosenthal
Selb 9

Rosenthal
Selb-Plössberg

Rosenthal
Selb-Plössberg

MADE IN ENGLAND
BONE CHINA
ROSINA
Longton 64

ROSINA
BONE CHINA
MADE IN
ENGLAND
Longton 64

ROSINA
QUEENS CHINA
GW&S LTD
ENGLAND
Longton 64

Roslyn
FINE
BONE
China
MADE IN
ENGLAND
Longton 65

Longton 65

Longton 65

Longton 63

Longton 63

Paris 126

Paris 126

Longton 2

Longton 3

Longton 66

Longton 66

Longton 66

Neuses

Bonn 1

Berlin 3

Brüx 2

Brussels 5

Stoke on Trent 2

Stoke on Trent 2

Longton 57

Longton 57

Worcester 1

Derby 1

Copenhagen 1

Copenhagen 1

Copenhagen 1

Burslem 2

Burslem 2

Burslem 2

Dux 1

Longton 45

Longton 45

Longton 45

Marktredwitz 1

Bruchmühlbach

Longton 37

Mitterteich 2

Tunstall 1

Longton 68

Longton 68

Fenton 10

Longton 21

Longton 76

Longton 76

Milan–San Cristoforo

Shelton 1

Galway

Tettau 1

Royal Vale
Longton 16

Longton 7

Longton 69

Longton 69

Longton 81

Kronach 3

Reichenstein

Tournay

Rozenburg

Hegewald

Berlin 4

Mannheim 1

Aussig

Schauberg 2

Tillowitz 2

Tillowitz 2

Milan–San Cristoforo

Fischhäusel

Suhl

Tillowitz 2

Tillowitz

Tillowitz 2

Tillowitz 2

Spechtsbrunn

Turn 5

Paris 41

Paris 94

Tillowitz 2

Saint-Uze 2

Paris 132

Paris 148

Limoges 73

St.-Denis 1

Freiwaldau 3

Freiburg

Magdeburg-
Neustadt 2

Longton 61

Rudolstadt
Volkstedt 21

Rodach

Kirchenlamitz 2

Kirchen-
lamitz 2

Rudolstadt
Volkstedt 20

Wunsiedel

S

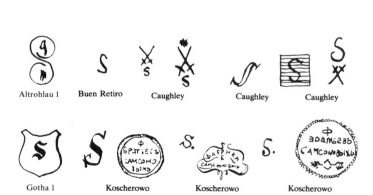

Altrohlau 1

Buen Retiro

Caughley

Caughley

Caughley

Gotha 1

Koscherowo

Koscherowo

Koscherowo

Köppelsdorf-Nord

Moscow 12

Paris 135

Szopienice

Paris 140

Paris 140

Paris 140

Paris 140

Sausenhofer

Schlaggen-wald 1

Sèvres 1

Sèvres 1

Sèvres 1

Sèvres 1

Sitzendorf

Sitzendorf

Schauberg 1

Scheibe-Alsbach

Scheibe-Alsbach

Schney

Schney

Schlaggenwald 1

Schlaggenwald 1

Schlaggenwald 1

Le Cateau

Paris 135

Gotha 1

Gotha 1

Tiefenbach

Villenauxe 3

Strasbourg 3

Paris 128

Sitzerode

Kronstadt-Brasow

Lubenz 2

Tiefenfurt 1

Tiefenfurt 1

Schlaggenwald 1

Selb/Berlin

Tiefenfurt 1

Meissen 5

Paris 131

Paris 131

Dresden 33

Turn 6

Eisenach

Limoges 42

Schönfeld 3

Saint-Amand-les-Eaux 1

Saint-Amand-les-Eaux 1

Kusnetzoff

Paris 129

Gustavsberg 1

Oberhohndorf

Limoges 59

Longton 69

Longton 69

Longton 69

Longton 70

Caughley

Caughley

Paris 131

Lowestoft

Hanley 13

Saint-Amand-les-Eaux 1

Ponsas-sur-Rhône 2

Sargadelos

Saint-Amand-les-Eaux 1

Budweis

Nieder-
salzbrunn 1

Meissen 2

New York

Fraureuth 1

SAXE
L H
Possneck 2

Schmuz
Baudiss

Paris 138

Schwarzenbach 2

Schwarzen-
bach 2

Longton 59

Sceaux 1

Schwarzenhammer

Rehau 1

Wallendorf

Paris 134

Schirnding 1

Schlaggenwald 1

Schlaggenwald 1

Schlaggenwald 1

Schlaggenwald 1

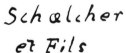

Suhl

Eisenach

Paris 135

Paris 135

Paris 135

Köppelsdorf-
Nord

Paris 113

Schönwald 2

Köppelsdorf-Nord

Velten

Moabit

SCHUMAN A MOABIT.
Moabit

Gotha 2

Rehau 1

Arzberg 4

Moabit

SCHWARZBURG
Rudolstadt
Volkstedt 20

Schwarzenhammer

Schwarzenhammer

SCHWEIG

WEISSWASSER
Weisswasser

Köppelsdorf-Nord

Schwarzen-bach 2

SCR
Milan–San Cristoforo

St. Cloud

S C RICHARD
Milan–San Cristoforo

S.D.
Dessendorf 1

Sèvres 1

PRUSSIA
Suhl

Stoke on Trent 10

Segovia

Seltmann Erbendorf
BAVARIA
Erbendorf 1

Seltmann Weiden
Weiden 2

SELTMANN WEIDEN
Weiden 2

Eisenberg 1

Konstanz 2

Mitterteich 1

Turn 9

Milan–San Cristoforo

Sèvres 1

 Sesták János Kolozsvárt

Kolozsvar

SESZTAK J.

Kolozsvar

SÈVRES 1848.

Sèvres 1

Sèvres 30

Sèvres 1

Sèvres 1

Sèvres 1

Sèvres 1

Sèvres 1

Sèvres 1

Sèvres 1

Coalport

Sèvres 1

Sèvres 1

Sèvres 5

Foecy 5

Tiefenfurt 2

Longton 74

Gotha 1

Seger porzellan

Creidlitz 3

Rudolstadt
Volkstedt 19

Derby 1

Longton 73

FINE BONE CHINA
Shelley
ENGLAND
Longton 73

Burggrub

Hüttensteinach

Charlottenbrunn 1

SILESIA
Tiefenfurt 2

SILESIEN
GERMANY
Tiefenfurt 2

SILESIEN
Tiefenfurt 2

SILESIA
Tiefenfurt 2

BAVARIA
Rehau 1

SIMON HALBIG
Gräfenhain

SIMON HALBIG
K & R
53
Waltershausen 1

SIPM
Stanowitz

Limoges 67

Salins

SCHRAMBERG
Schramberg 2

1775
Buen Retiro

S:L:PALME
IN SCHELTEN
BEI HAYDA
Schelten

S. M.
Schlaggenwald 2

LIMOGES
ELITE
FRANCE
Limoges 32

Limoges 48

Schmiedefeld 2

Lange-
wiesen

So
Caughley

SOCIETE
DES
ANCIENS
ETABLISSEMENTS
A.HACHE & C°
PARIS
VIERZON
Paris 117

SOMMER
HAND-
MALEREI
Garmisch-
Partenkirchen

France
SOCIETE FRANCAISE
de porcelaine
Paris 139

Sophienthal
b. Bayreuth
BAVARIA
Sophienthal

FEIN BAYREUTH
GERMANY
Sophienthal

SORAU
Sorau 1

S.P
Sceaux 1

Schelten

SPENCER
STEVENSON
ENGLAND
BONE CHINA
Longton 75

Neuhaldens-
leben 4

Meissen 4

Moabit

Moabit

Moabit

Eisenberg 5

Tiefenfurt 3

Bayreuth 3

Bayreuth 3

Stoke on Trent 11

Stoke on Trent 11

Stoke on Trent 11

Stoke on Trent 11

Stoke on Trent 11

Stoke on Trent 11

Stoke on Trent 11

Stoke on Trent 11

Stoke on Trent 11

Stoke on Trent 11

Stoke on Trent 11

Stoke on Trent 11

Stoke on Trent 11

Stoke on Trent 11

Stoke on Trent 11

Stoke on Trent 11

Stoke on Trent 11

Stoke on Trent 11

Korzec

Freienwaldau

Saint-Vallier 2

Fenton 13

Reichenbach 3

Longton 72

Paris 130

Longton 71

Longton 71

Kronach

Kronach

Mariaschein

Dresden 36

Stadtilm

Stadtlengsfeld

Longton 6

Fenton 2

Fenton 4

Shelton

Fenton 4

Longton 21

Longton 6

Longton 6

Gustavsberg 1

Longton 6

Vienna 17

Saint-Cloud

Kriebern

Bonn 1

Zwickuau 2

Derby 1

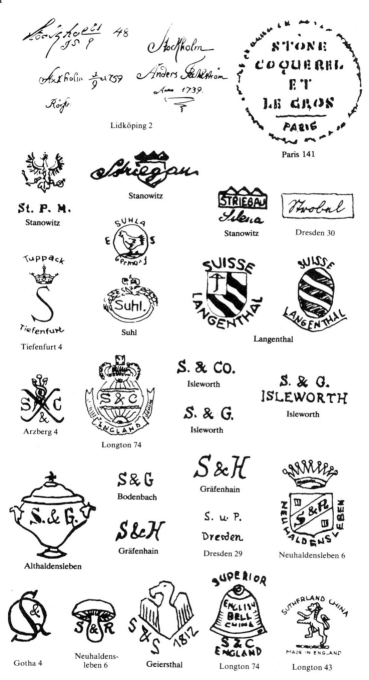

Lidköping 2

Paris 141

Stanowitz

St. P. M.

Stanowitz

Stanowitz

Dresden 30

Tuppack

Tiefenfurt

Tiefenfurt 4

Suhl

Langenthal

Arzberg 4

Longton 74

S. & CO.
Isleworth

S. & G.
Isleworth

S. & G.
ISLEWORTH
Isleworth

S & G
Bodenbach

S & H
Gräfenhain

S & H
Gräfenhain

S. u. P.
Dresden

Dresden 29

Neuhaldensleben 6

Althaldensleben

Gotha 4

Neuhaldens-
leben 6

Geiersthal

Longton 74

Longton 43

Longton 43

Schwarza-Saalbahn

Walterhausen 2

Sèvres 1

Köppelsdorf-Nord

Köppelsdorf-Nord

Köppelsdorf-Nord

Köppelsdorf-Nord

Swansea

Swansea

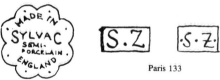

Sceaux 1

Sceaux 1

Sceaux 1

Longton 72

Paris 133

T

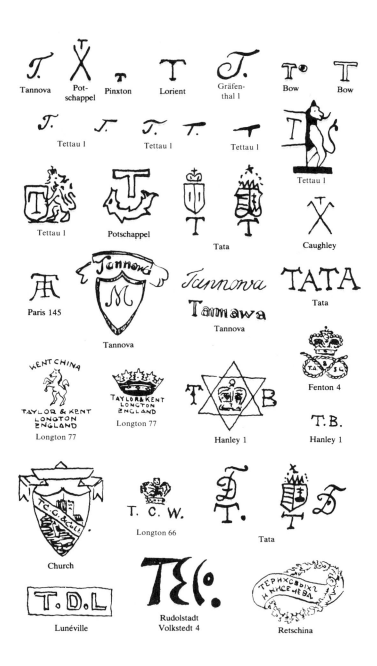

Tannova   Pot-   Pinxton   Lorient   Gräfen-   Bow   Bow
           schappel   thal 1

Tettau 1   Tettau 1   Tettau 1

                                                      Tettau 1

Tettau 1   Potschappel   Caughley

                                  Tata

Paris 145   Tata

        Tannova   Tannova

                            Tannova

                                                      Fenton 4

KENT CHINA

TAYLOR & KENT   TAYLOR & KENT   T   B   T.B.
LONGTON   LONGTON
ENGLAND   ENGLAND
Longton 77   Longton 77   Hanley 1   Hanley 1

Church   T. C. W.   Tata
                 Longton 66

T.D.L   Rudolstadt
Lunéville   Volkstedt 4   Retschina

Retschina

Saint-Uze

Saint-Vallier 1

Lunéville

TERRE DES ALPES rectifiée

Saint-Vallier 1

T.F.
Hanley 6

T.F. & S.
Longton 32

T.F. & S. L?
Longton 32

Tunstall 1

FEUTON T. G
Fenton 5

Choisy-le-Roi 2

Xanten

Théodore Haviland Limoges FRANCE
Limoges 38

Limoges 38

Porcelaine Mousseline Limoges FRANCE
Limoges 38

Porcelaine Theo. Haviland Limoges FRANCE
Limoges 38

Limoges 38

THARAUD
Limoges 85

THE FINE BONE CHINA OF ARTHUR BOWKER MADE IN ENGLAND
Fenton 2

THE FOLEY CHINA ENGLAND
Longton 73

PORCELAINE THOMARET Déposé
Montreuil 4

Thomas
Kirchen-laibach

Thu.E MR
Marktredwitz 4

THORLEY CHINA LTD. MADE IN ENGLAND
Longton 79

Thomas Thomas Bavaria
Marktredwitz 4

Thomas ..Sophienthal-Bavaria..
Marktredwitz 4

TILLOWITZ
Tillowitz 1

TILL DRESDEN
Dresden 31

TINET 32 Rue du Bac
Montreuil 5

TINET 29 x 32 rue du Bac
Montreuil 5

TIRSCHENREUTH
1838

HUTSCHENREUTHER
GRUPPE
GERMANY
Tirschenreuth 1

Titov Veles

TK
Klösterle 1

TK
Klösterle 1

Klösterle 1

Moscow 6

TK
Thun
Klösterle 1

TK
Klösterle 1

Klösterle 1

Longton 77

Königl.pr.Tettau
Tettau 1

Königl.pr.Tettau
Tettau 1

T.L.B.
LIMOGES
Limoges 82

LIMOGES
Limoges 83

Longton 55

TMR
Madeley
S
Magdeburg

T.M.
Longton 56

T°
Tebo

TN DV
Limoges
Paris 144

Tomás Momparler
Tomas Momparler
Valencia 1

Tomaszów Mezer.   Tomaszów

TOMASZÓW
Tomaszow

Tomaszow
Fabryka Kraiowa
Tomaszow

Tomaszow
Tomaszow

Tomaszow Mezer
Tomaszow

Tours·1782
Tours 1

Tournay quai des Salines
28
Tournay

Königsee 2

TPL
Longton 48

Tiefenfurt 4

TPM
Tiefenfurt 1

Turin

.MARK.
Mitterteich 2

Brüx 2

Portadown

TRADE MARK
CROSVENOR CHINA
Longton 44

TRADE MARK
Longton 30

Longton 80

ROYAL CROWN POTTERY
FINE BONE
CHINA
ENGLAND
Longton 80

Triptis
A-G.
Triptis

R T
Zwickau 1

ROYAL BAYREUTH
1794
GERMANY
Tettau 1

T. S.
DEP
L
Lessau

TSCHECHOSLOVAKEI
Jokes

T. Couchard
Rue de la Michaudière
No 12 a Paris
Paris 147

Turn 2

T.T. & CO.
Longton 78

T
&
C
Altwasser 2

T & CF
·X·
Hanley 6

T. & C.F.
Hanley 6

T. & K.
L.
Longton 77

TURNER
Caughley

TURN
VIENNA
Turn

Longton 81

Limoges 86

T.W. & CO.
Longton 66

U

U
DALWITZ

Dallwitz

Limoges 87

Limoges 87

Upsala

Upsala

Dresden 32

Paris 57

Nova Bana

Limoges 88

Ullersricht

U L
LIMOGES
FRANCE
Limoges 88

Ulm

Vierzon 15

Burslem 4

Union
Kleindembach

Kleindembach 1

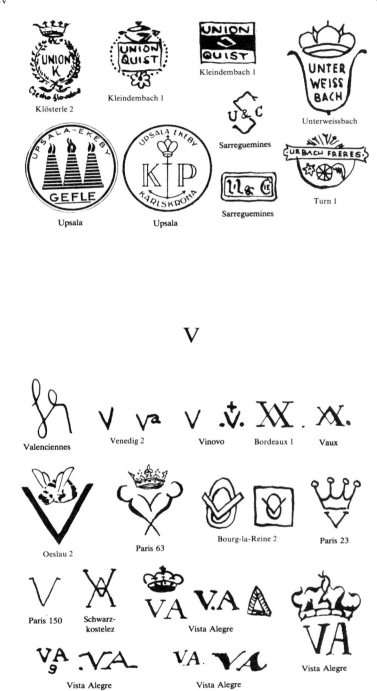

Klösterle 2

Kleindembach 1

Kleindembach 1

Unterweissbach

Upsala

Upsala

Sarreguemines

Sarreguemines

Turn 1

V

Valenciennes

Venedig 2

Vinovo

Bordeaux 1

Vaux

Oeslau 2

Paris 63

Bourg-la-Reine 2

Paris 23

Paris 150

Schwarz-kostelez

Vista Alegre

Vista Alegre

Vista Alegre

Vista Alegre

Vista Alegre

Vista Alegre

Vista Alegre

Vista Alegre

Vista Alegre

Vista Alegre

Vista Alegre

Vista Alegre

Vista Alegre

Vista Alegre

Vista Alegre

Vista Alegre

Vista Alegre

Vista Alegre

Vista Alegre

Paris 149

Paris 149

Varoslöd

Longton 16

Longton 16

Choisy-le-Roy 1

Valenciennes 1

Paris 152

CAR:
Vinovo

D 3 B
Vinovo

D G
Vinovo

D.G G
Vinovo

D G

D G
Vinovo

VDubois
Paris 45

VeL.

Ve LANGLOIS BAYEUX
Bayeux

LIMOGES
Limoges 53

Velvet china
Ilmenau 1

Jen:
Venedig 2

VEN^A
Ven:^a
Venedig 2

Ven=
Venedig 2

1765
Venezia
Fab: Geminiano
Cozzi
Venedig 2

Fortunato
ToLevazzi Fece
Venesia. 1163
Venedig 2

VENEZIA
Venedig 2

Ven^a

Venezia
Venedig 2

Laveno

VERBANO
Laveno

VETROCHINA R.G
Doccia

V.F
Venedig 2

Foecy 5

VH chunnong
Strasbourg 1

VICTORIA CARLSBAD AUSTRIA
Altrohlau 3

VICTORIA
Altrohlau 3

Stone Ware J.R VICTORIA
Shelton 1

VICTORIA CHINA CZECHOSLOVAKIA
Altrohlau 3

Altrohlau 3

Longton 20

Longton 20

Kronstadt-Brasov

Limoges 53

Paris 36

Cobridge 4

Chantilly 1

VINDOBONA

Vienna 8

Vista Alegre

SEVRES
Vin Sare
France

Sèvres 6

Schorndorf

Vohenstrauss

Vista Alegre

Vista Alegre

Est. 1824

Vista Alegre

Valenciennes 1

Berlin 7

V.L.
BX.

Bayeux

Venedig 2

Rudolstadt Volkstedt 11

Rudolstadt
Volkstedt 11

Rudolstadt
Volkstedt 15

Rudolstadt
Volkstedt

Chodau 1

Chodau 1

Rudolstadt
Volkstedt 7

Fismes

Fismes

Frankenthal 1

Vista Alegre

Villenauxe-
la-Grande 4

Villenauxe-
la-Grande 4

V . U.

Turn 9

Paris 41

VU
FRANCE

et

S E N

Paris 3

Bayeux

W

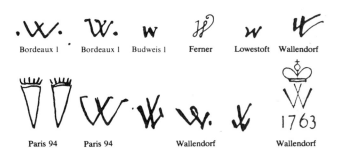

Bordeaux 1

Bordeaux 1

Budweis 1

Ferner

Lowestoft

Wallendorf

Paris 94

Paris 94

Wallendorf

Wallendorf

Vicenza 1

Weesp

Weesp

Berlin 1

Berlin 1

Berlin 1

Berlin

Weisswasser

Worcester 1

Worcester 1

Worcester 1

Fürstenberg

W. A. A. & Co.
Longton 3

W. A. A.
Longton 3

1763
Wallendorf

WACKERLE.
Wackerle

Wagner
Dresden 34

WALDERSHOF
BAVARIA
Waldershof 2

WALDERSHOF
BAVARIA
Marktredwitz 3

WALDERSHOF
F   N
BAVARIA
GERMANY
Marktredwitz 3

wallendorf
Wallendorf

WARBURTON'S
PATENT
New Hall 2

W.
AUSTRIA
Horn

W
AUSTRIA
Horn

W   B
Cobridge 2

W. B.

W.B &S.
Cobridge 2

Marktleuthen 2

W Cookworthy's
Factory Plymouth
. 1770 .
Plymouth

W. DUESBURY.
1803.
Derby 1

Duisdorf

WEETMAN GIFTWARE
ENGLAND
Tunstall 4

WEETMAN
SANDYFORD

WEETMAN FIGURES
SANDYFORD
Tunstall 4

WE
Berlin 1

WEDGWOOD
Wedgwood

Wehsner
Dresden 35

Blankenhain 1

Weimar Porzellan
SEIT 1790
Blankenhain 1

Blankenhain 1

WEIMAR
ORLA
Kleindembach 1

Weiß
Meissen 1

WEISS
25
Denkow

WEISSWASSER
Weisswasser

WELLINGTON CHINA
J.H.C&C°
LONGTON ENGLAND
Longton 27

WELLINGTON CHINA
J.H.C.&C°.
LONGTON ENGLAND
Longton 27

WERKST
KIRSCH
WIEN
Vienna 12

WE TOY
PARIS
Paris 148

WETLEY CHINA
LONGTON
LTD
Longton 71

WETLEY CHINA
ENGLAND
Longton 71

WETLEY CHINA
LTD
LONGTON ENG.
Longton 71

W. fter Snell
1776
Lowestoft

LIMOGES
W G
& C°
FRANCE
Limoges 32

WG
Thiersheim in Bavaria
Thiersheim

Waldershof 1

Ottweiler

W.H.GOSS
Stoke on Trent 8

W H G
Stoke on Trent 8

Waldershof 1

Porzellanfabrik Waldershof.
(BAVARIA)
Waldershof 1

W.H.&S.
Longton 86

WIENER
Budweis 1

Wien
Vienna 3

WIEN
Budweis 1

WIEN TEPLITZ
Turn 10

WIEN's TEPLITZ
Turn 10

WIENER H KIRSCH PORZELLAN
Vienna 12

WILHELMSBURG
Vienna 14

WILHELMS ~FELD~
Oeslau 2

WILHELMS FELDER JASPIS
Oeslau 2

WILHELMS FELD
Oeslau 2

Wilh. JÄGER Eisenberg s. Alba
Eisenberg 2

William Story à Paris
Paris 143

WILLOW ART CHINA LONGTON STAFFORDSHIRE
Longton 41

WILSON
Hanley 14

MADE IN BONE WINDSOR CHINA ENGLAND
Longton 26

BONE CHINA WINDSOR MADE IN ENGLAND
Longton 26

MADE IN BONE WINDSOR CHINA ENGLAND

WINTERLING GERMANY
Bruchmühlbach

Winterling Schwarzenbach BAVARIA GERMANY
Schwarzenbach 2

WINTERLING MARKTLEUTHEN BAVARIA
Marktleuthen 2

DECORE W.J.S EN DANEMARK
Copenhagen 7

W.KC. graefen X thal
Gräfenthal 4

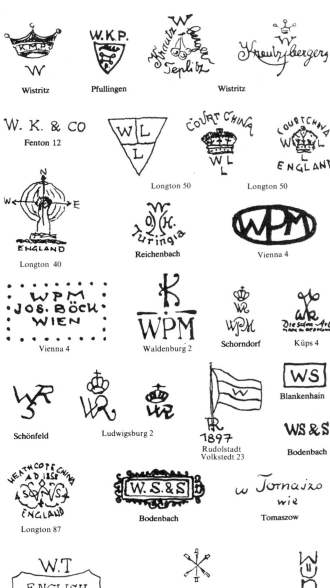

Wistritz

Pfullingen

Wistritz

W. K. & CO
Fenton 12

Longton 50

Longton 50

Longton 40

Reichenbach

Vienna 4

Vienna 4

Waldenburg 2

Schorndorf

Küps 4

Schönfeld

Ludwigsburg 2

Rudolstadt
Volkstedt 23

Blankenhain

WS & S
Bodenbach

Longton 87

Bodenbach

Tomaszow

Coalport

W TOMASZOWIE

4808

Tomaszow

Dresden 37

Longton 87

Lippelsdorf

Stoke on Trent 12

W.W. L.
DALWITZ

Longton 87

Dallwitz

Küps 5

Y Z

Ungvár

Schwarzen-
hammer

Rudolstadt
Volkstedt 17

Leipzig

Zürich

Z . . Z

Z. B.   Z. B. & S.

Zürich

Hanley 3

Rehau 1

ZELL
Zell

Rehau 1

Rehau 1

Zell

Höchst

Zeven

Budapest 6

Pécs

Pécs

Pécs

Pécs

Rehau 1

Rehau 1

Rehau 1

Tirschenreuth 2

Lichte

Zürich

Russian marks

These marks are arranged alphabetically
according to location

Baranowka

Baranowka

Baranowka

Baranowka

Barasze

Bielotyn

Bielotyn

Bronnitzi

Bronnitzi

Emilzyn

Frjasino

Frjasino

Frjasino

Frjasino

Frjasino

Frjasino

Frjasino

Frjasino

Frjasino

Frjasino

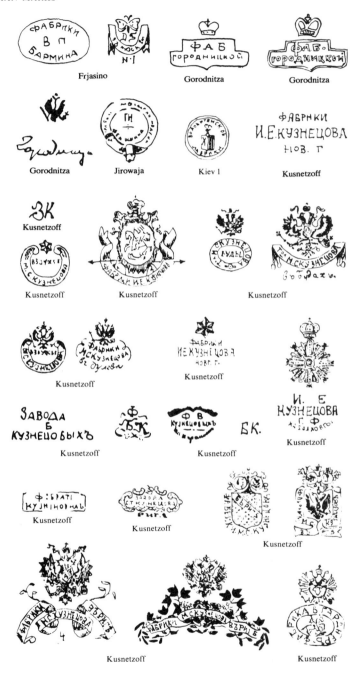

Frjasino

Gorodnitza

Gorodnitza

Gorodnitza

Jirowaja

Kiev 1

Kusnetzoff

Kusnetzoff

Kusnetzoff

Kusnetzoff

Kusnetzoff

Kusnetzoff

Kusnetzoff

Kusnetzoff

Kusnetzoff

Kusnetzoff

Kusnetzoff

Kusnetzoff

Kusnetzoff

Kusnetzoff

Kusnetzoff

Kusnetzoff

Kusnetzoff

Kusnetzoff

Kusnetzoff

Kusnetzoff

Kusnetzoff

Kusnetzoff

Kusnetzoff

Leningrad

Morje

Leningrad

Morje

Morje

Moscow 2

Moscow 2

Moscow 2

Moscow 2

Moscow 2

Moscow 2

Moscow 2

Moscow 3

Moscow 3   Moscow 4

ГАРДНЕРЪ

Moscow 4

Moscow 4   Moscow 4   Moscow 4

Moscow 4   Moscow 4   Moscow 4

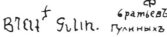

Moscow 5   Moscow 5   Moscow 5

Moscow 5   Moscow 5   Moscow 5

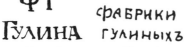

Moscow 6   Moscow 7

Moscow 6

Moscow 8

Moscow 8   Moscow 8

Moscow 8

Moscow 8   Moscow 8

БРАТЬЕВЬ НОВЫХЪ
Moscow 8

Moscow 8

Moscow 8

Moscow 8

Moscow 8

Moscow 8

Moscow 8

Moscow 8

Moscow 8

Moscow 8

Moscow 8

Moscow 8

ПОПОВЫ
Moscow 9

ПОПОВЫ
Moscow 9

БРАТЬЕВЪ РАУКИНЫХЪ
Moscow 10

Moscow 10

Moscow 10

Moscow 10

Moscow 10

Moscow 10

Moscow 10

ЗКРАУКНЯ
Moscow 10

Moscow 12

Moscow 12

Moscow 12

Moscow 12   Ratkowo   Retschina

ФАБРИКИ
П
ТЕРИХОВА

Retschina

Retschina   Retschina

ФАБРИКИ
ПЕТРА
ТЕРИХОВА.

Retschina   Retschina   Petersburg 1

Petersburg 1   Petersburg 1

Б   Б   ГИНТЕРЬ ∧ К°   ГИНТЕРЪ и Ко.

Petersburg 2   Petersburg 3

БР
Ко

Petersburg 4

Petersburg 4

Tambow

,Petersburg 4

Monogram marks

Niderviller

Chemnitz

Paris 41

Paris 41

Paris 41

Limoges 1

Arzberg 2

Weiden 1

Niderviller

Schorndorf

Niderviller

Niderviller

Meierhöfen 2

Frankenthal 1

Limoges 45

Montgat

Derby 1

Walders-
hof 1

Coburg 1

Limoges 30

Rudolstadt
Volkstedt 5

Köln-Kalk

Choisy-le-Roy 1

Paris 44

Dresden 7

Tata

Fulda 1

Rudolstadt Volkstedt 1

1762

1762

Neuhaldensleben 5

CHINA BLAU

Potschappel

1872

Vienna 12

Oeslau 1

Lauf

Rudolstadt Volkstedt 1

Nove

Nove

Lettin

Neuhaldensleben 1

Gmunden

Fischern 1

Lubenz

Ladowitz 2

RH

Bottengruber

1729

Bottengruber

Niderviller

Niderviller

Köppelsdorf-Nord

Dresden 14

Frankenthal 1

Metzsch

Paris 98

Vienna 12

Vienna 12

Paris 74/153

Paris 131

Paris 37

Paris 141

PAR BREVET D'INVENTION

PARIS

Paris 37

Paris 37

Paris 98

Etiolles

Hohenberg

Könitz

Limoges 58

Paris 109

Paris 109

Herend

Cobridge 2

Paris 118

Paris 98

Paris 98

Paris 98

Paris 37

Freienorla

Hermsdorf

Reichmanns-
dorf 3

Turn 5

Dresden

Potschappel

Rudolstadt
Volkstedt 21

Sèvres 1

Sèvres 1

Turn 5

Turn 6

St.-Amand-les-Eaux

Paris 131

Fenton 13

Sèvres 1

Longton 77   Niderviller   Triptis   Longton 85

Windischeschenbach   Denkendorf   Zeven   Gutenbrunn

Heraldic marks

Alexandrinenthal 1   Treviso 1   Iglo   Elbogen 2

Frankenthal 1   Ansbach   Baden-Baden   Neuhaus 1

Schlierbach   Wloclawek   Neuhaus 1   Eisenberg 3

Tillowitz 1   Gerona   Helsinki

Pössneck 1   Rehau 1   Sarreguemines   Suhl

Plaue

St.-Amand-   Schwarzenberg
les-Eaux 3

Helsinki

Kronach   Beleek

Herend

Ludwigsburg 2   Nymphenburg   Nymphenburg   Nymphenburg

Vienna 3   Vienna 1   Vienna 1

Vienna 1   Vienna 1   Vienna 1   Vienna 1

Eichwald   Eichwald   Suhl   Hohenberg   Rudolstadt Volkstedt 9

Vienna 1   Langewiesen   Vienna 6   Vienna 15   Hohenberg

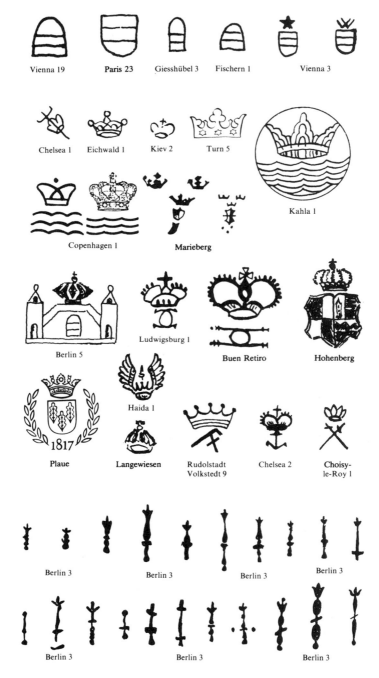

Vienna 19   Paris 23   Giesshübel 3   Fischern 1   Vienna 3

Chelsea 1   Eichwald 1   Kiev 2   Turn 5

Copenhagen 1   Marieberg

Kahla 1

Berlin 5   Ludwigsburg 1   Buen Retiro   Hohenberg

Plaue   Haida 1   Langewiesen   Rudolstadt Volkstedt 9   Chelsea 2   Choisy-le-Roy 1

Berlin 3   Berlin 3   Berlin 3   Berlin 3

Berlin 3   Berlin 3   Berlin 3

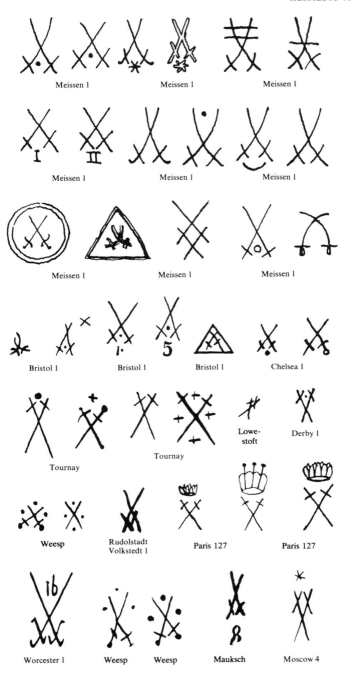

Meissen 1   Meissen 1   Meissen 1

Meissen 1   Meissen 1   Meissen 1

Meissen 1   Meissen 1   Meissen 1

Bristol 1   Bristol 1   Bristol 1   Chelsea 1

Tournay   Tournay   Lowe-stoft   Derby 1

Weesp   Rudolstadt Volkstedt 1   Paris 127   Paris 127

Worcester 1   Weesp   Weesp   Mauksch   Moscow 4

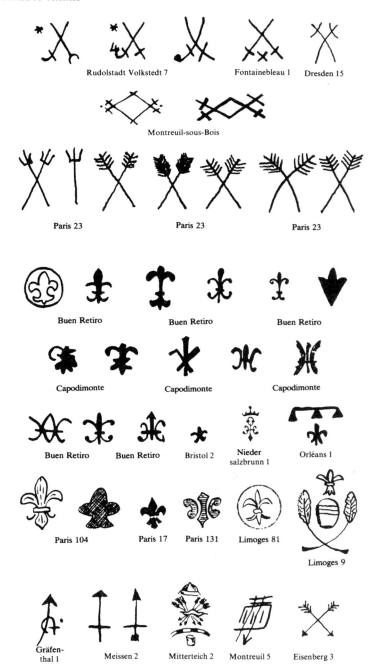

Rudolstadt Volkstedt 7   Fontainebleau 1   Dresden 15

Montreuil-sous-Bois

Paris 23   Paris 23   Paris 23

Buen Retiro   Buen Retiro   Buen Retiro

Capodimonte   Capodimonte   Capodimonte

Buen Retiro   Buen Retiro   Bristol 2   Nieder salzbrunn 1   Orléans 1

Paris 104   Paris 17   Paris 131   Limoges 81

Limoges 9

Gräfen-thal 1   Meissen 2   Mitterteich 2   Montreuil 5   Eisenberg 3

Bow   Bow   Bristol 2   Bristol 2   Bristol 2   Zwickau 1

Paris 44   Paris 44   Pinxton   Caughley

Bow   Rozenburg   Charlotten-
                                      burg

Frankenthal 1   Kassel   Elbogen 3   Nymphenburg

Köppelsdorf-   Neuhaus 1   Dresden 14   Paris 87
Nord

                                                          Unterweissbach

The Hague

                                                          The Hague

Gotha 1   The Hague   The Hague

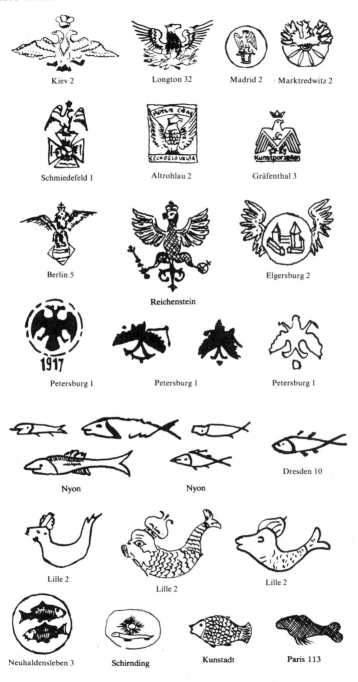

Kiev 2

Longton 32

Madrid 2

Marktredwitz 2

Schmiedefeld 1

Altrohlau 2

Gräfenthal 3

Berlin 5

Reichenstein

Elgersburg 2

Petersburg 1

Petersburg 1

Petersburg 1

Nyon

Nyon

Dresden 10

Lille 2

Lille 2

Lille 2

Neuhaldensleben 3

Schirnding

Kunstadt

Paris 113

Vienna 1   Köppelsdorf-Nord   Doccia   Paris 17

Erome   Limoges 85   Oberklingensporn   Ellwangen

Passau 3   Bischofs-werda   Ellwangen   Limoges 28   Elbogen 1

Elbogen 1   Haslach   Bordeaux 5   Schwarzen-feld   Limoges 55

Ludwigsburg 1   Pirkenhammer   Pirkenhammer   Schedewitz

Berlin 3   Leningrad

Other marks without inscription

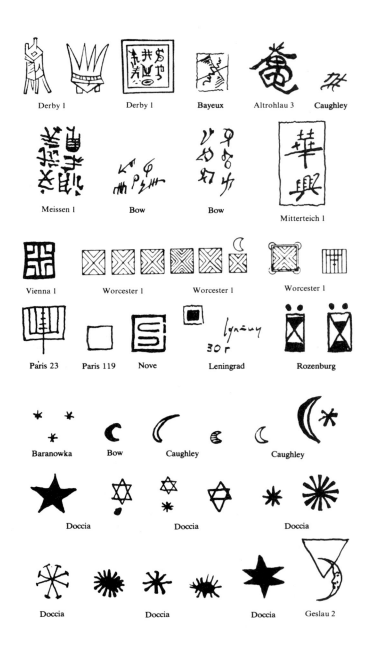

Derby 1

Derby 1

Bayeux

Altrohlau 3

Caughley

Meissen 1

Bow

Bow

Mitterteich 1

Vienna 1

Worcester 1

Worcester 1

Worcester 1

Paris 23

Paris 119

Nove

Leningrad

Rozenburg

Baranowka

Bow

Caughley

Caughley

Doccia

Doccia

Doccia

Doccia

Doccia

Doccia

Geslau 2

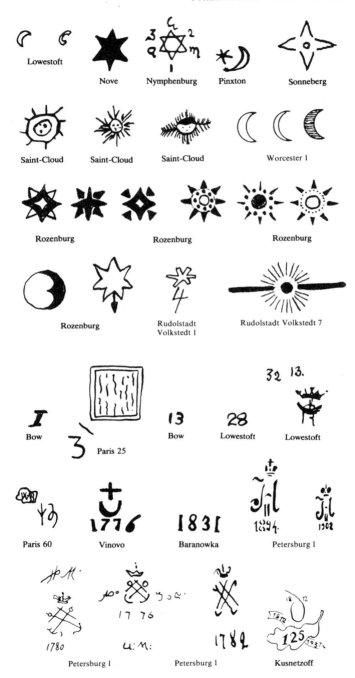

Lowestoft

Nove

Nymphenburg

Pinxton

Sonneberg

Saint-Cloud

Saint-Cloud

Saint-Cloud

Worcester 1

Rozenburg

Rozenburg

Rozenburg

Rozenburg

Rudolstadt
Volkstedt 1

Rudolstadt Volkstedt 7

Bow

Paris 25

Bow

Lowestoft

Lowestoft

Paris 60

Vinovo

Baranowka

Petersburg 1

1780

Petersburg 1

Petersburg 1

Kusnetzoff

Bow　　　　　　Bow　　　　　　Bow

Chelsea 1　　　　　Chelsea 1　　　　　Chelsea 1

Gorod-　Cologne 2　Long-　Sceaux 1　　Sceaux 1　　Paris 60
nitza　　　　　　ton 56

Paris 42　Rozenburg　Longton 7　Choisy-　　Paris 131　Magdeburg-
　　　　　　　　　　　　le-Roy 1　　　　　Neustadt 1

Chantilly 1　　Chantilly 1　　Chantilly 1　　Vierzon 10

Chantilly 1　　Chantilly 1　　　　Chantilly 1

Höchst　　Höchst　　Bock-　　Passau　　Schönwald 1
　　　　　　　Wallendorf

Stoke on
Trent 11　　Damm　　Arnstadt　　Bristol 1

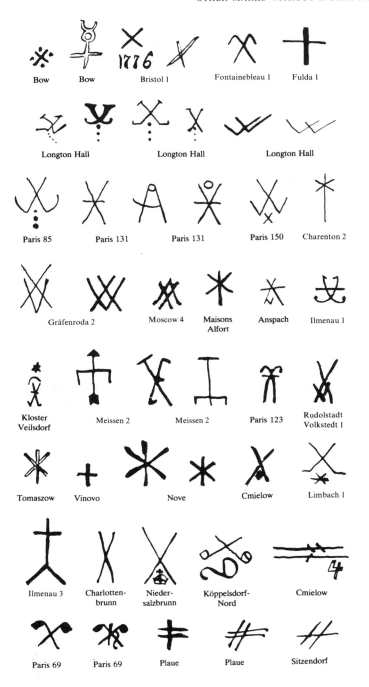

Bow   Bow   Bristol 1   Fontainebleau 1   Fulda 1

Longton Hall   Longton Hall   Longton Hall

Paris 85   Paris 131   Paris 131   Paris 150   Charenton 2

Gräfenroda 2   Moscow 4   Maisons Alfort   Anspach   Ilmenau 1

Kloster Veilsdorf   Meissen 2   Meissen 2   Paris 123   Rudolstadt Volkstedt 1

Tomaszow   Vinovo   Nove   Cmielow   Limbach 1

Ilmenau 3   Charlottenbrunn   Niedersalzbrunn   Köppelsdorf-Nord   Cmielow

Paris 69   Paris 69   Plaue   Plaue   Sitzendorf

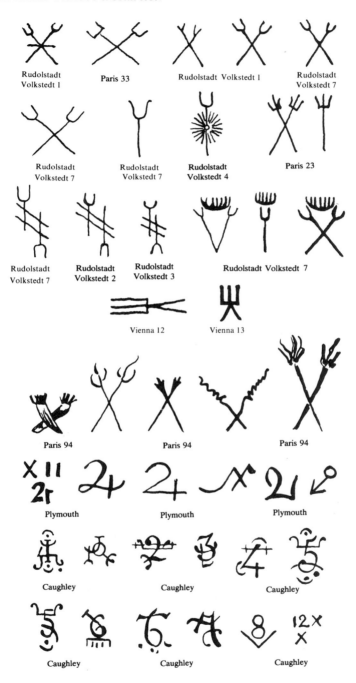

Rudolstadt Volkstedt 1

Paris 33

Rudolstadt Volkstedt 1

Rudolstadt Volkstedt 7

Rudolstadt Volkstedt 7

Rudolstadt Volkstedt 7

Rudolstadt Volkstedt 4

Paris 23

Rudolstadt Volkstedt 7

Rudolstadt Volkstedt 2

Rudolstadt Volkstedt 3

Rudolstadt Volkstedt 7

Vienna 12

Vienna 13

Paris 94

Paris 94

Paris 94

Plymouth

Plymouth

Plymouth

Caughley

Caughley

Caughley

Caughley

Caughley

Caughley

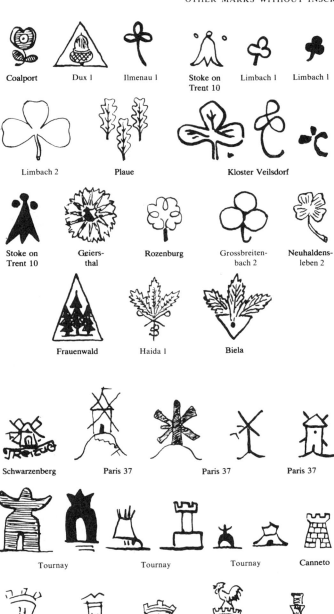

Coalport   Dux 1   Ilmenau 1   Stoke on   Limbach 1   Limbach 1
                                                    Trent 10

Limbach 2   Plaue   Kloster Veilsdorf

Stoke on   Geiers-   Rozenburg   Grossbreiten-   Neuhaldens-
Trent 10   thal   bach 2   leben 2

Frauenwald   Haida 1   Biela

Schwarzenberg   Paris 37   Paris 37   Paris 37

Tournay   Tournay   Tournay   Canneto

La Tour d'Aigue   La Tour d'Aigue   Ilmenau 7   Biela

Bristol 2   Bristol 2   Bristol 2

Lowestoft   Bow   Vincennes 2   Caughley   Orléans 1

Rozenburg   Copenhagen 1   Copenhagen 1

Paris 131   Paris 131   Paris 131   Paris 131

Oberköditz   Milan–San Cristoforo   Magdeburg Neustadt   Munich 7

Burlsem 3   Dieringhausen   Hildburghausen 2   Limoges 84

Vienna 7   Rozenburg   Cobridge 3

Bourg-la-Reine 2   Rozenburg   Knummennaab 3

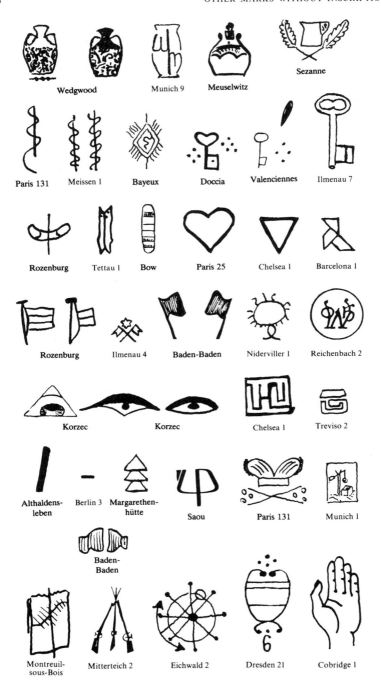

Unidentifiable marks

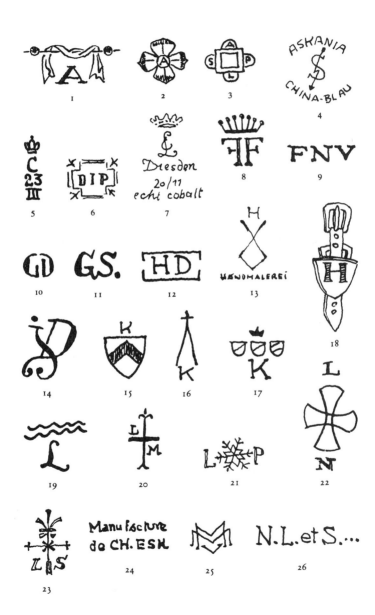

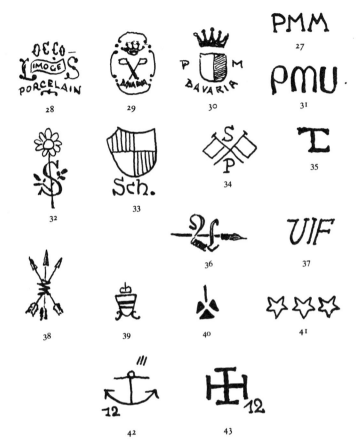

27

28   29   30   31

32   33   34   35

36   37

38   39   40   41

42   43

Trademark Register

The following porcelain marks were entered in the Trademark Register of the German Reich between 1875 and 1922.

1	KPM Berlin, all marks	10. 1. 1875	Königliches Amtsgericht Berlin
2	Hildenburghausen (2)	29. 4. 1875	Herzogliches Kreisgericht Hildenburghausen
3	Altwasser	8. 5. 1875	Königliches Handelsgericht Waldenburg
4	Meissen (1), all marks	20. 5. 1875	Königliches Amtsgericht Meißen. The Mark AR No. 1
5	Gotha	12. 6. 1875	Herzogliches Kreisgericht zu Gotha No. 2
6	Neuhaldensleben	30. 9. 1875	RWZR
7	Altwasser	18. 10. 1875	RWZR
8	Zwickau (1)	12. 11. 1875	Handelsgericht Zwickau
9	Potschappel	4. 1. 1876	Kreisgericht Döhlen
10	Unterneubrunn	28. 8. 1876	Landgericht Eisfeld
11	Hohenberg	16. 12. 1876	Königlicher Handelsgerichtshof
12	Rudolstadt Volkstedt (2)	20. 1. 1877	Fürstliches Amtsgericht Rudolstadt
13	Rudolstadt Volkstedt (12)	1. 4. 1878	Fürstliches Amtsgericht Rudolstadt
14	Hohenberg	23. 4. 1878	Königlicher Handelsgerichtshof
15	Königszelt	12. 6. 1880	Königliches Amtsgericht
16	Schaala	27. 11. 1880	Fürstliches Amtsgericht Rudolstadt
17	Dresden (21)	27. 5. 1881	Königliches Amtsgericht Dresden
18	Oberkassel	9. 2. 1882	Königliches Amtsgericht Krefeld
19	KPM Berlin	8. 3. 1882	Königliches Amtsgericht Berlin
20	Rehau (1)	3. 8. 1882	Königliches Amtsgericht Rehau
21	Weiden (1)	7. 11. 1882	Königliches Landgericht Weiden
22	Hohenberg	4. 12. 1882	Königliches Landgericht Hof
23	Meissen (1)	23. 12. 1882	Königliches Amtsgericht Meißen
24	Dresden (16)	7. 3. 1883	Königliches Amtsgericht Dresden No. 116
25	Dresden (5)	7. 3. 1883	Königliches Amtsgericht Dresden No. 117
26	Dresden (28)	7. 3. 1883	Königliches Amtsgericht Dresden No. 118
27	Dresden (10)	7. 3. 1883	Königliches Amtsgericht Dresden No. 119
28	Dresden (16)	12. 3. 1883	Königliches Amtsgericht Dresden No. 121
29	Niedersalzbrunn (1)	6. 8. 1883	Königliches Amtsgericht Waldenburg No. 25
30	Fischern (1)	19. 11. 1883	Königliches Amtsgericht Leipzig No. 3133
31	Oberhohndorf	22. 2. 1884	Königliches Amtsgericht Zwickau No. 2
32	Rudolstadt Volkstedt (2)	8. 3. 1884	Fürstliches Amtsgericht Rudolstadt No. 6
33	Hamburg (1)	23. 7. 1884	Landgericht Hamburg
34	Blankenhain (1)	15. 8. 1884	Großherzogliches Amtsgericht Blankenhain No. 2
35	Schlierbach	20. 11. 1884	Königliches Amtsgericht Wächtersbach No. 1

36	Waldenburg (2)	26. 10. 1885	Königliches Amtsgericht Waldenburg No. 29/30
37	Lauscha	14. 12. 1885	Herzogliches Amtsgericht Steinach
38	Meissen, Cölln	12. 12. 1885	Königliches Amtsgericht Meißen
39	Tiefenfurt	16. 2. 1886	Königliches Amtsgericht Bunzlau
40	Dresden (36)	3. 3. 1886	Königliches Amtsgericht Dresden
41	Rudolstadt Volkstedt (2)	27. 3. 1886	Fürstliches Amtsgericht Rudolstadt
42	Gehren	5. 8. 1886	Fürstliches Amtsgericht Gehren
43	Selb	17. 9. 1887	Königlich Bayerisches Amtsgericht Selb
44	Fürstenberg	16. 6. 1888	RWZR
45	Stadtlengsfeld	23. 3. 1891	Landgericht Stadtslengsfeld
46	Charlottenburg	28. 5. 1891	No. 14956 in the RWZR
47	Selb (9)	17. 11. 1891	RWZR
48	Mitterteich (1)	11. 4. 1892	Königliches Amtsgericht Leipzig
49	Haida (1)	29. 4. 1892	Königliches Amtsgericht Leipzig No. 5260
50	Paris (127)	20. 5. 1892	Königliches Amtsgericht Leipzig
51	Schwarzenbach (2)	7. 6. 1892	Landgericht Hof/Bayern
52	Poppelsdorf	10. 8. 1892	Königliches Amtsgericht Bonn
53	Schmiedefeld	18. 10. 1892	Königliches Amtsgericht Schleusingen
54	Hohenberg	29. 12. 1893	Königliches Landgericht Hof
55	Rudolstadt Volkstedt (7)	27. 3. 1894	Fürstliches Amtsgericht Rudolstadt No. 11
56	Freiwaldau	30. 5. 1894	Königliches Amtsgericht Sorau No. 68
56a	Sorau (2)	16. 7. 1894	Königliches Amtsgericht Sorau No. 68
57	Rudolstadt Volkstedt (7)	3. 9. 1894	Fürstliches Amtsgericht Rudolstadt No. 13
58	Rudolstadt Volkstedt (4)	15. 9. 1894	Fürstliches Amtsgericht Rudolstadt No. 12
58a	Rudolstadt Volkstedt (3)	29. 9. 1894	Fürstliches Amtsgericht Rudolstadt
59	Rodach	15. 10. 1894	Landgericht Sachsen-Coburg-Gotha
60	Lichte (2)	12. 1. 1895	No. 4 Bd. 1895 Kaiserl. Patentamt Berlin
61	Dresden (16)	12. 1. 1895	Königliches Amtsgericht Dresden No. 1719
62	Altwasser	22. 3. 1895	Königliches Handelsgericht Waldenburg
63	Ilmenau	10. 10. 1895	No. 10092 in the RWZR
64	Rudolstadt Volkstedt (7)	12. 10. 1895	No. 10137 in the RWZR
65	Rudolstadt Volkstedt (7)	25. 11. 1895	No. 11329 in the RWZR
66	Rauenstein	6. 12. 1895	No. 11749 in the RWZR
67	Rudolstadt Volkstedt (4)	16. 12. 1895	No. 12005 in the RWZR
68	Rudolstadt Volkstedt (1)	4. 1. 1896	No. 12514 in the RWZR
69	Elgersburg	25. 1. 1896	No. 13233 in the RWZR
70	Potschappel	10. 2. 1896	No. 13793 in the RWZR
71	Neuhaldensleben (1)	7. 3. 1896	No. 14596 in the RWZR
72	Rudolstadt Volkstedt (20)	22. 5. 1896	No. 16682 in the RWZR
73	Turn nr. Teplitz	2. 12. 1896	No. 20791 in the RWZR
74	Mannheim (2)	9. 12. 1896	No. 20946 in the RWZR
75	Rehau (1)	29. 12. 1896	No. 21268 in the RWZR
76	Weisswasser	11. 1. 1897	No. 21482 in the RWZR

77	Waldenburg	5. 2. 1897	No. 21974 in the RWZR
78	Tiefenfurt (1)	22. 2. 1897	No. 22320 in the RWZR
79	Tiefenfurt (1)	9. 4. 1897	No. 23505 in the RWZR
80	Fürstenberg	10. 4. 1897	No. 23545 in the RWZR
81	Rozemburg	9. 6. 1897	No. 24901 in the RWZR
82	Zell a. H.	14. 8. 1897	No. 25970 in the RWZR
83	Mitterteich (1)	21. 8. 1897	No. 26023 in the RWZR
84	Kronach	23. 3. 1898	No. 29660 in the RWZR
85	Mitterteich (1)	7. 4. 1898	No. 29956 in the RWZR
86	Hof-Moschendorf	30. 6. 1898	No. 31710 in the RWZR
87	Sorau (2)	11. 7. 1898	No. 31943 in the RWZR
88	Dresden (19)	13. 7. 1898	No. 31963 in the RWZR
89	Geiersthal	25. 7. 1898	No. 32080 in the RWZR
90	Marktredwitz (2)	5. 8. 1898	No. 32287 in the RWZR
91	Zell a. H.	23. 8. 1898	No. 32440 in theRWZR
92	Marktleuthen (1)	21. 9. 1898	No. 34281 in the RWZR
93	Suhl	10. 12. 1898	No. 34775 in the RWZR
94	Fraureuth	27. 2. 1899	No. 36312 in the RWZR
95	Wunsiedel	27. 2. 1899	No. 36313 in the RWZR
96	Turn nr. Teplitz	18. 9. 1899	No. 39741/2 in the RWZR
97	Rehau (1)	3. 10. 1899	No. 40029 in the RWZR
98	Mannheim (1)	9. 2. 1900	No. 42204 in the RWZR
99	Rudolstadt Volkstedt (6)	20. 4. 1900	No. 43314 in the RWZR
100	Rudolstadt Volkstedt	3. 5. 1900	No. 43595 in the RWZR
101	Marktleuthen (1)	8. 1900	No. 45675 in the RWZR
102	Meissen (1)	5. 4. 1901	No. 49332 in the RWZR
103	Dresden (12)	28. 8. 1901	No. 50256 in the RWZR
104	Burgau	26. 3. 1902	No. 53347 in the RWZR
105	Suhl	16. 5. 1902	No. 54161 in the RWZR
106	Munich	27. 12. 1902	No. 57308 in the RWZR
107	Passau (3)	13. 3. 1903	No. 58772 in the RWZR
108	Passau (3)	9. 4. 1903	No. 59442 in the RWZR
109	Dresden (14)	15. 4. 1903	No. 59557 in the RWZR
110	Potschappel	6. 8. 1903	No. 61992 in the RWZR
111	Passau (3)	15. 9. 1903	No. 62823 in the RWZR
112	Coburg	22. 10. 1903	No. 63821 in the RWZR
113	Dresden (5)	30. 10. 1903	No. 64101 in the RWZR (Crown)
114	Dresden (5)	30. 10. 1903	No. 64102 in the RWZR (Kron)
115	Dresden (10)	25. 11. 1903	No. 64713 in the RWZR
116	Ilmenau	15. 12. 1903	No. 65260 in the RWZR
117	Turn nr. Teplitz	3. 4. 1904	No. 68834 in the RWZR
118	Meissen (see under Fürsten)	1. 7. 1904	No. 70704 in the RWZR
119	Marktredwitz	5. 9. 1904	No. 71820 in the RWZR
120	Rudolstadt Volkstedt (20)	30. 9. 1904	No. 72544 in the RWZR
121	Berlin (3)	13. 10. 1904	No. 73022 in the RWZR
122	Schorndorf	9. 11. 1904	No. 73724 in the RWZR
123	Hohenberg	28. 11. 1904	No. 74373 in the RWZR
124	Suhl	27. 3. 1905	No. 77684 in the RWZR
125	Berlin (3)	24. 4. 1905	No. 78499 in the RWZR
126	Berlin (3)	10. 5. 1905	No. 78794 in the RWZR
127	Mitterteich (1)	26. 6. 1905	No. 80141 in the RWZR
128	Rudolstadt Volkstedt (11)	29. 7. 1905	No. 80963 in the RWZR
129	Ilmenau	20. 9. 1905	No. 81694 in the RWZR

130	Ludwigsburg (1)	28. 6. 1906	No. 89107/8/9/10 in the RWZR
131	Ludwigsburg (1)	2. 7. 1906	No. 89262 in the RWZR
132	Oberhohndorf	6. 9. 1906	No. 90606 in the RWZR
133	Roschütz	7. 9. 1906	No. 90622 in the RWZR
134	Creidlitz (1)	24. 9. 1906	No. 90942 in the RWZR
135	Kleindembach	9. 2. 1907	No. 94686 in the RWZR
136	Selb	23. 2. 1907	No. 95105 in the RWZR
137	Ilmenau	25. 4. 1907	No. 96979 in the RWZR
138	Rudolstadt Volkstedt (7)	8. 6. 1907	No. 98389 in the RWZR
139	Rudolstadt Volkstedt (21)	19. 8. 1907	No. 100367 in the RWZR
140	Zell a. H.	29. 1. 1908	No. 104648 in the RWZR
141	Passau (3)	30. 3. 1908	No. 106331 in the RWZR
142	Niedersalzbrunn (1)	26. 6. 1908	No. 108719 in the RWZR
143	Oeslau	1. 7. 1908	No. 108911 in the RWZR
143a	Rudolstadt Volkstedt (7)	9. 7. 1908	No. 109243 in the RWZR
144	Berlin (6)	15. 10. 1908	No. 111474 in the RWZR
145	Rudolstadt Volkstedt (7)	19. 12. 1908	No. 113264 in the RWZR
146	Marktredwitz	30. 12. 1908	No. 113484 in the RWZR
146a	Rudolstadt Volkstedt (12)	15. 2. 1909	No. 114951 in the RWZR
147	Altwasser	13. 5. 1909	No. 117665 in the RWZR
148	Neuhaldensleben	17. 5. 1909	No. 117809 in the RWZR
149	Schwarzenbach	28. 5. 1909	No. 118240 in the RWZR
150	Unterweissbach	7. 6. 1909	No. 118535 in the RWZR
151	Mannheim	8. 6. 1909	No. 118588 in the RWZR
152	Lichte (2)	30. 6. 1909	No. 119362 in the RWZR
153	Dresden (14)	20. 10. 1909	No. 121633 in the RWZR
154	Stadtlengsfeld	11. 10. 1909	No. 122318 in the RWZR
155	Waldershof (1)	29. 10. 1909	No. 122925/6 in the RWZR
156	Limoges (1)	1. 11. 1909	No. 122989/90 in the RWZR
157	Köppelsdorf	4. 1. 1910	No. 125146 in the RWZR
158	Weiden (1)	13. 1. 1910	No. 125483 in the RWZR
159	Kahla	21. 1. 1910	No. 125742 in the RWZR
160	Schönwald	24. 1. 1910	No. 125820 in the RWZR
161	Lichte (2)	4. 3. 1910	No. 127009 in the RWZR
162	Dresden (19)	26. 3. 1910	No. 127739 in the RWZR
163	Oberköditz	14. 5. 1910	No. 129734 in the RWZR
164	Tiefenfurt	17. 5. 1910	No. 129800 in the RWZR
165	Plankenhammer	18. 7. 1910	No. 132456 in the RWZR
166	Selb Zeidler	27. 7. 1910	No. 132725 in the RWZR
167	Stoke on Trent (8)	29. 8. 1910	No. 133667 in the RWZR
168	Ilmenau	19. 5. 1911	No. 144259 in the RWZR
169	Marktredwitz	24. 5. 1911	No. 144500 in the RWZR
170	Selb	24. 5. 1911	No. 144511 in the RWZR
171	Selb	18. 8. 1911	No. 147837 in the RWZR
172	Weiden	19. 9. 1911	No. 148638 in the RWZR
173	Weiden	7. 10. 1911	No. 149624 in the RWZR
174	Berlin (7)	20. 10. 1911	No. 150207 in the RWZR
175	Schönwald	25. 10. 1911	No. 151709 in the RWZR
176	Selb	8. 11. 1911	No. 159979 in the RWZR
177	Schönwald	16. 2. 1912	No. 155112 in the RWZR
178	Eisenberg	19. 2. 1912	No. 155178 in the RWZR
179	Copenhagen	22. 3. 1912	No. 156154 in the RWZR
180	Stanowitz	1. 4. 1912	No. 156858 in the RWZR
181	Schönwald	20. 5. 1912	No. 159201 in the RWZR
182	Schönwald	8. 6. 1912	No. 160260 in the RWZR

183	Marktredwitz	29. 7. 1912	No. 162570 in the RWZR
184	Elgersburg	26. 10. 1912	No. 165889 in the RWZR
185	Elgersburg	5. 11. 1912	No. 166255 in the RWZR
186	Dux	31. 3. 1913	No. 173047 in the RWZR
187	Königsee (1)	5. 6. 1913	No. 176409 in the RWZR
188	Potschappel	26. 1. 1914	No. 187733 in the RWZR
189	Potschappel	28. 1. 1914	No. 187853 in the RWZR
190	Arzberg	21. 4. 1914	No. 192262 in the RWZR
191	Katzhütte	23. 4. 1914	No. 192330 in the RWZR
192	Copenhagen	9. 7. 1914	No. 196616 in the RWZR
193	Königszelt	3. 8. 1914	No. 198006 in the RWZR
194	Potschappel	26. 9. 1914	No. 199079 in the RWZR
195	Bockwallendorf	31. 12. 1914	No. 201073 in the RWZR
196	Krautheim	20. 4. 1915	No. 202919 in the RWZR
197	Katzhütte	7. 5. 1915	No. 203259 in the RWZR
198	Schwarzenbach	21. 7. 1915	No. 204789 in the RWZR
199	Rudolstadt Volkstedt (1) and (5)	8. 9. 1915	No. 205638 in the RWZR
200	Rudolstadt Volkstedt (5) and (8)	27. 10. 1915	No. 206619 in the RWZR
201	Eichwald	18. 12. 1915	No. 207647 in the RWZR
202	Tiefenfurt	18. 12. 1915	No. 207660 in the RWZR
203	Rudolstadt Volkstedt (1) and (5)	13. 4. 1916	No. 209661 in the RWZR
204	Sitzendorf	17. 5. 1916	No. 210321 in the RWZR
205	Tillowitz	23. 5. 1916	No. 210505 in the RWZR
206	Vohenstrauss	23. 6. 1917	No. 218445 in the RWZR
207	Krummennaab	19. 9. 1917	No. 219774 in the RWZR
208	Weimar	28. 11. 1917	No. 221178 in the RWZR
209	Munich (8)	6. 7. 1918	No. 225106 in the RWZR
210	Schramberg (2)	20. 9. 1918	No. 226288 in the RWZR
211	Weiden	6. 1. 1919	No. 228403 in the RWZR
212	Schorndorf	24. 1. 1919	No. 228751/2/3 in the RWZR
213	Rehau	4. 2. 1919	No. 229018 in the RWZR
214	Selb-Plössberg	5. 2. 1919	No. 229122 in the RWZR
215	Limbach	15. 2. 1919	No. 229485/6 in the RWZR
216	Schorndorf	15. 2. 1919	No. 229487 in the RWZR
217	Selb (4)	18. 2. 1919	No. 229582 in the RWZR
218	Limbach (2)	13. 3. 1919	No. 230181 in the RWZR
219	Dux	14. 3. 1919	No. 230219 in the RWZR
220	Rudolstadt Volkstedt (6)	1. 4. 1919	No. 230665 in the RWZR
221	Fraureuth (1)	4. 4. 1919	No. 230728 in the RWZR
222	Wunsiedel	22. 4. 1919	No. 231192 in the RWZR
223	Tiefenfurt	11. 6. 1919	No. 232989 in the RWZR
224	Oeslau (2)	11. 8. 1919	No. 234408/9/10 in the RWZR
225	Selb	15. 9. 1919	No. 235330 in the RWZR
226	Gotha	24. 9. 1919	No. 235574 in the RWZR
227	Zwickau (2)	9. 2. 1920	No. 242259 in the RWZR
228	Longton (78)	13. 2. 1920	No. 242542 in the RWZR
229	Kleindembach	27. 2. 1920	No. 243236/7/8 in the RWZR
230	Selb	8. 4. 1920	No. 245243 in the RWZR
231	Waldsassen	11. 5. 1920	No. 246872 in the RWZR
232	Waldsassen	19. 5. 1920	No. 247307 in the RWZR
233	Plankenhammer	1. 6. 1920	No. 247904 in the RWZR
234	Plankenhammer	1. 6. 1920	No. 247905 in the RWZR
235	Chemnitz	28. 6. 1920	No. 249336 in the RWZR

236	Dresden (15)	12. 10. 1920	No. 253868 in the RWZR
237	Erkersreuth	21. 10. 1920	No. 254375 in the RWZR
238	Weiden (1)	25. 4. 1921	No. 263927 in the RWZR
239	Mitterteich	11. 6. 1921	No. 267061 in the RWZR
240	Grossbreitenbach	27. 9. 1921	No. 272489 in the RWZR
241	Tiefenfurt	6. 2. 1922	No. 279384 in the RWZR
242	Schorndorf	18. 2. 1922	No. 280774 in the RWZR
243	Aachen (1)	22. 2. 1922	No. 281169 in the RWZR
244	Mitterteich	9. 3. 1922	No. 281859 in the RWZR
245	Freienwaldau	17. 3. 1922	No. 282532 in the RWZR
246	Rehau	3. 4. 1922	No. 283526 in the RWZR
247	Königszelt	18. 5. 1922	No. 286423 in the RWZR
248	Nymphenburg	16. 6. 1922	No. 287972 in the RWZR
249	Schmiedeberg	11. 11. 1922	No. 293938 in the RWZR
250	Gräfenthal (1)	11. 3. 1879	Herzogliches Landsgericht Gräfenthal
251	Ohrdruf	13. 6. 1919	No. 233082 in the RWZR
252	Schorndorf	4. 6. 1918	No. 224480 in the RWZR
253	Stadtlengsfeld	20. 4. 1895	Landgericht Stadtlengsfeld
254	Tettau (1)	27. 5. 1895	Kgl. Landgericht
255	Tettau	20. 4. 1920	No. 245792 in the RWZR
256	Vohenstrauss	3. 4. 1911	No. 141909 in the RWZR
257	Schwarza	10. 9. 1895	Landgericht Schwarza
258	Ladowitz	14. 9. 1900	No. 45494 in the RWZR
259	Niedersalzbrunn	29. 8. 1910	No. 133665 in the RWZR
260	Köppelsdorf	2. 1903	No. 58176 in the RWZR

Sèvres artists and their Signatures

Asterisks indicate artists who signed with their full names

Alanord: female decorator 1920–30
Alaurent: decorator 1923–38
Allard: repairer 1832–41
Aloncle: birds, animals 1758–81
André: landscapes 1840–69

Anthaume: landscapes 1752–8

Apoil: figures 1851–64

Apoil (Mme): figures 1865–92

Archelais: modeller 1865–1902

Armand cadet: flowers 1746–88

Asselin: portraits, miniatures 1765–1804

Astruc: biscuit repairer 1903–50

Aubert aîné: flowers 1754–8

Avisse: decorator 1848–84

Bailly père: gilder 1753–67

Baldisseroni: figures 1860–79

Ballanger: decorator 1905–12

Barbin: decorator 1815–49

Bardet: flowers 1751–8

Barrat l'oncle: festoons, flowers 1769–91

Barré: flowers, gilding 1773–8

Barré: flowers 1844–81

Barriat: figures, ornaments 1848–83

Baudoin: ornaments, gilding 1750–1800

Beaudoux: female decorator 1932–40
Becquet: flowers 1749–65

Belet Adolphe: decorator 1881–2

Belet Emile: flowers 1879–1900

Belet Louis: decorator 1878–1913

Béranger: figures 1807–46

Bergeret: figures 1804–18

Berlin: decorator 1920–51
Berthault: decorator, then sculptor, modeller since 1943

Bertrand: bouquets 1757–74

Bestault: sculptor 1889–1929

Bieuville: decorator 1886–1925

Bienfait: decorator 1756–62

Binet: bouquets 1750–75

Bisson (M.): decorator 1943–50

Blaise: female decorator 1929–31

Blanchard: decorator, gilder 1848–80

Blanchard (A.): decorator 1878–1901

Bocquet: decorator 1899–1920

Boileau: repairer 1773–81

Boitel: gilder 1797–1822

Bollé: repairer since 1949
Bonnet (Melle): flowers 1834–54

Bonnuit: decorator, gilder 1858–94

Boquet: landscapes 1809–10

Boquet: sculptor 1815–60

Boquet (Melle V.): figures 1865–9

Boterel: biscuit repairer 1889–1933

Bouché-Leclercq: decorator 1902–19

Boucher: flowers and festoons 1754–62

Bouchet: landscapes, figures, ornaments 1763–93

Boucot: flowers, birds 1785–91

Bouillat fils: flowers, landscapes 1785–93

Boulanger père: gilder 1754–84

Boulanger fils: rustic scenes, children 1778–81

Boullemier (A. G.): gilder 1802–42

Boullemier (F. A.): gilder 1806–38

Boullemier (H. F.): gilder 1813–55

Boullemier (Melle): gilder 1814–42

Boulmé: decorator since 1953

Bourdois: sculptor 1773
Bourgeois: flowers 1846–8

Boutaleb: decorator since 1948

Bouvrain: ornaments 1826–48

Brachard aîné: sculptor 1782–1824

Brachard jeune: sculptor 1784–1827

Brécy: sculptor-modeller 1881–1928

Briffaut: sculptor 1848–90

* Brunel Roques: figures 1852–83

Bulidon: bouquets 1763–92

Bulot: flowers 1855–83

Bunel (Mme, née Buteux): flowers 1778–1816

Buteux aîné: figures 1756–82

Buteux jeune: bouquets 1759–66

Buteux, fils cadet: flowers, landscapes 1773–90

Buteux Théodore: ornamental decorator 1786–1822

Cabau: flowers 1847–85

Caille: painter 1943–50

Cantin: biscuit repairer 1902–11

Capelle: landscapes 1746–1800

Capronnier: gilder 1812–19

Cardin: bouquets 1749–86

* Caron: genre-painter 1792–1815

Carrié: flowers 1752–7

Castel: landscapes, hunting scenes, birds 1772–97

Caton: arcadian scenes, children 1749–98

Catrice: flowers 1757–74

Catteau: decorator 1902–4

Célos: decorator 1865–95

Chabry: miniatures 1765–87

Chambon: female painter 1930–40

Chanou (J. B.): repairer 1779–1825

Chanou (Melle S.): flowers 1779–98

Chanou (Mme, née Durosey): female gilder 1779–1800

Chaponet-Desnoyez: flowers 1788–1828

Chappuis aîné: flowers, birds 1761–87

Chappuis jeune: bouquets 1772–7

Charpentier: gilder 1852–79

Charrin (Melle): figures, portraits 1814–26

Chauvaux aîné: gilding 1753–88

Chauvaux fils: bouquets 1773–83

Chevalier: flowers, bouquets 1755–7

Choisy (A. J. de): flowers, arabesques 1770–1812

Chulot: flowers, arabesques 1755–1800

Cieutat: biscuit repairer 1894–1928

Cirot: biscuit repairer 1903–17
Collet: sculptor 1784–1809

Commelin:bouquets, festoons1768–1802

Constans: painter and gilder 1803–40

Constantin: figures 1813–48

* Cool (Mme de): figures 1860–70

Cornaille: flowers 1755–1800

Cosson: repairer since 1932
Cotteau: decorator 1780–4

Courcy (de): figure painter 1865–86

Coursajet: gilder 1881–6

Courval: female gilder 1919–66

Couturier: flowers 1762–75

Dailhat: repairer since 1934

Dammouse: figures, ornaments 1852–80
Daniel: sculptor since 1945

David: decorator 1844–81

Davignon: figures 1807–15

* Degault: figures 1808–17

Delachenal: arcanist and painter 1924–46

Delafosse: figures 1804–15

Delahaye: repairer 1818–52

Delatre cadet: repairer 1754–8

* Demarne: landscapes 1809–13
Demarne (Melle C.): landscapes 1822–5

* Denois (Melle J.): portraits 1817–28

Depérais: ornamental decorator 1794–1822

Depiere: repairer since 1945

Depoorter: sculptor 1920–35

Derichweiler: decorator 1855–84

Derny: sculptor since 1938

* Des Isnards: flower painter 1835–48

Desvignes: biscuit repairer 1902–23

Deutsch: decorator and gilder 1803–19

Develly: landscapes 1813–48

�⅁ⅅ	Devicq: sculptor and modeller 1881–1928
ⅅ.I	Didier: ornamental decorator 1819–48
⚿	Dieu: Chinese decorating, gilding 1777–1811
ⅅ	Doat: decorator 1879–1905
K..	Dodin: figures, portraits 1754–1802
ⅅ	Doré: ornamental decorator 1829–65
ⅅⅬ	Drand: Chinese figures, gilding 1764–80
*	Drolling: figures 1802–13
⅏Έⅅ	Drouet (Emile): decorator 1878–1920
ⅅ⅌	Drouet (Gilbert): flowers, birds 1785–1825
Ⅺ	Dubois (Alexandre): biscuit repairer 1896–1915
ⅅ	Dubois (Edmond): biscuit repairer 1906–23
	Dubois (J. C. T.): landscapes and seascapes decorator 1842–8
ⅉ	Dubois (J. R.): flowers, festoons 1756–7
⅍ⅅ	Ducluzeau (Mme A.): figures, portraits 1818–48
ⅅE	Dufossé: biscuit repairer 1901–21
ⅅⅅ	Dumain: biscuit repairer 1884–28
ⅉⅅ	Dumeyniou: repairer 1932–45
ⅅ.ⅵ	Durosey: gilding 1802–30
ⅅ..	Dusolle: bouquets 1768–74
ⅅT	Dutanda: bouquets, festoons 1765–1802
⅌'	Eaubonne (L. d'): decorator 1902–14
Æ	Escallier (Mme): flowers, birds 1874–88
⅍	Evans: birds, butterflies, landscapes 1752–1806
⅍⅐	Even: repairer since 1938
⅀ⅅ	Fachard: biscuit repairer 1889–1934
F	Fallot: arabesques, birds 1773–90
HF	Faraguet (Mme): figures 1857–79
MF	Ferry: biscuit repairer 1907–14
Æ	Ficquenet: flowers and ornaments 1864–81
ⅉⅉ	Fischbag: sculptor 1834–50
.Ⅻ	Fontaine (J. J.): painter 1825–57
∴	Fontaine (J.): painter 1752–1807
ANF.	Fontaine (A. M.): female decorator 1928–38
♡	Fontelliau: decorator 1753–5
F.Forgeot	Forgeot: sculptor 1856–87
Y	Fouré: flowers 1749–62
Ⅎ	Fournerie: decorator 1901–3
ⅎ	Fournier: decorator 1878–1926
⅏Ⅳⅉ	Fragonard (Th.): flowers, landscapes 1839–69
ⅉF	Freyssinges (J. B.): painter 1916–35
⅌	Freyssinges (C.): decorator 1919–71
☀	Fritsch: figures, children 1763–4
⅏. ⅎ	Fritz: decorator 1902–50
EF	Fromant: figures 1855–85
⅌⅌fx	Fumez: bouquets 1777–1804
*	Gallois (Mme): figures 1871
Gu.	Ganeau: gilder 1813–31
*	Garneray L.: seascapes 1839–48
P.G	Gaucher: decorator 1933–67
⅌	Gauthier: figures, landscapes 1787–91
⅁	Gauvenet: sculptor 1908–47
⅍⅁	Gauvenet (A. J.): sculptor since 1950
⅌	Gébleux: decorator 1883–1928
J.G	Gély: decorator 1851–89
G	Genest: figures 1752–89
ⅉ	Genin: flowers, festoons, friezes 1756–7
⅍⅁	Gensoli: decorator 1921–57
⅁.⅁.	Georget: figures, portraits 1801–23
⅁ⅉ.	Gérard (C. C.): pastoral scenes, miniatures 1771–1824
ⅶⅼ	Gérard (Mme, née Vautrin): flowers 1781–1802
*	Giboy: decorator 1806
⅍	Girard: arabesques, Chinese figures 1772–1817
⅁ⅼR	Gobert: figures enameller 1849–91
⅍	Gobled: decorator 1902–5
*	Goddé: gilder, enameller 1856–83
ⅅ.G.	Godin (Mme): female gilder 1806–28
⅁	Godin (F. A.): sculptor 1813–48
⅏	Gomery: flowers and birds 1756–8
F.S – F.G	Goupil: figures 1859–78

Gt Grémont: festoons, bouquets 1769–81

𝒳 Grison: gilding 1749–71

L G Guéneau: biscuit repairer 1885–1924

J.G Guignard: repairer since 1949

𝕲 Guillemain: decorator 1864–85

ℋ Hallion, E.: landscapes 1870–93

ℋ Hallion, F.: gilder, decorator 1865–95

* Hamon: figures 1849–57

(J.H. Hébert-Coeffin (J.): sculptor 1938–47

jℎ Henrion: festoons, bouquets 1770–84

ℋ⋀ ℋ Herbillon: decorator 1901–41

ℎ Herbillon (Mme J.): female decorator 1933–41

ℎe. Héricourt: festoons, bouquets 1770–7

𝔴 Hileken: figures, rustic scenes 1769–74

ℋ Houry: flowers 1754–5

ℎ.∂. Huard: ornaments 1811–46

· ε·ȝ· Humbert: figures 1851–70

ℎ Huny: decorator and sculptor 1791–9

JP Huré: decorator 1915–52

ℋℰ Huss: sculptor 1929–55

* Isabey: figures 1808–17
Jacobber (Mele, Mme Worms): flowers and fruits 1835–9

Jα' Jaccober (M.): flowers and friezes 1814–48

* Jacques: figures 1812–14

J2 Jacquotot (Mme): figures 1801–42

* Jadelot (Mme S.): figures 1852–70

ℰ Jardel: decorator 1886–1913

Ƶ Joyau: bouquets 1766–75

r-J Jubin: decorator 1772–5

ℰ Julienne: Renaissance ornaments 1837–49

ƙ Kiefer, F.: ceramist 1936–47

ℋ Kiefer: female painter 1947–54

PK Knipp (Mme P.): flowers and birds 1808–26

Λ Labbé: flowers 1847–53
Lacour: biscuit repairer 1895–1911

℈ Lagriffoul: decorator 1907–21

* Lamarre: landscapes 1821–4

ℋ Lambert: flowers and ornaments 1859–99

* Lamprecht: figures and animals 1784–7

L·Ꮆ Langlacé: landscapes 1807–44

lꝣ Langle: flowers 1837–45

* Langlois (Paul): landscapes 1891–7

* Langlois (Polyclès): landscapes 1847–72

ᏗᏢ Lapierre: repairer 1833–43

ᏂᏒ Laroche (J. F. L. de): flowers, festoons 1759–1802

ℋ. Lasserre: decorator 1886–1931

ℰ Latache: gilder 1867–79

* Laurent (Mme M. P.): figures 1838–60

ᏂᎠᎠ Léandre: children, presentations 1779–85

Ꮐℒ Lebarque: biscuit repairer 1895–1916

Ꮲꝣ Le Bel aîné: figures, flowers 1766–75

ᏞᏰ Le Bel jeune: festoons, bouquets 1773–93

£·Ꭾ Le Bel (Nicolas): landscapes, portraits 1804–45

L Leclerc: biscuit repairer 1897–1911

ℒ Leclerc, S.: repairer 1911–55

ll,ll Lecot: Chinese decorating, gilding 1773–1802

∪ Ledoux: landscapes, birds 1758–61

⌐Ꮑ˪ꟼ Leduc: decorator 1923–54

ℒ Legay: repairer 1861–95

Λ - Ꭲ Léger: decorator 1905–19

ℒ.Ꮆ. Le Grand: gilder and decorator 1776–1817

£.Ꮆ. Le Guay père: gilder 1749–96

L G Le Guay (E. C.): figures, portraits 1778–1840

ℱ Le Guay (P. A.): miniatures 1772–1818

ᏞᎡ Le Riche: sculptor 1757–1801

ℰℒ Leroy: gilder 1855–91

* Lessore: figures 1853–5

ℐ Letourneur: sculptor, 1756–62

LT Le Tronne: sculptor 1753–7

L Levé (Denis): flowers, arabesques 1754–1805

ℱ Levé (Félix): flowers, chinoiseries 1777–9

* Levy: female decorator 1930–40

JL	Liancé: sculptor 1769–1810
AL, A.	Ligue: decorator and gilder 1884–1911
A	Longuet: repairer 1840–76
C.L, Ch.L	Lucas: decorator 1878–1909
*	Lyngbye: landscapes 1841–2
R.B	Maqueret (Mme, née Bouillat): flowers 1796–1820
⊲A	Martinet: flowers 1847–78
MA	Mascret: ornaments 1836–46
Mas	Mascret (J. E.): sculptor 1810–48
M.C	Mascret (L.): sculptor 1825–64
M6	Masy: flowers, birds 1779–1803
Ma-ME	Maugendre: sculptor 1879–87
ЄdeM.	Maussion (Melle de): figures 1862–70
S	Méreaud aîné: friezes 1754–91
9	Méreaud jeune: bouquets, festoons 1756–79
ₒM	Mérigot: ornaments, flowers 1845–92
E.M.	Métayer: female painter since 1947
JAR	Meyer (Alfred): decorator 1858–71
*	Meyer-Heine (Jacob): ornaments, enameller 1840–73
X	Micaud (J.): flowers, bouquets 1757–1810
M.C	Micaud (P. L.): painter and gilder 1795–1834
M	Michel: bouquets 1772–80
M	Milet (Optat): decorator 1862–79
LM M.	Mimard: decorator 1884–1928
LM	Mirey: gilder 1788–92
M	Moiron: bouquets 1790–1
5	Mongenot: flowers 1754–64
M.R.	Moreau: gilder 1807–15
CAJ	Moreau-Jouin: female decorator c. 1928
M	Morin: marine and military scenes 1754–87
M.R.	Morin: gilder 1805–12
AM	Moriot: decorator 1843–4
*	Moriot (N. M.): figures, portraits 1828–48
EM	Moriot (Melle): figures, ornaments 1881–6
m .f	Moyez (P.): repairer 1827–48
M	Moyez (J. L.): gilder 1818–48
V	Mutel: landscapes 1754–73
M	Naret: decorator 1907–14
A . N ·	Naudy: decorator 1928–34

4	Né: female decorator c. 1928
ng·	Nicquet: bouquets 1764–92
⁀l⁀	Noel: figures 1755–1804
SD	Nouailhier (Mme née Dorosey): flowers 1777–95
og	Oger: sculptor 1784–1821
o⏀	Ouint (C.): decorator gilder 1879–90
P	Paillet: ornaments 1879–93
🦅	Pajou: figures 1751–9
*	Parant (L. B.): figures 1806–41
P	Parpette: flowers 1755–1806
PP	Parpette (Melle): flowers 1788–98
LP	Parpette (Melle L.): flowers 1794–1817
P	Peluche: decorator 1881–1928
ap	Percheron: repairer 1827–64
*	Perlet (Melle): portraits 1825–30
fP	Perrenot: figures 1804–15
R	Petit: biscuit repairer 1902–14
P.T.	Petit: flowers 1756–1806
f	Pfeiffer: bouquets 1771–1800
P.H.	Philipp: copper enamelling 1846–77
	Philippine aîné: rustic scenes, children 1778–1825
Ph.	Philippine cadet: flowers and animals 1783–1839
PP	Piédagnel: figures 1861–90
P·	Pierre aîné: gilder 1759–75
Pg.	Pierre jeune: bouquets, festoons 1763–1800
P	Pihan: sculptor and decorator 1879–1910
P	Pine: gilder 1854–70 Piquet: decorator 1920–2
Pt.	Pithou aîné: portraits, historical scenes 1757–90
P.j.	Pithou jeune: figures, flowers, ornaments 1760–95
R	Planchais: modeller, repairer since 1948
t.RP	Plantard: painter since 1928
P	Porchon: decorator 1880–4
&	Pouillot: bouquets 1773–8
P	Poupart: landscapes 1815–48
HP.	Prévost le second: gilder 1757–97
P	Prince: decorator 1920–5
QM	Prunier: decorator 1920–59

Œ Quennoy: decorator 1901–7

∴.. Raux: bouquets 1766–79

R. Régnier (J. F.): decorator 1812–48

JR Régnier (Hyacinthe): sculptor 1825–70

R Réjoux: decorator and gilder 1858–93

R Rémy: decorator 1886–1928

RH Renard (Emile): decorator 1852–82
Renard (Henri): decorator, landscapes 1879–82

RR Renault: biscuit repairer 1920–52

A Richard (Auguste): gilder 1811–48

EMR Richard (Emile): flowers 1859–1900

ER Richard (Eugene): flowers 1833–72

R Richard (François): decorator 1832–75

JhR Richard (N. J.): ornaments 1831–72

LR Richard (Léon): decorator 1902–25

✳ Richard (Paul): gilder, decorator 1849–81

R.. Richard (Pierre): gilder 1815–48

R Richard (Melle M.): female decorator 1930–4

RL Rigolet: biscuit repairer 1895–1935

Rx Riocreux (I.): landscapes 1846–9

R Riocreux (D. D.): flowers 1807–28

JR Risbourg : biscuit repairer 1895–1925
Riton: ornaments 1821–60

CR Robert (C.): biscuit repairer 1889–1930

R.B Robert (J. F.): landscapes, hunting scenes 1806–43

HR Robert (H.): biscuit repairer 1889–1933

PR Robert (P.): ornaments 1813–32

CR Robert (Melle L.): flowers and landscapes 1835–40

XX Rocher: figures, miniatures 1758–9

R Roden: decorator since 1947

✳ Rodin (A.): sculptor, decorator 1879–83 and 1888

✳ Rogeard (Melle): female decorator 1817–19

JR Roger: sculptor 1852–86

↙ Rosset: landscapes and flowers 1753–95

ER Roucheret: biscuit repairer 1901–41

RL Roussel: bouquets 1758–74

PMR Roussel: figures 1850–71

R Roy (Melle): female decorator 1920–30

S Samson: biscuit repairer 1897–1918

S Sandoz: sculptor 1890–1920
Sauve: decorator 1919–22

✳ Schilt (Abel): figures 1847–80

✳ Schilt (Léonard): figures 1877–93

P. S. Schilt (Louis P.): flowers 1818–55

S. h. Schrade: birds, landscapes 1773–86

S Sère: decorator 1949–55

S S Serré: decorator 1902–20

S Sieffert: figures 1881–98

HS Sill: decorator 1881–7

EJ Simard: decorator and gilder 1884–1909

N Sinsson (Nicolas): flowers, festoons 1773–95

S. S Sinsson (Jacques): flowers, ornaments 1795–1846

SSp Sinsson (Pierre): flowers 1818–48

SSl Sinsson (Louis): flowers 1830–47

R Sioux: flower painter 1752–92

O Sioux jeune: flowers, festoons 1752–9

R√ Sivault: decorator 1924–68

M Solon: figures 1857–71

✳ Solon (Melle): figures 1861–9

Sw Swebach: military scenes 1802–13

◆ Tabary: birds 1754–5

✳ Taillandier: bouquets, festoons 1753–90

• • • Tandart: flowers, festoons 1754–1803

⊡ Tardy: bouquets 1755–95

• • • • Théodore: decorator and gilder 1765–79

| Thévenet père: flowers 1741–77

Jt Thévenet fils: flowers 1752–8

T Tissier: biscuit repairer 1900–16

J.T Trager (J.): flowers, birds 1847–73

HT Trager (H.): decorator, flowers 1887–1909

Ⅼ   Trager (L.): decorator 1894–1934

✳   Tréverret (Melle de): figures 1820–42

Ꭹ   Tristan: decorator, figures 1837–82

ᴦ   Troyon: decorator and gilder
      1801–17

✳   Turgan (Mme C.): portraits 1830–52

ℋℐ   Uhlrich: gilder 1879–1925

ᐯᕍ   Vande père: gilder, flowers 1753–79

Ⅴᗪ   Vande (P.): gilder 1779–1824

✳   Van Marcke (J. B. J.): landscapes
      1825–32

✳   Van Marcke (E.): landscapes,
      animals 1853–70

✳   Van Os: flowers and fruits 1811–22

✳   Van Spaendonck: flowers 1795–1809

ℱⅤ   Vast: decorator 1902–9

ℐ Vaubertrand: gilder and decorator
      1822–48

W   Vasasseur aîné: arabesques and
      flowers 1753–70

ᴗᴗ   Vieillard: landscapes 1751–90

ᵞ ᵿ   Vignol: decorator 1884–1909

Ⅴ   Villion (P.): biscuit repairer
      1886–1934

ⅭⅤ   Villion (C.): biscuit repairer
      1894–1941

2 000   Vincent: gilding 1753–8

W   Walter: flowers 1859–70

W   Weydinger père: flowers and gilder
      1757–1807

W   Weydinger 2 fils: ornaments, gilder
      1778–1824

ℋℙ   Weydinger 3 fils: decorator and gilder
      1781–1816

✚   Xhrouet: landscapes 1750–75

ᵼ   Yvernel: landscapes, birds 1750–9

Porcelain factories which decorated with the Meissen strawflower pattern

(See Ilmenauer strawflower pattern)

Porcelain factories which decorated with the Meissen onion pattern

Producers of dolls and dolls' heads

Modern-day place names of Czechoslovakia with the historical equivalents used in this book

Bibliography

Works mentioned specifically by the author in this edition are marked with an asterisk

Alfassa and Guérin, *Porcelaine française du 17ᵉ au milieu du 19ᵉ siècle* (Paris)
D'Agnel, G. A., *La Faïence et la Porcelaine de Marseille* (Paris-Marseille)
Albiker, C., *Die Meißnér Porzellantiere im 18. Jahrhundert* (Berlin 1935)
Angst, H., *Zürcher Porzellan* (Zürich 1905)
Anonym. Verf., *Porzellan und Porzellanbereitung. In: Okonomisch-technologische Enzyklopädie von J. G. Krünitz* (Berlin 1810)
Anonym. Verf., *Das Entdeckte Geheimnis des ächten Porcelains, so wohl des Chinesischen als Sächsischen, von einem Besitzer des Geheimnisses* (Berlin 1750)
Anonym. Verf., *Völlig entdecktes Geheimnis der Kunst, Fayence, englisches Steingut und ächtes Porcellain zu verfertigen* (Leipzig 1793)
Anonymus A. P. F. B., *Abentheur von Allerhand Mineralien in dem uralten Königreich Sina*
Auinger, H., *Meißner Porzellanmarken* (Dresden 1909)
Baeckström, A., *Rörstrand och dess tillverkningar 1726–1926* (Nordiska museet 1930)
Balet, L., *Ludwigsburger Porzellan* (Stuttgart u. Leipzig 1911)
Barbantini, N., *Le Porcellane di Venezia e delle Nove* (Venedig 1936)
Bayer, Adolf, *Ansbacher Porzellan* (Ansbach 1933)
Behse, A., *Deutsches Porzellanmarken-Brevier* (Braunschweig 1954, 1970)
Bemrose, G., *Nineteenth Century English Pottery and Porcelain* (London c. 1950)
*Bergmann, A., *Egerländer Porzellan und Steingut 1789–1945* (Amberg 1975)
*Berling, K., *Das Meißner Porzellan und seine Geschichte* (Leipzig 1900)
*Berling, K., *Festschrift der Kgl. sächs. Porzellanmanufaktur Meißen* (Dresden 1911)
Blacker, J. F., *The ABC of English Ceramic Art* (London c. 1920)
*Bott, G., *Kunsthandwerke um 1900 Jugendstil. Katalog des Hessischen Landesmuseums Nr. 1* (Darmstadt 1965)
Brongniart, A. and Riocreux, D., *Description du Musée Céramique de Sèvres* (Paris 1845)
Brüning, A., *Porzellan* (Berlin 1907)
Brunet, M., *Les Marques de Sèvres* (Paris 1953)
Burton, W., *A General History of Porcelain* (London 1921)
Burton, W., *Josiah Wedgwood and his Pottery* (1922)
Burton and Hobson, *Marks on Pottery and Porcelain* (London 1909)
Chaffers, W., *Marks and Monograms on European and Oriental Pottery and Porcelain* (London 1863 many subsequent editions)
Christ, H., *Ludwigsburger Porzellanfiguren* (Stuttgart and Berlin 1921)
Clemm, F., *Slg., Verst.-Kat. Lepke Nr. 1496* (Berlin 1907)
Cox, W. E., *The Book of Pottery and Porcelain Volume I and II* (New York 1944)
*Csányi, K., *Geschichte der ungarischen Keramik, des Porzellans und ihre Marken* (Budapest 1954)
*Cushion, J. P. and Honey, W. B., *Handbook of Pottery and Porcelain Marks* (London c. 1950)
*Cushion, J. P., *Pocket Book of French & Italian Ceramic Marks* (London 1965)
Cushion, J. P., *Animals in Pottery and Porcelain* (London 1974)
Danckert, L., *Manuel de la porcelaine européenne* (Fribourg 1973)
Dees, Otto, *Die Geschichte der Porzellanfabrik zu Tettau* (Saalfeld 1921)
Demmin, M. Auguste, *Guide de l'Amateur de Faïences et Porcelaines* (Paris 1867)
Dixon, J. L., *English Porcelain of the 18th Century* (London 1952)

685   BIBLIOGRAPHY

*Doenges, W., *Meißner Porzellan* (Dresden 1921)
Dolz, R., *Antiquitäten: Porzellan* (Munich 1969)
Ducret, S., *Zürcher Porzellan des 18. Jahrhunderts,* (Zürich 1945)
Ducret, S., *Deutsches Porzellan* (Baden-Baden 1962)
Ducret, S., *Deutsches Porzellan und deutsche Fayencen mit Wien-Zürich-Nyon* (Baden-
   Baden 1962)
Ducret, S., *Fürstenberger Porzellan (3 Bde.)* (Braunschweig 1965)
Ducret, S., *Würzburger Porzellan* (Braunschweig 1973)
Erichsen-Firle, U., *Figürliches Porzellan Katalog des Kunstgewerbe-Museums Köln, Bd. V*
   (Cologne 1975)
Ernst, R., *Wiener Porzellan des Klassizismus. Die Sammlung Bloch-Bauer* (Vienna 1925)
Esser, K. H. and Reber, H., *Höchster Fayencen und Porzellane* (Mainz 1964)
Falke, O. v., *Wiener Porzellansammlung Karl Mayer. Verst.-Katalog Glückselig* (Vienna
   1928)
Falke, O. v., *Sammlung P. V. Ostermann Verst.-Kat. Cassirer-Helbing* (Berlin 1928)
Fischer, C. H., *Altmeißner Porzellan Sammlung Heberle, Verst.-Kat.* (Cologne 1906)
Fisher, St. W., *The Decoration of English Porcelain* (London 1954)
Folnesics, J. and Braun, E. W., *Geschichte der K. K. Wiener Porzellanmanufaktur* (Vienna
   1907)
Frantz, H., *French Pottery and Porcelain* (London)
Frei, Karl, *Zürcher Porzellan* (Basel 1930)
Gerhardt, G. v., *Slg., Verst.-Kat. Lepke Nr. 1623* (Berlin 1912)
Geiger, Benno, *Keramisches ABC* (Bern 1947)
*Godden, G. A., *The Handbook of British Pottery and Porcelain Marks* (London 1968)
*Godden, G. A., *Encyclopaedia of British Pottery and Porcelain Marks* (London 1970)
Godden, G. A., *Coalport & Coalbrookdale Porcelains* (New York 1970)
Graesse, J. G. Th., *Guide de l'Amateur de Porcelaines et de Faïences* (1st Edition 1869)
Graesse-Jaennicke, *Führer für Sammler von Porzellan usw., Neubearbeitung von A. und L.
   Behse, 21. Auflage* (Braunschweig 1967)
Graul, R. and Kurzwelly, A., *Altthüringer Porzellan* (Leipzig 1909)
Grollier, Ch. de, *Manuel de l'Amateur de Porcelaines, Manufactures européennes (France
   exceptée)* (Paris 1914)
Grollier, Ch. de, *Manuel de l'Amateur de Porcelaines, Manufactures françaises* (Paris 1922)
Hannover, E., *Keramisk Haandbog* (Copenhagen 1919)
Haug, H., *Les Faïences et Porcelaines de Strasbourg* (Strasbourg 1922)
Hayden, A., *Kopenhagener Porzellan* (Leipzig 1913)
Hayward, J. F., *Viennese Porcelain of the Du Paquier Period* (London 1952)
Hermann, F., *Glas-, Porzellan- und Email-Malerei* (Leipzig 1882)
Hernmarck, C., *Marieberg* (Stockholm 1946)
Heuser, E., *Die Pfalz-Zweibrücker Porzellanmanufaktur* (Neustadt a. d. H. 1907)
Heuser, E., *Porzellan von Straßburg und Frankenthal* (Neustadt a. d. H. 1922)
Hirsch, R. E., *Marcas antiguas de Porcelanas Europeas* (Barcelona 1949)
Hobson, R. L., *Porcelain,* (London 1906)
Hofmann, F. H., *Das europäische Porzellan des Bayer. Nationalmuseums* (Munich 1908)
Hofmann, F. H., *Das Porzellan der europ. Manufakturen im 18. Jahrhundert* (Berlin 1932)
Hofmann, F. H., *Frankenthaler Porzellan* (Munich 1911)
Hofmann, F. H., *Geschichte der Bayer. Porzellanmanufaktur Nymphenburg* (Leipzig 1922)
Honey, W. B., *Dresden China* (New York 1946)
Honey, W. B., *English Pottery and Porcelain* (London 1947)
*Honey, W. B., *European Ceramic Art from the end of the Middle Ages to about 1815*
   (London 1952)

Honey, W. B., *German Porcelain* (London 1947)
Honey, W. B., *Old English Porcelain* (London 1928)
Hughes, G. B., *The Story of Spode* (Stoke on Trent 1950)
Jacquemart, A., *Les Merveilles de la Céramique* (Paris 1879)
Jaennicke, F., *Grundiß der Keramik* (Stuttgart 1879)
Jaennicke, F., *Handbuch der Porzellan-, Steingut- und Fayence-Malerei über und unter Glasur* (Stuttgart 1898)
Josten, H. H., *Fuldaer Porzellanfiguren* (Berlin 1929)
Jedding, H., *Europäisches Porzellan, Band I* (Munich 1974)
*KAB, *Adreßbuch der Keramindustrie seit 1883 – 26te Auflage* (Coburg 1971)
*KAB, *Keramos, Zeitschrift der Gesellschaft der Keramikfreunde e. V.* (Düsseldorf, erscheint laufend)
*Klein, A., *Europäische Keramik des Jugendstils. Katalog der Außtellung im Hetjens-Museum, Düsseldorf* (Munich 1974)
Köllmann, E., *Berliner Porzellan 1751–1954. Kuntsgewerbemuseum der Stadt Köln* (Cologne 1954)
Köllmann, E., *Berliner Porzellan (2 Bde.)* (Braunschweig 1960)
Köllmann, E., *Meißner Porzellan* (Braunschweig 1965)
Kolbe, G., *Geschichte der königl. Porzellanmanufaktur zu Berlin* (Berlin 1863)
*Kovel, R. M. and T. H., *Dictionary of Marks, Pottery and Porcelain* (New York 1953)
*Kronberger-Frentzen, H., *Altes Bildergeschirr* (Tübingen 1964)
Kunstgewerbemuseum der Stadt Köln, *Berliner Porzellan 1751–1954*, Kollmann, E. (Cologne 1954)
Lachavery, H., *Tentoonstellung van Belgische Kunstceramiek* (Antwerpen 1948)
Lechevallier-Cheviguard, *La Manufacture de Porcelaine de Sèvres* (Paris 1908)
Leistikow-Duchardt, A., *Die Entwicklung eines neuen Stiles im Porzallan* (Heidelburg 1957)
Lenz, G., *Berliner Porzellan* (Berlin 1913)
Liers, L. and Neumeister, J., *Die Gothaer Porzellan-Manufaktur. Museen der Stadt Gotha* (Gotha 1975)
Lindgren-Fridell, M., *Rörstrand of Today* (Stockholm 1952)
Lukomskij, G., *Russisches Porzellan* (Berlin 1924)
Marryat, M. S., *Histoire des Poteries, Faïences et Porcelaines* (Paris 1866)
Meyer, H., *Böhmisches Porzellan und Steingut* (Leipzig 1927)
Mottu, A., *Porcelaine de Nyon* (Geneva 1940)
*Neuwirth, W., *Porzellan aus Wien* (Vienna 1974)
*Neuwirth, W., *Wiener Keramik Historismus-Jugendstil-Art Deco* (Braunschweig 1974)
*Neuwirth, W., *Meißener Marken und Wiener Bindenschild* (Vienna 1977)
*Nikiforowa, L., *Russian Porcelain in the Hermitage Collection* (Leningrad 1923)
Nowotný, A., *Pražský Porcelán* (Praze 1949)
Papillon, G. and Savreux, M., *Musée Céramique de Sèvres* (Paris 1921)
Pauls Eisenbeiss, E., *German Porcelain of the 18th Century, 2 Bde.* (London 1972)
Pazaurek, G. E., *Deutsche Fayence- und Porzellan-Hausmaler* (Leipzig 1925)
Pazaurek, G. E., *Meißner Porzellanmalerei des 18. Jahrhunderts* (Stuttgart 1929)
Pazaurek, G. E., *Nordböhmisches Gewerbemuseum, Keramik* (Reichenberg 1905)
Pelka, O., *Chinesisches Porzellan* (Leipzig 1914)
Pelka, O., *Keramik der Neuzeit* (Braunschweig 1924)
Penkala, M., *European Porcelain* (Bern c. 1950)
Pfeiffer, B., *Album der Erzeugnisse der ehem. württ. Manufaktur Alt-Ludwigsburg* (Stuttgart 1906)
*Plinval de Guillebon, R. de, *La Porcelaine de Paris 1770–1850* (Fribourg 1973)

Poche, E., *Böhmisches Porzellan* (Prag 1956)

Pottery Gazette, *The Story of Royal Worcester* (1951)

Pottery Gazette and Glass Trade Review, Reference Book (London)

Reckham, B., *Catalogue of the Schweitzer Collection* (London 1915)

Richard-Ginori, *Primo Trentennio della Società Ceramica*

Richard-Ginori, *Società Ceramica* (Milan 1953)

Röder, K., *Das Kelsterbacher Porzellan* (Darmstadt 1931)

*Röder, K. and Oppenheim, M., *Das Höchster Porzellan* (Mainz 1930)

Rosenthal, E., *Pottery and Ceramics* (Harmondsworth 1949)

Rostock, X., *The Royal Copenhagen Porcelain Manufactory and the Faïence Manufactory Aluminia past and present* (Copenhagen 1939)

Rozembergh, A., *Les Marques de la Porcelaine Russe* (Paris 1926)

Rückert, R., *Franz Anton Bustelli* (Munich 1963)

Rückert, R., *Meißener Porzellan 1710–1810* (Munich 1966)

Rupé, H., *Katalog süddeutscher und mitteldeutscher Fayencen Sammlung Dr. P. Heiland* (Munich 1934)

Sandström, G. E., *Beauty in the Making* (Stockholm 1947)

Sauerlandt, M., *Deutsche Porzellanfiguren des 18. Jahrhunderts* (Cologne 1923)

*Scharer, J., *Meißen 75, Informationen über dad gegenwärtige Schaffen der ersten europäischen Porzellanmanufaktur. VEB Porzellanmanufaktur Meißen* (Meissen 1975)

Schätzer, L., *Keramik* (Berlin 1954)

Roh- und Werkstoffe, Prüfmethoden

*Scheffler, W., *Berlin im Porzellanbild seiner Manufaktur* (Berlin 1963)

*Scheffler, W., *Kunstgewerbemuseum Berlin Bd. II: Werke um 1900* (Berlin 1966)

Scherer, Chr., *Das Fürstenberger Porzellan* (Berlin 1909)

Scherer, Chr., *Fürstenberger Porzellan* (Halberstadt 1923)

*Scherf, H., *Alt-Thüringer Porzellan* (Leipzig 1969)

Schnorr v. Carolsfeld, L., *Europäisches Porzellan des 18. Jahrhunderts* (Berlin 1925)

Sammlung Darmstaedter, Verst.-Kzat. Lepke Nr. 1933

*Schnorr v. Carolsfeld-Köllmann, *Porzellan der europäischen Fabriken (2 Bde.)* (Braunschweig 1974)

Schmidt, R., *Das Porzellan als Kunstwerk und Kulturspiegel* (Munich 1925)

Schönberger, A., *Deutsches Porzellan,* (Munich 1949)

Soil de Moriamé, E. J., *Les Porcelaines de Tournay* (Tournay 1910)

Sponsel, J. L., *Kabinettstücke der Meißner Porzellanmanufaktur von Johann Joachim Kändler* (Leipzig 1900)

Staatl. Porzellanmanufaktur Nymphenburg, *Zweihundert Jahre Nymphenburg* (Munich 1948)

Stazzi, F., *Italienisches Porzellan* (Frankfurt/M. 1964)

Stieda, W., *Die Anfänge der Porzellanfabriken auf dem Thüringer Walde* (Jena 1902)

Stieda, W., *Die Keramische Industrie in Bayern während des 18. Jahrh.* (Leipzig 1906)

Strohmer-Nowak, *Altwiener Porzellan* (Vienna 1950)

Swinarski, M. and Chrościcki, L., *Znaki Porcelany Europejskiej i Polskiej Ceramiki* (Poznán 1949)

*Tardy, *Les Porcelaines Françaises* (Paris 1950/75)

Tardy, *Poteries – Faïences – Porcelaines Européennes* (Paris 1953)

The Royal Doulton Potteries Burslem, *Ceramics in Art and Industry* (London 1947)

*Treskow, I. v., *Berliner Jugendstilporzellan Die KPM 1890–1904* (Munich 1972)

Tronitzki, *Porzellan der Eremitage* (St. Petersburg 1911)

Vernet – Grandjean – Brunet, *Sèvres* (Paris 1953)

Walcha, O., *Porzellan* (Heidelberg 1963)

*Walcha, O., *Meißner Porzellan* (Dresden 1973)

Wanner-Brandt, O., *Album der Erzeugnisse der ehem. württ. Manufaktur Alt-Ludwigsburg* (Stuttgart 1906)

Wedgwood, H. and Graham, J. M., *Wedgwood – A Living Tradition* (1948)

Weiß, G., *Ullstein Porzellanbuch* (Berlin/Frankfurt/Vienna 1964/73)

Wiese, O., *200 Jahre Porzellanfabrik zu Schloß Fürstenberg* (Fürstenberg 1947)

Winter, H., *An Introduction to European Porcelain* (New York 1972)

Zimmermann, E., *Die Erfindung und Frühzeit des Meißner Porzellans* (Berlin 1908)

Zimmermann, E., *Meißner Porzellan* (Leipzig 1926)

Zimmermannn, E., *Chinesisches Porzellan und die überigen keramischen Erzeugnisse Chinas* (Leipzig 1923)